ISBN 978-0-332-22926-3
PIBN 11013438

AMERICAN

NEGLIGENCE REPORTS

CURRENT SERIES

[CITED AM. NEG. REP.]

ALL THE CURRENT NEGLIGENCE CASES DECIDED IN THE FEDERAL COURTS OF THE UNITED STATES, THE COURTS OF LAST RESORT OF ALL THE STATES AND TERRITORIES AND SELECTIONS FROM THE INTERMEDIATE COURTS

TOGETHER WITH

NOTES OF ENGLISH CASES AND ANNOTATIONS

EDITED BY
JOHN M. GARDNER
OF THE NEW YORK BAR

VOL. XII

NEW YORK
REMICK & SCHILLING.
1903

PREFACE.

The cases reported in this volume of the series of AMERICAN NEGLIGENCE REPORTS (VOL. XII) relate to INJURIES TO PERSONS AND PROPERTY, decided in the State and Federal Courts during the year 1902, being Negligence cases arising out of the relations of CARRIER AND PASSENGER, LANDLORD AND TENANT, MASTER AND SERVANT, MUNICIPAL CORPORATIONS, STEAM AND STREET RAILROAD COMPANIES, and all other branches of the LAW OF NEGLIGENCE. Additional cases, prior to those decided in 1902, are appended to the numerous Notes and Annotations to the current decisions reported in this volume.

Among the SPECIAL NOTES on the various topics of NEGLIGENCE LAW are the following: Liability of Carriers for Loss of Baggage; Liability of Connecting Carriers for Negligence; Recent cases on Furnishing Servant Safe Place to Work; Recent cases of Defective Appliances; Recent cases on Proximate Cause of Injury; Recent cases arising from Injuries to Trespassers, which notes are contributed by MR. ALFRED J. HOOK, Librarian of the Law Library in Brooklyn, N. Y. The complete list of Special and other Notes in this volume will be found at the end of the TABLE OF CASES REPORTED.

Annotations and Notes of English Cases are added to many of the cases reported herein, with numerous cross-references to various topics and cases reported in the series of AMERICAN NEGLIGENCE REPORTS.

The cases reported in this volume comprise decisions in the highest Courts of Alabama, Arizona, Arkansas, California, Colorado, Connecticut, Delaware, District of Columbia, Florida, Georgia, Idaho, Illinois (Supreme and Appellate Courts), Indiana (Supreme and Appellate Courts), Indian Territory, Iowa, Kansas (Supreme and Appellate Courts), Kentucky, Louisiana, Maine, Maryland, Massachusetts, Michigan, Minnesota, Mississippi, Missouri (Supreme and Appellate Courts), Montana, Nebraska, Nevada, New Hampshire, New Jersey (Supreme and Errors and

Appeals), New York (Court of Appeals and Appellate Division of Supreme Court), North Carolina, North Dakota, Ohio, (Supreme and Intermediate Courts), Oklahoma, Oregon, Pennsylvania, Rhode Island, South Carolina, South Dakota, Tennessee, Texas (Supreme and Civil Appeals), Utah, Vermont, Virginia, Washington, West Virginia, Wisconsin, Wyoming, and the United States Supreme, Circuit Courts of Appeals, Circuit and District Courts.

Reference to the TABLE OF CASES CLASSIFIED ACCORDING TO FACTS, which precedes the INDEX, will enable the practitioner to see at a glance the nature of the case reported, and thus act as a ready guide to a case in point.

The editor cordially acknowledges the able services of MR. WALTER J. EAGLE in the preparation of the cases and the general notes and annotations thereto, and the compilation of the Tables of Cases and Index in this volume of AMERICAN NEGLIGENCE REPORTS.

JOHN M. GARDNER.

NEW YORK, *January*, 1903.

TABLE OF CASES REPORTED.

[Notes of current cases are designated by the letter n preceding the number of the page on which the same appears in this volume, as, for instance: Andrews v. Kinsel, 114 Ga. 390....................n 486].

D

E

F

G

H

N

O

P

Y

Z

NOTES.

TABLE OF CASES CITED.

[Where a case is cited in a note, the number of the page on which it appears in this volume is preceded by the letter n; as, for instance: Andrews v. Kinsel, 114 Ga. 390................n486].

A

B

H

N

Y

Z

AMERICAN NEGLIGENCE REPORTS.

GREEN v. LOS ANGELES TERMINAL RAILWAY COMPANY.

Supreme Court, California, July, 1902.

PERSON CROSSING TRACK AT STREET CROSSING STRUCK AND KILLED BY TRAIN — LOOKING AND LISTENING — CONTRIBUTORY NEGLIGENCE. — Where plaintiff's intestate, when about thirty feet from a crossing on defendant's track, stopped, looked up the track, and finding it clear for the space of 800 feet, proceeded to cross without again looking for train, but as she stepped upon the track was struck and fatally injured by a train which was running at a rapid and dangerous rate of speed, no signal having been given, it was *held* that the facts shown did not constitute negligence, as a matter of law, on the part of deceased (1).

1. *Collisions and Crossings.* — For actions arising out of Accidents at Crossings, see vols. 11 and 12 AM. NEG. CAS., where the cases relating to "Collisions and Crossings" are chronologically grouped, from the earliest period to 1897, and arranged in alphabetical order of States. Subsequent actions on the same topics to date appear in vols. 1-12 AM. NEG. REP., and the current numbers of that series of Reports.

See also the following recent cases relating to Pedestrians injured at Crossings or on Track:

Person run over and killed by train. — In LOUISVILLE & NASHVILLE R. R. Co. *v.* MITCHELL, *(Alabama, June, 1902),* 32 So. Rep. 735, person run over by train on track, judgment for plaintiff for $9,000 was reversed, the facts, as per opinion by HARALSON, J., being stated as follows: "The facts of this case without conflict are that Elmore station is a village of about 300 inhabitants, and is not a scheduled station for the train that passed, — the fast mail. The crossing at which plaintiff's intestate was killed was not a street or public thoroughfare. The public crossings, of which there were two, were above and below the depot, some 200 yards or more. The tracks of the railroad, running north and

COMMISSIONERS' DECISION. Department 1. Appeal from Superior Court, Los Angeles County.

From a judgment for $5,000 for plaintiff in action for negligent killing of his wife by railway company, and an order denying a motion for a new trial, defendant appeals. *Judgment affirmed.*

GIBBONS, THOMAS & HALSTED and GOODRICH & McCUTCHEN, for appellant.

R. A. LING and EDWIN A. MESERVE, for respondent.

south at this point, were fenced; the fences opened by two gates, one on the east and the other on the west, and a pathway from one gate to the other ran across the railroad tracks, which path was used without objection on the part of the railroad company, so far as appears, by people, generally, of Elmore or from the country, who desired to go from one part of the village to the other, and was much frequented for such purposes. At no time was it used, so far as appears, as a matter of right but only for convenience without objection on the part of the railroad company. The train, as the evidence tends to show, ran through, at from forty to sixty miles an hour, as estimated by different witnesses; that one coming in at the east gate, could see up the track, north, about half a mile, and not so far when outside of the gate; that there is a curve eastward in the track coming from the north, before reaching the depot, which curve was some 200 or 300 yards from the depot. Intestate approached the track from the east gate, and the evidence tends to show that he looked up the track north as he crossed the switch track, — which is a few feet away, on the east from the main line. One witness testified that he told him to look out or the train would kill him, but intestate made no reply and went on and was caught and killed just before he got across the main line. There was no evidence that the engineer saw the deceased before the collision occurred, or knew that he was in proximity to the track. Treating the third count, as we must, as one for simple negligence, and not for wantonness or intentional injury of the deceased, it is apparent that under the principles above stated, the plaintiff's intestate was guilty of negligence which proximately contributed to his own death, and, on the case if tried upon such a count, the affirmative charge might have been properly given for defendant." * * * The court also said: "As to persons walking on or crossing a railroad track, it is held that " the mere fact that persons living in the neighborhood of a railroad track have become accustomed to use it to walk upon (or across) without any objection on the part of the railroad company, does not in any manner alter or change the duty of the railroad company to such persons. They are simply trespassers " (Glass *v.* Railroad Co., 94 Ala. 586, 10 So. Rep. 217); and " one who is injured in consequence of being negligently on a railroad track cannot recover, unless the railroad employees are guilty of such gross negligence or recklessness as amounts to wantonness or intention to inflict the injury; and that this wantonness and intention to do wrong can never be imputed to them, unless they actually know (not merely ought to know) the perilous position of the person on the track, and with such knowledge, fail to resort to every reasonable effort to avert disastrous consequences. And this doctrine applies to densely populated neighborhoods in the country, and to

SMITH, C. — This is a suit brought by the plaintiff to recover damages for the death of his wife, alleged to have been the result of the negligent operation of the defendant's railroad. The plaintiff recovered judgment for the sum of $5,000 and costs; and the

the streets of a town or city, as to the solitudes of the plains or forest." Nave *v.* Railroad Co., 96 Ala. 267, 11 So. Rep. 391; Railway Co. *v.* Lamb, 124 Ala. 172, 26 So. Rep. 969; Railroad Co. *v.* Robbins, 124 Ala. 113, 27 So. Rep. 422; Railroad Co. *v.* Crawford, 89 Ala. 240, 8 So. Rep. 243; Railway Co. *v.* Foshee, 125 Ala. 199, 27 So. Rep. 1006. In the case last cited, after announcing the well-understood doctrine, that it is the duty of a person approaching the track of a railway for the purpose of crossing it, to stop and look and listen if need be, for the approach of a train, and that the omission of this duty followed by injury in collision with a train, locomotive or car, while attempting thus heedlessly to cross over the track is as matter of law negligence on the part of the person so contributing to the result, as to defeat his action counting on the injury as having been produced by the simple negligence of the company, or its employees, the court states what seems to be axiomatic, that "It is not possible to conceive that any foot traveler need or could with the proper use of his senses ever go upon a railway in ignorance of the approach of a train sufficiently near to strike him before he crosses over it. No curve even in a deep cut that a train can be operated upon, can be so acute as to deprive him of the opportunity while standing beside the track, to refrain from attempting to cross in front of it." * * *

Boy run over by train at street crossing. — In O'DONNELL *v.* CHICAGO, ROCK ISLAND & PACIFIC R'Y CO. (*Nebraska, July, 1902*), 91 N. W. Rep. 566, an action for injuries to plaintiff, a boy eight years old, who, in attempting to cross track at street crossing where train was standing was thrown under wheels of car and his leg injured, judgment for defendant was reversed, the syllabus by the court stating the case as follows:

"1. An instruction confining the plaintiff's recovery to the results of negligence in the specific acts alleged, and directing the jury to consider other acts at other times and places only as bearing upon the acts and injury complained of, *held*, in connection with the other instructions, not to narrow unduly the issues, nor to prevent the showing of any negligence directly connected with and tending to cause the injury.

"2. Whether or not it is negligence on the part of a locomotive engineer to fail to stop his train, moving at not exceeding three miles an hour, on seeing a boy of eight years jumping on and off a ladder at the side of a freight car, is a question to be determined by the jury in view of all the circumstances.

"3. To instruct the jury that all material allegations of plaintiff's petition must be established by a preponderance of the evidence is erroneous where material allegations are admitted, but prejudice will not be presumed where it is hardly possible the jury were misled.

"4. To instruct the jury that all material allegations must be proved, without indicating what they are, is error; but, to be available to the losing party, a more specific instruction must have been requested, or there must have been in the case a distinct failure of justice.

"5. Acts of a witness merely going to show how he knows that a train appeal is from the judgment, and from an order denying the defendant's motion for new trial.

It is found by the court that at the time of the accident the defendant's train "was being run and operated in a very dangerous and grossly negligent and careless manner, as to its rate of speed

stood on a crossing thirty minutes or more, which are otherwise immaterial, should generally be admitted, at least in outline, but it is not error to strike them out as unresponsive, when volunteered in detail in answering a question as to the time of the train's standing there.

"6. In the absence of a distinct admission of the precise statement tendered to be proved, a party who has laid the proper foundation may prove a previous statement made by a witness materially contradicting his testimony."

Boy run over by street car. — In BAIER *v.* CAMDEN & SUBURBAN R'Y CO. *(New Jersey Supreme Court, June, 1902)*, 52 Atl. Rep. 215, it was held that "a motorman is not chargeable with negligence because he fails to apprehend that a boy who is riding on the back of a wagon will jump from the wagon and run under his car while he is engaged in looking at the wagon in order to pass it without a collision." On the trial there was a verdict for plaintiff. Rule to show cause why a new trial should be granted made absolute.

Boy stealing a ride jumping from street car and run over. — In MEMPHIS STREET R'Y CO. *v.* NEWMAN *(Tennessee, May, 1902)*, 69 S. W. Rep. 269, boy, eleven years old, who was stealing a ride on a street car, jumping off car and run over and killed by car on other track, judgment for plaintiff for $500 was reversed for failure of trial court to instruct jury in reference to defendant's theory of the accident where there was conflicting evidence as to the cause of same.

Run over by street car. — In NORFOLK RAILWAY & LIGHT CO. *v.* CORLETTO *(Virginia, June, 1902)*, 41 S. E. Rep. 740, person run over by street car, judgment for plaintiff was reversed for erroneous instruction where there was no evidence tending to prove the facts upon which the instruction was based. As to overruling of demurrer to declaration the court, (per BUCHANAN, J.), said: "The objection made to the declaration is that it does not allege facts from which there could be inferred any duty owing by the defendant to the plaintiff. The declaration only contains one count. It alleges that at the time of the injury complained of the railway and light company was possessed of, and was operating by electricity, a certain street railroad, on Church street, one of the public highways of the city of Norfolk, and that whilst operating the same it so carelessly, recklessly, negligently, and improperly managed its cars that by reason of its carelessness and negligence one of its cars ran and struck with great force and violence upon and against the plaintiff, who was then and there in and upon the street, whereby his left hand and the forefinger of his right hand were so fractured and injured that they had to be, and were, amputated, and that the plaintiff was otherwise greatly injured. It may be that the averments of the declaration would not be sufficient to make a *prima facie* case of negligence against the defendant if it had been an ordinary steam railway company, operating its cars on its own premises. But the defendant company was not operating its cars upon its own land, but upon a public street, where the plaintiff had and failure to sound ordinary signals of warning," and that the accident to the deceased was the result of the negligence of the defendant and its employees; "that before crossing or attempting to cross the defendant's railroad track [the deceased] used ordinary care, and did what an ordinarily prudent person would have done

the right to be. He was neither a trespasser nor a licensee. 2 Shear. & R. Neg. (5th ed.), sec. 485c; Elliott, Roads & S., sec. 765. Having the legal right to be upon the street, it was the duty of the defendant to exercise reasonable care to avoid injuring him; and if, as the declaration alleges, the defendant negligently and carelessly ran its car upon him, it was clearly liable for the injury inflicted, unless he was guilty of contributory negligence; and this does not appear from the averments of the declaration. The demurrer was properly overruled." * * *

Person killed while crossing railroad bridge or trestle.—In Chesapeake & Ohio R'y Co. *v.* Rogers' Adm'x. *(Virginia, June, 1902)*, 41 S. E. Rep 732, judgment for plaintiff for $4,000, in action for negligent killing of plaintiff's intestate while crossing a certain bridge or trestle of defendant company, was reversed for erroneous instruction based upon a fact that there was no evidence tending to prove. Harrison, J., stated the facts as follows: "It appears that Thomas W. Rogers was employed by the Virginia Carolina Chemical Company, and that in going to and from his work he, with others working in that vicinity, but living on Church Hill, in the city of Richmond, was accustomed, morning and evening, to pass over the bridge or trestle of the defendant company, which extends from Nicholson street to Church Hill, a distance of about 1,300 feet, and varies in height, being some twenty-five or thirty feet from the ground at the highest point. This elevated track is supported by bents about twelve feet apart, and at each bent there is what is called a 'cap sill,' which extends out on both sides of the structure between two and three feet. There is no plank or walkway on any part of this structure; nothing but the ties, a few inches apart, on which a person can walk. At each end of this trestle is a warning board placed, with the following large conspicuous letters thereon: 'Caution. Keep Off the Bridge.' These warning boards are so placed as to be plainly in view of every person who approaches the structure with the intention of crossing. Below this structure, and close beside it, there is a lower trestle, which comes from the gas house on an ascending grade to a point east of Nicholson street, where this lower track joins the upper one. Near the Fulton end of the bridge there are signals placed, which control the running of trains over these trestles. These signals are for the safe running of the trains, and not for the information of the public, and are worked from a tower several squares distant, and have to be changed back and forth as circumstances may require. On the night of January 31, 1901, between the hours of 8:30 and 9 o'clock P. M., Rogers met his death. He had been engaged at the chemical works several hours overtime, and was on his way home with a companion. The engine which ran over and killed Rogers and his companion was going in the same direction they were, and was running with the tender in front The point where the men were run over is about 360 feet from Gillies' creek. There was also on the trestle, at or near Gillies' creek, a colored man, going in the same direction as Rogers. As the engine approached, under the circumstances;" and that she "did not by her own carelessness or negligence in any way contribute to said accident." But it is claimed by the appellant, in effect, that these are inconsistent with the more specific findings, and that upon the latter the conclusions of the court and the judgment should have been different. The case, as presented by the specific findings, is as follows: The defendant's railroad runs easterly along Humboldt street, in Los Angeles city, crossing at right angles Avenues 21 to 26, inclusive, and from the last crossing leaving the street by a sharp curve to the northward. Humboldt street, between Avenues 22 and 23, is crossed at an angle of thirty degrees by "a wide, hard-beaten path, regularly traveled by pedestrians," which runs from a point on Avenue 23 south of Humboldt street, northwesterly, across vacant lots, to Avenue 22, in the vicinity of the house where the plaintiff and deceased lived. The distance along the path from its intersection with the south line of Humboldt street to its intersection with the railroad track is about thirty feet; and from the former point, looking easterly, one can see the track to the curve at Avenue 25, a distance of about 800 feet, but not beyond. The deceased was killed at the intersection of the path above described with the railroad in the afternoon of November 15, 1899, while it was still light, by a train coming from the east. She was then passing along the path to her home; and when she came to Humboldt street, and had entered thereon, "she looked up defendant's track in the direction from which the train * * * was coming," and "there was [then] no train on the defendant's track in sight from where she

this colored man got out on a cap sill, and thus saved himself. These cap sills appear from the evidence to be places of safety, under such circumstances, and available to persons situated as Rogers was. It appears that when the plaintiff's intestate approached the upper trestle, over which he was about to cross, there was exhibited at that point a stop signal, which indicated that over the lower trestle a train was expected, and that trains over the upper trestle were blocked; that a few minutes after Rogers started over the upper trestle the signal was changed from the lower to the upper trestle, giving the right of way to trains over the latter; and that almost immediately the engine and tender came at a rapid speed over the upper trestle. It appears that the night of the accident was unusually clear and bright; that it was possible to see a long distance. The fact is established by the evidence that, notwithstanding the dangerous character of this structure as a walkway, and the conspicuous warning constantly displayed cautioning persons to keep off the bridge, it had been constantly used for some years by numerous persons working at the chemical works and in that vicinity, and that this habitual use of the trestle as a walkway was well known to the defendant company. These are the salient facts which the evidence tends to prove." * * *

was." The deceased then, without again stopping or looking up or down the track, proceeded to cross the street and railroad, following the path, and as she stepped upon the track was struck by the engine of defendant's train coming from the east, and fatally hurt. The train at the time of the accident was running down grade, without using steam, and making but little noise, — "at an excessively high and dangerous rate of speed" (between twenty-five and thirty miles per hour). No whistle was blown on the engine from the time it passed a point beyond the curve, out of sight of the deceased, until within ten or fifteen feet of her, and just as the engine was about to strike her; nor was the bell rung before or while crossing any of the streets until just above where the accident occurred. As the train rounded the curve "the engineer in charge of the engine * * * saw [the deceased], and knew that she was walking on said path, and crossing said Humboldt street, ahead of said train, and that she gave no evidence of knowledge of the approach of said train," and, "notwithstanding said facts, * * * did not slacken or lessen the speed of said train, or attempt to give [deceased] warning of its approach, * * * until the train was within ten or fifteen feet of the point of the accident," though it is found he could have stopped the train within 200 feet after starting to do so.

The above facts are not disputed by the appellant's counsel, except as to the rate of speed, the failure of the engineer to sound the signals required of him, and his failure to slacken speed until within ten or fifteen feet of the deceased. But on the last point the engineer's own testimony is explicit to the same effect as stated in the finding, and as to the others it is admitted that the evidence is conflicting. The facts found must therefore be taken as established. We do not understand that this is disputed by the appellant; but the point made is that the deceased, after stopping at the south line of the street and looking up the track for an approaching train, should have again looked and listened for the approaching train, and that, as a matter of law, her failure to do so in itself constituted negligence. But it is difficult to imagine on what principle this contention could be sustained, or, if it could, how it could be material. On the question of contributory negligence the burden of proof is on the defendant; and here there was absolutely no evidence of such negligence, except that she did not look up the track for an approaching train in passing from the south line of the street to the track. Certainly we cannot say that the inference of negligence from these facts is irresistible, or, as a matter of law, that they constituted negligence; and, unless this can be said, the contention must fail. For, to set aside the finding of the court that there was no contributory negligence on the part of the plaintiff, "such negligence must affirmatively appear as a conclusion of law from the undisputed facts." Schneider *v.* Railway Co., 134 Cal. 482, 487, 66 Pac. Rep. 734 *et seq.* Indeed, in this case the evidence tended to show that the deceased took all the care to avoid danger required of her. When she looked up the track and found it clear for the space of 800 feet, she was near enough to cross with safety, had the train been running at any but an excessive rate of speed.

I advise that the judgment and order appealed from be affirmed.

We concur: CHIPMAN, C.; HAYNES, C.

PER CURIAM. — For the reasons given in the foregoing opinion, the judgment and order appealed from are affirmed.

ROWELL v. CROTHERS.

Supreme Court of Errors, Connecticut, July, 1902.

DRIVING ON HIGHWAY — COLLISION — TREBLE DAMAGES — STATUTE — PLEADING AND PROOF. — In an action to recover damages for injuries to plaintiff's wagon caused by collision with defendant's wagon on highway, it was held that in order to recover treble damages under sections 2689 and 2690 of the General Statutes which provides that when "the drivers of any vehicles for the conveyance of persons shall meet each other in the public highway each shall turn to the right and slacken his pace," etc., and that every driver of such vehicle who neglects to conform to such provision, and drives against another vehicle and injures it or its owner, shall pay to the injured party treble damages, the party injured must allege and prove that defendant was driving "a vehicle for the conveyance of persons," and designation of the vehicle as a wagon or team is not sufficient.

APPEAL from Court of Common Pleas, Fairfield County.

Action by Charles E. Rowell against John G. Crothers for injuries from the negligent driving of defendant against the plaintiff's wagon on a highway. From judgment of the City Court of Stanford for plaintiff for $25.80 (that being treble the amount of damages found to have been sustained by plaintiff), defendant appealed to the Court of Common Pleas, where there were verdict and judgment for plaintiff for $10, the court denying his motion for treble damages, from which latter judgment plaintiff appeals. *Judgment affirmed.*

GEORGE P. ROWELL, for appellant.

GALEN A. CARTER, for appellee.

HALL, J. — The complaint in this case alleges that the plaintiff "was driving in a wagon belonging to him along the westerly or right-hand side" of a certain public highway, and that the defendant was driving another wagon along the same side of the same highway, so that "said team of the defendant was approaching that of the plaintiff from the opposite direction, and that the teams of the defendant and the plaintiff were about to meet;" that the plaintiff was driving at a moderate pace, and that he thereupon slackened the same, and turned further to the right, giving the defendant more than half the traveled path, and affording him a fair and equal opportunity to pass on the highway; that the defendant was driving at a high rate of speed, and that he did not turn to the right and slacken his pace, so as to give half of the traveled path to the plaintiff, although it was practicable for him to do so, and did not give the plaintiff a fair and equal opportunity to pass on said highway, contrary to the statute in such case made and provided, and that "in consequence thereof, and by neglecting to conform thereto, the defendant carelessly and negligently drove against the wagon of the plaintiff, and thereby broke and injured the same, and the plaintiff was thrown out of his wagon and much bruised and injured." The complaint stated that the plaintiff claimed, "in treble damages and costs, pursuant to the statute in such case made and provided, $500 damages." The answer admitted that the defendant's team was approaching that of the plaintiff from the opposite direction, and that said teams were about to meet, and denied the remaining allegations of the complaint. By way of counterclaim, the defendant asked for judgment for the damages which he claimed to have sustained; alleging that the collision was due to the plaintiff's negligence. The plaintiff's reply denied the principal averments of the counterclaim. Upon these pleadings the jury rendered a verdict in favor of the plaintiff for $10 damages.

The court properly denied the plaintiff's motion for treble damages. Section 2689 of the General Statutes provides that when "the drivers of any vehicles for the conveyance of persons shall meet each other in the public highway each shall turn to the right and slacken his pace," etc., and that "any driver who shall violate this section shall forfeit fifteen dollars to the town * * * and pay to the injured party his damages;" and section 2690 provides that "every driver of such vehicle who shall, by neglecting to conform to the preceding section, drive against another vehicle and injure its owner or any person in it, or the property of any person, * * * shall pay to the party injured treble damages and costs," etc. An essential element of the offense described in these sections, for the commission of which the payment of treble damages may be imposed as a punishment upon the offender, is the driving of "a vehicle for the conveyance of persons;" and, to justify a judgment for such treble damages, that element must be both alleged and proved. While the plaintiff might have properly alleged that the vehicle driven by the defendant was one for the conveyance of persons, without using the precise words of the statute, it was necessary for him, in order to recover treble damages, to so describe the vehicle in the complaint as to clearly bring it within the class named in the statute. The substituted complaint describes the vehicle driven by the defendant, and that in which the plaintiff was driving as a "wagon." They are also referred to in the complaint as "teams." Since either of these words may as properly be used to designate a vehicle for the carriage of goods as one for the conveyance of persons, neither of them nor both of them constitute a sufficiently specific description of the vehicle named in the statute to entitle the plaintiff to a judgment for treble damages. The complaint is, however, not demurrable, as it states a good cause of action for negligence at common law, and the defendant properly took advantage of the absence of an allegation that he was driving a vehicle for the conveyance of persons by opposing the plaintiff's motion for treble damages (which motion could only be made to the court) after the verdict fixing the actual damages. Practically the same question raised by this appeal (as to the sufficiency of the description of the vehicle to entitle the plaintiff to treble damages under this statute) was decided by this court in the recent case of Stevens *v.* Kelley, 66 Conn. 570. In that case, and in the cases of Broschart *v.* Tuttle, 59 Conn. 1, and Hotchkiss *v.* Hoy, 41 Conn. 568, the question of what allegations must be contained in the complaint to justify a judgment for such damages has been so fully considered as to require no further discussion here.

The plaintiff in the present case, who was a physician, having testified upon the trial, upon his direct examination, that the collision occurred when he was driving to call on a patient was asked upon cross-examination if he had not a very large practice and also, upon cross-examination, whether he had not talked about the case with a certain person who witnessed the collision, and whose deposition was afterwards taken, and whether he (the plaintiff) had any ill feeling toward the defendant, and whether he had had any trouble with him, or had told the defendant that he would get him removed from his place in the post office. The last two questions were answered by the witness in the negative. All said questions were admitted against the plaintiff's objection. We discover no error in any of these rulings. Certainly the plaintiff has no cause to complain of them. The verdict was in his favor, and, although it was for a smaller sum than the amount claimed by him, we fail to see how these rulings could have in any way affected the amount of damages awarded to him.

There is no error. The other judges concurred.

MANCHESTER MANUFACTURING COMPANY v. POLK.

Supreme Court, Georgia, June, 1902.

MINOR EMPLOYEE INJURED BY DEFECTIVE MACHINERY — VOLUNTEER — INSTRUCTION. — 1. Other than as indicated below, the grounds of the motion for a new trial do not show any error which requires a reversal of the judgment.

2. In the trial of a case brought by a servant against a master to recover damages for personal injuries received by the servant in the use of defective machinery furnished by the master, it was error to charge, in effect, that the master was liable for the injuries so received if he was negligent in failing to provide machinery reasonably safe for the work, or to keep the machinery in proper repair, and that if the master had been negligent in either of these particulars, and the servant was injured in consequence of that negligence, the master would be liable, without instructing the jury, in the same connection either literally or in substance, that, before the servant could recover for such injuries, it must appear that he did not know, and had not equal means with the master of knowing, such fact, and by the exercise of ordinary care could not have known thereof. In a case where the injured servant was a minor, the instructions should be so qualified as not to require of him more diligence than should be expected of one of his age and capacity (1).

3. In a suit of the nature above indicated, it was error so to charge the jury that a verdict for the plaintiff would under any circumstances, be authorized, if he were not a servant, but a mere volunteer, at the time of the injury.

(Syllabus by the Court.)

1. As to knowledge of defect in machinery, see the following recent Georgia cases:

In CHARLESTON & WESTERN CAROLINA R'Y CO. *v.* MILLER, *(Georgia, April, 1902)*, 41 S. E. Rep. 252, where judgment for plaintiff was affirmed, the syllabus by the court held that "a petition by a servant against his master for injuries resulting from defective machinery, which alleges that the plaintiff did not know the fact that defects existed in the machinery, and could not have discovered the same by the exercise of ordinary care and diligence, but that the defendant did know this fact, or could have known it by the exercise of such care and diligence, in effect states that the servant had not equal means of knowing such fact." * * * "The suit was for damages on account of personal injuries received

ERROR from City Court of Macon.

From a judgment for plaintiff, defendant brings error. *Judgment reversed.*

DESSAN, HARRIS & HARRIS, for plaintiff in error.

LANE & PARK and RYALS & FELDER, for defendant in error.

by the plaintiff while in the employment of the defendant as a train hand. and negligence was attributed to the company in having and maintaining a defective coupling apparatus and defective bumpers on its train, which, it was alleged, caused the plaintiff's injuries. The amendment which was allowed, and by which it was sought to supply the allegations necessary to complete the cause of action, was an addition to the petition in the following words: 'That the plaintiff did not know of the defective coupling and defective bumpers, nor could he have discovered said defects by the exercise of ordinary care and diligence; but said defendant company knew of said defects, or could have known of them by the exercise of ordinary care and diligence.'" * * * (See former decision in the Miller case, 113 Ga. 15, 38 S. E. Rep. 338.)

In STEWART *v.* SEABOARD AIR LINE R'Y *(Georgia, June, 1902)*, 41 S. E. Rep. 981, judgment for defendant was affirmed, the court (per COBB, J.), stating the facts as follows: "Stewart sued the railway company for damages. At the trial the court granted a nonsuit, and to this judgment the plaintiff excepted. It appeared from the evidence that the plaintiff was a mechanic employed by and at work in the shops of the railway company. On a hill near the shops, timber to be used in the shops was stored by the defendant; and, to convey this timber from the place where it was stored to the shops, a hand or push car was used, which was propelled along a track running from the place where the timber was located down an incline to the shops. This push car consisted of trucks, and an open frame above the same; there being no floor on the car. The timber was placed upon this frame, and the speed of the car in going down the incline was regulated by brakes, which were controlled by a lever on the side of the car. The plaintiff was directed to take the car, go up the hill, and bring to the shops a heavy piece of timber. In obedience to this direction he repaired with the car to the top of the hill, and, with another employee, placed the piece of timber upon the car, seated himself on the end of the timber, which was at a point on the car near the lever, and placed his foot between the end of the timber and one of the crossbeams of the car. The other employee placed himself upon the timber behind the plaintiff. While the plaintiff was in this position the car was started down the hill, and, when it had attained a speed which was considered by the plaintiff to be as high as was safe, the lever was used by him to control the speed of the car and prevent it from being increased. It was then found that the brakes would not control the car. The speed increased, and the car was propelled, by running at a high rate of speed, against some trucks which were on the track, and plaintiff's leg was broken by being crushed between the end of the timber and the crossbeam of the car. The plaintiff did all he could to stop the car, and the brakes would not hold the wheels. Plaintiff had been working for the railway company for more than a year, and had used this car frequently; sometimes using it every day, and then not using it for a week at a time. The plaintiff testified that there was nothing the matter with the

LITTLE, J. — Polk, a minor, by his next friend instituted an action against the manufacturing company to recover damages for personal injuries. He alleged that the corporation owned and controlled a cotton factory; that on a named date, while he was an employee and servant of the company, and under its direction and control, he was injured in working in defendant's factory, without fault on his part, by the negligence of defendant in not furnishing proper machinery, and because the company, with knowledge thereof, permitted the machinery to get out of repair, and failed, after reasonable notice, to repair and make the same safe. His injuries he alleged were permanent, in that his hand was mashed by certain cogwheels used to apply power to the machinery, which were not suitably protected. At the time he was injured he was thirteen years of age. His capacity to labor by reason of the injury was permanently diminished, etc. At the time he sustained the injury he was acting within the scope of his employment, and did not know of the defective condition of the machinery; nor did he have the same means of knowing the defects in the same that the company had, etc. The defendant denied all the allegations of the petition,

car, other than the brake, that he knew of; that, so far as he knew, the car was in good condition, and equipped with the proper machinery. The brake appliances would not stop the car on the occasion that he was hurt. That was all he knew. They had held the car before when he operated it, and had not failed to hold prior to that occasion. He had not used the car on the day on which he was hurt, previous to the time he was hurt. He had used it the week previous, but did not remember the day. He had opportunities to see it frequently. He used it, you might say, daily, and sometimes more than once a day. He never noticed anything wrong with the brake before that day, and did not notice anything wrong with it before the accident that day. If there was anything wrong he never knew it. The car had been operated by him without any trouble before, and its movements were controlled by the same brake all the time up to that time. He had the brakes on when he first started down, and when he got to the crest of the hill he lost control of the movements of the car. There was testimony from an employee of the railway company that after the accident he examined the car, and found that some of the nuts needed tightening up, which was done, and that it was necessary to take up 'some slack in the brake. The slack was in the rod that goes from the brake beam to the lever.' This witness also testified that 'if the rod was slack, you would have to pull the lever a little farther than if it was tight, and, if the iron rods were slack, you might pull the lever clean back, and it would not give power enough to stop the wheel;' that when he worked on the brake, which was two days after the accident, there was nothing the matter with the car, except the slack above referred to; and that the effect of this slack would be that the lever would have to be pushed farther back. There appear in the record photographs of the car and the tracks and the place at which the accident occurred. The plaintiff alleged in his petition that the defendant was negligent in two particulars:

except the facts that the plaintiff was a minor, and that he was injured by one of the machines in its factory, and, as a special defense, averred that the plaintiff was not in its employ at the time he received his injuries, but was under the care of his father, who was employed in the mill. for the purpose of working under his instruction in order to learn the business of a mill operative, and that the injuries were occasioned entirely by the negligence of the plaintiff. By amendment the plaintiff averred, as an additional ground of negligence on the part of the defendant, that the covering to certain cogwheels (being the machinery by which he was injured) was, at the time he received the injury, made with wooden boxes, and that iron or metal caps should have been provided by the defendant to cover such cogwheels. The defendant objected to the amendment on the ground that it set forth a new and distinct cause of action. The objection was overruled and the amendment was allowed, and the defendant excepted *pendente lite*, and in its bill of exceptions assigns error on the allowance of the amendment. The trial resulted in a verdict for the plaintiff in the sum of $875.

First, that the defendant negligently furnished unsafe machinery and appliances for the use of the plaintiff, and an unsafe place for him to work; that the appliances, means, and brakes for stopping the car which were furnished to him were not sufficient for that purpose; and, second, that the defendant negligently failed to inspect and superintend the machinery and appliances which were furnished to the plaintiff, and, if these appliances and machinery had been inspected, the defect in them could have been discovered by the defendant." * * * It was held (as per syllabus by the court) as follows:

"1. Even if the defendant was negligent in furnishing to the plaintiff an improper appliance, the plaintiff had equal opportunity with the defendant of discovering the defect in the appliance furnished, and the defendant was therefore not liable for an injury resulting from this defect.

"2. Considering the evidence as a whole, it appears that the injury to the plaintiff was not occasioned by negligence on the part of either the defendant or the plaintiff, but that it was the result of an accident.

"3. Whether the case be considered in the light of the evidence introduced, or in the light of the evidence admitted as well as that which was rejected, the railway company was not liable to the plaintiff, and the court did not err in granting a nonsuit."

In DE LAY *v.* SOUTHERN R'Y CO. *(Georgia, July, 1902)*, 42 S. E. Rep. 218, judgment for defendant was affirmed (PER CURIAM), the syllabus by the court holding as follows: "Though there was evidence showing that the plaintiff was injured by reason of a defect in the implement furnished him with which to work, by his master, the defendant, yet, as it did not appear that the latter either knew, or, in the exercise of ordinary care and diligence, ought to have known, of such defect, and it did appear from the plaintiff's own testimony that he had equal means with the master of ascertaining the existence of the defect, the judgment of nonsuit was right. Civ. Code, secs. 2611, 2612."

The defendant submitted a motion for a new trial on forty-three grounds. Among them, complaint is made that the verdict was contrary to the evidence and the law, and was excessive. Inasmuch as the judgment overruling the motion for a new trial is reversed, and another trial of the case will be had, we do not deal with these grounds of the motion. Neither do we pass on the grounds of the motion, in which we find no error in any other than in a general way.

1. The evidence was conflicting on the material issues raised by the pleadings, and, of course, a nonsuit should not have been granted. We do not think the trial judge erred in refusing to enforce the rule as to the separation of witnesses, so as to exclude Polk, the father of the minor and his next friend, by whom the suit was instituted, from the court room, while the witnesses were being examined. Aside from being a matter largely in the discretion of the court, it would seem that the presence of the father and next friend might be necessary in the conduct of the case for the plaintiff. We do not find any error, under the explanation of the trial judge, in the admission of the evidence of Polk in relation to the defective condition of the boxing over the cogwheels, except possibly that part in which he testified from information received from another employee. While this was erroneous, it does not afford a sufficient reason to cause a reversal. We are not prepared to say that the court erred in instructing the jury in relation to the rule for determining what is ordinary or due care in the case of a minor; nor in the general rule which was announced, that the master owes to the servant the duty of furnishing machinery reasonably safe and suitable for the work being carried on; nor in relation to the duty of the company to instruct a minor of tender years as to the dangers incident to the operation of the machinery where he was employed; nor as to what would or would not constitute the plaintiff a servant of the company; nor that the fault of the father would not be attributable to the son if he was in the employment of the defendant; nor in the charge on the subject of damages; nor the instructions given in relation to the impeachment of witnesses. While the rulings set out in the grounds of the motion referring to the above subjects may in a few instances be the subject of legitimate criticism, they are not, as they appear, sufficient to authorize a reversal of the judgment; and, without further reference to them, we pass to those grounds which we think present sufficient merit to authorize the grant of a new trial.

2. The thirteenth ground of the amended motion for a new trial complains that the judge erred in instructing the jury as follows: "The law is that a master is liable to a servant for injuries that may

be inflicted upon the servant by reason of defective machinery, if the master has been negligent, whether in failing to provide machinery reasonably safe for the work, or to keep the machinery in proper repair. If a master has been negligent in either of these particulars, and the servant is injured in consequence of that negligence, then the master would be liable for the damages incurred by reason of the injury." This proposition is not sound, as a matter of law, because one very important and essential element in determining the right of a servant to recover from the master for injuries received because of the use of defective machinery is omitted. It is declared by sec. 2612 of the Civil Code that, in suits for injuries arising from the negligence of the master in failing to furnish machinery reasonably safe to be operated with ordinary care and diligence, it must appear not only that the master knew or ought to have known of the defects or dangers in the machinery supplied, but "it must also appear that the servant injured did not know, and had not equal means of knowing, such fact, and by the exercise of ordinary care could not have known thereof." The same criticism is applicable to the sixteenth and seventeenth grounds of the amended motion for a new trial. The propositions stated in the charge excepted to in each of these grounds were too broad, and are not the law of the case, unless they are coupled with the qualification which appears in the Code. As a matter of law, if the injured servant did know or had equal means of knowing the defects in the machinery, then, notwithstanding the master may have known of them, and been negligent in not furnishing machinery reasonably safe to be operated by employees using ordinary care and diligence, the servant cannot recover. In this connection it may be said that the care and diligence which are required of a minor employee thirteen years old are not left to be determined by an arbitrary rule based on age alone, nor is it a sound proposition of law that none is required of him. On the contrary, such a minor, if he has sufficient capacity to know the danger and to observe due care for his own protection, and voluntarily goes into danger, cannot recover (Railroad Co. *v.* Rylee, 87 Ga. 495); and the jury, in the case of a minor of this age, who, having been injured, sues to recover damages, must find from the evidence whether the child has sufficient capacity to know the danger and to observe due care for his own protection. (Id.) See also Rhodes *v.* Railroad Co., 84 Ga. 320; Wynne *v.* Conklin, 86 Ga. 40. We have examined carefully the entire charge, with a view of ascertaining whether the qualification above referred to was anywhere so made as that the jury could have understood that the parts of the charge above referred to were to be taken and construed with any qualification; and, while we find in other parts of the charge some reference to the rule that, if the servant had equal means with the master of ascertaining the defects of the machinery, he could not recover, we have reached the conclusion that the proposition contained in the charges above mentioned, not being coupled with this qualification, were error. The propositions charged as the law governing the rights of the parties, as contained in these grounds of the motion, are concisely stated, and made in plain and emphatic language, and so prominently set forth that we are unable reasonably to assume that the jury did understand that they were to be accepted with the qualifications mentioned, which were only incidentally referred to in another part of the charge. As they stand, they are error, and the error is material. They should not have been given without qualification, and, in order to prevent a misunderstanding of the law by the jury, the important principle of law which controls their application should have been given in the same connection.

3. It is further complained that the court erred in giving to the jury the following charge: "If you find from the evidence in this case that this plaintiff * * * was, at the time of the injury, thirteen years of age, and if you further find from the evidence that the plaintiff was only a volunteer in the factory of the defendant at the time of the injury, he (the plaintiff) would, though a volunteer, not be held responsible for his acts and conduct at the time of the injury, unless it be shown you by the proof that he knew at that time the distinction between good and evil, and also had capacity to comprehend the danger and avoid the same." Aside from any other criticism of this part of the charge, it is sufficient to say that the plaintiff in this case based his right to recover on the allegation that he was in the employment of the company at the time he was injured, and that the latter was negligent in failing to furnish him, as an employee, machinery reasonably safe for the work in which he was engaged, and to keep the same in good repair. Under the petition, if plaintiff was entitled to recover, he could only do so on the ground that he was an employee, and injured by the negligence of the master. There is no allegation that the company owed him any other duty than as its employee. It is true that defendant denied the employment, and averred that plaintiff was, at the time he was injured, a mere volunteer. This averment was in direct response to the allegation that he was in the employment of the company when injured, and, if it was sustained by the evidence, then the plaintiff could not lawfully have recovered in this action, because no negligence was charged against the master, from which

injuries resulted to the plaintiff, except as an employee; and while the question whether he was an employee or a volunteer was raised by the answer, and while the issue thus raised was a proper subject-matter of inquiry, if it had been satisfactorily proved that the plaintiff was a volunteer, and not a servant of the defendant, he would have had no right of recovery under the allegations in his petition. The jury might well have understood from this charge that, even if the evidence showed that the plaintiff was a volunteer, he could recover under given circumstances. So understood, the charge was error. Whether so understood or not, it was at least susceptible of such construction, and should not have been given in this case.

In view of the errors specifically referred to, the trial judge erred in overruling the motion for a new trial. Judgment reversed. All the justices concurring, except LEWIS, J., absent on account of sickness.

YORK v. PACIFIC AND IDAHO NORTHERN RAILWAY COMPANY.

Supreme Court, Idaho, June, 1902.

CHILD FATALLY INJURED WHILE PLAYING ON TURNTABLE — DAMAGES. — 1. A motion for a nonsuit should not be granted when there is any evidence to sustain the allegations of the complaint.

2. Where there is a substantial conflict in the evidence, the verdict of the jury will not be disturbed.

3. Where it is shown that the death of a child is caused by negligence of the defendant, and the jury find a verdict for the sum of $2,000, *held* not to be excessive damages (1).

SULLIVAN, J., dissenting.

(Syllabus by the Court.)

APPEAL from District Court, Washington County.

Action by George B. York against the Pacific & Idaho Northern Railway Company. From judgment for plaintiff, defendant appeals. *Judgment affirmed.*

J. H. RICHARDS and N. M. RUICK, for appellant.

RHEA & LOVEJOY, for respondent.

STOCKSLAGER, J. — This is an appeal from an order overruling a motion for a new trial and from the judgment. The complaint

1. See note on LIABILITY OF RAILROAD COMPANIES FOR ACCIDENTS TO CHILDREN ON TURNTABLES, in 9 AM. NEG. REP. 611–616, in which many of the authorities referred to in the opinion in the case at bar are cited.

alleges that defendant is a corporation existing under the laws of Idaho; that on the 13th day of May, 1900, defendant owned and operated a railroad and equipments, including tracks, depots, turntable, etc., between the city of Weiser and town of Cambridge, all in said county of Washington, State of Idaho; that among the equipments of said railroad so owned and operated by defendant was a turntable, theretofore, to wit, prior to May 30, 1900, unlawfully, carelessly, and negligently constructed and placed by said defendant in a public and much-frequented place by men and women and children in the said town of Cambridge, and there suffered to remain by defendant, so carelessly, unlawfully, and negligently constructed and so owned and operated by it, said defendant, as to make the same a dangerous machine to all persons, but more especially children frequenting said place; that said turntable, when constructed in the manner aforesaid, was, and on said 13th day of May, 1900, remained and was, a large oblong frame, mostly iron, forty-nine and one-half feet in length by thirteen and one-half feet in width, rounded slightly at the ends so as to permit it to revolve past the respective ends of the main track, with an iron railroad track upon its top for locomotives to rest upon while being turned around, and revolving upon a central pivot by means of hand levers at the ends, the frame part planked on the cross-ties on the ends and sides for walking or sitting upon, and the whole resting in a pit or round hole in the ground, and the ends of the stationary railroad track at the place of approach at each end of said turntable square, while the ends of the turntable were slightly rounded as aforesaid to permit the revolving of same, leaving a space between the revolving ends and the said stationary ends of seven and one-half inches at the four rounded corners, and two and one-half inches where the tracks came together in place, and said turntable thus constructed, owned, and operated by defendant became and was at all times hereinbefore stated an attractive, alluring, and very dangerous object and machine for all persons, and especially children of tender years, to play with and ride upon, as a merry-go-round, and in any manner; that defendant well knew, through its officers, agents, and employees, at all times when it so constructed, owned, and operated and maintained said turntable, that a child sitting upon either corner end of said planks upon said turntable, with its feet and legs hanging downward, and said turntable being turned, and its legs could not pass between the ends of said turntable and the main stationary track at such ends without crushing its legs, and defendant, notwithstanding such knowledge, by and through its said officers, agents, and employees, did wrongfully, unlawfully, carelessly, and negligently so construct, own, operate, and maintain said turntable in a public place in said town of Cambridge in the manner aforesaid without warning signs, danger signs, and without fence, shield, or protection about said turntable, and without lock, and without any fastening whatever to prevent the same from being turned by children or others, except a rude wooden slot and wedge easily movable and unwedged by a child of tender years; that plaintiff on said 13th day of May, 1900, was a married man and the head of a family, and as such the father of an infant male child four years old, living at plaintiff's home in said county, named Joseph William York, now deceased, and who prior to said date had been and was a strong, healthy child, bright and smart in all ways, and a comfort to plaintiff, and capable of earning for plaintiff before its age of maturity large sums of money with physical and mental labors and energies, and thus adding much to the wealth, welfare, comfort, and happiness of plaintiff; that on said 13th day of May, 1900, without any fault or negligence on the part of plaintiff, and without knowledge on his part of the dangerous construction and character of said turntable, said infant child was carelessly, unlawfully, negligently, and wantonly permitted by defendant, its officers, agents, and employees, to go upon said turntable, and there sit upon the corner of one of said end planks, with its feet and legs hanging down while said turntable was carelessly, negligently, unlawfully, and wantonly permitted and allowed by defendant, its said officers, agents, and employees, to be turned, and there so permitted to remain until both of its legs were crushed by the close jam of said turntable, and from which said crushing said child soon thereafter, and on said 13th day of May, 1900, died, and plaintiff thereby became and was deprived of the services of said child during its minority, and the comfort, support, and happiness of its society, to his damage in the sum of $5,000. Then follows prayer for judgment. Complaint verified. The answer "denies each and every allegation in said complaint contained."

Upon these issues a trial was had, and the jury returned a verdict in favor of the plaintiff for the sum of $2,000. A statement of the case was settled by the court, and thereafter, and on the 7th day of January, 1902, the motion for a new trial was overruled, and an appeal from said order taken to this court.

There are four assignments of error. The first is:

"1. Excessive damages, appearing to have been given under the influence of passion or prejudice, and in particular as follows: First. That the verdict, as to the amount of damages given, is not sustained by the evidence.

"2. Insufficiency of the evidence to justify the verdict, and in particular as follows: First. The evidence shows that the child killed was less than five years of age, and there is no evidence showing the probable life of such child, or condition of the parents of such child, as to whether such parents were likely to become in any manner dependent upon such child for support, or what were the conditions of the parents or child as to the probable earning capacity of said child.

"3. That such verdict is against the law, and in particular as follows: First. That the evidence in no wise shows that the defendant in any manner failed to construct or maintain the turntable in question in a manner or in a location that rendered the same dangerous, or that it failed to keep said turntable fastened as such turntables should be fastened to render it reasonably safe. Second. That such evidence shows that the turntable in question was, immediately prior to the accident alleged, fastened in such manner as to render the same safe and as such turntables are usually fastened. Third. That the evidence shows that the child sustaining the injury alleged was less than five years of age, and was taken by the plaintiff and the mother of such child near such turntable, and permitted to play upon such turntable with other children, with the full knowledge of plaintiff and the mother of such child, and without any one to look after or guard such infant from danger; and the evidence further shows that both the plaintiff and the mother of such child knew that said turntable was a dangerous thing, when unfastened, for little children to play with; and the evidence further shows that said plaintiff and the mother of such child knew that said turntable was unfastened while such child was playing there; and the evidence fails to show that the defendant has any knowledge that such children were playing with such turntable, or that such turntable was unfastened at or about the time of said alleged injury.

"4. Errors of law occurring at the trial, and excepted to by defendant, and in particular as follows: First. The court erred in admitting in evidence, and over the objection of defendant, the testimony of H. M. St. Cyr as to whether or not, prior to the time of the alleged accident, he had seen any men, women, or children playing on that turntable. Second. The court erred in admitting in evidence, and over the objection of defendant, the testimony of Charles A. Colson as to whether he had ever seen any ladies on the turntable in question at any other time than the day of the alleged accident. Third. The court erred in refusing to admit the evidence of —— Briggs as to the kind of fastening the turntable in Boise had to keep it from turning when an engine goes on or off, and to which refusal counsel for defendant excepted. Fourth. The court erred in overruling the motion of defendant to enter a judgment of non-suit against the plaintiff. Fifth. The court erred in refusing the instructions to the jury requested by the defendant and refused by the court."

We will consider the errors assigned as urged by counsel for appellant in their brief. The first is that the court erred in the admission of the testimony of witness St. Cyr at folios 48 to 53. This testimony relates to the fact that prior to the time of the accident to the deceased child witness had some ladies on the turntable, and it was being revolved by young men, using it as a merry-go-round. This was on Sunday, a week prior to the day of the accident. There were no inclosures or signs about the table at that time. Was familiar with the trail leading from road from Salubria across the railroad track. The turntable pit as it was constructed cut the path in two, and it was necessary to go around it. This evidence was introduced as shown by the record, to show that the turntable was in a public place frequented by people residing in that community, and that there were no danger signs or anything to warn the people of danger. We see no error in this ruling of the court for the purposes for which it was admitted. The court said: "If it was to show that it was frequented by people for amusement, and by reason of that fact was enticing to children, it was proper for that purpose." It is true that defendant was engaged in a lawful business, as urged by counsel for appellant, but that does not relieve it of the duty it owes to the public to use all reasonable means to protect the people from injury. This obligation rests on all alike, corporations as well as individuals.

The next contention is that deceased was a trespasser upon the property of appellant at the time of the injury complained of. It is not shown that there was any reason for any one to think that it was a trespass to go upon this turntable any more than to walk upon the track of appellant. It is shown that there were no obstructions to any one going upon the turntable, and that there were no signs warning people of danger. It is also shown that people were in the habit of going upon the turntable and using it as a merry-go-round, and that it was an attractive place for children.

The next contention is that there was no attempt on the part of respondent to show that appellant had any knowledge that any person had ever trespassed upon such property or played upon such table at any time. It is clearly the duty of appellant or any other corporation or individual to protect life and property in all reasonable ways, and under this rule was it not the duty of appellant to so construct its turntable as to protect even trespassers (if one entering thereupon was a trespasser) from injury, and is this not especially true when it is shown that the turntable was located in a community thickly populated? We think it was. It is true that the evidence is conflicting as to the manner of construction of the turntable, but the jury passed upon that question as well as all the questions of fact submitted to them, and we do not feel authorized to disturb their findings.

The next assignment of error to which our attention is called by appellant is that "the court erred in overruling the motion of defendant to enter a judgment of nonsuit against plaintiff." This motion was presented to the trial court, and by it overruled. Thereafter the defendant introduced a number of witnesses, and hence did not stand upon the motion and order of the court overruling it. The question arises, when the appellant refused to stand on the order of the court overruling the motion for a nonsuit, and thereafter introduced evidence in the case, is not all the evidence in the case before us for review? To say the least, under the rule laid down that, where there is any legal or competent evidence to support a verdict, a motion for nonsuit should be overruled, we think the rule should prevail in this case. Our attention is called to Railroad Co. *v.* Holt, 40 Pac. Rep. 56, a decision of this court. The syllabus says: Where damage is claimed for death of a minor child by reason of the negligence and carelessness of defendant, it must affirmatively appear from the evidence that the accident resulted from the negligence and carelessness of the defendant, and that the imprudence or negligence of the plaintiff did not contribute to the result. This is undoubtedly the correct rule. In that case a child was drowned in a well "on the private grounds of defendant, and remote from any street or sidewalk, and at the time of the accident the child was not traveling on any public street or sidewalk but was on the private land of defendant, without the knowledge, invitation, or consent of defendant. Nor is it shown that the defendant had any machinery or other improvements upon said lot whatever that would attract children there." It was also shown that the well had been frequently covered with planks and cord wood, and the danger thus obviated, but removed by campers, etc. Our attention is next called to McEachern *v.* Boston & Maine R. R. Co., 150 Mass. 515. In this case it was alleged that defendant left a freight car standing on a side track, and left the door, which it knew was not properly attached to the car, to remain open and unlocked, knowing that it would be an enticing object to children, and that a boy eleven years old passing by saw the door open, and looked in, and in so doing carefully touched the door, which fell upon him, and it was held to state no cause of action. This car was only temporarily upon the side track, likely to be removed at any time, and we do not think the rule there enunciated applicable to this case. In Curley *v.* Railroad Co., 98 Mo. 13, a boy ten years old, with others, entered an empty box car, standing upon a railroad track, which was being made up into a train, and was pushed off by one of his companions after the train was in motion, the trainmen having no knowledge of their presence, and it was held he cannot recover. We cannot see where this case applies to the case at bar. Counsel cite Railroad Co. *v.* McLaughlin, 44 Ill. 215. We find no such case reported in that volume. In Nolan *v.* Railroad Co., 53 Conn. 461, it is held that the question of negligence is a mixed one of law and fact; that a railroad should always be diligent to prevent accidents, but owes no duty as such to run its trains so as to prevent accidents to persons unnecessarily and unlawfully on its tracks. The fact that a child is but seven years of age does not create a duty toward him on the part of the company that would not otherwise have existed. The care which plaintiff must have exercised to be free from the imputation of contributory negligence is reasonable care, which is that degree of care which may reasonably be expected from a person in his situation. Railroad Co. *v.* Bell, 81 Ill. 76, holds that where a turntable not covered with planks or walled, except where the rails of the switch intersected, was constructed, not near to any public street or place where the public were in the habit of passing, but in an isolated place, and a boy was seriously injured while he, with others, was turning and riding upon it, it also appearing it was latched, but not locked, that, in view of the isolated position of the table, the railway company was not guilty of such negligence as to render it liable. See Boland *v.* Railroad Co., 36 Mo. 484; Bransom's Adm'r *v.* Labrot, 81 Ky. 638; Powers *v.* Harlow, 53 Mich. 507; Meeks *v.* So. Pac. R. R. Co., 56 Cal. 513, 11 Am. Neg. Cas. 226; Kan. Cent. R'y Co. *v.* Fitzsimmons, 22 Kan. 686; Keffe *v.* Mil. & St. P. R'y Co., 21 Minn. 207; Sioux City & P. R. R. Co. *v.* Stout, 17 Wall. 657; Barrett *v.* So. Pac. Co., 91 Cal. 296; Atch. & Neb. R. R. Co. *v.* Bailey, 11 Neb. 332 (1).

The next question urged by appellant is that respondent was negligent and imprudent, and thereby contributed to the accident complained of, and that it affirmatively appears from the testimony of respondent that such negligence and imprudence bars a recovery, and hence the motion for nonsuit should have been sustained. A

1. See abstracts of the cases cited in the opinion in the case at bar, in the NOTE ON TURNTABLE CASES, 9 AM. NEG. REP. 611–616.

review of the evidence discloses that the turntable was constructed near the village of Salubria; that tents were close by, in which people lived; it was close to the public highway, and near the ball ground; that there were no danger signs or warnings to "keep off;" that people were in the habit of using it; that it was fastened with a slot or piece of board two by four inches, two feet long, and that it was dangerous, as shown by the testimony of witness St. Cyr, that respondent went there on the day of the accident with his wife and the deceased; that after remaining in the wagon awhile he got out, and engaged in the game of ball, leaving his wife and the deceased in the wagon; that the child got out of the wagon, got upon the turntable, and received the injury which caused its death. The father and mother saw other people upon the turntable at the time or just before the injury. Did they contribute to the injury by their carelessness or negligence under such circumstances, and was it a question of fact for the jury to determine? We are of the opinion that it was, and the motion for a nonsuit was properly overruled. Deering, Neg., sec. 403; Carter *v.* Oil Co., 34 S. C. 211; Deans *v* Wilm. & W. R. R. Co., 107 N. C. 686, 12 Am. Neg. Cas 401; Thoresen *v.* La Crosse City R'y Co., 87 Wis. 597 (12 Am. Neg. Cas. 657n).

The next question urged is that the court erred in refusing to instruct the jury to return a verdict in favor of appellant, and cites Thomas *v.* Irrigation Co., 63 Pac. Rep. 595. This case holds that when an action is brought to recover damages for the negligent and careless construction and maintenance of a foot bridge, and the evidence wholly fails to establish the allegations of the complaint in that regard, the judgment for plaintiff must be reversed; also when there is no substantial conflict in the evidence, and the verdict of the jury is contrary to such evidence, a judgment based upon said verdict will be reversed upon appeal. We think this opinion correctly states the law, but the facts in that case and the one at bar differ very materially, as we construe the record in the case at bar and the facts in that case. We do not think the evidence shows that appellant was blameless in the construction and maintenance of the turntable. On the other hand, we think it establishes that the appellant was careless and negligent in the construction, and especially the maintenance of the turntable, in that it did not have proper and sufficient appliances for fastening the turntable, and that it had no danger signs or anything to warn the people to keep off, and when we consider the public place on which it was constructed, and the fact that it was frequented by the people in that community, it was the duty of appellant to take every precaution to warn people of the danger of going upon or riding thereon, even though it be a trespass to do so.

Appellant complains that the damages were excessive, and that the verdict should have been set aside, and a new trial awarded on this ground, if no other. We cannot agree with this contention. The evidence shows that the child was a stout, healthy child, with ordinary faculties, and less than five years of age. Plaintiff asked for $5,000 damages, and the jury awarded him $2,000, and we see no good reason why this court should disturb the judgment of the lower court upon the showing made by appellant. An inspection of the entire record and the authorities cited by both appellant and respondent does not justify us in saying that appellant's motion for a new trial should have been sustained.

The judgment of the lower court is affirmed. Costs to respondent.

QUARLES, CH. J. — I concur in the conclusion reached in this case, and agree with the reasoning of my associate who has written the main opinion, and think the authorities fully sustain the conclusion reached. I have carefully read and reread the evidence in this case. In my opinion, the claim of the appellant that the death of the deceased child is attributable to contributory negligence on the part of the plaintiff is not sustained by the evidence. The plaintiff testified that he went with his family to Cambridge to witness a game of baseball; that he, his wife and children and the hired man remained in his wagon for awhile before the game commenced; that he was chosen to play on one side, and left his wagon and engaged in the game; that he did not permit the deceased, a boy less than five years old, to leave the wagon; that while he was playing ball he heard some children laughing and making a noise, and looked back of where he was standing, and saw about twenty-five children playing on the turntable, and thought he recognized his little boy among them, and then started to the wagon, when immediately he heard his wife screaming, and saw a lad carrying his little son, and went to him, and found him crushed and so injured that he died about three hours afterwards; that he did not know up to that time the dangerous nature of turntables. There was evidence contradictory to the statements of plaintiff, but it is apparent that the jury were authorized to and did believe and accept the statements of the plaintiff as true. I am not in sympathy with the idea that it is the duty of a parent to keep his child in sight all of the time, and hold it by the hand, in order to protect it from unsuspected dangers. Nor can I give my assent to the establishment of a rule which would preclude a recovery in cases like the one before us, because forsooth a parent could have prevented the injury by keeping his child at home or imprisoned in some way so that he could not go upon a highway and witness games of sport and indulge in other innocent amusements. If the plaintiff knowingly sent his little son into danger, or knowingly permitted him to go upon the turntable knowing it to be dangerous, he could not and should not recover in this case.

The turntable in question was a dangerous instrument, insecurely fastened, in its very nature attractive to children, was located in a public place, and the agents and employees of the defendant corporation knew its dangerous character, and knew that it was frequented by people in the vicinity and used by them for amusement.

The construction of the machine was such that the distance between it and the frame in which it revolved was greater on one side than on the other, so much so that the limb of a person, and the body of the deceased, could be caught between the table and the frame around it. This fact, and the fact that children could revolve it, made it so dangerous that it became the duty of the defendant to keep it so secured that it would be safe. It would be no more difficult or inconvenient to keep this turntable locked than it is to keep a switch which is in constant use locked. It is usual, if not universal, for railroad companies to keep switches which are in constant use locked. The use of a lock upon this turntable would have prevented the accident, and the failure of the defendant to so secure the said turntable is negligence. My attention has been called to the decision in Edgington *v.* Burl., C. R. & N. R'y Co., 90 N. W. Rep. 95 (1), recently decided by the Supreme Court of Iowa, and which is directly in point, where all of the authorities

1. In EDGINGTON *v.* BURLINGTON, CEDAR RAPIDS & NORTHERN R'Y CO. *(Iowa, April, 1902)*, 90 N. W. Rep. 95, an action for injuries received by plaintiff, a child between seven and eight years of age, while playing on defendant's turntable, judgment for plaintiff rendered in the District Court, Muscatine county, was affirmed. The facts of the case, as stated in the opinion by WEAVER, J., were as follows: "The defendant company owns and operates a line of railroad entering the city of Muscatine, Iowa. In connection with its station and yards at this place, it maintains and uses a turntable, a well-known machine or device for turning locomotives. This table turns about a central point or axis, and, when unfastened, is easily revolved by hand power applied to bars or levers. At and prior to the time of the accident upon which this action is based the table, when not in use, was ordinarily fastened by a pin, bolt, or latch of some kind, the exact description of which is not disclosed by the record before us. This machine stood upon an unfenced lot, owned by the defendant, near the line of a public alley, and at a distance from the street variously estimated at from 80 to 300 feet. Children of the neighborhood were to some considerable degree in the habit of passing through the alley, and at times loitered and played upon and about the turntable. This practice does not seem to have been with the express knowledge or consent of the defendant, and upon at least one occasion its employees drove the children away. There was a box factory not far distant,

that support the conclusion reached in this case, as well as those opposed, are carefully reviewed.

SULLIVAN, J. — I dissent from the conclusion reached by my associates. The deceased child was taken by its parents to witness a game of baseball. The father entered the game, and left the child in the wagon with the mother and older children. It also appears that said turntable was locked with a piece of wood two by four inches, and from sixteen to twenty-four inches long, and some meddler had removed it. Had it been left as the appellant left it, the accident could not have occurred. It also appears that the older brother or brothers of the deceased child were revolving the turntable when the accident occurred. The rule laid down by my associates charged the duty of protecting children upon every member of the community except upon their parents, which I do not believe to be the correct rule.

The judgment ought to be reversed.

to which also children resorted by way of the alley, and near the turntable, to gather scraps of wood for fuel. On the 16th day of June, 1899, the plaintiff, then a child of seven years and eight months, living in that neighborhood, started from her home, with several little girls somewhat older, intending to go to the box factory for wood. Passing down the alley, they stopped to play about the turntable. One of them removed the bolt or catch which fastened the machine, and soon afterward two small boys arrived, and began to revolve it, while the other children rode upon the platform or frame. Under these circumstances the plaintiff in some manner stepped or fell into the space between the outer edge of the table and the wall of the pit in which it revolved, receiving severe, painful, and permanent injuries. Negligence is charged against the defendant upon the theory or claim that the turntable was a dangerous machine, and of such nature and construction as to be specially attractive to children; and that, having placed it upon an open lot near a public way, where they might reasonably be expected to pass or gather to play, it was defendant's duty to use reasonable care to so guard or fasten said machine as to prevent injury to young and inexperienced children who might be tempted to play upon it. Defendant denies that it was charged with any such duty, and denies that it failed to exercise all reasonable and proper care in the premises. It further insists that the children, in playing upon the turntable, were trespassers, and the law imposed upon the defendant no duty to exercise any care for their safety except to refrain from wilful or wanton injury to them after discovering them upon its property. It also claims that in entering upon the company's property without permission and in playing upon the turntable the plaintiff was guilty of contributory negligence, and therefore is not entitled to recover damages." * * *

The learned judge, in the course of his opinion, entered into a long and exhaustive discussion on the liability for "turntable accidents," and in an able review of the authorities covered the American decisions during the last thirty years, and also treated the question of duty which a property owner may owe to an infant, citing numerous American and English authorities.

CHICAGO, ROCK ISLAND AND PEORIA RAILWAY COMPANY v. DURAND ET AL.

Supreme Court, Kansas, July, 1902.

COLLISION BETWEEN PUBLIC HACK AND TRAIN AT STREET CROSSING — PASSENGER INJURED — NEGLIGENCE OF DRIVER — PARTIES — SIGNAL — GATES. — 1. A driver of a hack carrying passengers, who negligently drives in front of an approaching train of cars at a street crossing, may be joined in an action against the railway company for negligently running into his hack to the injury of one of his passengers.

2. In an action against a railway company for negligently running its train on a traveler at a city street crossing without giving any signal of the train's approach, it is error to admit evidence of a like failure of the train to signal its approach to another street crossing in the city. Atch. Top. & S. F. R. R. Co. *v.* Hague, 54 Kan. 284, *overruled.*

3. In an action against a railway company for negligently running one of its trains on a traveler at a city street crossing, where the company was in the habit of operating gates across the street at certain hours of the day, but not at the time of the accident, it is error to refer to the jury the question whether the single isolated circumstance of failure to operate the gates at that time was negligence in the company (1).

(Syllabus by the Court.)

IN BANC. Error from Superior Court, Sedgwick county.

Action by C. G. Durand and others against the Chicago, Rock Island & Peoria Railway Company. From judgment for plaintiffs, defendant brings error. *Judgment reversed.*

M. A. LOW, W. F. EVANS and STANLEY, VERMILION & EVANS, for plaintiff in error.

HOUSTON & BROOKS, for defendants in error.

DOSTER, Ch. J. — This was an action for bodily injuries negligently inflicted upon plaintiff at a railroad and street crossing in the city of Wichita. There was a circus entertainment in the outskirts of the city. Albert Wilson was a hack driver carrying people to and from the city and circus grounds. The plaintiff and others were passengers in his conveyance. He negligently drove in front of a train as it was running over the crossing near the depot. The train approached the crossing without warning signals, and ran over it at

1. *Collisions and Crossings.* — See vols. 11 and 12 Am. Neg. Cas., where the cases relating to Collision and Crossing Accidents are chronologically grouped, from the earliest period to 1897, and arranged in alphabetical order of States. Subsequent actions on the same topics to date are reported in vols. 1-12 AM. NEG. REP., and the current numbers of that series of Reports.

a dangerously rapid speed, and struck the conveyance in which plaintiff was riding. These were the allegations of the petition made against the railway company and Wilson jointly. The defendants defended separately A verdict and judgment were rendered against them together, from which the company on its part has prosecuted error.

The counsel for the railway company intended to file a demurrer to the petition for misjoinder of causes of action, but inadvertently filed an answer. The making of this mistake was satisfactorily shown to the court, and leave asked to withdraw the answer and file a demurrer. The leave to do so was refused. This refusal constitutes the first claim of error. It will not be necessary to consider, in its ordinary aspect, the question of the court's abuse of discretion in refusing to allow the one pleading to be withdrawn and the other to be substituted. The court did not abuse its discretion if the demurrer, when filed, could not have been sustained; and that such could not have been done is reasonably clear. The objection is that the petition charges a separate independent tort on the part of both defendants, — Wilson for negligently driving the plaintiff into danger, the railway company for negligently running over him. It is true that the drivers of public conveyances, whether railway coaches or common vehicles, are individually responsible for the safety of their passengers; but so likewise are the drivers of other conveyances responsible to the former's passengers at points of collision or common danger. At such points there is a common and mutual duty of diligence and caution, because there, to the knowledge of each, a dangerous juxtaposition of their respective vehicles is liable to occur. In the case of a railroad and highway crossing there is a common point of danger against which there is a mutual and concurrent obligation to guard. That common point is the one of contact between the train and the vehicle. It is as though the injured person stood at that point, and the two rushed upon him with mutual design to crush him between them. From one he might escape, but not from the two together, seeking to compass his injury by the impact of their opposing forces. The rule of joint liability in such cases is stated in 3 Thomp. Negl., sec. 2781, with citations to many supporting decisions. The case of City cf Kansas *v.* File, 60 Kan. 157, applies the same general principle to a somewhat different state of facts. That the carrier of the passenger may be under a greater obligation of prudence and caution than the driver of the train or other vehicle does not change the rule of joint liability. The carrier may be required to use extraordinary care; the other only ordinary care. That, however, does not excuse the latter from using such measure of caution as the law imposes on him. It is no answer to him to say that, while he failed to observe the minor degree of prudence required of him, the other party failed to observe the greater degree required of him. The question of joint liability in such cases cannot be affected by the comparative culpability of the offenders. If the neglect of one to exercise the extraordinary degree of diligence required of him conjoins with the neglect of another to use the lesser degree of diligence required of him, to the injury of a third person, such injury is none the less the single result of the two negligent acts or omissions of duty. It is well settled that the law will not undertake to apportion consequences between two or more persons jointly guilty of wrongful conduct towards another, though their contributions to the injury were in unequal degrees, or from different motives, and it must be that the same rule applies where the injury was wrought by the neglect of differing degrees of responsibility.

There is no statute or ordinance of the city of Wichita requiring trains to give warning signals of their approach to street crossings. It was, of course, a disputed question whether the trainmen gave any signals of their approach to the crossing of the street at which the accident occurred. About two-fifths of a mile before reaching that crossing there is another street, likewise running at a right angle with the track. Witnesses were allowed to testify that the employees operating the train in question failed to give any warning of their approach to that crossing. The admission of this character of evidence is defensible on the authority of the majority opinion in Atch., T. & S. F. R. R. Co. *v.* Hague, 54 Kan. 284, 38 Pac. Rep. 257 (11 Am. Neg. Cas. 570n), although in that case the two crossings were about a mile apart, and were in the country, where there is a statutory duty to give signals of approach to highway crossings. We think, however, the rule is the same in both kinds of cases. In one, as in the other, the evidence is offered for the purpose of laying a foundation from which to argue that, inasmuch as the railway company was negligent at one crossing, it was, therefore, negligent at the other one. It cannot be any the more admissible to prove the violation of a statutory duty at one place, or under one set of circumstances, in order to deduce the conclusion of a violation of the same kind of duty at another place, or under another set of circumstances, than it is to prove the violation of a merely moral duty at one place, or under one set of circumstances, in order to deduce the conclusion of its violation elsewhere, or under other circumstances. We are constrained to think that the majority holding in the case of Hague was wrong. Although supported by the decision of another State, it seems to us to be violative of a fundamental rule of evidence. "Ordinarily, when a party is sued for damages flowing from negligence imputed to him, it is irrelevant, for reasons already given, to prove against him other disconnected, though similar, negligent acts. Thus, in an action against a bailee for the loss of property intrusted to him, evidence of independent acts of negligence not connected with the loss is inadmissible. So, where the question, in a suit against a railway company, is whether a driver was negligent on a particular occasion, it is irrelevant to prove that he had been negligent on other occasions." 1 Whart. Ev., sec. 40. Analogous to this rule is the more familiar one which prohibits the proof against defendants in criminal trials of different and disconnected offenses, though of the same particular class. But these instances are applications of the general rule of inadmissibility of collateral incidents and circumstances to convict the party on trial, unless they, with the main incident, form connected parts of a common and designed system. Id., sec. 29. Now, two failures of a locomotive engineer to sound crossing signals, though quite closely connected in point of distance and time, do not evidence a systematic inattention to duty; nor do we think, as counsel do, that the inference of systematic neglect is aided by the fact that the engineer was slightly behind time, and was running through the city at more than usual speed, there being no evidence that such circumstances were conducive to the neglect of the duty in question.

There is no statute of the State or ordinance of the city requiring the maintenance of gates at street crossings. The court, however, gave to the jury the following instruction: "It is for you to determine, from all the circumstances surrounding the case, whether it was necessary for the defendant railway company, in the exercise of ordinary care by the company, to keep and maintain and operate gates after six o'clock in the evening on said railroad crossing. And if you so find, — that the exercise of ordinary care by the company required such maintenance and operation, — then it becomes the duty of the railway company to use reasonable care and foresight to avoid leaving said gates in such position, or managing them in such manner, as to needlessly mislead a traveler on the highway to his injury, and without his fault, into attempting to cross said railway track at a time when there was danger from approaching trains; that is, the company should do as a person of ordinary care and prudence would do under like circumstances." This instruction was erroneous, because it singled out a particular circumstance, not directly connected with the operation of the train, but collateral to its operation, and gave it to the jury as a fact upon which they might predicate a conclusion of wrong. There is much dispute as to the soundness of instructions of the character of the one above quoted. The court was not without abundant precedent for giving it. 2 Wood R'y Law, pp. 1313, 1314; 2 Thomp. Negl., sec. 1537. The better opinion, as it seems to us, is that the court should not submit isolated facts, apart from the main act of negligence, to wit, the careless operation of the train, as sufficient to justify a verdict. The point to the instruction in question is that under it the railway company was made liable for failure to shut down its gates, though it moved its train never so cautiously. In Grippen *v.* N. Y. Cent, R. R. Co., 40 N. Y. 34, (12 Am. Neg. Cas. 361n), the trial court said to the jury: "I leave it to you to say, under all the circumstances, whether a flagman at this station, as a measure of proper caution, was or was not required of defendant." This instruction was held to be erroneous, and the ruling there made has been followed in many subsequent cases in the courts of New York. The argument in one of these cases — McGrath *v.* N. Y. Cent., etc., R. R. Co., 63 N. Y. 522, (12 Am. Neg. Cas. 396n) — appears to us so strong and convincing that we quote much of it. Said the court: "Where there has been a collision at a railroad crossing with a traveler upon the highway, and the railroad company is sued for negligence in causing the collision, its negligence is made out generally by proving all the circumstances surrounding the transaction, and submitting them, with proper instructions, to the jury. It may be proved that the collision took place in the night-time, in a rainstorm; that the way to the accident would make the defendant liable, no matter how careful it may have been in running and managing the train, and in all other respects. Such effect is given to that omission of duty because the law imposes the duty and enacts the consequence for its omission. Under such a charge as I have supposed, the jury is put in the place of the legislature, and its decision as to the duty has the force of statute law; and hence such a charge has properly been condemned by the courts of this State. In another case the evidence is received, and the jury is charged that the defendant owed no duty to any one to keep a flagman at the crossing, but that its sole duty to travelers upon the highway was to run and manage its trains with proper care, so as not to injure them in the exercise of their lawful rights; and that upon the question whether such care was exercised they must consider all the circumstances existing at the time and place of the accident, and among them the fact of the absence of a flagman at the crossing. In such a case a proper use is made of the evidence, and the charge is liable to no just criticism. If the jury find such care was exercised, they will find for the defendant, whether there was a flagman at the crossing or not." The same holding has been made by other courts. Heddles *v.* Chicago & N. W. R'y Co., 74 Wis. 239 (12 Am. Neg. Cas. 658n); Winchell *v.* Abbot, 77 Wis. 371 (12 Am. Neg. Cas. 658n); Chicago & Iowa R. R. Co. *v.* Lane, 130 Ill. 116 (11 Am. Neg. Cas. 428n); Railroad Co. *v.* Luebeck, 157 Ill. 595, 41 N. E. Rep. 897; Lesan *v.* Me. Cent. R. R. Co., 77 Me. 85 (11 Am. Neg. Cas. 657n); Md. Cent. R. R. Co. *v.* Neubeuer, 62 Md. 391 (12 Am. Neg. Cas. 9n). To hold, as some courts have done, that the non-use of the accustomed gates at street crossings is a notice of safety to approaching travelers, and tantamount to an invitation to cross, impinges very closely upon, if not in reality abrogates, the rule which requires persons about to cross railway tracks to look and listen, and in some instances to stop in order to better do so. The doctrine that the single circumstance of leaving gates open may be accepted by the jury as sufficient evidence of negligence in the company in of a piece with that which acquits the traveler of negligence if he sees the gates open. They are both wrong. Of course, evidence in proof of the negligent omission to maintain gates at a street crossing is admissible, and in Kan. Pac. R'y Co. *v.* Richardson, 25 Kan. 391, (11 Am. Neg. Cas. 570n), it was held that such omission, although not specially alleged in the petition, was nevertheless included in the general charge of negligent operation of the train, and might be proved as one of the circumstances constituting the *res gestæ*. The implications from the language of the opinion in that case harmonize with the ruling we make in this one.

Many other claims of error are made. None of them impress us as substantial enough to constitute of themselves grounds for reversal, if, indeed, they be even technically correct. However, in one instance a witness was allowed to give his opinion as to the speed at which the train approached the crossing, without showing a sufficiently close observation of it, or thought at the time concerning it.

The judgment of the court below is reversed, and a new trial ordered. All the justices concurring.

CITY OF WICKLIFFE v. MORING.

Court of Appeals, Kentucky, June, 1902.

DEFECTIVE SIDEWALK — NOTICE TO CITY. — In an action to recover damages for injuries sustained by plaintiff, a girl twelve years of age, who fell on a sidewalk caused by a loose plank in such walk, it was held that it was for the jury, where there was conflicting evidence as to the length of time the defect had existed, to determine the question whether the city had notice of the defect or by the use of ordinary diligence might have had such notice, and could have repaired the defect before the injury occurred to plaintiff (1).

1. *Injured on defective sidewalk — Knowledge of defect — City not liable.* — In CITY OF COVINGTON v. MANWARING (*Kentucky, June, 1902*), 68 S. W. Rep. 625, judgment for plaintiff for $500 was reversed, the facts being stated in the opinion by HOBSON, J., as follows: "The plaintiff at the time of the injury was about nineteen years of age, and had worked for five or six months in a grocery store fronting on Greenup street. A large tree stood on the sidewalk just on the property line of this store lot, and a few feet beyond this tree from the store sat a barrel on the curb, in which were put ashes. The sidewalk was perhaps fifteen feet wide. About ten feet of it next to the fence was in excellent condition, and here was where most of the travel went. Around the tree the roots had raised the bricks in places, making them uneven. Some of the bricks were raised in this way from one-half inch to an inch, or something over. The plaintiff's main business was delivering the goods from the grocery, but he also swept out the store, swept off the sidewalk, and put ashes into the barrel at times. He says he did this about once a week. His employer says he did it four or five times a week. At the time he was injured he was going from the store to the ash barrel with some ashes in a dustpan to empty into it, holding the pan in front of him. As he passed along by the tree he struck his toe against one of the bricks that were raised, and fell upon the pavement with his knee in such a manner as to inflict a serious injury on the knee joint. The injury occurred at two o'clock in the afternoon, and, of course, if he had looked, he could have seen the condition of the bricks, and avoided falling over them. He testifies that he did not know that the bricks were raised or the pavement in a bad condition; but as he had worked in this store five or six months, and it was a part of his business to sweep off the sidewalk in front of it, which ran up to the tree on the side next to the store, he must be charged with knowledge of the condition of the pavement, and we must take his statement as meaning that he had never thought of the pavement as dangerous, or anticipated that he might fall over it as he did. For it is entirely incredible that one who had been about this store as long as he had, and had swept off the pavement as often as he had, could have failed to observe the effect of the roots of this tree on the brick. It was a large tree, and there was nothing to prevent his seeing the condition of the pavement, which was such as is not uncommon under such circumstances. The question then arises, is such a condition of

APPEAL from Circuit Court, Ballard County.

Action by Motelle Moring, by next friend, against the city of Wickliffe, to recover damages for personal injuries. From judgment for plaintiff, defendant appeals. *Judgment affirmed.*

BUGG & WICKLIFFE, for appellant.

WM. DANCE, for appellee.

BURNAM, J. — The appellee, Motelle Moring, a girl twelve years of age, brought this suit by next friend to recover damages for injuries alleged to have resulted from a fall caused by a loose plank in the sidewalk on Front street, in the city of Wickliffe. She testified that whilst coming from school with one of her companions she met a colored woman, who stepped upon one end of a loose plank in the sidewalk as she stepped upon the other end; that the plank flew up, caught her leg, and threw her down. She also testified that there were three or four loose planks in the sidewalk near the one which threw her down; that, as a result, her spine was seriously hurt. Her statements are fully corroborated by her companion, Gracie Bayne. And there is testimony to the effect that this defect in the sidewalk had existed for some time, although the mayor, street superintendent, and other officials of the city testified that they were not aware that such condition existed. The trial court gave

a pavement in a city a ground of recovery against the city, in favor of one who has notice, or must be charged with notice, of its condition, and in daylight stumbles over it from inadvertence? In Town of Gosport *v.* Evans, 112 Ind. 134, the court said: "While a municipal corporation is required to exercise vigilance in keeping its streets and sidewalks in a reasonably safe condition for public travel by night as well as by day, it is by no means an insurer against accidents; nor can it be expected to maintain the surface of its sidewalks free from all inequalities, and from every possible obstruction to mere convenient travel. A contrary rule would or might burden municipal corporations beyond endurance. That a pavement may have become uneven from use, or that bricks therein may have become loose or displaced by the action of the elements, so that persons are liable to stumble or be otherwise inconvenienced in passing, does not necessarily involve the municipality in liability, so long as the defect can be readily discovered and easily avoided by persons exercising due care, or provided the defect be of such a nature as not of itself to be dangerous to persons so using the sidewalk." * * * In Nicholas *v.* Peck, 20 R. I. 533, the plaintiff in daylight struck her foot against a stone projecting above the surface of the pavement, when she knew the condition of the pavement. It was held she could not recover. The court said: "In these circumstances, the necessary inference is that she stumbled over the stones because she was not looking for them, as she was bound to do if they were dangerous, and she knew of the danger. Though ordinarily the question of contributory negligence is for the jury, we think the plaintiff's negligence is sufficiently clear for the court to hold that she was negligent as a matter of law." In City of Richmond *v.* Courtney, 32 Gratt. 792, where the injury occurred from to the jury the following instructions, which fairly and correctly stated the law: "1. If the jury believe from the evidence that defendant's sidewalk at the time and place at which plaintiff claims to have been hurt was not in a reasonably safe condition and repair for use by the public, and that she was injured by reason thereof, and that the defendant city of Wickliffe, through its mayor or councilmen or street commissioner, had knowledge or notice of such unsafe condition of said sidewalk, or might have had knowledge or notice by the use of ordinary diligence on the part of such officers, and that a reasonable length of time had elapsed in which it could have repaired said sidewalk after it received such knowledge or notice and before the injury occurred to the plaintiff, then the law is for her, and the jury should find for her compensatory damages for any injury to her person, and for any physical or mental pain or anguish which she suffered or endured by reason of such injury. Unless they so believe, they should find for the defendant. 2. Before the jury are authorized to find for the plaintiff in this case, they must believe from the evidence not only that the sidewalk, where she claims to have been hurt, was in an unsafe and dangerous condition, and that she was thereby injured, but they must further believe from the evidence that the defendant, through its mayor,

loose bricks lying around, over which the plaintiff stumbled and fell in daylight, a recovery was likewise refused. The court said: "It is not to be expected, and ought not to be required, that a city should keep its streets at perfect level and even surface. Slight obstructions, produced by loose bricks in the pavement, or by the roots of trees which may displace the pavement, from the very nature of things, cannot be prevented. And so there cannot be perfect uniformity of a level surface where curbstones and culverts are necessary to be constructed on the streets. In a large city, with many miles of paved streets, it must often happen, from the very nature of the material out of which the pavement is constructed, that the bricks, from the very wear and tear of the use to which they are subjected, will become broken and displaced, so as to cause the fall of a person not careful in walking over them. Certainly, if the obstructions are of such a character as those indicated, and which would not cause the fall of a person exercising ordinary care, the city in such case could not be held liable." To the same effect, see Shallcross *v.* City of Philadelphia, 187 Pa. St. 143 (5 Am. Neg. Rep. 272n), and City of Indianapolis *v.* Cook, 99 Ind. 10; Schaefler *v.* City of Sandusky, 33 Ohio St. 246; City of Quincy *v.* Barker, 81 Ill. 300; Corlett *v.* City of Leavenworth, 27 Kan. 673. We have found no conflict of authority on the subject, and under the universally recognized rule, which seems to us both just and sound, the plaintiff was not entitled to recover, and the peremptory instruction to find for the defendant should have been given, under the evidence. Judgment reversed, and cause remanded for further proceedings consistent with this opinion." Duffy, Ch. J., dissented. (F. J. Hanlon, appeared for appellant; W. McD. Shaw, for appellee.)

councilmen, or street commissioner, had knowledge or notice of the defect in its sidewalk which caused her injury, or by the use of ordinary diligence might have had such notice, and that a reasonable time had elapsed in which it could have repaired its walk after it received such notice, and before the plaintiff was injured. 3. The court instructs the jury that the defendant, city of Wickliffe, is not required to foresee or to provide against every possible danger or accident that might occur to the public, and is only required to exercise reasonable prudence and diligence in the construction of its sidewalks, and in keeping them in a reasonably safe condition for use by the traveling public."

The jury found a verdict for the appellee for $210, which we are asked to reverse upon the sole ground that it is so palpably against the weight of evidence as to import passion and prejudice in the minds of the jury. The statements of plaintiff as to how the injury occurred are not contradicted, and the evidence is quite conflicting as to the length of time the sidewalk had remained in the condition in which it was, and, giving fair weight to all the testimony in the case, this court would not be warranted in reversing the judgment.

Judgment affirmed.

PARSONS v. LEWISTON, BRUNSWICK AND BATH STREET RAILWAY.

Supreme Judicial Court, Maine, July, 1902.

PRACTICE — NEW TRIAL — NEWLY-DISCOVERED EVIDENCE — STATUTE — DISCRETION OF COURT — HORSE FRIGHTENED AT SNOW PLOW ON STREET-CAR TRACK. — 1. In granting a new trial upon motion based on newly-discovered evidence the true doctrine is that the newly-discovered testimony must be of such character weight, and value, considered in connection with the evidence already in the case, that it seems to the court probable that on a new trial, with the additional evidence, the result would be changed; or it must be made to appear to the court that injustice is likely to be done if the new trial is refused.

2. It is not sufficient that there may be a possibility or chance of a different result, or that a jury might be induced to give a different verdict. There must be a probability that the verdict would be different upon a new trial. But it is not necessary that the additional testimony should be such as to require a different verdict.

3. If it were true that such new evidence must be of such a character as to require a different verdict upon a new trial, as stated in Linscott *v.* Insurance Co., 88 Me. 497, and State *v.* Stain, 82 Me. 472, then it would follow

as a logical sequence that none but a different verdict would be allowed by the court to stand.

4. The rule stated in those two cases is too strict. It would deprive a party of the privilege of having his evidence passed upon by a jury, whose peculiar province it is to decide controverted issues of fact, even in cases where the court is of opinion that the new evidence would probably change the result, or that injustice would be likely to be done if a new trial was not granted.

5. It is not an absolute and unqualified rule that a new trial will not be granted under any circumstances upon newly discovered cumulative evidence.

6. When the newly-discovered evidence is additional to some already in the case in support of the same proposition, the probability that such new evidence would change the result is generally very much lessened, so that much more evidence, or evidence of much more value, will generally be required when such evidence is cumulative; but if such newly-discovered testimony, although merely cumulative, is of such a character as to make it seem probable to the court that, notwithstanding the same question has already been passed upon by the jury, a different result would be reached upon another trial with the new evidence, then such new trial should be granted.

7. The provisions of the statute (Rev. St., c. 89, sec. 4), applicable to petitions for review, that "newly-discovered cumulative evidence is admissible and shall have the same effect as other newly-discovered evidence," should have some effect upon the value of such testimony upon motions for a new trial; otherwise a party who had lost a verdict would have greater rights upon a petition for review after judgment than upon a motion for a new trial before.

8. While it is important to have general rules in regard to granting new trials upon this ground, which may be known to the profession, and by which the court will be governed so far as practicable, each case differs so materially from every other that the decision of the question as to whether or not a new trial should be granted in any particular case must necessarily depend to a very large extent, but of course within the limits of such general rules, upon the sound discretion of the court, which will always be actuated by a desire, upon the one hand, to put an end to litigation when the parties have fairly had their day in court, and, upon the other hand, to prevent the likelihood of any injustice being done.

Linscott *v.* Insurance Co., 88 Me. 497, and State *v.* Stain, 82 Me. 472, *criticised.* (Official.)

ON MOTION by plaintiff for new trial.

The facts and points decided appear in the opinion. *New trial granted.*

Argued before WISWELL, Ch. J., and EMERY, WHITEHOUSE, STROUT and PEABODY, JJ.

E. M. BRIGGS, for plaintiff.

W. H. NEWELL and W. B. SKELTON, for defendant.

WISWELL, Ch J.—While the plaintiff was driving a horse attached to a long covered vehicle on runners across the bridge between the cities of Lewiston and Auburn, in the direction of Auburn, he met the defendant's rotary snowplow coming towards him from Auburn.

His horse became frightened at the appearance of the snowplow and the noise caused by it to such an extent as to become unmanageable. Finally, the horse bolted towards one side of the bridge, and, after striking that side, started diagonally across the bridge to the other side. The plaintiff in the meantime was thrown out, dragged some distance, and sustained severe injuries (1).

The plaintiff, claiming that the accident was attributable to the negligence of the defendant's employees in the management of the snowplow, brought this suit to recover the damages sustained by him. The trial resulted in a verdict for the defendant, and the plaintiff brings the case here upon two motions for a new trial, — one because the verdict was against the weight of the evidence; the other upon the ground of newly-discovered evidence. The plaintiff's counsel admits in argument that the jury was authorized in finding a verdict for the defendant upon the evidence introduced at the trial, so that it only becomes necessary to consider the second motion and the newly-discovered testimony presented under it, in connection with the case as submitted to the jury.

The contention of the plaintiff at the trial was that his horse showed signs of fright when about 100 feet distant from the snowplow as the two were slowly approaching each other; that the fact that his horse was greatly frightened and was becoming unmanageable was so apparent that it should have been seen, and in fact was seen, by the motorman, a sufficient length of time before the horse bolted, for him to have stopped his plow, and allow the plaintiff to drive past; that by doing so the accident would have been avoided, but that he failed to stop the snowplow, and that this failure was the proximate cause of the accident resulting in the injury to the plaintiff. The defendant's answer to this proposition is, and was at the trial, that the motorman did stop his plow as soon as the horse showed any signs of fright. Defendant's counsel, in their brief, say, "Coincident in point of time with the first appearance of real fright on the part of the horse, the motorman shut off the current, applied the brake, and stopped the plow."

Upon this issue the plaintiff testified that the snowplow did not stop until after the accident, and one witness called by him, whose means of observation, on account of his distance from the scene of

1. *Horse frightened.* — See vols. 11 and 12 AM. NEG. CAS., for actions arising out of accidents caused by horses being frightened by noise of trains, etc., the same being chronologically grouped from the earliest period to 1897 and arranged in alphabetical order of States. Subsequent actions to date appear in vols. 1-12 AM. NEG. REP. and the current numbers of that series of Reports.

the accident, were not particularly good, to some extent substantiated the plaintiff, stating it as his impression that the snowplow did not stop. Upon the other hand, four witnesses called by the defense, all of whom were on the snowplow at the time, and in the employ of the defendant corporation, and three of whom were still in its employ at the time of the trial, all testified in substance that the motorman stopped his plow as soon as the horse appeared to be frightened. A jury certainly would be authorized to find that it was negligence upon the part of those managing the rotary snowplow, such as this one was described and shown by the photographs to be, to continue its movement along the track in such a situation as this, when an approaching horse displayed signs of great fright and of becoming unmanageable. But, upon the other hand, the jury was authorized to find from the testimony in the case that the motorman seasonably stopped his plow, and did all that he could do to prevent the accident. So that the important issue of fact at the trial was as to whether or not the plow was seasonably stopped, in view of the situation.

Since the trial the plaintiff has discovered three additional witnesses who saw the accident, and who will testify, with varying degrees of positiveness, that the snowplow did not stop until after the accident. These witnesses are entirely disinterested. They had no acquaintance with the plaintiff. Their opportunities for seeing what happened were good. The testimony of these three witnesses is newly-discovered within the well-established rule in this state. Its discovery subsequent to the trial was accidental; and the failure of the plaintiff or his counsel to be earlier aware of its existence cannot be attributed to any negligence upon their part, because diligence upon their part would not have been likely to have put them in possession of it.

The question, then, is whether the court, in the exercise of its sound discretion, but within the rules which have been adopted relative to granting new trials upon this ground, should grant a new trial in this case. But first, inasmuch as there may be some confusion as to what the true doctrine is governing the court in the exercise of its discretion in cases of this kind, growing out of the language used in two decisions of this court, it may be well to carefully state it.

The true doctrine is that, before the court will grant a new trial upon this ground, the newly-discovered testimony must be of such character, weight, and value, considered in connection with the evidence already in the case, that it seems to the court probable that on a new trial, with the additional evidence, the result would be changed; or it must be made to appear to the court that injustice is likely to be done if the new trial is refused. It is not sufficient that there may be a possibility or chance of a different result, or that a jury might be induced to give a different verdict. There must be a probability that the verdict would be different upon a new trial. But it is not necessary that the additional testimony should be such as to require a different verdict.

The correct doctrine has been so repeatedly stated by this court that we quote the language used in numerous earlier decisions relative to the character of the newly-discovered evidence necessary and sufficient to justify the court in granting a new trial upon this ground. "A new trial to permit newly-discovered testimony to be introduced should only be granted * * * when there is reason to believe that the verdict would have been different if it had been before the jury" (Handly *v* Call, 30 Me. 10); "unless the court should think it probable the new evidence would alter the verdict" (Snowman *v.* Wardwell, 32 Me. 275). "A review will never be granted to let in additional testimony, when such testimony would not be likely to change the result" (Todd *v.* Chipman, 62 Me. 189); "nor unless there be reason to believe that it would change the result" (Trask *v.* Inhabitants of Unity, 74 Me. 208). In Linscott *v.* Insurance Co., 88 Me. 497, the court stated the rule, citing various earlier cases, in these words: "It has long been the settled doctrine of this court that a new trial will not be granted on the ground of newly-discovered evidence, unless it seems to the court probable that it might alter the verdict." In Stackpole *v.* Perkins, 85 Me. 298, nothing is said in the opinion in regard to the new evidence being of such a character as to require a different verdict. The court does say in that case: "If believed [the newly-discovered witness], his testimony must substantially destroy the evidence of a witness at the trial, whose testimony may have been considered of controlling weight." A new trial was granted in this case, although the effect of the newly-discovered testimony was stated by the court to depend upon the weight given to it by the jury.

It is true that in Linscott *v.* Insurance Co., *supra*, where the correct doctrine of this State was very distinctly stated as above quoted, and in accordance with the previous authorities, the court, at the conclusion of the opinion, said that the question was "whether the legitimate effect of such evidence would require a different verdict." The case of State *v.* Stain, 82 Me. 472, was cited in support of this doctrine. But we do not find the rule so stated in any case, other than in these two, in this State. If it were true that such new evidence must be of such a character as to require a different verdict upon a new trial, then it would follow as a logical sequence that none but a different verdict would be allowed by the court to stand. The rule thus stated in these two cases is too strict. It would deprive a party of the privilege of having his new evidence passed upon by a jury whose peculiar province it is to decide controverted issues of fact, even in cases where the court is of opinion that the new evidence would probably change the result, or that injustice would be likely to be done if a new trial was not granted.

In this case we cannot say that the new evidence, in connection with the former evidence, would require a different verdict. After this evidence is submitted, it then becomes a question for the jury to pass upon. But it does seem probable to the court that the verdict will be different when the case is submitted anew with the additional evidence.

It is true that this evidence is cumulative, but it is not an absolute and unqualified rule that a new trial will not be granted under any circumstances upon newly-discovered cumulative testimony. Snowman *v.* Wardwell, 32 Me. 275. When the newly-discovered evidence is additional to some already in the case in support of the same proposition, the probability that such new evidence would change the result is generally very much lessened, so that much more evidence, or evidence of much more value, will generally be required when such evidence is cumulative; but if the newly-discovered testimony, although merely cumulative, is of such a character as to make it seem probable to the court that notwithstanding the same question has already been passed upon by the jury, a different result would be reached upon another trial with the new evidence, then such new trial should be granted.

The provision of the statute (Rev. St., c. 89, sec. 4), applicable to petitions for review, that "newly-discovered cumulative evidence is admissible and shall have the same effect as other newly-discovered evidence," should have some effect upon the value of such testimony upon a motion for a new trial; otherwise a party who had lost a verdict would have greater rights upon a petition for review after judgment than upon a motion for new trial before.

And after all, while it is important to have general rules in regard to the granting of new trials upon this ground, which may be known to the profession, and by which the court will be governed so far as practicable, each case differs so materially from every other that the decision of the question as to whether or not a new trial should be granted in any particular case must necessarily depend, to a very large extent, but, of course, within the limits of such general rules, upon the sound discretion of the court, which will always be actuated by a desire, upon the one hand, to put an end to litigation when the parties have fairly had their day in court, and, upon the other, to prevent the likelihood of any injustice being done.

In the exercise of this discretion, and within the rules as above laid down, the court is of the opinion that this plaintiff should have the opportunity to again submit his case, with the additional testimony, to the determination of a jury.

New trial granted.

WILKINS v. MONSON CONSOLIDATED SLATE COMPANY.

Supreme Judicial Court, Maine, April, 1902.

PROPERTY DAMAGED — BLASTING — OVERFLOW — ESTOPPEL — EVIDENCE — DAMAGES — INSTRUCTION. — 1. In an action to recover damages resulting from rocks thrown upon the plaintiff's land by blasting in defendant's quarry, and injury from water pumped from the quarry and allowed to flow on plaintiff's land, the defendant asked an instruction that, plaintiff having conveyed the premises occupied by the defendant, with knowledge that they were to be opened and used as a quarry, he was estopped from claiming any damages arising from the proper use of the quarry as a quarry, when carried on in the ordinary, usual, and proper business of a slate quarry.

This request was refused, and the jury was instructed that "plaintiff could maintain the action, providing he proves damages, although he sold the land with the understanding that it was to be used as a slate quarry," and that it was not necessary for the plaintiff to prove negligence or carelessness on the part of the defendant. Upon exceptions taken to the refusal to instruct, and to the instruction given, *held*, that the refusal was correct, as was also the instruction given (1).

2. Evidence is not admissible to show that between the date of the writ and the time of trial rocks had been thrown upon plaintiff's land by defendant.

3. The plaintiff also claimed to recover for probable future damages, but the court instructed the jury that no damages subsequent to the date of the writ could be recovered. *Held*, that the instruction is correct.

(Official.)

EXCEPTIONS from Supreme Judicial Court, Piscataquis County.

Action by Fred J. Wilkins against the Monson Consolidated Slate Company. Verdict for plaintiff, and both plaintiff and defendant file exceptions. *Exceptions overruled.*

1. For other actions for injuries to person and property resulting from blasting operations, from 1897 to date, see vols. 1–12 AM. NEG. REP., and the current numbers of that series of Reports.

Argued before WISWELL, Ch., J., and EMERY, WHITEHOUSE, STROUT, SAVAGE and POWERS, JJ.

H. HUDSON, for plaintiff.

J. B. PEAKS, for defendant.

STROUT, J. — This case comes up on exceptions by both parties. It is a suit to recover damages resulting from rocks thrown upon plaintiff's land by blasting in defendant's quarry, and injury from water pumped from the quarry and allowed to flow upon plaintiff's land. The quarry, which lies on the opposite side of the road from plaintiff's residence, was conveyed by the plaintiff to defendant's grantor with knowledge that it was to be used as a quarry.

Defendant's exceptions: An instruction was asked that plaintiff, having conveyed the premises occupied by the defendant with knowledge that they were to be opened and used as a quarry, he was estopped from claiming any damages arising from the proper use of the quarry as a quarry, when carried on in the ordinary, usual, and proper business of a slate quarry. This request was refused by the presiding justice, who instructed the jury that the plaintiff could "maintain the action, providing he proves damages, although he sold the land to the predecessor in title of the defendant with the understanding that it was to be used as a slate quarry," and that it was not necessary for the plaintiff to prove negligence or carelessness on the part of the defendant. The defendant excepts to the refusal to instruct, and to the instruction actually given.

The owner has the right to use his property in any manner he pleases, provided such use is lawful and inflicts no injury upon another. The maxim, "*Sic utere tuo ut alienum non lædas*," expresses not only the law, but the elements of good neighborhood and mutual right. The fact that plaintiff granted the quarry, to be used as a quarry, cannot be regarded as conferring a right upon defendant to make an illegal use of the quarry to his detriment, nor as a release of damages resulting therefrom. With suitable precautions, blasting can be done in the quarry without throwing rocks upon plaintiff's premises. Such noise as necessarily results from blasting may be supposed to have been considered at the time of the grant, and been an element in making the price. But the unnecessary throwing of rocks or other debris upon plaintiff's land cannot be so regarded. The plaintiff might well rely upon the assumption that defendant would conduct his operations in compliance with law, and with that regard to his rights which the law imposes. The elements of estoppel do not exist upon the facts of this case. Lyman *v.* Railroad Corp., 4 Cush. 288; Wilson *v.* City of New Bedford, 108 Mass. 261. The cases of Vickerie *v.* Buswell, 13 Me. 289, and Francis *v.* Milling Corp., 4 Pick. 365, cited by counsel, are not applicable to the facts of this case. These principles are elementary. The instructions given were in accordance with them.

Plaintiff's exceptions: The writ bore date January 24, 1900. Plaintiff introduced evidence tending to show that from December 1, 1898, to the date of the writ, rocks were blasted from the quarry by defendant, and thrown upon the dwelling house of plaintiff and upon his land. He also offered evidence to show that, between the date of the writ and the time of trial, rocks had been so thrown upon plaintiff's land by defendant, which was excluded, and exception taken. It was claimed that such evidence tended to show that rocks were so thrown prior to the date of the writ, but this was clearly a *non sequitur*. Evidence of a wrong or trespass of this kind at one time has no legitimate tendency to prove a like wrong or trespass at some prior time. The offered evidence was clearly inadmissible.

Plaintiff also claimed to recover in this suit not only damages to the date of writ, but probable future damages. The court instructed the jury that no damages subsequent to the date of the writ could be recovered. That this instruction was correct is too plain for argument. *Non constat* that any more rocks would ever be thrown upon plaintiff's land. The quarry might not be operated, or precautions might be taken to prevent a recurrence of the injury complained of. There was no basis upon which future damages could be assessed. If they occur, it is matter for a subsequent suit.

Exceptions of plaintiff and of defendant overruled.

PELLERIN v. INTERNATIONAL PAPER COMPANY.

Supreme Judicial Court, Maine, April, 1902.

EMPLOYEE INJURED BY FALLING FROM STAGING — DEFECTIVE APPLIANCE — PRESUMPTION — FELLOW-SERVANT. — 1. In an action to recover damages by the plaintiff who was injured by the falling of a stage upon which he was at work, the declaration alleged that: "The staging was insecure and unsafe. The iron rods were unable to sustain the weight, and broke, and precipitated the plaintiff a distance of fifteen feet — to the floor of the room."

After verdict for the plaintiff, and on motion for a new trial, it appeared that there was no affirmative proof of culpable negligence on the part of the defendant company. *Held*, that no presumption of such negligence arises from the mere fact that an accident happened. If there is any presumption in such a case, it is that the defendant has complied with the obligations resting upon it equally with other men. The fact that two of the dependent hooks broke may be some evidence tending to show that they were not suitable for the use to which they were applied, but it is not alone sufficient to establish negligence on the part of the defendant company.

2. The defendant kept in its storehouse sufficient materials for the construction of the staging required by the workmen in painting the ceilings, and there was no direct evidence that these materials were not suitable for that purpose. There was no evidence that the defendant undertook to furnish the staging in question for the workmen as a completed structure. The company did not assume the responsibility of adapting specific hooks or planks to the construction of a particular staging. The plaintiff's fellow-workmen obtained the hooks and the planks from the company's storehouse, and erected the staging themselves, and there was no suggestion that they were not competent workmen. *Held*, that if the plaintiff's fellow-workmen failed to exercise due care in the adjustment of the planks to the hooks, and the accident resulted from that cause, the defendant company is not responsible (1).

(Official.)

1. *Employee injured by defective machinery — Assumption of risk.* — In DRAPEAU *v.* INTERNATIONAL PAPER CO. (*Maine, March, 1902*), 52 Atl. Rep. 647, defendant's motion for new trial on verdict rendered for plaintiff for $510.19 was overruled, the official syllabus stating the case as follows:

"1. An inexperienced laborer is not held to assume the risk of perils which are not called to his attention, and of which he has no knowledge, but of such only as he knows, or by the exercise of ordinary care ought to know.

"2. The plaintiff was directed by the assistant superintendent to take a position near the capstan on the left-hand side of a wire cable seven or eight feet from the mill, used in drawing logs from a large pile into the water, and communicate to the operator of the drum winder the signals received from the man at the log pile. But all the power that could be applied proved insufficient to move the logs to which the cable had been attached, and there was evidence to justify the plaintiff's contention that at the last attempt the cable slipped off the capstan, vibrated against the corner of the building, rebounded over the head of the plaintiff, and then swept back with resilient force against the plaintiff's left leg, causing a fracture of both bones below the knee.

"3. After a patient study of all the evidence in the case, it is the opinion of the court that the conclusion of the jury cannot be deemed unmistakably wrong in finding that such a capstan or winch head, without an effectual guard to hold the cable in place, was not a reasonably suitable appliance to perform the work required under the circumstances existing at the time of the accident. It might reasonably have been anticipated by those in charge of the work, who had frequently seen the cable fly off from the capstan under similar conditions, and observed its tendency to vibrate to some extent after it left the capstan, that an accident would happen to the signalman, either in the way it did happen, or in some similar manner.

"4. *Held*, that there was sufficient evidence to support the conclusion which the jury probably reached, — that the plaintiff had not performed any regular service as a signalman in connection with the working of this cable prior to the day of the accident, that his knowledge of the working of it prior to that time was only of that

ACTION by Philip Pellerin against the International Paper Company. Plaintiff recovered a verdict of $431.59, and defendant moved for a new trial. *New trial granted.*

Argued before WISWELL, Ch. J., and EMERY, WHITEHOUSE, STROUT, PEABODY and SPEAR, JJ.

D. J. MCGILLICUDDY and F. A. MOREY, for plaintiff.

GEO. D. BISBEE and RALPH T. PARKER, for defendant.

WHITEHOUSE, J. — In this action the plaintiff seeks to recover damages for personal injuries sustained by reason of the fall of a staging upon which he was at work for the defendant company. The jury returned a verdict for the plaintiff for $431.59, and the defendant asks the court to set it aside as against law and evidence.

The plaintiff introduced testimony tending to establish the following facts. The plaintiff was employed in painting the ceiling of a room in the defendant's pulp mill, and at the time of the accident was standing or sitting with three other workmen upon a staging suspended about five feet below the ceiling by six iron rods, or painters' hooks, attached to the ceiling. The staging was about twenty feet long and ten feet wide, with three of the depending iron rods on each side. The lower ends of these rods were bent in the form of rectangular hooks or loops, into which were placed edgewise three planks, two inches thick, to serve as stringers or floor timbers. Upon these stringers were laid the planks constituting the stage upon which the workmen were seated while engaged in painting, but, as these planks were only about eleven or twelve feet long, it required two of them to reach the entire length of the stage; the ends lapping over on the middle stringer. Thus constructed, the staging could be readily taken apart and removed, or set up in another part of the room, as necessity or convenience might require in the progress of the work.

The defendant company furnished the iron rods and the planks to be used in the erection of such stagings, and when not in use they were stored with like materials in the company's storehouse.

general and indefinite character which might be derived from the casual observation of a laborer who was not charged with any special duty in regard to it, and that he did not comprehend and fully appreciate the perils incident to the operation of it under the conditions existing at that time, but unhesitatingly assumed that no danger would be incurred in following the directions of his superior. Under these circumstances, his conduct is entitled to be viewed in the light of reasonable charity, and he should not be deprived of the benefit of a verdict in his favor which is not shown to be clearly wrong." Opinion rendered by WHITEHOUSE, J. (D. J. MCGILLICUDDY and F. A. MOREY, appeared for plaintiff; G. D. BISBEE and R. T. PARKER, for defendant.)

The plaintiff's fellow-workmen brought the rods and planks from the storehouse for the erection of the staging in question, and, although the plaintiff himself took no part in the selection of the materials, he had several times assisted in moving the staging, by taking it down and putting it up again. At the time of the accident the plaintiff was engaged in painting with a fellow-workman at one end of the stage, when the two workmen at the other end, having finished painting there, went over to that part of the stage where the plaintiff sat. Thereupon two of the iron rods broke — one at the inner angle of the hook and the other at the outer angle — and the stage fell and caused the injuries to the plaintiff of which he complains. There was evidence tending to show that the planks placed edgewise in the rectangular iron hooks filled only about five-eighths of the space between the rods of some of the hooks, and were not secured in a vertical position, but allowed to incline outward, as shown by the following diagram [omitted here].

The defendant introduced no evidence, contending that the plaintiff had failed to show any actionable negligence on the part of the company.

It is the opinion of the court that this contention on the part of the defense was justified by the evidence, and that a nonsuit might properly have been ordered by the presiding justice.

The action set forth in the plaintiff's writ rests upon the allegation that: "The staging was insecure and unsafe. The iron rods were unable to sustain the weight, and broke, and precipitated the plaintiff a distance of fifteen feet — to the floor of the room." But there is no affirmative proof of culpable negligence on the part of the defendant company, and no presumption of such negligence arises from the mere fact that an accident happened. "If there is any presumption in such a case, it is that the defendant has complied with the obligations resting upon it equally with other men." Nason *v.* West, 78 Me. 253. The fact that two of the dependent hooks broke may be some evidence tending to show that they were not suitable for the use to which they were applied, but it is not alone sufficient to establish negligence on the part of the defendant company. Coleman *v.* Mechanics' Iron Foundry Co., 168 Mass. 254, 2 Am. Neg. Rep. 374. The testimony is silent respecting the size and condition of the iron rods. There is no direct evidence of any patent or visible defect or imperfection of any kind in the hooks that broke. All the testimony is entirely consistent with the theory that, if any defects existed in those hooks, they were latent ones, which were not discoverable by the exercise of ordinary care in the inspection of them.

The defendant kept in its storehouse sufficient materials for the construction of the staging required by the workmen in painting the ceilings, and there is no direct evidence that these materials were not suitable for that purpose. There is no evidence that the defendant undertook to furnish the staging in question for the workmen as a completed structure. The company did not assume the responsibility of adapting specific hooks or planks to the construction of a particular staging. On the contrary, it satisfactorily appears that that duty was intrusted to the workmen engaged in painting the ceiling, and assumed by them as within the scope of their employment. The plaintiff's fellow-workmen obtained the hooks and the planks from the company's storehouse, and erected the staging themselves. There is no suggestion that they were not competent workmen. Under such circumstances, if the plaintiff's fellow-workmen failed to exercise due care in the adjustment of the planks to the hooks, and the accident resulted from that cause, the defendant company is not responsible. Kelley *v.* Norcross, 121 Mass. 508; Adasken *v.* Gilbert, 165 Mass. 443; Dube *v.* City of Lewiston, 83 Me. 211; Small *v.* Manufacturing Co., 94 Me. 551, 48 Atl. Rep. 177.

There was evidence tending to show that the two-inch planks set edgewise in the hooks filled only about five-eighths of the space inside of the hooks, and that they were not firmly held in an upright position by wedges or otherwise, but allowed to sway back and forth with the swinging movement of the stage. It is obvious that the strong outward pressure which was thus liable to be exerted against the arm of the hook would easily break an iron rod fully capable of sustaining the same weight if the plank were securely held in a vertical position against the depending rod. If any want of proper care is affirmatively shown by the evidence, it is on the part of the plaintiff's fellow-workmen.

It is accordingly the opinion of the court that, upon well-settled principles of law, the verdict was manifestly not warranted by the evidence.

Motion sustained. Verdict set aside. New trial granted.

UNITED RAILWAY AND ELECTRIC COMPANY OF BALTIMORE CITY v. FLETCHER.

Court of Appeals, Maryland, June, 1902.

PERSON STANDING NEAR TRACK INJURED BY COMING IN CONTACT WITH CONDUCTOR ON FOOTBOARD OF MOVING OPEN STREET CAR — RAILWAY COMPANY NOT LIABLE. — In an action to recover damages for personal injuries sustained by plaintiff, who, while standing on a street near the car track, came in contact with the body of a conductor who was passing along the footboard at the side of a moving open summer car collecting fares, it appeared that plaintiff was employed in filling in a trench or ditch which was about three feet from the track, and as street cars passed he stood between the trench and the track, but when the car in question was passing was struck by the action of the conductor as aforesaid. *Held*, that there was no evidence of negligence on the part of defendant company or its servants directly contributing to plaintiff's injury as to entitle the case to go to a jury, and judgment for plaintiff reversed.

APPEAL from Baltimore City Court.

Action by John T. Fletcher against the United Railway and Electric Company of Baltimore City. From judgment for plaintiff, defendant appeals. *Judgment reversed.*

Argued before McSHERRY, Ch. J., and BOYD, PAGE, PEARCE, SCHMUCKER and JONES, JJ.

FIELDER C. SLINGLUFF, for appellant.

JOHN H. WALRAVEN and FREDERICK C. COOK, for appellee.

SCHMUCKER, J. — This is an appeal from a judgment of the Baltimore City Court in favor of the appellee against the appellant for damages resulting from personal injuries. The plaintiff was injured, while standing on a public street near the car track, by coming in contact with the body of a conductor who was passing along the footboard at the side of a moving open summer car. At the close of the plaintiff's testimony in the court below the defendant offered a prayer taking the case away from the jury for the want of evidence legally sufficient to entitle the plaintiff to recover. The court rejected the prayer, and the defendant then introduced its testimony. At the close of the whole evidence the plaintiff offered four prayers, and the defendant offered seven, the first of which was a renewal of the prayer taking the case away from the jury. The court granted three of the plaintiff's prayers, and rejected one of the plaintiff's and all of the defendant's prayers, and granted two instructions of its own to the jury. It is unnecessary for us to review in detail the action of the learned judge below on these prayers and instructions, because, for reasons which we will state, we are of opinion that he should have granted the defendant's prayer taking the case away from the jury for want of legally sufficient evidence to enable the plaintiff to recover. Three witnesses, who were present at the happening of the accident, testified in the case. They were the plaintiff and two laborers, who were at the time engaged with him in the service of the city water department in laying a water pipe. These witnesses agree that a long trench, two or three feet wide at the top and about four feet deep, had been dug by them in the street between the car track and the sidewalk, and distant three feet from the nearest track. They had been engaged in digging this trench and laying a six-inch pipe therein during the entire day up to the time of the accident, which occurred at about four o'clock in the afternoon. Cars had been passing the men engaged in the work at intervals throughout the day, and the workmen had stood in safety on the strip of ground between the trench and the tracks as the cars went by. At the time of the accident the pipe had been laid, and the workmen were engaged in filling up the trench. The several accounts given by the witnesses of the accident are substantially as follows: The plaintiff testified that he and the witness Burk were working on the side of the trench next to the track, when, as he says, "I saw the car was coming, and the car had rung up get out of my way, and I was standing there — standing on the side of the ditch — and if I had been let alone the car would have had plenty of room to pass me. The ditch was three feet from the railway track. * * * I stepped aside to let the car pass me, and as I did, why I felt the blow from the conductor where his body struck me." "I saw the conductor on the car. I saw him come up the track, and he passed Burk, and just as he got to me he swung, and when he swung himself he struck me, and therefore I know it was the conductor." He also testified that, although he saw the conductor on the footboard of the approaching car, he did not watch it as it was coming up, because he was satisfied that he was out of its way. He said that he saw no difference between the rate of speed of this car at the time when he was struck and that of the other cars which passed the place where he was working. John Kelbaugh, one of the two laborers who testified for the plaintiff, did not see him actually struck, but corroborated his evidence as to the local conditions at the place of accident, and said, "The ditch was about three feet from the railroad track, and there was plenty of room for any man to get out of the way of the car." He also saw the conductor on the footboard as the car approached. He thought the car was going at an unusually high rate of speed. Louis Burk, the other laborer, testified that he saw the conductor on the footboard of the passing car, collecting fares, as he thought, and that as the car neared the plaintiff the witness saw the conductor swing out, and that some part of his body struck the plaintiff, and knocked him down in the ditch. The testimony of this witness as to the local conditions of the place of the accident agreed with that of the other two. He also thought the speed of the car was very rapid. No other witnesses testified as to any facts bearing directly upon the happening of the accident. We fail to find in this testimony such evidence of negligence on the part of the defendant or its servants directly contributing to the injury of the plaintiff as to entitle the case to go to the jury. It has been repeatedly held by this court that the negligence of a defendant will not be presumed, nor will a surmise or a scintilla of evidence that there may have been negligence on his part justify a court in sending a case to the jury. There must be some reasonable evidence of well-defined acts of negligence or breach of duty on the part of the defendant causing the injury complained of. No one is responsible for injuries resulting from unavoidable accidents while engaged in a lawful business. Annapolis & Balt. S. L. R. R. Co. *v.* Pumphrey, 72 Md. 85 (12 Am. Neg. Cas. 11n); Baltimore & O. R. Co. *v.* State, 71 Md. 599; Cumberland P. R. Co. *v.* State, 73 Md. 77; Railroad Co. *v.* Burkhardt, 83 Md. 522, 523, 34 Atl. Rep. 1010. The evidence in the case at bar goes only so far as to show that the body of the conductor, while passing the footboard of the moving car, struck and injured the plaintiff. The conductor not only had the right to pass along the footboard of the car when it was in motion, but the discharge of his duty required him to do so very frequently. It is a well-known fact that the footboard is a narrow one, and a conductor, in order to pass along it in safety, especially if he has to lean in between the successive seats to collect fares, must, in passing by the upright standards of the car, give to his body a swaying or swinging motion. There is no evidence that the conductor in this case acted in a negligent or unlawful manner when passing along the footboard. The entire space between the railway track and the ditch was but three feet, a considerable part of which must have been occupied by the overhanging part of the car and the footboard. Under these circumstances the mere fact that the plaintiff, while standing in the narrow space between the car and the ditch, came in contact with the body of the conductor, is not *per se* even *prima facie* evidence of negligence on the part of the latter. If the plaintiff and the conductor were both small men, they may have passed each other in this narrow space with safety. If, on the other hand, they were both large men, they may have come in contact without any negligence on the part of the conductor. The evidence showed that the plaintiff stood between the ditch and the track in safety when other cars passed by, but it does not appear that in any of those cases the conductor was upon the footboard of the car as it passed. In the absence of reasonable evidence of any act of negligence or failure of duty on the part of the conductor, it was improper to let this case go to the jury to be determined by surmise or conjecture.

There were a number of exceptions taken by the defendant in the course of the trial in the court below to the court's action in admitting evidence, but, as the case will not go back for a new trial, it is unnecessary for us to pass upon the propriety of the court's rulings thereon. The judgment appealed from will be reversed, without a new trial.

Judgment reversed, without a new trial.

KEARNS ET AL. v. SOUTH MIDDLESEX STREET-RAILWAY COMPANY.

Supreme Judicial Court, Massachusetts, June, 1902.

EXCAVATION MADE BY STREET-RAILWAY COMPANY — TRAVELER INJURED — EVIDENCE. — In an action by husband and wife to recover damages for personal injuries caused by an excavation in the highway made by a street-railway company, it was *held* that the evidence was sufficient to justify a finding that the railway company made and maintained the excavation for its own purposes, where it was shown that before the excavation was made water ran down the track to defendant's switch; that the excavation had the appearance of having been made by digging and not of having been washed out; and that while it was there defendant's employees were at work upon the track within a few yards of the same.

EXCEPTIONS from Superior Court, Middlesex County.

Actions by Katherine Kearns and her husband against the South Middlesex Street-Railway Company for personal injuries and loss of services. From a judgment for plaintiffs, defendant brings exceptions. *Overruled.*

GEORGE L. MAYBERRY and JOHN J. SCOTT, for plaintiffs.

N. SUMNER MYRICK and J. ALBERT BRACKETT, for defendant.

BARKER, J. — In each declaration there were three counts, and each verdict was a general one, and may have been rendered upon either count. Without so deciding, we assume in favor of the defendant that upon the evidence neither plaintiff could recover upon the first count of his or her declaration. But no request was made for a separate ruling upon those counts. The three requests of the defendant were for general rulings that upon the evidence the plaintiffs were not entitled to recover; that under the provisions of St. 1898, c. 578, they could not recover; and that the actions should have been brought against the town, and not against the defendant. Assuming in favor of the defendant that an exception was taken to the refusal to give these three requests, and was intended to be saved by the bill, it must be overruled if, upon the evidence, the plaintiffs were entitled to go to the jury upon the second or third counts. The distinctive allegation of the second count is that the defendant, in the repair of its railway, negligently produced and allowed to remain in the highway a deep excavation dangerous to travelers. This count is founded upon the liability imposed upon street-railway companies by the provisions of St. 1898, c. 578, sec. 11. That section requires the companies to replace surface material disturbed by it in the making of repairs, and to restore the street to as good condition as existed at the time of such disturbance, and makes the company liable for any loss or injury suffered by any person in the repair of its railway, or while replacing the surface of any street so disturbed, and resulting from the carelessness, neglect, or misconduct of its agents or servants engaged in the work. The third counts proceed upon the common-law liability of any person who creates and maintains a dangerous excavation in a public way, and they allege that the defendant negligently created and caused or permitted to be maintained a deep excavation in the highway, dangerous to travelers. Although the evidence would not justify a verdict upon the first counts, the three requests were refused rightly if the evidence would justify a finding that the defendant made the excavation in the repair of its railway as alleged in the second counts, or created the excavation and caused it to be maintained as alleged in the third counts. Although there was no testimony that any workman of the defendant was seen to make the excavation, nor that it was ordered to be made by any one in the defendant's service, we think the evidence justified a finding that the excavation was made and maintained by the defendant, and in the repair of its tracks. It was in evidence that before the excavation was made water ran down near the north rail to a railway switch nearby. The natural tendency of water so running would be to carry sand and gravel into the switch, and impede its operation. The excavation started at the north rail, and went towards and under the south rail, and connected with a gutter beyond the south rail. It deepened gradually in its course from the north rail, and it had the appearance of having been made by digging, and not of having been washed out. While it was there, employees of the defendant were at work upon the track replacing old ties with new ones within a few yards of the excavation. This would justify the inference that the excavation had been made for the purpose of diverting a flow of water from the defendant's switch, and, as that would be serviceable to the defendant, and to no one else, that it was made by the party whose interest it would serve. Besides this, the defendant, although it introduced evidence, made no attempt to show that it did not cause the excavation to be made, or by whom it was made, except to show by the cross-examination of one of the plaintiff's witnesses that there was a hydrant south of the track, near the excavation, and that the hydrant had been repaired several weeks before the accident. It is matter of common knowledge that the motormen and conductors of a railway company, if no others of its servants, pass over and have the opportunity to observe its tracks daily. In the absence of any evidence introduced on the part of the company, the evidence justified a finding that the company made and maintained the excavation for its own purposes. For this reason the three instructions stated were rightly refused. The same considerations dispose of the refusal to rule that there was no evidence on which the plaintiffs could go to the jury upon the third counts, and to the submission to the jury of the question, answered by them in the affirmative, whether the alleged defect between the rails was made by the defendant's servants while in the construction, alteration, or repair of its railway.

Exceptions overruled.

PEARL v. BENTON TOWNSHIP.

Supreme Court, Michigan, June, 1902.

COLLAPSE OF BRIDGE — FLOOD — DEFECT — NOTICE TO TOWNSHIP. — In an action to recover damages for personal injuries caused by the fall of a bent under the end of a bridge, at a time of exceptionally high water when the stream overflowed its banks, it was *held* that a township is not

liable for the collapse of a bridge, three years after its construction, unless it had notice of a defect in the same (1)

DEFECTIVE BRIDGE — NOTICE — QUESTION FOR JURY. — In such case, however, where there was testimony tending to show that there was an imperfection in the bridge and that it was visible and generally known for a long period, the question of notice to the township** was for the jury to determine.**

ERROR to Circuit Court, Berrien County.

Action by Arthur L. Pearl against the Township of Benton. From judgment for defendant, plaintiff brings error. *Judgment reversed.*

GORE & HARVEY (JAMES O'HARA, of counsel), for appellant.

F. H. ELLSWORTH and G. M. VALENTINE (M. L. HOWELL, of counsel), for appellee.

HOOKER, Ch. J. — The plaintiff was injured through the fall of a bent under the end of a bridge. This bridge was built by the town-

1. *Pedestrian injured on defective bridge.* — In LENZ *v.* CITY OF ST. PAUL *(Minnesota, July, 1902)*, 91 N. W. Rep. 256, an action by a minor for damages for personal injuries sustained while crossing a defective bridge, judgment for plaintiff was affirmed, the opinion by COLLINS, J., being as follows: "The gist of the complaint in this, a personal injury case, was that while the defendant city was reconstructing its Wabasha street bridge its employees connected a newly constructed part with a section of the old by means of a negligently placed plank, and that in crossing this structure the plaintiff, a pedestrian, stepped upon this plank; that it slipped from under her; and that one foot and leg went into an aperture causing the injuries complained of. The case was twice tried, with a verdict for the plaintiff in each instance; the first being set aside for error committed at the trial. The present appeal is from an order denying a new trial after the second verdict. The contest in the court below was very clearly and sharply drawn; the plaintiff testifying that the plank which seems to have been placed across the sidewalk, inclining from one part to the other a few inches lower, slipped as she stepped upon it, early in the morning; her counsel contending that it had never been nailed or fastened at all, while defendant's witnesses testified that just before quitting work the night before the workmen securely and firmly nailed the plank in position, so that it could not move or slip at all. If defendant's testimony was true the plank could not have been in the condition contended for by plaintiff, for it could not have slipped when she stepped on it the next morning after it was so fastened. This was a well-defined issue, and without any objection whatever from either party, or any suggestion that there was any mistake or error, the court, when instructing the jury, charged that, if the plank was securely and firmly nailed or fastened by the men the night before, plaintiff could not recover; and further charged that if the plaintiff, while carefully walking over this plank, placed her foot, as she had testified, upon it, and it slipped 'because it had never been securely fastened,' causing her to fall and to receive the injuries, she was entitled to a verdict. Thus was the issue presented by the testimony placed clearly

ship over a drain many years ago, and in the fall of 1892 it was rebuilt. The north posts rested upon the old mudsill, which was sound, and was not disturbed. The men who rebuilt it stated that the bed of the mudsill was below the bottom of the drain. The negligence complained of is that in rebuilding the bridge the contractor left the mudsill some inches above the bottom of the drain, and that they were afterwards undermined by water; and plaintiff claims that the bridge was never properly constructed in that respect, and that the township was chargeable with notice of the condition because it was a defect in repairing or reconstruction. The plaintiff relied upon the testimony of one Stone to prove that the bottom of the drain was below the mudsill. This witness said that he was employed to clean out this drain, and in doing so deepened it; that the bridge was rebuilt in the fall of 1892, just after he had cleaned and deepened the drain; that he worked to a profile; that the ditch

and fairly before the jury by the trial court, and their finding was for plaintiff. The verdict will have to be sustained, for the evidence in plaintiff's behalf tended to support her contention. While the testimony preponderated in favor of the city upon this point, we cannot say that there was no testimony tending to warrant the jury in concluding that the plank was not fastened; and, if it was not, inclining it without fastening, over an aperture in the walk, was, it seems to be conceded, a negligent act for which the city would be liable. After the jury had been in consultation some time they returned into court, and through the foreman asked if they were satisfied that the plank in question was insufficiently spiked in the evening, could they, on that ground, find a verdict for the plaintiff? The court immediately replied that there was no evidence whatever from which the jury could find that the plank was insufficiently spiked. They must either find it was spiked, or that it was not, said the court, with some elaboration upon the question at issue before referred to. There was no suggestion by counsel at the time that this was not strictly true, nor was it claimed upon appeal that there was any evidence which would justify a finding that the plank was insufficiently spiked; but it is now claimed by counsel for the city that the jury should have been charged, when asking this question, that they could find for the plaintiff if of the opinion that ordinary care did not require the city, under the circumstances shown, to have taken the precaution to have the plank sufficiently spiked, and that the failure so to charge was error which prejudiced the city. If this instruction to the jury would have been to the interest of the defendant city, its counsel should have proposed it; but a moment's thought will show that the instruction already given, and adhered to by the court when the jury asked this question, was more favorable to the city than the one suggested. Had such an instruction been given, counsel for plaintiff might have complained, but no ground exists for counsel to say that the defendant city was prejudiced by the omission. There are no other questions which need comment. Order affirmed." (JAMES E. MARKHAM and FRANKLIN H. GRIGGS, appeared for appellant; OTTO KUEFFNER and ALBERT SCHALLER, for respondent.)

was two feet on bottom and eight feet across top, slope one to one. On direct examination he said, "I should think I dug from twelve to sixteen inches below the bottom of the mudsill." On cross-examination he admitted that he might have said on a former trial that it might have been four or five inches below the sill. He stated further on cross-examination: "Q. I understand you to say now, when you had completed it, the bottom of the ditch was twelve to sixteen inches below the bottom of the mudsill. Is that right? A. I said I dug the ditch fifteen or sixteen inches. Q. You dug it down fifteen or sixteen inches? A. Fifteen or sixteen inches under the bridge. Q. Do you say that carried it below the bottom of the mudsill? A. It carried it below the bottom of the mudsill several inches; more than four or five inches. Q. About how many inches? A. I should think at the least calculation ten inches, or somewhere along there. I don't know as I did testify before it was four or five inches. Q. Explain how it was you said before it was not more than four or five inches. How much below the bottom of the mudsill was the bottom of the ditch when you was there a year ago? A. I could not say exactly. It was considerable lower. I went regardless of the old ditch at all. I went by the grade stakes, and dug down to the grade. Some places I would have to dig out more than ever was taken out before. You understand, out of the old ditch. Got down below the bottom of the old ditch. Other places I wouldn't have so much to dig out. Take out what was caved in and filled in. I say in places. I think some sand washed in at the bridge. Most always does. I have an idea, when I last saw it the ditch was some lower than the mudsill. I could not say exactly how much. I could not tell anywhere near. I don't suppose how deep it was. It was below the bottom of the mudsill more than four inches. I could not say how much more. Q. Six or eight inches? A. I could not say whether it was or not. Q. Twelve or fifteen inches? A. Might have been. Q. Might have been twelve or fifteen inches? I will ask you this: How much below the mudsills — the bottom of the mudsills — did you actually dig? A. Below the bottom of the old mudsill fifteen or sixteen inches. Somewhere in that neighborhood." It was shown that upon a former trial he testified that he dug twelve or fifteen inches, and when through it was four or five inches below the bottom of the mudsills. There was other testimony similar to that of Stone. The undisputed testimony in the case shows that this bridge stood three years after rebuilding, that during that time it was subjected to severe and repeated tests, and that heavy threshing outfits crossed it without trouble. The description of the drain as given by Stone, and of the bridge as given by all, permit a conclusion as to the condition of the bridge, when rebuilt, with something like mathematical certainty.

It is shown by the diagram [omitted here], which is predicated on the testimony, that it was sixteen inches below the bottom of the sill, and is therefore a favorable view of plaintiff's proof. The law requires that highways be made reasonably safe and fit for travel. If once put in such condition, there can be no liability for a defect until the municipality can be said to be chargeable with notice of such defect. Not only does the diagram show that the center of the mudsill was five feet and more distant from the edge of the ditch at the bottom, and four feet and three inches from the ditch at the level of the bed of the sill, but it also shows that the whole bent was taken out and floated down the stream, at a time of exceptionally high water, when the stream overflowed its banks. We are of the opinion that the court did not err in holding that the evidence failed to show that this bridge was not, as constructed, reasonably safe and fit for travel. A township is bound to anticipate only the things that are reasonably probable, and it is not proper to hold the public to a stricter account than private persons. In the history of the country it has been no uncommon thing for floods to undermine and wreck bridges, the construction and cost of which must bear some reasonable and practicable relation to the ability of a community, which is restricted in some respects as to the money at command for such purposes. The public is not an insurer. It is apparent that this township endeavored to maintain a reasonable bridge, and did so until from extraordinary conditions it was weakened, and settled when plaintiff crossed it. The rule for which counsel contends is a severe one. It is not that the liability is for a defect which is at once a source of danger, but one which may at some time in the future become so. It is not a construction that will necessarily become dangerous, but one which may or may not, depending on the nature of prospective events. All roads are subject to wear, and to washouts through the action of floods. It goes without saying that townships know this. Yet, until apprised of the defect caused by wear or washout, there is no liability. The legislature has said that the traveler must take the risk of danger of these things until the municipality not only has notice, but an opportunity for repair. When this bridge was rebuilt, it had every semblance of a good and stable structure. Moreover, by three years' use it was proved to have been so when erected. Not only the township, but every one else, plaintiff included, believed it to be so. It was only when in the course of time it became out of repair by the fortuitous undermining of its foundation that it became defective and dangerous. It is too strict a rule to say that the township should have anticipated this possibility, as it would be to say that it should anticipate that nails will rust and break, beams become affected by dry and invisible decay, or iron girders and supports become crystallized and weakened. Everything is subject to these changes, and every one knows it. Either of two policies may be adopted: One to compel the township to know and protect against these dangers, — *i. e.*, insure the traveler against them; the other to require diligence, as our law does, but to limit liability to cases where knowledge or notice exists. The rule contended for nullifies the statute. In the case of Rochefort *v.* Inhabitants of Attleborough, 154 Mass. 140, it was held that a town was not liable for an accident caused by a defect in a culvert so constructed that the defect was likely to occur in the remote future, where the defect had not existed for such a length of time as to make the town chargeable with notice thereof, and there had been no such defect at that place for more than a year previously," etc. See also Stoddard *v.* Inhabitants of Winchester, 154 Mass. 149. The case of Wakeham *v.* St. Clair Tp., 91 Mich. 27, is in point. There the township maintained a causeway built of logs, and covered with dirt along a river. It was a common occurrence for the dirt to drop through, leaving holes, owing to the action of water; and the township knew every time that it repaired the way, if it did not when it was constructed, that this would inevitably happen if that method of construction was adopted or retained. Held, that notice was necessary to create liability. We think, however, that the judgment should be reversed upon the ground that the question of notice was for the jury, there being some testimony tending to show that the imperfect condition of the bridge was visible, and generally known for a long period.

LONG, J., did not sit. The other justices concurred.

AMORY v. WABASH RAILROAD COMPANY.

Supreme Court, Michigan, April, 1902.

PASSENGER'S BAGGAGE — MERCHANDISE SAMPLES — THEFT — NOTICE TO CARRIER. — Where there was evidence that the plaintiff had been a traveler over defendant's road for six years, carrying samples of merchandise in trunks that differed from the ordinary trunk, and that on one of these trips recently made the baggage master stated to a witness that plaintiff was a dress man and that he had ladies' dresses, but received and checked the trunks as passenger's baggage, and some of the contents

were stolen, there was sufficient to warrant the jury to infer knowledge on the part of the defendant as to the character of the contents, and a verdict and judgment for plaintiff was affirmed (1).

ERROR to Circuit Court, Wayne County.

Action by William R. Amory against the Wabash Railroad Company. From a judgment for plaintiff, defendant appeals. *Judgment affirmed.*

"This is an action to recover the value of merchandise or samples, shipped by plaintiff as a passenger, and lost or stolen in transit. In the conduct of his business the past six or seven years, Wm. R. Amory, a ladies' tailor and milliner of Detroit, had been making semi-annual visits to Paris, to secure the latest fashions, bringing back with him suits, single garments, and millinery. With these he made quarterly trips to St. Louis, Cincinnati, and Cleveland, and occasionally to Chicago, Pittsburg, and Toledo, where he exhibited the samples or models for the purpose of sale, or the taking of orders for duplication. These goods were carried in trunks, originally procured in Paris, of which he had ten, of about the same size, — three feet five inches long, one foot eleven inches wide, two feet two and one-half inches high. On May 12, 1900, he started from Detroit for St. Louis, Mo., on one of his trips, with four employees, taking his entire stock of garments and millinery, of a total approximate value of $10,015, packed in six trunks, — five of the same size, and one a little larger, with square top. These were sent to the Union station baggage room by an omnibus line wagon about 12:30 P. M., receipted for by a porter, and placed upon a transfer truck, where they remained until checked and loaded on the 3:30 P. M. Wabash train for St. Louis. The party of five persons arrived at the depot about three o'clock, and, before boarding the train, Mr. Amory attended personally to the checking of the trunks, going to the baggage room and presenting to the Union station baggage master five mileage books for their transportation. He said nothing to Baggage Master Jones, who checked the trunks, as to what they contained, and no inquiry was made. If plaintiff had notified Jones of the character and value of the contents of the trunks, or, if Jones knew that they contained merchandise, it would have been the duty of Jones, before consenting to check them, to require of Mr. Amory a shipping contract, or release, reading as follows: 'In consideration that said company has consented to carry the property covered by this agreement upon its passenger

1. See NOTES OF RECENT CASES AS TO LIABILITY OF CARRIERS FOR BAGGAGE, at end of this case.

trains, and for a rate based upon the valuation thereof hereinafter given, I agree that the value of said property does not exceed the sum stated, and that no claim beyond its value as herein stated shall be made against said company, or any of its connecting lines, on account of any injury to, or loss or destruction of, such property from any cause whatever.' For six years Mr. Amory had been making trips with his trunks over this road, four times a year. Jones, the baggage master, had been employed by the defendant in that capacity during all this time. An employee of the omnibus line delivered the trunks, and testified that he said to the employees at the baggage room, to whom he delivered them, that he had six trunks for Mr. Amory, the ladies' tailor. Mr. McCormick, one of these men, testified that Mr. Jones said to him that 'Mr. Amory was a dress man; he had ladies' dresses, and brought them over from Paris.' The trunks had European baggage stamps on them. At the same time four empty hat boxes were sent with the trunks to the depot, to be sent by express, with the name, business, and address of Mr. Amory upon them. The testimony of Mr. Jones is evasive. When asked whether the trunks differed in any way from the ordinary run of trunks containing baggage, he replied, 'Well, I took them to be personal property.' Again, when asked if they differed in their general appearance from ordinary trunks, he replied, 'Well, all I could see, some of them had canvas covers on.' Again he said, 'They were something like show baggage or family baggage; that is what I took them for.' Upon arrival at the Southern hotel, St. Louis, the following morning, one of the trunks was found to have been broken open, the contents disarranged, and goods to the amount of $385 were missing. Verdict and judgment for plaintiff."

THOMAS W. PARKER (ALFRED RUSSELL, of counsel), for appellant.

E. T. WOOD, for appellee.

GRANT, J. (after stating the facts). — Counsel do not disagree as to the law of the case. The statute provides for compensation for transporting any passenger and his ordinary baggage, not exceeding in weight 150 pounds. Comp. Laws, sec. 6234, subd. 9. All the authorities agree that the baggage which a passenger is entitled to have carried is the articles which are necessary and requisite for his personal convenience. Story, Bailm., sec. 499. If a passenger ships merchandise in his trunk without notice to the railroad company, or knowledge on its part of the contents of the trunk, the company is not responsible for its loss. It is the duty of the passenger to give the carrier notice that his trunk contains merchandise, or things which cannot be included as baggage, unless the carrier has knowledge that the contents of the trunk are not baggage, but merchandise. Knowledge is equivalent to notice. The question, therefore, is, in this case, was there any probative testimony from which a jury could infer that Mr. Jones, the agent of the defendant, knew that these trunks contained merchandise? We think this question must be answered in the affirmative. If the jury believed Mr. McCormick, Mr. Jones did know that Mr. Amory's trunks contained merchandise, and that he was transporting such merchandise for business purposes. Were it not for the testimony of Mr. McCormick, the question would be more doubtful. But, in connection with that, the fact that Mr. Amory had traveled over this road so often for several years, using these same trunks; that they were delivered by an employee of the omnibus line as the trunks of Mr. Amory, the ladies' tailor: that Mr. Jones knew Mr. Amory and his business, and the large and uniform size of the trunks — were competent for the jury to consider in connection with Mr. McCormick's testimony in determining Jones' knowledge of the character of the contents of the trunks. Sloman *v.* Railroad Co., 67 N. Y. 208; Jacobs *v.* Tutt (C. C.) 33 Fed. Rep. 412; Railroad Co. *v.* Swift, 12 Wall. 262; 2 Fetter, Carr. Pass., sec. 606; Ft. Worth & R. G. R. Co. *v.* I. B. Rosenthall Millinery Co. (Tex. Civ. App.) 29 S. W. Rep. 196; Oakes *v.* Railroad Co., 20 Ore. 392. See also Railway Co. *v.* Hochstim, 67 Ill. App. 514.

Judgment is affirmed.

LONG, J., did not sit. The other justices concurred.

NOTES OF RECENT CASES AS TO LIABILITY OF CARRIERS FOR BAGGAGE.

1. **Baggage injured or stolen before being checked.**
2. **Baggage injured or stolen after arrival at station or landing or from wagon.**
3. **Merchandise checked as baggage.**
4. **Limiting liability.**
5. **Connecting carrier.**
6. **Passenger's effects stolen from car berth or stateroom.**
7. **Passenger carrying prohibited articles into car.**

1. Baggage injured or stolen before being checked.

In MCKIBBIN *v.* GREAT NORTHERN R. Co. (Minn. 1899), 78 Minn. 232, plaintiff's traveling salesman had an expressman carry four of his sample cases to the defendant's station, where the expressman left them at ten o'clock at night, on one side of the station platform, some distance from the station house. The station agent was in the station house and the expressman told him that "there were four trunks out there," and went away. The salesman was provided with a thousand-mile ticket, and with what are called "excess baggage tickets," to pay for the excess weight of the trunks that were thus permitted by the company to be carried on passenger trains as excess baggage. When the salesman arrived at the station soon after the delivery of the trunks and applied to the agent to have them checked, one was found missing, and it was afterwards found to have been stolen and the contents abstracted. The court below directed a verdict for the plaintiff for the full amount. On appeal the court reversed the judgment and said that the question of whether there had been a delivery to the station agent should have been submitted to the jury. The court further said that it was competent for the carrier to contract to carry as baggage, merchandise or other property not designed for personal use or property not belonging to the passenger, and if it does so it will be liable as a common carrier. But there must be evidence to justify the court to hold as matter of law that such a contract was entered into.

In CORRY v. PENNSYLVANIA R. R. CO. (Pa. 1900), 194 Pa. St. 516, the plaintiff intending to become a passenger sent her trunk by an expressman to defendant's railway station, where it was left and was broken open and the contents stolen before the plaintiff arrived, and who became a passenger thereafter. The lower court rendered judgment for the plaintiff that was reversed on appeal, the court saying that at the time the articles were taken she had not become a passenger, and hence the company never did undertake to carry her and her missing baggage. That the cause of action should have been for the negligent and careless keeping of the trunk before the plaintiff became a passenger.

In GOLDBERG v. AHNAPEE & W. R. CO. (Wis. 1899), 105 Wis. 1, one of the plaintiffs, a traveling man, sent his trunks, containing merchandise and not baggage, to defendant's railway station in the evening about five o'clock, intending to check them the next morning on a train that left about six o'clock. During the night they were destroyed by fire, without fault or negligence of defendant. A verdict was rendered by the jury for defendant. A rule of the company prohibited the checking of baggage until a half hour before train time, which plaintiff knew. On appeal the court said that as matter of law it could not be said that such rule was unreasonable, nor that twelve hours was reasonable or was rendered necessary by the circumstances, and that the submission to the jury of that question was proper. That whether the defendant had accepted the trunks was a disputed question of fact, and a finding in the negative had abundant support in the evidence. Parol proof of the rule of checking a half hour before train time that was printed on a card that was hung in the depot and was burned in the fire was proper.

In the case of THE PRISCILLA (U. S. D. C. of N. Y., Jan'y, 1901), 106 Fed. 739, it appeared that the plaintiff's expressman delivered to and received a receipt for two trunks from defendant's company's agent at the pier from which the steamboat Priscilla was to sail that afternoon. About two hours afterwards plaintiff arrived at the pier and then purchased two tickets for passage for himself and wife. He presented the tickets to the agent and asked that the trunks be checked to his destination. One of the trunks could not be found then nor since. The court said that upon the long-established usage in evidence the reception of the baggage was an incident of the company's maritime business, and in anticipation of its subsequent maritime contract of transportation, and formed part of the contract from the moment the ticket was purchased. The court held that the contract printed on the ticket limiting the company's liability to $100 was binding on the passenger, and directed judgment for that amount. On appeal to the Circuit Court of Appeals Second, Circuit, Feb'y, 1902, 114 Fed. 863, the court held that as the carrier did not know to whom the baggage belonged or upon what particular vessel it was to be carried, or whether it was to be carried at all, it was in no sense within the control of any particular vessel or its officers, and therefore the maritime lien upon the vessel was not created, and the court below was directed to dismiss the libel. The court further said that it was consequently unnecessary to consider whether the company assumed the liability of a carrier or only that of a warehouseman.

2. Baggage injured or stolen after arrival at station or landing or from wagon.

In SOUTHERN R. Co. *v.* WOOD (Ga. 1901), 39 S. E. 922, it appeared that after plaintiff had purchased tickets and had checked her baggage to her intended destination the agent asked her for the check for one of her boxes, that he refused to send as baggage, as it was overweight, but promised to send the next day as freight on a freight train. The plaintiff gave up the check, relying on the promise which was not kept, and when the box was received by her it had been exposed to the weather and the contents were much injured. The plaintiff recovered a verdict, and the judgment was affirmed.

In GEORGIA R. Co. *v.* JOHNSON (Ga. 1901), 113 Ga. 589, plaintiff, upon arriving at her destination, presented her baggage check for her trunk and was informed that it was not there. She presented the check from time to time, until two months had elapsed, before she received the trunk, and when received the clothing therein had been ruined by the decaying of about a dozen apples, which were in the trunk. The plaintiff obtained a verdict which the Supreme Court reversed. The court said that articles perishable in their nature, such as fruit, are not baggage.

In WERNER *v.* EVANS (Ill. App. Ct. 1901), 94 Ill. App. 328, a valise and its contents delivered to an express company for transportation was lost. The valise belonged to a nurse and contained, besides wearing apparel and toilet articles, certain record books used by the nurse in her vocation. The court said that she could recover for the loss of the books at such valuation as from the evidence the jury should find. That the books were, as it appeared from the evidence, implements used in her vocation as nurse and such as she might properly include with her garments, also used in such employment, as part of her reasonable baggage. It was not necessary to show that the books had a general market value in order to prove what they were reasonably worth to appellee. A judgment for plaintiff was affirmed.

In MARSHALL *v.* PONTIAC, O & N. R. Co. (Mich. 1901), 126 Mich. 45, plaintiff purchased a ticket for the sole purpose of checking his trunk. He did not intend to go on the train and did not go, but went by his own private conveyance to the place to which the trunk was checked and for which the ticket was purchased. The trunk arrived at the place to which it was checked and remained on the station platform from ten o'clock in the morning until noon, when it was placed in the baggage room, which was burglarized on that night or the following night, and the trunk and contents were stolen. The plaintiff was not a passenger over defendant's road until more than four months had elapsed. The court said that baggage implies a passenger who intends to go upon the train with his baggage, and receive it upon the arrival of the train at the end of the journey; that the defendant was not in fault in checking the baggage, as plaintiff had not disclosed his intention of not accompanying it. The court held that plaintiff was not a passenger, that defendant was a gratuitous bailee, and was not guilty of gross negligence, and not liable.

In BLACKMORE *v.* MISSOURI PAC. R. Co. (Mo. 1901), 162 Mo. 455, plaintiff's trunks were left by him in the station baggage room, to remain there until the next day, when he intended to resume his journey, as it was more convenient than to have the trunks taken to the hotel. About three o'clock the next morning the depot room was consumed by fire, and the trunks were destroyed. There was evidence tending to show that the fire was caused by a spark from a locomotive that had passed just before the fire was discovered. The court held that the statute holding a railroad company liable for injury to property by fire communicated by sparks from a loccomotive, which was the statute invoked in this case, did not apply to goods in the possession of the company for transit or for delivery to the owner, but for those cases only where the owner of the property had no other remedy.

In FELTON *v.* CHICAGO G. W. R. Co. (Kansas City Ct. App. 1900), 86 Mo. App. 332, the plaintiff alighted from a night train at a station where there was no night agent, and going to the baggage car, found that his trunk was not on the train, and no one could tell him when it would arrive. The trunk arrived the following afternoon and was burglarized the same night in the station. Plaintiff had gone to the country and did not call for the trunk until the day after the burglary occurred. The court held that the plaintiff was not guilty of contributory negligence, that he had applied for his baggage within a reasonable time, and that the carrier's liability was not reduced to that of a warehouseman.

In PARKER *v.* NORTH GERMAN LLOYD S. S Co. (N. Y. Sup. Ct. App. Div. 1902), 76 N. Y. Supp. 806, the plaintiff, upon arrival of the steamship upon which he was a passenger at Bremen, directed that his trunks be forwarded to a town in England, for which a receipt was given him by the defendant's agent who forwarded the trunks in the usual way by way of London. On their arrival in England the trunks were detained at the custom house, and while on the pier were, with the pier, destroyed by fire. The court held the defendant not liable, and a verdict for plaintiff was reversed. The court said that the transportation of the plaintiff and his baggage was complete on the defendant's steamer when they reached Bremen, and the further contract was to forward, not to carry.

In TEXAS & PACIFIC R'Y Co. *v* MORRISON FAUST Co. (Tex. Civ. App. 1898), 20 Tex. Civ. App. 144, the plaintiff's trunk, containing sheet music used by them in their business, was lost from the platform of defendant's station. The court held that if the railroad company desired an instruction that it would not be liable if after the trunk was safely unloaded on the platform the plaintiff had taken charge of it, the instruction should have been asked, and cannot complain on appeal of the omission. The court further said that the manuscript music was entitled to be regarded and carried as baggage when the company traveled as passengers by train.

8. Merchandise checked as baggage.

In CENTRAL OF GEORGIA R. Co. *v.* JOSEPH (Ala. 1900), 125 Ala. 313, the plaintiff, an Armenian unable to speak English, entered the station of defendant to take passage on its train. She had a valise containing merchandise that she showed to the station agent, and some of which he bought. She afterwards bought her ticket of the same agent, who checked the valise to her destination. The valise after arrival at the destination was not called for within twenty-four hours, and when called for could not be found in the baggage room where it had been placed and was lost or stolen. A verdict was rendered for plaintiff and judgment entered which the court reversed on appeal on the ground that the valise did not contain wearing apparel, but merchandise, and that that fact was not known by the company. That the knowledge of the station agent was gained in his individual capacity and not while engaged in his business as an officer of the company, and therefore was not binding on it.

In WEBER CO. v. CHICAGO, ST. P., M. & O. R. CO. (Iowa, 1901), 113 Iowa, 188, plaintiff, knowing of a regulation forbidding baggagemen to receive jewelers' sample cases for transportation as baggage without a bond releasing the company from liability in case of loss, induced a baggageman to check two sample cases known to the baggageman to contain jewelry. One of the cases disappeared before it was put on the train, and this action was brought for its value. The court held that the defendant was not liable because of the fraudulent act of the plaintiff. That a common carrier of passengers may refuse to check as baggage that which is merchandise and may make any regulations in regard to the waiver of those objections which it sees fit to adopt. If there is no waiver, then the carrier is not liable to any extent for merchandise checked as baggage. Defendant's refusal to refund the sum paid for excess baggage was not a waiver, as it had not contracted to carry jewelry. A judgment on a verdict directed for defendant was affirmed.

In SHERLOCK v. CHICAGO, ROCK ISLAND & P. R. CO. (Mo. 1900), 85 Mo. App. 46, the plaintiff tendered to defendant's agent as baggage a pine box containing 165 copies of a book of which he was author and publisher and which he intended to take with him for sale and delivery at his destination. The agent was told what the box contained, and after it was weighed the agent charged and was paid for the excess in weight over the 150 pounds allowed each passenger. The agent had no authority to check the said box of books, but the plaintiff was not aware of the want of authority. When the plaintiff's destination was reached the box was found broken open and the books scattered over the floor of the car, and much damaged. The court said that though a carrier without special contract is only liable for such baggage as a traveler usually carries, it is liable where the agent chooses to treat other articles as baggage and a loss occurs if the passenger is ignorant of the agent's want of authority to accept merchandise as baggage. A verdict for plaintiff was affirmed.

In TRIMBLE v. N. Y. CENTRAL & H. R. R. CO. (N. Y. 1900), 162 N. Y. 84, the plaintiff's salesman checked a trunk containing samples of the goods he had for sale and that had every appearance of being a sample trunk without informing the baggage agent that it was a sample trunk. He paid eighty-five cents for excess of baggage and received a card known as "Excess Baggage Check," and for another small trunk he received an ordinary metallic check. The sample trunk and contents were destroyed while in possession of defendant, and the suit was brought by the owners. A rule of the defendant company provided that a release of liability would be required of all who carried sample cases. The release was not asked for by the baggage agent. The court said the evidence warranted the submission to the jury of the fact whether defendant was charged with knowledge of the character of the trunk, and a judgment for plaintiff was affirmed. The court said that the recovery was not on the contract of passage, but on an independent agreement for the transportation of the sample trunk as freight.

4. Limiting liability.

In MERRILL *v.* PACIFIC TRANSFER CO. (Cal. 1901), 131 Cal. 582, plaintiff on a train gave his baggage checks to defendant's agent and received in return a receipt containing his name, address where the trunks were to be sent, numbers of the checks, and also some printed matter that limited the liability of the carrier to $100, unless a special contract was made, and a notice that if the condition was not acceptable to notify the agent. The plaintiff read the pencilled memoranda, saw the address was correct, and without reading the printed matter put the receipt in his pocket. One of the trunks was stolen from a wagon of defendant. A verdict for the full amount was rendered by the jury. The judgment was reversed upon appeal because of a refused instruction as to whether the plaintiff had actual or constructive notice of the condition on the receipt was for the determination of the jury. The court also held that the admission of evidence of the expenditures for wearing apparel to replace that lost in the trunk should have been excluded.

In AIKEN *v.* WABASH R. CO. (Mo. App. 1899), 80 Mo. App. 8, the plaintiff checked her trunk through and traveled from Massachusetts to St. Louis, Mo., over three lines of roads. On the first she had a pass. Her ticket was purchased for her at a reduced rate from the next railroad for passage over it and the defendant's line. The ticket contained a limitation of the liability of the railroad from which it was purchased as to recovery for loss of baggage. The trunk was destroyed by fire in the baggage car that was burned by dynamite being carried as baggage, unknown to defendants, exploding in the car. The court on appeal said that, viewing the ticket as a contract, the presumption obtained as in other contracts that the plaintiff read or was advised of its conditions and assented thereto, and that the printed conditions on the face of the ticket being part of the contract, the liability of the railroad from which the ticket was bought for loss of baggage was limited to $100, and that this special contract was founded on a valuable consideration, viz., the reduced rate, and further that the limitation in the contract was available to the defendant as a connecting carrier, as it was acting as agent of the road from which the ticket was bought and was entitled to the benefit of the original contract of shipment.

In TALCOTT *v.* WABASH R. R. CO. (N. Y. 1899), 159 N. Y. 461, plaintiff purchased from defendant's agent a ticket having coupons attached for passage over defendant's and connecting roads. With his ticket he went to the baggage master and asked to have his sample trunks and personal trunk checked through to his destination. The baggage master was informed as to the character of the trunks and charged for excessive weight, which plaintiff paid. The plaintiff's ticket contained a provision that the defendant company selling the ticket acted as agent and did not intend to become responsible beyond its own line. The trunks were destroyed by fire on the first line connecting with defendant's road. The court held that the baggage master had authority to make the contract with the plaintiff in respect to the sample trunks, and that it was a conract independent of the purchase of the ticket, and that a nonsuit as to that, cause of action was improper. That as to the personal baggage of the plaintiff the ticket controlled, and that although he had not read it or the conditions, he testified that he knew what a coupon ticket meant, and that he was to travel over connecting roads, and this warranted the inference of notice to him of what was stated in the condition, and having failed to prove a contract as would enable him to recover, a dismissal of the complaint as to the last cause of action was proper.

In SPRINGER *v.* WESTCOTT (N. Y. 1901), 166 N. Y. 117, plaintiff, a passenger on a railway train, delivered her check to defendant's solicitor and agent for a trunk then on the train approaching New York, and received from him a receipt which she did not read, but that contained a stipulation that limited the liability of the express company for loss of the trunk to $100. The trunk arrived in New York, and while in the baggage car the agent placed the check he had received from plaintiff on the trunk strap that contained the duplicate check, and then pasted upon the trunk the label of the express company entitling it to remove the trunk from the baggage room. Before the defendant took possession of the trunk after it reached the baggage room, the trunk was stolen and rifled of its contents. It was returned to the baggage room by the agent of another company, who had found it, and it was then delivered by the defendant to the plaintiff. The court held that the premature surrender of the check to the railroad company by the defendant made the former the bailee of the latter and the latter having assumed control, was bound to make safe delivery of the trunk and its contents to the owner. The court also held that if the plaintiff knew the contents of the paper containing the stipulation, she could only recover the amount specified, but otherwise she could recover the full amount. That it was a question for the jury.

In HOUSTON, E. & W. T. R'Y CO. *v.* SEALE (Tex. Civ. App. 1902), 67 S. W. Rep. 437, plaintiff purchased tickets of defendant for transportation over its line and other lines that it connected with to a point in another State. On arrival at the plaintiff's destination the contents of his trunk were found to have been ruined by wet, and he brought suit for the damage to the articles and for being deprived of their use and for the mental distress occasioned thereby. The defendant set up the contract contained in the ticket limiting its liability to $100 on account of baggage. The court held that though the contract was interstate the state statute prohibiting carriers from limiting their liability as it existed at common law applied; that the measure of damages was the actual value of the articles destroyed, and that the allowance of damages for the deprivation of their use and the mental distress occasioned thereby was erroneous, and on the latter ground the judgment for plaintiff was reversed.

In MEXICAN NATIONAL R. CO. *v.* WARE (Tex. Civ. App. 1900), 60 S. W. Rep. 343, plaintiff purchased two tickets for himself and wife from a railroad company in Texas, of which the defendant was a connecting line, for transportation to Mexico and return, with stop-over privileges. The tickets contained a clause limiting the amount of recovery for wearing apparel to $100 for each ticket. The trunk was delivered to defendant in Mexico, to be transported to Texas, and was lost. It contained, besides clothing, some jewelry, a Bible, a Spanish dictionary, and toilet articles. The court said that the laws of Mexico did not apply, as the contract was made in Texas and began there, and was to end there; that by the laws of Texas common carriers cannot limit their liability as it exists at common law, and cannot restrict the right of a passenger to carry baggage necessary for his comfort or convenience by calling it "wearing apparel." A judgment for plaintiff for $750 was affirmed.

In THE NEW ENGLAND (U. S. Dist. Ct. of Mass. 1901), 101 Fed. 415, the libellant, who was a passenger on defendant's steamship from Boston to Liverpool. had delivered her trunk at the dock of the company in Boston, and it was not to be found when the steamship arrived in Liverpool. Several days afterwards the trunk was forwarded to the libellant's address, but it was empty. The defendant failed to explain delay in delivery or to introduce any evidence concerning the treatment of the trunk while detained in its hands. The court held it was justified in finding that the trunk was broken open and rifled by the company's servants. The court also held that a stipulation contained in the passenger's ticket issued by an English steamship company to the passenger in the United States, that the contract shall be governed by the English law that permits a common carrier to exempt itself by express contract from responsibility for the negligence of its servants, was void as contrary to the public policy of the United States. The court also held that a provision limiting the liability of the company for loss of baggage to $50 was not reasonable and would not be enforced.

5. Connecting carrier.

In MOORE *v.* N. Y., NEW HAVEN & H. R. Co. (Mass. 1899), 173 Mass. 335, plaintiff had her trunk checked and traveled over six distinct railroads, for each of which roads she had a separate coupon, but all forming one ticket. The trunk was in good condition and properly packed when delivered to the first railroad, and she did not see it again until it was delivered to her at her destination by the defendant. Upon opening the trunk, it was found that the contents had been wet with water in some unknown manner and greatly damaged, but she was unable to show when, where, or how the damage was done, or in whose possession the trunk was when the damage was done. In the lower court the judge refused to rule that the presumption was that the damage occurred while the trunk was in the possession of the last connecting line of railroad and rendered judgment for defendant. On appeal the court reversed the judgment and ordered judgment for plaintiff, and said the rule asked should have been given, and that the presumption was justified as a true presumption of fact.

In LESSARD *v.* BOSTON AND MAINE R. (N. H. 1899), 69 N. H. 648, plaintiff bought a ticket from defendant's agent for passage over it and connecting roads to his destination. The ticket had a coupon for each road and contained the stipulation that in selling it and checking baggage the company was acting only as agent and was not responsible beyond its own line. The plaintiff could not read, did not know what was on the ticket, and made no inquiry about it. The trunk was lost on one of the connecting lines that was an independent road. The court below found a verdict for defendants upon the ground that they were not liable beyond their own line when they had given express notice to that effect. The court on appeal said that whether the printed matter was express notice to the purchaser, who was unable to read it, was a question not necessary to consider. That it was incumbent on the plaintiff to prove that the defendants made a contract to carry his baggage beyond their own line. That under the law of the State no presumption arose that they made such a contract. That the case differed where the carrier attempted to limit the liability that ordinarily attached to the contract of carriage. That the finding that the defendants gave express notice that they would not contract in a certain way necessarily included one that it was not proved that they did so contract.

In TOLEDO AND OHIO CENT. R. CO. *v.* BOWLER AND BURDICK CO. (Ohio, 1900), 63 Ohio St. 274, 9 Am. Neg. Rep. 156, plaintiff's two trunks that the station agent of a connecting line knew contained only watches and jewelry were checked to a point on defendant's road and were destroyed in a collision of trains on that road. The court said, where the only authority given by a railroad company to the baggage agent of a connecting road is to check baggage to all stations on the line of the former road, no presumption follows that such agent has authority to check merchandise over the line of said road under the guise of baggage, and knowledge on the part of such agent that a passenger's trunks contain merchandise and not baggage is not sufficient to charge such company with knowledge.

In ST. LOUIS SOUTHWESTERN R. CO. OF TEXAS v. FRENCH (Tex. Civ. App. 1900), 23 Tex. Civ. App. 511, plaintiff brought an action for mental distress, pain, and anguish caused him and his wife by the alleged negligence of the railroad company in delaying the shipment of the corpse of their child. The plaintiff purchased through tickets for himself, wife and body of the child from the agent of a railway company for passage over its line and that of the defendant company, a connecting carrier. Plaintiff saw the corpse on a baggage truck near the door of the express car of defendant's train at the transfer station, but did not inform any one that he wanted the corpse shipped on that train, supposing that it would be so shipped. It was not shipped by that train, but was shipped by an extra train and arrived at plaintiff's destination an hour and forty-five minutes late. A verdict for $300 was rendered for plaintiff. The court said that an inspection of the coffin would no doubt have disclosed its destination, and the company's servants were negligent in failing to do so.

6. Passenger's effects stolen from car berth or stateroom.

In MCMURRAY v. PULLMAN PALACE CAR CO. (Ill. 1899), 86 Ill. App. 619, the plaintiff, a traveling salesman, placed his money in a card case, the card case in his vest, and his vest under the pillow of the lower berth in a sleeping car belonging to defendant. When he arose in the morning the card case and money were gone. There was no proof that there was no watch kept during the night by either the conductor or porter. The court said that there was no proof that the plaintiff's money was lost by reason of defendant's negligence, and that the mere proof of the loss of the money, without showing some such negligence, was not sufficient to sustain a recovery. A judgment for defendant was affirmed.

In PULLMAN PALACE-CAR CO. v. HUNTER (Ky. 1900), 54 S. W. Rep. 845, the plaintiff, while asleep in a lower berth in one of defendant's sleeping coaches, had three diamond rings stolen from her fingers and brought this action for their value. The car was in charge of the same porter for the entire distance, and there was evidence that twice he absented himself from the car for at least twenty minutes on each occasion, and that just before taking charge of the car he had completed a long trip on another route. The court said that there was sufficient evidence conducing to show negligence on the part of the agents of the company, and that the question had been properly submitted to jury. A judgment for plaintiff for $250 was affirmed.

In WAMSLEY v. ATLAS STEAMSHIP CO. (N. Y. 1901), 168 N. Y. 533, the plaintiff brought an action against defendant for conversion of a box of negatives and photographic prints that he had delivered to the steamship company when boarding one of their vessels and that could not be found when the vessel arrived at his destination. There was a verdict and judgment for plaintiff which was affirmed by the Appellate Division. The Court of Appeals reversed the judgment, holding that the mere failure to deliver because the article was lost would not work a conversion; that there might have been a cause of action for negligence as the relation of carrier and passenger existed.

In LINCOLN *v.* N. Y. & CUBA MAIL S. Co. (N. Y. Sup. Ct., Appellate Term, 1900), 30 Misc. 752, the plaintiff, a passenger on defendant's steamship, went to his stateroom that had been assigned to him, and placed some money in his traveling bag, which he locked and finding no key in the stateroom door closed it and went to the purser for a key. On his return he found the money had been stolen. The court below dismissed the complaint. On appeal the court said that having assigned him a stateroom the defendant had taken entire charge of the plaintiff, and that the latter having placed the bag in the stateroom, locked the bag, and closed the door of the room and then gone for a key for the door, had done all that could be reasonably expected of him. The judgment was reversed.

In PULLMAN PALACE CAR CO. *v.* ARENTS, (Tex. Civ. App., 1902), 66 S. W. 329, it appeared that plaintiff entered defendant's car at a station in Texas from which place he had a ticket, to a point in Mexico, but the ticket was not taken up nor his car fare collected until the train was in Mexico. At a station in Mexico plaintiff left the car temporarily, and when he returned found that his valise that he had left on a seat near an open window had been stolen. The court held that plaintiff was a passenger from the Texas station, and the contract was practically entered into there, and an action might be maintained in that State though neither he nor defendant resided there, where the latter had an agent there, and that the question of plaintiff's negligence in leaving the satchel near an open window, and of defendant company's employees in not taking precautions were properly left to the jury. A judgment for plaintiff was affirmed.

In THE HUMBOLDT (U. S. Dist. Ct., Wash., N. D., 1899), 97 Fed. 656, the libelant having purchased a ticket that entitled him to a stateroom and meals en route went on board the libelee's vessel just before sailing time, and placed his valise in the stateroom assigned to him and from which the valise was stolen. The court said that as there was no negligence or breach of duty charged, and the baggage had not been delivered to or taken into the custody of the carrier's servants the libelee was not liable. The court further said that a steamship company that provides rooms and meals for its passengers as well as transportation does not thereby assume the liability of an innkeeper.

7. Passenger carrying prohibited articles into car.

In RUNYAN *v.* CENTRAL R. CO. (N. J., 1900), 65 N. J. L. 228, 9 Am. Neg. Rep. 97, the plaintiff, who had a first-class ticket, was not permitted to enter defendant's train because he carried some parcels that defendant's agents said should be sent by express. The court said that there was sufficient eidence of usage to support a verdict that the defendant company, a common carrier, had adopted a rule that passengers might carry with them in the passenger cars their small parcels of merchandise.

In DOWD *v.* THE ALBANY RAILWAY (N. Y. Sup. Ct., App. Div. 1900), 47 App. Div. 202, the plaintiff boarded defendant's street car carrying two rifles with bayonets attached, and a valise, and when told by the conductor that it was against the rules for passengers to be allowed to ride when encumbered with such articles, the plaintiff refused to get off. The conductor then told the plaintiff he must get off and forced the plaintiff off by taking him by the collar of the coat and forcing him off. A verdict was rendered for plaintiff and judgment entered. The court said that the court below should have charged, as matter of law, that the rule of the company was reasonable instead of leaving it to the jury to say, and that the conductor had the right to eject the plaintiff, and that the only question for consideration for the jury was whether unnecessary force was used.

DENE v. ARNOLD PRINT WORKS.

Supreme Judicial Court, Massachusetts, June, 1902.

EMPLOYEE INJURED WHILE PASSING BETWEEN MACHINES — KNOWLEDGE OF DANGER — WARNING. — Where plaintiff, an operator in defendant's mill, while passing between two machines, slipped, and, to save himself from falling, threw out his hand, which was caught in the gears of one of the machines, and it appeared that he was familiar with the surroundings, and that the accident might have been caused by oil which was on the floor, and the passageway was unlighted, it was *held* that these facts were not sufficient to hold defendant liable, neither was defendant required to warn plaintiff of the danger in so passing between the machines (1).

EXCEPTIONS from Superior Court, Berkshire County.

Action by Ignes Dene, by next friend, against the Arnold Print Works. From a verdict for defendant, plaintiff brings exceptions. *Overruled.*

CROSBY & NOXON, for plaintiff.

BROOKS & HAMILTON, for defendant.

MORTON, J. — As the plaintiff went to pass through a passageway between two machines, on one of which he worked, in the defendant's mill, he slipped, and, to save himself from falling, threw out his hand, and it was caught in the gears of one of the machines and injured. This action is brought to recover for the injury thus sustained. At the time of the accident the plaintiff was between fourteen and fifteen years old, and had worked about two months on the machine on which he was working when injured. A few minutes before the accident he had started to go to the water-closet, passing on his way between these two machines, and had reached the stairs, when he turned back to speak of his intended absence to a man in the room whom he was required to notify of the absence. He went back the same way that he had come, and it was while going back that he met with the accident. There was testimony tending to

1. See notes of recent Massachusetts cases arising out of relation of Master and Servant, at end of this case.

show that the slipping might have been caused by oil on the floor. There was also testimony tending to show that the place where the plaintiff slipped was not lighted. The plaintiff contends that the defendant was negligent in these respects, and that his injury was caused thereby, and also that the defendant was negligent in not instructing him as to the danger of using the passageway.

If the slipping was caused by oil on the floor, and was not a pure accident, there is nothing to show how long the oil had been there, or what caused it to be there. It would be holding parties to a liability altogether too strict to say that the presence of oil on the floor of a mill was itself evidence of negligence. Regard must be had to what is practicable and reasonable, and it would hardly be possible to operate a mill without more or less oil getting on the floor, especially under and around different machines. We do not see how the absence of light can be said to have caused the injury. The plaintiff went through the passageway on his way to the stairs, and it was then unlighted, and was so when he returned. His familiarity with the machine and its surroundings was such that he needed no artificial light. Moreover, if there was negligence on the part of any one in not lighting the gas, it would seem that it was the negligence of a fellow-servant, and not of the defendant, or of one whose sole or principal duty was that of superintendence. It is manifest, we think, that the plaintiff needed no warning or instruction as to the danger, if any, in using the passageway, or of getting his hand caught in the gears.

Exceptions overruled.

SEE THE FOLLOWING RECENT MASSACHUSETTS CASES RELATING TO INJURIES TO EMPLOYEES:

Employee injured by washing machine.

In ROCHE *v.* LOWELL BLEACHERY *(Mass. May, 1902)*, 63 N. E. Rep. 943, action under Employer's Liability Act (Rev. Laws, c. 106, sec. 71, clause 2), to recover for injuries to employee, defendant's exceptions to verdict for plaintiff were overruled. HOLMES, Ch. J., stating the facts as follows: "The plaintiff ran a washing machine for the defendant. In connection with this machine were certain cylinders called "binders," which revolved and dragged the cloth along as it came through the plaintiff's machine. These binders frequently became loose, and it was the plaintiff's duty to tighten them. In order to do so he had to stop his machine and go up to another floor out of sight of the machine. At the time of the accident the binders had become loose and the plaintiff was tightening them in this way, having first stopped his machine, when the superintendent came along and set the machine running, by reason of which the plaintiff was caught in the shafting above. It is well understood that an employer is not liable for every act done by a person engaged in superintendence, even if done to help in carrying out an order which the latter himself has given, and that different minds may differ as to where the line shall be drawn. Joseph *v.* George C. Whitney Co., 177 Mass. 176, 177. But we are of opinion that the jury was warranted in finding, if not bound to find, for the plaintiff in this case if it found the facts to be as the plaintiff contended. The negligence, if there was any, did not consist in the mechanical details of carrying out a proper order; it consisted in setting the machine in motion at that time. If the superintendent had told another workman to start it up, probably the case would not be here. It is true, perhaps, that that could not be accepted as a universal test, because often the negligence is due to the consciousness of the party not having been directed to the point of complaint, which the hypothesis of a direction assumes it to have been. But the test seems to be of use when, as here, the precise object of the superintendent's conception was improper. In such a case the proximity between the brain that conceived and the subordinate ganglion that carried out the thought seems not to be a ground of exoneration. See O'Brien *v.* Look, 171 Mass. 36 (6 Am. Neg. Rep. 225n). Supposing the order to have been given, it would have been of sufficient importance and would have risen enough above merely mechanical execution of the work that might have come from any workman to be matter of superintendence. Indeed one might say shortly that, except as superintendent, Royer had no business to meddle with the machine. Exceptions overruled."

Employee injured by fall of stones — Act of fellow-servant.

In REAGAN *v.* LOMBARD ET AL. *(Mass. May, 1902)*, it appeared, as per syllabus to the report in 63 N. E. Rep. 895, that "plaintiff was injured by the fall of curbstones piled in tiers on a wharf. The stones were lifted onto the wharf by a crane, and piled by plaintiff's fellow-servants in tiers, with sticks or pieces of wood, selected by plaintiff's fellow-servants, between the stones. The stones in the piles were moved at various times, as occasion required, to get particular stones in each pile as they were wanted; and it did not appear how long the pile which fell had been piled, or had been in a dangerous condition. *Held* that, in the absence of such proof, the negligence, if any, was the improper piling, or the furnishing of improper dunnage between the stones, both of which were acts of fellow-servants, and plaintiff was therefore not entitled to recover." Defendant's exceptions to verdict for plaintiff sustained.

Defective machinery — Assumption of risk.

In DOBBINS *v.* LANG ET AL. *(Mass. May, 1902)*, 63 N. E. Rep. 911, defendant's exceptions to verdict for plaintiff were sustained, BARKER, J., stating the case as follows: "The danger of such an accident as that by which the plaintiff was hurt was not only obvious, but was so clearly and fully known to him and so clearly appreciated by him, that solely because of it he stopped work, left his machine, and went to find one of the defendants, in order to have the cause of danger removed. Not finding the person whom he sought he went back to the machine and resumed work, perfectly aware of the danger. This was not due care, and was an assumption of the risk. He was old enough and intelligent enough to have known better, and, as he acted under neither ignorance nor constraint, he has no cause of action, and the jury should have been so told. Exceptions sustained."

Scaffolding accident — Master not liable.

In MORRIS *v.* WALWORTH MANUFACTURING CO. *(Mass. May, 1902)*, 63 N. E.

Rep 910, defendant's exceptions were sustained, LATHROP, J., rendering the following opinion: "The plaintiff was injured while in the employ of the defendant. The declaration contains two counts — one under St. 1887, c. 270, sec. 1, and the other at common law. The case comes before us on the defendant's exception to the refusal of the judge to rule at the close of the evidence that the plaintiff could not recover. The plaintiff was between twenty-nine and thirty years old. He had been in this country between five and six years. Before coming here he had done farmer's work, and work as a helper in iron foundries. After his coming, he worked on farms about five months, and the rest of the time in factories, on iron work, and for three years of the time he helped put up fire escapes on finished and unfinished buildings. He worked on stagings, on platforms, and on planks. The plaintiff was employed by the defendant as a helper at its works in South Boston, and had been so employed a little more than five months, working as a helper for everybody. At the time of the accident he was at work on a new building belonging to the defendant. The outer walls were up, and it was roofed in. On the outside of the building was a platform which extended the whole length of the building, and was about twenty-five feet wide, and five feet high from the ground, with steps leading to the ground. There was an opening about six feet wide in the wall of the building onto this platform, and there was a brick retaining wall on the inside of the building, extending from the corner of the opening at a right angle; and all the floor space beyond this retaining wall had been filled with ashes, level with the top of the wall. For three days before the accident there had been but one plank, connecting the opening in the outer wall with the retaining wall inside. The plaintiff testified that some of the men put it there; that on the morning of the injury there were three planks laid across this corner, each five or six inches wide, and six, seven, or eight feet long, fastened together by a piece of wood nailed underneath in the middle, and projecting slightly beyond the planks; that he was set to work by one Riddell, and directed to take pipe into the place where the ashes were, and lay them there; that he took one piece in and set it, and on coming out, in walking over the planks, one of them tipped or bent, his toes caught, and he fell and broke one of his legs; and that he noticed after the accident that some of the nails had come out of the cleat. It is contended that Riddell was either a superintendent, or that he was acting as superintendent with the authority or consent of the employer, under St. 1894, c. 499. All the evidence on this point comes from the plaintiff, who, when asked, 'What did John Riddell do about there?' said, 'He is boss,' and, in answer to another question, said he had perhaps six or seven, perhaps more, under him. Without stopping to consider whether this is enough to show more than that he was merely a foreman in charge of a gang, we are of opinion that there is nothing to show that Riddell had anything to do with the planks, or that there was any negligence on his part in respect to them. For aught that appears, the planks were fastened together by some of the fellow-workmen of the plaintiff. We are also of opinion that the planks cannot be considered as ways or works, within the statute. They were used merely for a temporary purpose. Lynch *v.* Allyn, 160 Mass. 248; Burns *v.* Washburn, 160 Mass. 457; Adasken *v.* Gilbert, 165 Mass. 443, 445; Beique *v.* Hosmer, 169 Mass. 541. Nor do we find any evidence that would warrant the jury in finding a verdict for the plaintiff on the count at common law. The plaintiff failed to show negligence on the part of the defendant. Exceptions sustained."

Injured in saw mill.

In McLEAN *v.* PAINE ET AL. *(Mass. May, 1902)*, 63 N. E. Rep. 883, defendant's exceptions to judgment for plaintiff were overruled, MORTON, J., stating the case as follows: "This is an action of tort to recover for personal injuries sustained by the plaintiff's intestate while in the defendant's employment, and from which he died two days after. There was a verdict for the plaintiff, and the case is here on exceptions by the defendants to the exclusion of certain testimony and to the refusal of the presiding justice to give certain rulings that were asked for. Apart from the question of evidence, the case has been argued by the defendants on the footing that the questions are whether the plaintiff was in the exercise of due care, whether there was any evidence of negligence on the part of the defendants, and whether the plaintiff assumed the risk; and we shall so treat it. It seems to us that there was evidence of negligence on the part of the defendants. There was testimony tending to show that the saw 'wobbled,' and that the accident was caused by this 'wobbling.' It is true that there was also evidence tending to show that the accident was caused by the carelessness of the plaintiff's intestate in dropping a piece of wood onto the saw, but it was for the jury to say how the accident happened. It cannot be said, we think, that there was no evidence justifying the conclusion that it was caused by the 'wobbling' of the saw. We also think that there was evidence tending to show that the 'wobbling' of the saw was due to carelessness on the part of the defendants. There was testimony tending to show that the saw might have been sprung, so that it might have been improperly set on the arbor, or the arbor improperly set in the boxes, or the boxes so worn that the saw would not run smoothly, and that these things could have been discovered by proper care on the part of the defendants. And there was an admission, on cross-examination, by the man whose duty it was to put on the saw, and who did put it on, 'that he did not pay any particular attention to ascertain whether the saw was true, and in perfect running order.' This clearly warranted a finding that the defendants did not exercise proper care in seeing that the saw ran as it should run. There was evidence warranting a finding that the plaintiff's intestate was in the exercise of due care, and that he did not assume the risk. The testimony tended to show that he 'put the lumber in the saw as [he] had always put it in, and that the saw kicked and threw it back at him;' and there was nothing to show that he knew, or in the exercise of reasonable care ought to have known, that the saw was out of order. It would not be held therefore, that he assumed the risk, or was not in the exercise of due care. The remaining question relates to the matter of evidence. One Buffum, called as a witness by the defendants, was asked on cross-examination in regard to conversations with Margaret McLean. As we interpret the bill of exceptions, he stated fully all the conversation that he had had with her, and then was asked if he had not made certain specific statements to her, which he denied. Miss McLean was called in rebuttal, and was allowed to testify that Buffum had made the statements which he denied. This was the extent of the rebuttal. Thereupon Buffum was recalled by the defendants, and was asked to state what conversation he had had with Miss McLean. This was objected to, and was excluded. He was allowed to contradict the specific statements testified to by her. We think that the ruling was right. At the stage of the case at which the question was put it was clearly, we think, within the discretion of the presiding justice to admit or exclude it. Howes *v.* Colburn, 165 Mass. 385, 388.

43 N. E. Rep. 125. The case is clearly distinguishable from Mullins *v.* Peaslee (Mass.), 61 N. E. Rep. 811, on which the plaintiff relies. If the plaintiff, on calling Miss McLean in rebuttal, had been limited to the specific questions finally asked Buffum on cross-examination, the case presented would have been exactly parallel to that. But this case is entirely different. Buffum testified fully on cross-examination to the conversations with Miss McLean, and, if there was anything that the defendants had desired to bring out more fully, or correct, they could have asked Buffum about it when the cross-examination was concluded. To have allowed him to testify on surrebuttal would have been to permit him to testify again to a conversation which he had already given, and which there had been full opportunity to direct his attention to in case there had been any omissions or corrections which the defendants desired to have supplied or made. Whether he should be allowed to do so was, it seems to us, plainly within the discretion of the presiding justice as to the conduct of the trial. Exceptions overruled."

Injured by fall of iron metal bars.

In LANGLEY *v.* WHEELOCK ET AL. *(Mass. May, 1902)*, 63 N. E. Rep. 944, plaintiff's exceptions to judgment for defendants were overruled, the points of the case being stated in the syllabus to the report in 63 N. E. Rep. 944, as follows: " Where it was the regular custom of iron merchants to keep their stock of metal bars standing against the walls of their store, between racks made of pegs set in the walls, a servant who was familiar with this custom assumed the damages incident thereto. The servant assumed, also, the risk of the falling of a metal bar which was placed in a rack wherein there was not sufficient room for it, where there was no evidence as to what made the bar fall, and the only evidence of negligence was that half of the bar stood out beyond the ends of the pegs constituting the rack."

BIEBER v. CITY OF ST. PAUL.

Supreme Court, Minnesota, June, 1902.

PERSON INJURED ON DEFECTIVE SIDEWALK — EVIDENCE. — 1. Where personal injury occurs through an alleged defect in a sidewalk, which it is the duty of a municipality to maintain in a reasonably safe condition, such duty must be commensurate with the risks and dangers incurred by those who have a right to use the walk.

2. Evidence considered, and *held* that a depression of an inch and a quarter in a hexagonal cement block in a city sidewalk, in view of the extent and peculiar incidents of its necessary use at the place of an accident, might constitute such a defect as to render the municipality liable for damages for failure to remedy the same (1).

LEWIS, J., *dissenting.*

(Syllabus by the Court.)

1. See notes of recent cases relating to Liability of Municipal Corporations for Personal Injuries, at end of this case.

See also the following recent Minnesota cases against Municipal Corporations:

In KOPLITZ *v* CITY OF ST. PAUL *(Minnesota, June, 1902)*, 90 N. W. Rep.

APPEAL from District Court, Ramsey County.

"Action by Esther Bieber against the City of St. Paul. Verdict for plaintiff. From an order denying a new trial, defendant appeals. *Affirmed.*"

JAMES E. MARKHAM, FRANKLIN H. GRIGGS and THOMAS MCDERMOTT, for appellant.

SAMUEL A. ANDERSON, for respondent.

LOVELY, J. — Action to recover for injuries sustained from a fall upon an alleged defective sidewalk in the city of St. Paul. At the close of the evidence defendant requested an instructed verdict in its favor, which was refused. After verdict for plaintiff, defendant moved for judgment, or for a new trial in the alternative, which was denied. This appeal is from an order refusing a new trial.

The undisputed facts may be stated as follows: Near the hour of eleven o'clock on the morning of May 29, 1900, plaintiff was walking upon the sidewalk on the north side of Wabasha, between Seventh and Ninth streets, which was at that place very extensively used by pedestrians. As plaintiff approached the entrance to a provision store she observed a fish in the window, which she desired to purchase. She turned to enter, and attempted to go in. To do

794, judgment for plaintiff for $300 was affirmed, the syllabus by the court stating the case as follows:

"1. Negligence in the conduct of another will not be imputed to a party if he neither authorized such conduct, nor participated therein, nor had the right or power to control it.

"2. If, however, two or more persons unite in the joint prosecution of a common purpose under such circumstances that each has authority, expressed or implied, to act for all in respect to the conduct or the means or agencies employed to execute such common purpose, the negligence of any one of them in the management thereof will be imputed to all of the others.

"3. The plaintiff, a young lady, was one of a picnic party consisting of young men and ladies. The latter furnished the lunches, and the former the transportation, — an omnibus drawn by four horses, as to the hiring or driving of which the ladies had nothing to do. The conveyance was overturned, and the plaintiff injured, by the negligence of the defendant as to one of its streets, and the contributory negligence of one of the young men, who was driving at the time. *Held*, that his negligence cannot be imputed to the plaintiff."

In GRANT *v.* CITY OF BRAINERD (*Minnesota, May, 1902*), 90 N. W. Rep. 307, order denying plaintiff new trial, in action for injury sustained while driving horse and buggy over one of city's public highways at approach to bridge, was reversed, syllabus by the court stating the case as follows:

"1. It is the duty of a municipality having control of its public thoroughfares to construct and maintain suitable approaches to its bridges therein intended for public travel, and to provide suitable barriers or guards thereon to prevent persons lawfully using such places from injury.

"2. Evidence considered, and *held*, that it was a question for the jury whether the public authorities of a city had failed to perform their full duty in so it was necessary to pass over an elevated stone step raised somewhat above the sidewalk to the level of the store. The walk along the entire front of the store was constructed of hexagonal cement blocks. Some of these, through the operation of the frost, had become depressed, and were sunken below their original level, particularly one at the entrance of the building, which was six inches from the step. It had fallen below the general surface of the walk at its outer side an inch and a quarter, while at the inner side to a less extent. The evidence shows that in going into the store plaintiff placed her right foot upon the step, and in transferring her weight thereto inadvertently put her left foot on the perfect and depressed portion of the walk at the same instant, when it tripped and turned. She slipped by this mischance, and fell upon the sidewalk, receiving serious injuries to her ankle, with consequent illness and pain, for which she had a verdict. It was conceded upon the argument that the evidence tended to show that this imperfect condition of the walk had continued for a sufficient length of time to establish notice thereof to the city, and, if there was a defect which

the maintenance of barriers on the sides of an embankment used as a public highway leading to a bridge in a populous and well-settled portion thereof; also, whether such neglect was the proximate cause of plaintiff's injury."

In WEISER *v.* CITY OF ST. PAUL *(Minnesota, April, 1902)*, 90 N. W. Rep. 8, order denying defendant's motion for new trial was affirmed, the syllabus by the court stating the case as follows:

"The person injured by falling into an unprotected ravine along a public highway within the limits of the city of St. Paul served notice upon the city council, as provided by Laws 1897, ch. 248, pleaded that fact in the complaint, and the service of such notice was admitted in the answer of the city. At the trial plaintiff secured a verdict for damages. Upon a motion by defendant for judgment notwithstanding the verdict, the court granted a new trial upon the question of notice only, and that issue was tried by the court. Findings upon that question having been filed by the court, judgment was ordered for defendant notwithstanding the verdict, upon the ground that the notice was insufficient. This order was filed, and notice served upon the plaintiff, but no judgment in pursuance thereof was ever entered. More than one year thereafter, plaintiff, upon an order to show cause, obtained orders vacating the previous order for judgment, requiring a hearing *de novo*, and finally denying the motion absolutely. This action of the court was presumably induced by the decision in Nicol *v.* City of St. Paul, 80 Minn. 415, which had been published in the meantime, and which held the notice admitted by the answer to be sufficient. *Held*, 1. The order for judgment not being appealable, and no judgment having been entered thereon, the court had jurisdiction to vacate or modify it. 2. If it was error to order a new trial on the separate issue of notice, it was error without prejudice. *Held*, also, that the verdict was justified by the evidence."

the municipality, in the exercise of its duty to maintain reasonably safe and suitable sidewalks for use, should have repaired, the order appealed must be affirmed. In this State, where a municipality having charge of the repairs of its walks permits a sidewalk designed for the use of pedestrians to continue and be thus used, it is its duty to exercise reasonable care to maintain it in a suitable state for use, and is liable to persons injured from defects therein, where the city has actual or constructive notice thereof. Furnell *v.* City of St. Paul, 20 Minn. 117 (Gil. 101); Graham *v.* City of Albert Lea, 48 Minn. 201, 50 N. W. Rep. 1108. Defendant insists, however, that as a matter of law the depression of the hexagonal block where the accident occurred of only an inch and a quarter below the surface of the walk was not such a defect as required attention and repair by the city, and hence that it was not wanting in ordinary care for its failure in that respect. Obviously, the degree of care to be exercised by a municipality in maintaining suitable walks for pedestrians on its public thoroughfares is to be tested by the rule applicable in other cases where the obligation is imposed to provide structural conditions for the benefit of those required or privileged to use the same. The degree of duty in such cases is to be measured by the liability of accident, and should be commensurate with the risks and dangers incurred. While we might not hold that a depression of a stone in a walk of only an inch and a quarter below its ordinary level at all places would require attention and repair by the city, or that the municipality would be liable in damages for permitting such a depression to continue after notice, where the probability of accident would not be apparent to those having charge of the duty to remedy the imperfection — as in places where such walk is not extensively used by travelers — yet it is reasonably conceivable that such a defect might in certain instances be the proximate cause of injury. The depression of the hexagonal block occasioning this accident was upon a sidewalk very extensively traveled. It was below a raised step at the entrance of a store, over which patrons of both sexes were accustomed to pass. In doing so a person would naturally turn from the stream of travel outside, and be likely, in entering, to place one foot upon the defective part of the walk while transferring the other to the step above, which was the course pursued by plaintiff. Hence the accident which happened to her does not seem to us to be so improbable in the ordinary course of utilizing the walk by the public as to justify the city in entirely disregarding the sunken block which caused the injury to plaintiff. In other words, the characteristic use of the walk at this place indicated an unusual danger from the defect, and upon the ordinary relation of cause and effect might reasonably have been anticipated by the city and should have been remedied.

Cases have been cited from other States which hold that structural protrusions above the surface of the walk, or the depression of a stone in a sidewalk to the extent of even two inches, would not be regarded as a defect of which the municipality must take notice and repair; but there are features in these cases distinguishing each from this, and we cannot adopt the conclusion that there is any inflexible rule which determines, without regard to the extent or necessary character of the reasonable use of a city sidewalk by pedestrians, that municipal responsibility to repair it is dependent upon an estimation of defects by inches or parts of inches. Each case must rest upon its own peculiar facts, and to say this plaintiff should have given particular attention to the walk at the entrance to the store to see whether it was defective in any respect would be exacting more than the ordinary class of pedestrians at such a place would bestow. Nine out of every ten of the patrons of the store would assume that at such a place the walk would be maintained in a safe condition, and intuitively rely upon that supposition in going in. That its condition was defective would seem apparent from the consequences which occurred, and to say that the depression of the block as shown to exist was not a defect to relieve the city would result in the palpable *non sequitur* that where there is a probability of accident, upon which recovery must depend, and the accident occurs, the cause thereof is not in reality an actionable defect — a mere legal juggle to avoid responsibility. Neither is it a reasonable inference from the rule of duty applicable in such cases that, because similar defects existed at other places, and were numerous, that this one need not have been corrected; for if the extent and nature of the use made it probable that an accident would occur, similar defects elsewhere, though very frequent, would not justify the municipality in ignoring its obligations, and excuse one act of negligence by others.

In view of these considerations, and the fact that the cause was very impartially submitted to the jury in the instructions given by the learned trial court upon the proper rules of duty and care, we hold that its order refusing a new trial should be affirmed.

LEWIS, J. — I dissent. The degree of care exacted from municipal authorities by this decision is altogether out of proportion to the standard dictated by ordinary prudence. If a depression to the extent of one inch and a quarter of a hexagonal cement block constitutes a dangerous sidewalk, then any depression or slight projection is dangerous. If it is negligence to permit such unevenness at the entrance to a store, it is likewise negligent to permit it in the middle of the sidewalk anywhere in the business part of the city and, if in the business portion, why not in the residence district? Should a person be required to exercise more care in stepping from an uneven block to his private sidewalk than when stepping from the walk into a store down town? One may count such depressions, projections, and inequalities by the hundred all along the business as well as the residence streets in this and other cities. Common prudence never has required any such limit as is set down by the decision in this case. The time may come when the people will require that degree of perfection in respect to streets and walks which is adopted in public parks or in the private grounds of the wealthy, but, according to the standard now prevailing, by common consent the wayfarer should assume the responsibility and risk of danger to be encountered in walking into the yawning gulf of destruction presented by a cement block in the sidewalk depressed on one side to the extent of an inch and a quarter. Those who care to know what the courts have said on the subject may read with profit: Raymond *v.* City of Lowell, 6 Cush. 524; Jackson *v.* City of Lansing (Mich.), 80 N. W. Rep. 8; Morris *v.* City of Philadelphia (Pa.), 45 Atl. Rep. 1068; Haggerty *v.* City of Lewiston (Me.), 50 Atl. Rep. 55; Weisse *v.* City of Detroit, 105 Mich. 482, 63 N. W. Rep. 423; Beltz *v.* City of Yonkers, 148 N. Y. 67, 42 N. E. Rep. 401; Morgan *v.* City of Lewiston, 91 Me. 566, 40 Atl. Rep. 545; Tubesing *v.* City of Buffalo (Sup.), 64 N. Y. Supp. 399; and Getzoff *v.* City of New York, 64 N. Y. Supp. 636.

SEE THE FOLLOWING RECENT CASES RELATING TO LIABILITY OF MUNICIPAL CORPORATIONS FOR PERSONAL INJURIES:

Defective sidewalk — Notice.

In CITY OF DENVER *v.* HUBBARD *(Colorado, May, 1902)*, 69 Pac. Rep. 508, judgment for plaintiff for $5,000 was reversed, for failure of court to instruct as to degree of care required of plaintiff, and also as to question of notice of defect in sidewalk being for jury. On these points STEELE, J., said "We are of opinion that the court erred in refusing to give the substance of request No. 16. The defect, such as described in the notice given to the mayor, was a slight defect; and we think the city should not be held liable for defects of this character, except upon the finding of a jury that the defect was such as would justify one in reasonably anticipating an accident therefrom. Even if we concede that much of the language employed in the instruction is argumentative, the substance of the instruction is correct, and should have been given." * * * (Citing Beltz *v.* City of Yonkers, 148 N. Y. 67; City of Denver *v.* Hyatt, 28 Colo. 129). Continuing, the court said: "We are also of opinion that the court erred in refusing to give the instruction requested in reference to the exercise of greater care under the conditions shown to have existed. The court, in instruction No. 4, did not discriminate between the degree of care required under ordinary circumstances and under conditions of increased danger; and this court has announced that, in cases where the sidewalk is slippery by reason of being covered with snow or ice, more than ordinary care is required of the pedestrian, and that unless greater care is exercised the city is not liable. In the case of City of Boulder *v.* Niles, 9 Colo. 415, this rule was announced: 'Upon persons using the sidewalks the duty imposed is that of ordinary care. Under conditions of increased danger, there is imposed a duty of increased care. These are general principles, to be understood and applied to the light of the circumstances of each particular case,' — and quoted with approval the following from Dill. Mun. Corp., sec. 1006: 'Where there is snow upon a sidewalk, and it is rendered slippery, there is danger from slipping and falling even on the best constructed walks; at such times there is imposed upon foot travelers the necessity of exercising increased care; and, where the city uses reasonable diligence, it will not be liable.' The testimony shows that the plaintiff had been living in the building in front of which this sidewalk existed for several months prior to the accident; that she was familiar with the condition of the sidewalk; that the defect in the sidewalk was about the middle thereof; that there was a way on either side of the defect for pedestrians; that the accident occurred about midday; that there was melting snow and ice upon the sidewalk: and we think the court should have instructed the jury that the plaintiff was required to exercise increased care, and that, when the court failed to so instruct the jury, it relieved the appellee of a burden which in this jurisdiction she must assume. For the reasons assigned, the judgment will be reversed."

Bicycle rider injured in defective street — Defective pleading.

In CITY OF LOGANSPORT *v.* KIHM *(Indiana Supreme Court, June, 1902)*, 64 N. E. Rep. 595, where plaintiff was injured by a fall from a bicycle alleged to have been caused by a defect in a street, judgment for plaintiff was reversed for defective pleading. The court (per DOWLING, Ch. J.), said: "The ground of objection to the first paragraph is that it is not shown by proper averment that the injury was caused by the defect in the street; and to the second, that it fails to state wherein the grade of the street on which the accident occurred was improper. The point made against the first paragraph seems to be well taken. It is averred that the street was paved with brick, and that the appellant had negligently suffered it to get out of repair, and to become worn by travel, and sunken at a certain point so that a hole had formed four inches in depth, two feet in width, and three feet long; three sides of such hole sloping outward, and the east end thereof being nearly perpendicular. It is then alleged 'that, while she [appellee] was riding her bicycle as aforesaid upon said street, she approached the said street, so out of repair as aforesaid, from the west end, traveling towards the east, using care and caution, and having full control of her wheel while so doing, and traveling at a reasonable rate of speed; that while so traveling as aforesaid, using care and caution, and having no knowledge of the defect in said street as aforesaid, and not seeing the same, and, on account of the character of the defect, it was such that it could not be seen in time to avoid her injury hereinafter set out, she, riding her wheel as aforesaid, struck said defective, unsafe, and out of repair street, and by reason of said street being out of repair as aforesaid, defective, and unsafe, she was thrown violently from her bicycle upon the brick pavement of said street,' etc. It does not appear that the appellee 'struck' the street at or near the defective part thereof, or that her bicycle struck the dangerous cavity, or that it ran into or across the hole, or that the hole in the street had any connection whatever with the accident. The appellee struck the defective street when she entered it, as she alleges, at some point near its west end: but it is not shown where she came upon it, nor how far from the hole described in the pleading. The street may have been half a mile or a mile or more in length. The averment 'that, by reason of the street being out of repair, she was thrown from her bicycle,' leaves the cause of the accident entirely to conjecture. Was she attempting to guide her bicycle around the obstruction? Or did she stop it suddenly to avoid running into it? Did she ride into the defective place in the street, and did the fall or obstruction cause the bicycle to turn over? Or did she attempt to leap from the wheel when she found she could not steer it around the dangerous spot? None of these questions is answered by the first paragraph of the complaint. While the paragraph describes a specific defect in the street, and alleges that the accident occurred by reason of that defect, it wholly fails to show that the defect in the street was the proximate cause of the accident and injury, or how or in what manner the accident was occasioned by it. * * *

"The second paragraph of the complaint contains all of the averments of the first, with the further allegation that the grade of the street, from its crown to the curbing on each side, was so steep and great as to be dangerous to persons riding bicycles, and that it had been in this state for a considerable time, as the appellant and its officers knew, but that the appellee was ignorant of its condition. The fact that the street was dangerous to persons riding bicycles, because of its steep slope or grade from its middle line to the curbing, is probably averred with sufficient certainty; but it does not appear that the bicycle slipped or became unmanageable in consequence of the abruptness of the slope, or that the nature of the grade of the street caused or contributed to the accident. This paragraph, in its description of the accident, is quite as indefinite as the first. In almost the same words it alleges that the appellee 'struck the defective * * * street' somewhere west of the hole, 'and by reason of the said dangerous and unsafe grade of said street, and being out of repair, as aforesaid, she was thrown violently from her bicycle.' etc. The fault of this paragraph, like that of the first, is not mere uncertainty. It fails to connect the alleged negligence of the appellant with the injury sustained by the appellee. Such connection between the condition of the street and the accident to the appellee not being shown, the paragraph does not state a cause of action against the appellant." * * *

Defective street crossing — Pleading.

In CITY OF INDIANAPOLIS *v.* CRANS *(Indiana Appellate Court, Division No. 2, April, 1902)*, 63 N. E. Rep. 478, where plaintiff was injured by falling on defective street, judgment for plaintiff for $400 was reversed for defective pleading. The court (per COMSTOCK, Ch. J.), said: "The first error assigned and argued challenges the sufficiency of the complaint to state a cause of action. It is argued that the complaint contains no allegation to the effect that the place where the accident occurred was within the limits of the city of Indianapolis. The complaint is as follows: 'Margaret E. Crans complains of the city of Indianapolis, and says that she was a citizen of Indianapolis, and on September 1, 1896, about half-past eight o'clock, she was walking with her husband on Orange avenue, across Hamilton avenue, at the intersection of said avenues;

that there had been heavy rainfalls on the 7th and 23d days of August, and also during the months of May, June, and July of said year; that the drainage and grading of said avenues was faulty and imperfect, and insufficient to properly carry off the rainfall on said avenues; that by reason of said faulty, imperfect and insufficient means of drainage, the water had caused an excavation and washout to the depth of thirteen or fourteen inches at said intersection, the north bank or side of the said washout being perpendicular and dangerous and unsafe; that the defendant had full knowledge of said washout, and of the unsafe condition of said avenue, or might have had knowledge by the exercise of reasonable diligence and supervision over said avenue; that said condition had existed for some time prior to September 1, 1897, but that she could not state how long; that the only light furnished at said place was given by an electric light located on Hamilton avenue, 350 feet south of said Orange avenue, and that said light was insufficient to afford any warning to said plaintiff, or to others passing on said avenue; that while walking on said avenue as aforesaid, holding the arm of her husband, who was to the north of her, and exercising all caution, walking slowly and carefully, and using her sense of sight as best she could in said darkness, she, without any fault on her part, and without knowledge of the existence of said excavation, stepped into it, and was thrown violently down, causing a sprain to, and fracture of, the ankle, and a fracture of some of the bones of the foot,' etc. We find no averment that the street on which the plaintiff was injured was within the corporate limits of Indianapolis. The allegation that the appellee had resided in Indianapolis twenty years last past, and at the date named was walking upon 'Orange avenue, across Hamilton avenue, at the intersection of said streets,' does not locate these streets in the city of Indianapolis. Municipal corporations are only required to maintain public streets in a reasonably safe condition for travelers when they are within their corporate limits, and this obligation must appear from the averments of the complaint. Railroad Co. *v.* Griffin, 100 Ind. 221; Thiele *v.* McManus, 3 Ind. App. 132, and cases cited. It is insisted that the complaint does not aver that the defect was caused by the negligence of the appellant, or that it was its duty to repair. It is averred that the 'drainage and grading of said Orange and Hamilton avenues was faulty and imperfect, and insufficient to properly carry off the rainfall on said avenues, as the defendant well knew,' and that by reason of said faulty and imperfect means of drainage there was an excavation or washout as set out, and the defendant had, or might have had, full knowledge of the dangerous condition of the avenue. The knowledge of the conditions charged would apply to a private right of way or private walks which had never been dedicated to the public, as well as to a public street. The averment of facts is wanting, showing that the faulty drainage was caused by the acts of omission or commission of appellant." * * *

Defective plank in board sidewalk.

In BEAVER *v.* CITY OF EAGLE GROVE *(Iowa, April, 1902)*, 89 N. W. Rep. 1100, judgment for plaintiff, in District Court, Wright county, was affirmed, the opinion as rendered by SHERWIN, J., being as follows: "While passing over one of the defendant's walks, the plaintiff stepped on a loose board, which tripped and threw her. There was evidence tending to show that the general condition of the walk for some distance along there was bad, and had been for some time before the accident to the plaintiff. In the seventh paragraph of its charge the court told the jury that the city would not be liable for the plaintiff's injury unless it was found that the defect in the walk, if any, had existed for such length of time as that the city should have had notice of it, if it had exercised reasonable care and watchfulness over the walk. The converse of this proposition was also stated in the same paragraph. In the ninth paragraph of the charge the jury was told that if the walk had been inspected by the defendant's officer immediately before the accident, with reasonable care, and no defects were found, the city would not be liable. This instruction, appellant concedes, is correct; but in the next paragraph the court said that if the defect complained of actually existed at the time of the inspection, and was such that it ought to have been discovered by the exercise of ordinary care, the city would be liable. Both the seventh and ninth paragraphs of the charge state the law correctly, as applied to the facts in the case. It is true, there is no direct evidence as to the previous condition of the particular board over which the plaintiff tripped; but there is abundant evidence tending to show the dilapidated general condition of the entire walk along there, and this was competent on the question of notice to the city of its condition at the point in controversy. Smith *v.* City of Des Moines, 84 Iowa, 685; Armstrong *v.* Town of Ackley, 71 Iowa, 75; Wilberding *v.* City of Dubuque, 111 Iowa, 484. The cases relied on by the appellant are cases where single defects in the walk were charged, and are not within the rule governing this class of cases. Cook *v.* City of Anamosa, 66 Iowa, 427; Ruggles *v.* Town of Nevada, 63 Iowa, 185. The plaintiff's evidence conclusively showed a permanent injury, and of such a peculiar nature that pain and suffering would necessarily accompany it. In the thirteenth paragraph of its charge, the court instructed that the plaintiff's recovery was limited to 'the actual injury to her person, and the pain and suffering already endured from her injury, if any, or to be endured therefrom in the future.' This is criticised because it authorized the assessment of double damages, and because it permitted the jury to enter the realm of speculation as to future pain and suffering. While the instruction is not couched in the most apt language, we do not believe the jury was misled into giving the plaintiff double damages, or more than she was fairly entitled to under the evidence. And in the succeeding clause of the instruction the jury was told that it must determine from the evidence the amount that would actually compensate the plaintiff for her injury, taking into consideration its character, and the pain and suffering endured 'and to be sustained in the future, if any.' Taking the instruction as a whole, the jury could hardly have understood otherwise than that it must be guided by the evidence exclusively, and form its judgment as best it could therefrom. Moreover, the defendant asked an instruction on this point which embodies practically the same language, and for this reason alone cannot now successfully complain. Campbell *v.* Ormsby, 65 Iowa, 518. The thought expressed in instruction 1 asked by the defendant was substantially given in the court's charge; hence there was no error in refusing it. The verdict finds ample support in the evidence, and, under well settled rules, we cannot disturb it. The judgment is therefore affirmed." (EUGENE BRYAN and C. M. NAGLE, appeared for appellant; A. R. LADD, SYLVESTER FLYNN and T. D. HEALY, for appellee.)

Injured by spike in plank walk.

In RUSCH *v.* CITY OF DUBUQUE *(Iowa, April, 1902)*, 90 N. W. Rep. 80, personal injury sustained on defective sidewalk, judgment for plaintiff was affirmed, the facts (as per opinion by LADD, Ch. J.), being as follows: "The plaintiff, while walking on the sidewalk along the east side of Windsor avenue, between Lincoln avenue and Providence street, in the city of Dubuque, caught her foot on a spike protruding from the plank one and one-half to two inches, and fell. The evidence tended to show that the boards and the runners beneath them at that place were somewhat decayed, and also other nails sticking up. She had been over the walk several times during the fall, but had taken no notice of its condition. Nor was she observing the walk at the time of the injury. She 'walked as usual and looked ahead.' Appellant insists that in failing to observe the projecting spike and avoid it she was guilty of negligence, and ought not, for that reason, to recover. All required of plaintiff was that she exercise the care an ordinarily prudent person would in passing over the walk. Though in the daytime protruding nails and loose planks, unless out of place, would not necessarily be so obvious as inevitably to arrest the attention of the passing travelers, holes in the way, or obstructions, such as boxes, might be noticeable without effort; but few of the thousands using sidewalks would be likely to think of defects such as these. Pedestrians intent on other matters, and looking out for their general course, usually act on the presumption that the city has performed its duty and is maintaining its streets in a reasonably safe condition. While bound to make use of their senses and exercise the caution ordinarily displayed by persons of prudence, they are not required at their peril to discover every defect, even though open and visible. Barnes *v.* Town of Marcus, 96 Iowa, 675; Baxter *v.* City of Cedar Rapids, 103 Iowa, 599. Clearly, the defects in question were not so obvious that the plaintiff may be charged, as a matter of law, with notice of their existence; and whether, in failing to observe them, she was negligent, was properly left to the jury." * * * *Held*, also, that the notice of place of accident was sufficiently definite.

Defective highway — Person riding in vehicle injured — Negligence of driver — Imputed negligence — Notice.

In BARNES *v.* INHABITANTS OF RUMFORD *(Maine, March, 1902)*, 52 Atl. Rep. 844, judgment was rendered on the verdict for plaintiff for $1 304.33, and defendant's exceptions from Supreme Judicial Court, Oxford county, were overruled. The official syllabus (the opinion being delivered by WHITEHOUSE, J.), is as follows:

"1. A town is made chargeable by statute with the consequences of the neglect of its officers to make necessary repairs of its highways after receiving notice of the defect; and it is immaterial whether the notice is to one of the officers for the municipal year in which the accident occurred, or for some previous year, provided the defective condition of the way remained unchanged.

"2. It is provided by section 80, c. 18, Rev. St., that, 'if the sufferer had notice of the condition of such way previous to the time of the injury, he cannot recover of a town unless he has previously notified one of the municipal officers of the defective condition of such way.'

"3. In an action to recover damages caused by a defect in the highway, there was evidence tending to show that the driver, who had control of the carriage in which the plaintiff was riding, prior to the accident, had not given notice of the defect to any one of the municipal officers; but there was no claim that the plaintiff, who was the sufferer, had any notice of the condition of the way prior to the accident.

"4. *Held* that while this requirement of the statute imposes upon the traveler a distinct personal duty, as a condition precedent to his right to recover for njuries suffered on account of such defect, yet, with respect to the discharge of this particular statutory obligation, it would be an unwarranted construction of the act to hold that the sufferer was chargeable with the knowledge of the driver of a public carriage in which the plaintiff was a passenger, and thus responsible for his failure to notify the municipal officers.

"5. This express statutory duty is, of course, clearly distinguishable from the obligation imposed by the doctrine of contributory negligence or concurring causes, which, under the construction placed upon the statute by our court, has uniformly been held specially applicable to this class of actions against towns for defective highways.

"6. Upon this question of contributory negligence, the plaintiff was held responsible for the conduct of the driver, and in that respect she was chargeable with his knowledge of the existence of any defect at the point where the accident happened. But a breach of this distinct statutory duty of the traveler, to give to the municipal officers the benefit of any knowledge he may have of the existence of the defect, is sufficient to defeat his right to recover, independently of the doctrine of contributory negligence or concurring causes. In that respect the sufferer in this case was not chargeable with the knowledge which the driver had, but which she did not have, and was not responsible for his failure to communicate it to the municipal officers.

"7. *Held* that, while a declaration made by the driver out of court is admissible for the purpose of impeaching his credibility as a witness, it cannot be considered by the jury as evidence of the fact stated, tending to show how the accident happened. Said declaration was made three or four minutes after the accident happened. The driver was not then performing any act. The occurrence had terminated. His statement was not a spontaneous exclamation accompanying an act, and tending to explain or illustrate it, but a simple narration of a past event. It was not a part of the *res gestæ*.

"8. Whether the condition of the way at the point of the accident, in this case, was reasonably safe and convenient within the meaning of the statute as construed by our court, is a question of fact not entirely free from difficulty. A jury of practical men, a majority of whom had doubtless had experience in repairing highways, evidently found the road defective for want of an appropriate railing or guard to prevent travelers from driving into the ravine in the night-time, and the court considers that their conclusion was not unmistakably wrong. The evidence appears to have satisfied the jury that the municipal officers must have observed the condition of the road at that point unless grossly inattentive to their duty, and in the absence of any positive testimony to the contrary from these officers the jury drew the inference that they had actual notice of the defective condition which caused the accident. It is the opinion of the court that this question of notice is attended with less difficulty than that respecting the existence of a defect, and that the verdict of the jury should not be disturbed on this ground." (JAMES S. WRIGHT, appeared for plaintiff; GEO. D. BISBEE and RALPH T. PARKER, for defendants.)

Defective sidewalk — Crossing — Ice and snow.

In WATERS *v.* KANSAS CITY *(Court of Appeals, Kansas City, Missouri, May, 1902)*, 68 S. W. Rep. 366, judgment for defendant in Circuit Court, Jackson County, was reversed, the opinion by ELLISON, J., stating the case as follows: "This action is for personal injuries said to have been sustained by plaintiff by reason of defects in one of defendant's sidewalks. The verdict and judgment in the trial court was for defendant. The evidence was short, and tended to show a defective street crossing connecting the sidewalks, in that boards were out of it. It showed also that snow was on the ground, and at the time of the accident was still falling. The snow at least partially concealed the defect in the crossing. Plaintiff was traveling along the walk, and in stepping off the walk onto the crossing stepped into the vacant place made by the absence of the boards. This threw her forward and over cross-pieces, which threw her to the ground. Thereby she broke her arm, and was otherwise injured. The court gave ten instructions for defendant. We regard the objections made by plaintiff to some of them as being well taken. It is evident that the defendant was trying to protect itself from liability for the defective crossing by reason of the snow covering it, and it is clear that an attempt was made to impress the jury with the idea that, if the defect was such as it would have been seen and avoided if there had not been snow on it, then defendant was not liable. It would be strange if a city could excuse itself from liability for negligence by so usual an occurrence as an ordinary snow falling on the ground. Snow, in this climate, is no extraordinary occurrence, and does not afford the slightest excuse for negligence of cities charged with the duty of keeping the streets in repair. The following cases are applicable in principle: Bassett *v.* City of St. Joseph, 53 Mo. 290; Hull *v.* City of Kansas, 54 Mo. 598; Yocum *v.* Town of Trenton, 20 Mo. App. 489; Fairgrieve *v.* City of Moberly, 29 Mo. App., *loc. cit.* 156. Instructions on this head should not have been given, especially No. 8. Instruction No. 5 is erroneous in assuming that plaintiff 'was caused to slip and fall' by reason of snow. There was no evidence that she slipped and fell by reason of the snow, except as it connected with the defect in the walk. The instruction, as worded, would mislead a jury into the belief that she may have fallen on account of slippery snow. Instructions 8 and 9 are based upon the idea that, if the defects were obvious, it was plaintiff's duty to avoid them, but they assume that the defects were obvious, and were therefore improper. The different instructions repeat that defendant should only be required to keep its walks and crossings in reasonably safe condition for ordinary travel in ordinary circumstances, which we may concede; but it was wrong to have the jury believe that an ordinary snow was something more than an ordinary circumstance, and that it would, therefore, afford an excuse for defendant's neglect to keep the crossing in proper reasonable repair. The judgment is reversed, and the cause is remanded. All concur." (FYKE, YATES, FYKE & SNIDER, appeared for plaintiff in error; R. B. MIDDLEBROOK, for defendant in error.)

Falling over obstruction on sidewalk.

In OWEN *v.* TOWN OF DERRY *(New Hampshire, June, 1902)*, 52 Atl. Rep. 926, personal injury sustained by falling over piece of sewer or drain pipe lying on sidewalk, demurrer to petition was sustained and plaintiff's exceptions overruled. The court (per PARSONS, J.), said: "To entitle the plaintiff to maintain his action, he must therefore establish that his injury was due to the defect or insufficiency of a bridge, culvert, or sluiceway, or was caused by a dangerous embankment defectively railed. Unless the plaintiff alleges his injury was so caused, he does not state a claim against the town, and he cannot suffer manifest injustice by the refusal of permission to litigate a groundless claim. A culvert so constructed that the highway over it is unsuitable is within the statute, and for damage resulting therefrom a town may be liable. Gale *v.* Town of Dover, 68 N. H. 403; Boyd *v.* Town of Derry, 68 N. H. 272; Drew *v.* Town of Derry (N. H.), 51 Atl. Rep. 631. It may be that unevenness of the path caused by projections above the surface, would constitute a defect in a culvert, as well as depressions below the highway surface. But the petition does not allege as the cause of the injury any defect, insufficiency, or want of repair of the culvert, or any other cause within the statute, and therefore no error appears in the ruling of the Superior Court sustaining the demurrer. The only connection alleged between the accident and the culvert is that the broken pipe over which the plaintiff fell was once a part of the culvert. But the ground of liability is not the manner in which repairs were made six months before, but the condition at the time of the injury. The neglect of the surveyor to care for the fragments of pipe is immaterial, except as constituting an existing defect. If the facts warrant the claim made in the brief, that the injury was caused by an obstruction or defect in the covering of the culvert, the petition can be amended. Gitchell v. Andover, 59 N. H. 363, 364."

Bicycle rider running into pile of bricks in street — Contributory negligence.

In PINNIX v. CITY OF DURHAM *(North Carolina, June, 1902)*, 41 S. E. Rep. 932, judgment for defendant was affirmed, the case being stated by FURCHES, J., as follows: "On the 23d of November, 1900, about nine o'clock at night, the plaintiff received an injury which he alleges was caused by the negligence of the defendant, and this action is brought to recover damages therefor. The evidence discloses the facts that the defendant was engaged in paving its sidewalks on one of the main streets of the city of Durham, and was using brick for that purpose. For that purpose it had piled brick on the side of this street next to the sidewalk that was being paved. One of these piles, and the one where the plaintiff was injured, was about four feet high and about five feet square. This pile of brick had been piled there two or more months, but the work of paving the sidewalk had not been completed. This street was lighted with electric lights, and one of these lights — an arc light — was within about 150 yards of the place where the injury occurred; and the evidence shows that it lighted the street for 150 yards, and the pile of brick could be 'seen good for fifteen feet,' and the plaintiff testified that if he had seen the brick eight or ten feet before the collision he could have avoided it. There is an ordinance of the city requiring a red light to be kept at night on material left in the streets, and there was no red light on this pile of brick that night. The plaintiff was a young man, nineteen years old at the time of the injury; was reared in the city of Durham, and had lived there all his life; and his boarding house was in thirty yards of this pile of brick, but he had only gone to that house to board that day; and he testified that he had never seen that pile of brick. He was riding a bicycle at the time he received the injury, which was caused by his running into the pile of brick. He testified that he was looking, and did not see the pile of brick. The plaintiff, in his argument, contended that the defendant leaving the brick in the street for so long a time was a nuisance, and the defendant could not defend itself against an injury caused by a nuisance. However that may be, we do not think it was a nuisance for the defendant to pile bricks along the side of its streets for the purpose of repairing them; and the evidence is that the work of repairing had not been completed, and it was then at work paving the street a short distance from where the injury occurred. But the defendant was guilty of negligence in not having a red light on the pile of brick that night, and the jury so found. They also found that the plaintiff was guilty of contributory negligence. This street was forty feet wide between the curbstones, which leaves thirty or thirty-five feet of clear street outside of the pile of brick." * * * Commenting on the failure to have a red light, and whether this negligence was the proximate cause of plaintiff's injury, the court said: "Suppose the city ordinance had required a red light to be kept on this pile of brick in the daytime, and the defendant had not kept it there, and the plaintiff carelessly ran his bicycle into the pile of brick and was injured. The defendant might have been negligent in not having the red light on the brick, but would any one say that was the cause of the plaintiff's injury? Then take this case: A pile of brick four feet high and five feet across, so big that it looks like one could hardly keep from seeing it; an arc electric light in 150 yards that lighted the street to the pile of brick to such an extent that one could see the brick plainly for fifteen feet, and the plaintiff says that he could have averted the injury if he had seen the pile of brick eight or ten feet before he ran into it. Can it be that it was the want of the red light that caused the injury? It seems to us that any reasonable man would say that his injury was caused by his own negligence in running his bicycle into the pile of brick, and that defendant's negligence was not the proximate cause of the injury. The defendant's negligence was passive, inactive, while the plaintiff was the moving, active agency in producing the injury. He had, so to speak, the last clear chance. But the jury have found that the plaintiff was guilty of contributory negligence; that is, the plaintiff was guilty of negligence that contributed to his injury. This is sufficient to prevent him from recovery without showing that his negligence was the proximate cause, as we think it was. The injury was the concurrent negligence of the plaintiff and the defendant. Walker *v.* Town of Reidsville, 96 N. C. 382; Manly *v.* Wilm. & W. R. R. Co., 74 N. C. 655 (12 Am. Neg. Cas. 405n); McAdoo *v.* Rich. & D. R. R. Co., 105 N. C. 140 (12 Am. Neg. Cas. 411n); Rigley *v.* Railroad Co., 94 N. C. 604."

Defective plank in board sidewalk.

In TOWN OF NORMAN *v.* TEEL *(Oklahoma, July, 1902)*, 69 Pac. Rep. 791, action for damages for personal injuries sustained on defective sidewalk, judgment for plaintiff, in the District Court, Cleveland County, for $1,407.29 was affirmed, the facts, as stated by HAINER, J., being as follows: "It appears from the evidence in this case that the plaintiff, Mrs. Teel, was sixty-six years of age; that she resided just outside of the limits of the town, on the north; that on the evening of April 21, 1898, between sunset and dark, she, in company with another lady and her granddaughter, were on their way to her daughter's home, who resided in the south part of town, and while walking on the west side of Peters avenue, on the sidewalk, her companion, Miss Rogers, stepped on a loose board, and caused it to fly up, which threw Mrs. Teel on her face, and resulted in the breaking of both of her arms; that she had passed over the sidewalk every few days in going and returning from her daughter's home; that she had observed the sidewalk to be in a poor condition, but had no notice or knowledge that the board was loose where the accident occurred. The plaintiff, in answer to the question, 'What rate of speed were you going?' answered, 'A usual walk.' And again, to the question, 'What care, if any, were you taking in walking?' she answered, 'The usual care; I was always careful to notice holes, of course; this one board, I did not know anything about that when I stepped.' The evidence tended to show that the sidewalk where the injury occurred was in an unsafe and defective condition for public travel at the time of the accident and for several weeks prior thereto; that the stringers under the boards of the sidewalk at and near the point where the plaintiff sustained the injuries had become decayed and rotten; that the walk had been repaired several times, but that the stringers were in such a rotten and decayed condition that they would not hold the nails, and, consequently, the boards from time to time became loose, and that such was the condition of the walk for some time prior to the accident; that the town trustees or council had instructed the city marshal, in conjunction with the street commissioner, to look after the condition of the sidewalks, and to notify the property owners to build new walks or repair the same; that the city marshal, a short time before the accident occurred, notified the occupant of the property where the accident occurred to repair the sidewalk in front of said lot. There was no evidence offered by the defendant." * * * The points decided are stated in the syllabus by the court as follows:

"1. A municipal corporation is bound by law to use ordinary care and diligence to keep its streets and sidewalks in a reasonably safe condition for public use in the ordinary modes of traveling, and if it fails to do so it is liable for injuries sustained by reason of such negligence, provided, however, that the party injured exercises ordinary care to avoid the injury.

"2. Ordinary care, as applied to personal injury cases, means that degree of care and caution which might reasonably be expected from an ordinarily prudent person, under the circumstances surrounding the party at the time of the injury; and this is a question of fact for the jury to determine.

"3. As a general rule, notice to a city marshal of a town or city of the detective condition of a street or sidewalk is insufficient to charge the municipality with actual notice, but where the city marshal is instructed by the city council or board of trustees to look after the condition of the streets and sidewalks, and to repair them or cause them to be repaired, it is not error to admit testimony to show that such officer had actual notice of the condition of the sidewalk a short time before the accident occurred.

"4. The sufficiency of notice to fasten liability upon a city for a defective sidewalk is a question of fact to be determined by a jury under all the circumstances surrounding the particular case. It is not essential that the corporation shall have actual notice. If the defective condition of the street or sidewalk has existed for such a period of time that by the exercise of ordinary care and diligence the city authorities could have repaired the defect, and placed the street or sidewalk in a reasonably safe condition, and it fails to do so, then it is liable for any injuries that may be occasioned thereby by reason of such negligence, provided the injured party was in the exercise of ordinary care." (B. F. WILLIAMS, B. F. WOLF, S. H. HARRIS, A. W. FISHER and JOSEPH G. LOWE, appeared for plaintiff in error; J. R. KEATON and JOHN FRANING, for defendant in error.)

Defective street crossing — Contributory negligence.

In BOHL *v.* CITY OF DELL RAPIDS *(South Dakota, July, 1902)*, 91 N. W. Rep. 315, it was held (as per syllabus to report in 91 N. W. Rep.), that "where one familiar with a dangerous place in a sidewalk at a street crossing, and with such defect in mind at the time, attempted, on a dark night, when the street lamps were not lighted, to go down such sidewalk instead of going down the middle of the street, as she might have done, she was guilty of such contributory negligence as would bar a recovery for injuries caused by a fall from the sidewalk."

Child falling through grating in sidewalk.

In CITY OF DALLAS *v.* LENTZ *(Texas Civ. App., June, 1902)*, 69 S. W. Rep. 166, personal injuries sustained by a child from falling through a broken grate over a cellar in sidewalk, judgment for plaintiff was reversed, on the statutory provision under the City Charter 1899, sec. 159, which was in force when this event occurred, and which expressly exempts the city of Dallas from liability for injuries such as were sustained in this case, "in the event that because the sidewalk adjoins a homestead or for any other reason the city is unable to lawfully compel the owner to construct or repair a sidewalk by fixing a lien on his property for the cost."

Person tripped up by obstruction on sidewalk.

In ARTHUR *v.* CITY OF CHARLESTON *(West Virginia, March, 1902)*, 41 S. E. Rep. 171, judgment for $1,000 for plaintiff, who was tripped up by a rope stretched across the pavement on the south side of Kanawha street and fastened to a telephone pole for the purpose of holding the wharf boat during a flood in the Kanawha river, was affirmed, the syllabus by the court stating the case as follows:

"1. It is the positive duty of a municipality to keep its highways free from obstructions and defects dangerous to travel thereon in the ordinary modes to those using reasonable care and prudence, and it is not necessary to allege or prove that the city had notice of such obstructions or defects.

"2. In cases of temporary necessity a municipality may allow obstructions on the public sidewalks or streets, but the traveling public should be warned of and protected against the same in some proper manner.

"3. Whether a person is so intoxicated as to be unable to exercise ordinary care or prudence is a question of fact for the jury, and, unless plainly against the preponderance of the evidence, its finding will not be disturbed.

"4. Though proper instructions may be refused, yet if other instructions are given covering the same questions, and to the same effect, such refusal is not reversible error."

Falling into hole on sidewalk — Ice and snow.

In FOLEY *v.* CITY OF HUNTINGTON *(West Virginia, April, 1902)*, 41 S. E. Rep. 113, plaintiff falling into hole on sidewalk and foot and nose injured, the ground being covered with snow, and the opening being made for a sewer pipe, judgment for plaintiff for $1,200 was affirmed, the syllabus by the court holding as follows:

"1. In an action on the case for damages for personal injuries, where there is conflicting evidence as to the facts supposed to constitute contributory negligence, the question is one for the jury, and their verdict should not be disturbed unless it is clearly contrary to a decided preponderance of the evidence.

"2. Point 1, Syl., Kay *v.* Glade Creek & Raleigh R. R. Co., 47 W. Va. 467, 8 Am. Neg. Rep. 636, *reaffirmed* and *approved*."

In KAY *v.* GLADE CREEK & RALEIGH R. R. CO., 47 W. Va. 467, 8 Am. Neg. Rep. 636, 35 S. E. Rep. 973, referred to in the FOLEY case, *supra*, it is held, as per syllabus, point 1, that, "Where a stenographic report of evidence is made part of the certificate of evidence upon a motion for a new trial, and it shows objections to questions or evidence, and rulings of the court thereon, and that such rulings were excepted to, and the particular question or evidence complained of is specified distinctly in the motion for a new trial, or in an assignment of error, or in brief of counsel, so that the appellate court can readily and safely find the particular question or evidence to which the exception relates, the appellate court will consider the matter excepted to, though there is no formal bill of exceptions thereto; but such matter will not be considered without such specification, even though such report of evidence notes such objection and exception."

JACOBSON v. JOHNSON.

Supreme Court, Minnesota, August, 1902.

EMPLOYEE INJURED BY FALL OF CRANE — DEFECTIVE APPLIANCE — DUTY OF MASTER. — 1. The rule laid down by this and other courts, that it is the absolute duty of the master to furnish reasonably safe appliances for the use and protection of employees in his service, recognized and applied to the facts of this case.

2. Where an employee is required to work upon and about dangerous instrumentalities, the master cannot shield himself from liability for injury caused from a neglect of this duty by reliance upon the opinion of an expert as to the safety of an appliance provided by him, when it does not appear that his examination of such expert was thorough and efficient, which is a question of fact for the jury.

3. Evidence considered, and *held* sufficient to sustain the finding of the jury that an employer failed to provide reasonably safe guy rods or stays to support a heavy iron crane, by reason of which neglect the stays broke, whereby the crane fell upon an employee while engaged in the master's service, at his proper place, in the line of his duty (1).

(Syllabus by the Court.)

APPEAL from District Court, Hennepin County.

Action by Annie Jacobson, as administratrix of the estate of Mons E. Jacobson. Verdict for plaintiff. From an order denying a new trial or judgment in the alternative, defendant appeals. *Order affirmed.*

TRAFFORD N. JAYNE and HENRY C. BELDEN, for appellant.

BENTON & MOLYNEAUX, for respondent.

LOVELY, J. — The widow of Mons Jacobson brings this action as administratrix to recover damages sustained through the death of her husband from the alleged negligence of defendant. She had a verdict. Defendant moved for a new trial or judgment in the alternative, which was denied. From this order defendant appeals.

1. See notes of recent *Minnesota* of Master and Servant, at end of this cases arising out of duty and liability case.

There are twenty-eight assignments of error. A careful examination of these assignments, upon a review of the entire record, leads to the conclusion that the only question worthy of consideration on this review is the sufficiency of the evidence to sustain the verdict. This is one of the instances where counsel has deemed it important to require this court to examine every exception in the record, and, as is usual in such cases, the imposition of much unnecessary labor upon the court fails to realize the result that it has been profitable to appellant.

It was reasonably made to appear by the evidence that defendant was at the time of the accident the owner and operating a dredge boat on Lake Minnetonka, used in the work of dredging and pulling piles. Plaintiff's intestate was one of the deck hands on the boat. An instrumentality in this work was a heavy iron crane weighing 4,000 pounds, extending from the deck of the boat to an angle into the air. At its extreme outside end was suspended a dipper and other appliances for the work of dredging and pulling the piles. The crane was held in place at the requisite angle by means of two guy rods of iron attached to either side thereof. These rods were stationary, they kept the crane suspended, and prevented it from falling. Plaintiff's intestate at the time of the accident was at work at his proper place on the deck of the boat. The crane and its appliances were operated by means of an engine, when, under the effect of some severe strain produced by use of the crane or engine, the guy rods both broke, and the crane fell upon plaintiff's husband, inflicting such injuries that he died therefrom.

The dredge boat had been constructed by defendant two years before the accident. The engine and boiler had been purchased from second-hand dealers of machinery. The guy rods had been in use on the steamer City of St. Louis, on Lake Minnetonka, as braces, or what are called "hog chains," for the period of eighteen years, and when that boat was broken up these rods were taken therefrom and adapted to the purpose of stays, as above stated, by defendant, who personally possessed no special knowledge or capacity to judge of their strength or fitness for that use. A competent expert in machinery was, however, after the stays were placed upon the crane, called to do some work on the dredge boat, and informed the defendant, in answer to a question regarding the suitability of the guy rods for the new use made of them, that they were sufficient; but it does not appear that any critical scrutiny was made of such rods by this expert, or that a careful inspection thereof was given by him or any one else. The examination was, at best, casual and perfunctory.

The cause went to the jury under instructions from the court upon the duty of defendant to supply reasonably safe guy rods of sufficient strength to sustain the weight of the crane in the essential and necessary work required to be done in its use. Evidence of an expert character was received to support the claim of defendant that greater weights than that which the crane was sustaining at the time of the accident had previously been applied thereto in its actual use, from which it is urged, upon the showing thus made, that the tensile strength of the iron guy rods was demonstrated as a matter of fact; hence that the absolute conclusion follows that the breakages were not attributable to the weakness of the material therein, and the disaster was not the result of structural defects or their incapacity, but due to some cause unknown. Upon the whole evidence we are of the opinion that the adequacy of these stays to hold the crane in place was a question of fact. It appears that they had been used for twenty years; that they were not manufactured for the purpose to which defendant applied them, when they were newly subjected to extraordinary burdens and excessive strains; and we are not inclined to adopt the theory of defendant that iron will not wear out through the process of time, nor can we hold that this conclusion should have been adopted by the jury, and if there was expert testimony tending to justify this view it seems so at variance with experience that we should not reverse this case because the jury did not accept it. It would be but a fair result from the counsel's reasoning that the guy rods were strong enough and could not have broken under strain, to suggest that they actually did break after years of long service, which might have exhausted their power of endurance, unless the natural inference that all material things will wear out cannot be applied to the iron material of which the stays were composed.

It is but a repetition of the usual legal rule of duty imposed upon the employer, so often laid down by this and other courts, to hold that he must furnish reasonably safe appliances to those engaged in his service. In the structural arrangements by which the guy rods were applied to the heavy iron crane, their purpose and utility was so necessary and apparent that the sudden breakages, as in this case, were out of the usual or ordinary course of things, and not to be expected. This accident was an extraordinary one, and such as might upon its happening impose the duty upon the master of showing that the appliances he adopted were suitable and proper. But the evidence does not leave the master's liability upon this presumption alone. The size and length of the guy rods, the purpose for which they were adapted, the previous history of their use, the amount of strain continually imposed upon them, as well as their inherent strength, upon the evidence were fully submitted to the jury, and, in our judgment, afforded sufficient means by which to determine whether the defendant had performed his absolute duty to provide suitable instrumentalities for the use and protection of intestate, whose life may have been forfeited through a neglect to perform such duty, which we must hold was for the jury to determine.

Defendant invokes the benefit of the rule that an employer may select from a competent and skilled manufacturer instrumentalities of an approved pattern, and in common use, and if he has done so it is to be presumed that he has fulfilled his duty to his employee in that respect. We cannot give the benefit of this presumption to defendant in this case, for it does not apply. The defendant was the manufacturer of his boat; he adapted the guy rods to a novel use, without having, as appears, made any test of their capacity, or having shown that he possessed the requisite skill to determine whether they were suitable to meet the exigencies required in the new purposes to which they were adapted.

Neither can the defendant shield himself from liability upon the ground that he submitted the question of the sufficiency of these appliances to the opinion of a person who was competent to determine their capacity. The most that can be said of this inspection by the expert whose opinion was obtained is that it was superficially made, upon a casual view, and the master cannot exculpate himself, where the duty to inspect exists, by anything less than a sufficient inspection, which is also a question of fact. Tierney *v.* Railway Co., 33 Minn. 311, 23 N. W. Rep. 229.

Upon review of the entire record, under a fair and impartial submission to the jury of the issues by the trial court, which gave the defendant all that he was entitled to have, we have easily reached the conclusion that the verdict must be sustained.

Order affirmed.

SEE THE FOLLOWING MASTER AND SERVANT CASES, RECENT DECISIONS IN MINNESOTA:

Railroad employee clearing wreck.

In KREUZER *v.* GREAT NORTHERN R'Y CO. *(Minn. June, 1902)*, 91 N. W. Rep. 27, railroad employee injured while clearing railroad wreck, judgment for plaintiff for $3,500 was affirmed. See also former decision in the KREUZER case, 83 Minn. 385, 10 Am. Neg. Rep. 293 (June, 1901).

Dangerous premises — Trapdoors — Employee injured.

In DIETERS *v.* ST. PAUL GASLIGHT CO. ET AL. *(Minn. June, 1902)*, 91 N. W. Rep. 15, judgment for plaintiff was affirmed, the syllabus by the court stating the case as follows:

"1. In an action to recover damages for personal injuries alleged to have been caused by the negligence of defendants, it appears that both defendants are corporations organized for the purpose of furnishing electric light and power to their patrons, in the conduct of which business they occupied the same premises, employed the same servants, and were otherwise more or less jointly associated, though separate and distinct corporations, and distinct accounts of transactions and expenses were kept. At the time complained of, and for some time prior thereto, plaintiff was in the employ of both defendants, performing services for each company portions of the time, and being paid by each for the time employed for each separately. He was injured while engaged in the work of his employment, and brought this action to recover damages therefor. The evidence presented in the record is examined, and held to justify the verdict of the jury to the effect: 1. That plaintiff was in the employ of both defendants, and engaged in the performance of his duties as such, at the time of his injury; 2, that the evidence is sufficient to sustain a finding that defendants were guilty of negligence; and, 3. that plaintiff did not assume the risks, nor was he chargeable with contributory negligence.

"2. The premises occupied by defendants were leased from a third person, and were also occupied in part by other tenants. The negligence causing plaintiff's injury was in the alleged failure of defendants to keep certain trapdoors leading to the basement of the building in proper repair for use. It is held that, as defendants furnished the premises in question as a place in and about which plaintiff was to perform his work, it was their duty to keep the same in reasonably safe repair, and they cannot absolve themselves from liability for failure to do so by showing that the premises were also occupied by other tenants and as to such tenants it was the duty of the owner of the premises to keep the same in repair.

"3. Various assignments of error considered, and held to present no reversible error."

Railroad employee clearing snow from switch struck by "kicked" car.

In MURRAN *v.* CHICAGO, MILWAUKEE & ST. PAUL R'Y CO. *(Minn. June, 1902)*, 90 N. W. Rep. 1056, an action for injury to a railroad employee, order denying plaintiff new trial was reversed, the question of negligence of the parties being for the jury to determine. The facts (as per opinion of COLLINS, J.) were as follows: "The plaintiff had been in defendant's employ as a section man in a part of its yard contiguous to the Union station in St. Paul for about one week before the accident occurred. It was in the winter season, and most of the time he had been engaged in cleaning out snow and ice from the yard switches. In the forenoon of this particular day he went with the foreman and one or two other laborers to a switch upon one of the tracks some 200 feet east of the station shed, and was set at work cleaning out snow and ice which had accumulated therein. The foreman and other men were at the same kind of work not far distant. A very brisk easterly wind was prevailing, blowing about twenty-four miles an hour. Snow was falling, and to some extent was being blown about in the air, and there was already four or five inches on the ground. While he was thus at work, a switch engine, with eight or ten cars attached, passed easterly, stopping some 300 feet beyond the switch. The engine then commenced to "kick" cars onto defendant's side tracks on the south, between where plaintiff was at work and the river. There was some dispute as to whether cars were kicked westerly over the switch and track at which plaintiff was or over a switch and track nearer the river, but it is not very material where these cars were sent. There was sufficient notification, in any event, for plaintiff admitted that enough transpired to warn him of the risk, and also admitted that he appreciated and understood the danger of working at that point while an engine was east of him throwing cars onto the side tracks. He testified that he kept a careful lookout, knowing that no one was by to warn him of approaching danger, and fully understanding that it was his business, as a section man, to look out for himself while at work in the yard. He kept a constant watch to the east. He then saw the train motionless, about where it first stopped, and, for convenience in getting the snow and ice out from under a cross bar which connected the two rails, turned his back to the east, and was struck within a half minute by a single car, which had been thrown over the switch he was cleaning out. It appeared that just about the time he turned his back this car was sent in his direction, starting with a speed of ten miles an hour and slowing down to about three miles, when it struck him. No notice or warning was given that it was coming, although the switchman in charge stood on the ground, within a few feet of the car as it ran along, saw that plaintiff had turned his back, and was in a stooping position. This man could easily have stopped the car before it reached plaintiff if he had tried, but he did not make any effort so to do. When the car was within about 150 feet of plaintiff, he did exert himself sufficiently to shout, although he knew, as he expressed it on the witness stand, that his voice was not "in it" as against the wind. The shouting was not heard by plaintiff." * * *

Fireman falling from pilot and foot crushed by engine.

In KERRIGAN *v.* CHICAGO, MILWAUKEE & ST. PAUL R'Y CO. *(Minn. June, 1902)*, 90 N. W. Rep. 976, judgment for plaintiff for $8,475, in action for injuries to foot which was crushed by being run over by engine from the pilot of which plaintiff fell, was affirmed, the facts being stated in the syllabus by the court as follows:

" 1. Plaintiff was in defendant's employ as a fireman, engaged as such on an engine equipped with a certain step, — an appliance placed on the pilot to be used by the employees in lighting or adjusting the headlight. The step became out of repair, and plaintiff was injured while using it in the discharge of his duties. *Held*, that the evidence is sufficient to sustain the verdict of the jury to the effect, 1, that defendant had notice that the step was defective and unfit for use in ample time to have enabled it to repair the same before the accident to plaintiff; 2, that it was guilty of negligence in failing to do so; and, 3, that plaintiff was not guilty of contributory negligence, nor did he assume the risks incident to the use of the step.

" 2. Gen. St. 1898, sec. 3072, of the State of Wisconsin, provides, among other things, that when an action is removed from the Circuit to the Supreme Court of that State by defendant, and the order or judgment appealed from is reversed, and a new trial granted, the plaintiff shall pay the taxable costs, and proceed with such new trial within one year, in default of which the action may be dismissed. *Held*, that a dismissal of an action under said statute for failure of plaintiff to comply therewith is not a judgment on the merits, and is not a bar to another action in this State based upon the same cause of action."

Injured by machinery.

In WALKER *v.* GRAND FORKS LUMBER CO. *(Minn. May, 1902)*, 90 N. W. Rep.

573, judgment for plaintiff was affirmed, COLLINS, J., stating the case as follows: "The plaintiff was in the employment of defendant corporation as an oiler in its sawmill. He was an experienced man, but had worked in this particular mill only seven days when his foot was caught in a large wheel — a part of a log-chain gearing — and crushed so that amputation below the knee became necessary. This action was brought to recover damages, and plaintiff had a verdict. The appeal is from an order denying the alternative motion, made under the provisions of Laws 1895, c. 320. In the course of the performance of plaintiff's duty as an oiler, it became necessary for him to walk on certain beams some eight or ten feet above the floor of the mill, in order to reach and oil the wheel in which he was caught and another of the same size, both with beveled gearing, the teeth meshing at right angles, and running upon separate shafting. These wheels were of cast iron, with arms and, of course, arm spaces. One of them ran parallel with and near to the beam on which plaintiff had to step from another beam at right angles with it, in order to oil the machinery. Both wheels had been guarded with boards shaped into a box or hood, but on the side toward plaintiff, as he stepped onto the beam, the covering board did not fit down close to the beam. An aperture of from one and one-half to three inches wide had been left between the lower edge of this board and the top surface of the beam, and in stepping onto the latter the plaintiff's foot slipped through the aperture and into one of the arm spaces of the wheel, which was revolving with dangerous rapidity. His foot did not get into the cogs, but was simply caught in this arm space and the injury resulted." * * * The syllabus by the court states the ruling as follows:

"1. Upon an examination of the testimony in this, a personal injury case, it is held that the questions of defendant's negligence in failing to fully guard certain machinery in its saw mill, in which plaintiff, an employee, was injured, and of the latter's contributory negligence or assumption of risk, were for the jury to pass upon and determine.

"2. The court instructed the jury, in substance, that machinery such as that in which plaintiff was injured should be, as far as practicable, properly guarded or otherwise protected. *Held*, in view of the character of this particular machinery, that the instruction was not erroneous."

Section man injured by hand car.

In LINDGREN *v.* MINNEAPOLIS & ST. LOUIS R. R. CO. *(Minn. May, 1902)*, 90 N. W. Rep. 381, section man injured by hand car, overruling of demurrer to complaint was affirmed, the syllabus by the court stating the point as follows: "In an action brought to recover for personal injuries, it is *held* that a cause of action is stated in the complaint, in which it is alleged that, while plaintiff was in defendant's employ as a section hand, he was injured by the carelessness and negligence of fellow servants, also section men, while they were engaged, with plaintiff, in removing a hand car from the railway track to make way for an approaching freight train."

Employee cleaning windows injured by falling — Assumption of risk.

In ZEIGLER *v.* C. GOTZIAN & CO. *(Minn. May, 1902)*, 90 N. W. Rep. 387, judgment for plaintiff for $600 was affirmed, the question of assumption of risk being properly for the jury. The opinion, as rendered by START, Ch. J., is as follows: "The plaintiff, a minor of sixteen and one-half years of age at the time he was injured, was employed by the defendant in its factory in the city of St. Paul, and assigned to the work of inserting eyelets in shoes. He had been engaged in this work for about five months, when he was ordered by the defendant's foreman to wash the windows in the third story of its factory. This, so far as appears from the record, was the first time he was required to do work of that kind. The windows were about three feet wide, and twice as high as the plaintiff was tall; and each window consisted of two panes of glass, — one in each of the lower and upper sashes thereof. In order to wash the outside of the window, it was necessary for the plaintiff to stand on the ledge or sill thereof. While he was so standing for such purpose, he pulled down the upper sash of one of the windows, washed the glass therein, and attempted to shove it back to its place; but it did not go up easily, and he "gave it a good jerk, and it flew up," and he lost his balance and fell to the ground, whereby his right thigh was fractured, and he was otherwise seriously injured. He claimed that the defendant's superintendent ordered him to wash the outside of the windows, and brought this action, by his guardian ad litem, to recover damages for such injuries, on the ground that the defendant negligently ordered him into such place of danger, the hazards of which he, by reason of his youth and inexperience, did not understand and appreciate. The answer of the defendant denied that the plaintiff was ordered to wash the outside of the windows, and alleged that he was ordered not to do so, and in violation of such order he attempted to so wash the windows, and by reason of such disobedience and his own negligence he fell and was injured, and, further, that he then fully appreciated the dangers incident to the situation he voluntarily placed himself in. The jury returned a verdict for the plaintiff in the sum of $600, and the defendant appealed from an order denying its motion for judgment notwithstanding the verdict, or for a new trial. The only question for our decision is whether the verdict is sustained by the evidence. The evidence is unquestionably sufficient to justify a finding by the jury that the plaintiff was ordered by the defendant to wash the windows on the outside, and that in so ordering it was guilty of negligence. But the defendant insisted that it conclusively appears from the undisputed evidence that the plaintiff fully understood and appreciated the dangers and risks incident to the work he was ordered to do, and the place thereof; hence it must be held, as a matter of law, that he assumed such risks. To justify such a holding, it must appear from the undisputed evidence and all reasonable inferences therefrom that the plaintiff not only knew that the place in which he was required to work was dangerous, but also that he fully understood, or ought, in the exercise of ordinary prudence, to have understood, all of the risks incident to the doing of the work assigned to him in such place. From a consideration of the whole evidence, we have reached the conclusion that, in view of the plaintiff's youth and inexperience, reasonable men might fairly draw from the evidence different inferences as to whether the plaintiff fully understood the risks to which he exposed himself in complying with the defendant's order. Therefore it was a question for the jury whether he did so understand and assume such risks. This question was clearly and fairly submitted to the jury by the trial judge, and their finding thereon is sustained by the evidence. Order affirmed."

Injured by laundry mangle — Assumption of risk.

See BLOM *v.* YELLOWSTONE PARK ASSOCIATION *(Minn., May, 1902)*, 90 N. W. Rep. 397, where the question of assumption of risk was held to be for the court, the syllabus by the court stating the point as follows:

"Action to recover damages sustained by the plaintiff while operating, as the employee of the defendant, an unguarded mangle in its laundry. The trial court directed a verdict for the defendant, on the ground that, upon the undisputed evidence, the plaintiff fully understood and assumed the risks incident to the operation of such machine. *Held*, that the instruction was correct."

Minor employee injured by machinery.

In TORSKE *v.* COMMONWEALTH LUMBER CO. *(Minn., May, 1902)*, 90 N. W. Rep. 532, minor employee, a boy fifteen and one-half years old, injured by machinery, judgment for plaintiff was affirmed on conditions, the syllabus by the court stating the case as follows:

"While bracing his foot against the end piece of a molding machine for the purpose of pulling a board out of it, plaintiff was injured by having his toes caught by the revolving knives of the machine. Evidence examined, and *held*

"1. That he was not, as a matter of law, guilty of contributory negligence.

"2. Whether or not it was negligence to brace the foot against the machine in such a position as to come in contact with the knives was a question for the jury, considering the age and experience of plaintiff.

"3. Defendant was not guilty of negligence by its mere failure to guard the knives in the machine at the point where plaintiff was hurt, but, when considered in connection with the manner in which the molder operated, the duties of plaintiff, his age, and lack of experience, it was a question for the jury to determine whether defendant was guilty of negligence in failing to warn plaintiff of the danger in working around the machine.

"4. Where the instructions of a court are susceptible of two possible constructions, an exception will not be deemed to have been taken by virtue of c. 113, Laws 1901, but in such case it is the duty of counsel to direct the court's attention to the possible misinterpretation, in order that it may make the necessary correction.

"5. Verdict of $2,500 *held* to be excessive, and is reduced to $1,500; otherwise the order appealed from is affirmed."

CITY OF GENEVA v. BURNETT.

Supreme Court, Nebraska, July, 1902.

DEFECTIVE SIDEWALK — PLEADING — NEGLIGENCE — X-RAY PICTURES — EVIDENCE. — 1. A petition in an action for personal injuries that states facts and circumstances from which the inference of negligence by the defendant is inevitable is not defective for omitting the use of the word "negligent," or its derivatives (1).

2. Under the proper precautions, and with necessary explanations, what are known as "X-ray pictures" are admissible in evidence for the purpose of showing the condition of the internal tissues of the body.

(Syllabus by the Court.)

1. *See the following recent Nebraska cases on liability of Municipal Corporations:*

In CITY OF SOUTH OMAHA *v.* BURKE *(Nebraska, July, 1902)*, 91 N. W. Rep. 562, judgment for plaintiff was re-

COMMISSIONERS' OPINION. Department No. 3. Error to District Court, Fillmore County.

Action by Mary E. Burnett against the city of Geneva. From judgment for plaintiff, defendant brings error. *Judgment affirmed.*

J. D. HAMILTON and CHAS. H. SLOAN, for plaintiff in error.

ROBT. J. SLOAN, for defendant in error.

AMES, C. — The defendant in error (plaintiff below) alleged in her petition that on the 12th day of December, 1898, she suffered personal injury from a loose board forming part of the structure of one

versed, the opinion by HASTINGS, C., stating the facts as follows: " From a verdict and judgment in favor of James Burke, plaintiff below, the city of South Omaha brings error to this court. The action was to recover $15,000, alleged damages for an injury caused to the plaintiff by being thrown from a milk wagon, as he claims, through negligence of the defendant city. He says that on November 25, 1897, a trench two and one-half feet wide and four to ten feet deep had been dug near the center of N street and Twenty-third to Thirtieth, in the defendant city, and left open and unguarded for several months, and was in a dangerous condition, of which the city officials had notice, and that such condition existed long enough for the city in the exercise of ordinary care, to have rebuilt or erected safeguards; that in riding in the milk wagon with Edward Burke, his father, along Twenty-third street, the horses became frightened and started to run; that the driver was unable to control his horses sufficiently to cross in safety the narrow space left between the ends of the trench; the right wheels of the wagon ran into the ditch, throwing the plaintiff ten or twelve feet upon a hard pavement; that the fall injured the right side of his face and head, right eye, right arm, and right leg, caused nervousness affecting his entire system and destroying control of his muscles, affected his disposition, and rendered him irritable, caused him to wake in the night with terror, and produced spasmodic movements of the face and arm, drawing his mouth to the left side, and permanently injuring the right eye and the right side of the face; that the injury was without negligence on plaintiff's part, and through negligence of defendant in leaving the trench open, and the injury to his eye and nervous system are permanent. The city admitted its incorporation; admitted the plaintiff's filing a claim for damages; denied generally; and alleged that any injury sustained by plaintiff was due to his own negligence. The jury returned a verdict for $3,000. Motion for new trial was made, among other grounds, for excessive damages, and plaintiff was required to file a remittitur of $1,500, which was done, and judgment thereupon rendered in plaintiff's favor for $1,500 and costs." * * * " In the present case the following instruction was given and excepted to: ' It is the duty of a city to keep its streets in a reasonably safe condition for public travel in the ordinary modes, and if it fails to do so, and a person lawfully thereon is injured thereby, the city is liable unless the person injured was guilty of negligence which contributed to his injuries, and this is true although a person be injured because of a defect in such street caused by another than the city.' In City of Lincoln *v.* Calvert, [39 Neb. 305], injury resulted from the presence of a stone lying across the pathway. The plaintiff in that of the sidewalks in the city of Geneva, and "that said board was lying loose across the stringers in said sidewalk; not being nailed to any of them. And that said board was loose, and that said sidewalk was in bad condition and repair, was well known to the mayor and council of said city, and to the officers whose duties it was to repair and oversee the same. And that for a long time previous to the

case stumbled upon the stone and fell, suffering a severe injury. An instruction in terms almost identical with those of the one above, indicating a requirement that the city maintain reasonably safe sidewalks, and that if the walk was in a dangerous condition and plaintiff was injured upon it without negligence on his part the city was liable, was held erroneous. The charge as to the general duty to maintain a reasonably safe condition was held to be ordinarily accurate, but as having no application to a street undergoing improvements. The instructions objected to in the case at bar are such as are applicable to a street in which no improvements are under way. As is stated in City of Lincoln *v.* Calvert, the city had the right for a reasonable time and to a reasonable extent to render its streets unsafe in the effort to make them safer. It would have the same rights in an effort to make them lighter. The question submitted to the jury by the instructions in this case was not whether the city has been reasonably cautious in making this improvement and reasonably expeditious in completing it, but whether the street in its then condition was reasonably safe for travel. This was just as erroneous in the present case as in that of City of Lincoln *v.* Calvert, [39 Neb. 305]. It is clear that the above instruction, that the city was liable if an injury, owing to an unsafe condition of the street, occurred to one not guilty of contributory negligence, completely ignores the whole question of the right of the city to repair or improve the street, and impair its safety in so doing. It can only be upheld in this case by assuming, as the trial court evidently did, that the condition was due to negligence, and was not a reasonably necessary result of the laying of the gas pipes." * * * "For the failure to note the right of the city to reasonably interfere with the safety of its streets in making improvements, it is recommended that the judgment of the trial court be reversed, and the cause remanded for further proceedings."

In VILLAGE OF PLAINVIEW *v.* MENDELSON *(Nebraska, June, 1902)*, 90 N. W. Rep. 956, person injured on sidewalk, judgment for plaintiff for $2,400 was affirmed, the ruling being stated in the syllabus by the court as follows:

"1. The duty devolving on cities and villages to keep streets and sidewalks reasonably safe and fit for travel applies to defects in construction as well as neglect to repair, and the safety required extends to travel by night as well as by day.

"2. Where a sidewalk is built or suffered to remain on a part of the street only, its ends or termini must be so graduated to the natural level of the street as to permit pedestrians to safely pass from it to the street. Village of Ponca *v.* Crawford, 23 Neb. 666 followed.

"3. When facts relied upon to prove negligence are undisputed, but are of such a character that different minds might reasonably draw different conclusions from them, the question of negligence should be submitted to a jury for its determination.

"4. Unless the testimony fairly shows the damages awarded by a jury to have been excessive, the judgment

12th day of December, 1898, and ever since said date, the authorities above mentioned allowed said sidewalk to be and to remain in a dangerous condition." A general demurrer was interposed to this petition, supported by the argument that it does not sufficiently allege that the city authorities were negligent with respect to the matter complained of. The demurrer was properly overruled. If the circumstances were such as the petition narrates, the inference of negligence is inevitable. The use of the word "negligence" would not have made the charge any more specific or emphatic. Its omission from the pleading, therefore, did not render the pleading defective. The answer denied "that the said walk was unsafe and dangerous, or that it had any notice of such defect in the walk, and that the defect, if any, which caused the injury, was latent and unknown to it, although it had used diligence in the premises." This is an admission of the defect charged, coupled with a denial of notice and negligence. It is like a denial that a note is genuine, coupled with an allegation that, if genuine, it was obtained by fraud. A party cannot deny and confess and avoid the same cause of

of the jury and of the trial court on the amount of damages will not be disturbed by this court.

"5. Instuctions examined and approved."

In RAYNOR *v.* CITY OF WYMORE *(Nebraska, May, 1902)*, 90 N. W. Rep. 759. person injured by falling on sidewalk, judgment for defendant was reversed, DAY, C., stating the case as follows: "One of the errors complained of by the plaintiff relates to instruction No. 8, given at the request of the defendant, which is as follows: 'The court instructs the jury that it is negligence for a person knowingly and unnecessarily to expose himself to danger, and if you believe from the evidence that the plaintiff before and at the time of the alleged injury knew of the defect in the sidewalk by reason of which she claims to have been injured, and that in going to and from her place of business plaintiff could have gone with equal convenience by some other sidewalk or sidewalks, if the same were in a safe condition, and thus have avoided the defect above mentioned, and failed to do so, then she was negligent, and if you so find then the plaintiff cannot recover.' This instruction is erroneous because it assumes as a matter of law that the defect in the sidewalk was of such a dangerous character that its use by the plaintiff was negligence, if she could have gone with safety and equal convenience to her place of destination by some other route. The record shows that the sidewalk in question was constructed of planks laid across wooden supports extending lengthwise of said sidewalk, to which supports the planks were fastened by nails; that the planks in several places had been permitted to become loosened, and at the point where the injury occurred one of them had become broken, and about one-half thereof entirely removed thereby causing a hole in said sidewalk about nine inches wide, six inches deep, and extending about one-half of the width of the sidewalk. The plaintiff had been over the walk a great many times, and knew of its defective condition. It also appears that on the morning of the injury the sidewalk and the hole therein were covered by snow, so that action in the same pleading. Dinsmore *v.* Stimbert, 12 Neb. 433. The answer also alleged that, if the plaintiff had suffered any injury, it was incurred by her own carelessness, without the fault or negligence of the defendant. The reply was general denial. The evidence concerning all matters in issue was conflicting. The plaintiff recovered a verdict and judgment, which the defendant seeks to set aside by this proceeding.

The plaintiff testified that her foot and ankle, which were injured by the accident, were previously thereto in a sound and healthy condition, and that the injury had produced a permanent, or at least prolonged, disability. Some medical men testified that one of the consequences of the injury was, or might probably be, a calcareous deposit in the tissues of the foot, and that they had examined the foot of the plaintiff, who was a young person, by means of an apparatus for making or taking what are called "X-ray pictures" of it, which disclosed the presence of such a deposit, and that, in their opinion, the deposit was the result of the injury (1). Plaintiff in

a person walking thereon could not see the defect.

"We do not think the mere using of the sidewalk in the condition and under the circumstances presented in this case would, as a matter of law, constitute negligence on the part of the plaintiff. Whether it was negligence for her to attempt to pass over the walk would depend upon whether she exercised ordinary care in selecting her route, and exercised ordinary care in using the sidewalk; that is, such care as an ordinarily prudent person would have exercised under similar circumstances. This is a question for the jury to determine from a consideration of all the facts and circumstances of the case.

"This instruction is also erroneous because it is not responsive to the evidence. There is no testimony in the record that there was any other sidewalk or route which the plaintiff could have selected in going to and from her place of business. The instruction assumed the possible existence of a state of facts which the jury had no right to find from the evidence. This was error. City of Crete *v.* Childs, 11 Neb. 252; Hitchcock *v.* Shager, 32 Neb. 477; Trust Co. *v.* Montgomery, 30 Neb. 33; Bowie *v.* Spaids, 26 Neb. 635." * * *

In CITY OF CRETE *v.* HENDRICKS *(Nebraska, April, 1902)*, 90 N. W. Rep. 215, person injured on defective sidewalk, judgment for plaintiff was affirmed. On the question of exhibiting injured part to jury, the court (per ALBERT, C.) said: "The injury alleged to have been sustained by the plaintiff was to his foot. He was permitted, over defendant's objection, to exhibit the injured foot to the jury. This is assigned as error. The foot was exhibited to the jury after the introduction of evidence to the effect that it had been permanently injured as and in the manner alleged in the petition, and that its condition at that time was wholly due to such injury. There was no error in the ruling of the court on this point."

1. See note on X-ray evidence, in 11 AM. NEG. REP. 73-74.

See also KANE *v.* ROCHESTER R'Y CO. (N. Y. Sup. Ct., App. Div, July, 1902), reported in this volume, *post*.

error objects because some of the pictures so obtained were admitted in evidence. There was a very thorough and complete explanation of the time, manner, and circumstances of the taking of the pictures, and of the condition of the foot which they were supposed to indicate; but it is insisted that they were secondary evidence, and so not admissible. From the testimony of the witnesses, we are convinced that no better evidence of the condition of the interior tissues of the foot could have been obtained, without a surgical operation, to which the plaintiff was not called upon to submit. We do not think that the ruling complained of was erroneous.

Complaint is also made of the refusal by the court to give certain instructions requested by the plaintiff in error, but we think they are all of them substantially embodied in a series of instructions given by the court of its own motion, which fairly stated the law, and submitted the issues to the jury.

The verdict and judgment are moderate in amount, and we recommend that they be affirmed.

DUFFIE and ALBERT, CC., concur.

PER CURIAM. — For reasons stated in the foregoing opinion, it is ordered that the verdict and judgment of the District Court be affirmed.

KNUTTER v. THE NEW YORK AND NEW JERSEY TELEPHONE COMPANY.

Court of Errors and Appeals, New Jersey, June, 1902.

LINEMAN INJURED WHILE STRINGING WIRES — FELLOW-SERVANT — "SUPERIOR SERVANT RULE" DOES NOT PREVAIL IN NEW JERSEY. — 1. Plaintiff was a lineman in the employ of a telephone company, and was injured while engaged in work, with others, under the charge of a foreman. One Runyon was with the party, exercising general supervision and control of the others, including the foreman, and at the same time actively participating in the work. Runyon was called the "district manager," and had general charge of the business of the telephone company throughout a large territory, including the place where the work in question was in progress. In that territory he was intrusted with the hiring and discharge of the employees of the company, including the linemen. There was evidence tending to show that the plaintiff's injuries were the direct result of negligence on the part of Runyon while he was co-operating with the plaintiff in the work, and at the same time was supervising and directing the work.

Held, that Runyon was a fellow-servant of the plaintiff, for whose negligence the common employer cannot be held liable.

2. The "superior servant rule," as a limitation upon the master's exemption from liability to a servant for the negligence of a fellow-servant, does not obtain in this State.

3. Where there is negligence in the performance or nonperformance of some duty that is imposed by law upon the master for the safety of the injured servant, the master is responsible, irrespective of the rank of the negligent employee; but, where the negligence is in the performance or nonperformance of some duty that is merely incidental to the general employment, the master is not responsible, although the negligent servant was superior in rank to him who was injured.

(Syllabus by the Court.)

ON ERROR to Supreme Court.

Appeal from judgment for plaintiff. The facts appear in the opinion. *Judgment reversed.*

EDWARD A. & WILLIAM T. DAY, for plaintiff in error.

WILLARD P. VOORHEES, for defendant in error.

PITNEY, J.—The plaintiff was a lineman in the employ of the defendant, and brought this action to recover damages for personal injuries sustained by him while engaged in the performance of his duties. At the time of the occurrence in question he was working in company with two other linemen, one of whom, named Chamberlain, was the foreman. They were putting up a line of wire upon poles in the streets of Somerville for the purpose of making a connection between the residence of a subscriber and the central telephone exchange in that town. One Runyon was with the party, and had general charge of its operations, besides participating actively in the work. He was called the "district manager," and there was evidence from which the jury had a right to infer that he had general charge of the telephone exchanges of the defendant at Westfield, Plainfield, Bound Brook, and Somerville, and of the lines communicating with each exchange, and the lines connecting the several exchanges together, and that he was intrusted with the hiring and discharging of all employees within the territory indicated. Runyon himself was called as a witness for the defendant, and testified that his duties were "to overlook all the work, and help out if they were pushed." He said: "I look after the whole business — everything that goes on; sometimes have to go up poles." The evidence, in short, tended to show that he was in general charge of defendant's business throughout the district in question, occupying a position of superiority over all the linemen, yet engaging at times personallv in the work of line construction:

As to the cause of the accident, plaintiff's evidence was to the effect that under the immediate supervision and command of Runyon, the manager, plaintiff ascended a pole, and stepped from it into the branches of a neighboring tree, about twenty feet above the ground; that Runyon stood upon the ground with the wire in his hand; that it was necessary to throw or swing the wire over a limb of the tree, in order that the wire might be raised to its proper position upon the poles; that thereupon Runyon directed the plaintiff to bear down upon the limb, in order to enable him to throw the wire over it. Plaintiff complied, and Runyon succeeded in getting the wire over the limb, but it caught upon a twig. Runyon then directed the plaintiff to get hold of the wire, and place it where it should go. Plaintiff at this time was standing upon the same limb on which the wire was lodged, and was preserving his balance by the grasp of his hand upon a limb that extended over his head. In obedience to Runyon's command, plaintiff "reached out upon the limb for the wire," when Runyon suddenly and without warning pulled down upon the wire, breaking the limb and precipitating the plaintiff to the ground. For the injuries thus received, he sued his employer in the present action. Plaintiff claimed that the limb would have borne his weight, had it not been for the added strain caused by Runyon's act in pulling upon the wire; the insistment being that this was negligence for which the employer was liable.

There was no dispute as to the relation occupied by Runyon to the general business of the defendant company; nor was it disputed that he was co-operating with the gang of linemen, and at the same time guiding and directing them in their work. It was denied that Runyon had caused the plaintiff's fall by pulling down upon the wire or otherwise, but upon this point there was sufficient evidence to go to the jury.

There was a motion to nonsuit, and a motion that the jury be directed to render a verdict in favor of the defendant. Both were denied. One of the grounds on which these motions were based was that Runyon was a fellow-servant engaged in a common employment with the plaintiff, so that for his negligence the common employer could not be held liable. A request made by the defendant that the trial judge should instruct the jury that Runyon was a fellow-servant of the plaintiff, so that for his negligence the plaintiff could not recover, was also refused. On the other hand, the court charged the jury that it was for them to determine from the evidence whether Runyon was a fellow-workman of the plaintiff, or was an official of the defendant company for whose acts it should be held liable, at the same time giving the jury to understand that from the fact that Runyon, in respect to the work in question was the superior and manager, the others being subject to his orders and that by his orders the plaintiff was sent into the tree, the jury would have a right to find that Runyon was an official of the defendant company, in such a sense that the company should be held responsible for his acts, if negligent in any way.

The jury having rendered a verdict in favor of the plaintiff, and judgment having been entered thereon, the defendant now assigns for error the above-mentioned rulings of the trial judge and that part of his charge just referred to.

The only question requiring consideration is whether the defendant can be held liable at the plaintiff's suit for the negligence of Runyon, in view of the familiar rule of law that exempts the master from liability for personal injuries received by one of his servants in consequence of the carelessness of another, while both are engaged in the common employment.

It is manifest that, in order to sustain this judgment, we must hold that Runyon, by reason of being a district manager, placed by the defendant in entire charge of its plant, working force, and operations within that district, with power to employ and discharge subordinates, and being at the same time in direct command of the work in which the plaintiff was engaged, became the representative of the defendant — its vice-principal or *alter ego*, — in such a sense and to such an extent that for his negligence, either in co-operating with the other workmen, or in controlling and directing their work, the defendant can be held liable to the plaintiff.

In some jurisdictions a tendency has been manifested to hold the master liable to a servant who sustains personal injuries through the negligence of a general superintendent or department manager, or of a servant of any grade superior to that of the servant injured; and this irrespective of the character of the work in the performance of which the negligence occurs. The rule that admits of such liability is commonly called the "superior servant rule." It obtains in Ohio and some other States. Little Miami R. R. Co. *v.* Stevens, 2 Ohio, 415; Cleveland, etc., R. R. Co. *v.* Keary, 3 Ohio St. 201; Berea Stone Co. *v.* Kraft, 31 Ohio St. 287, 27 Am. Rep. 510. But the courts of our own State have never adopted this rule. There are expressions in some opinions indicating a recognition of such a limitation upon the master's exemption from liability to his servant for the negligence of a fellow-servant. But the liability has not in any case been imposed upon the master on the mere ground that the negligent servant occupied a position of superiority or control over the party injured. In Smith *v.* Oxford Iron Co., 13 Vr. (42 N. J. L.) 467; O'Brien *v.* American Dredging Co., 24 Vr. (53

N. J. L.) 291, and Gilmore *v.* Oxford Iron Co., 26 Vr. (55 N. J. L.) 39, all of which were decided by the Supreme Court, the relative rank of the negligent servant and the injured servant was referred to; but the decision in each instance turned upon the question whether the negligence arose in the performance of a mere servant's duty, or in that which the law imposed upon the master. In the Smith case the liability was sustained because the negligence consisted in the failure to perform a duty which the common employer owed to the injured servant, and which could not be delegated. In the O'Brien and Gilmore cases the liability of the employer was denied notwithstanding the negligent servant was superior to him who was injured, and this on the ground that the negligence occurred in the performance of the work of a mere fellow-workman.

Numerous recent decisions in this court proceed upon the same general principle, viz., that, where the negligence is in the performance or nonperformance of some duty that is imposed by law upon the master for the safety of the injured servant, the master is responsible, irrespective of the rank of the negligent employee, but, where the negligence is in the performance or nonperformance of some duty that is merely incidental to the general employment, the master is not responsible, although the negligent servant was superior in rank to him who was injured, or may at other times have been intrusted with the performance of the master's duties. Some of these decisions are cited in an opinion delivered at the present term of this court (1), in the case of Smith *v.* Erie R. R. Co. (N. J.

1. *Baggage master acting as brakeman injured in derailment of train — Fellow-servant — Liability of master.* — In SMITH *v.* ERIE R. R. Co. *(New Jersey Errors and Appeals, June, 1902)*, judgment for plaintiff was affirmed, the facts as stated in the opinion by PITNEY, J, being as follows:

At the time of the occurrence which gave rise to this action, plaintiff was in the employ of the defendant in the capacity of baggage master and acting brakeman, and in the performance of his duties was traveling upon one of defendant's passenger cars over the Greenwood Lake branch of its railroad. This car, together with a locomotive and tender, made up the train. The occurrence took place on the evening of Saturday, January 14, 1899, shortly after seven o'clock. The train was running at some speed down a grade of about sixty feet to the mile, when, in rounding a curve, the passenger car became derailed, and, after bumping for some distance over the crossties, broke away from the tender, and was thrown down a steep embankment and demolished. The plaintiff sustained serious personal injuries, to recover damages for which he brought this action. The verdict and judgment in the court below having gone in his favor, the defendant now asks for a reversal because of alleged errors committed by the trial judge.

Plaintiff's insistment at the trial was that the derailment was occasioned by the non-repair of the track. Evidence was introduced tending to show that the inspection and repairs of this part of the railroad were customarily done

Err. & App., June, 1902; 52 Atl. Rep. 634). The quotations there given from the opinions in Maher *v.* Thropp, 30 Vr. (59 N. J. L.) 186; McLaughlin *v.* Camden Iron Works, 31 Vr. (60 N. J. L.) 557, 4 Am. Neg. Rep. 69, and Curley *v.* Hoff, 33 Vr. (62 N. J. L.) 758, 5 Am. Neg. Rep. 668, are equally applicable to the present case.

by a section gang of which one Duffy was foreman, and Sloat and two others were members; that during this particular week the section gang worked only on the alternate days; that at least as early as the afternoon of Friday, the day before the accident, a noticeable depression, called by the witnesses a "low joint" or "low spot," was found in the outer rail of the track at or near the curve in question; that this depression was observable by a person walking the track, and was sufficient to cause a decided lurch in a car passing over it; that on Friday afternoon Sloat reported this low joint to Duffy, yet the section gang was laid off duty from Friday night until Monday morning. Duffy, the track foreman, was called as a witness by the plaintiff, and testified that he was at work on Saturday, the 14th, but that his men were not, they having been laid off by him on the orders of Mr. Lynch, the supervisor of that division; that none of the trackmen were on duty on the 14th except Duffy himself; and that he walked over the section twice that day, but did nothing towards the repairs of the low joint in question; it being conceded that he could not repair it without help.

The plaintiff also produced the printed book of rules of defendant company, from which he introduced in evidence, without objection, the following rules:

" Supervisors. The supervisor has charge of the repairmen and other laborers employed on his subdivision, and must see that they perform their duties properly, and discipline them for neglect of duty. It is the supervisor's duty to keep the track, roadbed, bridges, culverts, buildings, and other property of the company on his subdivision in repair. He must pass over his subdivision daily; observe the condition of the track and bridges; see that the proper slopes and ditches are preserved, * * * that ties are of a standard size, evenly spaced, and properly tamped, and that the rails are in proper surface and securely fastened; * * * and do everything necessary to secure the safety of the road."

" Track Foremen. Track foremen report to, and receive their instructions from, the supervisor. They have charge of repairs on their respective sections, and are responsible for the proper inspection and safety of the tracks, bridges, and culverts. They must see that the track is in good line and surface, and properly spiked; that it is in true and uniform gauge; that the cross-ties are properly spaced, lined, and tamped; that the roadbed is in good order," etc.

Upon this evidence, and other to the same effect, the plaintiff claimed that the proximate cause of the accident was the bad condition of the track; that the defect was such that reasonable vigilance and proper inspection would have discovered it, and reasonable care required its reparation; and that in fact it was discovered by the trackman in ample time to enable them to mend it before the accident, so that there was negligence of the trackman, for which the defendant was responsible to the plaintiff. Defendant's insistment was that the low spot in the track was not the cause of the derailment of the car, and that the disaster was the result of the reckless speed of the

It has not been forgotten that Runyon, at the time of the occurrence in question, not only held a position of superiority to the plaintiff, but was actually exercising his authority by guiding and directing the plaintiff's movements at the moment of the accident. Although in so doing Runyon did, in a sense, represent the common

train, for which the locomotive engineer, a fellow-servant of the plaintiff, was responsible. With respect to the speed of the train the testimony was quite variant. There was evidence from which the jury would have been at liberty to believe that it was not exceeding twenty miles an hour, and other evidence from which they might believe its speed was far in excess of thirty miles per hour. It was claimed by the defendant that the low spot was sixty feet or more above the point where the wheels of the passenger car left the track; it being argued that this distance, of itself, demonstrated that the low spot did not cause the derailment. It was further insisted that in a derailment resulting from such a low spot the wheels would jump over the outer rail, whereas in this case several lengths of the outer rail rolled over under pressure of the wheels, thereby causing a spreading of the track, and permitting the wheels to settle down upon the cross-ties. As corroborating the defendant's theory, and negativing the theory which attributed the derailment to the low joint, it was pointed out that the locomotive remained on the track, and that the tender remained attached to the locomotive, although the rear wheels of the tender left the track. It is also claimed that after the passenger car became derailed it remained attached to the tender, and that its wheels bumped along the cross-ties for a distance of over 200 feet before the car broke from the tender and pitched down the bank. From all this it is argued that the occurrence resulted not from the car leaving the track by reason of roughness, unevenness, or any low joint, but by the locomotive and cars remaining on the track, clinging to it and destroying it. But the evidence tends to show that the low joint indicated that the track was being heaved by the frost, and so it cannot be said to be a necessary conclusion that the weakness of the track was confined to the immediate vicinity of the low joint. Nor can it be said that a derailment which occurs by the overturning of the rails, caused by the weight of a train consisting of a locomotive, a tender, and a single car driven at a speed less than that which would cause them to jump the track, necessarily excludes the notion that the rails spread by reason of the nonrepair of the tracks.

There were motions for nonsuit and for directions of a verdict for the defendant. The refusal of these motions raises the questions on which the principal stress was laid in the argument before this court. The motions were based in part on the ground "that the accident was due to the negligence of a fellow-servant of the plaintiff." As we have already seen, there was evidence from which the jury had a right to infer that the occurrence was due to negligent non-repair of the track, and not to excessive speed of the train. Therefore the question is raised whether the employees whose duty it was to inspect and repair the track were fellow-servants of the plaintiff, engaged in a common employment with him, within the meaning of the rule that absolves the master from liability to a servant for the consequences of a fellow-servant's negligence. It is entirely clear that as between a railroad company and such of its

master, yet, according to the great weight of authoritative decisions, such conveyance of orders is merely incidental to the common employment, and is not a duty for whose nonperformance or negligent performance the master can be held liable in damages to one of his servants who may be injured thereby.

employees as are required, in the performance of their duties, to travel upon its trains, the company is bound to exercise reasonable care to so construct and maintain the tracks and roadbed as to make them reasonably safe for the purposes of such travel. So far as the trainmen are concerned, the tracks and roadbed come within the familiar rule that imposes on the master the duty of taking ordinary care that the places in which and the appliances with which the servant is required to work shall be reasonably safe for the purpose. The cases of Harrison *v.* Central R. R. Co., 31 N. J. L. 293, and Paulmier *v.* Erie R. R. Co., 34 N. J. L. 151, are instances in which the Supreme Court asserted the master's liability where the supports of the track were insecure, and the master had notice thereof. The recent decisions of this court furnish numerous illustrations of the general principle. Among them are Mills *v.* Ice Co., 51 N. J. L. 342; Steamship Co. *v.* Ingebregsten, 57 N. J. L. 400; Telegraph Co. *v.* McMullen, 58 N. J. L. 155; Van Steenburgh *v.* Thornton, 58 N. J. L. 160; Day *v.* Donohue, 62 N. J. L. 380, 41 Atl. Rep. 934; Cole *v.* Warren Mfg. Co., 63 N. J. L. 626, 7 Am. Neg. Rep. 93. In each of these cases the employer was held liable by reason of some neglect of the duty in question.

The defendant's insistment involves the proposition that the men in charge of inspection and repair of the track were fellow-servants of the plaintiff, so that for the consequences of their negligence he cannot recover against the common employer. This contention cannot prevail. It is true that in Harrison *v.* Central R. R. Co., 31 N. J. L. 293, where the imputed negligence was the failure to repair a railroad bridge known to be unsafe for want of repair, in consequence of which the bridge broke down under the weight of a train, thereby causing the death of a brakeman upon the train, the late Chief Justice BEASLEY said, in substance, that if the company had in fact directed its agents possessed of competent skill, to examine at stated periods the bridge in question, and they had reported it secure, the plaintiff could not recover, even if the agents making such report had acted carelessly in the discharge of their duties, or falsely reported their conclusions. But this remark was confessedly based upon a supposed state of facts precisely opposite to that presented by the case, nor was the remark necessary for the decision. This dictum has sometimes been treated as authority for the proposition that a master may fully discharge his duty with respect to providing a safe place of work and safe appliances for the work by employing competent agents to make inspections and repairs. But since the decision by this court in the case of Steamship Co. *v.* Ingebregsten, 57 N. J. L. 400, it must be taken as established that this duty may not be delegated by the master, except at his own risk; that those who are employed to make inspections and repairs for the purpose of keeping in proper repair the place of work and the tools and appliances of the work are not fellow-servants engaged in a common employment with those employees for whose reasonable safety the precautions are required. In that case Mr. Justice DIXON said: "The master's

What is known as the "superior servant rule," already adverted to, has for its foundation the notion that the superior servant embodies the authority of the common master, so as to impose a liability upon the latter for his defaults. As already shown, this rule has been distinctly repudiated in this State. It may be added

duty to his servant requires of the former the exercise of reasonable care and skill in furnishing suitable machinery and appliances for carrying on the business in which he employs the servant, and in keeping such machinery and appliances in repair, including the duty of making inspections and tests at proper intervals. So far the authorities are at one. Almost as unanimous are they in the proposition that if the master selects an agent to perform this duty for him, and the agent fails to exercise reasonable care and skill in its performance, the master is responsible for the fault."

It is now fully recognized in this State that the test for determining, in a given case, whether the master is liable to one servant for the negligence of another servant, is in the answer to the inquiry whether the negligent servant was in the performance of work which the law imposes as a positive duty upon the master, by way of preparation for the general employment, or whether, on the other hand, such negligent servant was at the time in the performance of some duty incidental to the general employment itself. In the former case the master is liable; in the latter case, not. It is the master's duty to exercise reasonable care in furnishing those things which go to make up the plant and appliances, so as to have them at the outset reasonably safe for the work of the servants who are engaged in the general employment, and, further, to exercise reasonable care, by means of inspections and repairs when needed to keep the plant and appliances reasonably safe. These duties the master cannot avoid by employing others for their performance. If the negligence of those who are charged with such performance results in injury to one of those servants for whose safety the precautions are required the master is liable, unless by reason of the obvious character of the consequent risk, or otherwise, it is assumed by the injured employee, or unless the injury is brought about by contributory negligence. Recent cases clearly recognize the distinction referred to. In Maher *v.* Thropp, 59 N. J. L. 186, Mr. Justice VAN SYCKEL, speaking for this court, said: "The master was charged with the duty to furnish to the plaintiff proper implements with which to do the work in which he was engaged. If he entrusted the discharge of that obligation to the foreman, he is undoubtedly responsible for the failure of the foreman to exercise due care in that respect. But the injury to the plaintiff is in no way chargeable to the failure of the master to furnish proper tools. On the contrary, the accident is attributable wholly to the fact that the plaintiff, under the advice of the foreman, laid aside the safe tool, and used in its place a chisel and a pair of tongs In doing that the foreman did not act as the vice-principal, standing in the place of the master, but he acted as a fellow-servant, performing, with the assistance of the plaintiff, the work in which both were engaged, and for which the master had provided the necessary implements with due care." In McLaughlin *v.* Camden Iron Works, 60 N. J. L. 557, 4 Am. Neg. Rep. 69, Mr. Justice COLLINS said: "Where appliances for work are needed, the duty is on the master to use reasonable care in their selection, and he cannot escape that it is now rejected almost universally in other jurisdictions. One of the most conspicuous decisions sustaining it was the Ross case, in the United States Supreme Court, decided in the year 1884 by a divided court (112 U. S. 377), where, principally on the authority of the Ohio and Kentucky decisions, a railroad company was

it by delegation. But carelessness in their use, or failure to use them on the part of his servant, whereby injury is received by a fellow-servant in the same common employment, is not chargeable to the master, no matter what may be the grade or authority of the servant." In Curley *v.* Hoff, 62 N. J. L. 758, 5 Am. Neg. Rep. 668, Mr. Justice COLLINS said at page 762, 62 N. J. L., and page 672, 5 Am. Neg. Rep.: "While delegation to others will not relieve the master from the consequences of negligence in the performance of what the law makes the master's duty, it will not charge upon the master the consequences of the negligence of his servants toward each other. The risk of that negligence, for reasons of public policy, the law places on the servant. The test always must be whether the negligent act or omission was in discharge of the master's or the servant's duty." In Cole *v.* Warren Mfg. Co., 63 N. J. L. 626, 7 Am. Reg. Rep. 93, the same distinction was taken.

It is plain, therefore, that, so far as the motions to nonsuit and for direction of a verdict were based upon the idea that the men charged with inspection and repair of the track were fellow-servants of the plaintiff, the motions were properly refused. This disposes at the same time of the principal remaining exceptions, they being intended to raise the same question upon the instructions of the trial court to the jury.

The motion to nonsuit and to direct a verdict were based on the further ground that the risk of derailment by reason of the low joint in question was assumed by the plaintiff, because he had passed over the same place many times before while traveling in defendant's trains, the last trip being about an hour before the accident. The low spot caused a sudden jolt or lurch, that was readily observed by passengers in the train. It is insisted, therefore, that the plaintiff assumed the risk. Regan *v.* Palo, 62 N. J. L. 30, 5 AM. NEG. REP. 63; Atha & Illingworth Co., *v.* Costello, 63 N. J. L. 27, 5 AM. NEG. REP. 655. But the risk of injury from a defect in a track or roadbed negligently permitted to remain in bad repair is not one of the ordinary and natural risks of the employment of a trainman. It was, therefore, not assumed by the plaintiff unless it was known to him, or was so obvious that by the exercise of ordinary care on his part it would have been known. A servant has the right to take it for granted that his master has performed his duty by the exercise of that reasonable care for the servant's safety which the law requires, until the servant is warned or notified of danger, or until the danger becomes so obvious that a reasonably prudent servant, under the circumstances, would observe it. But plainly it was far from obvious to one traveling upon the train that the roughness of the track indicated a weakness sufficient to cause derailment. The trial judge, therefore, could not say, as matter of law, that the plaintiff assumed the risk of the injury that he received; and so it was, at best, a question for the jury to determine whether the special danger was known to the plaintiff, or was so obvious that he ought to have known of it.

One of the assignments of error is

held liable to a locomotive engineer for injuries sustained through the negligence of the train conductor in failing to communicate running orders to the engineer; it appearing that by the general rules of the company the conductor had charge and control of the train and all persons employed on it, and was responsible for its movements while on the road, and that the conductor was specially charged with the duty of communicating the running orders to the engineer. But the Ross case, after being, in effect, seriously criticised by the same court in Balt. & O. R. R. Co. *v.* Baugh, 149 U. S. 368, was at last distinctly overruled in New England R. R. Co. *v.* Conroy, 175 U. S. 323, 7 Am. Neg. Rep. 182.

In an able article by Judge Dillon on the American Law Concerning Employer's Liability, in 24 Am. Law Rev., p. 189, after reviewing the history of the adjudications in this country, he uses the following well-considered language: "In the general American law, as I understand it, the doctrine of vice-principal exists to this extent, and no further, viz.: that it is precisely commensurate with the master's personal duties towards his servants. As to these, the servant who represents the master is what we may, for convenience, call a 'vice-principal,' for whose acts and neglects the master is

directed to the refusal to charge, as requested by the defendant, that "if the plaintiff was guilty of any negligence contributing to the injury for which recovery is sought, he cannot recover." The court charged, in substance, that in order to bar the plaintiff the defendant must show "that some negligence of the plaintiff contributed to the accident in such a way that, if the plaintiff had not been negligent, the accident would not have happened." The criticism is upon the use of the word "accident" instead of the word "injury," which was included in the request. The negligence imputed to the plaintiff was the failure to couple up the air brakes when the train was made up. This, admittedly, was his duty. The argument is that the "accident" refers to the derailment, while the "injury" — that is, the wounding of the plaintiff — occurred by the fall of the car to the bottom of the embankment. The answer is, that with respect to causation they are practically indistinguishable. If the derailment was not caused in whole or in part by the air brakes being uncoupled, neither was the fall of the car from the bank so caused. It is true, the evidence indicates that the car was dragged along the ties for 200 feet or more after leaving the rails, and that then the coupling between the tender and the car broke, leaving the car to pitch down the embankment. But it is not perceived that the use of air brakes after the car left the track could have averted the catastrophe. For the purposes of this case, it was proper enough to treat "accident" and "injury" as synonymous.

The other assignments of error have been examined, and found to be without support. The trial judge in his charge to the jury did no injustice to the defendant. His rulings upon questions of evidence, so far as complained of, were correct. The judgment should be affirmed, with costs. [CORTLANDT PARKER and CORTLANDT liable. Beyond this, the employer is liable only for his own personal negligence. This is a plain, sound, safe, and practicable line of distinction. We know where to find it and how to define it. It begins and ends with the personal duties of the master. Any attempt to refine, based upon the notion of 'grades' in the service, or, what is much the same thing, distinct 'departments' in the service, which departments frequently exist only in the imagination of the judges, and not in fact, will only breed the confusion of the Ohio and Kentucky experiments, whose courts have constructed a labyrinth in which the judges that made it seem to be able to 'find no end, in wandering mazes lost.'"

Now, it is obvious that the work in which Runyon was engaged, and wherein the jury have found him negligent, was the mere performance of the general service of the employer in common with the plaintiff. For all purposes of throwing the wire over the limb upon which the plaintiff stood, he was, to all intents and purposes, a lineman, like the plaintiff. The circumstance that at other times Runyon may have been called upon to perform duties that were "personal" to the master, in the sense that Runyon's negligence

PARKER, Jr., appeared for plaintiff in error; W. BRADFORD SMITH and ROBERT H. MCCARTER, for defendant in error.]

The ruling in the New Jersey case of SMITH v. ERIE R. R. Co. (of which the foregoing is the opinion), is stated in the syllabus by the court as follows:

"1. As between a railroad company and such of its employees as are required, in the performance of their duties, to travel upon its trains, the company is bound to exercise reasonable care to so construct and maintain the track and roadbed as to make them reasonably safe for such travel.

"2. For the negligence of the trackmen charged with the inspection and repair of the tracks and roadbed, where such negligence causes injury to a trainman traveling thereon, the railroad company is responsible.

"3. The master's duty to exercise reasonable care in furnishing a place for the work, and appliances for the work, that shall be reasonably safe for those engaged in the general employment, is not avoided by the employment of competent agents for its performance. Those servants to whom the duty is delegated are not fellow-servants engaged in a common employment with those for whose reasonable safety the duty is imposed upon the master.

"4. A servant has the right to take it for granted that his master has performed his duty by exercising reasonable care for the servant's safety in the respects above indicated, until the servant is warned or notified of a danger arising from the master's negligence, or until the danger becomes so obvious that a reasonably prudent servant, under the circumstances, would observe it.

"5. The risk of injury from a defect in a railroad track or roadbed negligently permitted to remain in bad repair is not among the ordinary and natural risks that are assumed by a trainman, and is not assumed unless it becomes known to him, or is so obvious that by the exercise of ordinary care on his part it would be observed."

in their performance or nonperformance would be chargeable to the employer, is immaterial upon the present case.

In behalf of the plaintiff it is argued that if the master in the case at hand had been an individual, instead of a body corporate, and, being personally present, had pulled the wire negligently, causing injury to the plaintiff, he would be liable. This may be readily conceded. So, also, it may be granted that, if Runyon was negligent to the injury of the plaintiff, Runyon was liable. In either case the liability would be imposed upon the individual for his own negligence, and without any resort to the maxim *respondeat superior*, which lies at the foundation of the master's liability for the defaults of his servants. This liability, on familiar principles, does not lie in favor of a fellow-servant.

It appearing clearly that Runyon was the fellow-servant of the plaintiff, the common employer could not be held liable for his negligence, in the absence of evidence tending to show that he was in general incompetent or unfit for the duty he was set to perform. It follows that the trial judge erred in refusing the motion to direct a verdict for the defendant.

The judgment should be reversed.

O'MALLEY v. GERTH ET AL.

Court of Errors and Appeals, New Jersey, June, 1902.

LIABILITY OF TRUSTEES FOR TORTS — PERSON INJURED BY STEPPING ON COAL-HOLE COVER IN SIDEWALK. — 1. Persons taking the possession, care, and control of real property under a trust devise in a will may be sued in tort, as individuals, for injuries resulting from their negligent acts or omissions in the management of the property. Whether such trustees may have indemnity out of the trust estate is of no concern as to the rights of a third party.

2. An abutting owner or occupart of premises who maintains a coal hole in a sidewalk in a city street, with a lid upon it, which he allows to become so insecure and unsafe that a traveler stepping thereon slips in the hole and is injured is liable to such injured person, irrespective of whether there be liability on the part of the municipality (1).

(Syllabus by the Court.)

1. See NOTE ON LIABILITY OF LANDLORD AND TENANT FOR CONDITION OF COAL HOLE IN SIDEWALK, 3 AM. NEG. REP. 314-315.

See also the following recent *New York* cases arising out of injuries sustained by persons falling into coal holes on sidewalk:

In VIAL *v.* JACKSON ET AL. (*Supreme Court, New York Appellate Division,*

APPEAL from Circuit Court Essex County.

Action by Martin O'Malley against Lilly Gerth and others. From judgment for plaintiff, defendants bring error. *Judgment affirmed.*

SAMUEL KALISCH, for plaintiffs in error.

ELVIN W. CRANE and FRANCIS CHILD, for defendant in error.

FORT, J. — The defendant in error is a policeman of the city of Newark. While on duty on the 29th day of April, 1900, he was passing through Campbell street, and stepped on a cover over a coal hole. The cover turned, and he fell astride it into the hole, and was seriously injured. The premises in front of which the coal hole was were the property of Julius Gerth in his lifetime. By his will this property was made a part of the residue of his estate, and was left in trust to his executors, to let and rent it, and to collect the rents

First Department, June, 1902), 76 N. Y. Supp. 668, a coal-hole accident case, the question decided was as to examination of defendant before trial. LAUGHLIN, J., said: "The action is brought to recover damages for personal injuries alleged to have been sustained by the plaintiff, owing to an insecure covering of a coal hole in the sidewalk adjacent to premises alleged to have been in the possession and under the control of the defendants as executors and trustees. The defendants in their answer deny that they were in possession and control of the premises. The object of the examination is "to enable the plaintiff to prepare for the trial." The examination is sought on the subject of the defendant's possession and control over the premises, sidewalk, coal hole, and grating covering it." * * * Order permitting examination affirmed.

In STURMWALD *v.* SCHREIBER ET AL. *(Supreme Court, New York, Appellate Division, Second Department, March, 1902)*, 74 N. Y. Supp. 995, judgment for plaintiff was affirmed, the facts, as stated in the opinion by JENKS, J., being as follows: "This action is based upon the failure of the defendants to provide and to maintain a safe and a secure covering to their cellar steps. On the night of September 1, 1899, the plaintiff, a traveler on the sidewalk in front of the premises of the defendants, stepped upon the covering and fell through it. There was evidence which warranted the jury in finding that the covering of the door was defective and out of repair, and that the defendants had notice." * * * "The premises in question was a tenement house, rented out in apartments. The learned counsel for the appellants contends that there was no liability upon his clients, because the first floor and basement of the house were rented to a tenant, who, by the terms of his lease, was required to make repairs. But the defendant testifies that he kept a janitor, who looked after the house, — who took care of it; that there were five families in the house, all of whom went by an inside door into the cellar to put ashes therein, but that the janitor always took the ashes out into the street for the tenants, and used the cellar door in question for such purpose; that Rubin (the said tenant) and the janitor had exclusive use of such door; and that the exclusive use was not in Rubin. I think that this testimony was sufficient to make the question of the liability of the defendants as owners one for the jury. Jennings *v.* Van Schaick, 108 N. Y. 530, 534. * * * ."

accruing from the same, and after paying taxes, insurance, repairs, and other charges, to pay the net surplus to the testator's widow. The executors have a power of sale. The three defendants are named as executors in the will, and all qualified. The accident occurred through the faulty condition of the coal hole, owing, undoubtedly, to the spreading of a cracked flagstone in which the rim of the lid or cover rested. Because of the enlargement of the hole, the lid at times would get in a position where it would slip in the hole, and turn upon its edge from pressure, and did when the defendant in error stepped upon it. Whether the defendants had knowledge of this condition of the hole and lid, and whether they had failed to repair within a reasonable time after notice thereof, was left to the jury, as a question of fact, which they must find in the affirmative before the verdict could be for the plaintiff. They so found. The additional lines of defense relied upon were: First, that the premises were occupied by a tenant, and that the fault was the fault of the tenant, and he alone was liable for the accident; no obligation being upon the defendants to repair. Second. That the damage resulted from a defect in the sidewalk, and that the city was charged with its repair, and it alone was liable for injuries resulting from non-repair. Third. That if the defendants were liable, they could not be held as individuals, but only as executors or trustees; their relation to the property being solely one of trust.

The trial judge properly declared the law as to the first proposition, and left it to the jury to determine whether the tenant had the exclusive possession of the premises, and whether it was incumbent upon the defendants to repair. He told the jury that if the premises were rented by a tenant, and the defendants did not reserve a right of entry for repair, or agree to repair, and the defective condition of the coal hole occurred during the tenancy, and while the defendants had no right or duty to repair, the plaintiff could not recover, but if the tenancy was uncertain, or monthly, or the like, and the defendants reserved or continuously exercised the right to repair, and had had their attention called to the defect in the hole, and had after this failed to repair, they were not, under that situation, relieved from liability. What the facts were in these respects was left to the jury, and they have found against the claim of the defendants. This states the rule of law correctly. Jennings *v.* Van Schaick, 108 N. Y. 530.

The second proposition is not tenable. Even if the city could be made liable in a case like this, it is still an undoubted legal rule that the owner of the premises or the occupant thereof, or both, are liable. The maintenance of a trap like this upon a sidewalk in front of one's premises is a nuisance. Busw. Pers. Inj., sec. 187; Cooley, Torts, p. 748; Davenport *v.* Ruckman, 37 N. Y. 568; Durant *v.* Palmer, 29 N. J. L. 544. Nor is the position that the defendants in this case cannot be held as individuals sustainable. The cases cited by counsel for the defendants were cases where receivers of railroads, appointed by the court, were sued as individuals for injuries happening to passengers or others upon trains operated under the receivership, and within the line of their duty. The case of Cardot *v.* Barney, 63 N. Y. 281, which was of this character, was relied upon by the defendant's counsel to sustain his contention. In Kain *v.* Smith, 80 N. Y. 458, that case was distinguished from cases of the class before us, and the rule in the class of cases where the trust is one voluntarily assumed is fully stated. A party having independent control is liable for the acts of persons under his control, whether of contract or tort. Rogers *v.* Wheeler, 43 N. Y. 598. Trustees for the benefit of bondholders of a railway, who assume duties under the terms of their trusteeship, are personally liable for torts arising from negligence or misconduct of the employees operating the road under them. Sprague *v.* Smith, 29 Vt. 421. The fact is unimportant that the defendants were acting as trustees or in a representative capacity in the care or control of the property. An action in a case of this kind lies against them as individuals. Whether they may have indemnity out of the trust estate is of no concern as to third parties. Mason *v.* Pomeroy, 151 Mass. 164, 167; Association *v.* McAllister, 153 Mass. 292, 297, 26 N. E. Rep. 862.

No error is found, and the judgment of the Circuit Court is affirmed.

LAND v. FITZGERALD.

Supreme Court, New Jersey, June, 1902.

DANGEROUS PREMISES — LIABILITY OF OWNER — PERSON INJURED BY FALL OF CHIMNEY — LICENSEE. — 1. There is no implied duty on the owner of a house which is in an unsafe condition to inform a proposed tenant that it is in a dangerous condition, and no action will lie against him for an omission to do so, in the absence of express warranty or deceit.

2. Where the owner invites another to come upon his premises, he is required to use reasonable care to have his premises in a safe condition.

3. An averment in the declaration that the plaintiff was lawfully upon the

defendant's premises does not show that he was there with any greater right than that of a mere licensee; the only duty the defendant owed to such a person was to refrain from acts wilfully injurious (1).

(Syllabus by the Court.)

ACTION by Thomas F. Land against Bartholomew Fitzgerald. *Demurrer to declaration sustained.*

Argued February term, 1902, before GUMMERE, Ch. J., and VAN SYCKEL, GARRISON and GARRETSON. JJ.

YOUNG & ARROWSMITH, for plaintiff.

MCEWAN & MCEWAN, for defendant.

VAN SYCKEL, J. — The declaration in this case contains three counts. The first count alleges that the defendant was the owner of a dwelling-house on which he had carelessly constructed and maintained a chimney which was insecure and dangerous by reason of its negligent and improper construction; that the danger was known to the defendant and was not patent or known to the plaintiff; that the defendant rented a portion of the said house to the plaintiff, who entered into possession and was injured in the falling of said chimney. The second count alleges that the defendant was the owner of a dwelling-house on which he had carelessly constructed and maintained a chimney which was insecure and dangerous; that the danger was known to the defendant, but was not patent or known to the plaintiff; that the plaintiff was upon the premises by the invitation of the defendant, and while so there the said chimney, by reason of its faulty and careless construction, fell upon and injured the plaintiff. The third count alleges that the defendant was the owner of a dwelling house on which he had negligently constructed and maintained a chimney which was insecure and dangerous; that the danger was known to the defendant, but was not patent or known to the plaintiff; that the plaintiff was lawfully upon said premises, and while so there the said chimney fell upon and injured him. To each of these counts the defendant demurred.

Mr. Justice Depue, in his elaborate opinion in Clyne *v.* Holmes, 61 N. J. L. 358, 4 Am. Neg. Rep. 180, shows that it is well settled law that on a demise of a house or lands there is no contract or condition implied that the premises shall be fit and suitable for the use for which the lessee required them. He cites with approval the declaration of Chief Justice Erie in Robbins *v.* Jones, 15 C. B. (N.

1. For actions from 1897 to date, arising out of accidents on dangerous premises, and the liability of landlord therefor, see vols. 1-12 AM. NEG. REP., and the current numbers of that series of Reports.

S.) 221 (1), that a landlord who lets a house in a dangerous state is not liable to the tenants, customers, or guests for accidents happening during the term, for, fraud apart, there is no law against letting a tumbledown house, and the tenant's remedy is upon his contract, if any. He also adopted the views of Mr. Justice Dixon in Mullen *v.* Rainear, 45 N. J. L. 520, that there is no implied duty on the owner of a house which is in a ruinous and unsafe condition to inform a proposed tenant that it is unfit for habitation, and no action will lie against him for an omission to do so in the absence of express warranty or deceit. In tnat case the injury was occasioned by the breaking of a balcony connected with the demised premises. The authority of these cases is fully recognized by the Court of Errors and Appeals in Del., L. & W. R. R. Co. *v.* Reich, 61 N. J. Law, 635, 4 Am. Neg. Rep. 522. To this count the demurrer is well taken; it shows no breach of duty for which an action will lie.

The second count presents a different question. The allegation there is that the plaintiff was upon the premises by the invitation of the defendant, not that the plaintiff was his tenant. The law is equally well settled that, where the entry upon the owner's premises is made by his invitation, either express or implied, he is required to use reasonable care to have his premises in a safe condition. Phillips *v.* Library Co., 55 N. J. L. 307; Del., L. & W. R. R. Co. *v.* Reich, 61 N. J. L. 635, 4 Am. Neg. Rep. 522. The invitation and the negligence being sufficiently alleged, the second count discloses a good cause of action, and the demurrer should be overruled.

1. The facts in Robbins *v.* Jones, 15 C. B. N. S. 221, were as follows: In 1830 houses were erected on land adjoining a new road constructed at a high level as an approach to a new bridge across the Thames. Between these houses and this road was a space which was covered over (as a means of access to the houses) by a flagging in which were gratings to let light and air to the lower part of the buildings, which formed separate tenements, the entrance to which was upon the lower level at the rear. The space so covered had become, by dedication, prior to the 5 & 6 Will. 4, c. 50, a part of the public footway, and was used as such by the public. In 1862, in consequence of a large number of persons congregating upon the spot, the flagging and grating in front of one of the houses (having become weakened by user) gave way, and several persons were precipitated into the area below (a depth of about thirty feet) and one of them was killed. *Held*, in an action by his widow, under 9 & 10 Vict., c. 93, that, there being under the circumstances no legal liability on the part of the lessees of the house to keep the surface of this way in repair, the action was not maintainable, the gulf at the side of the causeway being the result of the road being raised by the makers of it, not of the land at the side being excavated by the proprietors of it; and that the artificial character of the flagging and grating did not make it more or less a way to be repaired by the parish.

The third count alleges simply that the plaintiff was lawfully upon the premises at the time he was injured. In Matthews *v.* Bensel, 51 N. J. L. 30, Chief Justice Beasley delivered the opinion of the court, holding that, in an action for injuries received in the manufactory of the defendants, the general allegation that plaintiff was lawfully on the premises is sufficient to show that he was not a trespasser. The facts from which such right proceeds need not be stated, but such general allegation will not show that he was there with greater right than that of a mere licensee. The right, therefore, which the plaintiff shows by the third count, is the right to be upon the premises merely by license. The only duty which the owner of land owes to a person who is upon his premises as a licensee only is to refrain from acts willfully injurious. Phillips *v.* Library Co., 55 N. J. L. 307; Taylor *v.* Turnpike Co., 65 N. J. L. 106, 46 Atl. Rep. 757; Del., L. & W. R. R. Co. *v.* Reich, 61 N. J. L. 635, 4 Am. Neg. Rep. 522.

No injurious act of an intentional or willful character is imputed to the defendant in the third count, and the demurrer to that count is therefore sustained. Costs will not be allowed to either side.

CARROLL v. TIDEWATER OIL COMPANY.

Court of Errors and Appeals, New Jersey, June, 1902.

EMPLOYEE INJURED BY DEFECTIVE MACHINERY — LATENT DEFECT — DUTY OF MASTER. — 1. C., a common laborer in the employ of the defendant, was directed with other laborers by the general superintendent of the defendant company to assist in the moving of a large iron punching machine. In the course of the moving, a fly wheel at the end of the machine, which was loose upon the shaft, slipped off, injuring the plaintiff, who was in the performance of his work standing in front of the wheel. *Held*, that the failure to exercise reasonable care for the safety of the servant and properly to inspect the condition of the machine before ordering its removal was a breach of duty on the part of the company for which it will be liable (1).

2. If the injury is due to a latent defect, which the master either knew, or by the exercise of the care required of him might have known, he will be liable.

3. A servant is entitled to assume, in the absence of any notice to the contrary, that the master has exercised reasonable care and skill in providing for the safety of the servant.

(Syllabus by the Court.)

1. See the numerous recent MASTER AND SERVANT CASES in this volume of AM. NEG. REP.

ERROR to Supreme Court.

Action by Thomas Carroll against the Tidewater Oil Company. From a judgment for defendant, plaintiff brings error. *Judgment reversed.*

THOMAS F. NOONAN, JR., for plaintiff in error.

ALVAH A. CLARK, for defendant in error.

VROOM, J. — This was an action brought by the plaintiff below against the defendant, the Tidewater Oil Company, to recover damages for personal injuries sustained while in the employment of the said company. The plaintiff was a common laborer, and had not, up to the time of the accident, worked in any other capacity while in this employment. With a number of other laborers he was ordered on the day of the injury to move a large iron punching machine some 500 feet from the place where it lay into a new boiler shop. The work of moving was done under the supervision and direction of two foremen of laborers named Gregory and Parker. It appeared that the removal of the machine to the boiler house was ordered by the general superintendent of the company. The machine was moved on rollers and on planks and on skids, by means of a block and fall. Plaintiff testified that he took different parts in the moving of the machine — running out with the block and fall, laying it on and hooking the block, and running back and pulling on the rope. When they had moved the machine into the boiler shop, and while the plaintiff was assisting in placing it on a platform and putting it in position, the fly or balance wheel at the end of the machine, of great weight, and four feet in diameter, fell off its axle or shaft. The plaintiff was standing in front of the wheel, with his hands on it. Seeing it about to fall, he tried to get out of the way by jumping, but the wheel fell upon his left foot, causing the injury complained of. There was evidence showing that this fly wheel had never been properly put on the shaft; that it was too loose in the beginning, and had been too loose ever since it was put on. There was also evidence that the only proper way to put such a wheel on a shaft was first to put it in tight, which would require two or three tons to press it on the shaft; then it should be fastened with a key driven in with a heavy hammer of some eight or ten pounds' weight, the key going partly in the hub of the wheel and partly into the shaft; then to be fastened with set screws on the quartershaft, and, in order to make it more secure, with the shaft countersunk. At the close of the plaintiff's case the trial judge granted a nonsuit upon the grounds thus stated by him: "That from the time that it (the machine) was taken charge of by the foreman, who was a co-servant of the plaintiff, for the purpose of removal — that is, to make the removal of the machine — the company was guilty of no act of negligence towards the plaintiff. There was a machine plainly perceivable by the plaintiff there to be removed. There is no evidence that it was not in safe condition at the time. It may have been the duty of Gregory at that time, if it had been unfit for removal, perhaps, to make a report to the company, or to take such measures as would make it safe; but he was the co-servant of the plaintiff, and his negligence was one of the risks assumed by the plaintiff. The plaintiff cannot charge the defendant with any injuries which he received by reason of any act of negligence of Gregory, who was his co-servant." On error to the Supreme Court the judgment of the Circuit Court was affirmed, the Supreme Court holding that those in charge of moving the machine were fellow-servants of the plaintiff, and that no negligence was found for which the company was liable. The assignment of error relied upon in this court was the failure of the Supreme Court to reverse the judgment of nonsuit in the Hudson Circuit Court.

The principal ground for the motion of nonsuit and for the judgment of the Supreme Court in affirmance thereof was the familiar rule that a master is not liable to a servant for damages resulting from the negligence of a fellow-servant in the course of a common employment. Almost the only case pressed upon this court in the brief of the defendant in error was that of O'Brien *v.* Dredging Co., 53 N. J. L. 291, 21 Atl. Rep. 324, in which case it was held "that a master will not be liable to a servant in his employ for injuries occasioned by the negligence of a superior servant, who is also employed as a boss or foreman of other workmen with whom he labors, in the execution of work designed and directed by the master or his vice-principal." It is apprehended that the correctness of the law as laid down in that case, and afterwards in Gilmore *v.* Nail Co., 55 N. J. L. 39, 25 Atl. Rep. 707, will not be disputed. But, as was so aptly said by Adams, J., in Flanigan *v.* Guggenheim Smelting Co., 63 N. J. L. 662, in referring to the rule above stated: "This rule does not apply to this case. It springs from and is concerned with a breach of duty of a fellow-workman; not a breach of duty of the employer." And he further says that: "The true criterion is thus compactly stated in the opinion of this court in Curley *v.* Hoff, 62 N. J. L. 758, 763, 5 Am. Neg. Rep. 668: 'The test always must be whether the negligent act or omission was in discharge of the master's or the servant's duty.'" The very gist of the plaintiff's action in this case is in the negligent act or omission in the master's duty. The moving of this heavy machine called for the exercise of reasonable care and skill on the part of the master, including inspection, and the security of those instructed to effect its removal. It is not a question involving the ordinary risks and perils in working at or about the machine, but whether it was reasonably safe when the plaintiff and other ordinary laborers were set to work moving it. Such laborers would not, nor could they be expected to, know anything of the construction of such a machine; whether it was or was not in suitable repair or condition for removing; whether the fly wheel was loose, and liable to slip off the shaft or not, in the course of such moving. As was said in this court in Telegraph Co. *v.* McMullen, 58 N. J. L. 155, 33 Atl. Rep. 384, in defining the risks assumed by a servant (and the exposition is particularly applicable to this case): "A servant assumes only the ordinary risks incident to his employment, and also risks arising in consequence of special features of danger known to him, or which he could have discovered by the exercise of reasonable care, or which should have been observed by one ordinarily skilled in the employment in which he engages." And there is a positive duty imposed upon the master to take reasonable care and precaution not to subject the servant to other and greater dangers. Electric Co. *v.* Kelly, 57 N J. L. 100, 29 Atl. Rep. 427. If the defect in the putting of this wheel upon the shaft was one that could not have been discovered by careful and diligent examination, no responsibility would attach to the master; but he would be liable for a latent defect, which, by the exercise of the care and diligence required of him, he might have discovered. The fact that one of the witnesses testified that while they were moving the machine up grade one Cox came up behind the machine, and said the wheel was nearly off, and that they tried to fix it on so as to keep it on, but demonstrates, if true, that reasonable care and precaution on the part of the master before the moving was undertaken would have prevented the accident. The plaintiff testified that he did not see Mr. Cox there at all until after he was injured, and it appeared that at the time the statement as to the wheel was alleged to have been made the plaintiff was over fifty feet from the machine, running the block and fall to the railroad track. In discussing the question of the liability of the master for negligence, Mr. Justice Van Syckel, in the case of Smith *v.* Iron Co., 42 N. J. L. 467, 468, laid down the rule, which has been approved and followed: "If there has been negligence on the part of the master in selecting proper servants, or in furnishing safe appliances for the conduct of business, the master is responsible;" and he further adds, on page 473, 42 N. J. L.: "It has been universally conceded that there are certain duties which a corporation must perform towards its servants, such as the furnishing of proper instrumentalities, and using due care in selecting co-servants, which cannot be neglected without consequent liability." In Steamship Co. *v.* Ingebregsten, 57 N. J. L. 400, 31 Atl. Rep. 619, in this court, Mr. Justice Dixon said: "A master's duty to his servant required of the former the exercise of reasonable care and skill in furnishing suitable machinery and appliances for carrying on the business in which he employs the servant, and in keeping such machinery in repair, including the duty of making inspections and tests at proper intervals;" and he adds: "So far the authorities are at one," and "almost as numerous are they in the proposition that, if the master selects an agent to perform this duty for him, and the agent fails to exercise reasonable care and skill, the master is responsible for the fault." This declaration of this court has been approved and followed in the later cases of Telegraph Co. *v.* McMullen, 58 N. J. L. 157, 33 Atl. Rep. 384; Van Steenburgh *v.* Thornton, 58 N. J. L. 160, 33 Atl. Rep. 380; Maher *v.* Thropp, 59 N. J. L. 186, 35 Atl. Rep. 1057; Comben *v.* Belleville Stone Co., 59 N. J. L. 226, 1 Am. Neg. Rep. 117; McLaughlin *v.* Camden Iron Works, 60 N. J. L. 557, 4 Am. Neg. Rep. 69; Curley *v.* Hoff, 62 N. J. L. 758, 5 Am. Neg. Rep. 668; Cole *v.* Warren Manufacturing Co., 63 N. J. L. 627, 7 Am. Neg. Rep. 93; Flanigan *v.* Guggenheim Smelting Co., 63 N. J. L. 647, 663, 7 Am. Neg. Rep. 113. To the same purport are the decisions of the Supreme Court of the United States. Railroad Co. *v.* Daniels, 152 U. S. 684; Hough *v.* Railroad Co., 100 U. S. 213; Railroad Co. *v.* Herbert, 116 U. S. 642; Railroad Co. *v.* Baugh, 149 U. S. 368. But, as was said in the case of Flanigan *v.* Guggenheim Smelting Co., *supra:* "Even if the accident be thought of as the product of the co-operating negligence of the employer and fellow-servants of the plaintiff, the conclusion is the same." The court there cited with approval the rule laid down in Beven on Negligence, on page 743: "If the negligence of the master combines with the negligence of the fellow-servant, and the two contribute to the injury, the servant injured may recover damages against the master." Cole *v.* Warren Manufacturing Co., 63 N. J. L. 626, 631, 7 Am. Neg. Rep. 93. When we come to apply the principles above stated to the present case, it is clear that it was the duty of the defendant, through its general superintendent, who admitted that he had directed the removal of this machine into the boiler shop, to see that it was removed with care, that proper foremen were selected to superintend the work, and to see that it was in a safe condition before delivered over for removal. In this duty or service he was the representative of the defendant, and not acting in a common employment with the plaintiff. If negligence also can be attributable to the foreman for failure properly to inspect the machine and supervise the work of removal, it will not avail the defendant, even though such foreman may be held to be in a common employment with the plaintiff, if their negligence is combined with that of the defendant. Cole *v.* Manufacturing Co., *supra.* The evidence on the part of the plaintiff clearly tended to show that the duty thus stated as devolving upon the master had not been performed, and that the injuries sustained by the plaintiff were the result of this negligence, chargeable to the defendant. The burden of proof of negligence in this respect, it is true, is upon the plaintiff; yet if the question presented by the evidence is one upon which a reasonable difference of opinion might be entertained, the duty of the trial court is to submit it to the jury. Whether there was negligence on the part of the defendant in not exercising reasonable care and skill in supplying reasonably safe machinery and appliances, and in keeping them in a safe condition for the work to be performed, was a question for the jury, depending upon the facts of the case. Van Steenburgh *v.* Thornton, 58 N. J. L. 160, 33 Atl. Rep. 380; Comben *v.* Belleville Stone Co., 59 N. J. L. 226, 1 Am. Neg. Rep. 117.

The judgment of the Supreme Court affirming the judgment of the Circuit Court is reversed, and the record remitted to the Circuit Court, with the direction that a *venire de novo* be awarded.

TREMBLAY v. HARMONY MILLS.

Court of Appeals, New York, June, 1902.

PERSON INJURED BY FALLING ON ICY SIDEWALK — WATER DISCHARGED FROM ROOF OF BUILDING — OWNER OF PREMISES LIABLE. — Where a person was injured by slipping on ice on sidewalk formed by discharge of water from leader on roof of building, the owner of the building was liable, and it was not error for the trial court to instruct the jury that if the defendant was negligent in maintaining a leader from the roof of a building so as to discharge water on the sidewalk, by which ice was accumulated thereon, and the walk rendered dangerous, the plaintiff was entitled to recover (1).

PARKER, Ch. J., and O'BRIEN and GRAY, JJ., *dissented.*

1. See the following recent *Pennsylvania* case as to liability of owner of building for ice on sidewalk:

In BROWN *v.* WHITE *(Penn., April, 1902)*, 57 Atl. Rep. 962, judgment for plaintiff, who was injured by falling on ice on sidewalk, was reversed for erroneous admission of evidence, etc. The facts of the case, as stated by MESTREZAT, J., are as follows: "The

APPEAL from Supreme Court, Appellate Division, Third Department.

Action by Peter Tremblay against the Harmony Mills. From a judgment of the Appellate Division (68 N . Y. Supp. 1150), affirming a judgment for plaintiff, defendant appeals. *Judgment affirmed.*

JOHN H. GLEASON and JOHN E. MACLEAN, for appellant.

MARK COHN and JOHN SCANLON, for respondent.

CULLEN, J. — Assuming the sufficiency of the appellant's exception to raise the point, — which may well be doubted, — the question presented on this appeal is whether the trial court erred in instructing

defendant [White] and Mrs. Effie O. Gilbert own adjoining lots on the east side of North Main street, in the borough of Chambersburg. On these lots are erected two brick dwelling-houses, between which is an archway from the property line to the rear of the buildings, about three feet wide, and extending in height to the second story of the buildings. The archway is on the land of Mrs. Gilbert, and is formed by the second story of the defendant's house projecting over the way to Mrs. Gilbert's building. The defendant had the right to use the archway. In April, 1899, he constructed a one and one-quarter inch drain pipe from a sink in the second story of his house to the archway, by which the contents of the sink could be carried to and discharged upon the surface of the archway, through which it flowed to the pavement, and thence in an open gutter over the pavement to the street. The water from the roof of the adjoining property was carried to the archway in a four-inch pipe opening therein a short distance in the rear of the place where the waste water from the sink was discharged. The defendant did not live in his house, but leased it to various tenants. Four rooms on the second floor — one extending over the archway — were rented and occupied jointly by two tenants engaged in the millinery business. The sink referred to was in one of these rooms, and used by the occupants in disposing of the waste water 'that would come from ordinary housekeeping.' The plaintiff is a woman of seventy-one years of age, and at the time of the accident was, and for three years prior thereto, had been, engaged as a chambermaid at the Montgomery hotel, on North Main street, Chambersburg, a short distance south of, and on the same side of the street as, the defendant's property. She lived outside the borough, and spent her nights at home. On leaving the hotel in the evening for her home, she immediately crossed Main street, and then entered an alley leading off the street. In returning to her work in the morning, she usually came on King street to Main street, and along the opposite side of that street from defendant's property to the hotel. Before daylight, and in the early morning of December 30, 1899, the plaintiff, in going to her work, came up King street, and, contrary to her usual custom, crossed to the east or hotel side of North Main street. She then proceeded along the footwalk on that side of the street until she came in front of the archway, where, stepping on some ice, she fell, and was seriously and permanently injured. There was no ice on the pavements between her home and the archway. She says it had been a good while prior to the time of the accident since she had passed over the pavement in front of the archway. The testimony of the plaintiff showed that on the morning the jury that, if the defendant was negligent in maintaining a leader from the roof of a building so as to discharge water on the side-walk, by which ice was accumulated thereon, and the walk rendered dangerous, the plaintiff was entitled to recover. "At common law any act or obstruction which unnecessarily incommodes or impedes

of the accident there was a continuous ridge of ice extending from the mouth of the archway across the pavement to the curb. In the center of the ridge it was from three to five inches thick, and sloped to the sides. It is claimed by the plaintiff, and her evidence tended to show, that this accumulation of ice was produced by the water which passed through the defendant's drain pipe, and thence through the archway to the pavement, where it froze. This action was brought by the plaintiff to recover damages for the injuries she sustained by the alleged negligence of the defendant in causing the pavement to be obstructed by ice. She avers that the defendant "did so negligently and carelessly construct, keep, and maintain the buildings on his said lot of ground erected, and the pipes, drains, and gutters in, upon, and about the same, in such manner that large quantities of waste water, drainage, and water from rain and melting snow and ice were discharged over and upon the said pavement, and became frozen thereon, so that it obstructed the same, and rendered it dangerous and unsafe to persons passing upon and using the said pavement." The trial in the court below resulted in a verdict and judgment for the plaintiff, and the defendant has appealed.

"The first, fifth, sixth, seventh, and eighth assignments allege error in the court in rejecting evidence of the defendant offered for the purpose of showing the condition of the premises before and after the accident. Portions of some of these offers might have been admissible, but, contained in an offer with other incompetent matter, were properly excluded. The learned trial judge was right in excluding the offers to which these assignments relate. The liability of the defendant arises from the condition of the premises at the time of the accident. This could not be shown by their condition prior or subsequent to that time. It may be that the defendant offered to show that the surface water flowing through the archway from the rear of the building produced ice on the pavement the winter before the accident; that this condition of the pavement existed before the drain pipe had been constructed, and after it had been removed. But conceding these allegations to be true, they do not meet or tend to disprove the averments of the plaintiff, supported by her testimony that the ice on which she fell, or a material part thereof, was formed by the water which came from the drain pipe leading to the archway from the kitchen on the second floor of the defendant's building. The evidence of the plaintiff shows that a quantity of water had been discharged through the drain pipe the evening before the accident by the occupants of the defendant's premises, and that that water had produced the accumulation of ice on which the plaintiff fell. In addition to this, there was testimony that on the occasion of the accident there was no ice back of the drain pipe, but that it extended from the mouth of the drain pipe in the archway to the pavement. This was the issue which the defendant was called upon to meet, and evidence offered by him that ice on the pavement a year previous or at a time subsequent had accumulated from other causes would not negative the proposition of the plaintiff's averment.

the lawful use of a highway by the public is a nuisance" (Ang. Highw., sec. 223), and any party who sustains a private or peculiar injury therefrom may maintain an action to recover the damages sustained. Wakeman *v.* Wilbur, 147 N. Y. 657, 42 N. E. Rep. 341.

On former and subsequent occasions when the drain pipe was not in use. ice could have formed on the pavement at this point from water coming from the hydrants and the roofs of the houses, or from surface water collected in the rear of the buildings and carried to the pavement through the archway, as claimed in the plaintiff's offers; but that fact of itself would not show, nor tend to show, that water from another source might not have been discharged on the pavement, and formed the ice which caused the plaintiff's injuries. In the absence of evidence that water did flow to the pavement from other than the drain pipe, it cannot be presumed that water from such source did produce the ice on the occasion of the accident. After affirmative evidence of the fact on the part of the plaintiff, it was incumbent upon the defendant to show that the plaintiff was not injured by ice that had accumulated from water discharged through the drain pipe; and his offers, if admitted, would not have aided the jury in arriving at such a conclusion.

"The second, third, and fourth assignments complain of the court's refusal to admit testimony to show that in the borough of Chambersburg it is customary to drain water from lots, roofs, and waste pipes for domestic use in the houses of the borough, over and through uncovered drains across pavements to the gutters in the street, in the same manner as was done in the case on trial. The learned trial judge very properly sustained the objection to the offers, and excluded the testimony. In support of these offers the learned counsel for the defendant cite King *v.* Thompson, 87 Pa. St. 369. There it was held that an opening in the sidewalk such as is usual in a city for the purpose of light and ventilation to a dwelling is not, *per se*, a nuisance. The second point for charge, the refusal of which was held to be error, requested the court to instruct the jury that the defendant was not guilty of negligence or nuisance in maintaining an opening in the pavement if such opening was not only usual and customary in Allegheny City for lighting and ventilating cellars, but also was reasonably necessary for those purposes. In the opinion it is said that if it was customary, time out of mind, for property holders to have such opening, and "if reasonably necessary for light and ventilation, the property owner is not chargeable with negligence for placing and keeping it there." In the case at bar the offers did not propose to show, nor would it even be pretended, that the ice bank in question was necessary for any legitimate or lawful purpose; nor was it suggested in the offer that running water from the lots, roofs, and waste pipes over uncovered drains across pavements was a necessary, or the only practicable, way of disposing of such water. There is no averment by defendant that any necessity existed for using the pavements of the borough of Chambersburg for carrying to the gutters along the streets surface or waste water or water that might have flowed from the roofs of houses. It is therefore apparent that, had the testimony been admitted, it would have disclosed the single fact that the custom of the people of the borough was to conduct the water from the premises on the pavement, and permit it to congeal there, which was negligence, resulting in a nuisance, dangerous and

This is unquestionably the general rule. That the jury could have found that the discharge of water and drippings from the leader in winter weather, when the water so discharged was liable to freeze

unsafe to all who had occasion to use the streets. Regardless, therefore, of any necessity for thus disposing of the surface water by the property owners, the ice permitted to form in front of the archway, and on which the plaintiff fell, was, as shown by plaintiff's testimony, a public nuisance; and in the language of the court in McNerney *v.* Reading City, 150 Pa. St. 614, neither the lapse of time, nor the existence of like nuisances elsewhere with the consent of the municipality, will legalize it. Obstructions on the footwalks of the streets of a municipality, whether created by the accumulation of ice or otherwise, except such as are temporarily permitted for a lawful purpose, are a nuisance, and the party responsible therefore is liable to the individual injured by his illegal act. The public have a right to the use of the street in the condition in which the municipality has left it, and no person, whether an adjoining owner or not, is justified in placing or permitting an obstruction thereon which renders it dangerous or insecure. The custom of the citizens or the acquiescence of the municipality will not excuse such conduct. What has just been said applies to, and disposes of, the thirteenth assignment of error." * * *

"In the twelfth and fourteenth assignments the defendant denies his liability in this action because his house was, at the time of the accident, occupied by tenants, who used the sink and drain pipe which carried the waste water to the archway. In support of this position the defendant contends that it was the duty of the tenant to use the premises so as to injure no one, and to remove the ice and snow from the pavement. We are not here concerned with the duty and liability of the tenant to the plaintiff. It may be that the tenants who put the waste water in the drain pipe were liable to the plaintiff, but that fact does not relieve the defendant in this action. After purchasing the property, he constructed the sink and drain pipe for the purpose of carrying the waste water from the rooms in the occupancy of his tenants to the archway, with a knowledge that it would flow thence on the pavement. The condition of the building was therefore attributable to the act of the defendant, and not to that of the tenant, and its use by the latter was in conformity with the defendant's intention when he leased the premises. " We do not doubt," said GORDON, J., in Knauss *v.* Brua, 107 Pa. St. 88, " but that, in the absence of an agreement to repair, the landlord is not liable to a third party for a nuisance resulting from dilapidation in the leasehold premises whilst in the possession of a tenant. To make the lessor so liable, the defect must be one that arises necessarily from a continuance of the use of the property as it was when the tenant took possession of it. But the converse of this proposition is also true. If the premises are so constructed or in such a condition that the continuance of their use by the tenant must result in a nuisance to a third person, and a nuisance does so result, the landlord is liable." To the same effect are Fow *v.* Roberts, 108 Pa St. 489; Wunder *v.* McLean, 134 Pa. St. 334; Reading City *v.* Reiner, 167 Pa. St. 41." * * * Judgment for plaintiff in Court of Common Pleas, Franklin county, reversed. (J. A. STRITE and GILLAN & GILLAN, appeared for appellant; HORACE BENDER and SHARPE & ELDER, for appellee.)

and form ice, rendered the sidewalk dangerous, and constituted an obstruction, and that the defendant was negligent in not carrying his leader under the sidewalk to the carriageway, seems to me quite plain. To exonerate the defendant from liability it must establish one of two propositions: First, that it had the lawful right to discharge the water which it had collected on the roof of its building upon the highway, regardless of the effect of that action upon the highway; or, second, that because the municipality was liable to any one injured by the defective character of its highway, no action could be maintained against the abutting owner, though his act may have created the danger or defect. I think that neither proposition can be sustained. "Highways are public roads, which every citizen has a right to use." Ang. Highw., sec. 2. "The primary and dominant purpose of a street is for public passage, and any appropriation of it by legislative sanction to other objects must be deemed to be in subordination to this use, unless a contrary intent is clearly expressed." Hudson River Tel. Co. *v.* Watervliet T. & R'y Co., 135 N. Y. 393, 32 N. E. Rep. 148. *A fortiori* the use of the highway without legislative sanction must be subordinate to the public right of safe passage. A highway is not laid out or maintained either as a drain or as a sewer. In urban districts the easement acquired by the public includes the right to lay sewers, water pipes, and similar conveniences under the highway. But the highway itself remains devoted to its paramount purpose of public travel, and no action can be maintained against the municipality because it does not construct a sewer in a street. Nor can any right of the appellant to discharge the water from the roof of its building be predicated of its ownership of the adjacent land. As between private owners, as long as one leaves his land in its natural condition he is not required to adopt measures to prevent the flowage of surface water from his premises on those of his neighbor. Vanderwiele *v.* Taylor, 65 N Y. 341. But when he puts a structure on his land a contrary rule prevails, and he must take care of the rain or snow that falls thereon, except in case of extraordinary storms. Bellows *v.* Sackett, 15 Barb. 96; Jutte *v.* Hughes, 67 N. Y. 267; Davis *v.* Niagara Falls Tower Co., 171 N. Y. 336. Even when such an owner erects no structure he cannot "collect the surface water into channels, and discharge it upon the land of his neighbor to his injury. This is alike the rule of the civil and criminal law." Barkley *v.* Wilcox, 86 N. Y. 140. "He may consume it, but must not discharge it to the injury of others." Forbell *v.* City of New York, 164 N. Y. 522, 58 N. E. Rep. 664. The same principle obtains against the public authorities when they so grade a highway or construct a sewer as to collect water and discharge it to the injury of adjacent lands. Moran *v.* McClearns, 63 Barb. 185; Noonan *v.* City of Albany, 79 N. Y. 470. Why is not the converse of the proposition equally true? In the opinion of my Brother Gray, it is said of municipal corporations: "They owe the duty to the public of preventing the accumulation of ice from house conductors or leaders overhanging or near to the sidewalk." Surely, the abutting owner cannot be authorized to do that which it is the duty of the municipal authorities to prevent.

The fact that the city may have been liable to the plaintiff did not relieve the defendant from liability if the negligent or wrongful act of the latter created the dangerous condition of the highway. On the city there rested the duty of maintaining its streets reasonably safe for the passage of travelers. So far as the street may become unsafe from natural causes, that obligation is solely on the city; and, even if an ordinance imposes upon the abutting owners the duty of removing snow from the sidewalk, an action will not lie by a third party against an abutter for failure to comply with the ordinance. City of Rochester *v.* Campbell, 123 N. Y. 405, 25 N. E. Rep. 937. In the case cited the snow which caused the injury had fallen upon the sidewalk, and the abutter had not contributed to its presence there. The doctrine of the case has no application where the affirmative act of the abutter created the obstruction. On the contrary, "when corporations have been compelled to pay damages for a wrongful act perpetrated by another in public highways, they become entitled to maintain an action against such persons for indemnity from the liability which the wrongful act of the tort feasor has brought upon them." Opinion of Ruger, Ch. J., citing authorities, same case. It is contended that we are concluded by the decisions of this court in Wenzlick *v.* McCotter, 87 N. Y. 122, and Moore *v.* Gadsden, 87 N. Y. 84. We think they do not control the determination of the present case. In the Wenzlick case some broad statements were made by the learned judge writing the opinion which are in conflict with the views we have announced. These statements, however, were not necessary to the disposition of the case, and a careful reading of the opinion will show that the decision proceeded on the ground that the defendant had neither erected nor used the leader, and that, therefore, he was not liable for the creation of a nuisance, or its continuance, until he had been requested to abate it. In the Moore case the defendant had not changed the natural surface of his highway, from which it was alleged surface water or the drippings from melting snow had fallen on the sidewalk.

The judgment appealed from should be affirmed, with costs.

BARTLETT, MARTIN and VANN, JJ., concurred with CULLEN, J.

GRAY, J. (*dissenting.*) — The action was brought to recover for personal injuries sustained by the plaintiff from a fall upon an ice-covered sidewalk in front of the defendant's building. The complaint alleged the duty of the defendant to keep the sidewalk in a safe condition for travel; that it had constructed a water pipe leading from the roof of its building, the spout of which extended over the sidewalk; that it did "negligently, carelessly and unlawfully omit to erect a tunnel or raceway through or underneath said sidewalk to conduct the water off and from said sidewalk that flowed through said water pipe and spout, and negligently omitted to exercise any care or take any means whatever to conduct said water from said sidewalk;" that it did "negligently, carelessly and unlawfully suffer and permit ice to form, accumulate, and remain on said sidewalk near said water spout, in an unfit, dangerous, unsafe, and improper condition, and did at the time, * * * and for a long time prior thereto, negligently and unlawfully suffer and permit water to flow from said building through said water pipe and spout on said sidewalk, and accumulate and freeze thereon, * * * rendering it exceedingly dangerous, unsafe and hazardous for travel." The answer admitted the ownership of the building and the erection of the pipe and spout and denied that the latter extended over the sidewalk, or that the defendant was liable for the injuries. The defendant offered no evidence, and the case being submitted upon the plaintiff's evidence to the jury, the plaintiff had a verdict. From the unanimous affirmance by the Appellate Division in the Third Department of the judgment upon the verdict an appeal by the defendant has been allowed to this court.

The question for our consideration arises upon the exception taken by the defendant to the charge of the trial judge upon the subject of its liability. A motion to dismiss the complaint upon the plaintiff's evidence had been denied, and the trial judge, in instructing the jury, prior to the submission of the case, after adverting to what was the claim of the plaintiff, made the following remarks: "Now, you can see very well that it was possible for the rains to have descended, for the snows to have melted and to have accumulated on the top of that roof, and come down through that leader to the sidewalk, and every drop of it ran away into the gutter so far off from the street, leaving the sidewalk entirely clean and clear of any snow, or of any ice, or of anything that was dangerous. If that was the situation, then the fact that the leader was maintained there is a matter of no possible account to you, because it did not result in any damage to Tremblay. If, on the other hand, it had come down there, and by degrees had piled up something in the way of ice that was dangerous, and in fact a nuisance there, then the reverse would be the situation. * * * If you find that the Harmony Mills maintained a pipe there, which was negligence on their part, and this ice was in fact accumulated by reason of the water coming down out of that pipe, and you find the other facts which I will state to you in a moment in favor of the plaintiff, then the plaintiff is entitled to recover." At the close of the charge the defendant's counsel excepted "to that part of the charge in which the court said, if the defendant allowed this water to flow ou this sidewalk from the pipe, and become dangerous or frozen, it was a nuisance, whatever was said on that subject; that the Harmony Mills was in any wise liable for the maintenance of this pipe upon the building in question, or for any discharge of water therefrom upon the sidewalk in question." The building of the defendant was a tenement house in a street of the city of Cohoes, and had been unoccupied for some months prior to the time of the accident. A conductor led from a gutter, along the front of the roof, down to a point near the ground, where a spout projected eleven inches from the building. It had been there eighteen years under the same conditions. The evidence fails to show that the spout in fact projected over the sidewalk itself. It was not alleged, nor did it appear, to have been negligently or improperly constructed, and there was no proof that its maintenance was contrary to any municipal ordinance. On the day of the happening of the accident, in the month of December, there was an accumulation of ice upon the sidewalk, covering a large area, and extending from where the spout had discharged its water to the curb line. The sidewalk was flagged, and was graded down towards the curb line. The conditions were, therefore, simply these, to put it the most strongly for the plaintiff: Of a house owner having suffered ice to accumulate upon the sidewalk in front of its house as the result of the discharge of roof water through a conductor upon the sidewalk; where there was no defect in construction shown, but where the fault of the defendant, if any, was in its failure to provide some mode of carrying off the water, and thus to make that part of the street less dangerous to passersby, of whom plaintiff happened to be one. The conditions cannot be unusual in the cities of the State. The trial judge, consistently with his denial of the motion to nonsuit the plaintiff, presented the case to the jury upon the theory, as to the defendant's negligence, in the passages cited, that liability might be predicated upon the maintenance of the water pipe when its use caused or brought about a situation of danger to the traveler upon the sidewalk. I think that this was a mistaken view of the law, and that the defendant's exception is available here to point out the error. Municipal corporations are liable, as a general rule, for injuries caused by defective streets and sidewalks, because the control is vested in them, and it is their duty to keep them in a reasonably safe condition. They owe the duty to the public of preventing the accumulation of ice from house conductors or leaders, overhanging or near to the sidewalk. Todd *v.* City of Troy, 61 N. Y. 506; Allison *v.* Village of Middletown, 101 N. Y. 667, 5 N. E. Rep. 334; McGowan *v.* City of Boston, 170 Mass. 384, 49 N. E. Rep. 633. But, whatever our personal opinion might be upon the case, I think that we are concluded by authority, and, unless we are going to lay down another rule of liability than that which has received the sanction of this court, we must follow the case of Wenzlick *v.* McCotter, 87 N. Y. 122. The facts there were quite parallel with those of the present case. In that case the defendant was the owner of a house in the city of Brooklyn. It was built in connection with the adjoining house, and had a leader connected with the roof of the porch, which extended across the front of both houses. This leader ran down through the center of a column, between and partly upon both houses, until it reached the stoop. It then turned entirely onto defendant's premises, came through a hole in the baseboard of his stoop, and extended onto the sidewalk in front of his house. This leader had been there for twenty years, and had originally been used to carry off the water from both houses; but, at the time of the accident in question, only the water from the adjoining house passed through it. The defendant, at the time of the accident, was not in possession of the premises, having leased them to a tenant. Upon a day in the month of December, in the evening, the plaintiff, while passing in front of the house, stepped on a mound of ice, formed from the water discharging from the mouth of this pipe onto the sidewalk, and, slipping, fell, and broke her ankle, and for the injury thus occasioned the action was brought. Judgment was given for the plaintiff on the ground that the conductor was a nuisance, and defendant's liability the same as if the water had come from his own premises. Danforth, J., writing the opinion, said: "It is well to observe that the proof failed to sustain the averment of the complaint as regards the position and extent of the pipe upon the sidewalk. It did not reach the street, nor did it abridge the area of the walk. Nor does the decision below or the contention of the respondent rest upon that averment. Both stand upon the fact that it was the medium through which water was discharged thereon.

I do not, however, find the law to be that a conductor pipe, designed to convey water from the roof to the ground, when constructed with due care and proper precaution, is in itself unlawful, so that it can be deemed a nuisance, even if its mouth is toward the walk, and it discharge upon it. * * * The water itself caused no injury. Nor was the owner forbidden by any ordinance to relieve his roof in that manner. * * * As the care of streets and sidewalks is intrusted to the municipality, if they do not object to the discharge, I do not see how an individual can. Once upon the walk, and there frozen, and permitted to remain, it may subject the municipality to an action for omission of duty." In this opinion all the judges of this court concurred. In Moore *v.* Gadsden, 87 N. Y. 84, the action was brought to recover damages for injuries caused by slipping and falling upon the sidewalk in front of a vacant house of the defendant's in the city of Brooklyn, where ice had accumulated, and had not been removed. On the trial it appeared that a portion of the ice was formed from snow melting in defendant's yard, and flowing thence onto the sidewalk; also that snow, which had fallen ten days before the accident, had not been cleared away, and that all the other walks in the same block had been cleared. Danforth, J., writing the opinion of the court, said: "The general doctrine is that the public are entitled to the street or highway in the condition in which they placed it, and whoever renders the use hazardous by placing anything upon it is guilty of a nuisance. Congreve *v.* Smith, 18 N. Y. 79. The plaintiff's case is not within it. The sidewalk was constructed to receive the drip from the steps and yard, and so graded as to discharge itself into the gutter. If, by reason of obstruction, which it was the duty of the city or its officers to remove, it failed to do its office, the defendant cannot be made liable." The doctrine was reiterated later, upon a second appeal, in Moore *v.* Gadsden, 93 N. Y. 12.

I think the judgment should be reversed, and that a new trial should be ordered, with costs to abide the event.

PARKER, Ch. J., and O'BRIEN, J., concurred with GRAY, J.

Judgment affirmed.

GRIFFEN, ADM'X v. MANICE.

Supreme Court, New York, Appellate Division, First Department, July, 1902.

PERSON KILLED BY FALL OF ELEVATOR — REASONABLE CARE — CONSTRUCTION, OPERATION, AND INSPECTION OF ELEVATOR. — On appeal from judgment for defendant dismissing the complaint entered upon an order setting aside a general verdict in favor of plaintiff and special findings of the jury, in action for damages for death of plaintiff's intestate caused by fall of elevator weights in defendant's building, judgment was affirmed, it being held that where defendant had shown reasonable care in the construction, operation, and inspection of the elevator, he was not liable for the accident, even where it was shown that there had been an occasional bumping of the elevator upon the springs, such an incident not being an uncommon thing, and it did not appear that any accident had ever occurred by reason of it (1).

BURDEN OF PROOF. — In such action it was held that the burden of proof was upon plaintiff to show that the intestate's death was due to negligence on part of defendant.

O'BRIEN, J., and HATCH, J., *dissented.*

APPEAL from a judgment dismissing the complaint entered on an order setting aside a general verdict for $7,500 in favor of the plaintiff and special findings in connection therewith. The facts appear in the dissenting opinion by O'Brien, J. *Judgment affirmed.*

ROBERT M. BOYD, JR., for appellant.

ALBERT STICKNEY, for respondent.

MCLAUGHLIN, J. — This appeal is from the judgment in favor of the defendant dismissing the complaint entered upon an order setting aside a general verdict in favor of the plaintiff and special findings of the jury rendered in connection therewith.

The facts, so far as the same are material to the plaintiff's alleged cause of action, were fully stated on the former appeal to this court (47 App. Div. 70, 7 Am. Neg. Rep. 117), and on appeal therefrom to the Court of Appeals (166 N. Y. 188, 9 Am. Neg. Rep. 336), and it is, therefore, unnecessary to restate them in this opinion.

The law as laid down by the Court of Appeals is the law of the case and binding upon this court in so far as the facts are the same as upon the former appeal. The Court of Appeals, in reversing the

1. See former decisions in GRIFFEN v. MANICE, 47 App. Div. 70, 7 Am. Neg. Rep. 117 (January, 1900); and 166 N. Y. 188, 9 Am. Neg. Rep. 336 (March, 1901).

See NOTE ON ELEVATOR ACCIDENTS, 8 AM. NEG. REP. 146–157.

judgment of this court, held that the defendant owed the plaintiff's intestate the duty of using reasonable care to guard him against and protect him from injury. We are, therefore, to determine whether the judgment appealed from is right, when the rule as thus declared is applied to the facts as developed upon the trial. Upon the former trial the defendant offered no evidence, and we held that the trial court correctly instructed the jury that the doctrine of *res ipsa loquitur* applied, and whether or not the defendant had offered a sufficient explanation of the cause of the plaintiff's injuries was a question for the jury when subjected to the rule that the defendant was obligated "to use the utmost care and diligence" with reference to the appliances used in connection with and in operation of the elevator in which the intestate was at the time he was killed. This instruction was held to be erroneous, in that the defendant was only obligated to exercise ordinary care. The sole question presented therefore, on this appeal is whether or not the evidence justified a finding that the defendant was remiss in his duty in exercising that degree of care which the law imposed upon him., viz., ordinary care for the intestate's protection. And in this connection, it appeared that the elevator, and all the appliances used in connection therewith, was installed by a reputable dealer; that there had been provided all of the means then known for the prevention of accidents similar to or caused by the one that here occurred. To that end there had been provided the automatic stop and the slack cable device, either one of which was sufficient in and of itself, in case the operator was remiss in his duty, to cut off the power to stop the car. The evidence offered on the part of the plaintiff, as well as that offered on the part of the defendant, established beyond contradiction that the machinery used for operating the elevator was in perfect order at the time the accident occurred; that the operator had performed his duty; that each of the devices referred to had played the part designed for it; that, notwithstanding these facts, the power had continued to work after the car had reached the bottom of the shaft, and by reason thereof the counterbalance weights were forced from the frame in which they were placed, causing the injury complained of. The continuance of the power by which the drum was operated under such circumstances none of the witnesses were able to explain. But the defendant established not only by the cross-examination of the experts offered on the part of the plaintiff but also by its own witnesses, the fact that the machinery was in perfect order; that nothing was broken, out of repair or that its servant had failed to perform the duty assigned to him, and the plaintiff's witness Thorpe testified upon cross-examination that he had never known nor heard of an accident of this kind; that he did not know, and was then unable to state, how any precaution could have been taken in the shape of improvements to the machinery which would have prevented it. In addition to this it appeared that frequent inspections had been provided for not only by the dealers who originally installed the elevator, but also by two different insurance companies and by the authorities of the city, and that an inspection was made by one of them on the very day and only a few hours before the accident occurred, the result of which was to the effect that the elevator, including the appliances used to operate it, was in good order.

Under such circumstances, how could the trial court do otherwise, if defendant's duty was to be measured by ordinary care, than set aside the verdict and special findings of the jury and dismiss the complaint? There was no proof, either actual or constructive, of any defect in the machinery or of a threatened or apprehended danger by reason of its operation. It is true that there was some proof to the effect of an occasional bumping of the car upon the springs, but in this connection it appeared, and the fact was not contradicted, that this was not an uncommon thing, where an elevator was operated as this one was, nor was there any proof that it was an indication of danger or that the machinery was not properly adjusted. One of the plaintiff's witnesses testified that the bumping was due to the setting of the automatic stop, but this manifestly could not be changed at every trip which the car made, nor was there any satisfactory proof that there was any bumping intermediate the last setting of the automatic stop and the accident, and, if there had been, it would not have established liability on the part of the defendant, because, as already said, it was not an uncommon thing, and, so far as appears, no accident had ever occurred by reason of it (McGrell *v.* Buffalo Office-Building Co., 153 N. Y. 265, 2 Am. Neg. Rep. 598; Burke *v.* Witherbee, 98 N. Y. 562); nor was there any proof which would have justified a finding that the accident was due to the oiling of the brake band.

The defendant, under the rule laid down by the Court of Appeals, was bound to exercise such a degree of care as a man of ordinary prudence would have exercised under similar circumstances. The plaintiff, before she could recover, was bound to show that the intestate's death was due to and resulted from some neglect on the part of the defendant; in other words, that the defendant failed to exercise ordinary care for the protection of her intestate. This she failed to do. Upon the facts developed upon the trial a man of ordinary prudence could not have foreseen that injury was liable to be sustained as it was here. It must, therefore, be held, in view of the care used by the defendant, in the selection, inspection and maintenance of the elevator, under the rule laid down by the Court of Appeals, that he did all that an ordinary man could be required to do under the same conditions and circumstances.

The judgment appealed from, therefore, must be affirmed, with costs.

VAN BRUNT, P. J., and INGRAHAM, J., concur.

O'BRIEN, J. (*dissenting*). — This action, which is to recover for the death of the plaintiff's husband, who was killed by the fall of elevator weights in defendant's building, No. 55 William street, in the city of New York, was before this court on appeal from a judgment in plaintiff's favor (47 App. Div. 70, 7 Am. Neg. Rep. 117), and before the Court of Appeals, where the judgment of affirmance by this court was reversed (166 N. Y. 188, 9 Am. Neg. Rep. 336), on the ground that the trial court erred in charging that the defendant was required to use the utmost care and diligence, and is liable for the slightest neglect which foresight might have guarded against, and it was held that he was required to use only reasonable care. The Court of Appeals held, further, that upon the facts herein appearing the doctrine of *res ipsa loquitur* applied, and that the covenant in the lease of the defendant, who was a tenant of the building, releasing the owner from liability, does not release him from responsibility, since the right to use the elevator was based on the general invitation to do so. On the new trial the defendant endeavored to show that no reasonable care could have prevented the accident, and that there was no assignable cause for it, and it was shrouded in mystery. At the close of the case a motion to dismiss the complaint was made, as well as one to direct a verdict for the defendant, and the court reserved decision until after the verdict of the jury. The jury were then charged, and it appears that they made the following answers to questions submitted to them:

1. Do you find from the evidence that the dropping of the weights on Griffen came from the impact of the lower weights upon the upper ones? A. Yes.

2. Do you find from the evidence that the cause of such impact on the occasion of the accident can be discovered by human intelligence? A. Yes.

3. Do you find from the evidence that the bumping caused such impact? A. Yes, partly.

4. Do you find from the evidence that an unexplained continuance of the electric power after the car would have stopped but for such continuance caused such impact? A. No.

5. Could such impact have been foreseen in the way it occurred by the exercise of the proper intelligence required? A. Yes.

6. Did any omission of proper care in the descent of the elevator cause the injury to Griffen? A. Yes.

7. Did the negligence of the defendant cause the death of Griffen? A. Yes.

8. Did any negligence of Griffen contribute to his injury? A. No.

The jury gave further a verdict of $7,500 for plaintiff.

Thereafter, decision of the court upon the motions having been reserved, the court rendered its decision that the findings of the jury, except the first, with the general verdict, should be set aside, the complaint dismissed and verdict directed for the defendant. From judgment so entered the plaintiff appeals.

The manner in which the questions are presented on this appeal is somewhat unusual, but the final ruling of the court seems to have been on the motion to dismiss the complaint after both sides had rested, rather than on the motion to set aside the verdict on the grounds stated in section 999 of the Code of Civil Procedure. The plaintiff's rights, therefore, are to be considered, bearing in mind the rule that if there is evidence sufficient to support the inferences of defendant's negligence and the plaintiff's freedom from contributory negligence it is the province of the jury, and not of the court, to draw them (McDonald *v.* Met. St. R'y, 167 N. Y. 66).

The law of this case being that the defendant was required to use only reasonable care, the facts must be examined to determine whether upon this issue there was sufficient evidence to go to the jury. In defining, however, what is reasonable care, Judge Cullen, writing for the majority in the Court of Appeals, said (166 N. Y. 188, 9 Am. Neg. Rep. 336): "The care must be commensurate with the danger."

There being no suggestion that the plaintiff was guilty of contributory negligence, the single question presented is, would the evidence warrant an inference by the jury that the defendant was guilty of negligence? The plaintiff made out a *prima facie* case by showing the nature and attending circumstances of the accident which justified the application of the doctrine of *res ipsa loquitur*. To meet this *prima facie* case, the defendant sought by cross-examination of plaintiff's and by his own witnesses to show that no explanation could be given as to what was the cause of the accident, and that consequently it did not appear what care, if any, could have guarded against the fall of the weights.

As to the maintenance and operation of the elevator, it appeared that in the basement there was a drum moved by electricity supplied from an outside source, to which was attached a rope winding about it, which extended to the top of the shaft and over a wheel or pulley down to the top of the car, the revolution of the drum thus raising the car. Attached to this drum was another rope which moved in the opposite direction from the first rope and passed to the top of the shaft and over a wheel or pulley down to a set of lower weights, which ran up and down between vertical bars, moving up as the elevator descended, and *vice versa*, and serving to counterbalance the drum and steady the motion. There was another rope attached to the top of the car, which ran up the shaft and over a wheel or pulley, down to what are called the upper weights, which also moved between vertical parallel guides and were adjusted so as to go up and down and always three feet above the lower weights. These upper weights counterbalanced the car and went up as the elevator descended. It was not intended that they should come nearer than within two feet of the top of the shaft, where there were horizontal permanent beams.

On the day of the accident, after the car fell or descended rapidly from the floor above to the landing floor, the lower weights were found pressing against the upper weights, which in turn were pressing against the horizontal beams, and thus had forced apart the vertical bars or guides so as to permit weights to fall out into the shaft and upon the elevator car below, causing the death of plaintiff's intestate It was testified that, although the momentum of the weights in their upward course might, when the car stopped, cause the weights to continue on less than a foot, it would not cause the lower weights to go upwards at least five feet, pushing the upper weights upwards against the horizontal beams. Hence it appears that the only other possible force must have been force applied through the rope attached to the lower weights, which rope passed down to the drum which was moved by electricity. It was testified that the drum, after the power had been shut off, might, by momentum, revolve perhaps half or quarter of a revolution if the brake was in proper condition and this might raise the car a foot. The weights, however, were raised more than a foot and to the extent at least of five feet; so that it appears that they were raised either because the power was not shut off or because the brake was out of order. Three ways were provided for shutting off the power and applying the brake — by the operator in the car, by the automatic stop or clutch device and by the slack cable device. The two latter were designed to stop the car should it fall or the cables beoome slack. It was testified that if the car came to the bottom and the operator failed to shut off the power and the automatic stop failed to work, then the slack cable device would shut off the power and apply the brake; and it is evident that if the power was still on, the car being at the bottom, the rope above the car would become slack while the lower weights were being raised. Under such conditions, it was testified, the weights might rise about three feet six inches. Even this, however, does not account for the five feet covered by the lower weights; and, therefore, it follows either that the slack cable device was out of order or wrongly adjusted, or else that the power was continued in spite of it.

It is conceded that this elevator, which was of the Otis make, was a first-class machine, and it is not disputed that the various parts were properly and skillfully made. But in all the testimony sought to be elicited by the defendant and offered as to the different devices and safeguards, the matter of adjustment was lightly touched upon. It appears that the brake should be rightly adjusted in order to work in time, and that the automatic stop depended for its efficiency upon adjustment, and that the slack cable device required adjustment and was dependent upon the adjustment of the brake. In this connection it was brought out that for some time previous to the accident the elevator had been heard to bump when it reached the first floor, and it was testified that on one occasion it had bumped so hard that an electric light bulb was shattered. It thus appears that for a considerable period of time prior to the accident in question the elevator had at intervals come to the bottom of the shaft with a bump similar to, but not as violent as, that which preceded the accident.

It was testified that unless the machine was out of order it was not possible for it to bump; and again, "It is not possible for a car to bump hard if the machinery is properly adjusted." At the time of the accident the elevator bumped and rebounded eighteen inches. As to the automatic stop, it was testified: "It is supposed to operate of itself when the elevator gets to a certain point at the bottom of the shaft. If it is properly adjusted it does." Here it did not operate, as evidenced by the fact that the power must have continued to lift the weights which were lifted; and a fair inference seems to be that the stop was not properly adjusted, and this independently of the bumping. And it was testified that if there was a heavier weight than usual in the car, it would be apt to bump if the brake was out of adjustment. The car did bump, and hence it would seem to be demonstrated that the brake was out of adjustment and had been for some time.

Although, therefore, the defendant showed that he had furnished a modern and scientifically constructed machine, the evidence would justify the inference that at the time of the accident it was not properly adjusted, and had not been for a considerable period prior thereto.

To meet this evidence the defendant showed that it was the duty of the Otis elevator people, who constructed the elevator, to adjust it when it was put in, and thereafter to inspect it; and that the Employer's Liability Corporation regularly inspected it and had done so on November 25, 1898, the accident occurring on December 5, 1898, and their report was that the elevator was found to be in good condition. It was this evidence which, no doubt, had a controlling influence upon the learned trial judge; and it may be said to be the dividing line at which different minds considering the testimony will conclude in favor of or against the view that the defendant did not use reasonable care. But it is because different inferences can be drawn that we think the question of the defendant's negligence should have been submitted to the jury.

Upon this subject, bearing in mind the rule "that the care must be commensurate with the danger," we think that where an owner of an elevator has notice of its defective condition — and here, not only had the bumping been heard all over the building, but the engineer who represented the defendant in the building testified that he knew of it — his duty is not discharged in providing by contract for the mere inspection of the elevator from time to time by a liability company or the persons who constructed it, without calling the attention of the inspectors to the particular defects of which he had knowledge. The dropping of the car below the lower floor and into the bottom of the shaft, causing the bumping to which we have alredy referred, was sufficient to apprise those having charge of the elevator that something was wrong with the machinery, and we think, in that connection, it was incumbent upon the defendant, in the discharge of his duty of exercising reasonable care to protect those whom he permitted to use the elevator, to have remedied the defect which he knew or should have known existed, or, at least, to have called it to the special attention of those who were experts in the elevator business. Although it was shown that the elevator was regularly inspected at stated times and under some general arrangement, it does not appear that the defendant gave to the inspectors any notice of the bumping which was going on, or in any way sought to have it corrected.

Upon the proof, therefore, as it stood at the end of the case, we think that the course pursued by the learned trial judge in submitting the question of the defendant's negligence to the jury was right; and that after the verdict in plaintiff's favor his special ruling dismissing the complaint — because, as we take it, that is what was finally done — was erroneous; and that this error required a reversal of the judgment appealed from.

The judgment should be reversed and judgment ordered for the plaintiff on the verdict.

HATCH, J., concurs.

KANE v. ROCHESTER RAILWAY COMPANY.

Supreme Court, New York, Appellate Division, Fourth Department, July, 1902.

PERSONAL INJURIES — X-RAY EXAMINATION — EVIDENCE. — In an action to recover damages for personal injuries sustained in a collision between plaintiff's wagon and defendant's street car, it was *held* that an instruction, requested by defendant, to the effect that where a physician made an X-ray examination of plaintiff's fingers and wrist, at plaintiff's request, and such physician having been called to the witness stand by plaintiff, but the latter omitted to ask what was discovered from such examination, the jury had a right to assume that such testimony, if given, would have been adverse to plaintiff, should have been given, even though the defendant called out the fact that such X-ray examination had been made, and might have asked the result of such examination (1).

APPEAL from Special Term, Monroe County.

Action by James Kane against the Rochester Railway Company. A verdict was returned for plaintiff, and from an order granting a new trial plaintiff appeals. *Order affirmed.*

"The action was commenced on the 31st day of October, 1899, to recover damages for injuries alleged to have been sustained by the plaintiff on the 25th day of June, 1899, by coming in collision with one of defendant's cars at Franklin street, where it crosses defendant's tracks at Clinton avenue, in the city of Rochester, N. Y., alleged to have been caused solely through the negligence of the defendant."

Argued before ADAMS, P. J., McLENNAN, SPRING, WILLIAMS and HISCOCK, JJ.

CHARLES ROE, for appellant.

CHARLES J. BISSELL, for respondent.

McLENNAN, J. — The order appealed from was granted by the

1. See NOTE ON X-RAY EVIDENCE, in 11 AM. NEG. REP. 73-74.

See also City of Geneva *v.* Burnett (Neb., July, 1902), reported in this volume, page 104, *ante*.

learned trial justice upon the ground, as appears by his opinion, that error was committed in refusing to charge the jury as requested by defendant's counsel, which request was substantially as follows: It appearing that Dr. Weigel made an X-ray examination of plaintiff's fingers and wrist, at the request of the plaintiff, and the plaintiff having omitted to ask Dr. Weigel, when called to the witness stand by him, what he discovered from such examination, the jury have the right to assume that Dr. Weigel's testimony, if given, would have been adverse to the plaintiff upon that point.

At about 10:30 in the evening of the 25th day of June, 1899, the plaintiff and one Hanify were riding with one Johnson in a wagon drawn by one horse, which was being driven by Johnson along Franklin street, in the city of Rochester, N. Y. In crossing Clinton avenue one of the defendant's cars collided with the wagon, overturned it, and threw the occupants out; and the plaintiff alleges that he thereby sustained serious injury. He testified or gave evidence tending to show that his side was injured in such manner that a hernia resulted; that three fingers of the left hand and two of the right were put out of joint, and that his wrist was seriously injured, constantly pained and troubled him, and was in such condition at the time of the trial, two years after the accident, that he had to keep a leather bandage constantly around it when at work — stating that he could not use the wrist in his work without such bandage which was exhibited to the jury. There was a sharp controversy between the medical experts, as is usual in such cases, as to whether or not any hernia existed; but, remarkable as it may seem, they all agreed that at the time of the trial there were no objective symptoms of injury to the fingers or wrists that would account for the weakness and pain complained of and testified to by the plaintiff, and that, if there was any difficulty with the bones, an X-ray examination would disclose it. Upon the cross-examination of the plaintiff, it appeared that Dr. Weigel made an X-ray examination of the plaintiff's wrist and fingers, and Dr. Weigel, who was called as a witness by the plaintiff, testified upon his cross-examination that he did make such examination, and that he took X-ray photographs of the same, and that he then had such photographs, or the plates, in his possession; that he made the examination and took the photographs in December, 1899, or January, 1900. Plaintiff's counsel did not ask the plaintiff or Dr. Weigel what the X-ray examination disclosed as to the condition of the fingers or wrist, nor offer to produce the photographs showing their condition. The omission so to do was the basis of the request to charge made by defendant's counsel; and because of its refusal, to which an cxeepiton was duly taken, the order appealed from was made. Whether or not the refusal by the learned trial justice to charge as requested was reversible error presents the only question which need be considered upon this appeal.

Clearly, the request had reference to a material question of fact. The nature and extent of plaintiff's injuries were sharply contested. The character of the evidence given in respect to the injury to plaintiff's side was such as to leave it entirely problematical as to whether or not he had a hernia. One or two physicians testified that he unquestionably had, and another, eminent in his profession, testified positively that he had not; so that it is impossible to say what part of the verdict, if any, was awarded by the jury on account of the injury to the side, or that substantially all of it was not awarded because of the injury which the plaintiff claimed resulted to his fingers and wrist. Under those circumstances, if the defendant was entitled, as matter of law, to have the jury instructed that they had a right to assume that the bones of the fingers or wrist were in their normal condition, from the fact that the physician called by the plaintiff, who had examined them with the X-rays, did not disclose the result of such examination, it cannot be said that the refusal to charge as requested was not prejudicial to the defendant. Was the defendant entitled to have the jury charged as requested? Fair play and common sense would certainly dictate an affirmative answer. Facts were within the knowledge of the witness called by the plaintiff for the purpose of establishing the seriousness of the injury which he sustained, which concededly would demonstrate whether such injury was as serious as claimed or not. Under those circumstances, plaintiff ought not to be permitted to withhold such information from the jury. It is very natural to suppose that if such information would have tended to corroborate plaintiff's claim, it would have been called out by him; and the conclusion is almost irresistible that he omitted so to do because he knew the information possessed by the physician as the result of the examination made by him would be hurtful to his claim if communicated to the jury. It is no answer to the proposition that the defendant called out the fact that the X-ray examination had been made, and might have asked what the result of such examination was. The defendant was not called upon to take the chances of an answer by a hostile witness. The question whether or not the plaintiff's fingers and wrist were seriously and permanently injured was evidently regarded as important, and one which would materially affect the plaintiff's right to recover, or, at least, the amount of the verdict; and early in the course of the trial, before Dr. Weigel, who had made the X-ray examination, had been called by the plaintiff and sworn, it appeared that such examination had been made by him; and upon his cross-examination the plaintiff's attention was again called to the fact, so that the omission to inquire as to what the X-ray examination disclosed cannot be attributed to oversight or mistake.

The precise question involved was decided by this court in Milliman *v.* Railway Co., 3 App. Div. 109, 39 N. Y. Supp. 274. That was an action brought to recover damages for injuries sustained by the plaintiff, who was riding with his daughter along one of the streets of the city, which was also occupied by defendant's railroad. One of the cars, which was following the phaeton, collided with it, and the injury resulted. The important issue litigated was whether the collision occurred immediately after the horse entered upon the track, or whether the car followed the phaeton for a distance of 125 feet or more, overtook it, and ran it down. The plaintiff's daughter, who was called as a witness by him, and who, as appeared by her testimony, had opportunity to know the relative positions of the horse and car when the horse entered upon the track, was not interrogated by counsel for either litigant, in regard to such positions. In his charge the learned trial justice called the attention of the jury to the fact that the daughter had not been examined upon this issue, although she had the same opportunity of knowing the facts as the plaintiff, and charged, in substance, that such omission might be taken into account by the jury in determining on which side the truth lay. Plaintiff's counsel duly excepted to the charge, and upon appeal urged that it presented such error that the plaintiff's motion for a new trial should have been granted. In considering the question, Justice Follett, in writing the opinion for the court, said: "In case a litigant fails to produce a person known to be friendly to him and to his cause, who is so situated that he must have knowledge of the facts in issue, the jury is permitted to presume that the testimony of that person would not have been favorable to the party. Kenyon *v.* Kenyon, 88 Hun, 211, 34 N. Y. Supp. 720, and cases there cited; Thomp. Trials, secs. 989, 1045; Tayl. Ev., 8th ed., sec. 117. * * * I think the rule is applicable to a case in which a party fails to interrogate a friendly witness, so situated as to be presumed to have knowledge of the existence or non-existence of the vital facts in issue, as it is to the case of a failure to produce such a witness. Indeed, I think the omission to interrogate a friendly witness in respect to facts presumably within his knowledge is more significant than the failure to call such a person as a witness, and that the presumption that the testimony would not have been favorable to the party's case is stronger than the one which arises from the failure to produce such a person as a witness."

The learned counsel for the plaintiff in the case at bar concedes, as did the plaintiff's counsel in the Milliman case, *supra*, that the rule, as stated, applies to a party who fails to produce a friendly witness who has knowledge of facts material to an important issue. The cases of Kenyon *v*. Kenyon, 88 Hun, 211, 34 N. Y. Supp. 720; Sherlock *v*, Insurance Co., 21 App. Div. 18, 47 N. Y. Supp. 315; and Carpenter *v*. Railway Co., 13 App. Div. 328, 43 N. Y. Supp. 203, fully sustain the correctness of that proposition; but plaintiff's counsel contends, as was urged in the Milliman case, that it does not apply to a party who fails to interrogate a friendly witness, called and sworn by him, as to facts material to an important issue, although known to be within the knowledge of such witness. There is no reason for such a distinction, and, if made, it would only enable a party to avoid the effect of the rule adverted to by calling a friendly witness who had knowledge of facts pertinent to a material issue, or by compelling his adversary to take the hazard of interrogating the witness as to such facts. The defendant was not bound to prove its defense by plaintiff's expert physician, who, at plaintiff's request, made a careful examination of the injured parts to ascertain the extent of their injury; and the burden was upon the plaintiff not only to produce him, but also to interrogate him as to facts within his knowledge relating to the important issue, or expose himself to the hazard of unfavorable inferences. A party seeking to recover for serious injury to his side and wrist ought not to be permitted to call as a witness an expert physician, who, at his request, examined and learned the condition of both, and interrogate him only as to the condition of one, without exposing himself to the hazard of having the jury infer that, if the witness had been asked as to the condition of the other, his answer would have been unfavorable to the party calling such witness. The rule laid down in the Milliman case, *supra*, is logical. Its application will tend to prevent the suppression of the truth in the trial of causes and should be adhered to and followed. It follows that the order appealed from should be affirmed, with costs.

Order affirmed, with costs. All concur.

BRAHAM v. NASSAU ELECTRIC RAILROAD COMPANY.

Supreme Court, New York, Appellate Division, Second Department, May, 1902.

PERSON CROSSING STREET STEPPING ON STREET-CAR RAIL — ELECTRIC SHOCK — EVIDENCE. — Where plaintiff, while crossing a street, stepped on one of defendant's street-car rails and received an electric shock, and it was clearly established that the accident would have been impossible if the track was in good order, and it was also proven that close to the place where plaintiff was walking was a joint where two rails met, which, if not properly bonded or welded, would permit the infliction of an electric shock upon any one whose foot should be placed upon it, and there was some evidence that the rails at the time were so laid as not to allow in the usual manner for expansion and contraction, and that such manner of laying the rails was calculated to result in imperfect joints, *held*, that such evidence established defendant's liability.

APPEAL from Trial Term, Kings County.

Action by Emanuel Braham against the Nassau Electric Railroad Company. From a judgment for plaintiff, and from an order denying a new trial, defendant appeals. *Judgment affirmed.*

Argued before GOODRICH, P. J., and JENKS, WOODWARD, and HIRSCHBERG, JJ.

I. R. OELAND, for appellant.

JAMES C. CROPSEY, for respondent.

HIRSCHBERG, J. — The plaintiff, while crossing Bergen street on the afternoon of December 28, 1898, stepped on one of the defendant's rails and received an electric shock, which resulted in injuries for which a jury has awarded him an amount not claimed to be excessive. The defendant, however, claims that the complaint should have been dismissed — First, because no negligence on its part was established; and, second, because, if a *prima facie* case of negligence was established in the first instance, the circumstances were conclusively rebutted by the proof that no defect existed at the place of the accident which would permit the escape of the electric current. These claims are untenable. It was clearly established that the shock which the plaintiff received would have been impossible if the defendant's track was in good order. It was further proven that close to the place where the plaintiff was walking was a joint where two rails met, which, if not properly bonded or welded, would permit the infliction of an electric shock upon any one whose foot should be placed upon it; and there was some evidence that the rails at the time were so laid as not to allow in the usual manner for expansion and contraction, and that such manner of laying the rails was calculated to result in imperfect joints. This evidence, together with that of the shock actually received by the plaintiff, established the defendant's liability, and called upon it for an explanation of the occurrence, in order to relieve it from the charge of negligence, on the principle of *res ipsa loquitur.* Clarke *v.* Railroad Co., 9 App. Div. 51, 41 N. Y. Supp. 78; Jones *v.* Railway Co., 18 App. Div. 267, 46 N. Y. Supp. 321. The presumption of negligence arising from the proof referred to was not so far overborne by the defendant's evidence as to make the question one of law. The explanatory evidence was principally that of an employee of the defendant whose duty it was to keep the tracks in order, and who testified that they were in order at the time and place of the accident. Waiving the question whether this evidence could be regarded as explaining the occurrence, it is clear that, in view of the position and employment of the witness, a submission of the charge of negligence to the jury for determination was required. Volkmar *v.* Railroad Co., 134 N. Y. 418, 31 N. E. 870; O'Flaherty *v.* Railroad Co., 34 App. Div. 74, 54 N. Y. Supp. 96; Smith *v.* Railroad Co., 59 App. Div. 60, 69 N. Y. Supp. 176. The happening of the accident under the circumstances tended to prove the existence of conditions necessary to cause it which could not arise without either negligence on the defendant's part, or a defect of some kind, for which, if such a thing be possible, it was not to blame; and proof merely that no defect whatever existed would not serve to remove the case from the province of the jury, where the proof was furnished by an interested witness in the defendant's employment, and the question of credibility was accordingly a factor. The judgment and order should be affirmed.

Judgment and order affirmed, with costs. All concur.

KNIGHT v. LANIER.

Supreme Court, New York, Appellate Division, Second Department, March, 1902.

HORSE FRIGHTENED BY AUTOMOBILE ON HIGHWAY — DUTY TOWARDS LICENSEE. — Where plaintiff was driving a horse and surrey along a private lane which was tacitly open to public use, and the horse becoming frightened by the approach of defendant's automobile, plaintiff got out of his vehicle and held his horse by the head, the automobile having stopped before the two vehicles met, and the automobile then proceeded and the horse broke away, upsetting the vehicle and the occupants were thrown out, and the evidence was conflicting as to whether plaintiff signaled the defendant to proceed when he was in peril, it was *held* that the question of defendant's negligence in so going ahead was for the jury to determine (1).

In such case it was also *held* that, although plaintiff was a mere licensee, the defendant owed him a duty to abstain from injuring him, either intentionally or by failing to exercise reasonable care.

AUTOMOBILE ON HIGHWAY — DEGREE OF CARE — While the automobile is a lawful means of conveyance, and has equal rights upon the road with the horse and carriage, its use cannot be lawfully countenanced unless accompanied with that degree of prudence in management and consideration for the rights of others which is consistent with safety.

1. *Horses frightened.* — For actions arising out of accidents caused by horses being frightened by noise of trains, steam, etc., obstructions on highway, etc., see vols. 11 and 12 AM. NEG. CAS., where the same are chronologically grouped from the earliest period to 1897, and arranged in alphabetical order of States. Subsequent actions to date appear in vols. 1-12 AM. NEG. REP., and the current numbers of that series of Reports.

Child run over and killed by automobile - Duty of operator of vehicle. — In THIES *v.* THOMAS *(Supreme Court, Trial Term, New York County, May, 1902)*, 77 N. Y. Supp. 276, an action for damages against Thomas for running over with his automobile and killing plaintiff's intestate, a boy between six and seven years of age, the jury rendered a verdict for plaintiff for $3,125. In the course of his charge to the jury, Mr. Justice FREEDMAN charged as follows: * * * "Now, the deceased was killed by an automobile in charge of the defendant at the time. It is claimed by the plaintiff that the automobile at the time was run at an excessive speed. But that is not the most important point. The mere rate of speed, whether high or low, lawful or unlawful, is immaterial, unless it entered into the cause of the accident. In the case at bar there is not even any evidence showing what the lawful rate of speed is for an automobile. An automobile is a vehicle of quite recent times, carrying its motive power within itself, but as such it has the same duties to perform, when meeting pedestrians, or other vehicles, in the streets of this city, which other vehicles are subjected to. There are vehicles drawn by horses, and there are trolley cars moved by electricity conveyed either overhead or under ground, and each is permitted to go at a certain rate of speed; but it has never been the law, and it never will be the law, that the driver of a horse and wagon or the motorman of a trolley car may escape responsibility for a collision by simply showing that at the time of the collision he did not exceed the limit of speed fixed by law or the ordinances of the city, as a general rule. On the contrary, the law has always been, and yet is, that every driver of a horse and wagon and every motorman of a trolley car is bound to anticipate that persons on foot or in other vehicles may be met at any point in a public street, and therefore bound to look out for them, and to keep his horse and wagon or his trolley car constantly under such control as will enable him to avoid a collision with another, if possible. Even steam railroads, owning their own roadbed, have been held liable in

APPEAL from Trial Term, Nassau County.

Action by Charles W. Knight against James F. D. Lanier. From a judgment for plaintiff, and from an order denying a new trial, defendant appeals. *Judgment affirmed.*

FREDERICK HULSE (ERNEST F. EIDLITZ, on the brief), for appellant.

GEORGE B. STODDART, for respondent.

HIRSCHBERG, J. — The plaintiff has recovered a small judgment on the theory of negligence, and the question presented on the appeal is whether, at the time of the occurrence complained of, the defendant owed him the duty of exercising care. The accident occurred on Sunday, May 27, 1900, in the daytime, on a private lane belonging to Mr. Whitney, at Wheatly Hills, in Nassau county. The lane appears to connect public highways and to be tacitly open to public use. The plaintiff was driving a horse and surrey, and was accompanied by his daughter and two other ladies. He was engaged at the time as landscape gardener for Mr. Foxhall Keene, and was on his way from the latter's place to his own home at Glen

damages for any collision which could have been avoided by the exercise of proper care and caution on their part, provided there was no contributory negligence in the person injured. No owner or operator of an automobile is, therefore, exempt from liability for a collision in a public street by simply showing that at the time of the accident he did not run at a rate of speed exceeding the limit allowed by law or the ordinances. On the contrary, no matter how great the rate of speed may be which the law and the ordinances permit, as a general rule — although in this case there is no evidence — he still remains bound to anticipate that he may meet persons at any point in a public street, and he must keep a proper lookout for them, and keep his machine under such control as will enable him to avoid a collision with another person also using proper care and caution. If necessary, he must slow up, and even stop. No blowing of a horn or of a whistle, nor the ringing of a bell or gong, without an attempt to slow the speed, is sufficient, if the circumstances at a given point demand that the speed should be slackened or the machine be stopped, and such a course is practicable, or, in the exercise of ordinary care and caution proportionate to the circumstances, should have been practicable. The true test is that he must use all the care and caution which a careful and prudent driver would have exercised under the same circumstances. On the other hand, every such operator of an automobile has the right to assume, and to act upon the assumption, that every person whom he meets will also exercise ordinary care and caution according to the circumstances, and will not negligently or recklessly expose himself to danger, but, rather, make an attempt to avoid it. It is only when such an operator has had time to realize, or by the exercise of a proper lookout should have realized, that a person whom he meets is in a somewhat helpless condition, or in a position of disadvantage, and therefore seemingly unable to avoid the coming automobile, that the operator is required to exercise increased exertion to avoid a collision. This applies peculiarly when children of tender years are met." * * *

Cove, and was using the lane as a shorter route, in accordance with his daily habit during the two years of his employment. The defendant was operating an automobile or motor carriage on the lane in an opposite direction from the plaintiff's. He had been visiting the Steven's place, to which the lane furnished the only access and was returning accompanied by a lady. When the automobile was within 100 or more yards, the horse became frightened, and before the two vehicles met the defendant stopped the machine. The plaintiff says that he shouted to the defendant to stop, and in this he is corroborated by his companions. The defendant says he did not hear the shout, but he did see that the horse was frightened, and that he stopped in order to give the plaintiff an opportunity to get out and hold his horse, or do what he might choose. The plaintiff did get out and took his horse by the head, whereupon, as he claims, the defendant, while the horse was still frightened, snorting, prancing, and plunging, started up the machine and attempted to pass, causing the horse to break from the plaintiff's hold, and to overturn, and throw out the occupants of the surrey.

The negligence of the defendant, if any, must obviously be predicated upon the act of starting the machine again when the plaintiff was in plain peril. He says, and his companion corroborates him, that the plaintiff beckoned him to do so. The plaintiff and his witnesses assert that no such sign was given, and that nothing was said except that at the time the horse became fractious the plaintiff shouted: "For God's sake, stop that machine and let us get out before you kill us all." He further testified that immediately after the accident the defendant said: "I am awful sorry. I ought not to have started up." This the defendant did not deny, except as his story may in itself involve a denial. Under the circumstances the question of negligence, assuming that care was due, was one of fact, and it cannot be said that the conclusion reached by the jury is without support. But the defendant claims that he owed the plaintiff no duty which was violated, inasmuch as he was a guest or visitor of one lawfully entitled to use the lane, while the plaintiff was at most a mere licensee. The learned trial justice charged the jury that each party had a right to be in the lane, and no exception was taken. Assuming, however, the correctness of the defendant's premises, the conclusion that no duty of care would follow is not correct. The rule applicable is indicated in the cases cited on his behalf, and would seem to extend the liability for affirmative negligence, such as that charged against the defendant, even as to the owner of the property, had he been in the defendant's place. Thus in Larmore *v.* Crown Point Iron Co., 101 N. Y. 391, 395, it was said:

"The duty of keeping premises in a safe condition, even as against a mere licensee, may also arise where affirmative negligence in the management of the property or business of the owner would be likely to subject persons exercising the privilege theretofore permitted and enjoyed to great danger. The case of running a locomotive without warning over a path across the railroad which had been generally used by the public without objection furnishes an example. Barry *v.* N. Y. Cent., etc., R. R. Co., 92 N. Y. 289 (12 Am. Neg. Cas. 313n). See also Beck *v.* Carter, 68 N. Y. 283."

The rule is perhaps more explicitly stated in Walsh *v.* Fitchburg R. R. Co., 145 N. Y. 301, at page 305, viz.: "The plaintiff was not on the land by invitation of the defendant, nor in its business, but for his own purposes, totally disconnected with the defendant's business. He was not a trespasser in the sense of his being unlawfully upon the premises, because the defendant, by its course of conduct, had impliedly granted a license to the public to use the land for the purpose above mentioned. This license, of course, could at any time have been revoked, and then any one going upon the land would have been a trespasser. But under the circumstances, treating the plaintiff as an adult, and simply upon the question of the invitation held out to him, he was there by sufferance only. The defendant had no right intentionally to injure him, and it would be liable if it heedlessly or carelessly injured him while performing its own business. It owed him a duty to abstain from injuring him either intentionally or by failing to exercise reasonable care, but it did not owe him the duty of active vigilance to see that he was not injured while upon its land merely by permission for his own convenience. Nicholson *v.* Erie R'y Co., 41 N. Y. 525 (12 Am. Neg. Cas. 388n); Byrne *v.* N. Y. Cent., etc., R. R. Co., 104 N. Y. 363 (12 Am. Neg. Cas. 313n); Splittorf v. State, 108 N. Y. 205; Cusick *v.* Adams, 115 N. Y. 55."

The doctrine was followed by this court in De Boer *v.* Warehouse Co., 51 App. Div. 289, 64 N. Y. Supp. 925, and is in accordance with the uniform current of authority.

No error was committed at the trial. The court refused to charge as matter of law that the indications of fright exhibited by the plaintiff's horse did not cast upon the defendant the duty of halting his automobile until the fear subsided, but left the question to the jury, saying: "You might see a horse in front of you in such a state of excitement that the situation would be one of such danger that the law might say as a matter of prudence you ought to stop for the time being. Whether that was the situation or not I leave for the jury."

This must be the law. The rules governing the degree of care which individuals upon the highway should exercise for mutual safety are well settled, and relate in their application to the danger to be reasonably apprehended under ever varying conditions of exposure and peril. While the automobile is a lawful means of conveyance, and has equal rights upon the road with the horse and carriage, its use cannot be lawfully countenanced unless accompanied with that degree of prudence in management and consideration for the rights of others which is consistent with safety. If, as the jury has found, the defendant was aware that the machine in his possession and control had so far excited the plaintiff's horse as to render him dangerous and unmanageable, and if, having stopped at the urgent solicitation of the occupants of the surrey in order to afford them an opportunity to alight, he, before they could do so, started the machine again, and so caused the horse to run away, a question of fact was clearly presented for determination whether under all the circumstances his conduct was characterized by ordinary care. While men may possibly differ in the solution of the question, it is surely not within the province of an appellate court to say that a determination adverse to the defendant is without support or justification. The judgment and order should be affirmed.

Judgment and order affirmed, with costs. All concur.

CLEVELAND, AKRON AND COLUMBUS RAILWAY COMPANY v. WORKMAN.

Supreme Court, Ohio, June, 1902.

RAILROAD EMPLOYEE, A BOY, RIDING ON HAND CAR, STRUCK AND KILLED BY TRAIN — LICENSEE — SIGNAL — STATUTE — INSTRUCTIONS — EVIDENCE — DAMAGES. — 1. An employee of a railroad company, whose duties in the performance of his employment do not require him to be on the main track of the railroad with a three-wheeled hand car, called a "speeder," but who so goes upon the main track without any invitation or inducement therefor by the company, but with no objection on the part of the company, is, at most, a mere licensee; and his use of the track in such manner is subject to all the risks incident to the use of the track by the company in the same manner as it was used at the time the license was granted, and the company does not owe him the duty to especially look out for and protect him when running its trains, except to use reasonable care to avoid injuring him after discovering him upon the track.

2. Rev. Stat., secs. 3336, 3337, are intended for the protection of such persons only as are crossing the track, or are about to do so; and they do not inure

to the benefit of persons who are on the track, and not at a crossing. Railroad Co. *v.* Depew, 40 Ohio St. 121, approved and followed.

3. Where the evidence shows that the deceased was struck by a train and killed at a point about 600 feet from the crossing, it is error to charge the jury that it is for them to determine from the evidence whether the statutory signals were given or not, and that their conclusion on that subject would be one of the elements which they should consider in determining whether the defendant was guilty of negligence that produced, in whole or in part, the death of the deceased; and in such case it is also error to charge the jury that the deceased was bound to use reasonable precautions to detect the approach of trains, and to know that the defendant might run a train over the road at that point at any time, " unless lulled into a feeling of security by a failure of the defendant's employees in charge of its train to observe the statutory regulations and rules of the company in the manner of running and management of the train at the time and place of the accident, and under the circumstances shown by the evidence."

4. Where it is an admitted fact that at the time of the accident it was so foggy that it was difficult, if not impossible, to see objects on the railroad more than a few rods distant, and there is evidence tending to show that the deceased took the " speeder " upon the main track for no reason connected with his employment, other than his convenience; that after lighting one switch light he rode down the main track toward another switch light on the speeder, with a companion, in violation of the orders of his superior, the station agent; that there was a side track or " passing track " from a point near the station to where the other switch light was to be placed; that the deceased could have easily placed the speeder upon said side track, and reached his destination easily and with safety; and that, instead of doing so, he went down the main track, without keeping any lookout behind him, —it is error to refuse to charge the jury that, if they find such facts, the deceased was guilty of such negligence as would prevent the plaintiff from recovering in the case, unless the defendant could have avoided the injury after discovering the deceased upon the track.

5. Where there is evidence tending to show that the father of the deceased was guilty of negligence directly contributing to the death of his son, and the court charged the jury that, in arriving at the amount of damages, they should consider the pecuniary injury to each separate beneficiary, first determining the value of the life of the deceased to his father, etc., but that the verdict should be for a gross sum, not exceeding $10,000, it is error to refuse to charge the jury, as requested, that if they should find that the father of the deceased was guilty of negligence directly contributing to the death of his son, the plaintiff could not recover for any pecuniary loss suffered by the father, for the death of his son. Wolf *v.* Lake Erie & W. R'y Co., 55 Ohio St. 517, approved and followed.

6. An issue in the pleadings being whether an ordinance existed or not, it was error to permit parol proof of the passage of the ordinance; and the error was not cured by the court saying to the jury that the ordinance was a circumstance to be taken into consideration, in connection with the other facts and circumstances, in determining whether the defendant was guilty of negligence or whether the deceased was guilty of negligence which contributed to cause his death.

(Syllabus by the Court.)

ERROR to Circuit Court, Knox County.

Action by one Workman, administrator of Arleigh J. Mead, deceased, against the Cleveland, Akron and Columbus Railway Company. From judgment for plaintiff, defendant brings error. *Judgment reversed.*

The defendant in error, as the administrator of Arleigh J. Mead, deceased, sued in the Court of Common Pleas of Knox county to recover damages from the plaintiff in error for the death of his intestate, caused, as alleged, by the negligence of the plaintiff in error. The negligence charged was that the conductor and engineer of the train were negligent in running the train without a headlight, and in violation of the village ordinance, at a high and dangerous rate of speed; that the bell was not rung, or any notice or warning given of its approach in any way whatever: that the train was not run on schedule time, but was an extra. It is alleged that the said afternoon was very foggy, making it very dark, so that it was "very difficult, if not impossible, to see objects on the said railroad more than a few rods in front of the engine." The answer denied the allegations of negligence, and denied specifically the passage or existence of the alleged ordinance, and charged the deceased with contributory negligence. A verdict and judgment were rendered for the administrator, which was affirmed in the Circuit Court, and the cause comes into this court for review.

The facts are substantially as follows: The railway of the plaintiff in error passes through the northern part of the corporate limits of Buckeye City in an almost east and west direction, crossing the highway at right angles; the general direction of the road, however, being north and south. At the southeast corner of the crossing is Danville station. The railroad is perfectly straight east and west of the crossing for more than a mile each way. There is a descending grade from a point something over a mile east of the station. A switch extends along the south side of the main track, starting at the station and running east a distance of 1,020 to 1,040 feet; and a passing track, starting at the west side of the highway, 100 to 150 feet north of the station, and running west about 2,050 feet. This passing track was entirely clear on the day of the accident. The whistling post for the crossing is about a quarter of a mile east of the station. The west corporation line of Buckeye City was 582 feet from the west end of the platform, and 603 feet from the station. The accident happened about 683 feet from the station. It happened on the 13th day of January, 1899. For many years the father of the decedent, J. H. Mead, had been station agent for the defendant company at this place. It was a part of his duty to light the switch lamps in the evening, and bring them in in the morning. He was partially crippled, and, to assist him in the performance of his duties, he purchased, for his own convenience, and used, a "speeder," or three-wheeled vehicle, which could be run on the track, propelled by hands and feet. He did this without objection on the part of the company. The speeder at the time of the accident had a brake, but the brake had been lost or broken off, so that there was no way of stopping it except by the hands. The deceased at the time of the accident was about sixteen years old, and was in the employ of the company, at $5 per month, as his father's assistant and night man. His duties were to light the switch lamps in the evening and bring them in in the morning, attend to the two night trains at the station, and, when not in school, carry the mail. Mr. Mead, the father, permitted his son, the deceased, to use the speeder in doing his work, but cautioned him to be careful and to look out for trains when on the track. He had forbidden him to allow any one else on it with him, but had seen him once or twice take another boy with him. It appeared in evidence that every two or three days, and sometimes oftener, extra trains ran through Danville without stopping and that one of the rules of the road provided: "Extra trains may pass over the road at any time without previous notice and foremen must always be prepared for it. Anything that interferes with the safe passage of trains at full speed is an obstruction." At the time of the accident one J. P. McCaskey, a telegrapher out of employment, was temporarily helping Mr. Mead in the office. While Mr. Mead and Mr. McCaskey were in the office together during the afternoon McCaskey who was sitting at the instrument table, heard orders going over the wires, and turned to Mead and told him that an extra would meet No. 23 at a station east of Danville — either Brinkhaven or Baddaw Pass. No. 23 passed Danville going north at 2:52. The extra coming south (west) actually passed at Brinkhaven. Mead, who was busy at the time, paid little attention to the matter, and it passed out of his mind. Neither he nor McCaskey communicated the fact of the extra being on the road to Arleigh, the deceased. Mr. Mead, the station agent, left the station about three o'clock and went home, but, before he left, the deceased came in. Shortly after his father had left, the deceased took the speeder and a boy companion (one Herbert Parrish), and started out to light the switch lamps. It does not appear that Mr. Mead, the father, knew that the deceased was going on the speeder that day nor did he or McCaskey, nor any one, so far as the evidence discloses, inform the deceased that an extra was on the road. The boys backed up the main track to the north switch light, and, having lighted it, they turned towards the station, where they stopped for a moment to "hello" to Mr. Burrows' horse to get off the track, and then went on their way down the main track, towards the south switch light. They sat side by side, with their faces towards the south, talking together, and did not at any time, until just before the accident occurred, so far as known, look behind them. They both worked the handle-bars, and made the speeder go as fast as they could. The extra had no orders to stop at Danville, nor any reason to expect any. The rule of the company required each train, when running after sunset or obscured by fog, to display a headlight. But there was no headlight burning. The engineer testifies that a headlight would not have thrown a glare through the fog to enable parties to see that there was something coming, but there is other testimony on the subject. The train was going at full speed. There is some conflict in the testimony as to the rate of speed. The trainmen put it at twenty-five to thirty miles an hour, and plaintiff's witnesses about double that. The engine whistled, but whether it whistled for the crossing or not, or whether it gave an alarm whistle before the accident occurred, is a matter of some dispute. It does not appear that the boys heard the whistle. McCaskey, being in the station, heard the whistle, and running out, called to the boys as loud as he could. They were then some fifty feet beyond the west side of the crossing. Failing to attract their attention, he stood upon the corner of the platform, and tried to give the engineer a signal to make him stop the train or whistle. The engine was then right up to him. The target was white, which indicated there were no orders there for the train, and no occasion to stop, and the road was clear. As the engineer passed he saw McCaskey give a signal. He did not understand it, and turned for an instant to look again at the target, and then at once turned his face down the track; and at the same instant the fireman saw the boys at the distance of one and one-half telegraph poles ahead of the train. The boys were facing south then, with their backs to the train. The engineer claims to have given the alarm whistle at this time, applied the air brakes to the engine, gave a signal for the brakes, reversed his engine, and did everything in his power to stop the train. The conductor and two brakemen were in the caboose, and, at the whistle for brakes, they ran out and set them as fast as they could. Parrish, the boy who accompanied the deceased, says that the first he knew of the danger was the rumbling of the train. They both looked back, but the train was close upon them. The trainmen say that immediately upon blowing the alarm whistle the boys turned and looked back,

Parrish, sitting on the left side, succeeding in getting off, but the deceased fell back upon the track and was instantly killed. A witness who was at the station had seen the boys come down the track on the speeder. He heard the whistle for the station as he was getting on his wagon, and drove across the track, and called to the boys as loud as he could, and failed to get their attention. They were then a telegraph pole and a half from the crossing.

The existence of the alleged ordinance of Buckeye City prohibiting the running of cars through its corporate limits at a speed exceeding eight miles an hour was distinctly put in issue by the pleadings. On the trial the plaintiff called as a witness the mayor of Buckeye City to prove that he had given some notice to the company as to the speed of trains through the corporation. The defendant objected, and the court ruled that the plaintiff should first prove the ordinance, if there was one. Thereupon the witness produced the ordinance book containing the record of the supposed ordinance. Objection was made for the reason that the book was not the minutes of the proceedings of the council, nor did the record show that the supposed ordinance had ever been signed by the mayor. Thereupon the former mayor was called, and a piece of paper handed to him, signed by himself, and, as he says, by the city clerk, both in the presence of the council. He says it was passed one evening, and posted the next day. The paper was not at that time offered in evidence, but thereupon the plaintiff again offered the book of ordinances, and was permitted to read therefrom the ordinance as it appeared therein, to which ruling the defendant excepted. The record did not show that the ordinance had ever been signed by the mayor, nor that it had been published. Thereupon counsel for the defendant moved that it be stricken from the record for those reasons, and because the ordinance was not evidence of the passage of an ordinance, which could only be proved by the minutes of the proceedings of council. The motion was overruled, and the defendant excepted. Later in the trial the plaintiff offered the original piece of paper on which the ordinance was written, signed by the mayor and the clerk, which had been identified by the witness. Thereupon the paper was admitted in evidence, to which the defendant excepted. The minutes of the council were not produced or offered.

The defendant asked the court to charge the jury as follows: "That there having been testimony adduced tending to show that the defendant's station agent at Danville station, James Mead, was guilty of negligence that contributed to the death of his son, Arleigh J. Mead, the court charges you that the plaintiff cannot recover in this case on account or by reason of any negligence on the part of the said James Mead," — which the court refused to give, and the defendant excepted. But the court upon that subject charged the jury as follows at the request of the plaintiff: "If the jury find negligence of the defendant, its agents and servants, and also that there was negligence of the said J. H. Mead as agent and servant of the defendant, the fact of such negligence of said J. H. Mead, which, combined with the negligence of other agents and servants of the company, caused the injury, would not prevent recovery if such negligence of the defendant, its agents and servants, was the proximate cause of said injury, and said Arleigh J. Mead was not guilty of negligence contributing directly to his injury." And the court also said to the jury upon that subject: "In actions of this kind, gentlemen of the jury, the administrator is a mere nominal party, having no interest in the case for himself or his estate he represents, as such actions are for the exclusive benefit of the beneficiaries named in the section of the statute that I referred to at the beginning of this charge. In arriving at the total amount of damages in the case, the jury should consider the pecuniary injury to each separate beneficiary, but the verdict should be for a gross sum, not exceeding ten thousand dollars. * * * What has each separate beneficiary lost in money in the death of Arleigh J. Mead? will be your inquiry. First, determine the value of his life to the father; next, the value of his life to his mother, and then to each of the seven sisters; and, after you have found the value of his life to them all, you will return your verdict for the aggregate sum. In considering what each beneficiary is entitled to recover, you are to consider the age, the health, and the ability of the deceased to perform labor and earn money; * * * the health and circumstances of the parents, and the disposition and good will of the deceased to the beneficiaries, as likely to result in gifts or inheritances." * * * The defendant also asked the court to charge the jury in that connection as follows: "The plaintiff is not entitled to recover in this action for any pecuniary loss suffered by James H. Mead, the father of Arleigh J. Mead, on account of the death of the said son, if the jury shall find that the said James H. Mead was guilty of negligence directly contributing to the death of his son." This was refused, and the defendant excepted. The defendant also asked the court to charge the jury as follows: "1. That the character of Arleigh J. Mead's employment considered, and the means which he used at the time of the accident to reach the point at which he intended placing the switch light, and the other facts and circumstances surrounding the transaction, considered, that the employees of the defendant upon and in charge of and in the management of the train which caused his death were not obliged to regulate the speed of said train with reference to the possibility of injury to said Arleigh J. Mead, provided said employees, in the exercise of proper care and caution in the management and running of said train to accomplish the purpose of their employment, used all proper care and diligence to avoid said accident after they became aware of the presence of said Arleigh J. Mead upon said railroad track." "4. It is alleged in the amended petition that the afternoon or evening upon which the accident occurred was very foggy, making it very dark, so that it was very difficult, if not impossible, to see objects on the railroad more than a few rods in front of the engine. If you find such to be the fact, and that the deceased, Arleigh J. Mead, took the speeder out upon the main track, and chose that means of travel for no reason connected with his employment, other than his own convenience, and, after lighting the north switch light, returned to the station and passed with the speeder down the main track to light the south switch light, taking with him a companion, in violation of the order of his superior, the station agent, said James Mead; and if you shall find that from the street crossing adjoining the station there was a side track connected at that point with said main track, which led directly to the south switch where the second light was to be placed, and that the said Arleigh J. Mead could have easily used the said side track with the speeder for reaching the point where the light was to be placed; and if you shall find that by so doing he would have been in a position of safety from passing trains, and that, instead of so doing, he chose to so go down the main track without keeping any lookout behind him, or using other precautions to insure his own safety from passing trains — then I charge you that such conduct was negligence upon the part of said Arleigh J. Mead, and such negligence, the court charges you, as will prevent the plaintiff from recovering in this case unless they, the jury, shall further find that the defendant's agents and employees upon and in the management of the said train that caused the accident could have avoided said accident after they became aware of the presence of the said Arleigh J. Mead upon said track." These requests were refused, and the defendant excepted.

The court charged the jury as follows: "Evidence has been offered in this case on the part of the plaintiff tending to show that the defendant neglected and failed to sound the whistle of the locomotive for the public crossing, and failed to ring the bell, as provided by law, on approaching and passing the public crossing, a short distance from the point where the deceased met his death. Whether the bell was rung or the whistle sounded, or both, is a question for you to determine from a consideration of all the evidence offered; and your conclusions on this subject would be one of the elements that you are to consider in determining whether the defendant was guilty of negligence that produced, in whole or in part, the death of the deceased. In this connection I will only add that it was the duty of the company to make and enforce reasonable rules and regulations to guard against danger at public road or street crossings and in dangerous places, and that the deceased, while in the employment of the company, and when at or near a public street crossing, had a right to expect the performance of that duty." And also as follows: "A railroad track is commonly a place of danger. Whoever undertakes to walk along a railroad track or to travel thereon with a speeder, or other means of locomotion, must take such precautions as to ascertain the presence of danger as the ordinarily prudent person would take under like circumstances. The deceased, Arleigh J. Mead, on going on the defendant's track, was bound to use all reasonable precautions to detect the presence or approach of danger from passing trains. He was bound to know that the defendant might run a train over its road at that point at any time; and ordinary care would require him to look and listen for the approach of trains, and to continuously keep alive to the approach and presence of danger from passing trains, while on the defendant's track, unless lulled into a feeling of security by the failure of the defendant's employees in charge of its train to observe the statutory regulations and rules of the company in the matter of the running and management of the train at the time and place of the accident, and under the circumstances shown by the evidence." The court also charged the jury as follows with respect to the ordinance: "Evidence has been offered tending to show that some time prior to the accident the village of Buckeye City had passed an ordinance limiting the speed of trains through the corporate limits, which it had a right to do, under the statutes. The issue is made in the pleadings that this ordinance is not a valid ordinance, but the court is of the opinion that the issue is not material in the case. It does not depend on the fact whether the ordinance is valid or not. If the village council have passed an ordinance, or attempted to pass an ordinance, which they supposed was valid, and notice of its passage had been communicated to the railroad authorities, and they had acted upon the assumption that the ordinance was valid, and had regulated the speed of their trains accordingly, and also if knowledge of the passage of the ordinance had come to the deceased, it would be, for the purposes of this case, equivalent to a valid ordinance; and the deceased would have a right to presume that the company would conform to such regulation; and if he acted in accordance with such presumption, in the absence of knowledge of the fact that the railroad company had exceeded such limit in running its trains, it would not, of itself, be an act of negligence on the part of the deceased. But if, on the other hand, the village had passed a valid ordinance, or had attempted to pass an ordinance, without conforming to the requirements of the statute, and the provisions of the ordinance had been ignored by the company, and they had exceeded the limits prescribed by the ordinance in running trains through the village, and this fact had come to the knowledge of the deceased, the mere fact that the ordinance had been passed would not give the deceased a right to assume that the company at the time of the accident would regulate the speed of its train in conformity to the ordinance. Running a train in violation of an ordinance limiting the speed of trains is not of itself negligence on the part of the railroad company. After all, gentlemen of the jury, it is a mere circumstance for the jury to take into consideration, in connection with all the other facts and circumstances, in determining whether the defendant was negligent in the running of its train in the manner in which you find the evidence shows it was run at the time and place of the accident, and also in determining whether the deceased was guilty of negligence that contributed to cause his death."

Upon the trial several of the rules of the company were given in evidence. After the parties had rested, and after the jury had risen to their feet, and some of them had left the jury box, but before any of them had retired to their room, counsel for the plaintiff requested that the book of rules of the defendant, which had been referred to, and offered during the progress of the trial, be sent to the jury, to be used by them during their deliberations. This was objected to for the reason that only a small portion of the book had been offered in evidence, the plaintiff claiming that the whole book had been offered. The court said that only certain rules or parts of the book had been offered in evidence, and instructed the jury as follows: "Of course, the jury will understand that only such rules as have been offered in evidence and read to the jury during the trial will be considered by them." Thereupon the jury retired to their room. The book of rules was subsequently sent to them, and was in their possession during the time of their deliberations.

COOPER & MOORE and WATSON, BURR & LIVESAY, for plaintiff in error.

W. STILWELL and D. F. & J. D. EWING, for defendant in error.

DAVIS, J. (after stating the facts). — In the theory of this case which seems to have been entertained by the trial court there are several radical errors. Nearly all of them result from a misconception of the relation of the deceased to the plaintiff in error. That he was an employee of the railway company is not disputed, but at the time of the accident his position and his conduct were not within the scope of his duty. He was on the main track with the speeder for his own convenience, and under circumstances which made his presence there uncalled for and dangerous in the extreme. Such acquiescence in the occasional use of the speeder by the deceased and his father as may be implied in this case, at best, amounts to no more than a permission for that purpose, and constituted the deceased a bare licensee. The company did not object to the use of the speeder, if it knew of it, nor did it offer any inducement or invitation therefor. 2 Thomp. Neg. (2d Ed.), secs. 1722, 1723. The deceased took the license with its concomitant perils. The acquiescence in the use of the track with a speeder did not involve an undertaking on the part of the company to modify its rights as to the user of its own property, nor could it change its obligations to the public as a common carrier of passengers and freight. The trial court in this case, not without some warrant of authority, it must be admitted, took the view, and so instructed the jury, that it was the duty of the railway company to exercise reasonable care not only to avoid injury to the deceased after it discovered him upon the track, but that it was its duty to keep a careful lookout to discover and avoid injury to any person who might happen to be on its track at that place and at that time, and that this duty was implied in the license to the deceased and his father. It was in this view, apparently, that the court refused to give to the jury the defendant's first request to charge, and instructed the jury, instead, that the defendant "had a right to run its cars at the time and place of the accident at any speed and in any manner consistent with safety which was necessary in the conduct of its business in the usual and ordinary manner, taking into consideration, however, all circumstances surrounding the locality, and having a due regard to the safety of persons who might be upon its tracks. It was required to use ordinary care in running its train, having due regard to the rights of others." Such a conception of the law is opposed to reason, because a bare licensee must know that his license is subject to all the risks incident to the use of the track by the company in the same manner in which it was used at the time the license was granted, and that the company assumes no new obligation or duty toward him. Therefore the company owed him no duty of active vigilance to especially look out for and protect him. Railway Co. *v.* Aller, 64 Ohio St. 192, 60 N. E. Rep. 205; 3 Elliott, R. R., sec. 1250. It is believed that it is also contrary to the weight of authority. 3 Elliott, R. R., secs. 1250, 1251; 2 Thomp. Neg. (2d Ed.), secs. 1709, 1711, 1712, 1723, 1724; Railway Co. *v.* Vittitoe's Adm'r (Ky.), 41 S. W. Rep. 269. It may be added here that the rule is substantially the same as to trespassers and mere licensees; that is, licensees without invitation or inducement. An employee who goes upon the track or elsewhere upon the company's premises, not in the line or discharge of his duty, and without any invitation, express or implied, is at most a mere licensee, to whom the company owes no duty to keep such place safe. 3 Elliott, R. R., sec. 1251, and cases cited; Id., sec. 1303, and cases cited; Cleveland Terminal & Valley R. R. Co. *v.* Marsh, 63 Ohio St. 236, 9 Am. Neg. Rep. 167; Baker *v.* Railway Co., 95 Iowa, 163, 63 N. W. Rep. 667; Railroad Co. *v.* McKnight, 16 Ill. App. 596; 1 Thomp. Neg. (2d Ed.), secs. 945, 946. The doctrine of Harriman *v.* Railway Co., 45 Ohio St. 11, 12 N. E. Rep. 451, does not apply here, because there was in this case no pretense of acquiescence in the public use of the railway track in the way in which it was used by the deceased, nor was there any invitation or inducement held out to the deceased to so use it. There was at most only a failure to object to such user. We cannot think, therefore, that the trial court was right in instructing the jury as it did in this regard, and in refusing to instruct as requested in the defendant's first request.

In this connection we will consider the instructions of the court to the jury in regard to signals. Seemingly having in mind the erroneous theory criticised above, the trial court called the attention of the jury to the fact that evidence had been introduced by the plaintiff tending to show that the defendant had neglected and failed to give the statutory signals required on approaching and passing a public crossing; and the jury were instructed that it was for them to determine from the evidence whether such signals were given or not, and that their conclusion on that subject would be one of the elements which they should consider in determining whether the defendant was guilty of negligence that produced, in whole or in part, the death of the deceased, and, further, that the deceased was bound to use reasonable precautions to detect the approach of trains, and was bound to know that the defendant might run a train over the road at that point at any time, "unless lulled into a feeling of security by the failure of the defendant's employees in charge of its train to observe the statutory regulations and rules of the company in the matter of running and management of the train at the time and place of the accident, and under the circumstances shown by the evidence." It was also charged that the deceased, while in the employment of the company, and when at or near a public street crossing, had a right to expect the performance of that duty. The accident did not happen at or near the crossing, but more than 600 feet west of it, and not while the deceased was crossing the track, but while he was traveling longitudinally upon it. Independently of the theory of liability to a bare licensee, which we have already discussed, this raises the question whether the statutory duty to give signals when approaching a crossing inures to the benefit of persons on the track and not at a crossing. The statute obviously is not for the protection of persons who are not crossing the track, or about to do so; for not only is the whistle to be sounded before reaching the crossing, but the bell is to be continuously rung until the crossing is passed. The signals are not required at any other time. This is the construction which has been adopted in almost, if not quite, every jurisdiction where the question has arisen. It was fully considered and distinctly decided in Railroad Co. *v.* Depew, 40 Ohio St. 121, 127-129 (12 Am. Neg. Cas. 512n); also in the following cases: O'Donnell *v.* Providence & W. R. R. Co., 6 R. I. 211 (12 Am. Neg. Cas. 578n); Harty *v.* Central R. R. of N. J. 42 N. Y. 468 (12 Am. Neg. Cas. 397n); Williams *v.* Railroad Co., 135 Ill. 491, 26 N. E. Rep. 661; Railroad Co. *v.* McKnight, 16 Ill. App. 596; Rohback *v.* Railroad, 43 Mo. 187; Toomey *v.* Railroad Co., 86 Cal. 374, 24 Pac. Rep. 1074; Hale *v.* Columbia & G. R. R. Co., 34 S. C. 292 (12 Am. Neg. Cas. 582n); Atlanta & Charlotte Air-Line R'y Co. *v.* Gravitt, 93 Ga. 369 (11 Am. Neg. Cas. 330); 2 Thomp. Neg. (2d Ed.), sec. 1707. There being no legal duty in that regard due from the defendant to the deceased this instruction to the jury was erroneous.

Up to this point we have endeavored to consider the questions of law which were under review without complicating them with the subject of contributory negligence. It becomes necessary now to look at that phase of the case. The court refused to instruct the jury as requested in the defendant's fourth request. This instruction was sound, and ought to have been given. If it were found to be true that the deceased chose to travel with the speeder upon the main track for no reason connected with his employment, other than his convenience; that he rode down the main track with a companion on the speeder in violation of the order of his superior, the station agent; that from the station to the south switch light there was a "passing track," on which he could have placed the speeder, and easily and with absolute safety have reached his destination; and that instead of doing so he chose to go down the main track, without keeping any lookout behind him — there can be no doubt that he was guilty of negligence which proximately contributed to his own injury, unless the defendant could have avoided the injury after discovering the deceased upon the track. The authorities sustaining this proposition are so numerous that it would be practically impossible to cite them all here. We content ourselves with citing a few pertinent cases and leading text-writers, with the cases collected and cited by them: 3 Elliott, R. R., sec. 1303, and cases cited in notes thereto; 2 Thomp. Neg. (2d Ed.), secs. 1734, 1738, 1747, 1748, 1774, and cases cited in notes thereto; Ream *v.* Railroad Co., 49 Ind. 93; Railroad Co. *v.* Depew, 40 Ohio St. 121 (12 Am. Neg. Cas. 512n); Burling *v.* Ill. Cent. R. R. Co., 85 Ill. 18 (11 Am. Neg. Cas. 429n). It will be seen from these authorities that the instruction, as requested, states the law more strongly against the company than was necessary. It makes the qualification that "unless the jury shall further find that the defendant's agents and employees * * * could have avoided said accident after they became aware of the presence of the said Arleigh J. Mead upon said track." Strictly speaking, the law would require the defendant, after discovering the deceased to be upon the track, to use reasonable care under the circumstances to avoid the accident, not absolutely to avoid it; but, this being an error against the party asking the instruction, it should not have been refused for that reason. Besides, the instruction which was asked specifically challenged the attention of the jury to some very important circumstances affecting the claim of contributory negligence, and the error of refusing this is nowhere cured in the charge as given.

Again, the defendant asked the court to charge the jury that the plaintiff could not recover on account of or by reason of any negligence on the part of James H. Mead, the father of the deceased, at that time the agent of the defendant, and also that plaintiff could not recover for any pecuniary loss suffered by the father of deceased on account of the death of his son, if the jury should find that the father was guilty of negligence directly contributing to the death of his son. These requests were refused. There was, it is true, no issue in the pleadings upon this subject; but the court did charge the jury that, "in arriving at the total amount of damages in the case, the jury should consider the pecuniary injury to each separate beneficiary, but the verdict should be for a gross sum, not exceeding ten thousand dollars," and that, "what has each separate beneficiary lost in money in the death of Arleigh J Mead? will be your inquiry. First, determine the value of his life to the father;

next, the value of his life to his mother," etc. Having done this, and having given the jury the plaintiff's requests numbered 13 and 19, the defendant's request that the jury should also be instructed that the plaintiff would not be entitled to recover for any pecuniary loss of the father, if the jury should find that the father was guilty of negligence directly contributing to the death of the son, could not properly be refused. Wolf *v.* Lake Erie & Western R'y Co., 55 Ohio St. 517, 12 Am. Neg. Cas. 508, 45 N. E. Rep. 708.

The trial court and the counsel for the defendant in error seem to have entertained the view that the question raised concerning the ordinance of Buckeye City related to the validity and effect of the ordinance, but the issue in the pleadings was as to the legal passage and existence of the ordinance. The evidence to show the existence of the ordinance was clearly incompetent and insufficient, and the charge of the court did not cure the error of admitting it. It left the ordinance with the jury, as if it were a proven fact, instructing them that it was a circumstance to be taken into consideration, "in connection with all other facts and circumstances, in determining whether the defendant was negligent in the running of the train in the manner in which you find the evidence shows it was run at the time and place of the accident, and also in determining whether the deceased was guilty of negligence that contributed to cause his death." Nothing more needs to be said on that subject.

Another manifest error was the sending of the book of rules to the jury, to be used by them in their deliberations; only a few of the rules having been offered in evidence. Upon this record we would not reverse for that error, because it does not clearly appear that the company was prejudiced thereby; but we mention it in order that we may not seem to have approved it, and for the guidance of the trial court hereafter.

The judgments of the Circuit Court and the Court of Common Pleas are reversed.

BURKET, SPEAR, SHAUCK and PRICE, JJ., concur.

HEISS v. CITY OF LANCASTER.

Supreme Court, Pennsylvania, June, 1902.

PERSON INJURED AT GUTTER CROSSING IN STREET — EVIDENCE. — In an action to recover damages for injuries sustained by plaintiff at a gutter crossing, it was *held* that testimony that there were many other

crossings in the same condition as the one in question was competent on the question whether to keep it in that condition was negligence, and it also had a bearing on the question of plaintiff's contributory negligence.

CROSSING — DUTY OF CITY. — **A city is not bound to cover its crossings at all places, and the absence, therefore, of a crossing at the place of the accident was not of itself negligence (1).**

APPEAL from Court of Common Pleas, Lancaster County.

"Action by Levius Heiss against the City of Lancaster for injury received by plaintiff by stepping on the crossing of a street as it sloped to the gutter, the gutter not being bridged over from the crossing to the sidewalk." From judgment for defendant, plaintiff appeals. *Judgment affirmed.*

J. W. BROWN and MR. HENSEL, for appellant.

A. B. HASSLER, CHAS. R. KLINE and E. M. GILBERT, for appellee.

MITCHELL, J. — The first and second assignments of error are to the admission of evidence that other gutter crossings in the city were in a similar condition to the one where the accident occurred. The evidence, while not weighty, was competent. A general or common method of performance of a common duty may nevertheless be negligent, but the natural inference is to the contrary. Thus, the usual and common practice of travelers to stop at a certain place before crossing a railroad is evidence that it is a proper place to stop. The witnesses in the present case had given testimony tending to show that the crossing was dangerous, and the testimony that there were many other crossings in the same condition had some bearing on the question whether to keep it in that condition was negligence on the part of the city. It had also a bearing on the question of plaintiff's contributory negligence. If these places were dangerous, and there were many of them in the streets of the city, the plaintiff was under a proportionate obligation to be on the lookout, and use special care in crossing them.

The third assignment is to the charge of the court that: "A city is not bound to keep its highways in the condition of absolute safety; nor is it obliged to cover its crossings at all places, if it does not see fit to do so. This, like all other city improvements, may be done or not, as the municipal authorities see proper; and the absence, therefore, of a crossing at the place of the accident, was not of itself negligence in the corporation." This was a correct statement of the law. See Canavan *v.* City of Oil City, 183 Pa. St. 611, 38 Atl. Rep. 1096. On the authority of that case and the

1. See notes of recent Pennsylvania cases arising out of liability of municipal corporations for personal injuries, at end of this case.

well-settled law, the learned judge would have been justified in giving a binding direction for the defendant.

The last assignment is to the charge that: "A burden rests upon the plaintiff, even though the city was negligent. If he could have seen the defect which was here alleged had he looked, and he did not look, he cannot recover in this action. He must make out a case of negligence on the part of the city, free from contributory negligence on his own part. Has he done so?" It is admitted that this was a correct statement of the law, except for the use of the word "burden." The word was perhaps not happily chosen, but it was not inaccurate. The plaintiff was bound to make out a case clear of contributory negligence, and this may be properly described as a burden, though a negative one. The context immediately following shows the sense in which the word was used, and states the law with such entire accuracy that the jury could not have been misled.

Judgment affirmed.

NOTES OF RECENT CASES ON LIABILITY OF MUNICIPAL CORPORATIONS, DECIDED IN PENNSYLVANIA.

Falling on sidepath along township road — Nonsuit.

In SIEGLER *v.* MELLINGER ET AL. *(Penn., June, 1902)*, 52 Atl. Rep. 175, action against defendants, supervisors of Upper Leacok Township, for injuries received by plaintiff, who fell while walking on a sidepath along a township road, judgment of compulsory nonsuit was affirmed, MITCHELL, J., in the course of his opinion saying: "There was no evidence to warrant a jury in finding the defendants guilty of negligence. They were under no obligation to construct a footpath, and the one they permitted to be constructed and used there was not intrinsically dangerous. So far as shown, it was a smooth cinder path, about four feet wide, running at the side, and for the most part on a level with the roadway. At the point where this unfortunate accident occurred the path was between five and six feet above the road, and a man walking in the dark might, as in this case, make a misstep. But that did not make the place intrinsically dangerous for ordinary travel, which is the measure of defendant's duty in regard to it. The opinions of witnesses that the place was dangerous were properly excluded. There was nothing in the situation which a brief description would not enable the jury fully to understand. In such cases opinions of witnesses are not admissible. Graham *v.* Pennsylvania Co., 139 Pa. St. 149, 21 Atl. Rep. 151."

Defective pavement — Contributory negligence for jury.

In MUSSELMAN *v.* BOROUGH OF HATFIELD *(Penn., May, 1902)*, 52 Atl. Rep. 15, judgment of nonsuit was reversed, the opinion being rendered by DEAN, J., as follows: "Two villages, Hatfield and South Hatfield, were incorporated into one borough under the general borough laws on 27th of June, 1898. On December 23, 1900, Anna Musselman, the plaintiff, between nine and ten o'clock of a dark, stormy night by reason of a break in the pavement, fell and was seriously injured. At the time she was on her way home. The pavement where she fell was on Market street, a street thirty two feet between curb lines; the sidewalk or pavement on each side about twelve feet. The street leads from Union to Main street, and is much used by both pedestrians and vehicles. The walk in front of Snyder's lot on Market street was paved with large flagstones for about six feet of its width. The pavement in front of the adjoining lot (Kulp's) was a board walk, only three and one-half feet wide, — about one-half the width of Snyder's flagstone pavement. On each side of this narrow board walk there is an abrupt descent or offset of more than a foot, at its connection with the six and one half feet of Snyder's stone pavement. Plaintiff had a small child, her daughter, by the hand. Her son, a small boy, was walking in front of her. She knew of the break on each side of the board walk, and was watching for it; but, the night being dark, she did not see it, and consequently stepped outside the board walk and fell. There was one other way by which she could have reached her home, and that was by going around by Main street, a macadamized road with no sidewalks. Plaintiff, averring negligence in not maintaining a reasonably safe sidewalk, brought suit for damages against the borough. Defendant averred contributory negligence on the part of the plaintiff in choosing for her way home a pavement which she knew was unsafe, instead of a turnpike street, or in not carrying a lantern, as the night was dark and there was rain. The court below, being of opinion the case was ruled by City of Altoona *v.* Lotz, 114 Pa. St. 238, and Haven *v.* Bridge Co., 151 Pa. St. 620, directed a compulsory nonsuit which it afterwards refused to take off, and we have this appeal by plaintiff.

"We do not think the cases cited, or any others, will sustain the judgment, in view of the facts here presented. The true rule is: 'Where the risk is not obvious, it becomes a question of fact, for the determination of the jury, whether there was contributory negligence.' In City of Altoona *v.* Lotz, *supra*, the plaintiff knew of the unsafe condition of the board walk on which he was injured. The night was dark. He could have walked in the middle of the muddy street; could have gone another way some distance out of his course. It was a question of relative risk, and the court submitted the evidence to the jury. This was affirmed by this court. In Haven *v.* Bridge Co., *supra*, the accident was in broad daylight. The plaintiff was notified that the footway of the bridge was then being repaired. There were, also, danger signs at each end. She chose the footway. This court held that to be contributory negligence, because the danger was obvious, and the risk was voluntarily and unnecessarily assumed. We concede that it is often difficult to apply the law to the varying facts of different cases and say just which is for the court and which for the jury; but here the risk was relative. Whether she should, in the exercise of care, have walked in the middle of the street, or have gone by the turnpike, or have walked on Market street pavement, which she knew had the offset where the board walk joined the stone, depended on a comparison of risks. In an unlighted borough, on a dark, rainy, stormy night, a very prudent mother will probably stay indoors with her children. But this is a degree of care which the law does not impose upon the citizen. The law might as wel then hold that the duty of the borough extended no further than to provide reasonably safe ways for the citizen in fair weather and broad daylight. But its duty is more exacting, it must provide reasonably safe ways for the public, night and day. The citizen must only exercise reasonable care in their use

Whether the plaintiff exercised that care in this case was for the jury. Therefore the judgment is reversed, and a *procedendo* awarded."

Bicycle riders striking loose plank and falling over bridge.

In STRADER *v.* MONROE COUNTY *(Penn., May, 1902)*, 51 Atl. Rep. 1100, judgment for plaintiff for $15,000 was affirmed, the facts being stated in the opinion by DEAN, J., as follows: "The plaintiff and her son, the latter about thirteen years of age, residents of the borough of Stroudsburg, on the 8th of August, 1899, while riding bicycles, had occasion to cross a county bridge over Brodhead creek, the boundary of the borough on the east. The bridge was of three spans, two of 101 feet each and one of 116 feet. The bridge was twenty-eight feet wide, including a six feet wide footway on the north side, then a driveway thirteen feet wide, then six feet for a street railway, and then an unoccupied strip about three feet wide to the edge. The planks on the driveway were laid crosswise, those between the rails of the street railway longitudinally; thus making the latter much the smoother way. The mother and son reached the bridge about half-past seven in the evening, and rode on the driveway about two-thirds of the way across; then concluded to return on the planks between the rails because of the smoother condition of the floor. About twelve feet from the west end of the bridge the mother's bicycle struck a piece of loose plank, about twenty by five inches, which had been used to patch a break or rut in the floor. There was no guard rail from this point to where the bridge ended, a distance of fifteen feet. By the force of collision with the plank she and her bicycle were precipitated over the side of the bridge, and they fell fourteen feet upon rocks below. The fall broke her spine, with the consequence that she will be during life a confirmed invalid. She brought suit against the county for damages, averring negligence on the part of defendant in not keeping in repair the floor of the bridge, and in not maintaining a guard rail at the side. The defendant answered: That the proximate cause of the accident was the broken plank. That this she could have seen, if she had looked, 100 feet distant. She was negligent if she did not look. If she looked, and saw it, she was negligent in not avoiding it, either by getting over to the driveway or by steering around it on the route between the rails she had chosen. The court below, in an elaborate charge, submitted the evidence to the jury to find: First, whether defendant was negligent in permitting the piece of plank to remain for weeks on the floor of the bridge, and whether it negligently failed to protect the edge of the bridge, only five feet distant, with a barrier or guard rail; and, second, whether the plaintiff had contributed to the accident by her own negligence in not seeing the plank when she ought to have seen it, or, if she did see it, in not using ordinary care to avoid it. The jury found for plaintiff on both questions, and assessed her damages at $15,000.

"If plaintiff was entitled to a verdict at all, it could not, with plausibility, be argued that the amount was excessive. She was a comparatively young woman, only thirty-nine years of age, in excellent health, earning a good salary in a manufacturing establishment. She is now incapacitated for life. As to her alleged contributory negligence, there was some evidence to sustain the charge, but it was not of that undisputed character, as appellant argues, to warrant the court in withdrawing it from the jury. In view of it, it is scarcely worth while to spend time in reviewing the elaborate discussion of counsel as to what was the remote or what the proximate cause of the accident. If it unquestionably appeared that the piece of plank was the dominating cause, and therefore the proximate one, and that just as unquestionably plaintiff was guilty of contributory negligence in permitting her bicycle to strike it, it would, perhaps, be material to discuss the threadbare subject of proximate and remote cause; but in this case it is of no practical importance. The court below spoke thus to the jury: 'She was bound, gentlemen of the jury, to ride her bicycle with reasonable care and caution. She was bound to observe where she was going. She was bound to take notice of obstacles that may have been in the way. Now, then, was she exercising reasonable care and caution when she was riding her bicycle in the manner in which she did ride it? The evidence is that the boy, her son, was from twelve to fourteen feet in front of her; that she was riding along, following him; that they were riding slowly, as the evidence describes; perhaps four to five miles an hour, — we think the testimony is to that effect; and that when her attention was called to the rut or the plank by her boy, who had passed it by going around it, that she was then upon or at this plank or obstruction, and lost control of her bicycle, and the accident happened by reason of losing that control in passing that plank or obstacle.' This was the pith of the charge on the question of contributory negligence, and, although in different language, was repeated over and over to the jury. Undoubtedly, the cause of the deflection of the bicycle towards the edge of the bridge was the piece of plank, and if the occurrence had stopped there, it is highly probable very slight, if any, injury to her would have resulted. But she went over the edge, fell fourteen feet to the rocks below, and broke her spine. If the piece of plank caused the bicycle to turn, the absence of the guard rail was the cause of the serious injury. If defendant was — as is scarcely denied — guilty of negligence in not maintaining a guard rail at that point, as the jury has found, and was guilty of negligence in permitting the piece of plank to remain on the floor of the bridge, as the jury has also found, and plaintiff was not guilty of contributory negligence, it helps us not, in determining liability, to determine also which of the two operating causes was the dominating one. It must pay if either was." * *

Stepping into hole in pavement filled with dust.

In GLADING *v.* CITY OF PHILADELPHIA *(Penn., April, 1902)*, 51 Atl. Rep. 886, where plaintiff was injured by stepping into a hole filled with dust and sweepings, in the pavement of a crowded thoroughfare in the central part of the city, it was *held* that the question whether she exercised reasonable care, was clearly for the jury, and judgment for plaintiff was affirmed.

Falling over stake on highway at public crossing.

In ROWLAND ET AL. *v.* CITY OF PHILADELPHIA *(Penn., March, 1902)*, 51 Atl. Rep. 589, action by husband and wife for injuries to wife, judgment for plaintiffs was affirmed. POTTER, J., in the course of his opinion, said: "In his opening argument, counsel for the appellant calls attention to the fact that, while this suit was brought against the city of Philadelphia and two separate contractors as joint tort feasors, yet the evidence did not show concert of action, nor was there any attempt upon the trial to prove that the act complained of was the joint act of the defendants. Judgment of voluntary nonsuit was entered against the two contractors, and the action proceeded against the city alone. No exception was, however, taken upon the part of the city to proceeding with the case against itself alone after the entry of the judgment of nonsuit against the contractors, and the question is raised apparently for the first time in the case at the argument in this court." * * * After discussing the method of procedure and citing Weist v. City of Philadelphia, 200 Pa. St. 148, 49 Atl. Rep. 891, the court said: "In the present case, however, no objection was made in the court below to the course there pursued. The appellant took the chance of the verdict, without any exception to the trial proceeding against it as the sole remaining defendant after the entry of judgment of nonsuit in favor of its co-defendants. By so doing it must be held to have waived its right to raise the question, and we cannot now consider it here."

Continuing, the court said: "Turning now to the specifications of error, the only one which is pressed in the argument is to the refusal by the trial judge of binding instructions in favor of the defendant, the city of Philadelphia. In the statement of claim, the negligence charged was permitting a stake to exist and remain as an obstruction in the line of travel upon the public crossing of the highway at the intersection of Goodman street and Sedgeley avenue for an unnecessary length of time after the work upon the highway was completed; and this without guarding the obstruction in any way, or placing a light upon it, so as to give notice to pedestrians by night. The placing of the stake originally as a guide to the contractors for the street work was admittedly proper. But the plaintiff claims that the stake was left in the ground in such a way as to protrude above the surface, and was so left for a considerable time after the work was completed and the reason for its location had ceased. There was evidence tending to support this claim. Mrs. Rowland testified that she fell over a stake as she was walking across Sedgeley avenue about half-past eight o'clock in the evening. She describes the stake as being about two inches square, and protruding above the ground more than six inches. The contractor for the sewer testified that stakes were set for him by the city surveyor to show the line of the sewer, but that he had finished the work under his contract, and left the street, several days prior to the accident. It appeared by the terms of the contract with the city that the contractor was prohibited from removing stakes until authorized to do so. In submitting the case to the jury, the trial judge instructed them that the plaintiff could recover, unless she was guilty of contributory negligence, if they found that she fell over the stake put in by the city; otherwise not. The city was held responsible for nothing beyond the acts and omissions of its own officers. This being the case, no proof of notice to the city as to the existence of the stake was necessary. Had it been placed and retained in its position by third parties, a different question would arise. Neither does it appear from the evidence that the obstruction was so manifest, nor the condition of the street so obviously bad, that the court could say, as a matter of law, that it was contributory negligence to use the crossing. That was left for the determination of the jury. Under all the evidence in the case, it would have been manifest error for the trial judge to have taken the case from the jury and given binding instructions in favor of the city. The assignments of error are overruled and the judgment is affirmed." (SAMUEL CHEW, HOWARD A. DAVIS and JOHN L. KINSEY, appeared for appellant; JOHN CADWALADER, JR., FRANCIS FISHER KANE, D. STUART ROBINSON and JAMES M. BECK, for appellees.)

EHNI v. NATIONAL TUBE WORKS COMPANY.

Supreme Court, Pennsylvania, June, 1902

EMPLOYEE INJURED BY BREAKING AND FALL OF PLANK — INSPECTION — MASTER NOT LIABLE. — Where a plank in a scaffolding which plaintiff, an employee of defendant company, had used a great many times for more than two years, and had not seen any defect in it, suddenly broke while he and others were upon it, and he was injured, it was *held* that the fact of its use for so long a period without any defect being discovered was evidence of its original suitability, and defendant did not owe plaintiff the duty of an inspection by a third party, and was not liable for the injury to plaintiff (1).

APPEAL from Court of Common Pleas, Allegheny County.

Action by W. F. Ehni against the National Tube Works Company. From judgment for defendant, plaintiff appeals. *Judgment affirmed.*

PETTES & MCALLISTER and MARRON & MCGIRR, for appellant.

W. B. RODGERS, for appellee.

POTTER, J. — The plaintiff was in the employ of the defendant company as a belt repairer. In addition to mending belts when broken, it was his duty to replace them upon the pulleys whenever they had been removed for repairs or were off for any other reason. According to his own testimony, he had been engaged in this capacity some two or three years prior to the date of the accident. On July 11, 1898, it became necessary to place in position a rather heavy belt which was more than fifty feet in length. The shafting upon which the belt ran was at a considerable height above the floor — perhaps some seventeen or eighteen feet — and in order to reach it, and enable the men to care for the other machinery which was running overhead, scaffolds were erected and maintained in position through the mill. They were of simple construction, consisting of parallel planks, running longitudinally with the lines of belting, and connected at intervals by a cross plank running from one to the other. It does not clearly appear from the evidence whether the cross planks were permanently fastened in place or were movable, but this is not a matter of special importance. At the time of the accident the plaintiff and a fellow-workman were standing upon one of these cross planks, which was about fourteen inches wide and two inches in thickness, and at least sixteen feet in length. The

1. For other actions arising out of accidents caused by defective scaffolding, etc., from 1897 to date, see vols. 1–12 AM. NEG. REP., and the current numbers of that series of Reports.

men had just made a strong effort to place the belt upon the pulley, without success, and were resting quietly for a moment after their exertion. Suddenly the plank upon which they were standing broke beneath them, and the plaintiff fell, receiving the injuries for which recovery is here sought.

Upon the trial in the court below, at the close of the plaintiff's testimony, a compulsory nonsuit was entered, and the subsequent refusal to take off this judgment is made the subject of the first assignment of error. The facts of the case are perfectly simple. The plaintiff testified that he was very familiar with the plank which broke, and that he had used it a great many times during the two years or more of his employment by the defendant. He could not say specifically how many times he had stood upon it, but said that it might be half a dozen times in one day, and then not again for a month. It is perfectly apparent, however, that, if there was any defect in the plank, no one could have been in a better position to have ascertained that fact than the plaintiff himself. From its elevated position it must have been almost constantly before his eyes, as well as under his feet. If he, therefore, with his thorough familiarity with the plank, and his almost constant use of it, discovered nothing wrong with it, how could it with any reason be expected that any one else should discover that which he was unable to detect? The plank was apparently of ample size and strength. The fact that it had been in use for so long a period of time without breaking or showing any signs of being defective, is evidence of its original suitability. Where, as in this case, material of such apparent good quality was furnished to the employees, and was accepted as such by them, and used without objection for so long a period of time, it would be most unreasonable to hold the employer responsible for a break, in the absence of any testimony indicating any defect known before the accident. It was suggested in the argument that the employer owed to the plaintiff the duty of an inspection by a third party, in order to ascertain the safety of the plank upon which the plaintiff stood. This is a mistaken idea as applied to any such a condition as prevailed in this case. When suitable material is furnished by the employer, he does not engage that it will always continue in the same condition. It is the duty of the employee to discover and report to his employer any defect which may arise by reason or in course of the use made of the material. He has means of observing and ascertaining any such defect which the employer does not possess, and it is his duty to exercise reasonable care for his own protection. As is said in Mixter *v.* Coal Co., 152 Pa. St. 397, 25 Atl. Rep. 587, when reasonably safe tools or machinery have once been furnished, "it is not negligence in the master if the tool or machine breaks, whether from an external original fault, not apparent when the machine or tool was at first provided; or from an external apparent one produced by time and use, not brought to the master's knowledge. These are the ordinary risks of the employment, which the servant takes upon himself." The present case does not involve even the sufficiency of any tool or machine. The exercise of judgment required upon the part of the plaintiff was only that of determining the apparent strength and sufficiency of an ordinary plank, which calls for about as modest an exercise of discretion as can well be imagined. There was no occasion for the introduction of any expert testimony either as to the character of the plank when it was first selected for use or as to the effect upon it of the conditions under which it was used by the plaintiff. There was, therefore, no error in the rejection of testimony offered for this purpose, or to show the absence of inspection by any one else than the men who were daily using the plank.

The assignments of error are all overruled, and the judgment is affirmed.

HUGHES v. PENNSYLVANIA RAILROAD COMPANY.

Supreme Court, Pennsylvania, April, 1902.

CARRIER — LIMITING LIABILITY — CONFLICT OF LAWS — CONNECTING CARRIER — INTERSTATE COMMERCE ACT. — A stipulation in a contract that limits the liability of a carrier for damage to a horse from negligence to $100 is against the policy of the State, and will not be enforced though the contract was made in a State where such a contract was valid, for carriage from a point in that State to a point in this State where the damage occurred (1).

A contract to carry by connecting lines is a separable contract, where the carrier making the contract does not contract for itself beyond its own lines, acting only as agent for the connecting carrier, and the freight charges are distinct sums.

The Interstate Commerce Act is not violated by holding that the contract that stipulates a limitation upon the carrier's liability in case of injury from negligence within this State is invalid.

1. *Connecting carrier.* — See NOTE OF RECENT CASES OF LIABILITY OF CONNECTING CARRIER FOR NEGLIGENCE, at end of this case.

APPEAL from Court of Common Pleas, Philadelphia County.

Action by William Hughes and another, trading as Hughes & Fleming, against the Pennsylvania Railroad Company. From judgment for plaintiffs, defendant appeals. *Judgment affirmed.*

EDWIN JAQUETT SELLERS, DAVID W. SELLERS and JOHN G. JOHNSON, for appellant.

A. S. L. SHIELDS, for appellees.

POTTER, J. — The plaintiffs in this case were the owners of a valuable horse, which was shipped by their agent from Albany, N. Y., to Cynwyd, Pa. The contract for transportation was made in Albany with the New York Central Railroad, acting for itself and connecting carriers. The bill of lading provided that "no carrier shall be liable for loss or damage not occurring on its own road, or its portion of the through route." The horse was carried safely by the initial carrier to the end of its line, and delivered to the defendant company, by whom it was brought to Philadelphia. At this point the horse was badly injured by the negligence of defendant's servants, and the injuries thus received are the foundation of this action. The defendant admitted liability, but claimed that the plaintiff was not entitled to recover in excess of $100. In support of this claim, it relied upon a printed form of a shipping contract, which was signed by plaintiff's agent at the time of shipment, and retained by the carrier. This contract contained a stipulation that the liability of the initial carrier and any connecting carrier should be limited, in case of loss or damage to a horse or mule, whether through negligence or otherwise, to an amount not exceeding $100 each. At the trial the court below declined to charge the jury that such a limitation of the amount of the damages was lawful in this case. The jury, under the evidence, found a verdict for $9,900 — the full value of the horse.

The refusal of the court to charge that the contract of shipment, limiting the liability for negligence, was valid and binding upon the plaintiff, is here assigned as error. It is conceded that this contract is valid under the law of New York, and that, if the horse had been injured while in course of transportation through that State, the plaintiffs would have been limited to the sum of $100. It is also conceded that such a contract, made in Pennsylvania, for transportation between points within the State, would be void, as against the settled policy of this State. The question is not an open one with us. Nor does it matter whether the attempt be to limit the liability, as in Ruppel *v.* Railroad Co., 167 Pa. St. 166, or to claim exemption entirely from liability, as in Willock *v.* Railroad Co., 166 Pa. St. 184. But because the contract was made in New York, to be performed partly in New York and partly in Pennsylvania, it is contended that the law of New York should govern the case. It may be noted here that while the contract contains an acknowledgment that Grady had the option to ship the horse at a higher rate, with increased liability, yet, as a matter of fact, no such offer was made. The evidence shows that the freight agent at Albany did not know the amount of the charges, and the blanks for the amounts were not filled in. The case of Burnett *v.* Railroad Co., 176 Pa. St. 45, seems to be decisive of the question now before us. In that case the plaintiff was an employee of defendant at Trenton, N. J. He applied for and obtained free transportation from Trenton to Elmira, N. Y. He received two passes — one from Trenton to Philadelphia, which was not in evidence, and the other, an employee's trip pass, from Philadelphia to Elmira — by the terms of which he assumed all risks of accident. He was injured at Harrisburg, Pa., through the admitted negligence of the defendant's employees. It was proved at the trial that under the laws of New Jersey the contract by which the plaintiff, in consideration of free transportation, assumed the risk of accident, was valid, and that in that State he could not recover; and it was conceded by the defendant that in Pennsylvania the decisions are otherwise, and that such a contract will not relieve a common carrier from responsibility for negligence. There, as in this case, the contract was valid in the State where made. The transportation was safely performed into this State, and the injury occurred within this State through the negligence of the carrier. It was held that the responsibility of the defendant was to be determined by the law of the State where the contract was being performed, and where the negligence occurred, and recovery was allowed. In the present case the facts are more strongly against the defendant, in that it is not the initial carrier under the contract, and the stipulation upon the part of each carrier was against liability for damages not occurring on its portion of the through route. In Fairchild *v.* Railroad Co., 148 Pa. St. 527, there was a contract for the transportation of a horse from Washington, D. C., through Pennsylvania, to Harkimus, N. J. It was injured by the negligence of the defendant while in Baltimore, Md. The contract contained a stipulation limiting the value of the horse to $100. Suit was brought to recover damages for the injury. The court below held the contract to be valid, and, under instructions, a verdict was rendered for $105.50, and judgment entered thereon. This judgment was affirmed; this court saying, in a *per curiam*, "This written contract was made in the District of Columbia, and is to be interpreted by the *lex loci contractus.*" Forepaugh *v.*

Railroad Co., 128 Pa. St. 217. If, however, in the performance of the contract, the horse had been carried into Pennsylvania, and it had been injured in this State, the principle set forth in Burnett *v.* Railroad Co., *supra*, would, no doubt, have been applied, and the limitation of liability held void. In the Fairchild case, *supra*, nothing is said about the law of Maryland, where the injury occurred, though, as a matter of fact, the limitation of liability was valid in that State, as appears in Brehme *v.* Dinsmore, 25 Md. 328.

The Fairchild case, *supra*, when properly understood, is authority only for the proposition that a contract containing a limitation of liability, made in a State where it is valid, will be enforced in this State, when an injury occurs in the course of transportation through a State where such a contract is not contrary to public policy. It is only an application of the doctrine of Forepaugh *v.* Railroad Co., 128 Pa. St. 217, to a slightly differing state of facts. The reference to Hart *v.* Railroad Co., 112 U. S. 331, could only have been to show the law of the District of Columbia; for in Grogan *v.* Express Co., 114 Pa. St. 523, this court expressly refused to follow the Hart case.

A distinction may well be made between contracts of a general nature, and those of common carriers of goods through several States. Much stress is laid in the brief of appellants upon the opinion of Justice Bradley in Morgan *v.* Railroad Co., 2 Woods, 244, Fed. Cas. No. 9,804. The contract in that case was made in New York, to be performed, in an important part, there, and in part by the building of a railroad in Louisiana. Another important part was to be performed in Alabama, and perhaps other important parts in other States. The court held that, where a contract is to be performed in several jurisdictions, there could be no presumption that the parties had in view the laws of each of these jurisdictions, as the law that was to govern the contract, and therefore held that it was governed by the law of New York, where it was made. But it will be noticed that the case did not involve the law of common carriers, but only a contract relating to a matter about which the parties were free to contract, and against which there was no public policy of any State. The inquiry was therefore properly confined to ascertaining the intention of the parties to the agreement. But a contract for the carriage of goods is not one as to which parties are entirely free to contract. Judge Sulzberger, in his charge in this case, aptly said: "There are, however, limitations upon the right of contract. There is a certain field of human activity over which the State assumes supreme control by virtue of its sovereignty, and when the State declares its policy, which we call 'public policy,' upon these questions, then the right of private contract is utterly abolished to that extent." It will not do, therefore, to apply to the contracts of common carriers all the principles that may apply to other contracts. When courts declare a contract void as against public policy, they are not declaring the intention of the parties, as in the ordinary case, but are acting under the obligation of the higher law, which requires the enforcement of that which is for the public good. Where a contract containing a stipulation limiting liability for negligence is made in one State, but with a view to its performance by transportation through or into one or more other States, we see no reason why it should not be construed in accordance with the law of the State where its negligent breach, causing injury, occurs. If such a contract comes under construction in a State like Pennsylvania, whose policy prohibits such exemption, and the injury has occurred in a State where the contract is valid, the stipulation will be enforced, as in Forepaugh *v.* R. R. Co., *supra*, and in Fairchild *v.* R. R. Co., *supra*. But if the injury has taken place within its limits, it will declare the contract null and void, as in Burnett *v.* R. R. Co , *supra*. In the Fairchild case, *supra*, as the injury occurred in Maryland, this court enforced the law of that State. If the injury to the horse had been delayed until in the course of the journey it had reached Pennsylvania, our own law of public policy would have controlled. This principle is maintained in Barter *v.* Wheeler, 49 N. H. 9. In that case the transportation was from Toledo, Ohio, to Concord, N. H. The goods were lost on their passage through New York, and the court said that, if it is to "be executed partially in New York, we perceive no reason why, in respect to that part, the law of that State should not govern; and such is the doctrine laid down in Story, Cont., sec. 655." To the same effect is Pitts., Cin., C. & St. L. R'y Co. *v.* Sheppard, 56 Ohio St. 69, 1 Am. Neg. Rep. 517. This principle involves no greater difficulty, as to proof, than the attempt to recover under a limitation of liability. In either case, negligence is a fact to be proven as to time and place, as any other fact.

Careful consideration of the contract and of the evidence shows that the contract in this case was not entire, either as to the obligation of the carrier to transport, or of the shipper to pay the freight. The New York Central Railroad made no contract for itself beyond its own lines. It acted as agent only for the connecting carrier. It is the same as though each carrier had separately agreed to transport over its own line. And the freight charges were shown to be made up of two distinct sums; one being the amount from Albany to Jersey City, and the other from Jersey City to Cynwyd. No case has come under notice, directly deciding that such a contract is severable. But in Wells *v.* Thomas, 27 Mo. 17, the ruling is such as to indicate that, in the opinion of the court, the bill of lading issued in that case, covering lines of several carriers, was not an entire contract.

The third assignment of error suggests that the entry of judgment is in conflict with the interstate commerce act of Congress. This seems to be an afterthought, as there is no indication in the record that this question was raised or considered in the court below. It is not apparent how the act can have any application to this case. It contains nothing bearing upon the validity of a contract limiting the liability of a railroad for loss or injury caused by negligence. The object of the act seems to be to secure continuous carriage and uniform rates, and to compel the furnishing of equal facilities. We cannot see that the entry of judgment in this case interferes in any way with the legitimate exercise of interstate commerce.

Upon the case as a whole, there is nothing to show any bad faith upon the part of the shipper. He applied for the transportation of his horse upon a special car, and loaded him thereon, together with the traps and harness and a special attendant. There was no concealment, nor any misrepresentation as to value. The shipper paid the carrier the amount asked of him. It does not appear that any bargain was made in advance for a freight rate; nor was there any reason why the full rate, sufficient, in the opinion of the carrier, to cover the risk of transportation, should not have been charged and collected. The shipper should not be asked to pay for insurance against the negligence of the employees of the carrier. If protection of that nature was desired, the carrier was at liberty to procure it for itself, and at its own expense. It must be assumed, also, that both shipper and carrier knew the law of Pennsylvania, and had it in view when the contract was made. The facts were submitted to the jury in a charge which clearly and correctly stated the public policy of this State with regard to the question under consideration.

The assignments of error are overruled, and the judgment is affirmed.

MITCHELL and BROWN, JJ., dissent.

NOTES OF RECENT CASES OF LIABILITY OF CONNECTING CARRIERS FOR NEGLIGENCE.

1. **Delivery to next carrier.**
2. **Injury occurring before delivery to connecting carrier.**
3. **Delivery prevented by law.**
4. **Agent of connecting carrier.**
5. **Connecting carrier failing to limit liability.**
6. **Initial carrier not liable for negligence of connecting carrier.**
7. **Presumption that injury occurred on line of last connecting carrier.**
8. **Other cases.**

1. Delivery to next carrier.

In FELTON *v.* CENTRAL OF GEORGIA R. (Ga., 1902), 40 S. E. Rep. 746, where there was no contract between defendant and plaintiff as testified to by the latter, binding the carrier defendant to transport his goods beyond its own lines, the company was liable only to its own terminus and until delivery to the next connecting road.

In WASHBURN-CROSBY CO. *v.* BOSTON & A. R. CO. (Mass., 1902), 62 N. E. Rep. 590, a quantity of flour was shipped by plaintiff at Minneapolis consigned to parties at London, and over defendant's road as one of several connecting carriers. The defendant unloaded the flour on its pier that was used by the next carrier, a steamship company, for the reception of goods to be shipped. The flour was burned there. The defendant had given notice to the steamship company by a letter that remained unanswered and seemingly acquiesced in, that unloading of steamship freight at that place constituted delivery on the defendant's part, and that thereafter it assumed no responsibility for the same. The court said that the facts warranted a finding of an actual delivery by the defendant on the steamship pier named in the bill of lading, and which the notice to the steamship company required, and that the liability of the defendant had ceased.

In DUNBAR *v.* CHARLESTON & W. C. R. CO. (So. Car., 1902), 40 S. E. Rep. 884, the plaintiff shipped some barrels of melons over defendant's line and connecting carriers. The melons were injured by delay on one of the connecting carriers. The plaintiff received a receipt at the time of shipping which contained a provision that the shipment was received subject to the carrier's regular bill of lading, for which the receipt could be exchanged. The bill of lading, which the plaintiff did not obtain, provided that the carrier should not be liable for a loss not proved to have occurred on its own road or after the property was ready for delivery to the next carrier. The court said the plaintiff had notice from the receipt to put him on inquiry, and he was bound by the terms of the bill of lading that he failed to procure to inform himself of the conditions of shipment.

In SAN ANTONIO & A. P. R. CO. *v.* BARNETT (Tex. Civ. App., 1901), 66 S. W. Rep. 474, cattle shipped over defendant's line and that of a connecting carrier were injured before arriving at their destination. Plaintiff alleged and testified that there had been a verbal agreement for through shipment and that the written and printed contracts signed by him were obtained because the cattle would not be moved unless he signed them. The contracts provided that the defendant would not be liable beyond its own line and that the cattle were to be delivered to him at the point where the connecting carrier took them. The court stated that the verbal contracts were merged in the written ones and that they could not be repudiated by plaintiff as there was no proof of fraud, compulsion or want of time to read them.

In TEXAS AND PACIFIC R. Co. v. REISS (Sup. Ct., U. S., 1902), 183 U. S. 621, a number of bales of cotton was shipped over two railroads to a pier of the second railroad, where it was to be loaded on a steamship, the third carrier. The cotton was burned on the pier. The first carrier made out the bills of lado ing, which stated that they were on behalf of all three companies, and that no carrier should be liable for loss not occurring on its own road, nor after the said property was ready for delivery to the next carrier, and that no carrier should be liable for delay nor in any other respect than as warehouseman, while the said property awaits further conveyance, and that the contract was accomplished and all liability thereunder terminated on the delivery of the said property to the steamship. The usual manner of handling the cotton upon arrival at the pier that belonged solely to the second carrier was for the bales to be unloaded from the cars and checked, and the check list sent to the steamship company that then sent a vessel for the cotton that was pointed out to the steamship company's agent and it was loaded on the vessel. No such list of the cotton burned was sent, nor was the steamship company notified that the cotton had arrived. The court said that there had been no delivery to the steamship company, and that the second railway company, the defendant, was liable as a common carrier. That the clause "awaiting further conveyance" meant after notification that the cotton was ready for delivery.

In TEXAS AND PACIFIC R. Co. v. CALLENDER (U. S. Sup. Ct., 1902), 22 Sup. Ct. Rep. 257, a case arising from the same cause of action as Tex. & P. R. Co. v. Reiss, it was decided that the railroad company did not, by unloading the cotton on the pier that was under its sole and absolute control and possession, and after notifying the steamship company that was the succeeding carrier, of the arrival of the cotton, deliver the cotton "to the steamship company or on the steamship pier" within the meaning of a clause in the bill of lading that provided that the railroad company's liability should terminate on such delivery, though such pier should be assumed to be the place agreed upon between the two companies for the delivery of cotton to be thereafter carried by the steamship company, when it appeared that the railroad company still continued to retain full control of the cotton, and could, under certain contingencies, and at any time before the cotton was delivered to a steamship, send it by another steamer, and it also appeared that it was agreed between the two companies that the steamship company was not to take the cotton until it sent a steamer to the pier for that purpose.

2. Injury occurring before delivery to connecting carrier.

In SUSONG v. FLORIDA CENT. & P. R. Co. (Ga., 1902), 41 S. E. Rep. 566, a carload of horses was shipped by rail over the initial carriers' line, and the defendant's line, a connecting carrier. The car was unloaded and reloaded at different points, and at the place where the car was delivered to the defendant it was unloaded and reloaded, and the seals of the initial carrier placed on the doors of the car. The defendant did not receipt for the car "as in good order," but received the same without exception. The car reached its destination in the same condition as received by the defendant, and the horses were delivered to plaintiff as received, one of the horses originally shipped was not among them, and one other was in a damaged condition. The shipment was made under a special contract at a reduced rate of freight, and there was a provision that the plaintiff or some agent of his should ride on the train with the horses and assist in unloading and reloading them. The court said the defendant was not liable, first because the loss of the one animal and the injury to the other occurred before the car containing them was delivered to the defendant, and, second, that the loss and injury would probably not have occurred if the defendant had complied with the contract and accompanied the stock, or had some one do so. That though the Code provided that a connecting carrier would be liable when goods received without objection were found injured, yet the presumption that they were in good condition at the time might be rebutted.

In SAN ANTONIO & A. P. R. Co. *v.* THOMPSON (Tex. Civ. App., 1902), 66 S. W. Rep. 792, vegetables were delayed several days at a point on defendant's line. The court said that if such delay was the cause of the damage to the vegetables, the defendant would be liable for all the natural consequences thereof during the entire transit, even beyond its own line.

In MISSOURI, K. & T. R. Co. *v.* MAZZIE (Tex. Civ. App., 1902), 68 S. W. Rep. 56, a carload of grapes was shipped over a railroad at a certain point, and shipped then by the consignee at that point over connecting carriers to another point. This arrangement was not disputed to have been proper, and all the carriers concerned treated the consignment as one shipment. Each of the companies concerned was liable only for the damage which occurred on its own line. The plaintiffs proved that the goods were delivered in good condition to the initial carrier, and were delivered by the terminal carrier in a damaged condition. Evidence was introduced tending to show that the grapes were in the possession of the initial carrier for four or five days in a car not iced when the weather was hot, and that grapes so packed and under such conditions would mould and rot. The car was sealed when it started first on its journey, and was not opened until its final destination was reached. The court said that as the condition of the fruit at any intermediate point could not be shown by direct and positive evidence it was error for the trial court not to submit to the jury whether the damage or any part thereof occurred on the line of the initial carrier, so as to relieve the defendant terminal carrier that would otherwise be liable for the loss of the grapes.

8. Delivery prevented by law.

In FORT WORTH & D. C. R. Co. *v.* MASTERSON (Tex. Sup. Ct., 1902), 66 S. W. Rep. 833, the defendant, a connecting carrier, refused to receive from the previous carrier and transport two cars of cattle, to the next point mentioned in a through bill of lading. A section of the Revised Statutes provides that every railroad in the State must receive freight from connecting lines when tendered, and transport the same to the destination. The refusal of the defendant to transport was on the ground of a quarantine line of the State commission to protect domestic cattle extending to a point through which the said cattle would pass. There was also a quarantine line of the United States Department of Agriculture that did not extend as far as the State line. The suit was brought against the contracting carrier that impleaded the defendant. The court said that the line established by the State commission was void, as the commission had not power to establish one different in its location from the one established by the national authorities, and afforded no justification to the plaintiff for refusing to receive and carry the cattle.

In FARMERS' LOAN & T. CO. *v.* NORTHERN PAC. R. CO. (U. S. Circ. Ct., S. D., N. Y., 1902), 112 Fed. Rep. 829, a quantity of lead was accepted by defendant's agent for shipment over the railroad, and by ship to an eastern port. The railroad had an arrangement with the steamship company to accept freight for its line. The lead was delivered on board the ship, but the deputy collector of the port refused to clear the vessel with the lead on board, as the country to which it was consigned was at war with another one, and the lead was contraband of war. The lead was unloaded and the ship sailed without it. The master of the ship would have been liable to a penalty if he had sailed without clearance papers. The court said that the defendant was not liable for the depreciation in the value of the lead when it arrived at the point across seas, as the shipper could not complain of the failure to obtain clearance as the nature of the shipment was the cause.

4. Agent of connecting carrier.

In NASHVILLE, C. & ST. L. R. CO. *v.* SMITH, (Ala., 1902), 31 So. Rep. 481, where the defendant company delivered freight to a connecting carrier through whose negligence the freight was injured, the fact that whether the agent of the defendant had or had not authority to make the verbal agreement with the plaintiff to deliver the freight at a point where the defendant company did not take freight to be delivered was immaterial, when the defendant company undertook to carry out the agreement.

In MCLAGAN *v.* CHICAGO & N. W. R'Y CO. (Iowa, 1902), 89 N. W. Rep. 233, it was held, where an agent of a receiving carrier had told the shipper that the rates of a connecting carrier were lower than they turned out to be, and the shipper was induced to buy and transport goods over the lines of the receiving and connecting carriers, such receiving carrier was not bound by such statements in the absence of proof of any authority of the agent to so bind the receiving carrier, and it was not liable in an action to recover the difference between the amount alleged to have been stated by the agent as the rate over the lines of the connecting carrier and that actually charged.

In AIKEN *v.* WABASH R. CO. (Mo. App., 1899), 80 Mo. App. 8, the plaintiff checked her trunk through and traveled from Massachusetts to St. Louis, Mo., over three lines of roads; on the first she had a pass. Her ticket was purchased for her at a reduced rate from the next railroad for passage over it and the defendant's line. The ticket contained a limitation of the liability of the railroad from which it was purchased as to recovery for loss of baggage. The trunk was destroyed by fire in the baggage car that was burned by dynamite being carried as baggage unknown to defendants exploding in the car. The court, on appeal, said that viewing the ticket as a contract, the presumption obtained as in other contracts that the plaintiff read or was advised of its conditions and assented thereto, and that the printed conditions on the face of the ticket being part of the contract, the liability of the railroad from which the ticket was bought for loss of baggage was limited to $100, and that this special contract was founded on a valuable consideration, viz., the reduced rate, and further that the limitation in the contract was available to the defendant as a common carrier, as it was acting as agent of the road from which the ticket was bought, and was entitled to the benefit of the original contract of shipment.

In CHICAGO, R. I. & P. R. Co. *v.* WESTERN HAY & GRAIN Co. (Nebraska, 1902), 90 N. W. Rep. 205, the defendant carrier received goods for shipment over its own line and connecting carriers, and collected the charges for the whole distance to the point of destination. The bill of lading contained a clause that the defendant's liability terminated at the end of its line, and upon delivery of the goods to the next carrier. The goods were delivered in good condition to the next carrier after which they were lost or delayed. The court held that the contract was one to deliver goods, not to a connecting carrier, but at destination, and defendant was liable.

In LESSARD *v.* BOSTON AND MAINE R. R. (N. H., 1899), 69 N. H. 648, plaintiff bought a ticket from defendant's agent for passage over it and connecting roads to his destination. The ticket had a coupon for each road, and contained the stipulation that, in selling it and checking baggage, the company was acting only as agent, and was not responsible beyond its own line. The plaintiff could not read, did not know what was on the ticket, and made no inquiry about it. The trunk was lost on one of the connecting lines, that was an independent road. The court below found a verdict for defendants upon the grounds that they were not liable beyond their own line when they had given express notice to that effect. The court, on appeal, said that whether the printed matter was express notice to the purchaser, who was unable to read it, was a question not necessary to consider. That it was incumbent upon the plaintiff to prove that the defendants made a contract to carry his baggage beyond their own line. That under the law of the State, no presumption arose that they made such a contract. That the case differed where the carrier attempted to limit the liability that ordinarily attached to the contract of carriage. That the finding that the defendants gave express notice that they would not contract in a certain way, necessarily included one that it was not proved that they did so contract.

In TALCOTT *v.* WABASH R. R. Co. (N. Y., 1899), 159 N. Y. 461, plaintiff purchased from defendant's agent a ticket having coupons attached for passage over defendant's and connecting roads. With his ticket he went to the baggagemaster and asked to have his sample trunk and personal trunk checked through to his destination. The baggagemaster was informed as to the character of the trunks, and charged for excessive weight, which plaintiff paid. The plaintiff's ticket contained a provision that the defendant company selling the ticket acted as agent, and did not intend to become responsible beyond its own line. The trunk was destroyed by fire on the first line connecting with defendant's road. The court held that the baggagemaster had authority to make the contract with the plaintiff in respect to the sample trunks, and that it was a contract independent of the purchase of the ticket, and that a nonsuit as to that cause of action was improper. That as to the personal baggage of the plaintiff, the ticket controlled, and that, although he had not read it or the conditions, he testified that he knew what a coupon ticket meant, and that he was to travel over connecting roads, and this warranted the inference of notice to him of what was stated in the condition, and having failed to prove a contract as would enable him to recover, a dismissal of the complaint as to the last cause of action was proper.

In HARRIS *v.* MINNEAPOLIS, ST. P. & SAULT STE M. R. Co. (N. Y. Sup. Ct., Appellate Term. 1901), 36 Misc. Rep. 181, the defendant, a connecting carrier, received, transported and safely delivered to the next carrier goods that were held by the latter at their destination at the request of the consignee until he could communicate with the consignor. After the lapse of several months the consignee refused to accept the goods which were sold by auction at a loss to the consignor, who had been informed of the refusal of the consignee and who then directed such sale. The consignor brought this suit for such loss. The court said that the defendant was not liable for the delay of the last carrier in informing the consignor of the consignee's refusal; that the last carrier was not the agent of the defendant, but an independent carrier, for whose negligence the defendant was not liable.

In TOLEDO AND OHIO CENT. R. CO. v. BOWLER AND BURDICK CO. (Ohio, 1900), 63 Ohio St. 274, 9 Am. Neg. Rep. 156, plaintiff's two trunks that the station agent of a connecting line knew contained only watches and jewelry, were checked to a point on defendant's road, and were destroyed in a collision of trains on that road. The court said where the only authority given by a railroad company to the baggage agent of a connecting road is to check baggage to all stations on the line of the former road, no presumption follows that such agent has authority to check merchandise over the line of said road under the guise of baggage, and knowledge on the part of such agent that a passenger's trunks contained merchandise and not baggage is not sufficient to charge such company with knowledge.

In MEXICAN NAT. R. CO. v. WARE (Tex. Civ. App., 1900), 60 S. W. Rep. 343, plaintiff purchased two tickets for himself and wife from a railroad company in Texas, of which the defendant was a connecting line, for transportation to Mexico and return, with stop-over privileges. The tickets contained a clause limiting the amount of recovery for wearing apparel to $100 for each ticket. The trunk was delivered to defendant in Mexico to be transported to Texas, and was lost. It contained, besides clothing, some jewelry, a Bible, a Spanish dictionary and toilet articles. The court said that the laws of Mexico did not apply as the contract was made in Texas, and began there, and was to end there; that by the laws of Texas common carriers cannot limit their liability as it exists at common law, and cannot restrict the right of a passenger to carry baggage necessary for his comfort or convenience by calling it "wearing apparel." A judgment for plaintiff for $750 was affirmed.

In HOUSTON E. & W. T. R'Y v. SEALE (Tex. Civ. App., 1902), 67 S. W. Rep. 437, plaintiff purchased tickets of defendant for transportation over its line and other lines that it connected with, to a point in another State. On arriving at the plaintiff's destination the contents of his trunk was found to have been ruined by wet, and he brought suit for the damage to the articles, and for being deprived of their use, and for the mental distress occasioned thereby. The defendant set up the contract contained in the ticket limiting its liability to $100 on account of baggage. The court held that though the contract was interstate, the State statute prohibiting carriers from limiting their liability, as it existed at common law, applied; that the measure of damages was the actual value of the articles destroyed, and that the allowance of damages for the deprivation of their use and the mental distress occcasioned thereby was erroneous, and on the latter ground the judgment for plaintiff was reversed.

In GULF, C. & S. F. R. CO. v. LEATHERWOOD (Tex. Civ. App., May, 1902), 69 S. W. Rep. 119, two railroad agents agreed between them to transport plaintiff's cattle over their respective roads at a certain price stated, and the connecting carrier further contracted to deliver the cattle at a point on a road that connected with his road, but without consulting the last named road. The initial carrier made the usual bill of lading at the rate specified, and limiting its liability to its own road, and that no one carrier should be liable for the neglect of another, and safely deliver the cattle at the end of its route to the connecting carrier. The connecting carrier made out new bills of lading over its own lines, and also over the lines of the other carrier on whose line was located the point of destination. When the cattle arrived there the freight agent refused to deliver them to plaintiff without the payment of charges greatly in excess of those contracted for. After some delay the amount asked was paid and the cattle delivered, but because of the bad treatment they had received when confined at their destination without water or food, many died and many were depreciated in value. The court said that the connecting carrier having agreed to transport the cattle beyond its own line it was liable for the acts of the other carrier.

5. Connecting carrier failing to limit liability.

In PITTSBURG C. C. & ST. L. R. CO. *v.* VIERS ET AL. (Ky., May, 1902), 68 S. W. Rep. 469, cattle were shipped over a railroad the initial carrier with which the contract was made for shipment over it and connecting carriers without the contract specifying what carriers should complete the transportation. The initial carrier limited its own liability to damages as should occur on its own line, and also further limited its liability and provided that such limitations should inure to the benefit of connecting carriers. It was not shown that the connecting carrier sought to be charged for injury to the cattle on its line knew of these provisions, but it must have known that some contract existed by which the cattle were being transported, and it could have ascertained the terms, or it could have limited its own liability by the terms of the receipt which it gave for the cattle to the intermediate carrier. Having received the cattle without any such limitation the court said the defendant connecting carrier must be assumed to have accepted them under the terms of the original contract, and it was bound as if it had signed the original contract.

In TEXAS & PACIFIC R. CO. *v.* MCCARTY (Tex. Civ. App., June, 1902), 69 S. W. Rep. 229, two railroad companies were sued for damages to cattle occurring on the line of the one that was the connecting carrier of the other which was the initial carrier, and that did not limit its liability to its own line. Judgment was rendered against both companies with judgment in favor of the initial carrier over against the other that was primarily liable. The court held the judgment to be proper as rendered. That the initial carrier need not take advantage of the judgment in its favor if it did not wish, and the connecting carrier could not complain of the judgment against it, as it would have been liable if sued alone.

6. Initial carrier not liable for negligence of connecting carrier.

In HARTLEY *v.* ST. LOUIS, K. & N. W. R. CO (Iowa, 1902), 89 N. W. Rep. 88, some horses being transported by rail were injured on the line of a connecting carrier through the negligence of one of its employees. The contract of shipment by the initial carrier was from a point on its own line through to the destination of the horses, a point on the line of the connecting carrier. The contract also contained a clause limiting the liability of the initial carrier to its own line. The plaintiff signed and received from the connecting line bills of lading, in which the carrier assumed liability. The court said that the contract of limitation of the initial carrier was not invalidated by a section of the

Code providing that no contract shall exempt a railway corporation from a liability which would have existed had no contract been made, as under the common law a carrier is not liable for the negligence of an employee of a connecting carrier in the absence of a contract to that effect. That the contract exempting the carrier from liability for the negligence of the connecting carrier was not against public policy. That the signing and acceptance of the bills of lading from the connecting carrier was evidence that the plaintiff did not regard the initial carrier as having assumed a carrier's liability for the entire distance.

IN TAFFE *v.* OREGON R. Co. (Oregon, 1902), 67 Pac Rep. 1015, some perishable goods that were lost were consigned to New York by the printed bill of lading that contained a blank space for the place of destination with directions not to insert points not on the contracting carrier's lines, and the blank was not filled. It was provided in writing on the bill of lading for "fastest passenger train service consigned as above." A stipulation provided that the carrier would not be liable for loss or damage except on its own lines. The court, on appeal from a judgment for plaintiff, held that the defendant was not liable, that the blank space for insertion of destination was reserved for points on the carrier's own lines, and that the written part was a contract for general carriage only, and that the contract as a whole was to be taken as one to carry safely to the end of the defendant's own line, and there deliver in good order to the next carrier for whose negligence it was not liable.

7. Presumption that injury occurred on line of last connecting carrier.

In MOORE *v.* N. Y., N. H. & H. R. Co. (Mass., 1899), 173 Mass. 335, plaintiff had her trunk checked and traveled over six distinct railroads, for each of which roads she had a separate coupon, but all forming one ticket. The trunk was in good condition, and properly packed when delivered to the first railroad, and she did not see it again until it was delivered to her at her destination by the defendant. Upon opening the trunk it was found that the contents had been wet with water in some unknown manner and greatly damaged, but she was unable to show when, where, or how the damage was done, or in whose possession the trunk was when the damage was done. In the lower court the judge refused to rule that the presumption was that the damage occurred while the trunk was in the possession of the last connecting line of railroad, and rendered judgment for defendant. On appeal the court reversed the judgment, and ordered judgment for plaintiff, and said the rule asked should have been given, and that the presumption was justified as a true presumption of fact.

8. Other cases.

In ST. LOUIS SOUTHWESTERN R. Co. OF TEXAS *v.* FRENCH (Tex. Civ. App., 1900), 23 Tex. Civ. App. 511, plaintiff brought an action for mental distress, pain and anguish caused him and his wife by the alleged negligence of the railroad company in delaying the shipment of the corpse of their child. The plaintiff purchased through tickets for himself, wife, and body of the child, from the agent of a railway company for passage over its line and of that of defendant company, a connecting carrier. Plaintiff saw the corpse on a baggage truck near the door of the express car of defendant's train at the transfer station, but did not inform any one that he wanted the corpse shipped on that train, supposing that it would be so shipped. It was not shipped by that train, but was shipped by an extra train, and arrived at plaintiff's destination an hour and forty-five minutes late. A verdict for $300 was rendered for plaintiff. The court said that an inspection of the coffin would, no doubt, have disclosed its destination, and the company's servants were negligent in failing to do so.

In CROSBY *v.* PERE MARQUETTE R. Co. (Mich., 1902), 91 N. W. Rep. 124, plaintiff, a connecting carrier of defendant, sued for a statutory penalty "to be recovered by the party aggrieved." Goods were shipped over the line of defendant, who refused to take them if required to deliver them to plaintiff as connecting carrier, but accepted them when another connecting carrier was designated. The court said that the shipper was the "party aggrieved" under the statute that provided the penalty for a refusal of a carrier to take and transport a passenger or property offered for transportation, and that to hold that a connecting carrier was also the "party aggrieved" would be an enlargement of the statute, as not more than a single penalty was contemplated.

In GULF, C. & S. F. R. Co. *v.* CUSHNEY (Sup. Ct., Tex., 1902), an action for damages for delay of connecting carriers in shipping cattle over their roads, it was held that an instruction which in effect directed the jury to find first the whole amount of the damage done by all the defendants, and then "apportion" it among them, "according to and in proportion to their respective liability, as indicated by instructions already given," was not objectionable as authorizing the jury to fix the liability of each according to an arbitrary rule, and not according to the evidence when there were other instructions directing an apportionment of damage that was caused by each defendant solely, and that there should not be apportioned against one the damage caused by another.

TEXAS STATE FAIR v. MARTI.

Court of Civil Appeals, Texas, July, 1902.

ACCIDENT ON STATE FAIR GROUNDS — EXHIBITION OF FIREWORKS — FALL OF STAND — LIABILITY OF STATE-FAIR CORPORATION. — In an action to recover damages for injuries sustained by plaintiff's wife, caused by the fall of a stand while attending a fireworks display given by an exhibitor on the grounds of the defendant, a State-Fair corporation, it was held that, notwithstanding the negligent construction of the stand by the exhibitor, the defendant corporation was liable for the injury, as it was its duty to use ordinary care to see that the seats on the stand provided for use of persons attending the show given by the exhibitor were in a reasonably safe condition (1).

PERSONAL INJURIES — PLEADING — EVIDENCE. — Where a petition alleges injuries to specific parts of the body, it is error to admit evidence of injuries to other parts not set out in the petition.

1. See on this point Sebeck *v.* Plattdeutsche Volkfest Verein (N. J., June, 1900), 8 Am. Neg. Rep. 84, where it was held that "the owner of a private park, who invites the public to it for the purpose of looking at an exhibition of fireworks, is not relieved from all responsibility for the safety of his guests by reason of the fact that the exhibition is to be given, not by himself, but by an independent contractor. He is bound to use reasonable care to provide them with a safe place from which to view the exhibition. He is further bound, in making his contract, to use care to select a skilful and competent person to give the exhibition."

ERROR from District Court, Dallas County.

Action by Henry Marti against the Texas State Fair. From a judgment for plaintiff, defendant brings error. *Judgment reversed.*

PLOWMAN & BAKER, for plaintiff in error.

CRAWFORD & CRAWFORD, FORD & CRAWFORD and W. T. STRANGE, for defendant in error.

TEMPLETON, J. — This writ of error was sued out from a judgment recovered by Henry Marti against the Texas State Fair on account of personal injuries sustained by his wife while attending a fireworks exhibition given by Smith & Lucas on the grounds of the plaintiff in error. The injuries were caused by the falling of the stand upon which Mrs. Marti was seated. The plaintiff in error is a corporation organized for the purpose of conducting the Texas State Fair and Dallas Exposition. It owns extensive grounds in the city of Dallas, where it gives annual fairs, which are attended by great numbers of people, who are charged admission fees. Many attractions of various kinds are exhibited, some by the plaintiff in error and some by parties authorized by it to display their devices within the grounds. Part of the grounds of the plaintiff in error is known as the "old baseball park." On May 29, 1900, plaintiff in error entered into a written agreement with Smith & Lucas, by which it conceded to them the exclusive use of said park during the continuance of the fair to be held from September 29 to October 14, 1900, for the purpose of exhibiting a production designated as the "Great Chicago Fire," each night during that time. It was provided that Smith & Lucas should furnish at their own expense all ticket sellers and spielers, etc., and that the Texas State Fair should furnish at its own expense all ticket takers necessary for the proper conduct of the said entertainments; that no admission should be allowed except by tickets of admission, and that all complimentary tickets issued by each party should be charged up in full to the party issuing same; that the gross receipts from tickets of admission both into the gates as well as to the grand stand or reserved seats should be divided at the close of each night's entertainment between the parties, the plaintiff in error to receive twenty-five per cent. thereof and Smith & Lucas the remainder. At the time of the making of the aforesaid contract there were a considerable number of seats in the said park which had been placed there by the plaintiff in error, and it was agreed in the contract that Smith & Lucas should have the use of said seats. It was thought that the seating capacity provided was inadequate, and Smith & Lucas erected other seats. It was these last-named seats which fell. The plaintiff in error did not supervise the erection of said seats, or direct how the work should be done, and none of its officers or agents in any way assisted in the construction of the seats. The plaintiff in error extensively advertised the show to be given by Smith & Lucas in the newspapers, and invited the public to attend the same. It was while the fair was in progress, and the fireworks of Smith & Lucas were being exhibited under the aforesaid contract, that Mrs. Marti was injured. She had paid for admission to the grounds. A great crowd was in attendance that night, and the evidence indicates that the seats were caused to fall by reason of some negligence in not having the same properly constructed and safeguarded. Shortly before the accident occurred the tax collector of Dallas county approached the officers of the plaintiff in error, and sought to ascertain whether Smith & Lucas were liable for an occupation tax. He was informed by the said officers that the exhibition was a part of the fair, and came under the tax paid by the plaintiff in error. Soon after the accident the tax collector was notified by the plaintiff in error, through its officers, that the exhibition of Smith & Lucas was entirely independent of the fair, and that the tax paid by it did not cover the said exhibition.

The plaintiff in error contends that, if the injuries to Mrs. Marti were caused by the negligence of any one, the negligence was that of Smith & Lucas, who were independent contractors, and not its agents, and for whose acts it was in no way responsible. If this contention is correct, the plaintiff in error is not liable herein. We are of opinion that the position of plaintiff in error is not tenable. It permitted the exhibition to be given on its grounds, and invited the public to attend. All the tickets of admission were taken up by its agents, and one-fourth of the gross receipts of the show was paid to it. Under these circumstances it was the duty of the plaintiff in error to exercise ordinary care to prevent injury to those attending the entertainment. This is certainly true regarding the safety of the premises. The rule on this subject is stated in Cooley, Torts (2d Ed.), p. 718, in this language: "It has been stated * * * that one is under no obligation to keep his premises in a safe condition for the visits of trespassers. On the other hand, when he expressly or by implication invites others to come upon his premises, whether for business or any other purpose, it is his duty to be reasonably sure he is not inviting them into danger, and to that end he must exercise ordinary care and prudence to render the premises reasonably safe for the visit. Many cases illustrate this rule. Thus, individuals holding a fair, and erecting structures for the purpose, are liable for injuries to their patrons caused by the breaking down of these structures through such defects in construction as the exercise of proper care would have avoided." No matter by whom the seats were erected, it was the duty of the plaintiff in error to see that the same were in a reasonably safe condition before inviting the public to occupy them. Richmond & Manchester R'y Co *v.* Moore's Adm'r (Va.), 2 Am. Neg. Rep. 473, 27 S. E. Rep. 70; Conradt *v.* Glauve, 93 Ind. 478; Sebeck *v.* Plattdeutsche Volkfest Verein (N. J Err. & App.), 8 Am. Neg. Rep. 84, 46 Atl. Rep. 631. Our conclusion is that the trial court did not err in instructing the jury that it was the duty of the Texas State Fair to use ordinary care to see that the seats provided for the use of persons attending the show given by Smith & Lucas were in a reasonably safe condition.

On the trial the plaintiff was permitted to prove that Mrs. Marti was injured internally, and that her groins and ovaries were affected. This evidence was objected to on the ground that no such injuries were alleged in the petition. The objections were overruled, and exceptions duly reserved. We find that the testimony was improperly admitted. The allegations of the petition concerning the alleged injuries to Mrs. Marti read thus: "That her head, back, side, arms, and stomach were seriously injured, and her nervous system greatly shocked; that one of her ankles was strained and bruised and so injured that it cannot recover, and will be stiff and useless the balance of her life." The groins and ovaries are not included in any organ or part of the body alleged to have been injured, and the injuries thereto were not the result of the other injuries set out in the petition. It is, of course, well settled that no injuries can be proved except those alleged, and because this rule was not observed on the trial hereof the judgment must be reversed.

The defendant demurred to plaintiff's petition, which demurrers were overruled, and we are asked to revise the ruling of the trial court on that point. While we are not prepared to hold that the petition is subject to the exception, we are inclined to think that the objections to the plea could be wholly obviated, and that the better practice is that this should be done. We make this suggestion in view of another trial, and to avoid having the record, in case of another appeal, incumbered with a question which is not entirely free from doubt.

The testimony of Dr. Moseley as to the declarations made to him by Mrs. Marti concerning her injuries should be confined to involuntary expressions of present pain, and no statement made by her to him relating to any other matter should be admitted. Railway Co. *v.* Johnson (Tex. Sup.), 67 S. W. Rep. 768.

For the error in admitting evidence concerning internal injuries to Mrs. Marti and injury to her groins and ovaries, the judgment is reversed, and the cause remanded. Reversed and remanded.

NOLL v. CITY OF SEATTLE.

Supreme Court, Washington, July, 1902.

FALLING INTO EXCAVATION IN STREET — EVIDENCE — NOTICE TO CITY. — In an action to recover damages for injuries sustained by plaintiff who fell into an excavation made in a much-traveled street by a property owner, evidence tending to show that the excavation had been uncovered for several days, was unguarded and without barriers or sufficient light to show excavation, and that the city had given permission for it to be made, was sufficient to show knowledge on part of city of negligent condition of excavation (1).

1. *Liability of city for defective highway.* — In BRABON ET AL. v. CITY OF SEATTLE (*Washington, July, 1902*), 69 Pac. Rep. 3. judgment for plaintiffs was affirmed, the opinion by FULLERTON, J., showing the following facts: "Brabon was a member of the paid fire department of the city of Seattle. He was killed while on the way to a fire by the overturning of a hose cart on which he was riding. This action was brought to recover for his death. On the day of the accident he rode in his accustomed and proper place on the rear platform of the cart, which was being driven by its regular driver, whose duty it was to regulate the speed and select the route of the cart while on the road from the fire station to the place of the fire. While proceeding on his way at the time in question, the driver turned into an ungraded street, known as "East St. John street," where he ran onto a root extending from a stump on the side of the traveled way partially across the track, which caused the cart to overturn and fall upon Brabon, inflicting the injuries from which he died. From the judgment in favor of the respondents the city appeals. The appellant first contends that because the evidence fails to show that the city had graded the street, or had otherwise attempted to improve or prepare it for public travel, it is not liable for injuries caused by defects therein, claiming that as to the city it was a street only in name, and that any one using it did so without invitation from the city, either express or implied, and consequently at his peril. There are cases which maintain the rule that the mere fact of establishing a highway by judicial action does not of itself so open it to the public as to render the municipality liable for injuries that may occur to travelers thereon because of defects therein; and this perhaps is the general rule. There are cases also which hold that a dedication by a landowner of a public street, unaccepted by the municipality in which it is situated either by ordinance, resolution, or other appropriate formal action, or by user short of the period necessary to establish a highway by prescription, will not have that effect. But neither of these rules applies to the facts of the case before us. Here the street

APPEAL from Superior Court, King County.

Action by Frederick Noll against the City of Seattle for injuries received from an excavation in a city street. From a judgment for plaintiff, the defendant appeals. *Judgment affirmed.*

W. E. HUMPHREY and EDWARD VON TOBEL, for appellant.

FREDERICK R. BURCH, for respondent.

REAVIS, Ch. J. — Action to recover damages for personal injuries. It appears that defendant had given permission to a property owner who was operating a laundry to uncover or make an excavation in Main street. Such excavation was made, and, while without barriers or cover around it, the plaintiff fell into it, and sustained the injuries complained of. When the plaintiff's testimony was concluded, a motion for nonsuit was made by defendant. Two grounds for nonsuit were urged: 1. That the city had no notice of the unguarded condition of the excavation at the time the accident occurred; and, 2, that the plaintiff was guilty of contributory negligence.

Relative to the first ground, it may be said the evidence on the part of plaintiff tended to show that the excavation had been uncovered for several days, and was at times unguarded; that there was not sufficient light to show the excavation; and that when plaintiff was injured there were no barriers for protection of any sort around the excavation. It will also be noted that the city had given permission for the street to be uncovered and the excavation to be made. This permission, taken in connection with the other evidence that the excavation was in a public and much-traveled street, was sufficient for the jury to infer knowledge on the part of the city of the negligent condition in which the

was dedicated in 1875. The city has so far recognized it as a public street of the city as to change its name by ordinance, and to lay a sewer along it. It has graded the streets running at right angles to it on each end, and suffered and permitted it to be used without objection by vehicles of all kinds for a period long enough to establish a highway by prescription under the statutes of this state. It may be that the demands upon it did not require it to be graded or cleared for its full width; but the city, after having recognized it as a public street, and permitted its use thereafter, was bound to maintain a reasonably safe way along it sufficient to accommodate the travel upon it, and is liable, under the rule in this State, to one who, without fault, is injured thereon because of defects therein, while using it for a lawful purpose, and in the manner it was intended to be used. Rowe *v.* City of Ballard, 19 Wash. 1, 3 Am. Neg. Rep. 743n, 52 Pac. Rep. 321; Taake *v.* City of Seattle, 18 Wash. 178, 3 Am. Neg. Rep. 743n, 51 Pac. Rep. 362; Sutton *v.* City of Snohomish, 11 Wash. 24, 39 Pac. Rep. 273; Cowie *v.* City of Seattle, 22 Wash. 659, 62 Pac. Rep. 121; Einseidler *v.* Whitman Co., 22 Wash. 388." * * * Judgment affirmed.

excavation was left. For a pertinent discussion of the knowledge imputed to defendant, see Beall *v.* City of Seattle (Wash.), 69 Pac. Rep. 12 (1). Relative to contributory negligence, the evidence showed that plaintiff had engaged in a brawl some two blocks from the place of the accident, and ran away rapidly from the persons with whom the difficulty occurred and in his course ran into the front and out of the rear door of a saloon, and through an alley onto Main street, and into the excavation. The manner in which he got onto the street, and the rate of speed at which he was going, were facts to be submitted to the jury.

No error of law appearing on the record, the judgment is affirmed.

ANDERS, HADLEY, FULLERTON, MOUNT and DUNBAR, JJ., concur.

1. BEALL *v.* CITY OF SEATTLE (*Washington, May, 1902*), 69 Pac. Rep. 12, was an appeal from judgment on verdict directed for defendant in Superior Court, King county, in action by plaintiff for personal injuries received from an explosion which occurred underneath the sidewalk on which the plaintiff was walking, near the corner of Second Avenue South and Washington street, in the city of Seattle. Judgment reversed. The syllabus to the report in 69 Pac. Rep. 12, states the point as to notice to city, as follows: "A carpenter, employed to construct a sidewalk basement and place a heating apparatus therein, applied to the board of public works for a permit, and was referred to the assistant building inspector, who informed the carpenter that a permit to place the heating apparatus under the sidewalk was not required, and told him how to place it, and issued a permit to construct a stairway from the street to the basement of the building. The chairman of the board of public works testified, in an action against the city by a person injured, while walking on the sidewalk, by an explosion of the heating plant, that the assistant building inspector was the proper person to whom such applications should be made. The basement was not constructed as required by Seattle City Ordinance No. 2833, secs. 5, 22, specifying the manner of constructing sidewalk basements, and requiring the building inspector to visit every building in the course of erection, and require the construction to be in accordance with the ordinances. *Held*, to show actual notice to the city of alterations intended to be made under the sidewalk, as an attachment to the building, sufficient to raise a question for the jury, — whether the city should have known of the location and purposes of the heating plant, and of the nature of the entire work."

ZAHN v. MILWAUKEE AND SUPERIOR RAILWAY COMPANY.

Supreme Court, Wisconsin, April, 1902.

BRAKEMAN INJURED COUPLING CARS — ASSUMPTION OF RISK. — **In an action to recover damages for injuries sustained by plaintiff, a brakeman in defendant's employ, while coupling cars, it appeared that at the time of the injury the engine was in charge of plaintiff's brother, the fireman, the engineer having gone to dinner, and the train crew then consisted of the fireman, plaintiff and two other brakemen; that one of the brakemen gave a signal to back up to make a coupling, and two cars were coupled, and that while plaintiff ran to another car to adjust a link for the coupling, the engine continued backing and plaintiff's fingers were caught between the bumpers and crushed; that it was the custom on defendant's road on signal to back engine to make a coupling to continue backing until signal to stop was given; that plaintiff was familiar with the custom, having been in defendant's employ seven or eight years; and the fireman testified that he did not know plaintiff was making the coupling. *Held*, that plaintiff, knowing the custom, assumed the risk incident thereto. *Held*, also, that there was no evidence to justify finding of jury of negligence on the part of the fireman (1).**

1. See the following recent Master and Servant cases in Wisconsin:

Employee injured in coal yard — Fellow-servant. — In OKONSKI *v.* PENNSYLVANIA & OHIO COAL CO. (*Wisconsin, May, 1902*), 90 N. W. Rep. 429, judgment for plaintiff, an employee in defendant's coal yard, was reversed, the facts of the case, as stated by DODGE, J., being as follows: "Action for personal injuries suffered by the plaintiff as an employee in the coal yard of the defendant at Manitowoc. That yard was about 500 feet long north and south, bounded on the east by the slip into which the vessels entered. Immediately adjoining the water were a series of four towers on tracks parallel to the dock line, some thirty-five feet high, in each of which was situated a steam engine and its operator. Extending from each of these towers westward to the hard coal shed, a distance of about 150 feet, was a steel cable, upon which the buckets lifted from the vessel were transported by the engine located in the tower. The coal carried in these buckets might be delivered at various points between the tower on the east and the coal shed at the extreme western terminus of the cable. Thus, immediately west of the row of towers was an open space of perhaps seventy five feet in width, known as the 'platform,' upon which it was customary to dump soft coal, and which at times was piled up over its whole surface therewith, although at the time of the injury it was nearly free from coal. Next to this open space were a series of four hoppers, about twenty-eight feet from the ground, located one under each of the cables and each communicating over screens with a railroad track, onto which cars were customarily run to receive coal which it was desired to put immediately aboard cars. The buckets held about a ton of coal each. The usual method of causing them to

APPEAL from Circuit Court, Waukesha County.

Action by Albert Zahn against the Milwaukee and Superior Railway Company. From a judgment for plaintiff, defendant appeals. *Judgment reversed.*

Action under section 1816, Rev. St. 1898, to recover damages for personal injuries claimed to have been sustained by plaintiff while in the discharge of his duties as brakeman for defendant. The accident occurred a little after noon on November 3, 1899. The plaintiff was engaged in coupling cars on a side track in the yard at North Lake station. The negligence alleged is that the fireman, who was in charge of the engine while the engineer was at dinner, backed the engine, with several cars attached, without any signal

dump at one place or another was by placing upon the cable, at about the spot, a device called a 'tripper' or 'dumper,' which, coming in contact with the latch upon the bucket, caused it to empty. These trippers also ran on trolley wheels along the cable, being secured at the westerly end to the stanchions of the shed and running down by their own weight when the rope holding them was loosened. When it was desired to empty the buckets at any point between the tower and the shed, this tripper was, by certain of the employees, lowered down by this rope to the desired point, and the rope then secured. The method of doing this was for a man to go up to the roof of the shed to handle the rope, and another to stand in his sight upon the platform, and signal to him when the proper point had been reached. At a little after four o'clock on the day in question, to wit, the 30th day of November, 1897, the unloading of a new vessel was commenced, and the buckets, which from the preceding vessel had been emptying at their extreme western terminus into the coal shed, were desired to be emptied into the hoppers above spoken of, adjoining the railroad track. Accordingly, one Graham, who is designated as a foreman, directed two of the men on the dock to go up and lower the tripper on the southernmost cable, known as 'cable No. 1,' saying that he would signal to them when it had reached the right point. This process was called 'spotting.' They untied the rope, cast off a considerable amount of slack, and let the tripper run down. For some reason—whether because they did not keep sufficient control of it, or because Graham did not signal soon enough—it ran down to a point some ten or fifteen feet east of where it should be for the purpose of making the bucket empty into the hopper, and Graham immediately gave signals to haul it back, but before that could be done the engineer in the tower sent a bucket of coal westward on the cable, having no knowledge of what was going on at the other end. The bucket came in contact with the tripper, and its contents were precipitated onto the platform just as the plaintiff was passing under the cable in the performance of his duties in going toward the south end of the yard to aid in pushing down some railway cars. It was in proof that it was a stormy night, and quite dark, but that the yard was lighted by eight electric lights, so that the cable was easily in sight of those walking under it; but there was evidence also that it was customary to fix a gasoline torch near the eastern corner of the hopper when dumping coal there, which enabled the engineer in the tower to see when the bucket from plaintiff, and without any notice or signal to plaintiff, suddenly against a car that plaintiff was preparing with coupling links, and caught and crushed his hand. A motion for a nonsuit at the close of plaintiff's testimony was denied, as was also a motion to direct a verdict for defendant at the close of the testimony. Both rulings were duly excepted to. A special verdict was submitted, in which the jury found substantially as follows: 1. That plaintiff was injured while in defendant's employment; 2, that he was injured by having his right hand caught between the bumpers of the cars; 3, that the fireman was in charge of the engine; 4, that the engine and cars attached to it were pushed back against the car the plaintiff was preparing for coupling, without any signal from plaintiff; 5, that the

approached its destination, and slow it up somewhat before its collision with the tripper. Those torches were supplied, and it was the duty of certain members of the crew in the yard to put them in place when desired by the engineers. None had yet been placed on the hopper near which the plaintiff was injured. Plaintiff had worked about coal yards for twelve or fifteen years, but upon this particular yard, which varied somewhat in its apparatus, only about six days. The work done upon the dock and yard was various, consisting generally in the unloading of coal from the vessels, the distribution thereof to various parts of the yard both by the cables in question and by wheelbarrows, the incidental screening of it, the loading upon railway cars, and the removal of the screenings to other parts of the yard. Plaintiff was a common laborer engaged in such work as was indicated to him, and on the day in question had been wheeling soft coal from the north end of the platform to some other point. At the time of injury, as already stated, he had started with two other men to move cars down onto the railway track adjoining the hoppers. Motion to direct verdict for defendant was overruled, and a special verdict in answer to twenty-seven questions was taken upon which, after motion for new trial, judgment was rendered in favor of the plaintiff, from which the defendant appeals." * * * The court discussed the question of fellow-servants and held that the injury was occasioned by the negligent manner in which the work was done and that the foreman, in assisting in the work, was a fellow-servant of plaintiff, for which defendant was not liable. Judgment for plaintiff reversed.

Employee injured in coal yard — Unsafe place. — In NIX *v.* C. REISS COAL CO. *(Wisconsin, May, 1902)*, 90 N. W. Rep. 437, judgment for plaintiff, an employee in defendant's coal yard, was affirmed, the facts being stated by DODGE, J., as follows: "Action for personal injuries suffered by the plaintiff as an employee in defendant's coal yard at Sheboygan. That coal yard extended two or three hundred feet north and south along the water's edge, which was on its west. The westerly part of it consisted of a shed under which the hard coal was kept, and the easterly part was open dumping ground for soft coal, and bounded easterly by railroad tracks. The portions devoted to the two different kinds of coal were separated by a fence a short distance east of the eaves of the coal shed. The yard was completely traversed by a superstructure of tracks for the distribution of coal in small cars. This structure consisted of upright ten by ten posts, approximately twenty feet engine and cars were so pushed back without any notice to plaintiff; 6, that they were pushed back without any knowledge on the part of plaintiff; 7, that plaintiff was engaged in the capacity of brakeman; 8, that plaintiff was not then employed in the capacity of conductor; 9, that the plaintiff had no knowledge of the absence of the engineer; 10, that plaintiff did not notify the fireman he was going between the cars; 11, that plaintiff did not see the approaching car in time to have removed his hand from between the two drawbars; 11 1-2, that plaintiff did not hear the approaching engine and cars in time to have removed his hand; 12, that plaintiff was not injured in consequence of a movement of the cars in the usual and ordinary

high, and twenty feet apart in each direction. These posts were surmounted by eight by eight or eight by ten timbers, running over their tops from north to south, secured from slipping off by the spiking of two-inch plank onto the upright posts and onto the surmounting timbers, forming caps, so called. On top of, and at right angles to, these north and south timbers, and along each line of posts running east and west, were the tracks, which were supported by two planks, three by ten, set edgewise. The upright posts were braced to each other and to the ground. On December 31, 1900, the yard was mainly filled with coal extending to a height of some eighteen feet, or nearly up to the timbers on top of these posts. On that day a fire broke out which destroyed the coal sheds and burned down some of the superstructure of tracks, reaching in this respect about to the fence dividing the hard and soft coal, but leaving the track structure undestroyed from thence eastward to the ailroad tracks, although fire had run over it to some extent further eastward, charring and blackening it. The fire also communicated itself to the piles of coal, and apparently for some days afterward the fire department poured water copiously onto the coal, which in many places formed a thick coating or crust of ice, mingled, of course, with the upper portions of the coal. Commencing on the 1st of January, the defendant set to work a gang of men, who commenced on the east side of the yard, and proceeded to move the soft coal piled therein into cars on the railroad track above mentioned, working their way gradually westward. The plaintiff was amongst those employed; his business, like that of others, being to shovel the coal from the pile into a wheelbarrow, and wheel it to the railroad cars. In doing this it was continually necessary for some of the men to climb on top of the pile with picks and break down the icy crust, and the peril from such falling lumps or chunks was of frequent occurrence, and was obvious to all of the workmen. On the 19th of January the work had progressed so that the plaintiff and those immediately with him were working under the last section of the tram-track structure, which remained undestroyed by fire, and were within about twenty feet of the fence dividing the hard and soft coal. A few days before, the tram track structure immediately south of where they were at work had been pulled down by cutting off the upright posts, and by sawing off the north and south timbers on a line about six feet south of the uprights which were left standing. Plaintiff, together with other workmen, had participated in the taking down of such structure by pulling on ropes after the cutting away had been done. On the day in question, manner; 13, that the condition of the coupling apparatus was not the sole and proximate cause of plaintiff s injury; 14, that plaintiff was injured by the negligence of the fireman in charge of the engine; 14 1-2, that a person of ordinary care, under the circumstances, should not have known that the engineer was absent from the engine; 15, that plaintiff was not guilty of any want of ordinary care which contributed directly to produce the injury; 16, that the defendant's employee was guilty of negligence which was the natural probable cause of the accident, and which accident ought to have been foreseen by a person of ordinary care and prudence;

one of the crew with whom the plaintiff was at work went up on top of the pile to break down the icy crust, and succeeded in breaking off a mass of some sixty or seventy pounds' weight, which rolled down the inclined face of the coal pile, and struck the southwesternmost upright there standing, from about which the coal had been removed, so that only about three or four feet of it was still uncovered. The collision was followed immediately by the fall of the north and south horizontal timber resting on top of that upright, together with some of the superstructure above, whereby plaintiff was severely injured. The upright did not fall, but after the fall of the superstructure was found still standing, but the top leaning slightly westward; the timber having fallen on the easterly side of it. A special verdict of nineteen questions was taken, the material parts of which are to the effect that plaintiff was working at a place directed by one Roth, as foreman; that the support or fastenings of the beam which fell had been so far destroyed by the fire as to render the place where plaintiff was at work when he was injured an unsafe and dangerous place; that the fall of said beam was caused by such destruction of its supports and fastenings; that the defendant, through its proper representative, knew that the place was then unsafe and dangerous, and that by the exercise of ordinary care the defendant should have made the place in question reasonably safe before the time when the plaintiff was injured; that the defendant should 'reasonably have foreseen * * * that the natural and probable consequence of permitting the trestlework and the supports or fastenings of said beam or timber to remain in the condition in which they were at and before the time of the injury would be to cause said beam to fall upon and injure some of the coal shovelers;' that the condition of the trestlework and the supports or fastenings of said beam were the proximate cause of plaintiff's injury; that the plaintiff's injury was not the result of accident or misfortune which defendant could not have foreseen and prevented by the exercise of ordinary care; that the plaintiff did not have knowledge of the unsafe and dangerous character of the place, nor by the exercise of ordinary care should he have had such knowledge; and that no want of ordinary care on his part contributed to produce the injury. Defendant at the close of the evidence moved for the direction of a verdict in its favor, and afterwards moved to reverse the answers to most of the material questions, and also moved to set aside the verdict and for a new trial, all of which motions were denied, and judgment entered in favor of the plaintiff, from which the defendant appeals." Judgment for plaintiff affirmed.

17, damages, $2,500. Defendant submitted a motion "for an order setting aside the answers to questions numbered, respectively, 12, 14, 14 1-2, 15, and 16, in the special verdict rendered by the jury herein, for the reason that the same are unsupported by the evidence, and are against the uncontradicted evidence, and changing and perfecting the said special verdict in accordance with the uncontradicted evidence by answering question number twelve 'Yes,' question number fourteen 'No,' question number fourteen and one-half 'Yes,' question number fifteen 'Yes,' and question number sixteen 'No,' and granting judgment in favor of the defendant and against the plaintiff on the said special verdict as so changed and perfected, and upon the uncontradicted evidence." This motion was denied, and plaintiff's motion for judgment was granted Defendant's appeal is from the judgment.

SPOONER & ROSECRANTZ, for appellant.

RYAN, MERTON & NEWBURY, for respondent.

BARDEEN, J. (after stating the facts). — The plaintiff argues that, inasmuch as there was no motion for a new trial, the only question to be considered is whether there is any evidence to support the findings challenged. So far as relates to a decision of the question raised by the denial of the motion for a nonsuit, many of the cases say that, in absence of a motion for a new trial, the court will not review the evidence. The rule is this regard is sufficiently stated in Guetzkow *v.* Smith, 105 Wis. 94, 80 N. W. 1109. It rests upon the fact that evidence may have been admitted before the close of the trial sufficient to warrant a submission of the case to the jury. But when there has been a motion for a direction of a verdict, with due exception preserved in the record, the rule is different. In such a situation this court will review the testimony in order to determine whether the motion should have been granted.. Bank *v.* Larson, 80 Wis. 469, 50 N. W. 499; Plankinton *v.* Gorman, 93 Wis. 560, 67 N. W. 1128; McGinn *v.* French, 107 Wis. 54. 82 N. W. 724.

The points made by defendant are that the undisputed evidence shows that the engine was being operated in the usual and ordinary manner, and that the plaintiff was guilty of contributory negligence as a matter of law. The negligence upon which plaintiff's claim of recovery is based is that the engine and cars attached were pushed back against the car which plaintiff was preparing for coupling without a signal from or warning to the plaintiff. The evidence shows that at the time of the injury the engine was in charge of plaintiff's brother, who was the fireman. The engineer had gone to his dinner, and the fireman was operating the engine. The train crew then consisted of the fireman, the plaintiff, and two other brakemen. There were several cars on the side track near the east end, which were not coupled together. The evidence is somewhat vague as to their exact location. The engine was backed in on the switch at the east end. The brakeman, Sykes, gave a signal to back up to make a coupling, and two cars were coupled, Sykes making one and the plaintiff the other. There was yet one car to be attached, about two car lengths distant. Plaintiff ran to the stationary car to adjust a link for the coupling. While so engaged, the engine, with the cars attached, continued backing west, and plaintiff's fingers were caught between the bumpers and crushed. The undisputed evidence shows that it was the custom on defendant's road that when a signal is given to the person operating the engine to move backwards to make a coupling to continue backing until a signal to stop is given. The brakeman, Sykes, gave a signal to move backwards, and the two couplings were made. The engine continued moving slowly backwards, without any signal to stop until after plaintiff was injured. This was in conformity to the usual custom of the road. The plaintiff had been in the employ of defendant seven or eight years, and had had charge of a train for a year or two before the accident. He was familiar with the manner of operating its trains, and must be presumed to have known of the custom mentioned. Moreover, it is to be noted that after the engine had been cut off from the cars on the main line the plaintiff had not been in touch with the acting engineer in any way whatever. The signal for the movement of the engine had been given by the brakeman, Sykes, and the couplings made were in obedience to his directions. The fireman testified that he did not know his brother was making a coupling. In view of this fact, it is difficult to see any basis for the plaintiff's recovery. The engine was being handled and moved strictly in accordance with the established custom of the road. The plaintiff certainly knew of such custom, and, knowing it, assumed the usual and ordinary risk incident thereto. It is also difficult to see any ground for saying the acting engineer was negligent. If he did not know the plaintiff was making a coupling, he was not bound to give him a warning or to make a signal as the cars were moving. No ground is apparent for saying that he ought to have known the plaintiff was between the cars. There is no room for conflicting inferences from the facts disclosed. They all point one way. The jury, by its twelfth finding, say that plaintiff was not injured in consequence of a movement of the cars in the usual and ordinary way. The only testimony on the subject given by plaintiff's brother and the superintendent of the road was directly contrary to this finding. By the fourteenth finding they say plaintiff was injured by the negligence of the fireman in charge of the engine. Assuming the engine was being run in the usual and ordinary manner, we look in vain for anything in the record to support this conclusion. Without some showing upon which the finding of negligence can rest, there is no foundation for the verdict, and the other findings become immaterial. We may say, in passing, that the finding against plaintiff's contributory negligence has very little in the record to warrant it. The court should have granted defendant's motion to direct a verdict. Not having done so, it was his duty to have corrected the answers of the jury in the special verdict, and to have rendered judgment for defendant. Menominee River S. & D. Co. *v.* Milwaukee & N. R. Co., 91 Wis. 447, 65 N. W. Rep. 176; Conroy *v.* Chicago, St. P. M. & O. R'y Co., 96 Wis. 243, 2 Am. Neg. Rep. 98; Keller *v.* Schmidt, 104 Wis. 596, 80 N. W. Rep. 935; Stafford *v.* Railroad Co., 110 Wis. 331, 85 N. W. Rep. 1036.

The judgment is reversed, and the cause is remanded, with directions to the Circuit Court to correct the verdict by changing the answer to the twelfth question from "No" to "Yes," and the answer to the fourteenth question from "Yes" to "No," and the answer to the sixteenth question from "Yes" to "No," to conform to the facts, and to render a judgment on the verdict as so corrected in favor of defendant for costs.

FIREMAN FATALLY INJURED BY BEING SCALDED BY ESCAPING STEAM FROM BOILER OF ENGINE AGAINST WHICH HE WAS THROWN BY COLLISION BETWEEN TWO SECTIONS OF TRAIN — SUPERIOR SERVANTS — STATUTE.— In SOUTHERN PACIFIC COMPANY *v.* SCHOER (*United States Circuit Court of Appeals, Eighth Circuit, March, 1902*), 114 Fed. Rep. 466, judgment for plaintiff in United States Circuit Court for the District of Utah, was affirmed, SANBORN, Circuit Judge, delivering the opinion, and stating the facts as follows: "Between one and two o'clock on the dark and foggy morning of December 20, 1899, the second section of a passenger train of the Southern Pacific Company, upon which H. A. Schoer was a fireman, ran into the rear of the first section near the yard limits of the company at Terrace, in the State of Utah, threw this fireman against the boiler of the engine, and fastened him there under a mass of coal, which was thrown from the tender by the shock of the collision, until he was so scalded by steam that escaped on account of the breaking of the water gauge that he died. C. Schoer, the administrator of his estate, brought an action against this company for alleged negligence causing his death, and obtained a verdict and judgment which this writ of error has been sued out to review." * * *

The syllabus by the court states the points decided as follows:

"1. The states have the right to regulate within reasonable limits the relations between employers and employees within their borders, and to fix by legislative enactments the liabilities of the former for the acts and negligence of the latter.

"2. Sections 1342 and 1343 of the Revised Statutes of Utah make all servants employed in the service of a master doing business in that State, who are intrusted by him with authority to command his other servants, or with the authority to direct another of his servants in the discharge of his duties, vice-principals of their master, and charge him with liability for their negligence whether it was committed in the discharge of the positive duties of the master or in the performance of the primary duties of the servants.

"3. Those sections make the master liable for the negligence of superior servants committed in the discharge of their duties as employees, whether the negligence was committed while they were exercising their authority to command or superintend others or not.

"4. A writing which contains competent evidence upon a material issue cannot be lawfully rejected because it also contains evidence which is incompetent and irrelevant.

"5. Nothing less than such a fortuitous gathering of circumstances as prevents the performance of a duty, and such as could not have been foreseen by the exercise of reasonable prudence, or overcome by the exercise of reasonable care and diligence, constitutes an act of God which will excuse the discharge of duty."

SEGO v. SOUTHERN PACIFIC COMPANY.

Supreme Court, California, October, 1902.

PERSON KILLED WHILE CROSSING TRACK IN FRONT OF RAPIDLY MOVING TRAIN AT CROSSING—NEGLIGENCE OF RAILROAD COMPANY—CONTRIBUTORY NEGLIGENCE—NONSUIT.—In an action to recover damages for death of plaintiff's son who was killed while attempting to cross defendant's railroad track in front of a moving train which was run at great speed at a crossing much used by the public where no flagman was in attendance, it was *held* that the contributory negligence of the deceased barred recovery, notwithstanding the negligence of the railroad company in the particulars mentioned, and judgment of nonsuit was affirmed (1).

DEPARTMENT 1. Appeal from Superior Court, Solano County.

Action by F. F. Sego against the Southern Pacific Company. From a judgment for defendant, plaintiff appeals. *Judgment affirmed.*

1. *Accidents at Crossings.*—For actions arising out of accidents at crossings, see vols. 11 and 12 Am. Neg Cas., where the same are chronologically grouped from the earliest period to 1897, and arranged in alphabetical order of States. Subsequent actions to date, on the same topics, are reported in vols. 1-12 AM. NEG. REP., and the current numbers of that series of Reports.

Crossing street-car tracks. In KERNAN v. MARKET STREET R'Y CO. *(California, September, 1902)*, 70 Pac. Rep. 81, judgment for plaintiff for $1,000, in action for personal injuries caused by a street-car, was affirmed. The court (per McFARLAND, J.) in discussing the negligence of the parties said: "As to the negligence of appellant [the railroad company], the evidence was clearly conflicting, within the meaning of the rule that in such case a finding will not be here disturbed. No doubt, some juries would have found differently on this issue; but there was certainly considerable evidence that at the time of the accident the car was going at a high, unlawful, and dangerous rate of speed, and that no bell had been rung, nor other alarm given, at the crossing of Perry street, which was about one-half of a short block from the point where the respondent was struck.

"As to the alleged contributory negligence of respondent, we think that the evidence presented a case where it was for the jury to say whether the respondent exercised reasonable care in crossing the street, and not a case where a court can say, as it might in some instances, that, as a matter of law, there was contributory negligence. The accident occurred on a public street in a populous part of the city, along which appellant had its street railway track, over which it operated its street cars by electricity. In such case a person desiring to cross the street must, of course, exercise due care and caution, and if he does not do so, and his want of care contributes proximately to the injury, he cannot recover; but it has been repeatedly decided that he is not held to that high degree of care which is required in the case of an ordinary steam railroad running through the country, on which heavy trains of cars are moved at a high rate of speed, and cannot be quickly stopped or controlled.

ARTHUR W. NORTH, FRANK R. DEVLIN and GEORGE R. LOVEJOY, for appellant.

GEORGE A. LAMONT and FOSHAY WALKER, for respondent.

GAROUTTE, J. — Action for damages brought by the father for the death of his son, defendant's train having killed him at a highway crossing. Defendant relied upon contributory negligence, and at the conclusion of plaintiff's evidence he was nonsuited upon that ground. The appeal is taken from the judgment and a bill of exceptions containing the evidence.

For the purposes of this appeal it will be assumed that deceased was guilty of contributory negligence in attempting to cross the railroad track in front of the moving train. It will also be assumed for the purposes of the appeal that defendant was guilty of negligence by reason of the manner in which it was running its train at the place of the accident, in this: that the speed was excessive, and that the crossing was one greatly used by the traveling public, — no flagman being in attendance. In the face of the two concessions

Persons crossing a street railroad on a populous street are held only to what, under all the circumstances, is the exercise of reasonable care. See Strong *v.* Sacramento & P. R. R. Co., 61 Cal. 328, 11 Am. Neg. Cas. 196; Swain *v.* Fourteenth St. R. R. Co., 93 Cal. 184, 11 Am. Neg. Cas. 209, 28 Pac. Rep. 829; Driscoll *v.* Market St. Cable R'y Co., 97 Cal. 553, 11 Am. Neg. Cas. 186, 32 Pac. Rep. 591; Cross *v.* Railroad Co., 102 Cal. 316, 36 Pac. Rep. 673; Clark *v.* Bennett, 123 Cal. 278, 55 Pac. Rep. 908. In the case at bar there was evidence that the respondent, when she left the sidewalk to cross the street, which was a narrow one, had an unobstructed view of the street both ways, and that she looked both ways, and saw no car approaching, and heard no signal of its approach Considering all the evidence on the point, it cannot be correctly said that the jury was bound to find that the respondent was guilty of contributory negligence, or that the law must ascribe to her such negligence." * * *

COLEMAN *v.* LOWELL, ETC., STREET R'Y CO. *(Massachusetts, June, 1902)*, 64 N. E. Rep. 402, was an action of "tort for personal injuries caused by a collision between a car of the defendant and plaintiff's wagon. Plaintiff was crossing a street in Lowell, and saw the car coming. He thought he had time to cross, and when part way over the railway track was struck. Plaintiff walked his horse a portion of the way across the track. The motorman testified that he could have stopped the car and avoided the collision had the rails not been wet and slippery. In the Superior court, before Francis A. Gaskill, J., there was verdict for plaintiff, and defendant excepted." In delivering the opinion BARKER J., said: "The only contention now made in support of the bill of exceptions is that the plaintiff was not in the exercise of due care. He testified without objection that he judged the car to be a safe distance away. There was conflicting evidence as to the distance of the car from the team when the plaintiff attempted to cross the track, and also as to the speed of the car. In our opinion, the question whether the plaintiff was in the exercise of due care was for the jury. Exceptions overruled." (JOHN J. O'CONNOR, appeared for plaintiff; GEO. F. & GEO. R. RICHARDSON, L. T. TRULL, and F. N. WIER, for defendant).

suggested, involving the negligence of the defendant and the contributory negligence of the party killed, plaintiff claims that defendant was guilty of wanton and willful negligence in running its train at an excessive rate of speed at the place where the accident occurred, and therefore deceased's contributory negligence does not defeat a recovery. Whatever the law upon this question may be in some of the other States of the Union, we are not specially concerned, for in this State it may be said to be well settled. This question was directly involved in O'Brien *v.* McGlinchy, 68 Me. 552, where the court said: "Generally, it is a defense to an action of tort that the plaintiff's negligence contributed to produce the injury. But in cases falling within the foregoing description, where the negligent acts of the parties are distinct and independent of each other, the act of the plaintiff preceding that of the defendant, it is considered that the plaintiff's conduct does not contribute to produce the injury, if, notwithstanding his negligence, the injury could have been avoided by the use of ordinary care at the time by the defendant. This rule applies usually in cases where the plaintiff or his property is in some position of danger from a threatening contact with some agency under the control of the defendant, when the plaintiff cannot, and the defendant can, prevent an inquiry. Lord Ellenborough, in Butterfield *v.* Forrester, 11 East, 60,—a much-quoted case,—declared that 'one's being in fault will not dispense with another's using ordinary care' (1). Blackburn, J., in Radley *v.* London & N. W. R'y Co.. L. R. 10 Exch. 100, expresses the idea in this wise: 'A man is bound, when he puts himself in a place where he knows other persons are coming, not only for his own safety, but for that of his neighbors, to take reasonable care of himself and of his property; but, whether he does this or not, it does not relieve anybody else who comes there from the duty of also taking reasonable care.' * * * But this principle would not govern where both parties are contemporaneously and actively in fault, and by their mutual carelessness an injury ensues to one or both of them; nor where the negligent act of the defendant takes place first, and the negligence of the plaintiff operates as an intervening cause between it and the injury" (2). The law is well stated in this Maine case, and it has

1. In Butterfield *v.* Forrester, 11 East, 60, it was held that one who is injured by an obstruction in a highway, against which he fell, cannot maintain an action, if it appears that he was riding with great violence and want of ordinary care, but for which he might have seen and avoided the obstruction.

2. Radley *v.* London & Northwestern R'y Co., 1 L. R. App. Cas. 754, 46 L. J. Exch. Div. 573, 35 L. T. N. S. 637, 25 W. R. 147 (*reversing* 10 L. R. Exch. 100, 44 L. J. Exch. 73, 33 L. T. N. S. 209, which reversed 9 L. R. Exch. 71, 43 L. J. Exch. 73), was as follows: The plaintiffs were the owners of a colliery

been approved by several decisions of this court. It appeals to sound reason that, even conceding a railroad company to be guilty of willful and wanton negligence in handling its train, still those acts upon its part can be no excuse for the traveler to close his eyes to approaching danger and rush blindly into it. No conduct on the part of the company, no matter how willful and wanton, will release a person from using ordinary care in preserving himself from danger and consequent injury. As said in the case cited, under such circumstances both of the parties are equally at fault, and there can be no recovery. Even conceding the negligence of the company to be the greater negligence, still in this State the courts do not recognize the principle of law relating to comparative negligence which obtains in some of our sister States. The principle of law bearing upon a recovery when the defendant is guilty of willful and wanton negligence, notwithstanding the party injured may have been guilty of what may be called, in general terms, contributory negligence, finds

and of a siding connected with a line of railway, which siding was crossed by a wooden bridge about eight feet high, also belonging to the plaintiffs. The siding was used for the purpose of bringing loaded trucks of coal from the colliery upon the railway and of bringing them back when empty. The company was in the practice of bringing the empty trucks upon the siding, and the plaintiffs removed them whenever it was convenient. On Saturday afternoon, after working hours in the colliery were over, the company left several trucks on the siding, one of which had upon it another truck which had broken down, and the combined height of the two trucks was too great for them to pass under the bridge. The presence of this truck was known to the person left in charge of the colliery. On the following evening, after it was dark, the servants of the company brought some more trucks upon the siding, and the engine driver, in order to clear the main line, shunted the trucks against those which were already there, and thus brought the loaded truck into contact with the bridge. On finding that there was an obstruction, he did not go to ascertain its cause, but, assuming that it was caused by a brake, he drew back his engine and pushed up the whole train of trucks with such violence as entirely to carry away the bridge. In an action for the damage caused to the bridge the judge directed the jury that if there was any negligence or want of ordinary care on the part of the plaintiffs contributing to the accident the company would be entitled to the verdict. A verdict was found for the company. *Held*, that there was evidence of contributory negligence to go to the jury, but that the judge had misdirected the jury in not leaving to them the question whether, even if there had been contributory negligence on the part of the plaintiffs, the company might not have avoided the accident by the exercise of due care and diligence. In such action it was also held that the proposition that a plaintiff in an action for negligence cannot recover if he has been guilty of negligence or want of ordinary care contributing to the injury complained of, is subject to this qualification, namely, that if the defendant could, by the exercise of reasonable care and diligence, have avoided the injury, he is not excused by the plaintiffs' contributory negligence.

an apt illustration in Esrey *v.* Southern Pac. Co., 103 Cal. 544, 9 Am. Neg. Cas. 98*n*, 37 Pac. Rep. 500. There plaintiff, by reason of lack of ordinary care, placed herself in a position of danger. Defendant, knowing her danger, did not use ordinary care in protecting her from danger. In that case, technically speaking, plaintiff was not guilty of contributory negligence, for her negligence did not proximately contribute to the injury. In cases of that character it may be well said that the latter negligence is the proximate cause of the injury, and that the earlier negligence of the party injured is too remote to be classed as contributory negligence. In discussing this rule of law it is said in Everett *v.* Railway Co., 115 Cal. 128, 43 Pac. Rep. 210: "The rule can never apply to a case where, as here, the negligence of the party injured continued up to the very moment of the injury, and was a contributing and efficient cause thereof. For it is apparent by the slightest care and effort on the part of the deceased he could have put himself out of danger up to the last moment before he was struck." And that is exactly the case the court now has before it. The negligence of the party killed continued up to the very moment of time when he was struck by the approaching train. There is here no question of remote or earlier negligence upon his part. And conceding him guilty of negligence, that negligence necessarily contributed directly to his death. The case at bar is quite similar in its facts to Glascock *v.* Central Pacific R. R. Co., 73 Cal. 140, 11 Am. Neg. Cas. 203*n*, 14 Pac. 520, where this court said: "Mr. Glascock either saw the train before he reached the track, or he did not look toward the track as he approached it. * * * If he looked, he saw, and, having age and faculties to understand the dangers, is charged with a knowledge of them, and was bound to act upon that knowledge as a prudent and cautious man would under the circumstances. His failure so to act was negligence which, notwithstanding the negligence of the defendant, the law regards as such a contributory cause on his part as will make the injury his own misfortune, and relieve the other party from liability therefor."

For the foregoing reasons the judgment is affirmed.

We concur: VAN DYKE, J.; HARRISON, J

THUNBORG v. CITY OF PUEBLO.

Court of Appeals, Colorado, September, 1902.

ACCIDENT WHILE DRIVING — FIRE PLUG IN STREET CONCEALED FROM VIEW — NOTICE — NEGLIGENCE OF CITY. — In an action to recover damages for injuries sustained by plaintiff while driving, his vehicle striking against an obstruction in the street, it was *held* that the city's negligence was established, where it appeared that a fire plug, which was lawful and necessary in the place it occupied, but by reason of its being concealed from view, became a menace to the safety of travelers, was very close to the edge of the beaten roadway and a vehicle passing at that point could be avoided only by turning towards it, and the city had knowledge of the dangerous conditions (1).

CONTRIBUTORY NEGLIGENCE — DRIVING — INSTRUCTION. — In such action, however, a charge that if "plaintiff was traveling at a furious and rapid rate of speed and that such act on his part was the cause of the injury, and that he would not have suffered the same had he been driving at an ordinary and prudent rate of speed, then it is immaterial whether his so traveling was intentional on his part, or the result of his inability to restrain his horse," was erroneous, as if the horse was going excessively fast, it was quite material whether plaintiff was able to restrain him or not.

ERROR to District court, Pueblo County.

Action by C. A. Thunborg against the City of Pueblo from judgment for defendant, plaintiff brings error. *Judgment reversed.*

M. J. GALLIGAN, for plaintiff in error.

GEO. W. COLLINS, for defendant in error.

THOMSON, J. — C. A. Thunborg brought this action against the city of Pueblo to recover damages for injuries sustained by him on June 24, 1898, by coming into collision with a hydrant or fire plug hidden by weeds and sagebrush, while driving along Court street, a public street of the city, in the evening. The complaint charged negligence against the city in suffering a growth of weeds and brush to conceal the fire plug, and alleged want of knowledge in the plaintiff of its existence. The answer denied negligence on the part of the city, and alleged that the street was but little used, and that the plaintiff was guilty of contributory negligence in driving at a furious and unlawful rate of speed. The defendant had judgment, and the plaintiff appealed.

1. *Obstructions in streets and highways.* For other actions against municipal corporations involving the question of liability for obstructions in streets and highways, from 1897 to date, see vols. 1-12 AM. NEG. REP., and the current numbers of that series of Reports.

The following facts appeared from the evidence: The street was a public and much-used thoroughfare. The fire plug was but a few inches from the beaten roadway, which deviated towards it to avoid a puddle of mud, and was concealed by a thick growth of weeds and sagebrush. The same conditions had existed there for at least three years previous to the accident, the weeds being renewed every spring, and the sagebrush remaining constantly. The injuries received by the plaintiff were severe and permanent. It was dark, or nearly dark, when the accident occurred. The plaintiff testified that on the evening of the accident he was returning to his home in a cart; that when nearly opposite the fire plug, which he had never seen, and the existence of which he did not suspect, he saw another vehicle approaching him in the roadway, which he could not pass except by entering the weeds and brush; that, to avoid a collision, he turned to the right into the weeds and brush, struck the fire plug, and was thrown to the ground; and that when approaching the place where the fire plug was located his horse was going at an ordinary trot. It was testified that in the previous summer another person, meeting a team in the same locality, turned into the weeds and brush to avoid it, struck the fire plug, and broke his buggy; and that at still another time, at the same place, there was a narrow escape from the same kind of accident. Mr. E. Settles, the man in the buggy which the plaintiff turned out of the road to avoid, stated that he heard the rattle of the plaintiff's cart; that it seemed to him, from the great noise the cart was making, that some one was driving very fast, or that the horse was running away; that it was nearly dark, and he could not see whether the horse was trotting or loping; that, when almost opposite to him, the plaintiff left the road and struck the fire plug; and that he went to the plaintiff, and asked him why he was driving so fast, and the plaintiff answered that he was driving a new horse, and could not hold him. Witness also stated that the plaintiff was very much stunned by the fall. Two members of the police force of the city, who took the plaintiff to the hospital, said he told them that his horse was running away at the time of the accident. They also said he was suffering frightful pain. In rebuttal it was shown that, owing to the play of the spokes in the hubs, the plaintiff's cart, which was very old, was extremely noisy.

The fire plug was lawful and necessary in the place it occupied, yet, by reason of its being concealed from view, it became a menace to the safety of travelers. It appears that it was very close to the edge of the beaten roadway, and that a vehicle passing at that point could be avoided only by turning towards it; and this one having no reason to suspect that he would encounter anything more dangerous than weeds or sagebrush, would not hesitate to do. The plaintiff, being lawfully on the street, for the purpose, as he supposed, of preventing a collision, turned his horse into the harmless appearing growth of vegetation, with the result that he suffered permanent injury. That the city had actual or implied knowledge of the existence of the conditions which rendered its fire plug dangerous to travelers is not disputed, and we think its negligence was established beyond question. If, however, as to the question of the city's negligence, it could be said that the evidence left room for a difference of opinion, the court's third instruction, which was given by consent, contained a fair statement of the law, and, in so far as other instructions were inconsistent with it, they were erroneous. But while, respecting the duty and responsibility of the city in relation to the cause of the accident, the court correctly declared the law, on the question of contributory negligence it committed fatal error. In submitting that question to the jury the following language was used: "The jury are further instructed that if they find from the evidence that the plaintiff was traveling at a furious and rapid rate of speed, and that such act on his part was the cause of the injury; and that he would not have suffered the same had he been driving at an ordinary and prudent rate of speed, then it is immaterial, so far as this defense is concerned, whether his so traveling was intentional on his part, or the result of his inability to restrain his horse." Negligence is want of care. It consists in omitting to do something which should be done, or inconsiderately doing something in an improper manner. The term supposes the ability to do the thing omitted or to do the thing undertaken properly. It cannot be applied to an act or omission which is compulsory. There was no proof of rapid or furious driving by the plaintiff. The only evidence warranting a supposition that the horse was exceeding his ordinary speed is found in statements of the plaintiff made when stunned by the fall; and, according to the same evidence, the horse was, at the time, beyond control. If the horse was going excessively fast, it is quite material whether the plaintiff was able to restrain him or not; for, unless the plaintiff was himself responsible for the immoderate speed, it constitutes no defense to the city. City of Denver *v.* Johnson, 8 Colo. App. 384, 46 Pac. Rep. 621; City of Crawfordsville *v.* Smith, 79 Ind. 308; Ring *v.* City of Cohoes, 77 N. Y. 83; Baldwin *v.* Turnpike Co., 40 Conn. 238.

Let the judgment be reversed.

CENTRAL OF GEORGIA RAILWAY COMPANY v. DUFFY.

Supreme Court, Georgia, August, 1902.

LICENSEE INJURED BY DERAILMENT OF CAR—EVIDENCE—WITNESS—NEGLIGENCE OF RAILROAD EMPLOYEES—ILLUSTRATION OF RULE IN MORTALITY TABLES—DAMAGES.—In an action against a railroad company for damages on account of personal injuries sustained by reason of the derailment and overturning of a car which the plaintiff was in, evidence that another car of the defendant was overturned on a nearby but different track, three months prior to the time the plaintiff's injuries were received, was not relevant to prove negligence on the part of the defendant at the time and place alleged in the petition; but in this case it appears that the failure to rule out such evidence worked no harm to the defendant (1).

2. It is within the discretion of the trial judge to permit a witness who has been examined, and after conference with counsel, to take the stand a second time, and correct his testimony as originally given; and such discretion will not be controlled unless it has been manifestly abused.

3. A railroad company cannot avoid liability for injuring one who is rightfully upon its train, by showing that its servants notified his employer to have him leave the train by a certain time, and that if the employer had acted upon this notice, and the plaintiff had left the train before that time, the injuries complained of would not have been inflicted.

4. Ignorance by the servants of a railroad company of the presence in one of its cars of one who was rightfully there will not, without more, relieve the company of liability for damage done by reason of its negligence. The circumstance must be such that the servants of the company had no reason to suspect his presence in the car.

5. It is not error for the trial judge upon the trial of an action for damages against a railroad company, in illustrating to the jury the method of using the mortality and annuity tables, to use for example a figure approximating that shown by the evidence to be the plaintiff's age.

6. The requests to charge, so far as legal and pertinent, were covered by the general charge; the amount of damages awarded by the jury was not excessive; and the evidence supported the verdict.

(Syllabus by the Court.)

ERROR from City Court of Macon.

ACTION by William Duffy against the Central of Georgia Railway Company. From judgment for plaintiff defendant brings error. *Judgment affrmed.*

1. *Derailment of trains, etc.*—For actions arising out of injuries sustained by derailment of trains, etc., see vols. 9 and 10 Am. Neg. Cas., where the same are chronologically grouped from the earliest period to 1897, and arranged in alphabetical order of States. Subsequent actions to date are reported in vols. 1-12 AM. NEG. REP., and the current numbers of that series of Reports.

HALL & WIMBERLY and J. E. HALL, for plaintiff in error.

GUERRY & HALL and M. F. HATCHER, for defendant in error.

FISH, J. This was a suit for damages on account of personal injuries alleged to have been sustained by the plaintiff by reason of the negligence of the defendant. The petition alleged that, at the time the injuries complained of were inflicted, the plaintiff was employed by one Sanders as a laborer to sack and load corn in cars of the railroad company, which had been placed for that purpose on a track that was in its possession and under its control; that while he was in a car of the defendant, engaged in the performance of such work, the servants of the company, without warning to him, coupled an engine and cars to the car that he was in, and moved off with the train thus formed; that after going a short distance, and while moving at a moderate speed, the car that the plaintiff was in, owing to its defective condition and to defects in the track and roadway of the defendant, ran off the track and was turned over, as a result of which the plaintiff received the injuries on account of which he sued. The answer of the defendant denied all the material allegations of the petition. On the trial of the case the jury returned a verdict for the plaintiff for $1,000 damages. The defendant made a motion for a new trial, which was overruled and it excepted.

1. One ground of the motion for a new trial complained that the court erred in refusing to rule out, on motion of counsel for the defendant below, certain evidence to the effect that, about three months prior to the time the plaintiff received his injuries, another car of the defendant had been overturned on a different track, but in the vicinity of the place where the car in which the plaintiff was at work when injured was derailed. This testimony was given by a witness for the plaintiff on cross-examination. The evidence was not relevant to prove negligence on the part of the defendant at the time and place of the injuries complained of. But in view of the fact that there was ample evidence to support a finding that the railroad company was negligent on the particular occasion when the plaintiff was injured, and that no harm appears to have been done the defendant by the refusal to exclude the objectionable evidence, this ground of the motion furnishes no reason for reversing the judgment of the court below refusing a new trial.

2. It appears from the record that, at the conclusion of the cross-examination of a witness for the plaintiff, counsel for the plaintiff stated to the court that he had no further questions to ask the witness at that time, but that he might desire to recall him later. Subsequently, after a conference with this witness, plaintiff's counsel again placed him on the stand, and the witness changed his testimony

as originally given, stating that he had been mistaken in the answers that he had made to certain questions when first asked him. Counsel for the defendant objected to the reintroduction of this witness, on the ground that all the witnesses were under the rule, and that to allow a witness thus to correct his testimony after a conference with counsel would defeat the object of the rule. The court overruled the objection, and allowed the witness to testify a second time. Error was assigned upon this ruling. We are unable to see what bearing the rule of the separation of witnesses has upon the question of the right of a party to recall a witness to the stand after he has been once examined, and after he has conferred with counsel for the party so reintroducing him. There is no law in this state which forbids an attorney to confer with a witness, either before or after his examination in court, and certainly there is no law against recalling a witness to the stand for any legitimate purpose. It is so well settled as to need no citation of authority that matters pertaining to the reopening of a case, and the reintroduction of witnesses, are within the sound discretion of the trial judge, and that, unless such discretion is shown to have been manifestly abused (which was not done in this case), it will not be controlled by this court.

3. Error was also assigned upon the refusal of the court, upon request of counsel for the defendant, to charge, in effect, that if the jury should believe that the servants of the railroad company had notified Sanders, the plaintiff's employer, that the car in which the plaintiff was working would be moved by a certain time, and to finish sacking the corn by that time; that if the defendant's servants did not move the car until after the time specified; and that if the failure of the plaintiff to leave the car before it was moved was due to the failure of Sanders to notify him to leave it, — they would be authorized to find "that the injury was not caused proximately by the act or negligence of the defendant in not notifying him, and that the plaintiff would not be entitled to recover." This request was very properly refused. If the plaintiff was rightfully in the car, and the servants of the company knew or had reason to suspect his presence there, it was then the duty of the company to notify him that the car was about to be moved, and that duty could not be shifted to Sanders or to any one else not connected with the company. The warning to Sanders that the car would be moved at a certain time could in no sense be considered as a warning to the plaintiff, and the responsibility for the defendant's acts of negligence cannot be placed upon him. If the defendant made Sanders its agent for the purpose of notifying the plaintiff when the car would be moved, it would be liable for his failure to carry out the object of

his agency; if he was not its agent, the railroad company cannot escape liability to the plaintiff on account of a warning conveyed to Sanders which should have been communicated directly to the plaintiff.

4. Counsel for the defendant requested the court to charge the jury to the effect that, if the servants of the defendant did not know of the presence of the plaintiff in the car at the time the train was moved, the company would not be liable. The court instead charged, in substance, that if the defendant did not know of the plaintiff's presence in the car at the time mentioned, and was not negligent in failing to know that he was in the car, it would not be liable. The refusal to charge as requested, and the charge as given, are assigned as error. There can be no doubt as to the correctness of the instruction given by the court. To have charged without qualification that mere ignorance, on the part of the defendant, as to the presence of the plaintiff in the car, would have excused the defendant from liability, would have been manifestly erroneous; for it would have taken from the jury the consideration of one of the most important questions in the case, viz: whether the very ignorance behind which the defendant attempted to shield itself was of itself negligence. The charge as given was correct, and furnished no reason for granting a new trial.

5. Complaint was also made of the instructions given by the court as to the use by the jury of the mortality and annuity tables. The portion of the charge here excepted to is quite lengthy, but the chief objection interposed seems to be that the court, in illustrating to the jury the manner of using the tables, took for example an age differing only by one year from what the evidence showed the plaintiff's age to be. The charge as given was substantially correct, and we think there is no merit in the objection made to the method of illustration employed by the trial judge. We do not perceive how any harm could have been done the defendant simply because the judge, in demonstrating to the jury the use of the tables, used for example the figures 45, while the evidence showed that the plaintiff was 44 years old.

6. The foregoing disposes of all of the grounds of the motion for a new trial which in our opinion require discussion. The requests to charge, so far as legal and pertinent, were fully covered by the general charge. The amount of the verdict, in view of the evidence as to the extent of the plaintiff's injuries, was by no means unreasonable. There was ample evidence to establish the right of the plaintiff to be in the car at the time his injuries were received, and to support a finding that the defendant was negligent as charged

in the petition in bringing about those injuries. The judgment of the trial court overruling the motion for a new trial will, therefore, not be disturbed.

Judgment affirmed. All the justices concurring, except LEWIS, J., absent on account of sickness.

ROBERT PORTNER BREWING COMPANY v. COOPER.

Supreme Court, Georgia, August, 1902.

HORSE FRIGHTENED BY HARNESS BREAKING — LIABILITY OF MASTER FOR INJURY TO SERVANT DRIVING — PLEADING AND PRACTICE — EVIDENCE — INSTRUCTIONS.— 1. Where a motion for new trial and the rule *nisi* thereon have been served upon the respondent, and an amendment thereto is afterward regularly filed and approved by the trial judge, who overrules the amended motion upon its merits, this court cannot refuse to consider the amendment because it was not served upon the respondent.

2. Where the condition of a set of harness is the subject of inquiry, it is error to overrule a proper objection to evidence as to the condition of a set of harness which is not identified as the one under investigation (1).

3. It is error for a trial judge to instruct the jury that given facts would constitute negligence, when the facts are not such as are made by law to constitute negligence *per se*.

4. It is also error to charge that, where an employer has agreed to furnish an employee a harness sufficiently strong to enable him to control a certain horse, the employer is thereby made an insurer of the quality of the harness furnished, and that he is not in the exercise of ordinary care unless he makes his assurance good.

5. Other assignments of error are covered by the opinion.

(Syllabus by the Court.)

ERROR from City Court of Richmond County.

Action by J. J. Cooper against the Robert Portner Brewing Company and another. From judgment for plaintiff against the Brewing company, it brings error. *Judgment reversed.*

SALEM DUTCHER, for plaintiff in error.

W. K. MILLER and BOYKIN WRIGHT, for defendant in error.

SIMMONS, Ch. J. — Suit for damages for personal injuries was brought by Cooper against the Robert Portner Brewing Company and its manager. The plaintiff alleged that he was employed to deliver defendant's beer from a wagon which, with horse and harness, defendants were to furnish. He was given a horse which had run away, but he was assured by defendants that it would not run away if carefully handled, and that a strong set of sound and suitable harness would be supplied him. Relying upon the promise to furnish him a strong and sound harness, he used the horse. While he was proceeding quietly along the street, the horse shied, the harness broke and caused the horse to try to run away, then other portions of the harness gave away, and plaintiff was seriously injured by the kicking of the horse. Defendant had failed to supply such a harness as was reasonably safe with such a horse, had failed to keep the harness in proper repair, and, after having undertaken to repair the harness, had negligently stopped the repairs, to have work done on other harness. See Cooper *v.* Robert Portner Brewing Co., 112 Ga. 895, 9 Am. Neg. Rep. 457, 38 S. E. Rep. 91. The defendants answered that plaintiff had, in spite of their warning, used this horse rather than others offered him, because it was faster than the others, and that plaintiff's injuries were not due to the condition of the harness, which was sound, but resulted from plaintiff's own negligence. They also denied having agreed to supply plaintiff any unusually strong set of harness, and alleged that the harness furnished was reasonably safe and strong. The company's manager also denied that plaintiff was in his employment. On the trial the jury returned a verdict against the company, but in favor of its co-defendant. The company moved for a new trial, and the judge overruled the motion. The company excepted.

1. The original motion for a new trial contained but three grounds, and they were general in character. A rule *nisi* issued, in which it was provided that the movant should "have leave to amend said motion at or before" the hearing. Service of this motion and of the rule *nisi* was duly acknowledged by counsel for the respondent. Subsequently the movant amended his motion by adding quite a number of grounds, but this amendment was not served upon the respondent, so far as appears in the record. Counsel for the defendant in error claim that the matter contained in the amendment to the motion is not before this court, and cannot be considered. We are not aware of any requirement that such an amendment should be served, nor have we been referred to any case in which such a point has been decided. The original motion was duly served, or its service acknowledged, and the amendment was allowed and its grounds approved by the judge. The respondent, after acknowledging service of the original motion and the rule *nisi*, was bound to look after his case, and to take notice of all that was afterward regularly done therein. Further than this, the judge passed upon the merits of this amendment, and it does not appear that any objection was made to

1. See former decision in the case at bar, reported in 9 Am. Neg. Rep. 457

his doing so. See Fleming *v.* Roberts, 114 Ga. 637, 40 S. E. Rep. 792, in which, however, the question as to the necessity for service was not passed upon.

2. Error is assigned on the refusal of the judge to rule out the evidence of a harness repairer to the effect that the harness was considerably broken up, and from its appearance, had been considerably worn and in need of repair, and was not sufficiently strong for a spirited, "skittish" horse. On cross-examination the witness stated that he knew the harness about which he testified was that used by the plaintiff at the time of the injury, because witness "had been told so; that he did not know it of his own knowledge, only from the condition of the harness." It also appeared that his examination of this harness was after the time of the injury to plaintiff. The court ruled out what had been told witness. The latter then stated that the only knowledge he had that the harness was the same was derived from the fact that it was broken, and that at the time of repairing the harness in question he had repaired eight or ten other sets of harness for the defendant company,—all of them in need of repair. Counsel for the company then moved the court to rule out all of this evidence on the ground that the witness had no means of information as to the identity of the harness, except what had been told him, and that this was hearsay. The court admitted the evidence, and we think that so doing was error. The witness stated that the harness had been delivered to him by Johnson, who appears to have been on the wagon with plaintiff at the time of the injury, and that it was Johnson who told him that the harness was that used by plaintiff when he was injured. The court properly ruled out what Johnson had told the witness, and this left the statement that Johnson had delivered a set of harness to the witness. There was also evidence that there were eight or ten other sets of harness delivered to the witness for repair. Johnson was not present at the trial, and it was not shown that the harness delivered to the witness by Johnson was that the condition of which was under investigation. The fact that it was broken did not show this. There was nothing to show or to enable the jury to infer that the harness about which the witness testified was that used by plaintiff, and the evidence was therefore irrelevant, and should have been ruled out. See Turner *v.* Tubersing, 67 Ga. 161.

3, 4. The court charged the jury that if "both plaintiff and defendant knew that the horse was dangerous, and the defendant assured the plaintiff that if he would use this horse in its business it would furnish such harness as would enable him to control a horse of this character, then * * * the duty to furnish such a harness was manifest and imperative, and the defendant was not in the exercise of ordinary care unless nor until it made its assurance good. Moreover, if such assurance was made, it removes all ground for the argument that the servant by continuing the employment engages to assume the risk." In so far as this charge stated what facts would constitute negligence, it was erroneous. While the language is taken almost verbatim from Cooley on "Torts, as quoted in Cheeney *v.* Steamship Co., 92 Ga. 731, 19 S. E. Rep. 33, we think that it was not proper to give it in charge to the jury. Under our system a judge should not instruct a jury that any given facts constitute negligence, except in cases where such facts are by law made to constitute negligence *per se*. City of Milledgeville *v.* Wood, 114 Ga. 370, 40 S. E. Rep. 239. The charge was further erroneous in that, in fitting the quotation to the present case, the judge instructed the jury that the defendant would become practically an insurer of the quality of the harness furnished. We think that if the defendant had supplied plaintiff with a harness which to one reasonably and ordinarily prudent would have seemed to be of such quality as to enable plaintiff to control the horse, and the harness proved insufficient because of some defect hidden even from the ordinarily diligent, there could be no recovery.

5. Other complaints are made of the charge of the court. Portions of it are excepted to as intimating an opinion as to what had or had not been proved, as stating what facts would constitute negligence, as being unauthorized by the evidence, or as being given without sufficient qualification. After a careful study of these assignments of error, we find that none of them requires any special discussion. The errors, if any existed, are of minor importance, and of such character that they will probably not occur upon the next trial. Complaint is also made that the court erred in admitting evidence that the horse which plaintiff had been driving was used by the company in its business for some months after the injury to plaintiff. This evidence was objected to as irrelevant. This assignment of error was not argued or referred to by the counsel for the plaintiff in error, and apparently was abandoned. Inasmuch, however, as the case has to be again tried, we will say that this evidence seems to us to have been inadmissable. If offered to throw any light on the contract or arrangement of the plaintiff with the defendant, it was of course, irrelevant. If it was offered to show the use of the horse with a stronger harness, and to treat this as an admission by the company that the harness supplied the plaintiff had been negligently weak, then it was inadmissible under the ruling in Georgia Southern & Florida

R'y *v.* Cartledge (this term) 42 S. E. Rep. 405 (1). If it was offered for the purpose of showing the character of the horse, it was inadmissible, 1, because it was conceded by both parties that the horse was wild and not easily controlled; 2, because it did not sufficiently appear that the horse was afterward used under similar conditions as by plaintiff, or what was the difference in the harness, or how much skill had to be employed to manage the horse; and 3, the fact that the horse had run away with plaintiff may have induced defendant, in its subsequent use of the horse, to employ harness

1. In GEORGIA SOUTHERN & FLORIDA R'Y CO. *v.* CARTLEDGE *(Georgia, August, 1902)*, 42 S. E. Rep. 405, judgment for plaintiff, Cartledge, was reversed, the syllabus by the court stating the points decided as follows:

"1. That after an occurrence resulting in injury to one person, another who is sought to be held accountable therefor took additional precautions to prevent others from being likewise injured, can neither justly nor logically be regarded as an admission on his part that he was negligent in not sooner observing such precautions. Prior decisions by this court virtually to the contrary reviewed and overruled.

"2. It affirmatively appearing from the evidence in the present case that the proximate cause of the plaintiff's injury was his own independent act, for which there was no necessity, and which was in no way brought about by any default on part of the defendant company, he was not entitled to recover."

In the CARTLEDGE case *(supra)*, LUMPKIN, P. J., stated the case as follows: "This was a suit for damages against the railway company by Cartledge, who set forth in his petition the following allegations of fact: "On the 30th day of June, 1900, he was in the employment of the United States goverment in the railway mail service, and was, in the course of his employment on said day, riding upon the train and in a car of the said company." On that day, "while on the railroad train of said company in the discharge of his duties as mail clerk on his car furnished by said road, * * * the mail grab, which was fastened on the outside of said car, came in contact with a post standing upon the platform of said railway company at the station house at Sofkee." The result was that the "mail grab was turned from its fastenings to the side of said car and thrown down and upon the left hand of petitioner, who was at that time inside the car, where he had the right and where it was his duty to be, and where he then was in the exercise of all the care incumbent upon him. * * * Petitioner's hand was terribly mutilated, wounded, and crushed; the bone in the first finger of said hand being broken [and] made permanently useless." The injury thus sustained by him "was caused by the negligence of said railroad company in erecting the said post too near the track of said railroad company, and allowing it to remain there." A recovery was had by the plaintiff in the court below, and the company is here complaining of a judgment denying it a new trial." * * *

The court then reviewed the question as to the admission of evidence as to subsequent precautions at place of accident, with the result as stated in paragraph 1 of the syllabus to the CARTLEDGE case *(supra)*. Mr. Justice Lumpkin cited and reviewed numerous authorities in the several States in support of the overruling of previous Georgia decisions to the contrary.

stronger than even the most prudent would have thought necessary before the injury to the plaintiff.

Because of the errors pointed out in the second, third and fourth headnotes, a new trial should have been granted. Judgment reversed. All the justices concurring, except LEWIS, J., absent on account of sickness.

SOUTHERN RAILWAY COMPANY v. WEBB.

Supreme Court, Georgia, August, 1902.

PASSENGER THROWN FROM CAR BY SUDDEN JOLT OF TRAIN AND RUN OVER AND KILLED BY PASSING ENGINE—PROXIMATE CAUSE—INTERVENING ACT—EVIDENCE—1. While the general rule is that if, subsequently to an original wrongful or negligent act, a new cause has intervened, of itself sufficient to stand as the cause of the misfortune, the former must be considered as too remote, still if the character of the intervening act claimed to break the connection between the original wrongful act and the subsequent injury was such as its probable or natural consequences could reasonably have been anticipated, apprehended, or foreseen by the original wrongdoer, the causal connection is not broken, and the original wrongdoer is responsible for all of the consequences resulting from the intervening act.

2. There was no error in any of the rulings complained of which required the granting of a new trial. The evidence authorized the verdict, and the court did not err in refusing to grant a new trial.

(Syllabus by the Court.)

ERROR from City Court of Richmond County.

Action by Louis Webb against the Southern Railway Company. From a judgment for plaintiff, defendant brings error. *Judgment affirmed.*

JOS. B. & BRYAN CUMMING, for plaintiff in error.

H. C. HAMMOND and C. H. COHEN, for defendant in error.

COBB, J.—This was an action by the father of John W. Webb against the Southern Railway Company for damages alleged to have been sustained by the plaintiff on account of the homicide of his son. The trial resulted in a verdict in favor of the plaintiff, and the defendant complained that the court erred in refusing to grant it a new trial.

1. The petition alleged that John W. Webb was a passenger on one of the trains of the defendant; that while in one of the cars of the train, in the exercise of all ordinary care and diligence, and just as he was about to take a seat near the rear door of the car, the train was negligently, suddenly, forcibly, and with great violence

jerked, jarred and jolted, and as a result Webb was suddenly and without fault on his part thrown through the rear door of the car and fell across the platform at the end of the car onto the track on a bridge over which the train was passing at the time the jolt took place; that he was stunned by the fall, and rendered insensible; and that while upon the track in a stunned, insensible, and injured condition, and unable to walk or protect himself, he was negligently run over and killed by another engine passing along the track over the bridge. There was evidence authorizing the jury to find that Webb was a passenger upon a train of the defendant, and that while this train was going over a bridge a sudden and violent jolt occurred, sufficient to throw one from his feet who was standing in the train, and which had the effect of jostling the passengers and throwing down bundles from the racks of the car; that Webb was seen upon the train just before this jolt occurred, and he was then near the rear door of the car; that he was not seen afterwards by any one who was in the car; that shortly after the train upon which he was last seen had passed over the bridge an engine belonging to the Georgia Railroad Company ran over and killed Webb, who was lying across the track on the bridge just at the point where the train was when the jolt occurred; that, while the defendant had no control over this engine, the engines of the Georgia Railroad Company had a right to use this track, and it was known to the defendant that the engines of that company might pass along the track at any time when it was not otherwise in use. While the evidence was conflicting as to some of the points above referred to, there was ample evidence authorizing the jury to find all of the facts above stated. It is contended by the counsel for the plaintiff that from this evidence the jury could have inferred that Webb was thrown from the rear door of the car upon the track, and was there in a stunned condition at the time the engine ran over him. Counsel for the railway company contends that the jury were not authorized to draw any such inferences, and that the plaintiff has failed to establish the case made in the petition, but that, even if this position is not correct, and the jury were authorized to infer, from the facts above referred to, that Webb was thrown from the inside of the car through the rear door of the same upon the track, and stunned by the fall, still the plaintiff could not recover, for the reason that the negligence of the defendant which resulted in Webb being hurled upon the track was not the proximate cause of his death, but that the immediate cause of his death was the intervention of another independent agency — that is, the running of the engine of the Georgia Railroad Company upon the tracks at that point.

As we have reached the conclusion, for the reasons which will be hereafter stated, that the jury were authorized to infer, from the facts above detailed, that Webb was negligently thrown from the inside of the car through the rear door upon the track, it becomes necessary to determine whether this negligence on the part of the defendant was so far the proximate cause of the death of Webb that the defendant would be liable, notwithstanding the death was not actually brought about by the fall from the train, but by the running of the engine which ran over and killed him while he was lying in an insensible condition upon the track. See, in this connection, Hopkins, Pers. Inj., secs. 14–16. "No branch of the subject of personal injuries presents greater difficulty than the determination of liability for a specific loss, with reference to its naturalness and proximity as a consequence of the wrongful act complained of." Watson, Pers. Inj., sec. 25. As was said by Elbert, J., in Pullman Palace Car Co. *v.* Barker, 4 Colo. 344, 9 Am. Neg. Cas. 131: "What is the proximate cause of an injury in a legal sense is often an embarrassing question, involved in metaphysical distinctions and subtleties difficult of satisfactory application in the varied and practical affairs of life." Chief Justice Shaw, in Marble *v.* City of Worcester, 4 Gray, 397, said: "The whole doctrine of causation, considered in itself metaphysically, is of profound difficulty, even if it may not be said of mystery." In Scott *v.* Hunter, 46 Pa. St. 195, Strong, J., said: "Indeed, it is impossible by any general rule to draw a line between those injurious causes of damage which the law regards as sufficiently proximate and those which are too remote to be the foundation of an action." In Smith *v.* Telegraph Co., 83 Ky. 114, Judge Holt remarked: "The line between proximate and remote damages is exceedingly shadowy; so much so that the one fades away into the other, rendering it often very difficult to determine whether there is such a connection between the wrong alleged and the resulting injury as to place them, in contemplation of law, in the relation of cause and effect." It has been said that, notwithstanding the maze of doubt and difficulty with which this subject seems to be involved, still it is impossible to take a more practical and simpler view than the observations of learned jurists would indicate; that the practical administration of justice prefers to disregard the intricacies of metaphysical distinctions and subtleties of causation, and to hold that the inquiry as to natural and proximate cause and consequence is to be answered in accordance with common sense and common understanding. Watson, Pers. Inj., sec. 28. From the author just cited we quote the following: "A natural consequence is one which has followed from the original act complained of in the usual, ordinary, and experienced course of events; a result, therefore, which might reasonably have been anticipated or expected. Natural consequences, however, do not necessarily include all such as, upon a calculation of chances, would be found possible of occurrence, or such as extreme prudence might anticipate, but only those which ensue from the original act, without any such extraordinary coincidence or conjunction of circumstances as that the usual course of nature should seem to have been departed from." Section 33. "From the very outset the practical distinction between causes and consequences should be borne in mind in this particular: a consequence of an original cause may, in turn, become the cause of succeeding consequences. But such a cause should not, manifestly, be regarded as an intervening cause, which will relieve from liability the author of the original cause, but rather as only a consequence along with the other consequences. A tortious act may have several consequences, concurrent or successive, for all of which the first tort feasor is responsible. It is not intervening consequences, but intervening causes, which relieve. The test is to be found it has been said, not in the number of intervening events or agents, but in their character, and in the natural and probable connection between the wrong done and the injurious consequence. So long as it affirmatively appears that the mischief is attributable to the original wrong as a result which might reasonably have been foreseen as probable, legal liability continues." Section 58. "Some authorities have formulated rules on this subject designed for general application,—as that the defendant is not responsible where there has intervened the wilful wrong of a third person, or is liable where such act is of a negligent character merely. But the better doctrine is believed to be that whether or not the intervening act of a third person will render the earlier act too remote depends simply upon whether the concurrence of such intervening act might reasonably have been anticipated by the defendant." Section 71. In Railway Co. *v.* Taylor, 104 Pa. St. 315, Mr. Justice Paxson said: "In determining what is approximate cause the true rule is that the injury must be the natural and probable consequence of the negligence; such a consequence as, under the surrounding circumstances of the case, might and ought to have been foreseen by the wrongdoer as likely to flow from his act." In Lane *v.* Atlantic Works, 111 Mass. 139, Colt, J., said: "The injury must be the direct result of the misconduct charged; but it will not be considered too remote if, according to the usual experience of mankind, the result ought to have been apprehended. The act of a third person, intervening and contributing a condition necessary to the injurious effect of the original negligence will not excuse the first wrongdoer, if such act ought to have been foreseen. The original negligence still remains a culpable and direct cause of the injury. The test is to be found in the probable injurious consequences which were to be anticipated, not in the number of subsequent events and agencies which might arise." In Seale *v.* Railway Co., 65 Tex. 278, Chief Justice Willie said: "What character of intervening act will break the causal connection between the original wrongful act and the subsequent injury is also left in doubt by the decisions. If the intervening cause and its probable or reasonable consequences be such as could reasonably have been anticipated by the original wrongdoer, the current of authority seems to be that the connection is not broken." See, also, Investment Co. *v.* Rees (Colo. Sup.), 42 Pac. Rep. 42, 45; 21 Am. & Eng. Enc. Law (2d Ed.), p. 486 *et seq.*

Treating it as established in the present case that Webb was upon the track of the defendant in an insensible condition as a result of the negligence of the defendant, is it reasonable or unreasonable to hold that the defendant should have apprehended that a person in this condition, in such a place, might be injured or killed by the running of an engine upon the track? Was the defendant bound to anticipate that injury or death might result to a person in such a condition in such a place? The track was under the control of the defendant, and, if Webb had been killed by an engine of the defendant which came along the track after the train from which Webb was thrown had passed, the defendant would have been liable, although the employees in charge of the engine had been wholly free from negligence. Railroad Co. *v.* Nix, 68 Ga. 572. In that case Mr. Chief Justice Jackson said: "Suppose there had been a prosecution for murder, who would be found guilty thereof,—the conductor of the train who did the deed of throwing him off and under, or the conductor of the other train who ran unconsciously over him? Clearly, he who did the intentionally wrongful act, and whose act caused his death." The principle upon which the ruling in the Nix case is founded is that a railway company is bound to know that its tracks may be used at any time by the engines and trains of the company, and is bound to anticipate and apprehend any consequence that may result to one who, on account of its negligence, is left in a condition in which and in a place where he is liable to be injured by the running of such trains. If a railway company is bound to anticipate and apprehend that one left in a helpless condition in a perilous place upon its tracks through its negligence may be injured by one of its own engines or trains running thereon, is it not equally bound to so anticipate and apprehend any injury which might result to such a person from an engine of another company, which the first company knew had a right to and did actually use the tracks from time to time? It would, indeed, bring about a curious result if the defendant would be liable in such a case only when the second engine or train was owned by it. It must be kept in mind that in such cases no negligence is claimed against the persons in charge of the second train or engine. They are blameless. If there is any liability, it results from the negligence of those in charge of the train which left the person killed in a perilous situation upon the track. It would seem that ownership of the second engine or train would be entirely immaterial, and the only question to be considered would be whether the first company knew, or ought to have known, that the second engine or train, no matter by whom owned, had a right to, or did actually from time to time, use the track at the place at which the person was killed. When a railway company negligently leaves a person upon its track in a helpless condition, it will certainly be held liable for any injurious consequences which may result to such a person growing out of the running of trains along the track, without regard to the ownership of such trains, if the company knew or ought to have apprehended that the trains would pass along the track at that point. The present case is very similar to the case of Byrne *v.* Wilson, 15 Ir. C. L. 332 (1). That was a case brought in 1862, under Lord Campbell's Act, by William Byrne, as administrator of Mary Byrne, against a person who was alleged to be the proprietor of certain omnibuses, and as such engaged in the business of a common carrier of passengers. Mary Byrne was a passenger in one of the omnibuses, and through the negligence of the servants of the defendant the omnibus was precipitated into the lock of a canal, and Mary Byrne was there in an insensible condition, when the keeper of the lock turned the water therein, and she was drowned. It was held that, although the death of Mary Byrne was not caused immediately by the act of the defendant, it was such a consequential result of that act as entitled her representative to maintain an action. Lefroy, Ch. J., said (page 340): "It was not the negligence of the defendant that was the immediate occasion of her death, but it was the negligence of the defendant that put her into a position by which she lost

1. Byrne *v.* Wilson, 15 Irish Com. Law Rep. 332 (Court of Queen's Bench, Trinity Term, 1862) was as follows: Defendant was a carrier of persons in whose omnibuses passengers were conveyed from one part of Dublin to another. Plaintiff's intestate was a passenger, who was by defendant's negligence precipitated into a canal and drowned. Defendant claimed that the real cause of the death was the opening of the lock by the keeper, thus letting in the water. Held that although the death of the passenger was not immediately caused by the defendant's act, yet it was such a consequential result of defendant's act as would entitle the personal representative of the deceased to maintain an action.

her life, as a consequential injury resulting from that negligence; and although that death was not caused immediately by the act of the defendant, nor was the immediate and instantaneous result of his negligence, yet it was the consequential result of the defendant's act, and enables her representative to maintain this action." The defendant knew that the Georgia Railroad Company had a right to use these tracks. It also knew that it might use them at any time. When, therefore, Webb was negligently thrown upon the tracks, and left there in a helpless condition, the defendant was bound to apprehend and anticipate that injurious consequences would likely result to him from the use of the track by the servants and agents of the Georgia Railroad Company in charge of the engines and trains. This being so, the negligence of the defendant which resulted in leaving Webb helpless upon its tracks was in law the proximate cause of his death, notwithstanding his death was actually brought about by another agency.

We do not think this ruling is in conflict with any of the cases cited in the brief of counsel for the plaintiff in error. In Perry *v.* Railroad Co., 66 Ga. 746, the plaintiff had deposited his luggage in a car of the defendant, intending to go upon the train as a passenger, and left the car, and engaged in conversation with another person in the depot. While so engaged, his attention was called to the fact that the train had moved off, and he ran until he reached the end of the car shed. While passing through the gateway of the car shed, he came in contact with the engine of another company, which was coming into the shed, and as a consequence received serious injuries. It was held that the negligence of the railroad company in starting its train without giving a signal was not the proximate cause of the injury which the plaintiff subsequently received by running against the engine of another train in his effort to catch the defendant's train. The defendant could not have foreseen, nor was it bound to anticipate or apprehend, that, as a result of its negligence in starting its train without a signal, a passenger would, in attempting to catch the train, run against the engine of another train, and receive serious injuries. In the case of Mayor, etc. *v.* Dykes, 103 Ga. 847, 31 S. E. Rep. 443, a street car company had negligently constructed its track so that the rails were above the surface of the street. The plaintiff, while driving a horse attached to a two-wheeled road cart, attempted to drive across the track at an angle of about forty-five degrees. The wheels of his cart came in contact with the iron rails of the track, slipped along the track, and made a scraping noise, which caused the horse to take fright and run away. The cart collided with a wagon, and plaintiff was thrown to the ground and seriously injured. Although the street car company may have been negligent in the way it constructed its track, it certainly could not have foreseen that, as a result of this negligence, a scraping noise would be made, and that this noise would frighten a horse, and the horse would run away, and the vehicle to which he was hitched would collide with a wagon, and the plaintiff would, as a result, be injured. Of course, if the cart had been overturned as a result of the tracks being built too high above the surface of the street, and injury had resulted from an accident of this character, the case would have been different. In Railroad Co. *v.* Price, 106 Ga. 176, 32 S. E. Rep. 77, the plaintiff was a passenger who had been carried wrongfully beyond her station, and when this fact was discovered she was requested to alight at another station, which she did, and was carried to a hotel by the conductor. While at the hotel a lamp in her room exploded, and as a consequence she sustained damage. It was held that the railway company was not liable for the injury thus sustained. The defendant could not have foreseen, apprehended, or anticipated that the plaintiff would suffer injuries of the character received by her at the hotel; and hence its negligent act in carrying her beyond her station could not be said to be the proximate cause of the injuries thus received. In Central of Georgia R'y Co. *v.* Edwards, 111 Ga. 528, 8 Am. Neg. Rep. 595, 36 S. E. Rep. 810, the plaintiff was a brakeman on a freight train, and was ordered by the conductor to jump off the train for the purpose of changing the switch. In obedience to this order, the plaintiff jumped from the car on which he was standing, and, being unable to see the ground beneath him, his right foot was caught in a frog of the switch, the frog not having been blocked so as to prevent such an accident, and the wheels of the car ran over and crushed his foot. The distinction between that case and the present will be apparent when the following language of Mr. Justice Little in the opinion in that case is considered: "The direct and proximate cause of the injury which the plaintiff sustained was his jumping from the train, and, if he is entitled to recover damages from the defendant company therefor, it is because of some negligence on the part of said company which caused the jump from which the injury resulted, or negligence in not protecting the place where in fact he did jump. As we have seen, it is not charged in the petition that the railroad company was, through its conductor, negligent in directing the plaintiff to jump from the car at the time he did." It was held that the failure to block the switch was not an act of negligence.

In the determination of the question just presented we have been very much aided by the carefully prepared brief of counsel for the defendant in error. The brief shows not only laborious research, but ability and power of discrimination, and we take occasion to express our appreciation of the valuable aid thus brought to us in the decision of this puzzling question.

2. The motion for a new trial contains numerous assignments of error on rulings upon the admissibility of evidence. Several grounds complain that the court erred in not allowing testimony to be offered for the purpose of impeachment, which related to matters which were immaterial and irrelevant. While the judge seems to have permitted the cross-examination of different witnesses laying the foundation for impeachment to take a very wide range, we cannot say that any evidence he admitted was altogether irrelevant. But, even if it was, the error thus committed would not be sufficient to have required the granting of a new trial. The defendant offered in evidence a chain of title showing that the South Carolina & Georgia Railroad Company was the proprietor of the tracks at the point where the injury occurred and the yards adjacent thereto, and also offered a contract between the city council of Augusta and this railroad company; the purpose in offering this evidence being to show that the engine of the Georgia Railroad Company was upon the tracks at the point where Webb was injured, not by permission of the defendant, but in its own right under a contract made with the city council and the predecessor in title of the South Carolina & Georgia Railroad Company. This evidence was rejected, and error is assigned upon this ruling. It was immaterial who owned the tracks and the yards adjacent thereto. The defendant was shown to be in control of the tracks at the place where the injury occurred, and also the adjacent yards in the State of South Carolina. It was immaterial whether the Georgia Railroad Company ran its engine over the track by its own right or by permission of the defendant. It did not matter under whose authority the engine was operated upon the track. The only material question was whether the defendant knew or should have known that the Georgia Railroad Company was in the habit of using the tracks at that point. There was evidence authorizing the the jury to find that such was the case. What has just been said disposes of that ground of the motion which complains that the court erred in allowing a witness, who was an employee in charge of the Georgia Railroad engine, to testify, in effect, that the engine was on the tracks by permission of the defendant. Even if the judge committed any error in any of the rulings complained of in the motion for a new trial, we do not think, after a careful examination of the motion for a new trial and the entire record in the case, that there should be a reversal of the judgment for any of the reasons assigned in the motion.

It remains only to dispose of that assignment of error which complains that the verdict was not warranted by the evidence. It was earnestly argued by counsel for the plaintiff in error that there was no evidence authorizing a finding for the plaintiff. It was contended that, as the petition alleged that Webb was thrown through the rear door of the car across the platform at the end of the car and onto the tracks, and, as a result, was stunned and rendered insensible, the plaintiff cannot recover upon a general presumption of negligence against the company, but his recovery must be based upon evidence authorizing the jury to find that he was injured in the manner described in the petition; that is, by being thrown from the inside of the car through the door across the platform onto the tracks. Under the view we have taken of the case, it is unnecessary to determine whether a recovery could be had if the evidence failed to show to the satisfaction of the jury that Webb was thrown from the car in the manner described in the petition. There was abundant evidence authorizing the jury to find that Webb was upon the train as a passenger, and that while he was upon the train there was a jolt of the train, which was sudden, unusual, and violent, its character being such that the passengers were jostled in their seats, bundles were thrown from the seats and racks, and a person in the aisle of the car would probably have been thrown from his feet. There was no one who saw Webb actually thrown through the door to the platform and upon the track. The last that was seen of him, which was just before the jolt came, he was making his way towards the rear of the car, looking for a seat, and had reached a point near the door of the car. Nothing more was seen of him until he was found in a mangled condition by the employees in charge of the railroad engine which had run over him. All of the evidence in the record which bears upon the question as to whether Webb was thrown from the car as described in the petition is contained in the testimony of the witness Shinall, and we quote the exact language of this testimony: "We got on at Broad street together. John Webb got on the first step between the coaches, and I got on the next one, and he was on the platform; and I turned and went towards the back end of the car, and had a couple of bundles in my hand. As I was going along, Mr. Pardue asked me what I was doing there, and I sat on the side of the car, and was talking to him, when John Webb came through the train and passed by us, and went on toward the rear of the train. At or about that time the train stopped inside of the bridge all at once. I mean, by stopping all at once, it was going along ten or fifteen miles an hour, and all at once it stopped. It was a hard jerk. It would have jerked a man down if he had been standing on his feet. That occurred right immediately after I saw Mr. Webb standing up near the rear of the train. It was not more than a minute, or something like that. I was talking to Mr. Pardue, and then the jerk came, and people were making remarks about the jerk coming, and still I did not pay no attention to him. I did not know anything was the matter with him at that time. I did not find out for certain what had become of him until the next morning. After I got off at Bath, I asked for him, but nobody had seen him. I don't think I changed my position on that seat after I saw him. It is just a short run from Augusta to Bath, and I sat there talking to Mr. Pardue. The reason I didn't look around for John Webb, I was talking, and never put my mind on it. I thought maybe he was sitting behind us." To sustain the verdict it is not necessary for us to hold that this testimony of Shinall required a finding that Webb was hurled through the rear door of the car by the jerk of the train. If the jury could legitimately infer from this testimony that such was the case, we have no right to disturb their verdict after it has been approved by the trial judge. The able and learned counsel for the plaintiff in error presented the case to us in such a way that, if we had been sitting as a jury, or even as a court of appeals, with power to pass upon the weight of testimony, we would probably have decided with him at the close of his argument. It is, however, not within our province to pass upon cases like a jury, nor have we any desire to do so. Our authority extends simply to determining whether, under a given state of facts, the jury could legitimately arrive at a given result. While we do not think it is probable that Webb was thrown through the door of the car in the manner claimed, still it is possible that this took place, and under the evidence disclosed by the record we think the jury were authorized to so find. There is some mystery about the case, but, as was said by Mr. Chief Justice Bleckley in Railroad Co. *v.* Rouse, 77 Ga. 407, 3 S. E. Rep. 308, "juries have no more important function than to solve mysteries." The jury have solved this mystery to their own satisfaction. The trial judge has approved their solution, and we have no authority to interfere.

The judgment must be affirmed. All the justices concurring, except LEWIS, J., absent on account of sickness.

McLEAN ET UX v. CITY OF LEWISTON.

Supreme Court, Idaho, June, 1902.

PERSON FALLING THROUGH CELLAR OPENING IN SIDEWALK — LIABILITY OF CITY — PLEADING — DAMAGES. — 1. That part of the charter of the city of Lewiston which provides that said city shall be liable to any one for any loss or injury to person or property growing out of any casualty or accident happening to any such person or property on account of any "street or public ground therein," is broad enough to and does include the sidewalks on the streets.

2. Only ultimate facts need be pleaded, and allegations of complaint must be made sufficiently specific to enable defendant to make a full and complete defense to the action.

3. Permitting leading questions to one's own witness is largely in the discretion of the court, and the action of the court thereon will not be disturbed unless an abuse of discretion is shown. There are many exceptions to the general rule that leading questions are not permitted.

4. Hypothetical questions must be based on the facts admitted or established by the evidence, or both.

5. Allegation of great bodily injury, and that by reason thereof plaintiff was rendered an invalid and a cripple, is a sufficient allegation of permanent injury.

6. Great latitude is allowed in the cross-examination of expert and impeaching witnesses.

7. The law does not fix any precise rule of damages in actions for personal torts, but leaves their assessment to the unbiased judgment of the jury.

8. In such actions the verdict will not be disturbed on the ground of excessive damages, unless the amount of damages is so disproportionate to the injury proved as to justify the conclusion that the verdict is not the result of the cool, dispassionate consideration of the jury.

(Syllabus by the Court.)

APPEAL from District Court, Nez Perce County.

Action by J. A. McLean and wife against the city of Lewiston. From judgment for plaintiff, defendant appeals. *Judgment affirmed.*

McFARLAND & McFARLAND, for appellant.

MILES S. JOHNSON, for respondents.

SULLIVAN, J. — This action was brought by the respondents, who are husband and wife, for damages to the wife by reason of a defective sidewalk and of a cellar door opening therein (1). It is alleged

1. See NOTE ON LIABILITY OF MUNICIPAL CORPORATIONS FOR INJURIES caused by excavations and openings in streets and sidewalks, in 9 AM. NEG. REP. 552–556.

See also NOTE ON COAL-HOLE ACCIDENTS, in 3 AM. NEG. REP. 314–315.

that while said respondent, without fault or negligence on her part, was walking along said sidewalk, she was violently precipitated through said cellar door into the cellar underneath; that she was in an extremely delicate condition, being pregnant with child; was greatly bruised and injured, and received great bodily injury, and was made sick and sore, and received such injuries as to render her an invalid and a cripple. A demurrer was interposed to the complaint and overruled. Thereupon the appellant answered, denying all of the material allegations of the complaint except the corporate existence of appellant. The answer also averred contributory negligence on the part of respondents. A trial jury was had, and resulted in a verdict of $12,000 for respondents, on which judgment was entered. A motion for a new trial was denied. This appeal is from the judgment and the order denying the motion for a new trial.

Seventy-eight errors are assigned as grounds for a reversal of said judgment. The first is that the court erred in overruling the demurrer to the complaint. It is contended that this action was brought under the following provision of the city charter, to wit: "The city of Lewiston shall be liable to any one for any loss or injury to person or property growing out of any casualty or accident happening to any such person or property on account of the condition of any street or any public ground therein." It is contended that at common law an action for damages by a private individual against a municipal corporation for an injury sustained by a defect in a highway could not be maintained, and for that reason the respondents are held to the express terms of said quoted provision of the city charter; and that, as said provision makes no mention of the sidewalks, the complaint fails to state a cause of action. We cannot agree with this contention. This court held in Griffen *v.* City of Lewiston [Idaho], 55 Pac. Rep. 545, that the words "street or public grounds," as used in the above-quoted provision of the city charter, were broad enough to cover and include sidewalks; and, after considering the very able argument of counsel for appellant, we are not inclined to reverse said decision on that point. After a most careful consideration of all of the grounds of said demurrer, we cannot say that the court erred in overruling it. It is true that the complaint is not as specific as some pleaders would have made it, but we think the ultimate facts therein stated constitute a cause of action. In this class of cases the pleader must state all facts necessary to inform the defendant of all acts or omissions that are charged against the defendant, so as to enable him to make a full and complete defense thereto. It is an established rule of pleading that probative facts need not be pleaded.

On an examination of the answer and the proceedings at the trial we find that the attorneys for the appellant did all that could be done to protect the rights of the city, and were in no way misled because the allegations in the complaint were not more specific. This disposes of the second assignment of error.

Assignments Nos. 3 to 16, inclusive, and 26 to 29, inclusive, relate to the action of the court in overruling appellant's objection to questions propounded to witnesses, J. A. McLean and Dr. Brown, by counsel for respondents. It is contended that said questions are leading, and suggestive, and have for their object and purpose the proving of permanent injuries to respondent, Mrs. McLean; and it is earnestly contended that under the allegations of the complaint testimony of permanent injury was inadmissible, for the reason that such injury is not alleged in the complaint. On the point made as to said questions being leading and suggestive, we would say that under proper circumstances and conditions leading questions are permissible, — questions introductory in character; questions to a hostile witness; and cases where it is shown that the witness does not comprehend the import of the question propounded, or is embarrassed. There are many exceptions to the general rule on this subject. And as the permission to ask such questions is largely in the discretion of the court, such discretion will not be disturbed, unless an abuse of it is shown; which is not done in this case. And on the other point, to wit, that the allegation of permanent injury in the complaint is not sufficient to warrant the admission of evidence thereof, we are of the opinion that such allegation is sufficient. The main allegation on that issue is that respondent, Mrs. McLean, received such great bodily injuries as to render her an invalid and a cripple. That allegation, in connection with other allegations of injury showing permanent injury, is sufficient. The evidence called out by the questions last above referred to was as to the health of respondent Mrs. McLean prior to and after injury; as to her ability to nurse her child after the injury; as to her complaints of ill health before and after the accident; as to her disability and lameness; in regard to the rupture of respondent; as to her physical condition during the birth of her child; as to her ability to bear children after the injury; as to effect of injuries on her general health; and as to whether, in the opinion of the physician, she was permanently injured for life, — all of which evidence was admissible under the issues made by the pleadings.

Assignments 33 to 36 relate to a long hypothetical question propounded to medical witnesses of respondents. We have carefully examined said question, and, while we think it is more specific than was necessary, it is based on the facts shown by the evidence. Dr. Luhn's answer to said question was as follows: "I believe that a woman — such a one as described in the question — could not continue to be a healthy woman, and would probably be a wreck, a physical wreck." Other assignments of error go to the proof of the permanency of said injury, and the points therein involved are hereinabove disposed of.

Assignment No. 40 goes to the right of counsel for respondents, on cross-examination of a medical witness, to make out his case by such cross-examination. It appears that Dr. Shaff was called as a medical expert on the part of the city, and on cross-examination the hypothetical question above referred to was put to him. That question had been answered by the medical experts of respondents, and the answer of this witness corroborated the evidence of respondents' experts, and served to strengthen it. But respondents did not rely on that cross-examination to make out their case. Under the law a liberal range is allowed in the cross-examination of expert witnesses, and we do not think the court erred in said matter. This applies also to assignment of error 43, in regard to the examination of the witness Philips.

Objection was made to cross-examination of appellant's witnesses called to impeach one of respondent's witnesses, and on a careful examination of the interrogatories propounded we are unable to say that permitting such examination was error. Great latitude is allowed in cross-examination of impeaching witnesses.

Many other errors are assigned to the action of the court in the admission and rejection of evidence, which we have considered, and find no substantial error in them.

The leading counsel for respondents, in his argument to the jury, referred to one of the counsel for appellant, as we construe it, in a joking way, and counsel for appellant requested the court to require counsel to desist therefrom, and the court refused to do so, and stated, in the presence of the jury, that it would not interfere, and that counsel had a right to argue his cause from his own theory. While we do not consider such remarks proper, we do not think the refusal of the court to order counsel to desist from making them would warrant granting a new trial.

It is contended that instructions 19 and 20 given by the court on its own motion are objectionable on the ground that they do not give the jury any criterion on which to base the amount of damages to be awarded for the injury complained of, but license the jury to go outside of the testimony, and rely upon their judgment in other matters and business affairs in arriving at the amount of damages. Said instructions are as follows: "19. The jury are instructed that a party suing for an injury received can only recover such damages as naturally flow from, and are the immediate results of, the acts complained of. The jury should be governed solely by the evidence introduced before them, and they have no right to indulge in conjectures and speculations not supported by the evidence. If, from the evidence in the case, and under the instructions of the court, the jury shall find the issues for the plaintiffs, and that the plaintiffs have sustained damages, as charged in the complaint, then, in order to enable the jury to estimate the amount of such damages, it is not necessary that any witness should have expressed an opinion as to the amount of such damage, but the jury may themselves make such estimate from the facts and circumstances in proof, and by considering them in connection with their own knowledge, observation and experience in the business affairs of life. 20. If the jury believe from the evidence that the plaintiff, Miriam W. McLean, was injured by reason of the defendant negligently failing to keep its sidewalk in reasonably good repair, or negligently allowing the same to remain in an unsafe condition, as explained in these instructions, and without fault on her part, and that she has sustained damage, then the jury have a right to find for her such an amount of damages as the jury believe from the evidence will compensate her for the personal injury so received, and also for the pain and suffering undergone by her, and any permanent injury, if any such has been proved, not exceeding the amount claimed in the complaint." The last clause of said nineteenth instruction is objectionable, but, taking said instructions together, they correctly instruct the jury that they have a right to find for the respondent such an amount of damages as they believe from the evidence would compensate her for the personal injury so received, and also for the pain and suffering undergone, and for any permanent injury, if any such had been proved. In this character of cases the law does not prescribe any fixed or definite rule of damage, but, from necessity, leaves their assessment to the good, sound and unbiased judgment of the jury; and their verdict will not be disturbed unless the amount is so large as to suggest passion, prejudice, or corruption on the part of the jury. Aldrich *v.* Palmer, 24 Cal. 513; Horn *v.* Boise City Canal Co. (Idaho), 10 Am. Neg. Rep. 11, 65 Pac. Rep. 145.

The giving of other instructions is assigned as error, all of which we have carefully examined, and find no merits in such assignments, as they state the law of this case based on the facts as established by the evidence.

Counsel for appellant requested a number of instructions, one of which the court gave, and refused to give the others. One of said instructions the court gave, and is as follows: "The court instructs the jury in this action the burden is upon the plaintiffs to prove by a preponderance of the evidence that plaintiff Miriam W. McLean received the fall alleged; that her person was injured by said fall; that at, up to, and just prior to said fall said cellar doors were imperfectly or insecurely fastened or secured, or that said sidewalk at that point was dangerous or unsafe for persons to walk over or upon; that said Miriam W. McLean, at the time of or before said accident, did not know of such dangerous or unsafe condition of said cellar doors and cellar thereunder, or unsafe sidewalk, or, if knowing of such defect or dangerous condition of said cellar door or sidewalk, she used diligence or care in stepping upon or walking over or across the same; that the defendant had actual knowledge of such defect or dangerous or unsafe condition of said cellar doors or sidewalk, or that such defect or dangerous or unsafe condition of said cellar doors or sidewalk existed for such length of time before the accident that the defendant, if exercising proper care or diligence, would have known of it; and you are further instructed that, if plaintiffs fail to prove any one of said facts, they cannot recover in the action, and your verdict should be for the defendant." That instruction, with those given by the conrt, cover nearly all of the ground of those requested by appellant, and which the court refused to give, and all that were proper to be given of said instructions. There is nothing in the record to indicate that the verdict was rendered through prejudice or passion, and under all of the evidence in the case we do not think that the damages awarded are excessive. In this case it is shown that a strong, healthy, young woman has become an invalid and cripple, unfitted for marital or other duties of a wife, and we are not inclined to disturb the judgment on account of excessive damages.

The judgment is affirmed, with costs in favor of respondents.

QUARLES, Ch. J., and STOCKSLAGER, J., concur.

ILLINOIS STEEL CO. v. SITAR.

Supreme Court, Illinois, October, 1902.

MASTER AND SERVANT—SAFE PLACE TO WORK—Where it appeared that an employee was ordered by defendant's superintendent to remove a "bosh plate" from a blast furnace while the blast was on, and upon its

being removed a stream of fire, coke and gas was forced out by the pressure from the blast, and the employee was burned, the question of the negligence of defendant was for the jury (1).

APPEAL from Appellate Court, Second District.

Action by Stephen Sitar against the Illinois Steel Company. From a judgment for plaintiff (98 Ill. App. 300), defendant appeals. *Judgment affirmed.*

GARNSEY & KNOX and WILLIAM DUFF HAYNIE, for appellant.

DONAHOE & MCNAUGHTON, for appellee.

BOGGS, J. — This was an appeal from the judgment of the appellate court affirming the judgment, in the sum of $1,700, awarded the appellee in an action in case instituted by him against the appellant company in the Circuit Court of Will county. The appellee, an employee of the appellant company, together with one Harry Walsh, a pipe fitter, and others, also employees of the appellant company, was engaged, on the 22d day of May, 1899, in removing what is known as a "bosh plate" from one of the furnaces of the appellant company. The plate was removed while the blast or pressure was in the furnace. A stream of fire, coke and gas was forced out of the aperture by the pressure from the blast. Walsh, who stood nearer the furnace than the appellee, and the appellee, were burned and injured. Walsh subsequently died from his injuries, and his administrator, one John McFadden, brought an action against the appellant company in the Circuit Court of Will county to recover damages, under the statute, for the benefit of the next of kin of the deceased. He recovered a judgment in the Circuit Court, and the same was affirmed in the appellate court, and afterwards in this court. Illinois Steel Co. *v.* McFadden, 196 Ill. 344, 63 N. E. Rep. 671 (2). In that case and in this a motion was made, at the close of all the testimony, for an instruction directing a peremptory verdict for the appellant company. The motion was denied in each case. In the McFadden case, which was argued orally in this court by both parties, we fully considered the insistence the court erred in denying the motion, and reached the conclusion the motion was

1. See NOTES OF RECENT CASES ON FURNISHING SAFE PLACE TO WORK, at end of this case.

2. The case of ILLINOIS STEEL CO. *v.* MCFADDEN, ADM'R *(Illinois. April, 1902)*, 196 Ill. 344, is sufficiently stated in the opinion in the case at bar, and it is unnecessary to report the same in this volume of AM. NEG. REP. The Supreme Court affirmed the judgment of the Appellate Court, Second District, (98 Ill. App. 296) which affirmed a judgment in favor of plaintiff for $5,000. The opinion was rendered by MAGRUDER, J. (GARNSEY & KNOX, WM. DUFF HAYNIE, of counsel, appeared for appellant, the Illinois Steel Company; J. W. DOWNEY, for appellee).

properly denied, for the reason the evidence tended to establish that Walsh was in the exercise of ordinary care, and that the appellant company was negligent in ordering the workmen to work at the plate while the blast was on, and that the injury was not occasioned by any risk assumed by the workmen, but by the negligent acts of the employer. The pleadings in the two cases were not different in any material aspect. The facts disclosed upon the trial of the cases and the grounds of the motions for peremptory verdicts were the same. The facts are recited at length in the McFadden case. We hold here, as in that case, that the trial court correctly refused to direct a verdict for the appellant company.

It is urged that if there was any negligence to which the injury was due, it was that of Walsh in failing to observe and report to Conlon, the superintendent of the force of men then in the employ of the appellant company, if the plate was being loosened by the efforts to remove it, and Walsh was a fellow-servant of the appellee. In the case brought by McFadden, the administrator of Walsh, we found that Walsh was in the exercise of ordinary care, and that the injury to the workmen resulted from an improper and negligent order given by the superintendent, Conlon, to remove the bosh plate without directing the blast to be entirely withdrawn. As to this feature of the case, the evidence in the two cases is not different. Conlon did not bear the relation of fellow-servant to appellee, but occupied a position of superiority.

No error reversible in character occurred in the rulings of the court as to the admissibility of the opinion or "expectation" of the witness James, for, when all of the answers of the witness are considered together, it appears he was permitted to state, and did state, his opinion or his "expectation" on the point in question.

There is no complaint as to the action of the court in giving or refusing instructions to the jury.

The judgment is affirmed.

NOTES OF RECENT CASES ON FURNISHING SERVANT SAFE PLACE TO WORK.

1. Mines.
2. Quarries and tunnels.
3. Trench.
4. Saw mills.
5. Railroad.
Track.
Path.
Switchyard.
6. Machinery.
Belting.
Shafting.
7. Floor of factory, etc.
8. Scaffolding.
9. Telegraph poles.
10. Electric wires.
11. Stones or rails improperly piled.
12. Buildings in course of construction.
13. Miscellaneous.

1. Mines.

In PIONEER MIN. & MFG. CO. *v.* THOMAS (Ala. 1902), 32 So. Rep. 15, the plaintiff and another were driving a heading in defendant's mine and it was their duty to see that the roof of this heading was kept in proper and safe condition. The two men had braced one rock and after driving the heading past the timbering, they exposed another rock when the plaintiff was ordered to cut off the upper corner so that a tramway might curve in. The other man continued working at the heading and furthering uncovering the rock and neither put in any additional timber nor tested the roof. There was only one sledge hammer for both men and first one and then the other would use it. The plaintiff wanted to use it and as he passed under the unbraced rock to get it from the other man, the rock fell and injured him. A judgment for plaintiff was reversed. The court said that the injuries were due to the plaintiff's own negligence, that it was his duty to see that the roof was in proper condition.

In UNION GOLD MIN. CO. *v.* CRAWFORD (Colo. 1902), 69 Pac. 600, the plaintiff was a miner employed in defendant's mine. The mine was in levels and the fourth level had been leased by the defendant to a lessee. The plaintiff was at work at the bottom of the shaft which the defendant was at the time engaged in sinking, and was protected from falling articles by a heavy canopy. While at work a car loaded with ore in charge of an employee of the lessee of the fourth level fell from the fourth level to the bottom of the shaft, a distance of 700 feet, broke the canopy, killed two of the miners and seriously injured the plaintiff. The car while being loaded some distance back from the shaft on the fourth level had started of its own accord, and because of the slant towards the shaft had continued on to the shaft which was only protected at the opening by an iron chain drawn across and fastened at each side by hooks and had been placed there to protect the men from inadvertently stepping into the shaft as they were working in the level near it. A judgment for $15,000 for plaintiff was affirmed. The court said that the injuries were not caused by the negligence of a fellow-servant, and that the plaintiff from the evidence did not know the condition of the fourth level, that was in the same condition at the time of the injury as it was in when turned over to the lessee by the defendant that was therefore responsible for its condition. The law required the defendant to provide a reasonably safe place for its employees. The proximate cause of the injury was the excessive grade in the fourth level, and the absence of a proper barrier at the shaft opening.

In O'FALLON COAL CO. *v.* LAQUET (Ill. 1902), 64 N. E. 767, an action was brought under the act providing for the health and safety of persons employed in coal mines (Hurd's Rev. Stats. 1899, c. 93) to recover damages for the death of a miner due to the alleged wilful negligence of the coal company in failing to furnish "props and cap pieces" when requested by deceased, in order to make safe and secure the roof of a room in which he was at work in the mine, and which fell upon him. The evidence sustained the allegations of the complaint and the court affirmed a judgment for the plaintiff

In SPRING VALLEY COAL CO. *v.* ROWATT (Ill. 1902), 196 Ill. 156, the appellee was employed as a driver in appellants' mine and while passing along a certain passageway was caught by the roof of the mine and thrown or jerked to one side of a loaded "trip" of cars which he was driving and seriously injured. The roof at this point was from four feet to four feet six inches high and was extremely dangerous and had been reported to the company by appellee a few days before the injury, at which time the company promised to repair, but did not. A verdict was rendered for plaintiff and the court affirmed a judgment entered thereon. The court said that it was an elementary principle of law that the duty of furnishing a safe place to work was non-assignable and that the master could not escape liability by an attempt to place such duties on the shoulders of another. The court also said, where the owner wilfully disregards a duty enjoined on him by legislation and endangers those employed in the mine, he cannot say that because one enters a mine, as a miner, with knowledge that the owner has failed to comply with his duty, he is guilty of contributory negligence.

In CONSOLIDATED COAL CO. *v.* LUNDAK (Ill. 1902), 196 Ill. 594, appellee was employed as a driver of a mule hauling cars along a track in appellant's mine and was injured by the fall of a section of slate and rock from the roof of the mine upon the track where he was driving the mule. The day before the accident the attention of appellant's timberman was called to the dangerous condition at that place, and he proposed to put a bar up, but did not, because requested not to by a loader, who said it was intended to fire a shot which might disturb it. The timberman left it, trusting to the loader to secure the place. On the morning of the accident the loader put up a crosspiece and supported it by a post at each end. He was an experienced miner, but not employed for that kind of work. The appellee made six trips before he was hurt. On the last trip, when the place was reached, the mule balked because of a sore shoulder, and in some way one of the posts was knocked down, letting down the crosspiece, and several tons of rock and slate fell on the appellee. The court held that the setting of the prop that fell or was knocked down tended to prove a want of reasonable care on the part of the defendant. The court also held that notices posted throughout the mine in the guise of rules that the business was dangerous and every employee must take constant care to avoid injury, and that the duty of ascertaining the danger and avoiding it was on the employee, so far as they are claimed to operate as a contract against defendant's negligence, were void as against public policy.

In HIMROD COAL CO. *v.* CLARK (Ill. 1902), 197 Ill. 514, the plaintiff's intestate was employed as a machine runner in appellant's mine, and was killed while so employed by the fall of a portion of the mine roof that was not propped, as was known to the appellant. The appellant claimed that the deceased had an equal opportunity with appellant to ascertain the dangerous condition of the roof, and that it was a duty imposed upon him by rules of the company. The evidence showed that he had nothing to do with timbering or propping the roof; that this duty was performed by "timbermen" who were employed by appellant for the purpose; that the deceased would be in one place a short time at work when he would move to another place further along in the mine to continue his work, and that he had no time to inspect the roof. The court said that, under these circumstances, the deceased had a right to rely upon the appellant and its servants employed for that purpose to see that the roof of the mine was safe. While a servant must take notice of defects which are patent, he is not required to make an examination. He has the right to presume that the master has used reasonable care in making the place where he does his work reasonably safe. The rules that were posted in the mine requiring the employees to ascertain the safety of the roof before working under it were but attempts to make laws, and so far as they are claimed to operate as contracts against the negligence of the appellant, they are void as against public policy.

In ALASKA UNITED GOLD MINING CO. *v.* MUSET (U. S. C. C. A. 1902), 114 Fed. 66, plaintiff's intestate and another were employed at the bottom of a mine shaft and when about to blast would give a signal to the engineer who operated the elevator, who in turn would signify that he understood by raising and then lowering the bucket. They gave the signal and then ignited the fuse and signaled the engineer to hoist. They were raised a short distance and then lowered and the engineer shouted down the shaft that the compressed air by which the elevator was operated was cut off. The companion of the deceased climbed the elevator rope and escaped, but deceased was unable to do so and was killed by the blast. The air had been cut off by the foreman, who had the full charge and operation of the mine. There had been an iron ladder in the shaft, but it had been removed several weeks before and a new chain ladder was about to be placed there. A judgment for plaintiff was affirmed. The court said that the defendant owed a duty to provide adequate means of escape for its employees, and having failed to do so, it was liable.

2. Quarries and Tunnels.

In SOUTHERN INDIANA R'Y CO. *v.* MOORE (Ind. App. 1902), 63 N. E. 863, the appellee was employed in appellant's quarry, at the bottom of a ledge thirty or forty feet high, and received fatal injuries from large stones, that had been jarred from the ledge by explosions of dynamite, falling upon him. He had been warned to seek a place of safety before the explosions, but had been ordered to return to his work after the explosions took place. A verdict was rendered for the plaintiff, and the appellate court reversed the judgment entered thereon because of the erroneous charge of the trial judge, that it was the duty of the master to exercise care and diligence in the inspection of the work, its places, tools and machinery, so as to enable him to know that it was safe, so far as human foresight can know. The court said that it was only the duty of the master to furnish a reasonably safe place to work; to use the care of a reasonably prudent person.

In TRAPASSO v. COLEMAN (N. Y. Sup. Ct. 1902), 74 App. Div. 33. the plaintiff's intestate was employed in a quarry getting out rock that was loosened from time to time from a hillside by blasting. While he was at work upon a large rock at the base of the hill, another rock that had been loosened, probably by a previous blast, fell upon him, causing injuries from which he died. The court said that the danger was one which must have been as obvious to the plaintiff's intestate as to the defendants, and the latter having furnished him with all needful appliances and with competent fellow-servants, there could be no recovery. A judgment entered on a directed verdict for defendants was affirmed.

In WARD v. NAUGHTON (N. Y. Sup. Ct., June, 1902), 74 App. Div. 68, two gangs of workmen were engaged in drilling and digging rocks in trenches that had approached until a wall of rock of only two feet in thickness separated the two gangs. The plaintiff was a workman in one of these trenches, and was injured by a fall of the intervening wall of rock, caused by a blast set off by the other gang of workmen. The failure to give adequate warning of the firing of the blast was the alleged negligence. The court said that the defendants having provided a competent foreman and intrusted with the details of the work, they cannot be held responsible for the neglect of the foreman to give an adequate warning to the plaintiff. The giving of the warning was merely an incident of the work. A judgment for plaintiff was reversed, though by a divided court. The minority opinion cited with approval Belleville Stone Co v. Mooney (N. J. 1897), 61 N. J. L. 253, where the court held that the giving of the warning of firing the blast was embraced in the duty owed by an employer to his employees of furnishing and keeping a safe place to work.

In NEILSON v. NEBO BROWNSTONE Co. (Utah, 1902), 69 Pac. 289, where plaintiff employed by the defendant in its stone quarry was injured, it was alleged, by the negligence of the defendant in not providing him with a safe place to work; that on the day of the injury the defendant's foreman in charge, without affording the plaintiff reasonable time to retreat or escape from his work and while he was at work, blasted large quantities of rock, causing particles to fly, by some of which pieces of rock the plaintiff was struck and injured. The plaintiff was allowed to testify, after stating that he was twenty-three years old, that he had no experience in a quarry and had never been where they were blasting. The testimony was objected to as not within the issues and as being admissible only in rebuttal on the issue of contributory negligence. A judgment for plaintiff was reversed. The court said that, though it was in the discretion of the court to admit the testimony, a statement was not made to the jury limiting the testimony to the purpose for which it was admissible, and an asked instruction having been refused, the judgment was reversed.

In COCHRAN v. SHANAHAN (W. Va. 1902), 41 S. E. 140, the plaintiff, an employee of a firm engaged in the opening of a tunnel for a railroad, after, as directed, swabbing out a number of drill holes with a wooden stick and finding one obstructed, was ordered by the foreman to take a steel drill and open the hole. While doing so, with the foreman standing near by, an explosion occurred in the hole which destroyed one of the plaintiff's eyes. The evidence was wholly silent as to the cause of the explosion, whether it was a piece of dynamite, or one of the electric exploders, or whether it was a loaded hole that had failed to go off. As there was nothing in the evidence from which it could be inferred that the injury to the plaintiff resulted from the failure of the defendants to perform any of the duties which the law imposes on a master in respect to furnishing a safe place for the servant to work, proper appliances, etc., the law applicable to fellow-servants applied and governed the case. The plaintiff knew it was a dangerous work and assumed the risk.

In ROCKPORT GRANITE CO. *v.* BJORNHOLM (U. S. C. C. A. 1902), 115 Fed. 947, the plaintiff, an employee of the defendant, was injured by being struck by a piece of rock that was thrown in the air when a blast was set off in the defendant's quarry. The plaintiff knew the blast was going off, and was at a supposed safe distance. There was evidence that the defendant's superintendent failed to tap the stone to ascertain whether it was shelly and safe for powder. The court affirmed a judgment for plaintiff. The court said that when an employee assumes the known risks of his employment he assumes them with all their qualifications. While there is always danger of flying stones, yet it is plain from the record that as the danger here came mainly, if not wholly, from shelly rock, it was one which might have been largely, if not entirely, guarded against by care on the part of the superintendent of the kind which he was accustomed to exercise.

8. Trench.

IN MCLAINE *v.* HEAD & DOWST CO. (N. H. 1902), 52 Atl. 545, the plaintiff was a laborer in the employ of defendant, working at leveling and tamping the earth in a trench from fifteen to twenty feet deep, and was injured by a load of dirt being dumped upon him without warning. The boss of the gang, both before and after the accident, gave the warning, but failed to do so that one time. The plaintiff could not see the load from the trench and relied on the warning. A nonsuit was ordered and exceptions thereto were overruled. The court said that the plaintiff, the foreman and the teamsters were engaged in a common employment filling the trench. The only breach of the master's duty suggested was the failure to provide the plaintiff with a safe place to work, and to keep it safe. It is urged that the plaintiff could not safely work at the bottom of the ditch without warning, and the master's duty was not performed unless the warning was given. It is not suggested that the place itself was unsafe. The place and the danger varied as the work progressed. Having provided a safe place, the master is not liable upon the ground of that obligation if the place is made unsafe by the negligence of servants employed, not to provide the place, but to do the work in the place.

In LITCHFIELD *v.* BUFFALO, ROCHESTER & PITTSBURGH R. CO. (N. Y. Sup. Ct. 1902), 73 App. Div. 1, the plaintiff's intestate was one of a gang of men employed by the defendant to dig a trench across an embankment on top of which the defendant's trains were operated. After the trench was successfully dug, the plaintiff's intestate was retained as a helper to the masons who were to construct a culvert at the bottom of the ditch, and while so employed he was killed by the caving in of a quantity of earth from one side of the ditch caused by the jarring of the earth by heavy trains passing above. A judgment for plaintiff was reversed, the court saying that the trench or ditch was not a place in which to work, furnished by the master, but was made by deceased and his co-employees in the excavating gang, and the fact that the deceased at the time of the accident had finished his work as a member of that gang and was assisting another gang in the same ditch, did not render the defendant liable. If the deceased had commenced work in the trench as a mason's helper, and had not with his associates constructed it, the law of safe place would apply.

4. Saw mills.

In LINDSEY *v.* TIOGA LUMBER CO. (La. 1902), 32 So. Rep. 464 (107 La.), the plaintiff's intestate, a minor seventeen years of age, was employed in the defendant's mill and had been at work seven or eight days, when he was hurt. His employment consisted of catching lumber as it was dropped from the saws to the live rollers on its way to the edger. He was placed at a point between the edger and the live rollers, and the end of a piece of lumber struck him with sufficient force to shove him from his position, against the edger and inflicted a wound which caused his death about twenty-four hours afterwards. The evidence showed he was entirely unfamiliar with saw-mill machinery and had been employed outside in the yard until the morning of the day of the injury, when the foreman called him in and assigned him to the work without any warning or instructions. A judgment for plaintiff was affirmed. The court said that it was satisfied from the evidence that the place where he was at work and the work were both dangerous and that the company was liable for failing to give the warning the boy was entitled to receive.

In HILL *v.* BIG CREEK LUMBER CO. (La. 1902), 32 So. Rep. 372, (107 La.), the plaintiff's intestate was employed as a feeder of lumber to the edger in defendant's saw mill. He and another employee received the lumber from the gang saw and fed it to the edger behind which were stationed other employees, whose duty it was to keep the way clear for the lumber as it was passing through the edger, which is a table having small circular saws. If the table back of the edger was allowed to be clogged, imminent danger would result to those feeding the edger. One of the employees, whose especial duty it was to keep the table clear, had gone off somewhere, when the deceased and the other employee fed to the edger a large heavy plank, which went though all right except about two feet of the rear of the plank where the front end came in contact with a jam, a clog of lumber upon the table back of the edger, and as that stopped its progress, the plank turned a little and raised, and the small circular saws of the edger seized it and flung it with incredible force back out of the edger and against the deceased and crushed the life out of him. The case was tried before a judge without a jury, and a judgment was rendered for defendant. The court reversed that, and adjudged that the plaintiff recover $5,000. The court said that it was asked to hold that the deceased had assumed, as a risk of his employment, that the live rollers, the table and conveyor back of the edger would be kept unobstructed, would not be permitted to clog with lumber, and it refused to do so. A master must be held responsible not only for the employment of competent persons to do his work, but also for the failure to employ enough of them to do it safely, as respects others employed, at all times.

In HESSE *v.* NATIONAL BASKET CO. (N. J. 1902), 52 Atl. 384, the plaintiff, a minor sixteen years of age, was at work in front of a circular saw that ran through an iron table that was so high from the floor of defendant's shop that it was necessary for plaintiff while at work to stand upon a wooden bench, four and a half inches high. The bench stood upon the floor, and was not fixed to it in any way which the plaintiff knew. The accident occurred on the fifth day after he commenced work at the saw and was caused by the bench tipping, thereby causing him to lose his balance and fall towards the saw-mill table, thus bringing his hand in contact with the saw. Just what caused the bench to tip does not appear. The court said it is manifest that the tipping of the bench was caused by the plaintiff having assumed a position so near the end as to destroy the equilibrium of the bench, and that the position was assumed either of his own volition or by reason of a push given intentionally or unintentionally to the bench by a fellow-servant. If the fellow-servant pushed the bench, the master is relieved of liability. If it tipped because the plaintiff moved too near the end of the bench, the master is also relieved from liability. The plaintiff was old enough to fully appreciate the danger and the likelihood of the bench tipping, if he stood too near to one or the other of its ends, and took the risk to the same extent as a person of more mature age.

In HILDENBRAND *v.* MARSHALL (Tex. Civ. App. 1902), 69 S. W. 492, the plaintiff, a minor nineteen years of age, was employed in defendant's saw mill, and had been at work nine days, when the foreman, who was ripping up material for blinds with the circular saw, called the plaintiff and instructed him to remove the material that had accumulated. In doing so the plaintiff's hand came in contact with the saw that was set in a bench or table three feet high, and projected above about three inches, and his fingers were cut off. Some lumber piled near the saw and that fell against the plaintiff was alleged to have been the proximate cause of the injury. A judgment for plaintiff was reversed on the ground that it was error to refuse to give an instruction that if the condition and manner of the piling of the lumber that fell was open and obvious to the plaintiff, and he was of sufficient intelligence to know the danger, if any, he could not recover, even if defendant was negligent in piling the lumber.

5. Railroad.

Track.
Path.
Switch yard.

In CHICAGO & ERIE R. CO. *v.* LEE (Ind. App. 1902), 64 N. E. 675, the plaintiff's intestate was a brakeman on defendant's freight train, acting as switchman, and while walking sideways on the track before a slowly moving train that was backing he stepped into some interlocking switch wires that ran under the track and were uncovered, and he was run over and killed. A verdict was rendered for plaintiff, and a judgment entered thereon was reversed because of an instruction that railroad companies are required to use the "highest care" in providing persons in their employ a reasonably safe place to do their work. The court said that the deceased had the right to presume that his employer had invested the place where he was working with such safeguards as ordinary prudence required. He could not assume the risk attendant upon the use of an appliance of an unusual character where he was ignorant of its existence and had no notice of any danger.

In NEIDER *v.* ILLINOIS CENT. R. CO. (La. 1901), 32 So. Rep. 366 (107 La.), the plaintiff was a flagman in defendant's employ and alleged negligence of defendant in not providing a safe path for him to run on in doing his work. The defendant had five parallel tracks running through a very wide street and a cross-tie; a piece of lumber eight inches by ten inches thick and ten feet long had lain alongside the path and clear of it for several days. On the day of the accident some unknown person moved the tie to a position across the flagman's path, and soon after, as he was running in front of a slowly moving train to flag the cross streets, he tripped over the tie, fell, and was run over by the train. The court said there was no negligence shown on the part of the defendant, and the judgment for plaintiff was set aside.

In MURRAN v. CHICAGO, M. & ST. P. R. Co. (Minn. 1902), 90 N. W. 1056, 12 Am. Neg. Rep. 100, a section hand cleaning snow from a switch was struck by a car that had been kicked from a train that the section hand saw and that had been kicking cars, but that was motionless when the section hand turned his back to it, and within a half minute was struck by the kicked car that was allowed to approach him without warning though a switchman in charge saw the section hand's danger and could have stopped the car. A verdict was rendered for defendant, and an order denying plaintiffs's motion for a new trial was reversed.

In SOUTHERN R. Co. v. MCLELLAN (Miss. 1902), 32 So. Rep. 283, a flagman was employed by defendant on one of its local freight trains, and while walking at night alongside the train that was backing up to make a coupling to another car he stepped on a piece of slag, with which material the road was ballasted, and was thrown under the train, and both hands were so crushed that they had to be amputated. A judgment for plaintiff was reversed because of the rejection of some of defendant's offered evidence. The court said that the gravamen of the complaint was whether the roadway constituting the switch was or was not negligently constructed by reason of too large pieces of slag used in ballasting it, the servants of appellant being entitled to a reasonably safe roadway.

In SMITH v. ERIE R. Co. (N. J. 1902), 52 Atl. 634, 12 Am. Neg. Rep. 113, the plaintiff was in the employ of the defendant as baggageman and acting brakeman, and was injured in a derailment of the passenger car as the train was rounding a curve on a down grade of about sixty feet to the mile. Non-repair of the track was the alleged cause of the derailment. A judgment for plaintiff was affirmed. The court said: So far as the trainmen are concerned, the tracks and roadbed come within the familiar rule that imposes on the master the duty of taking ordinary care that the places in which and the appliances with which the servant is required to work shall be reasonably safe for the purpose.

In SMITH v. ATLANTA & C. R. Co. (N. C. 1902), 42 S. E. 139, the plaintiff was engaged in painting a switch target that was situated near a track of defendant in the switch yard and he was at times in danger of passing trains; the track was straight for several hundred feet and there was no obstruction in the view in either direction along the track. While so employed he was struck by a train that approached without warning and was injured. A judgment for plaintiff was reversed. The court said that the engineer had the right to assume that the plaintiff, in the possession of all his faculties and not hampered by any obstructions that would have prevented his instantaneous avoidance of danger. would have stepped out of danger, and that the judge's charge that allowed the jury to consider the continuing of his work by the plaintiff as evidence that he was engrossed with his work and on that account was inadvertent to the approach of the train, was error.

In MERCANTILE TRUST CO. *v.* PITTSBURGH & W. R'Y CO., LAKE, Intervener (U. S. Circ. Ct. App. 1902), 115 Fed. 475, a brakeman on the second section of a train was killed in a wreck at night caused by a landslide due to a storm of unusual violence. The train dispatcher knew of the landslides occurring along the line and notified the employees of the first section of the train, but failed to give any warning to those in charge of the second section that left the station twenty minutes later. The court held that the failure to warn the second section was a proximate cause of the accident by which decedent came to his death and was culpable negligence for which the respondent was liable. The court said that the duty of informing a servant of special or extraordinary risks connected with his service is a primary duty of the master, and the delegation thereof to any inferior servant cannot relieve him of the responsibility imposed upon him by law.

6. Machinery.

Belting.

Shafting.

In MYERS *v.* SAULT STE. MARIE PULP AND PAPER CO. (Canada App.), 3 Ont. Law, 600, the plaintiff, in the employ of defendants, had to climb a step-ladder and step over the unguarded rim of a revolving cog wheel to a plank in going to and from his work in the defendant's pulp factory. In coming from his work at the time of the injury a fellow-employee, for mischief, removed the step-ladder as the plaintiff was stepping on it, and, in recovering himself, the plaintiff's leg went through the spokes of the wheel and it was injured. The cog wheel was not guarded in any way. A judgment for plaintiff was affirmed. The court said the jury were warranted in finding that the providing a step-ladder upon which the workman had to go to and from his work, which was easily movable and which the defendants ought reasonably to have anticipated might at any time be removed by any one, whether a right or a wrong-doer, was not taking a reasonable precaution for the safety of the workman. The intervention of the workman in wrongfully taking away the ladder did not relieve the defendants, for their negligence still remained an operating cause of the plaintiff's injury.

IN CHICAGO & GRAND TRUNK R. CO *v.* SPURNEY (Ill. 1902), 197 Ill. 471, the plaintiff was in the employ of the defendant company as a laborer in its grain elevator, and it was his duty to guide and handle certain shovels which were connected with machinery, which was operated by steam. The shovels were moved by a rope, one end being attached to an automatic pulley geared on the shaft of the machinery, the other end of the rope being attached to the grain shovels that were guided by the plaintiff and others. At the time of the injury the machinery was started without any warning, and the plaintiff's leg was caught in the rope while he was adjusting it and he was severely injured. A judgment for plaintiff for $15,000 was affirmed. The court said that it could not be ruled as matter of law that the plaintiff assumed the risk of the danger from which he suffered the injury. The risks assumed by a servant are such only as cannot be obviated by the employment by the master of reasonable measures of precaution. Risks that are unreasonable or extraordinary or that arise from the master's negligence are not assumed.

In PRICE v. UNITED STATES BAKING CO. (Mich. 1902), 90 N. W. 286, the plaintiff was employed in the icing room of defendant's bakery, and it was her duty to attend to the making of marshmallow and to the mixing of icing. These two confections were in tanks that stood side by side, and were operated by machinery. In beating up icing, the plaintiff put the belt on with her hands, and when the icing was beat up she pushed the belt off with her foot; she was told to do so by the foreman. On the day of the accident the tanks were moved so close together that the plaintiff could not push the belt off with her right foot towards the right, as she had been accustomed, but had to push it off to the left with her right foot. She had only done it two or three times when her foot was caught by the belt, carried to the pulley and injured very severely. A judgment on directed verdict for defendant was affirmed. The court said that in operating the belt the danger was as apparent to the plaintiff as anyone, and in continuing to operate it after knowing the manner of its operation, she assumed any risk there might be in so doing.

7. Floor of factory, etc.

In CORNING STEEL CO. v. POHLPLOTZ (Ind. App. 1902), 64 N. E. 476, a complaint was held to be demurrable that stated that the appellee was a minor, eighteen years of age employed in defendant's steel works, and while at work stepped on the edge of an uncovered vat of molten metal, to hammer a cog-wheel into place, as directed, and struck at but missed the wheel, and was thus forced to swing round and fall into the metal. The averments showed negligence in failing to cover the vat and to inform appellee of the danger, and that missing a blow he would be thrown into the metal, but there was no averment that he did not know for what the vat was used, nor that he lacked the opportunity to observe it for himself. The court held that the complaint showed that he assumed an open and obvious risk, notwithstanding averments of inexperience and want of knowledge. A judgment for plaintiff was reversed.

In STEWART v. INTERNATIONAL PAPER CO. (Me. 1901), 51 Atl. 237, the plaintiff was in the employ of the defendant in the latter's pulp mill and he was injured by stepping into a drain, the cover of which had been taken off by a fellow-employee and not replaced. The drain, several inches deep, was in the basement and was used to carry off the waste pulp, and the cover had to be removed when the drain was to be used for its intended purpose. When the cover was on it formed a part of the floor of the basement. A verdict was rendered for plaintiff and the exceptions thereto by defendant were sustained. The court said that the servant whose duty it was to remove the plank in order that the drain might be used and then to replace it was not performing any of the personal duties which the master owed to his employee. The negligence was not in the construction or maintenance of a reasonably safe place for the servant to perform his work for which the master would be liable, but it was the fault of a co-servant in the operation of an appliance provided by the master.

In DENE v. ARNOLD PRINT WORKS, (Mass. 1902), 64 N. E. 203, 12 Am. Neg. Rep. 74, the plaintiff attempted to pass between two machines on one of which he worked in defendant's mill, when he slipped and to save himself from falling he threw out his hand and it was caught in the gears of one of the machines and injured. The plaintiff was between fourteen and fifteen years of age and had worked about two months on the machine. He had passed through the passage way twice a few minutes before he slipped. The testimony tended to show that the slipping might have been caused by oil on the floor, but there was no evidence how long the oil had been there, or how it came there. There was also testimony that the place where he slipped was unlighted. The court said that the absence of light could not have been the cause of the slipping, as the plaintiff had passed that way twice before. The presence of oil on the floor was not of itself evidence of negligence. Exceptions brought by plaintiff were overruled.

In RAIFORD *v.* WILMINGTON & W. R. Co. (N. C. 1902), 41 S. E. 806, the plaintiff was employed in defendant's machine shop dismantling an engine that had been in a wreck, and while engaged in removing an iron engine apron that covered the engine bumper that extended some two feet from the track where the plaintiff stood, he was injured by a large piece of iron that had been fastened underneath the bumper and that fell to the track below and in some unaccountable manner rebounded and struck him. The piece of iron was kept in place beneath the bumper by an iron rod extending from the top of the bumper and through it, and the rod was fastened underneath the piece of iron by a nut. Just before the plaintiff began his work another employee had removed the nut and withdrawn the rod. The pressure of wood against iron, probably rust of the iron and indentations of the wood, hold the piece of iron in place for a short time. The alleged negligence is the failure of the employee who removed the nut and withdrew the rod to remove the piece of iron. A judgment for plaintiff was reversed. The court said that the motion of defendant to dismiss the action should have been granted.

In SURLES *v.* KISTLER (Pa. 1902), 51 Atl. 887, the plaintiff had been employed in the defendant's laundry for years, and on the day of the injury was assisting, as was her duty, in scrubbing the floor. The floor was covered by wooden racks where the regular work of the laundry was going on, but these had been raised by the plaintiff and set on one side in order to scrub the floor. She testified that the floor gave way and her foot went through; that at the time there was nothing to indicate that the floor was unsafe to walk upon at the place where she was hurt. A judgment for defendant was affirmed. The court said that in cases of this character mere proof of the happening of the accident is not enough to justify a recovery. In this case the employer was bound to provide a reasonably safe place to work. He had apparently done so. The floor in question had been used by the plaintiff and others for years. If it was wearing out no one would be able to notice it more quickly than she. Yet she says she saw nothing wrong until the moment of the accident.

In DIRECT NAVIGATION Co. *v.* ANDERSON (Tex. Civ. App. 1902), 69 S. W. 174, the plaintiff was a deck hand on defendant's tug boat and part of his duties was to keep the deck clear. At the time of the injury he was, as directed, making a rope attached to a barge fast to the tug for the purpose of towing. As he stepped he put his foot on the end of a siphon pipe used for pumping water out of the hold, and that had been left on deck by another deck hand. As he leaned forward to take a turn with the rope around a cleat his foot slipped from the pipe into the coil of rope that was being taken up by the moving of the tug, and the rope tightening around the cleat caught his leg between the rope and cleat and crushed it so that it had to be amputated. A judgment for plaintiff was reversed. The court said that if it had not been a part of the plaintiff's duties to keep the deck clear he would not have assumed the risk, unless he should be charged with the risk of negligence of a fellow-servant or unless its being left on the deck was a mere detail of the work, but it being a part of his general work he must be charged with the risk, although owing to the darkness he did not see the siphon and was not aware of its presence.

8. Scaffolding.

In FROST MFG. CO. *v.* SMITH (Ill. 1902), 197 Ill. 253, the appellee was one of a number of carpenters engaged at work in one of the appellant's buildings in course of construction. He had been employed by appellant's superintendent and worked under his direction in framing timbers in the building. Other carpenters were at work putting in girders and used a platform that was put up and taken down as their work changed from one part of the building to another, as directed by the superintendent. The carpenters after a time reached the place where the appellee was at work and erected the platform over him. He proposed to move to another part of the building, but the superintendent directed him to continue his work at that place, and soon after the platform fell and injured him. A judgment for the appellee was affirmed. The court said that the principle applicable to the case would seem to be the duty resting upon the master to provide the appellee with a reasonably safe place to work. Whether appellee was a fellow-servant of the other carpenters was a question of fact which was settled against appellant. He had nothing to do with the construction or use of the platform.

In THOMPSON *v.* BARTLETT (N. H. 1901), 51 Atl. 633, the defendants were the builders of a gasometer tank for a lighting company, and plaintiff was employed by them to calk the edges of the iron plates after being riveted. It was the defendants' duty to prepare stagings for the calkers and to move the stagings from place to place as the work required. The stagings were erected by placing horses with projecting ledger boards near to the inside of the tank and laying a double row of planks upon the ledger boards so that the planks would project over the boards sufficiently to make them secure to walk upon. Before the day of the injury the plaintiff had calked all of the edges of the tank except those portions where the horses prevented. On the morning of the accident the defendants moved the horses away from the inside of the tank about eight inches, so that the plaintiff could get at the edges. The plaintiff walked once over the planks in their changed position without discovering anything wrong in the way the planks were placed. When he finished the calking he began to retrace his steps to the ladder that led from the staging to the top of the tank. The defendants had, in the meantime, again moved the horses back against the tank, but in such a way that a plank was insecurely placed, it resting on another plank instead of on a ledger board. The plaintiff knew the horses had been again moved, but not that the plank was insecurely placed. He could have seen the position of the plank had he looked at the farther end, but while retracing his steps his duty required him to examine the edges of the plates to see that the calking had been properly done. He took two or three steps on the insecure plank and it began to fall, and he was unable to save himself, and was injured. A judgment for plaintiff was affirmed.

In LANGAN *v.* TYLER (U. S. C. C. A., February, 1902), 114 Fed. 716, the defendant was the owner of a building containing an elevator that was run by his servant. On the day of the accident the servant thought the elevator was rnnning more slowly than usual and tried unsuccessfully to communicate with defendant's agent, whom he had been instructed to call upon in such cases. He then asked the plaintiff's intestate, who was in a similar employment in a building a short distance away, to come over, and after shutting-down time the two men took the machine apart, and after working at it awhile, put it together and started it. The intestate was shortly after killed by the giving away of a hanger. A judgment entered on a directed verdict for the defendant was affirmed. The court said that the deceased was not a servant of the defendant, being a volunteer, and that the defendant did not owe him the duty of providing a safe place to work, and was not liable for his death, though the defendant may have been chargeable with notice of the defective condition of the hanger.

9. Telegraph Poles.

In CLEVELAND, C. C. & ST. L. R. Co. *v.* SCOTT (Ind. App. 1902), 64 N. E. 896, the plaintiff was a lineman in the employ of the defendant company that was replacing old telegraph poles with new ones and then restringing the wires. It was the duty of the plaintiff to fasten the wires on the new poles and on those that had been left after having been inspected. The wires had to be stretched, and this was done by fastening them to the top of one of the poles. The pole so selected had to sustain a heavy strain and had to be braced, and in this instance being an old one, that was alleged not to have been inspected, it broke, and plaintiff who was on it fell and was injured. The pole proved to be rotten below the ground. A judgment for plaintiff was reversed because the complaint did not state that the pole fell because of a defect in its condition.

In WESTERN UNION TEL. CO. *v.* TRACY (U. S. C. C. A. 1902), 114 Fed. 282, the plaintiff was a lineman in the employ of the defendant, and was injured while removing wires from a pole that broke while he was on it. Three other poles were secured by guy ropes, but the fourth one was not, the foreman who made an inspection not ordering it done. The pole broke below the surface of the ground, and the defective condition could have been readily ascertained by the usual test by tools provided for the purpose. There was conflicting evidence as to whether the lineman was in duty bound to determine the safety of the pole or that the lineman could rely upon the inspection of the foreman. The court said the question was properly left to the jury, and a judgment for plaintiff was affirmed. The court said that as the jury had found that the duty of inspection was not that of the lineman, it was the positive duty of the company itself, and it was responsible for its non-performance, notwithstanding the fact that it had engaged another, however competent, to perform it.

10. Electric wires.

In THOMPSON *v.* NEW ORLEANS & C. R. CO. (La. 1902), 32 So. Rep. 177, (107 La.), the plaintiff intestate was a laborer employed with others in carrying heavy rails to the center of the street, where the company was about to lay them, and the company was also reconstructing its feeder system of electricity. The plaintiff intestate and his fellow-laborers had carried one rail and placed it as directed near the iron trolley pole. While carrying the second rail it came in contact with the trolley pole violently, according to the testimony of the defendant company, but this was denied by the plaintiff, and all the men received a shock which was severe enough to kill the plaintiff intestate. The defendant contended that the swinging of the rail violently against the pole broke the glass insulator, exposing an iron screw that cut the live wire and left it rubbing against the pole that thus became charged with electricity. The court said that it was led to believe from the facts that there was a live wire uninsulated or defectively insulated resting on the pole in question and that the company was liable for the death of the intestate.

In HOUGH v. GRANTS PASS POWER CO. (Oregon, 1902), 69 Pac. 655, a lineman was working under the supervision of the defendants manager on dead electric light wires, just before the time that the dynamos in the power house were usually started, when the manager directed another workman who had a bicycle, to hurry to the power house and notify the employees there not to start the current until they received further notice. The employee did not go immediately to the power house, and before he got there the current had been started and the lineman received the current in his body, fell to the ground and was killed. A judgment for damages for his death was affirmed. The court said that the vocation of a lineman may be classed as hazardous, but in this instance, neither the immediate work in hand, nor the place in which it was performed was hazardous or dangerous, and it was the duty of the defendant to take proper and reasonable precautions to guard against converting his position of safety into one of peril. The duty that the manager attempted to perform by the directions he gave the messenger, was one personal to the master, and it was not discharged by the mere selection of an agent with directions to give the notice, whether the agent was a competent and careful person or not. The manager was still responsible for any dereliction of duty on the part of the agent, because he was directed to discharge a part of the master's duties and therefore became vice-principal and in no sense a fellow-servant with the injured party.

11. Stones, rails, etc., improperly piled.

In GEORGIA R. & BANKING CO. v. RAYFORD (Ga. 1902), 42 S. E. 234, a demurrer to the petition was overruled where it was stated that the petitioner was one of a gang of men engaged in moving steel rails from one car to another, and that the foreman pointed out a certain rail to be moved, and that when it was lifted, it was the cause of one of the other rails in the pile to roll down on the petitioner's foot and crush it. The court said the contentions of the defendant that the petition showed that the danger of disturbing the equilibrium of the pile of rails was apparent to one man as another, was answered by the allegation in the petition that it was impossible for petitioner to see from his position that it was not safe to obey the order given him.

In MILLER v. MERCHANTS & MINERS TRANSP. CO. (Ga. 1902), 42 S. E. 385, a demurrer to the plaintiff's petition was sustained where it was stated that the plaintiff was defendants' employee, and that while he was going along between two piles of lumber on the deck of defendants' vessel that he was assisting to load, it listed and caused one of the pieces of lumber to fall on him and injure him; that he was in his proper place and was then unaware of any improper distribution of the cargo, and that he had the right to assume that the position he occupied was safe, and that the ship was in proper condition to be loaded; that the ship was defectively constructed and improperly loaded. The demurrer was on the grounds that it was not stated in what manner the ship's cargo was improperly distributed, or in what manner said ship was defective in construction. The demurrer was sustained, and the plaintiff failing to amend the petition was dismissed. The judgment entered was sustained. The court said that even if the plaintiff on account of his ignorance could be excused from specifying the improper loading and defective construction of the ship, the petition only alleges such ignorance at the time of the injury, and not at the time of beginning the suit.

12. Buildings in course of construction.

In BUTLER *v.* LEWMAN, (Ga. 1902), 42 S. E. 98, the owners of a building made a contract with contractors to remodel and repair the building that had suffered from a fire. The contractors employed sub-contractors to do parts of the work and the plaintiff was an employee of a firm that contracted to do the galvanized iron work. He was at work on the third floor and wanted a tool that was on a lower floor and approached a side wall that had three doors in it all alike, one led upstairs, one down stairs and the other opened into the elevator shaft. It was quite dark and he opened the elevator shaft door and tumbled through. The action was brought against the owners and the contractors. The court said that no action could be maintained against the owners as it appeared from the petition that they had surrendered all control of the building to the contractors, who were in possession at the time of the injury, The plaintiff's firm not being independent contractors, the contractors were bound to take reasonable measures to protect the employees of that firm from injuries likely to arise from hidden defects in construction or places of unusual danger about the building, though the relation of master and servant did not exist between them and the plaintiff. A demurrer by the owners was sustained and one by the contractors was overruled.

IN MORRIS *v.* WALWORTH M'F'G CO. (Mass. 1902), 63 N. E. 910, 12 Am. Neg. Rep. 76, the plaintiff was employed by the defendant as a helper or laborer, and while at work on a new building belonging to defendant was ordered by a foreman to do some work that required the plaintiff to walk over three planks fastened together on the under side by a piece of wood nailed to them in the middle. While he was walking over the planks one of them tipped or bent, his toes caught and he fell and broke one of his legs. The court said that without stopping to consider whether the foreman was merely a foreman or superintendent, there was nothing to show that he had anything to do with the planks or that there was any negligence on his part in respect to them. For aught that appears, the planks were fastened together by some of the fellow-workmen of the plaintiff. They could not be considered as ways or works within the statute. They were used merely for a temporary purpose.

IN HOGAN *v.* ARBUCKLE (N. Y. Sup. Ct., June, 1902), 73 App. Div. 591, the defendants entered into a contract with a firm of contractors for the alteration and reconstruction of their building. The contract specified that the contractors were to do all the work incidental to transforming the building. The plaintiff, an employee of an electrical company, while engaged in doing some electrical work in the building, fell through a hole in the floor to the floor below. He did not know the hole was there, and it was obstructed from view by an accumulation of rubbish piled up along the line of his approach. A verdict for $5,000 for plaintiff was sought to be upheld on the ground that the defendants were liable by reason of their failure to provide him with a reasonably safe place to do his work. The court reversed the judgment entered on the verdict, citing as sustaining their decision the case of Murphy *v.* Altman, 28 App. Div. 472, where the court said: "So far as the owner is concerned, each contractor or his workman takes the risk of fault on the part of his fellow-contractors, and his only recourse is against the party who, either personally or through his servants, has been guilty of fault."

13. Miscellaneous.

In CITIZENS' ST. R. CO. *v.* BROWN (Ind. App. 1902), 64 N. E. 98, appellee was employed by appellant to work in its barn to care for its mules. Appellant's agent directed appellee to move some iron frogs without instructing him as to the danger. And while performing the work he was pulled over, his hand caught and his fingers were mashed. The court said that the complaint did not show that the work was dangerous. The act of assisting to move a heavy piece of iron is not of itself dangerous. There was no averment that the danger was latent, and if it was a dangerous undertaking, the danger was as obvious to appellee as to appellant. A judgment for appellee was reversed and the court below was directed to sustain a demurrer to the complaint.

In SKINNER *v.* MCLAUGHLIN (Md. 1902), 51 Atl. 98, the plaintiff was a common laborer employed by the defendant, a shipbuilder, who ordered him to assist in launching a scow and did not warn him of the danger that attended his work, which was to hold, with three other men, the rope that was fastened to the scow and to allow the scow to go as little distance as possible when the water was reached. After the scow slid into the water the rope had to be taken in so rapidly that it could not be regularly coiled. When the scow started the men on deck had to haul in about eighty feet of the heavy rope which ran under the scow, and just as the rear end of the boat reached the water the rope was wrapped around the samson post once and the men were expected to hold on to it, paying it out as gradually as the speed of the scow and their strength would permit. The scow went so rapidly that it jerked the rope that had been piled up behind the men, forming kinks in it, one of which caught the plaintiff's foot and he was dragged in the kink to the samson post and his leg was crushed. There was evidence that the space between a pile of lumber on the dock and the samson post was not sufficient to permit the men to handle the rope without great danger. The court said that owing to the inexperience of the plaintiff, the defendant owed him a duty to warn him when he was directed to take part in work that was thus dangerous.

In ZEIGLER *v.* C. GOTZIAN & CO. (Minn. 1902), 90 N. W. 387, 12 Am. Neg. Rep. 102, the plaintiff, a minor, was ordered by defendant's foreman to wash windows, which was outside the plaintiff's regular employment, and while standing on the ledge of the window sill, he lost his balance, fell to the ground, and was injured. There was a judgment for plaintiff, which was affirmed. The court said, to justify a holding that the plaintiff assumed the risk, it must appear that the plaintiff not only knew that the place in which he was required to work was dangerous, but also that he fully understood, or ought to have understood, all of the risks incident to the doing of the work.

In KUECKEL *v.* O'CONNOR (N. Y. Sup. Ct. 1902), 73 App. Div. 594, the plaintiff, a carpenter, was at work at the bottom of a hoistway, through which the defendants were hoisting bundles of paper to the top of the building, and was injured by the fall of one of these bundles, which slipped out of the sling in which it was being carried up. The plaintiff knew of the danger. The court held that he assumed the risk, as there was evidence that he deemed it an unsafe place to work.

In McCORD *v.* SOUTHERN R'Y CO. (N. C. 1902), 41 S. E. 886, the plaintiff was assisting in digging a large well and the earth being banked mud, knee deep, all around except at the place where a cross-piece was laid over the well, and it being his duty to attend to a steam jet, which was reached by crossing on the cross-piece, he did so after being assured of its safety by the boss in charge, who made a show of fixing the cross-piece when the plaintiff said it seemed insecure. While crossing the cross-piece it turned, and he was thrown into the well and injured. A judgment for the plaintiff was affirmed, the court saying that the evidence tended to show negligence on the part of the master in failing to provide a safe place and appliance for the work.

In BAUMLER *v.* NARRAGANSETT BREWING CO. (R. I. 1902), 51 Atl. 203, an employee cleaning beneath vats of defendant and finding it necessary to assume a cramped position and to crowd into the space underneath until he found it impossible to extricate himself without injury, assumed the risk incident to the work. The court said there was not such an emergency connected with the work of scrubbing a floor as to prevent a person from looking out for his own safety, and a demurrer to the declaration was sustained.

In WELLS, FARGO & CO. *v.* PAGE (Texas Civ. App. 1902), 68 S. W. 528, the plaintiff was employed by the defendant as a guard to protect its express cars from robbers. At one of the stops of the train upon which he was on duty, he attempted to open the door of the express car, when he was injured by the fall of a piece of timber upon his foot. The timber was being carried by the express company, and had been negligently placed in an upright position against the side of the car by the express messenger. The court reversed a judgment for plaintiff on the ground that the duty to furnish a safe place to work extended only to the construction and equipment of the car, and the loading of express matter by another servant in a dangerous manner was not a breach of the duty.

In TEXAS & N. O. R. CO. *v.* GARDNER (Tex. Civ. App. 1902), 69 S. W. 217, the plaintiff was employed by defendant in its shop as a laborer, and his duties were to immerse pieces of machinery in a vat containing lye and caustic soda for the purpose of removing dirt and paint, and afterwards to submit the pieces of machinery to the action of a steam jet. The particles that adhered to the machinery would sometimes be blown back into the plaintiff's face when the steam jet was used, causing sores on his skin. After working at the employment eighteen months, he had to quit because of ill health, and brought suit against the company for the reason that the inhalation of the vapors from the vat had poisoned his system and caused his ill health. He had not been informed of the poisonous character of the contents of the vat, and was not aware of it. A judgment for plaintiff was affirmed. The court said that plaintiff had not assumed the risk, as the dangers were latent.

In OKONSKI *v.* PENNSYLVANIA & O. COAL CO. (Wis. 1902), 90 N. W. 429, 12 Am. Neg. Rep. 206, the plaintiff was a common laborer, and while walking along a platform in the performance of his duties he was injured by a bucket of coal being precipitated upon him. The bucket came in contact with a contrivance called a tripper, that had been placed too far from the hoppers where the coal was intended to have been dumped. The tripper had just been placed in the position by mistake, and was about to be moved to its intended place, but before it could be done the engineer, who did not know that the tripper was being shifted, had sent the bucket of coal along the wire cable. A judgment for plaintiff was reversed. The court said that there was no evidence that would warrant the jury in finding any failure on the part of the defendant in its duty to provide a safe place for plaintiff to work and safe appliance to work with as originally constructed. That the negligence charged was due to the act of a fellow-servant and the company was not liable.

CARTER v. TOWN OF LINEVILLE.

Supreme Court, Iowa, October, 1902

DEFECTIVE SIDEWALK — CONTRIBUTORY NEGLIGENCE. — Where it was shown that a town was negligent in failing to keep a sidewalk in proper repair, and plaintiff testified that she knew the condition of the walk, and that it was dangerous, but she also testified that all the other walks which she might take to reach her destination were also out of repair and dangerous, it was held that whether or not she should have gone out into the street and avoided all the walks, was a question of fact for the jury (1).

APPEAL from District Court, Wayne County.

"Action at law to recover damages for injuries sustained by plaintiff while passing along over one of the defendant's sidewalks. The trial court directed a verdict for defendant, and plaintiff appeals." *Judgment reversed.*

POSTON & SULLIVAN, for appellant.

G. T. WRIGHT, for appellee.

DEEMER, J. — That defendant was negligent in failing to keep the sidewalk upon which plaintiff was injured in proper repair is beyond the pale of reasonable discussion. Plaintiff testified, however, that she knew the condition of the walk, and that it was dangerous; but she also testified that all the other walks which she might take to reach her destination were also out of repair and dangerous. Whether or not she should have gone out into the street, and avoided all the walks, was a question of fact for the jury. The evidence is not such as to justify us in holding as a matter of law that her failure to do so constituted contributory negligence. Of course, if plaintiff knew the walk which she took was dangerous, and that it

1. For other actions against municipal corporations for personal injuries sustained on defective sidewalks, from 1897 to date, see vols. 1–12 AM. NEG. REP., and the current numbers of that series of Reports.

was imprudent to attempt to pass over the same, and there was another convenient walk by which she could have reached her destination, which was reasonably safe, then it was her duty to take the safe way, and avoid the danger. But this rule does not apply when all the convenient walks are dangerous. One is not required to stay indoors because the sidewalks are out of repair. There may be cases where he should use the middle of the street, but such cases are rare. In any event, the question, under the facts disclosed by the record before us, was one of fact for a jury. Barnes *v.* Town of Marcus, 96 Iowa, 675, 65 N. W. Rep. 984; Nichols *v.* Incorporated Town of Laurens, 96 Iowa, 388, 65 N. W. Rep. 335; Sylvester *v.* Incorporated Town of Casey, 110 Iowa, 256, 7 Am. Neg. Rep. 236, 81 N. W. Rep. 455; Hoover *v.* Town of Mapleton, 110 Iowa, 571, 7 Am. Neg. Rep. 237*n*, 81 N. W. Rep. 776; Cox *v.* City of Des Moines, 111 Iowa, 646, 82 N. W. Rep. 993, and cases cited; Barce *v.* City of Shenandoah, 106 Iowa, 426, 5 Am. Neg. Rep. 270*n*, 76 N. W. Rep. 747; Marshall *v.* City of Belle Plaine, 106 Iowa, 508, 5 Am. Neg. Rep. 270*n*, 76 N. W. Rep. 797; and Cosner *v.* City of Centerville, 90 Iowa, 33, 57 N. W. Rep. 636,—are exceptional cases; the facts being quite different from those appearing in the case now before us.

The trial court was in error in directing the verdict, and its judgment is reversed.

OLSON v. HANFORD PRODUCE COMPANY.

Supreme Court, Iowa, October, 1902.

EMPLOYEE INJURED IN DEFECTIVE ELEVATOR—ASSUMPTION OF RISK.—**In an action to recover damages for injuries sustained by plaintiff, an elevator operator in defendant's employ, caused by a projecting girder, it was *held* that plaintiff assumed the risks incident to the use of the elevator in its defective condition, where it appeared from his testimony that he had passed the projecting girder about 700 times before the accident; that he could have seen the girder if he had looked for it, but did not do so, and that at the time of the accident there was sufficient light to read a newspaper on the elevator (1).**

1. See NOTE on LIABILITY FOR ELEVATOR ACCIDENTS, in 8 AM. NEG. REP. 146–157.

Elevator operator killed. In WEBB *v.* D. O. HAYNES & Co. (*N. Y. Supreme Court, Appellate Division, Second Department, October, 1902*), 78 N. Y. Supp. 95, judgment of nonsuit was affirmed on the following facts (as per opinion by WOODWARD, J.,): "This is a judgment of nonsuit, and the plaintiff is entitled to the most favorable inferences which may be drawn from the evidence, but this liberal rule does not open the

APPEAL from District Court, Woodbury County.

From verdict and judgment for plaintiff defendant appeals. *Judgment reversed.*

WRIGHT, CALL & HUBBARD, for appellant.

JEPSON & JEPSON and GEO. W. ARGO, for appellee.

DEEMER, J. — This case was before us on a ruling on a demurrer to plaintiff's petition. [See 111 Iowa, 347, 82 N. W. Rep. 903.] When the cause was remanded defendant filed a general denial, and also pleaded plaintiff's contributory negligence, and his assumption of the risks incident to the use of the elevator. On these issues the case was tried to a jury, resulting in the verdict hitherto stated. No claim is made on this appeal that there was not sufficient evidence of negligence to take the case to the jury, but it is argued that the danger was open and obvious to plaintiff, and that he assumed the risks incident to the use of the elevator in its defective condition. The construction of the elevator is sufficiently described in the opinion when the case was first before us, and we need not again set out the facts with reference thereto. The questions of contributory negligence and assumption of risk were determined at that time on the allegations of the petition, and if there be any substantial evidence

way to a reversal of the judgment. Plaintiff's intestate was killed while operating an elevator for the defendant. The theory of the plaintiff is that her intestate was killed because of the fact that he was put at work running an elevator for which he had not been properly prepared by instructors, but the evidence does not show that he was not adequately instructed in the operation of a comparatively simple piece of machinery, or that his death was due in any measure to his lack of knowledge in this respect. All that is known is that after operating the elevator for a period of about one week some of his fellow-employees heard a cry or a groan, and on running to the elevator found him crushed between the floor and the car of the elevator; the injuries resulting in his death. No one saw the accident, and plaintiff's intestate lived only to say, in answer to the question how it happened, that he did not know. There was no evidence that the elevator was defective or out of repair, and there were no facts or circumstances developed by the evidence from which an inference could be drawn that the deceased was free from contributory negligence or that the accident was a result of any alleged lack of instruction. On the contrary, the plaintiff's own witnesses testify that the deceased was given instruction in the management of the elevator by a competent engineer, and by a fellow-employee who was accustomed to the operation of machinery, and it was not disputed that where the elevator was managed in the manner pointed out by these instructors it was perfectly in the control of the operator. The case is one which is nearly analogous with that of Palcheski *v.* Railroad Co., 69 App. Div. 440, 74 N. Y. Supp. 387, and it would have been entirely improper to permit the jury to speculate upon the matters which might have been suggested, but which were not proved by the evidence. The judgment appealed from should be affirmed, with costs." All concur.

in support of these allegations, there is, of course, no ground on which to disturb the verdict. The instructions given by the trial court were in harmony with the law announced in the opinion when the case was first before us, and the following, taken from the instructions, when considered with the evidence, presents the proposition for solution: "When the plaintiff entered upon the employment in question he did, as a matter of law, accept and assume the ordinary hazards and dangers of the work he was required to do, and such as are incident to it. He thus assumed all the open and obvious risks of his employment which could be reasonably discerned, and must use his sense of sight to the same extent that men of ordinary care and prudence would do under the same circumstances to discover the open and obvious dangers around them. And if, as a reasonably prudent man, so exercising his senses in the position in which he was placed, he should have seen the sill and its proximity to the platform, and have known of the danger arising from the proximity of the sill to the elevator platform, then such danger you will find to be one of the ordinary risks or hazards of his employment, which he had assumed, for the law holds him to have knowledge of those things which a man of ordinary skill and prudence, under the like circumstances, exercising ordinary care for his safety, should have known. It will be for you to say, from all the evidence before you, whether it appears therefrom by a preponderance of such evidence, that the danger which caused the injury of which plaintiff complains was one of the ordinary hazards of plaintiff's employment." Defendant contends that the evidence shows without dispute that plaintiff knew, or by the use of ordinary care should have known, of the defective condition of the elevator; while plaintiff insists that under the evidence this was a question for the jury, which specially found that the defect was not open and obvious, so that a man of ordinary caution should have seen the danger, and of necessity, in view of the general verdict, concluded that plaintiff did not know of the defect. The jury was fully justified in finding that plaintiff did not in fact know of the defect, but on the other question, to wit, as to whether or not he should have known of its condition in the exercise of ordinary diligence, we think the evidence is insufficient to sustain the verdict. In other words, it clearly appears from plaintiff's own evidence that by the use of ordinary care he should have known of the defect. We quote the following from the record, which it seems to us is conclusive on this proposition: Plaintiff testified that he had passed the projecting girder something like 700 times before the accident, and that: "When I got into the elevator, I turned my face to the south. If I turned my face in that direction I could have seen it. If I had turned my face in that direction during the 700 times I could have seen it if I had looked straight up or when I was passing by. The only reason I did not see it was because I didn't look at it." With reference to light in the building he said: "I think it was about 11:30 in the morning that I was hurt. There was one artificial light about five or six feet from the elevator. It was not lit that morning. We usually had lights in the building two or three hours in the morning when we first started to work, and let the lights run until about nine or ten o'clock. Then they were lit again about four or five o'clock in the afternoon. The windows did not furnish light to work all day without the aid of artificial light. I did not turn out the lights that morning myself. I suppose you could read a newspaper on the elevator after you had been in there a little while. You wouldn't have trouble to read a newspaper on the elevator most any time after you had been in there about an hour." In Bryce *v.* Railway Co., 103 Iowa, 671, 72 N. W. Rep. 782, we said: "If he could have ascertained by reasonable observation its dangerous proximity to the track it must be regarded as an obvious danger, which was assumed by continuing in the service of the defendant; in other words, what a man in law ought, by the exercise of reasonable diligence, to know, he does know." Way *v.* Railroad Co., 40 Iowa, 343; Heath *v.* Mining Co., 65 Iowa, 737, 23 N. W. Rep. 148. See, also, the cases cited in that opinion in support of the rule. The results to be arrived at in applying the conceded facts to this rule are so apparent that further argument is unnecessary.

We need only add that the special finding and general verdict are not supported by the evidence, and the judgment is therefore reversed.

KANSAS CITY v. GILBERT ET AL.

Supreme Court, Kansas, October, 1902.

BOY INJURED BY LIVE WIRE ON SIDEWALK—FAILURE OF POLICEMAN TO WARN PASSERS-BY—LIABILITY OF CITY.—1. Assuming, but not deciding, that a city policeman is a mere peace officer of the State, and not an agent of the municipality, competent in the lack of statute or ordinance to charge the latter with responsibility for his negligence in failing to properly remove dangerous obstructions to street travel, or to guard the public against them; yet, if a city negligently allows a broken and suspended electric wire to remain upon the sidewalk after falling down, it will be liable for injuries following the negligent act of a policeman in so moving the wire as to constitute it a conductor of the electric current from above,

and in failing to guard or warn passers-by against it, not because of the policeman's negligent performance of a legally imposed duty, but because of its own negligence in allowing the wire to remain down exposing the public to the hazard of being so misplaced or meddled with as to do harm (1).

(Syllabus by the Court.)

IN BANC. Error from Court of Common Pleas, Wyandotte County. Action by Edward Gilbert and others against the City of Kansas City. From judgment for plaintiffs, defendant brings error. *Judgment affirmed.*

T. A. POLLOCK and M. J. REITZ, for plaintiff in error.

L. W. KEPLINGER and C. W. TRICKETT, for defendants in error.

DOSTER, Ch. J. — This was an action for damages sustained by the plaintiff, a small boy, coming in contact with an electrically charged wire which had fallen down, and which, after falling down, the defendant, the city, had negligently allowed to remain upon one of its sidewalks. The accident occurred on a Saturday afternoon. According to some of the testimony the wire had been down since the preceding Thursday, and according to other testimony it had been down about eight hours; and the jury, in answer to a question whether it had been down "for at least several hours prior to the injury to plaintiff," answered that it had. The wire which caused the injury was a broken telegraph or telephone wire, which had fallen across or near by a "span wire" of an electric street-railway line, and which span wire had evidently become charged with electricity through some defective insulation. There was no evidence of actual notice to the governing officers of the city of the broken and dangerous condition of the wire. A few minutes before the accident a policeman discovered the pendent end of the wire lying on the sidewalk. He coiled it up and laid the coil at the foot of a post at the edge of the sidewalk, and started to report the fact of its being down. He should have remained in proximity to the wire, so as to warn passers-by against it until he could have been relieved from the duty. Such seems to be the charge of negligence, so far as he was concerned. The policeman did not receive any shock from the wire, but evidently it soon became charged, because, presently, the plaintiff came in contact with it and received his injuries. It is probable that the act of the officer in shifting the wire caused it to come in contact with the electrically charged span wire above, and received a current from that source. The jury returned a general verdict in favor of the plaintiff, and were also asked and made answers to special questions, of which those material to notice were as follows: "16. Did the police-

1. See NOTE ON LIABILITY FOR PERSONAL INJURIES CAUSED BY ELECTRIC WIRES, in 8 AM. NEG. REP. 213-221.

man, Mosby, remove the wire by which the plaintiff was injured from the sidewalk, and place it at the foot of pole of the street railway, at the place where the accident to the plaintiff occurred, about five minutes before the accident happened? Answer. Yes. 17. If you answer the preceding question in the affirmative, state if Police Officer Mosby was negligent in placing and leaving such broken wire as he did? Answer. Yes. 18. If you answer the last question, that Police Officer Mosby was negligent, state if such negligence was the direct cause of the plaintiff's injuries. Answer. Partly. 19. If you answer question No. 17 in the affirmative, state if the act of the policeman, Mosby, in placing the wire at the foot of the pole supporting the span wire of West Side Railway Company at the place of the accident, was one direct cause of the accident, without which it would not have occurred. Answer. Yes." No ordinance imposing upon policemen any duty in respect of dangerous conditions of street travel was introduced. Judgment went against the city, to reverse which it has prosecuted error.

The plaintiff in error claims that the petition charged the city with negligence in allowing the wire to remain down after sufficient lapse of time to impart constructive notice of its dangerous condition, whereas, as is further claimed, the above quoted findings and other incidents of the trial show that recovery was allowed for the negligence of the policeman, and that, such being the case, the judgment was erroneous, because as is also contended, a policeman, in law, is a mere peace officer of the State, and not an agent of the city, qualified, in the lack of statute or ordinance, to charge the latter with responsibility for his negligent acts. The criticism of the petition is not well founded. Its allegations were sufficient to permit a recovery on the theory of the city's liability for the negligence of the police officer, assuming him to have been a legally authorized agent, as well as to recover on the theory of constructive notice by lapse of time. There are many decisions holding cities exempt from liability for the negligent acts of a policeman in cases where they have not been constituted by statute or ordinance the agents of the municipality. Peters *v.* City of Lindsborg, 40 Kan. 654, 20 Pac. Rep. 490, is one, and City of Columbus *v.* Ogletree, 96 Ga. 177, 22 S. E. Rep. 709, and Cook *v.* City of Anamosa, 66 Iowa 427, 23 N. W. Rep. 907, are others. However, it is not necessary to determine the question of the city's liability for the negligence of policeman Mosby. The findings of the jury are not to be interpreted as founding the recovery on his acts. A charge of dangerous condition of the street, resulting from a broken electric wire falling and resting on the sidewalk, was made. The evidence and findings did nothing more than show that such generally dangerous condition was given specific character and force by the negligent act of the officer, just as such character and force might have been given by the like act of any other person. The general act of negligence charged and proved was the leaving of the broken wire to hang from above to the sidewalk below, exposing the public to those dangers which some specific occurrence, like the act of Policeman Mosby, might bring into play. The claim of negligence in this respect was submitted to the jury under appropriate instructions, and therefore a finding of the truth of the claim must be regarded as included in the general verdict. If one puts a dangerous mechanical contrivance in the public highway,— one liable to do harm if disarranged or meddled with,—and some meddler does disarrange or set it in motion to the injury of another person, it is no answer to say that the one whose act approximately in point of time or physical volition caused the injury was not the agent of the one who exposed the machine to the hazard of being meddled with. True, it was the act of the policeman in changing the position of the pendent wire so as to receive the electric current from the defectively insulated span wire above that produced the injury; but in law the responsible cause of the injury, or an equally responsible cause of it, was the negligent act of the city in allowing the wire to hang down, subject to the chances of being so moved about as to be made into a conductor of the electric current above.

Some other, but minor, claims of error are made, but none of them are well taken.

The judgment of the court below is affirmed. All the justices concurring.

MISSOURI, KANSAS AND TEXAS RAILWAY COMPANY v. MERRILL ET AL.

KANSAS CITY SURBURBAN BELT RAILROAD COMPANY v. MERRILL ET AL.

Supreme Court, Kansas, October, 1902.

RAILROAD EMPLOYEE INJURED WHILE LOADING CARS—CONNECTING LINES.— 1. A railway company, which delivers a defective freight car to a connecting line, is not liable in damages to an employee of the latter, who is injured by reason of such defects, after the car has been inspected by the company receiving it. The loss of control over the car and over the servants having it in charge relieves the delivering company from responsibility to the employees of the receiving company.

2. That part of the decision in Mo. Kan. & Tex. R'y Co. et al. v. Merrill, 61 Kan. 671, 7 Am. Neg. Rep. 620, 60 Pac. Rep. 819, indicated by the first paragraph of the syllabus, is overruled (1).

(Syllabus by the Court.)

IN BANC. Error from Court of Common Pleas, Wyandotte County.

Action by L. T. Merrill and others against the Missouri, Kansas & Texas Railway Company, and by the same plaintiffs against the Kansas City Surburban Belt Railroad Company. From judgment for plaintiffs, defendants bring error. *Judgment reversed.*

"Defendant in error L. T. Merrill, who was plaintiff in the court below, recovered a judgment against the Kansas City Surburban Belt Railroad Company and the Missouri, Kansas & Texas Railway Company for personal injuries sustained by him in attempting to pass from a flat or coal car to a box car in the yards of the Chicago Great Western Railway Company in Kansas City, Kan. He was a switchman in the employ of the latter company. The flat car belonged to the Missouri, Kansas & Texas Railway company. It was loaded with iron pipe at St. Louis, and the contents consigned to St. Joseph, Mo. The line of the latter company terminates at Kansas City, Mo. The car was provided with end gates, which were held in an upright position by wooden cleats, nailed to the inside of the side boards on the outside of the end gates. There were no iron hooks or eyebolts provided, which are generally used to hold the end gates in place. On the arrival of the car in Kansas City, Mo., it was sent from the yards of the Missouri, Kansas & Texas Railway Company to the yards of the Surburban Belt Railroad Company, there inspected by the latter company, placed in a train with about twenty-five others, and pushed a distance of about 2,000 feet across the state line, to a place where cars were usually left to be received by the Chicago Great Western Railway Company. There the car in question was inspected by an inspector of the latter companv. The switching crew of the Chicago Great Western Railway Company, of which plaintiff below was a member, then took charge of the string of cars, and hauled them to the yards of the latter company, and proceeded to make up a train destined for St. Joseph, Mo., and places beyond. Plaintiff below was near the engine on a box car, when, in the discharge of his duties, he started toward the rear of the train. Coming to the flat car, he walked over the iron pipe, which was about equal in height to the sides of the car and the end gates. The pipe had been pushed back from the end gate so that the top of it was about fifteen inches therefrom. Plaintiff stepped with his right foot from

1. See former decision in the MERRILL case (Kansas Supreme Court, April, 1900), reported in 7 AM. NEG. REP. 620.

the end of the pipe to the top of the end gate, and attempted to cross over to a box car attached. In doing so, the thrust of his body caused the end gate to give way, and he fell between the cars while in motion. It would seem that the load on the flat car had pushed the sides outwardly so that the cleats nailed thereto did not hold the end gate in an upright position, and permitted it to move past the cleats and topple over when stepped on."

LATHROP, MORRIS, FOX & MOORE and MILLER, BUCHAN & MORRIS, for plaintiffs in error.

ROBERT DUNLAP, for Atchison, T. & S. F. R'Y Co., as *amicus curiæ.*

ANGEVINE & CUBBISON, T. N. SEDGWICK, and SILAS PORTER, for defendants in error.

SMITH, J. — (after stating the facts). The question for consideration is whether a railway company which delivers a defective car to a connecting carrier is liable for injuries sustained by an employee of the latter, by reason of such defect, after the receiving company has inspected the car and taken it in charge for transportation over its line. In a former decision of this case it was held to be within the contemplation of the first carrier that the car would be delivered to another for transportation, and it was also known that connecting carriers employ switchmen to handle such cars, and that their services are necessary in the work of making up trains. It was said: "With this knowledge, it was the duty of both plaintiffs in error to provide a car which would be reasonably safe for the service to be performed and for the employees of connecting lines to handle, to the end that freight might be expeditiously carried to its destination. * * * Negligence on the part of the Chicago Great Western Railway Company will not excuse the plaintiffs in error either for their failure to inspect, or, having inspected the car, permitting it to be delivered to a connecting line in a condition which might be dangerous to switchmen and other employees engaged in the practical part of the business of railway transportation." Mo. Kan. & Tex. Ry. Co. et al. *v.* Merrill, 64 Kan. 671–675, 7 Am. Neg. Rep. 620, 60 Pac. Rep. 820. We are now fully convinced that the doctrine announced in the former decision on the subject in hand runs counter to an unbroken current of authorities, and fails to stand the test of reason. A critical examination of the cases cited in the former opinion to sustain the view then taken will show that they are distinguishable from the case at bar. We will review some of them.

In Railroad Co. *v.* Snyder, 55 Ohio St. 342, 45 N. E. Rep. 559, there was a traffic arrangement between the different railway companies forming a fast freight line by which they were to share in the earnings of the transportation in proportion to the distance the car should be hauled over their respective roads. Under the arrangement, the Pennsylvania Company, before delivering its cars to the Lake Shore Company, agreed to have them properly inspected and put into safe condition for hauling. The car, when delivered to the Lake Shore Company to be taken over its road, was defective and unsafe, which proper inspection would have discovered, and injury caused thereby to an employee of the Lake Shore Company. The case differs from the present one. It was argued in the briefs in that case that by reason of the traffic contracts between them the two railroads were partners, and it is stated in the opinion that under the arrangement the Pennsylvania Company, before delivering its cars to the Lake Shore road, was to have them properly inspected, and put in safe condition for hauling. While there is much said in the opinion favorable to the defendant in error on the question before us, yet the peculiar contractual relations of the two roads as to inspection and payment of the cost of repairs do not exist in this case. In the case just commented on, Moon *v.* Railroad Co., 46 Minn. 106, 48 N. W. Rep. 679, is cited and approved. That decision was given prominence as a precedent in the former opinion in this case. In the Moon case the Northern Pacific and Manitoba Railroad Companies were connecting carriers, and interchanged cars at certain common points under a traffic agreement. According to a rule adopted by the companies, cars received and delivered were required to be inspected by the car inspectors of both on the transfer track, and, if any repairs were needed, they were to be made by the Northern Pacific Company before they were transferred and received by the Manitoba Company. Accordingly, the car was so inspected by the car inspectors of both companies. It was examined by them together at the same time, and they agreed that it was in good order. Afterwards, while the car was being operated by the Manitoba Company, the plaintiff's intestate was injured by a defective brake. It was claimed that the brake staff was defective, and also that the car was not properly or carefully inspected by the inspectors of the respective companies. It is to be observed that in the Moon case the inspection by the two companies was substantially one act. The Northern Pacific Company, through its inspector, at the time the inspection was made, knew that no other or further inspection would be made for the protection of the employees of the Manitoba Company. Hence he is held in law to have anticipated that, if his inspection was careless or negligent, the employees of the Manitoba Company would be subjected to whatever dangers should arise therefrom. The court said: "In this case the inspection by the two companies was substantially one transaction, in pursuance of a mutual arrangement under which it was jointly made by the two car inspectors." The case of Heaven *v.* Pender, 11 Q. B. Div. 503 (1), was also cited in the former opinion, and is referred to in Moon *v.* Railroad Co., 46 Minn. 106. The facts on which that decision rested were as follows: The defendant, a dock owner, supplied and put up a staging outside a ship in his dock under a contract with the ship owner. The plaintiff was a workman in the employ of a ship painter, who had contracted with the ship owner to paint the outside of the ship, and, in order to do the painting, the plaintiff went on and used the staging, when one of the ropes by which it was slung, being unfit for use when supplied by the defendant, broke, and by reason thereof the plaintiff fell into the dock, and was injured. In that case the staging was supplied for immediate use, and it was not within the contemplation of the parties that the plaintiff's employer should make an inspection of the appliances to ascertain their fitness prior to their use. It was said by Brett, M. R.: "It must have been known to the defendant's servants, if they had considered the matter at all, that the stage would be put to immediate use; that it would not be used by the ship owner, but that it would be used by such a person as the plaintiff, a working ship painter." In Beven on Negligence (2d ed. vol. 1, p. 62), the author says: "It is submitted that the principle underlying the decision in Heaven *v.* Pender is that the dock owner, having undertaken to supply the staging, thereupon undertook the obligation to supply a fit staging, which obligation the plaintiff was justified in assuming he would discharge. Had there been a duty on the ship owner or on the ship painter to examine the staging, the chain of connection between the plaintiff and the dock owner would have been broken. The decision must, therefore, be taken to imply that there was no duty on the part of any one subsequent to the dock owner to test the staging supplied, but that, when the dock owner undertook to supply staging, there was an obligation that the staging supplied should be reasonably fit for the purpose for which it was to be used; so that those coming to use it might trust to the performance of the dock owner's duty without any independent examination of their own."

1. *Reversing* Heaven *v.* Pender, 9 Q. B. Div. 302, where it was held that defendant had no duty toward plaintiff to supply a reasonably safe staging, and therefore was not liable. See note of Heaven *v.* Pender, 11 Q. B. Div. 503, and other English cases, cited in former decision in the case at bar, in 7 AM. NEG. REP. 624–625.

In Railway Co. *v.* Booth, 98 Ga. 20, 25 S. E. Rep. 928, the deceased was an employee of a mill located on a railway company's switch. The latter placed cars on the switch to be loaded by the mill hands, and by reason of a defect in the car the employee was killed, and his representative recovered judgment therefor against the railway company, which was sustained. The railway company in that case selected and retained control of the car, and placed it in position, knowing the purpose for which and by whom it would be used; thus extending to the injured servant an invitation to use it. Had the master been a mere hirer, or the company exercised no right as to the selection of the cars to be used, the duty of inspection would have been upon the master, and, in case of injury to his servant in consequence of his furnishing an unsafe appliance, the loss would have fallen upon him.

A recovery has been denied in cases like the one at bar on two grounds: First. There being a positive duty resting on the receiving railway company to inspect the car turned over to it for transportation by another company, to the end that its employees may not be injured by defects existing before its receipt, the omission or negligent discharge of such duty breaks the causal connection between the negligence of the company tendering the defective car and the plaintiff's injury. In such cases the failure to inspect, or the negligent manner of doing it, is the proximate cause of the injury to the employee, and the negligence of the company turning over the unsafe car is the remote cause. The failure to discharge the obligation to inspect interposes an independent agency, which severs the causal connection between the company first guilty of negligence and the hurt. It was so held in Fowles *v.* Briggs, 116 Mich. 425, 74 N. W. Rep. 1046, a case very similar to this. See, also, Lellis *v.* Railroad Co., 124 Mich. 37, 82 N. W. Rep. 828. The duty of a railway company to inspect cars of other roads received by it is enjoined by law. Railway Co. *v.* Barber, 44 Kan. 612, 24 Pac. Rep. 969; Railroad Co. *v.* Penfold, 57 Kan. 148, 45 Pac. Rep. 574; Tex. & Pac. R'y Co. *v.* Archibald, 170 U. S. 665, 4 Am. Neg. Rep. 746, 18 Sup. Ct. Rep. 777. Wharton, in his work on Negligence (section 439), says: "There must be causal connection between the negligence and the hurt; and such causal connection is interrupted by the interposition between the negligence and the hurt of an independent human agency. Thus, a contractor is employed by a city to build a bridge in a workmanlike manner, and after he has finished his work, and it has been accepted by the city, a traveler is hurt when passing over it by a defect caused by the contractor's negligence. Now, the contractor may be liable on his contract to the city for his negligence, but he is not liable to the traveler in an action on the case for damages. The reason sometimes given to sustain such a conclusion is that otherwise there would be no end to suits. But a better ground is that there is no causal connection between the traveler's hurt and the contractor's negligence. The traveler reposed no confidence on the contractor, nor did the contractor accept any confidence from the traveler. The traveler, no doubt, reposed confidence on the the city that it would have its bridges and highways in good order; but between the contractor and the traveler intervened the city, an independent responsible agent, breaking the causal connection." The principle above stated is well illustrated in Carter *v.* Towne, 103 Mass. 507. There the defendant negligently sold gunpowder to a child, but the child gave all of the powder to its parents, who afterwards allowed the child to take some of it, by the explosion of which he was injured. The defendant was held not liable, because the effect of his negligence had been cured by the intervening breach of the child's parents in taking charge of the powder, and their consequent negligence in allowing the child to have it again could not restore the connection between the defendant's original negligence and the final injury.

A second, and, we think, better founded, reason for denying the right to recover in cases like the present is that the liability to a servant ceases with the control of the master over his actions. In Glynn *v.* Central R. R. of N. J., 175 Mass. 510, 7 Am. Neg. Rep. 442, 56 N. E. Rep. 698, the plaintiff was in the employ of the New York, New Haven & Hartford Railroad Company in Connecticut, and was injured while coupling a car belonging to a New Jersey railway company, which had a defective coupling apparatus. He sued the latter company. The court, in holding the defendant not liable, said: "There was no dispute that, after the car had come into the hands of the New York, New Haven & Hartford Railroad, and before it had reached the place of accident, it had passed a point at which the cars were inspected. After that point, if not before, we are of opinion that the defendant's responsibility for the defect in the car was at an end. * * * But when a person is to be charged because of the construction or ownership of an object which causes damage by some defect, commonly the liability is held to end when the control of the object is changed. Thus, the case of Clifford *v.* Cotton Mills, 146 Mass. 47, 15 N. E. Rep. 84, shows that the mere ownership of a house so constructed that its roof would throw snow into the street, and therefore threatening danger as it is, without more, whenever snow shall fall, is not enough to impose liability when the control of it has been given to a lessee, who, if he does his duty, will keep it safe. In the case at bar the car does not threaten harm to any one unless it was used in a particular way. Whether it should be used in a dangerous way or not depended, not upon the defendant, but upon another road. Even assuming that the car had come straight from the defendant at Harlem River, the defendant did no unlawful act in handing it over. Whatever may be said as to the responsibility for a car dispatched over a connecting road before there has been a reasonable chance to inspect it, after the connecting road has had the chance to inspect the car and has full control over it, the owner's responsibility for a defect which is not secret ceases. See Sawyer *v.* Railway Co., 38 Minn. 103, 35 N. W. Rep. 671; Wright *v.* Canal Co., 40 Hun, 343; Mackin *v.* Railroad Co., 135 Mass. 201, 206 (1)." In this case there was no contractual relation existing between the switchmen in the employ of the Chicago Great Western Railway Company and the plaintiffs in error. They did not employ them, and they had no power to discharge them. They could protect themselves against damages resulting to their own servants by reason of defects in the car by giving them notice of its condition, in which event their servants would have the option of assuming the risk or of quitting the service of their employers. There was no relation of confidence between Merrill and the plaintiffs in error. The latter owed a duty to their own servants to see that the cars put in their charge were in a reasonably safe condition and in proper repair, but to extend this duty to every servant of every other railroad in the United States under whose charge defective cars might come, would be to formulate a new rule of liability for negligence not sustained by reason or authority. In Sawyer *v.* Railway Co., 38 Minn. 103–105, 35 N. W. Rep. 672 — a case in many respects like the present one — the court said: "At the time of the accident the car was under the management and control of the company operating it, and not of the defendant. It did not come to the hands of the plaintiff through the agency or by the authority of the defendant, and there is no privity between them. It owed him no duty growing out of contract, and was not bound to furnish him safe instrumentalities. As to the defendant, the plaintiff was a mere stranger. [Citing authorities.] * * * The liability of the defendant in respect to the condition of its cars did not extend beyond those to whom it owed some duty by reason of its relation to them as master, employer, or carrier. Any other rule would be found impracticable of application in ordinary business operations." A railway company might have occasion to send a train of defective cars from San Francisco

1. See Glynn *v.* Central R. R. of N. J., 175 Mass. 510, 7 Am. Neg. Rep. 442, for numerous authorities bearing on the questions in the case at bar.

to Boston for repairs, to be hauled over several lines of road. Its own servants, knowing their bad condition, would use a high degree of care to avoid injury from them; but, under the theory of counsel for defendant in error, unless the company forwarding them gave express notice of their condition to every railway employee of the several roads transporting the cars, it would be liable for damages to them in the event they were hurt by reason of such defects. In Winterbottom *v.* Wright, 10 Mees. & W. 109–114 (1), the defendant had contracted with the postmaster-general to provide a coach for carrying the mail, and agreed to keep it in repair, and fit for use. Other persons had a contract with the postmaster-general to supply horses and coachmen for conveying the coach. The vehicle broke down, and injured the driver, by reason of the negligence of the defendant in failing to keep it in proper repair and fit for use. Lord Abinger said: "There is no privity of contract between these parties; and, if the plaintiff can sue, every passenger, or even any person passing along the road, who was injured by the upsetting of the coach, might bring a similar action. Unless we confine the operation of such contracts as this to the parties who entered into them, the most absurd and outrageous consequences, to which I can see no limit, would ensue." So a gasfitter was held not liable for damages for negligently hanging a chandelier in a public house, knowing that it would likely fall on plaintiff and others unless properly hung. It fell and injured the plaintiff. The court held that he had no cause of action, because the declaration did not disclose any duty by the defendant towards the plaintiff for the breach of which an action could be maintained. Collis *v.* Selden, L. R. 3 C. P. 495 (2). In Heizer *v.* Manufacturing Co., 110 Mo. 605–617, 19 S. W. Rep. 633, a servant of the purchaser of a steam boiler was injured by the explosion of it. He sought to charge the manufacturer

1. In Winterbottom *v.* Wright, 10 M. & W. 109, it appeared that A. contracted with the postmaster-general to provide a mail-coach to convey the mail bags along a certain line of road; and B. and others also contracted to horse the coach along the same line. B. and his co-contractors hired C. to drive the coach. Held, that C. could not maintain an action against A. for an injury sustained by him while driving the coach, by its breaking down from latent defects in its construction.

2. In Collis *v.* Selden, L. R., 3 C. P. 495, the declaration alleged that the defendant wrongfully, negligently, and improperly hung a chandelier in a public house, knowing that the plaintiff and others were likely to be therein and under the chandelier, and that the chandelier, unless properly hung, was likely to fall upon and injure them; and that the plaintiff being lawfully in the public house, the chandelier fell upon and injured him. Held, on demurrer, that the declaration was bad, as it did not disclose any duty by the defendant towards the plaintiff for the breach of which an action could be maintained.

of the boiler, and alleged that the latter, when he sold it, warranted it to be free from defects, and of first-class material; that the cylinder was made of poor material, was defective in construction, and too weak to stand the ordinary strain — all of which defects were known to the defendant's agents at the time of the sale, — and by reason thereof the explosion occurred. The court, in denying a right to recover, said: "Wharton thinks the better reason for the rule is that there is no causal connection between the negligence and the hurt; but, be this as it may, the rule itself is well established in England and in the United States, and we think the case in hand comes within it. It is true the defendant must have known, when it made and sold the machine to Ellis, that other persons would be engaged in operating it; but this is no reason why defendant should be held liable to such other persons for injuries arising from the negligent use of poor material or for defective workmanship. Such knowledge must have existed in the cases which have been cited as asserting the rule, and would have been as good an argument against the rule in those cases as in the case at hand. * * * The plaintiff's case tends to show no more than negligence, and an action based on that ground must be confined to the immediate parties to the contract by which the machine was sold. To hold otherwise is to throw upon the manufacturers of machinery not necessarily dangerous a liability which, in our opinion, the law will not justify." In the case quoted from, a large number of authorities, both English and American, are collected, which sustain the principle announced. See, to the same effect, Necker *v.* Harvey, 49 Mich. 517, 14 N. W. Rep. 503; Losee *v.* Clute, 51 N. Y. 494; Bragdon *v.* Perkins-Campbell Co., 30 C. C. A. 567, 87 Fed. Rep. 109.

One of the principal reasons given in the former decision in this case for holding plaintiffs in error liable was that they knew that this defective car, after it left their hands, must be switched about, and put into trains of connecting roads by switchmen employed by the latter, and, with such knowledge, they were negligent in permitting it to go into the charge of such railway employees in a defective condition. In the many cases cited and quoted from above it was equally well known by the manufacturer of a defective machine — like an elevator, for example — that employees of the purchaser would be called on to use it; yet, there being no privity between the maker of the machine and the vendee's servants who were injured by it, there could be no recovery by the latter against the manufacturer or builder. Heizer *v.* Manufacturing Co., 110 Mo. 605. If responsibility for defects in this car is to be fixed on the two railways or either of them, then the application of such a rule of liability must, of necessity, be extended to cover the case of a brakeman injured by a negligently constructed car wheel, and permit a recovery by him of damages against a foundry company which cast and furnished the wheel and sold it to the railway company; for it is within the contemplation of a manufacturer of car wheels that they will come into the charge and control of the servants of the railway companies using the cars. If such wheels are negligently constructed, the contemplated purpose of their future use being manifest, the liability of the maker would follow that use everywhere whenever they happened to cause injury to a railroad employee operating them. This liability of the maker could not be defeated by the fact that the defective appliances might have changed ownership and control many times after their first adoption to railway purposes. As we have seen, the liability of negligent parties so far removed from the injury as the manufacturer in the supposed case finds no support in the authorities. The defective car was not inherently dangerous. It was the manner of its use which caused the injury. The two railway companies that handled the car before its delivery to the Chicago Great Western Railway Company cannot be held to that strict account which the law imposes on one who negligently delivers poisonous drugs to another, imminently dangerous to human life, which fall into the hands of third persons to their injury. In Roddy *v.* Railway Co., 104 Mo. 234–247, 15 S. W. Rep. 1114, it is said: "It cannot reasonably be contended that a railroad car, though supplied with defective brakes, is an imminently dangerous instrument. Unless put in motion, it is perfectly harmless, and when in motion is not essentially dangerous." In Mastin *v.* Levagood, 47 Kan. 36–42, 27 Pac. Rep. 124, it is said: "There is a marked distinction between an act of negligence imminently dangerous and one that is not so; the guilty party being liable in the former case to the party injured, whether there was any relation of contract between them or not, but not so in the latter case." Glynn *v.* Central R. R. of N. J., 175 Mass. 510.

Counsel for defendant in error have invoked the rule *stare decisis*, and insist that the former decision must govern on the second appeal. This would come to us with more force if we were not now considering the same case with the same parties before the court. If an erroneous decision has been made, it ought to be corrected speedily, especially when it can be done before the litigation in which the error has been committed has terminated finally. We are fully satisfied that the rule of the former case is shattered by the pressing weight of opposing authority, and that reason is against it. In Ellison *v.* Railroad Co. 87 Ga. 691, 13 S. E. Rep. 809, the learned Chief Justice Bleckley uses the following forcible language: "Some courts live by correcting the errors of others and adhering to their own. * * * Minor errors, even if quite obvious, or important errors if their existence be fairly doubtful, may be adhered to and repeated indefinitely; but the only treatment for a great and glaring error affecting the current administration of justice in all courts of original jurisdiction is to correct it. When an error of this magnitude, and which moves in so wide an orbit, competes with truth in the struggle for existence, the maxim for a supreme court, supreme in the majesty of duty as well as in the majesty of power, is not '*stare decisis*,' but '*Fiat justitia ruat cœlum*.'"

The judgment of the court below will be reversed, with directions to enter judgment on the finding of the jury in favor of the defendants below. All the justices concurring.

DOSTER, Ch. J. (concurring specially). I believe we were in error in the former determination of this case, and therefore concur in the decision now made. However, I do not believe that our present judgment can be rested on the theory of the breaking of causal connection between the negligent acts of the railway company delivering the defective car and the one receiving it, caused by the latter's failure to inspect, or the making by it of an ineffective inspection. A failure to inspect, or a careless inspection, either one, was a simple failure to do a duty, — an omission, not an affirmative act of wrong-doing; and I think the breaking of causal connection between a series of negligent acts is accomplished only by the doing of something by somebody else which operates as a new and independent producing cause, diverting the first negligent act from its natural end, and giving it a direction and force it would not otherwise have. It is not philosophical to speak of causal connection between act and consequence being broken by a mere failure, though a negligent one, of some person, not the original actor, to do something. Causal connection is broken only by the intervention of active agencies, not the occurrence of passive conditions and qualities.

CITY OF COVINGTON v. JOHNSON.

Court of Appeals, Kentucky, September, 1902.

PEDESTRIAN FALLING OVER OBSTRUCTION MADE BY LOT OWNER ON SIDEWALK — LIABILITY OF CITY. — Where plaintiff was injured by falling over an obstruction on the sidewalk at night, not being aware of the defect, and it appeared that the obstruction was caused by a lot owner, it was *held* that the city was liable for injuries occasioned by its failure to

see that its streets and sidewalks were kept in reasonably safe condition for travel, and that the fact that another may be jointly liable is no excuse for the city's neglect of its duty (1).

APPEAL from Circuit Court, Kenton County.

Action by Thomas Johnson against the City of Covington to recover damages for personal injuries. From judgment for plaintiff, defendant appeals. *Judgment affirmed.*

F. J. HANLON, for appellant.

B. F. GRAZIANI, for appellee.

O'REAR, J.—Appellee was injured on March 8, 1900, by falling over an obstruction on the sidewalk on Fourth street in appellant city. The pavement had become out of repair, and had remained so for some time. It became so much worse on the 5th of March, because of the removal of a number of bricks from the pavement, and possibly the digging of a ditch or hole there,—for what purpose or by whom is not shown,—that a plank covering, nailed together in the shape and about the size of an ordinary door, was placed over the hole. This condition was permitted till after the 8th, the date of the injury. Appellee, a pedestrian, passing along this sidewalk at night, and not knowing of this unusual derangement, struck his foot against the plank, which projected above the level of the pavement, and fell, seriously injuring his ankle and shoulder. The night was dark, and the preponderance of proof is that there was no light near this point. Appellee sued for $6,000 damages because of pain suffered, loss of time, and of permanent impairment of his ability to earn money because of the injury. The jury returned a verdict for $558 for appellant. Both sides sought a new trial. The city alone has appealed.

The main contention made by appellant is that it did not create the condition through which appellee was injured, that it was the lot owner, and that he is liable primarily, and should be made to bear the damage. The lot owner was not before the court, so as to warrant a trial against him in a proceeding for personal judgment. It may be true that the lot owner is responsible for having dug the hole, and imperfectly or negligently covering it, so as to cause the injury sued for, but it is the duty of the city to see that its streets are kept in reasonably safe condition for travel upon them. If it fails to use ordinary care and diligence in the discharge of this duty to the public, it is liable for injuries occasioned thereby. That another is jointly liable is no excuse for the city's neglect of its duty. City of

1. For other actions against municipal corporations for personal injuries sustained by obstructions on sidewalk, from 1897 to date, see vols. 1–12 AM. NEG. REP., and the current numbers of that series of Reports

Covington *v.* Huber (Ky.), 66 S. W. Rep. 619. The finding of the jury that the covering of this hole, and leaving it so, for the length of time shown in this case (at least three days), was negligent, and that the city knew then, or, by the exercise of ordinary care, could have known, of it in time to remedy the defect, is fully sustained by the evidence. The court's proceedings are without error.

Judgment affirmed, with damages.

ILLINOIS CENTRAL RAILROAD COMPANY v. LALOGE.

Court of Appeals, Kentucky, October, 1902.

PASSENGER ASSAULTED AND INSULTED AT STATION — DUTY AND LIABILITY OF CARRIER — STATUTE — WHEN CARRIER NOT LIABLE.— In an action to recover damages for alleged assault and insult by a number of disorderly persons while plaintiff was waiting at defendant's station for a train, on which she contemplated passage, it appears that the assault and insult took place *two or three hours* before the train was due. *Held*, that the Kentucky statute, sec. 784, requiring railroad companies to keep their ticket offices and waiting rooms open for passengers at least *thirty minutes* immediately preceding the schedule time of departure of all passenger trains from regular passenger depots, fixed a *reasonable time* for the accommodation of intending passengers, and that in the absence of an agreement, express or implied, to accommodate the plaintiff beyond the reasonable time fixed by statute, the defendant was not liable (1).

APPEAL from Circuit Court, Muhlenberg County.

Action by Elizabeth Laloge against the Illinois Central Railroad Company, to recover damages for personal injuries. From judgment for plaintiff, defendant appeals. *Judgment reversed.*

JOHNSON & WICKLIFFE and PIRTLE & TRABUE, for appellant.

R. Y. THOMAS, JR., for appellee.

O'REAR, J.—Appellee claims to have been assaulted and insulted by a number of drunken and disorderly persons — loafers — while she was waiting at appellant's station for a train on which she contemplated taking passage over appellant's line of road from Central City to Paducah. She says that she arrived at Central City the morning of the 16th of February, 1900, her husband arriving later in the day. They did not stop at any hotel or other place, it seems,

1. *Assaults on passengers.* See vol. 8, Am. Neg. Cas., where cases arising out of ASSAULTS UPON PASSENGERS, from the earliest period to 1897, are reported. Subsequent cases to date are reported in vols. 1–12 AM. NEG. REP., and the current numbers of that series of Reports.

but loitered about appellant's depot at Central City, and at other points in the town, during the day. About eight o'clock in the evening they went to appellant's depot for the purpose, she says, of waiting for the train upon which she and her husband intended taking passage. That train was not due until about 1:05 o'clock the following morning. According to her testimony, she and her husband were in the public waiting room of appellant's depot after eight o'clock, when Mr. Nunsz, appellant's station agent, passed through the room; that her husband asked him what time the Paducah train would come along, and whether they would have time to go out in the town. She says the agent answered that the Paducah train would not be due till "12:05 or 1:05 in the morning,"—she did not remember which he said. They went out in the town, and returned about ten o'clock, or earlier; that no other notification was given to the company's agent, or any of them, of appellee's intention or purpose to become a passenger. She says she and her husband had money enough to pay their passage to Paducah, but it was taken from them or lost in the fight that occurred when they were assaulted at about 10:15 P. M., while still in the depot waiting room, waiting for the train. She claimed that the boys who assaulted her and her husband were making a great deal of noise, carousing and swearing. It was not shown that any agent of appellant knew of this disturbance before the assault, or that they could have known it by the exercise of ordinary diligence, except the opinion of appellee expressed, that the noise was loud enough for them to have heard it in the adjoining room, where a number of telegraph instruments were at work. The case was submitted to the jury, and a verdict was awarded appellee. Appellant asked for a peremptory instruction.

This appeal raises, first, the question, what was appellant's duty to appellee? It is argued for her that it was that duty owed by a common carrier to its passenger; that she was the passenger of appellant from the time she entered its depot with the intention to take passage on a train over a portion of its road. It may be stated that it is not necessary, always, that the person claiming the protection or privileges of a passenger shall have purchased a ticket. Section 558, Hutch. Carr. But at least such person must have a *bona fide* intention of taking a train shortly, to leave the carrier's station at the point where the complainant may be, and have the means at hand with which to pay his passage, and announce to the carrier's agent having such matter in charge, or that such agent shall be notified of such person's purpose. This must be true because the carrier must have some consideration to support its agreement or obligation to the proposed passenger; this consideration must be either the payment of the fare, which is of itself notice, or the communication of the fact of such purpose to the carrier, that it may know to whom it certainly owes the duties imposed by its contracts, and to whom it may lawfully look for such payment on demand. Section 565, Hutch. Carr. Even this statement must be subject to another qualification: The proposed passenger must present himself at the place appointed by the carrier for receiving such passengers, and within a reasonable time therefor.

By statute in this State it is made the duty of all common carriers to provide waiting rooms for their passengers. These rooms must of necessity be open to the public. Generally, the carrier cannot know who of those who attend them contemplate taking passage on its trains. Its waiting rooms are in consequence used more or less by persons not authorized. To this latter class the carrier owes no duty save such as it owes to licensees, — that is, to so conduct its business as to not wantonly or purposely or recklessly injure them. To the passenger, whether on its train or at its station, its duty is materially different. It must use every care to prevent their injury, and if it has notice of its passenger being in danger of violence, or indecent treatment, whether at the hands of a fellow-passenger, or another on its premises, or within its control, it must use its best endeavors to protect the passenger. Kinney *v.* Louis. & Nash. R. R. Co., 99 Ky. 59, 34 S. W. Rep. 1066, 8 Am. Neg. Cas. 295*n*. In Phillips *v.* Railway Co., 124 N. C. 123, 32 S. E. Rep. 388, the plaintiff was ejected from the carrier's waiting room although he had purchased his ticket for passage on one of its trains. The facts were: The train which plaintiff was to take was not due for some five hours after the act complained of. The carrier had a rule to close its waiting room till thirty minutes before the time of departure of each train. The plaintiff was ejected, and, it being a cold night, and he being thinly clad and having no place to go to, contracted a severe cold, and resultant illness. The court held that the rule of the railway company was not an unreasonable one. On the point pertinent to the case in hand, the court said: "A party coming to a railroad station with the intention of taking the defendant's next train, becomes, in contemplation of law, a passenger on defendant's road provided that his coming is within a reasonable time before the time for departure of said train. To constitute him such passenger, it is not necessary that he should have purchased his ticket, as seems to have been considered by his honor. 1 Fetter, Carr. Pass., sec. 223. But the purchase of the ticket would probably be considered the highest evidence of his intention. But still it is his coming to the station within a reasonable time before, with the intention to take the next train, that creates the relation of passenger and carrier."

But we have in this State what may be regarded as legislative construction of the length of time that should be considered reasonable for the carrier to be required to look out for, and safeguard, its passengers before they have taken actual passage. Section 784, Ky. St.: "All companies shall keep their ticket offices open for the sale of tickets at least thirty minutes immediately preceding the schedule time of departure of all passenger trains from every regular passenger depot from which such trains start or at which they regularly stop; and shall open the waiting room for passengers at the same time as the ticket office, and keep it open and comfortably warmed in cold weather until the train departs." The carrier is not an innkeeper. It cannot, in the discharge of its other duties required by the law, be held to furnish accommodation for the entertainment, for an indefinite length of time, of those who contemplate in the future becoming its passengers. It would have been just as reasonable to have held appellant liable for the safety and comfort of appellee at any time, while at its depot, from nine o'clock in the morning of the 16th to 12:30 in the morning of the 17th, as for the time sued for. We do not mean to hold that, if the carrier agrees to accommodate the proposed passenger by a longer time than the statute provides, it would not be liable for any injuries sustained because of its negligence during such time. But in the absence of such agreement, express or implied, we hold that the proposed passenger cannot claim the benefit of that relation by coming onto the carrier's premises an unreasonable length of time before the train which he expects to take passage on is due to depart, and that such reasonable time has been fixed by the statute above quoted. It follows that peremptory instruction asked for by appellant should have been given. In view of the conclusion to which we have arrived, the other errors complained of need not be noticed.

Reversed and remanded for proceedings consistent herewith.

McTIVER v. GRANT TOWNSHIP.

Supreme Court, Michigan, September, 1902.

DRIVING ON DEFECTIVE HIGHWAY—HORSE INJURED—KNOWLEDGE OF DEFECT—CONTRIBUTORY NEGLIGENCE.—In an action to recover damages for injuries to plaintiff's horse while driving on highway which was covered with corduroy, the horse stepping on a rotten piece of corduroy, it was *held* that plaintiff was not negligent, as matter of law, in attempting to pass over the highway which he knew to be defective, where the same was in constant use by others daily, and he did not know the exact point of danger.

ERROR to Circuit Court, Cheboygan County.

ACTION by Silas M. McTiver against the Township of Grant. From judgment for plaintiff defendant brings error. *Judgment affirmed.*

CROSS & HARPSTER, for appellant.

C. F. HULL (C. S. REILLEY, of counsel), for appellee.

MONTGOMERY, J. — The plaintiff recovered a judgment of $300 in an action against the defendant based upon the defendant's failure to keep a certain highway in a condition reasonably safe for travel. The testimony tended to show that the highway in question, on the west side of Black Lake, in defendant township, consisted, in one portion of its length, of a corduroy way some thirty to forty rods in extent; that the plaintiff had occasion to go to the farm of one John Grant to get some hay, which he had contracted for; that the usually traveled way was the one in question; that he started out two teams in charge of drivers, and that he himself followed with a single driving horse. The testimony further tended to show that the corduroy was not in good condition, and that while crossing this portion of the road the plaintiff's driving horse stepped on some rotten piece of corduroy and broke through, receiving injuries. Plaintiff repaired this place in the corduroy and proceeded to the residence of Mr. Grant, caused the hay to be loaded, and started the teams in charge of the drivers homeward, cautioning the drivers to use care in crossing the corduroy. In crossing one of the teams passed safely, but the other broke through. There was another road on the opposite side of the lake, but it was a much longer route, and there was some testimony to the effect that a bridge on this road was out of repair. Plaintiff testified as follows as to his knowledge of the condition of the road: "This road is a pretty bad piece of road. The corduroy is dangerous to drive over. I can't say that I ever drove over it when I considered it was not dangerous. I had not driven over it that summer since the snow went off. I told my men to be careful. I found enough to warrant me in telling them. I went down to look after the men, to see if they got through all right, and, if anything happened, to help them out. I told them to be careful on the corduroy when they started from home. Q. What did you say to them? A. Why, I told them to be careful in going over, and they would get over all right. Other teams had done the same, and I supposed I could, and charged them to be careful expressly on the corduroy. Q. You knew there was a poor road there, didn't you? A. Yes, but what difference did that make to me? How could I help it? Q. Then you was a little skittish about that highway? You stopped and tied your horse and went to help these other teams; is that the idea? A. No, I tied the horse, and followed them along, so that if anything happened I would be there to help them. Q. Why did you do that?

A. Why, I knew it wasn't altogether right. I knew that there might be a chance to get them horses in. I just tied my horse there, because, if one of the teams got hurt, I didn't want to get out and in again. I knew that there was a better chance of them getting in than her. Q. The first team got over all right? A. Yes." At the close of the defendant's case an amendment to the declaration was permitted in the statement of the number of the town and range. Plaintiff recovered for the injury to the driving horse and also for the injury to the team.

Two questions are raised by this appeal: First, was the amendment properly permitted; and, second, was the plaintiff guilty of contributory negligence, as a matter of law, in attempting to pass over the way? The amendment was properly allowed, as the declaration on its face showed that the attempt was to describe a highway in the defendant township, and the misstatement of the town and range was a clerical error, which could not have misled the defendant. We are not prepared to hold that the knowledge which the plaintiff had that this highway was in general in a dangerous condition precluded him from the right to attempt to pass over it, using care for that purpose. He knew that the highway was in constant use; that others were daily using it. And while he knew that it was not in perfect condition, we are not prepared to say that he must be held bound to have anticipated the exact danger encountered. There are cases in which one knowing of the existence of a hole in the way, or a particular defect, stepping into which would necessarily result in injury, has been held guilty of negligence in walking into such danger. In such cases the exact danger is known and assumed. Such cases are Black *v.* City of Manistee, 107 Mich. 60, 64 N. W. Rep. 868; Grandorf *v.* Railway Co., 113 Mich. 496, 71 N. W. Rep. 844; King *v.* Colon Tp., 125 Mich. 511, 9 Am. Neg. Rep. 311, 84 N. W. Rep. 1077. But the true test is, was the danger arising from the known defect obviously of such a character that no person in the exercise of ordinary prudence would attempt to pass over the highway at that point? If not, it is not negligence, as matter of law, for one to attempt to pass over a highway known to be defective. Lowell *v.* Watertown Tp., 58 Mich. 568, 25 N. W. Rep. 517; Laughlin *v.* Railway Co., 62 Mich. 220, 28 N. W. Rep. 873; Harris *v.* Clinton Tp., 64 Mich. 447, 31 N. W. Rep. 425; Schwingschlegl *v.* City of Monroe, 113 Mich. 683, 72 N. W. Rep. 7. See, also, 15 Am. & Eng. Enc. Law (2d ed.) 470. Had there been an accessible way to drive around the corduroy, or to turn the team out to pass it, the case might have been different. We think it was not error to submit the case to the jury.

Judgment affirmed.

LONG, J., did not sit. The other justices concurred.

ORTH v. VILLAGE OF BELGRADE.

Supreme Court, Minnesota, October, 1902.

FALLING OBJECT — PEDESTRIAN KILLED — NOTICE OF INJURIES — STATUTES. — 1. *Held*, following Maylone *v.* City of St. Paul, 40 Minn. 406, that the provisions of chapter 248, Laws 1897, requiring notice to be given to a municipality of injury caused by defects in its streets as a condition precedent to the maintaining of an action therefor, do not apply to an action by the personal representatives of a deceased person, whose death was caused by such defects.

(Syllabus by the Court.)

APPEAL from District Court, Stearns County.

Action by Michael Orth, as administrator of the estate of Christian Schreiber, deceased, against the Village of Belgrade. From an order overruling a demurrer to the complaint, defendant appeals. *Order affirmed.*

FRANK TOLMAN and CALHOUN & BENNETT, for appellant.

THEO. BRUENER and J. D. SULLIVAN, for respondent.

START, Ch. J. — This is an appeal by the defendant from an order of the District Court of the county of Stearns overruling the defendant's demurrer to the complaint herein. The plaintiff is the administrator of the estate of Christian Schreiber, deceased, and brings this action as such to recover damages for the death of his intestate by reason of the alleged negligence of the defendant, a municipal corporation, in the care of one of its streets. The complaint alleges that the defendant negligently permitted a decayed porch, which was insufficiently fastened, to overhang one of its streets, which, by reason of its defective condition, fell, on July 4, 1901, upon the deceased, while he was lawfully upon the street, whereby he sustained injuries resulting in his death on September 16th thereafter (1).

1. See the following Pennsylvania case relating to fall of a defective gate on land owned by a city:

In GILMARTIN *v.* CITY OF PHILADELPHIA (*Pennsylvania, February, 1902*), 51 Atl. Rep. 312, judgment for defendant was affirmed, the case being stated by FELL, J., as follows: "The negligence charged was, that the city allowed a gate which stood on its property to remain in a dangerous condition. The property was suburban, and consisted of a square of ground which had been acquired by the city for the purpose of establishing a public park, but had not been improved nor thrown open to the public as a park. The fence had been torn down and carried away by boys in the neighborhood, and the square was open on all sides to the streets which surrounded it, and was used to some extent as a ball ground and as a place for cleaning carpets. A building on the square which had formerly been

But it fails to allege that any notice, as provided by Laws 1897, c. 248, was served by him, or on his behalf, upon the defendant. This presents the sole question for our decision on this appeal, viz.:

a mansion house had been changed to a school house. Near the entrance of a driveway that led to this building, and beyond the line of the public highway, was an ornamental iron gate, with stone posts, which was open only when the driveway was used in hauling coal and supplies to the building. There was no occasion to open the gate at other times, as there was a passageway for pedestrians on either side of it, and as the whole square was open to the streets. Two of the bars at the top of the gate were eaten through by rust, and two of the lower ones were weakened from the same cause, so that the gate sagged when opened. It had been repaired by the use of wires which held the bars together and held the gate to the post to which the hinges were fastened. When the gate was closed, it was secure and safe; being supported by the hinges and wire at one end, and by the latch at the other. A boy of ten years of age, who was not attending the school, came on the lot from the street and climbed on the gate. His added weight broke or bent the lower bars and caused the gate to fall, and he was injured. On the proof of these facts a nonsuit was entered. As the land was unfenced, and, in a measure, thrown open to the public, it was the duty of the city to exercise ordinary care to keep it in a safe condition. Children attracted to it by curiosity, who, because of inexperience and indiscretion, might make an unusual use of objects on it, are not, in so doing, to be classed as trespassers. If an object was in itself dangerous, or might become dangerous if a child chanced to set it in motion while playing with it or by running against it, there was a duty on the city to take such precaution as was reasonable, under the circumstances, to prevent injury by it. On the other hand, the city was not required to anticipate and guard against dangers which might result from the improper use of objects safe in themselves, and for the use for which they were designed. There were many objects on this property which a childish impulse might make a source of danger. But if a child had climbed a tree that had a decayed limb, or an insecurely fastened water spout, or on the roof of a low building that would not sustain his weight, and had been injured, we should not think of holding the city liable. The gate was apparently strong enough for the use to which it was put. It was secure if used properly, and there was no danger of its falling if touched or run against. It was unable to sustain the added weight of fifty or sixty pounds. In principle, this case resembles Bridge Co. *v* Jackson, 114 Pa. St. 321, 6 Atl. Rep. 128, in which a boy seven years old, in crossing a bridge, walked outside of the ways provided for vehicles and pedestrians upon a gas pipe. In that case it was said: "It is not necessary to impute negligence to the child. It is sufficient that he was injured not as the result of the use of the bridge, but as the consequence of his venturing, in childish recklessness, where no one, child or adult, has anv business to be." The judgment is affirmed.

Falling object. See also the following Pennsylvania case:

In BOOTH *v.* DORSEY ET AL *(Pennsylvania, April, 1902)*, 51 Atl. Rep. 993, judgment for defendants in the Court of Common Pleas, Philadelphia county: was reversed, the opinion by MESTREZAT, J., stating the case as follows. "This is an action of trespass to recover damages for alleged negligence. It was brought against William Steele & Son, Rudolph Blankenburgh & Co.,

Can an administrator maintain an action against a municipality for the death of his intestate by reason of defects in its streets, where the deceased failed to give the notice required by the statute,

and Dorsey and Smith, the appellees. The statement avers that on January 14, 1899, the defendants were engaged in altering, repairing, and improving a building at the northwest corner of Twenty-Fourth and Ellsworth streets, in the city of Philadelphia, and that in the performance of the work the employes of the defendants negligently and carelessly permitted a brick or bricks used in said work to fall from said building, unknown to plaintiff, who was properly on the premises, and to strike him violently, thereby greatly injuring him. Each of the three defendant firms pleaded not guilty. The case was called for trial, and at the close of his testimony the plaintiff suffered a voluntary nonsuit as to Steele & Son and Blankenburg & Co. The counsel for the appellees then moved for a nonsuit as to his clients, "because they are joint tort feasors, and the action of the court in entering a nonsuit as to the other two sustains the fact shown by the evidence, that there was a single tort committed." The motion was overruled. The counsel for the appellees then declined to offer any testimony, whereupon the plaintiff's counsel moved to amend the statement. The appellees pleaded surprise, and the case was continued. The plaintiff's counsel stated that he would formally discontinue of record the action as to Steele & Son and Blankenburg & Co. On October, 15, 1901, the discontinuance was entered. On the same day an amended statement was filed by leave of the trial judge; which on October 29, 1901, the court struck off. On November, 22, 1901, the plaintiff took a rule on Dorsey & Smith to show cause why he should not be allowed to file an amended statement, charging them with the negligence averred in the original statement. This rule was supported by an affidavit of mistake. An answer was filed by the appellees, and on December 16, 1901, the rule was discharged. In this condition of the record, the case was again called for trial on January 28, 1902, the counsel for the appellees objected to the jury being sworn 'on the ground that, this suit having been brought against three several defendants, and the record showing a discontinuance as to two of the parties, and the statement of claim being as originally filed, there is no cause which can be properly tried at this time, and as to which the jury could be sworn.' Under exception, the court permitted the jury to be sworn. By agreement of counsel, 'the stenographer's notes of the case formerly tried shall be considered as having been taken at this time.' The evidence taken on the former trial was considered as admitted. The appellees moved for a nonsuit, which was granted, and which the court subsequently refused to take off. No opinion was filed by the court below giving the reasons for refusing, leave to file an amended statement, or for refusing to take off the non-suit. From what was said in the oral argument of counsel, however, we infer the learned trial judge thought that the action having been brought against the three firms, charging them as joint tort feasors, the pleadings could not be amended, and the action be prosecuted against the appellees, so as to charge them with a separate liability for the act resulting in the injury to plaintiff.

"The appellant has assigned for error the action of the court, 1, in making absolute the appellees' rule to strike off the amended statement, 2, in discharging the appellant's rule for leave to amend the statement; and, 3, in refusing to take off the nonsuit.

although he lived more than thirty days after the accident which caused his death? It is the confident contention of counsel for the

"The amendment proposed by the plaintiff did not change the cause of action. As we have seen, the original statement averred that the plaintiff's injuries were caused by the negligent performance of certain work on the building at Twenty-fourth and Ellsworth streets. The proposed amended statement alleges the same cause of action, to wit, that in the performance of the same work on the building the defendants carelessly and negligently permitted a brick or bricks to fall from the building, unknown to the plaintiff, who was legally on the premises, and to violently strike him, thus causing his injuries. The complaint or cause of action, therefore, as alleged in both statements, was the performance of the same act in the same negligent way. The only difference between the two statements was that in the original the tort was alleged to have been the joint act of the three firms, while in the amended statement it was laid as the separate act of the appellees. This did not constitute a change in the cause of action.

"The act of May 4, 1852, authorizes an amendment by changing or adding the name of any party at any stage of the proceedings when it appears that a mistake has been made in the name of such party. And this act is construed by the act of April 12, 1858, to authorize the court, where by reason of there being too many persons included as plaintiffs or defendants by mistake, as will prevent the cause from being tried on the merits, to permit an amendment by striking out from the suit such persons as plaintiffs or defendants. These statutes have always been construed liberally in furtherance of a trial upon the merits. Fidler *v.* Hershey, 90 Pa. St. 363. In Rangler *v.* Hummel, 37 Pa. St. 130, Thompson J., speaking for the court says: 'We have so often decided, under our several statutes of amendments, that parties might be stricken out or added whenever this was necessary to a trial on the merits of the case, that we do not deem it necessary to cite authorities on the subject. This is the plain requirement of the act of May 4, 1852, as construed by the act of April 12, 1858. Whenever the rights of a party are liable to be defeated by having joined too few or too many plaintiffs or defendants, these amendments may be made. In such circumstances, the fact of mistake is hardly debatable. It will be presumed, if without them the case may not be fully tried." The mistake for which an amendment should be allowed may be either of fact or law, and, when it is made to appear, it is the duty of the court to correct it. Kaylor *v.* Shaffner, 24 Pa. St. 489.

"It is apparent, therefore, that the plaintiff should have been permitted to file his amended statement. The nonsuit had eliminated the other parties from the case, and the proposed amendment to the statement did not change the cause of action. The plaintiff had brought himself literally within the acts of assembly authorizing amendments. He filed an affidavit in which it was made to appear that a mistake had been made in bringing the action, by including too many persons as defendants, and that such a mistake would prevent the cause from being tried upon its merits.

"Having disposed of the technical question on which the court below granted the nonsuit, we will refrain from expressing any opinion on the merits of the case, which will be fully developed on the retrial. The second and third assignments of error are sustained, the judgment is reversed, and a *procedendo* is awarded."

plaintiff that the question is answered in the affirmative by the case of Maylone *v.* City of St. Paul, 40 Minn. 406, 42 N. W. Rep. 88. Counsel for the defendant with equal confidence insist that the case has no relevancy to the question, for that case, neither in its facts nor the statute construed, is similar to the one at bar. That case was one by the administrator to recover damages for the death of his intestate, alleged to have been caused by the negligence of the city. A demurrer to the complaint was sustained in the District Court on the ground that the action was barred by reason of a provision of the city charter, which was this: "No action shall be maintained against the city of St. Paul, on account of any injuries received by means of any defect in the condition of any bridge, street, sidewalk or thoroughfare, unless such action shall be commenced within one year from the happening of the injury, or (nor) unless notice shall have first been given in writing to the mayor of said city, or the city clerk thereof, within thirty days of the occurrence of such injury or damage, stating the place where and the time when such injury was received and that the person injured will claim damages of the city for such injury; but the notice shall not be required when the person injured shall in consequence thereof be bereft of reason." Sp. Laws 1885, c. 7, sec. 19. Chapter 248, Laws 1897, here in question, is, so far as here material, as follows: "Before any city, village or borough in this State shall be liable to any person for damages for, or on account of, any injury or loss alleged to have been received or suffered by reason of any defect in any * * * street, * * * the person so alleged to be injured, or some one in his behalf, shall give to the city or village council, * * * within thirty days after the alleged injury, notice thereof, and shall present his or their claim to compensation to such council * * * in writing, * * * and such body shall have ten days' time within which to decide upon the course it will pursue with relation to such claim, and no action shall be maintained until the expiration of such time on account of such claim, nor unless the same shall be commenced within one year after the happening of such alleged injury or loss." The statute giving a cause of action to the personal representative of a deceased party was then the same as it is now, and was and is in these words: "When death is caused by the wrongful act or omission of any party or corporation, the personal representative of the deceased may maintain an action if he might have maintained an action, had he lived, for an injury caused by the same act or omission by which the death was caused." Gen. St. 1894, sec. 5913. The complaint in the Maylone case showed upon its face that the deceased died on the day of the occurrence of the accident which caused his death, and, further, that the action by his administrator was not commenced until more than one year thereafter. The question raised by the demurrer and decided by this court was whether the one-year limitation applied to the action by the administrator. In this case the complaint shows that the deceased lived for seventy-four days after he was injured. The claimed distinction between the two cases is that in the former case the deceased might have brought an action on the day of his death, because the time within which the notice of his injury was required to be given had not then expired, hence his administrator could bring the action; while in the latter case the time for giving the notice had expired before the injured party died, and he could not have brought the action; hence his administrator cannot. But the court, in its opinion in the Maylone case, reversing the order sustaining the demurrer, did not refer to the fact that the injured party died before the expiration of the thirty days, but based its decision upon the broad proposition that the provisions and limitations of the city charter applied only to the common-law action which the injured party had to recover for his injuries, and not to the very different right of action given by the statute to the personal representatives of deceased persons. Again, the injured party in the Maylone case could not have maintained an action on account of his injuries due to the neglect of the city without first complying with the conditions precedent as to the giving of the notice, nor, if he had lived, could he have maintained an action after one year from the happening of his injury. And yet the court held that his administrator might maintain the statutory action, although it was brought more than one year after the happening of the injury, and at a time when the injured party, if living, could not have maintained an action for his injuries. It is to be noted that the charter provision as to the time within which the action must be brought is absolute in its terms, and is not limited to an action by the person injured. Its language is, "No action shall be maintained against the city of St. Paul on account of any injuries received by means of any defect in the condition of any street unless the action is brought within one year from the happening of the injury." There is more reason for holding that the failure to bring an action within the year would be a bar to an action by a personal representative than there is for holding that the failure to give the notice would bar such action. Hence, if, as the court held, the failure to bring the action within the year is not a bar to an action by a personal representative, it follows that the failure to give the notice is not a bar to such an action. The statute giving the personal representative a cause of action (section 5913, Gen. St. 1894) limits the action to cases in which the facts are such that the injured party, if he had lived, might have maintained an action; that is, upon the merits. The conditions precedent to the right of the injured party to maintain his action are no part of the essential elements of his cause of action, but were prescribed by statute long after section 5913, Id., was enacted, and the decision in the Maylone Case necessarily holds that the words of this section, "if he might have maintained an action if he had lived," refer to the right of the deceased to have maintained, if he had lived, an action on the merits, for his injury; for otherwise it could not have held that the administrator's action could be maintained, although an action by the deceased, if he had lived, brought more than a year after his injury, would be barred. Now, the provisions of the General Statutes, chapter 248, Laws 1897, and the charter provisions construed in the Maylone Case, are, so far as here material, substantially the same, and the Maylone Case cannot be distinguished on principle from this case. It follows, unless we overrule the Maylone Case — and we know of no reason why we should do so,— that the question here under consideration must be answered in the affirmative. We therefore hold that the provisions of chapter 248, Laws 1897, do not apply to an action by the personal representative of a deceased person given by Gen. St. 1894, § 5913.

Order affirmed.

CHICAGO, BURLINGTON AND QUINCY RAILROAD COMPANY v. KRAYENBUHL.

Supreme Court, Nebraska, October, 1902.

BOY INJURED WHILE PLAYING ON TURNTABLE — EVIDENCE — DAMAGES — INSTRUCTION.— 1. Petition examined, and *held* good, as against a demurrer *ore tenus*.

2. When the owner of dangerous premises knows or has good reason to believe, that children, so young as to be ignorant of the danger, will resort to such premises, he is bound to take such precautions to keep them from such premises, or to protect them from injuries likely to result from the dangerous condition of the premises while there, as a man of ordinary care and prudence, under like circumstances, would take; approving Atch. & Neb. R. R. Co. *v.* Bailey, 11 Neb. 332, 336 (1).

1. See NOTE ON LIABILITY OF RAILROAD COMPANIES FOR ACCIDENTS TO CHILDREN ON TURNTABLES, in 9 AM. NEG. REP. 611–616, in which many of the authorities cited in the opinion in the case at bar are quoted.

3. In such cases, in the determination of the question of negligence, regard must be had to the character and location of the premises, the purpose for which they are used, the probability of injury therefrom, the precautions necessary to prevent such injury, and the relations such precautions bear to the beneficial use of the premises. If, under all the circumstances, the owner omits such precautions as a man of ordinary care and prudence would take, under like circumstances, he is guilty of negligence.
4. Ordinarily, the question of negligence is one of fact for the jury, to be determined from all the facts and circumstances shown in evidence, and it is error for the court to group certain facts in evidence together, and instruct the jury that they constitute negligence.
5. In an action, by an infant in the care and custody of its father, for personal injuries, it is error to instruct the jury that his lessened earning capacity is an element of damages, unless it be limited to the period from which he would be entitled to his earnings.
6. An instruction authorizing the jury, in arriving at a verdict, to bring to bear their own knowledge, observation and experience in the business affairs of life is erroneous when not limited to such knowledge, observation and experience as they share in common with men generally.
7. An instruction relative to the damages to be awarded the plaintiff, if any, closed with the statement that they should not exceed a specific amount, naming the amount claimed in the petition: *Held*, that the practice of thus referring to the amount claimed should be discountenanced.
8. Instructions tendered examined, and *held* properly refused.
9. Rulings on the admission of evidence examined, and *held* not erroneous.

(Syllabus by the Court.)

COMMISSIONERS' OPINION. Department No. 3. Error to District Court, Merrick County.

Action by Leo Krayenbuhl, by his next friend, against the Chicago, Burlington & Quincy Railroad Company for personal injuries. From judgment for plaintiff, defendant brings error. *Judgment reversed.*

J. W. DEWEESE, F. E. BISHOP, and JOHN PATTERSON, for plaintiff in error.

MATHEW GERING and MICHAEL O'DONAHUE, for defendant in error.

ALBERT, C. — This action was brought on behalf of Leo Krayenbuhl, whom we shall hereafter call the plaintiff, by his next friend, against the Chicago, Burlington & Quincy Railroad Company to recover for personal injuries received by the plaintiff while playing on a turntable belonging to the defendant.

It sufficiently appears from the evidence that on and prior to the 20th day of October, 1895, the defendant operated a line of railroad, which extended through the village of Palmer, at which point it maintained a passenger depot, roundhouse, coalhouse, water tank, and turntable. A few rods northwest of the depot the road branched, one branch taking a westerly and the other a northwesterly course. The turntable was situated between those two branches, at a point about 1,600 feet from the depot, and about 100 feet from each branch, and a track extended to it from the point of divergence of the two branches. A path or footway, beginning some distance northwest of the turntable, extended in a southeasterly direction, passed within about seventy feet of it, and crossed the track at the south. This path was in common use, not only by the members of the family to which the plaintiff belonged, but by the public generally, and there was no fence between it and the turntable. The turntable was provided with a movable bolt, which, by means of a lever, could be thrown into a socket in the surrounding framework, thus holding the turntable in position. Provision was also made for locking it with a padlock. The rules of the defendant in force at the time required the foreman of the roundhouse, or in his absence the station agent, to keep the turntable locked when not in use; but there is considerable evidence to the effect that this rule was frequently disregarded, and that, owing to the looseness of one of the staples used in connection with the lock, even when thus fastened, it could be unfastened by young children without much difficulty. The plaintiff's father was in the employ of the defendant as section foreman, and, with his family, occupied a small house on the right of way near the station, within about thirty feet of the track, and about 1,600 feet from the turntable. Another family resided on the right of way, a few rods from the turntable. The two families visited back and forth, using the right of way for a path. The plaintiff's father kept a cow, which was pastured on the right of way, sometimes near the turntable, and it appears from the evidence that his children drove it back and forth on the right of way as occasion required. There is evidence tending to show that it was the common practice for the children of the family and other children in the neighborhood to resort to the coalhouse, roundhouse, and turntable, and to amuse themselves by revolving the turntable, and riding on it while it was in motion, and that this practice was known to the defendant, who permitted it without protest.

On the 20th day of October, 1895, in the absence of his parents, the plaintiff, — he was then four years of age, — in company with some other members of the family, the oldest of whom was eleven years old, and some other children, the oldest of whom was fourteen, were playing with a push car, moving it up and down on the railroad track. The agent in charge of the station joined them, and rode a short distance on the car. He then left them, and went to his rooms in the station. The children continued to push the car, and finally reached the turntable. There is evidence sufficient to sustain a finding that they found the turntable unlocked and unguarded, but the evidence is conflicting on that point. The plaintiff and some of the other children got on the turntable, while two of the others set it in motion. While it was in motion the plaintiff's foot was caught between the rails, and severed at the ankle joint. The injury thus sustained is that for which damages is sought in this action. A trial was had to a jury, which resulted in a verdict and judgment for the plaintiff. The defendant brings error.

The first question raised is that the petition does not state facts sufficient to constitute a cause of action. The grounds of this objection, as stated in the defendant's brief, are as follows: "It does not allege the authority of any agent of the defendant to invite the plaintiff upon its turntable, or any facts which constitute such express invitation. It does not allege the characteristics either of location or construction of the table, which of themselves render the table an invitation to the danger." The petition is too long to set out at length. We think it will suffice to say that the allegations in these respects are that the plaintiff was induced by other small children, with the knowledge and consent of the defendant, its agents and servants, and by the invitation of the defendant, to come to and about the turntable. On the face of the petition, this is an allegation of an invitation by the defendant. If the plaintiff were invited by the defendant, he was invited by some agent of the defendant having authority in the premises. The allegation in that regard is sufficient. It is true the facts constituting such invitation are not set forth, nor do we deem it necessary that they should be for the purposes of the objection under consideration, which was first made by an objection to the introduction of any testimony, on the ground that the facts stated in the petition did not constitute a cause of action.

The question to which counsel have directed the greater portion of their arguments is whether the facts in this case are sufficient to sustain the verdict. On this question we have been favored with an exhaustive discussion of what is commonly known as the "doctrine of the Turntable Cases," which, applied to the facts in this case, would sustain the verdict. The leading case in support of this doctrine is Sioux City & Pac. R. R. Co. *v.* Stout, 17 Wall. 657 (9 Am. Neg. Rep. 614*n*). The doctrine was reaffirmed by the same court in Railroad Co. *v.* McDonald, 152 U. S. 262, 14 Sup. Ct. Rep. 619, and was expressly approved by this court in Atch. & Neb. R. R. Co. *v.* Bailey, 11 Neb. 336, 9 N. W. Rep. 50, and was approved and applied in the following among other cases: Barrett *v.* Southern Pacific Co., 91 Cal. 296, 9 Am. Neg. Rep. 611, 27 Pac. Rep. 666; Keffe *v.* Milw. & St. P. R'y Co., 21 Minn. 207; Twist *v.* Railroad Co. (Minn.), 39 N.

W. Rep. 402; Kan. Cent. R'y Co. *v.* Fitzsimmons, 22 Kan. 686; Ilwaco R'y & Navigation Co. *v.* Hedrick, 1 Wash. 446, 25 Pac. Rep. 335, 12 Am. Neg. Cas. 638*n;* Railroad Co. *v.* Skidmore (Tex. Civ. App.), 65 S. W. Rep. 215; Gulf, Colo. & S. F. R'y Co. *v.* McWhirter, 77 Tex. 356, 14 S. W. Rep. 26, 12 Am. Neg. Cas. 623*n;* Harriman *v.* Pitts. C. & St. L. R'y Co., 45 Ohio St. 11, 12 N. E. Rep. 451; Ferguson *v.* Columbus & Rome R'y Co., 75 Ga. 637, 9 Am. Neg. Rep. 612*n;* Nagel *v.* Mo. Pac. R'y Co., 75 Mo. 653 (1).

The doctrine, as we gather it from the cases cited, is that where a turntable is so situated that its owner may reasonably expect that children too young to appreciate the danger will resort to it, and amuse themselves by using it, it is guilty of negligence for a failure to take reasonable precautions to prevent such use. It has not been permitted to pass as law unchallenged. On the contrary, it has been expressly repudiated in many cases, among which are the following: Walsh *v.* Railroad Co. (N. Y.), 39 N. E. Rep. 1069; Daniels *v.* N. Y. & N. E. N. R. R. Co., 154 Mass. 349, 28 N. E. Rep. 283; Frost *v.* Eastern R. R., 64 N. H. 220, 9 Atl. Rep. 790 (2); Del., Lack. & W. R. R. Co. *v.* Reich (N. J. Err. & App.), 40 Atl. Rep. 682, 4 Am. Neg. Rep. 522. It has been criticised in others, among which are Ryan *v.* Towar (Mich.), 87 N. W. Nep. 644, and Dobbins *v.* Railroad Co. (Tex. Sup.), 41 S. W. 62. The latter case would seem to throw some doubt on the position of the courts of Texas in regard to the doctrine in question, but the case of Railroad Co. *v.* Skidmore, *supra*, appears to be the latest expression of the court on the question.

The defendant insists that the doctrine is unsound, and asks that it be repudiated by the court, and that the case of Atch. & Neb. Co. *v.* Bailey, 11 Neb. 332, 336, be overruled. The argument in this behalf rests on the proposition that the owner of dangerous premises owes no active duty to trespassing children. The assumption that the plaintiff was a trespasser might well be questioned. The right of way was his home and playground; it was where his father performed his daily labors; it was used as a path and for other purposes by the family. But, as the duty of the owner of dangerous premises to infant trespassers is raised by other assignments, it will shorten this opinion to allow the assumption to pass unchallenged. The proposition is not universally true, as is clearly shown, we think, by Sedgwick, J., in Tucker *v.* Draper, 62 Neb. 66, 10 Am. Neg. Rep. 307, 86 N. W. Rep. 913, wherein he says: "* * * There may be,

1. See notes of the cases cited in the opinion in the case at bar, in 9 AM. NEG. REP. 611–616.

2. See notes of these cases in 9 AM. NEG. REP. 615–616.

and often are, circumstances under which one owes some active duty to a trespasser upon his premises. If a man wilfully lies down upon a railroad track, the engineer must not wantonly run his engine over him. One may not set a snare or spring gun for trespassers, and, knowing that some stranger had placed the snare or spring gun, if he wantonly allows it to remain, he will be responsible for the consequences. A well may be so contrived as to act as a dangerous trap, and one who allows it to so remain upon his premises will, under some circumstances, be liable. If adults, or children of such age as to ordinarily be capable of discerning and avoiding danger, are injured while trespassing upon the premises of another, they may be without remedy, while under similar circumstances children of three or four years of age would be protected. If I know that there is an open well upon my premises, and know that children of such tender years as to have no notion of their danger are continually playing around it, and I can obviate the danger with very little trouble to myself, and without injuring the premises or interfering with my own free use thereof, I owe an active duty to those children, and if I neglect that duty, and they fall into the well and are killed, it is through my negligence. I cannot urge their negligence as a defense, even though I have never invited or encouraged them, expressly or impliedly, to go upon the premises."

The language amounts to a reaffirmance of the doctrine of the turntable cases, and, to our minds, suggests the true principle upon which cases of this character rest; that is, that where the owner of dangerous premises knows, or has good reason to believe, that children so young as to be ignorant of the danger will resort to such premises he is bound to take such precautions to keep them from such premises, or to protect them from injuries likely to result from the dangerous condition of the premises while there, as a man of ordinary care and prudence, under like circumstances, would take. At first sight it would seem that the principle, thus stated, is too broad, and that its application would impose unreasonable burdens on owners, and intolerable restrictions on the use and enjoyment of property. But it must be kept in mind that it requires nothing of the owner that a man of ordinary care and prudence would not do of his own volition under like circumstances. Such a man would not willingly take up unreasonable burdens nor vex himself with intolerable restrictions.

It is true, as said in Loomis *v.* Terry, 17 Wend. 497, "the business of life must go forward;" the means by which it is carried forward cannot be rendered absolutely safe. Ordinarily, it can be best carried forward by the unrestricted use of private property by the owner; therefore the law favors such use to the fullest extent consistent with the main purpose for which, from a social standpoint, such business is carried forward, namely, the public good. Hence, in order to determine the extent to which such use may be enjoyed, its bearing on such main purpose must be taken into account, and a balance struck between its advantages and disadvantages. If, on the whole, such use defeats, rather than promotes, the main purpose, it should not be permitted; on the other hand, if the restrictions proposed would so operate, they should not be imposed. The business of life is better carried forward by the use of dangerous machinery; hence the public good demands its use, although occasionally such use results in the loss of life or limb. It does so because the danger is insignificant, when weighed against the benefits resulting from the use of such machinery, and for the same reason demands its reasonable, most effective and unrestricted use up to the point where the benefits resulting from such use no longer outweigh the danger to be anticipated from it. At that point the public good demands restrictions. For example, a turntable is a dangerous contrivance, which facilitates railroading; the general benefits resulting from its use outweigh the occasional injuries inflicted by it; hence the public good demands its use. We may conceive of means by which it might be rendered absolutely safe, but such means would so interfere with its beneficial use that the danger to be anticipated would not justify their adoption; therefore the public good demands its use without them. But the danger incident to its use may be lessened by the use of a lock which would prevent children, attracted to it, from moving it; the interference with the proper use of the turntable occasioned by the use of such lock is so slight that it is outweighed by the danger to be anticipated from an omission to use it; therefore the public good, we think, demands the use of the lock. The public good would not require the owner of a vacant lot on which there is a pond to fill up the pond or enclose the lot with an impassable wall to ensure the safety of children resorting to it, because the burden of doing so is out of proportion to the danger to be anticipated from leaving it undone. Richards *v.* Connell, 45 Neb. 467, 63 N. W. Rep. 915. But where there is an open well on a vacant lot, which is frequented by children, of which the owner of the lot has knowledge, he is liable for injuries sustained by children falling into the well, because the danger to be anticipated from the open well, under the circumstances, outweighs the slight expense or inconvenience that would be entailed in making it safe. Tucker *v.* Draper, *supra*.

Hence, in all cases of this kind, in the determination of the question of negligence, regard must be had to the character and location of the premises, the purpose for which they are used, the probability of injury therefrom, the precautions necessary to prevent such injury, and the relations such precautions bear to the beneficial use of the premises. The nature of the precautions would depend on the particular fact in each case. In some cases a warning to the children or the parents might be sufficient; in others, more active measures might be required. But in every case they should be such as a man of ordinary care and prudence would observe under like cirstances. If, under all the circumstances, the owner omits such precautions as a man of ordinary care and prudence, under like circumstances, would observe, he is guilty of negligence. We are fully satisfied that the principle under consideration is sound, and that its application would not operate oppressively on the owner. We see no good reason for receding from the position already taken by this court in cases of this character.

The defendant tendered the following instruction: "The jury are instructed that in this case the plaintiff claims, in substance, that the railroad company was negligent in the manner in which it kept and used the turntable by which the plaintiff was injured, and that the turntable in question was a machine that was naturally enticing to children, and that children were tempted to play on and about this turntable. On this point the court instructs you that the law is that the railroad company has the right to the exclusive use of its own grounds and turntable and other machinery, the same as any other person has the exclusive right and use of his own property and premises, and that the company was under no obligations to keep its turntable in such a condition that it would be safe and convenient for children to play upon and to use as a plaything; and the court instructs you that the defendant was under no obligation to keep a watchman at and about said turntable for the purpose of excluding children therefrom; that the company was only required to exercise reasonable care in the placing and using of said turntable, and have the same fitted with such appliances as would make it reasonably safe and convenient for the purpose for which it was intended." The court refused the instruction as tendered, and modified it by omitting the concluding clause, and inserting the following: "But the company was required to exercise reasonable care in the placing and fastening of the turntable, and having the same fitted with such appliances as would make it reasonably safe in the situation where it was placed, under the circumstances as disclosed in this case."

The instruction as thus modified was given. The complaint of the refusal of the court to give the instruction as tendered is covered by what has been said on the sufficiency of the facts to sustain the verdict. But the defendant insists that the instruction as modified is erroneous, in that it submitted to the jury the proper construction and location of the turntable. Taking the instruction as a whole, we do not think it admits of that construction. The opening sentence informs the jury of the nature of the plaintiff's claim; that such claim is that the defendant "was negligent in the manner in which it kept and used the turntable by which the plaintiff was injured." In paragraph 7 of the instructions the jury were told that the action rests on the alleged negligence of the defendant in not keeping the turntable guarded, locked, or properly fastened. In the fifteenth paragraph they were told that the defendant "had a right to have and use the turntable in the carrying on of its business as a railroad company." The rejected clause of the instruction under consideration, as tendered by the defendant, uses the word "placing," the only word used in the substituted clause that could be construed as a reference to the location or construction of the turntable. From these considerations, we think the clause complained of has no reference to the location nor original construction of the turntable, but refers rather to the condition in which it was to be kept or left when not in use. In the light of the entire charge, the jury could hardly have understood it to refer to the location or construction of the turntable.

Another instruction tendered by the defendant is as follows: "If the jury find from the evidence that the turntable in question was a ponderous and powerful machine when set in motion, and that according to its mechanism it would turn easily, and when turned, even for a small space, it would accumulate a force of momentum of great power; and if you further find that the young people and children meddling with said turntable at the time of the injury complained of worked upon the levers of said machine back and forth through the small space in which the turntable could be moved, even when the fastenings were in proper place and held the machine; and that by the motion and momentum of the machine set in motion by the young people at the levers the fastenings became loosened so as to permit the turntable to go around — then you are instructed that under this state of facts the plaintiff could not recover, and your verdict should be for the defendant." It was refused, and its refusal is now assigned as error. The instruction entirely omits the question of due care. There was evidence to the effect that the lock used for the turntable was little, if any, obstacle to the use of the turntable by children, because one of the staples was loose, and could be easily removed. The instruction, if given, would have justified a finding of due care, however carelessly the turntable was fastened. That would have been erroneous. The instruction, in our opinion, was properly refused.

The court on its own motion gave the following instruction as part of the charge to the jury: "But if you find, from a preponderance of the evidence, that the turntable in question was a dangerous machine, and the defendants did know, or had reason to believe, under the circumstances of the case, the children of the place would resort to the turntable to play, and that if they did they would or might be injured, then, if they took no means to keep the children away, and no means to prevent accident, this would be evidence of negligence, and would be answerable for damages caused thereby to the children of tender years, and who did not possess sufficient knowledge or understanding to know the danger or dangerous character of such turntable. However, the defendants are not insurers of the limbs of those, whether adults or children, who may resort to their grounds, and there are many injuries continually happening which involve no pecuniary liability to any one." The defendant contends that there is no evidence to support the hypothesis that the defendant took no means to keep the children away, and no means to prevent the accident. The evidence of at least one of the children who was present at the time, and who assisted in revolving the turntable at the time, is to the effect that it was not locked, but yielded at once to their efforts to move it. There is other evidence to the same effect. Another witness testifies that it was never locked. As to the means taken to keep the children from the turntable, a considerable portion of the testimony offered on behalf of the plaintiff tends to show that no such means were taken. The defendant contends that the location of the turntable, at a distance from the town, was, in itself, a means of protection. But the instruction has reference to the circumstances as they existed at the time of the accident. The location of the turntable, as a means of protection, is important only as tending to show the improbability of children resorting to it, and that the defendant could not reasonably be expected to anticipate that they would do so. It becomes immaterial when, according to the hypothesis, the defendant knew, or had good reason to believe, that children would resort to the turntable and be injured by it. The instruction, we think, finds ample basis in the evidence.

Another criticism urged against this instruction is that it involves the province of the jury, in that it charges that if the defendant, under the circumstances stated, took no means to keep the children away, and no means to prevent the accident, it would be answerable in damages. The defendant insists that the question of negligence was one for the jury, and that it was not within the province of the court to say, in effect, that a certain state of facts constituted negligence. We are inclined to think this criticism is just. From the wording of the instruction, the jury could hardly draw any other conclusion than that, if they found the facts specifically stated therein, the verdict should be for the plaintiff; in other words, that such facts were to be considered by them, not only as evidence of negligence, but as negligence *per se*. It has been repeatedly held by this court that it is erroneous to single out and state a group of facts, and inform the jury that if such facts are found it establishes the existence of negligence. The question of negligence is seldom one of law, and the facts enumerated in the instruction should have been considered by the jury as evidence of negligence, to be considered in the light of all the other facts and circumstances shown in evidence. To thus single out and state a group of facts has been held by this court to amount to an improper comment on questions of fact by the court. We think the instruction was erroneous, and that the following cases support that view. Mo. Pac. R'y Co. *v.* Baier, 37 Neb. 235, 4 Am. Neg. Cas. 874, 55 N. W. Rep. 913; Railway Co. *v.* Morgan, 40 Neb. 604, 59 N. W. Rep. 81; Railroad Co. *v.* Oleson, 40 Neb. 889, 59 N. W. Rep. 354; Village of Culbertson *v.* Holliday, 50 Neb. 229, 1 Am. Neg. Rep. 111, 69 N. W. Rep. 853.

The nineteenth and twentieth paragraphs of the charge to the jury related to the measure of damages, and are as follows:

"19. The jury are instructed if from the evidence in the case, and under the instructions of the court, the jury shall find the issues for the plaintiff, and that the plaintiff has sustained damages, as charged in the declaration, then, to enable the jury to estimate the amount of such damages, it is not necessary that any witness should have expressed an opinion as to the amount of such damage, but the jury may themselves make such estimate from the facts and circumstances in proof, and by considering them in connection with their own knowledge, observation and experience in the business affairs of life.

"20. The jury are instructed that if, on the evidence in the case and under the instructions of the court, they find the issue in favor of the plaintiff, and that the plaintiff has sustained damages, as charged in the petition, then in assessing such damages they should take into consideration the age, expectancy of life of the plaintiff, his inability to labor as shown by the evidence, his mental anguish and bodily pain, if any has been shown, and whether or not the injury to the plaintiff is permanent. You should take all these elements into consideration, and allow him such a sum as will be fair and just compensation for the injuries sustained, not exceeding the sum of $25,000. But you cannot allow him exemplary damages; that is, damages by way of punishment of the defendants."

One objection urged against these instructions is that the jury were required to consider the facts and circumstances in evidence "in connection with their own knowledge, observation and experience in the business affairs of life." It is not only proper but necessary, that, in arriving at a verdict, the jury should make use of such knowledge as they possess in common with other men. But the instruction imposes no such limitation. We think the jury might have fairly inferred from it that they were required to bring to bear any special knowledge which they might have on the subject, or the result of their observations and experience in like cases, which would be manifestly improper.

Another objection to the instructions in this behalf is that the jury were required to take into account the plaintiff's inability to labor as an element of damage. The defendant insists that as the plaintiff is a minor, in the custody of his father, who is charged with his support and entitled to his earnings during minority, his inability to labor during his minority is not a proper element of damage in this case. The case of Railroad Co. *v.* Johnson (Tex. Sup.), 44 S. W. Rep. 1067, was an action for personal injuries to an infant, and an instruction not different in principle from those complained of was held reversible error for the reasons now urged by the defendant. The same principle was involved in an instruction considered in Decker *v.* McSorley (Wis.), 86 N. W. Rep. 554. The instruction was condemned.

A further objection is urged against these instructions, and that is that they instruct the jury that the damages shall not exceed $25,000. The defendant insists that an intimation was thereby conveyed to the jury that they might allow that sum, and that such intimation was prejudicial to the defendant. No authority is cited in support of this objection, nor are we aware that any exists. It is not unusual for courts to instruct the jury as to the limit of damages allowable under the pleadings in the case. As a matter of practice, we believe it should be omitted. If the damages awarded exceed the amount allowable, the remedy is simple. We believe that most lawyers will agree with us that the intimation conveyed to the jury by such a statement is dangerous to the defendant. We do not go to the extent of saying that it would constitute reversible error, but we believe the practice should be discountenanced.

In the course of the trial the court permitted the plaintiff to introduce in evidence a certain printed rule of the defendant which provided that turntables should be kept locked when not in use, and that it was the duty of agents at the stations where there was no engine house foreman to see that such turntables were locked after being used. Parol testimony was admitted to the same effect. It also admitted evidence to the effect that immediately after the accident the station agent went to the turntable and locked it. The defendant insists that the admission of this evidence was error. We do not think so. It was necessary to bring home to the defendant knowledge that children were likely to resort to the turntable. There is evidence tending to show that both employees mentioned in the rule introduced in evidence had knowledge of such fact, and the rule, taken in connection with the evidence in their relations to the defendant, tends to bring such knowledge home to the defendant. That the agent locked the turntable immediately after the accident had a bearing on the question of whether the turntable was locked before the accident, which was one of the issues in the case.

Another witness was permitted to testify that he went to the turntable after the accident, on the same day, and found the table unlocked. The defendant argues that it was not admissible to show the condition of the table after the accident occurred. This evidence, we think, is also admissible, as tending to show that the children found the turntable unlocked before the accident occurred.

Objection is also made to the admission of evidence of testimony to the effect that the roadmaster, or division superintendent, which one is not stated, was at the turntable after the accident, how long after does not appear. The objection to this evidence is not clear, nor are we able to see how it had any influence on the verdict one way or another. The objection that it was immaterial appears to be well founded, but we cannot see that its admission would constitute reversible error.

The defendant complains of the admission of testimony to the effect that the station agent on the day of the accident met the children, who were playing with the push car, rode a short distance on the push car, and said nothing to the children about playing with it. The ground of this complaint appears to be that playing with the push car, when the agent saw them and took part in the sport, and playing on the turntable, some 500 yards distant, were independent transactions, and the agent could not reasonably anticipate that they would go to the turntable from the place he left them, and therefore was not required to warn them of its danger. It seems to us that the station grounds as a whole were dangerous premises, especially for children of that age. The turntable was only one of its many dangers. The evidence objected to, it seems to us, was competent to show that the defendant had knowledge that children frequented these dangerous premises, and that they did so with its knowledge and consent. We think there was no error in the admission of this testimony.

Certain impeaching questions were addressed to one of the defendant's witnesses which were objected to by the defendant on the ground, among others, that no foundation had been laid. Before the questions were asked, the defendant's attention was directed to the time and place where the contradictory statements were made, and to the persons in whose presence they were made. Taken in connection with his testimony on direct examination, the witness could not fail to understand to what the questions related. We think the foundation was sufficient, and that his answers, some of them showing that he had made contradictory statements, were properly admitted.

We recommend that the judgment of the district court be reversed, and the cause remanded for further proceedings according to law.

AMES and DUFFIE, CC., concur.

PER CURIAM. For the reasons stated in the foregoing opinion, the judgment of the district court is reversed, and the cause remanded for further proceedings according to law.

FIVEY v. PENNSYLVANIA RAILROAD COMPANY (1).

Court of Errors and Appeals, New Jersey, June, 1902.

BRAKEMAN INJURED IN COLLISION — CONTRACT — RELEASE — FRAUD — BURDEN OF PROOF. — 1. Where a party attaches his signature to a contract otherwise valid, a conclusive presumption is created, except as against fraud, that the signer read, understood and assented to its terms.

2. Where a defense set up to an action upon a written contract is that the signature thereto has been obtained by fraud, the burden is upon him who raises such a defense to establish the alleged fraud by clear and satisfactory proof. The presumption of the law is in favor of innocence, and fraud is not to be assumed on doubtful evidence.

3. The plaintiff sued a railroad company for accidental injuries sustained while in its employ. The defense was a release arising by the acceptance of benefits from a relief fund established by the company, of which the plaintiff had become a member. The plaintiff replied, alleging fraud; the principal facts alleged being that, when he began to read the application, the medical examiner told him to sign it, saying it was only a matter of form, and was immaterial; that the association was a benevolent one, belonging to the employees, and sustained by deductions from the wages of the members each month; but failing to state that the acceptance of benefits

1. See former decision in Fivey *v.* Penn. R. R. Co. (N. J. Sup., February, 1901), 9 Am. Neg. Rep. 538.

for injuries would operate as a release; but it also appearing that the plaintiff knew that he was signing a contract, and that he could read and write, and that the agreement in question was printed in plain, legible type, and that he was furnished with a book containing a copy of his application and agreement, and of the regulations of the relief fund, which he had in his possession over two months before the accident. At the close of the evidence a verdict was directed for the defendant. *Held*, on review, that the proof of fraud failed, and that the direction was not erroneous (1).

(Syllabus by the Court.)

ERROR to CIRCUIT COURT, Hudson County.

Action by Patrick Fivey against the Pennsylvania Railroad Company. From judgment for defendant, plaintiff brings error. *Judgment affirmed.*

THOMAS P. WICKES, for plaintiff in error.

JAMES B. VREDENBURGH, for defendant in error.

HENDRICKSON, J.—The plaintiff brought suit against the defendant company to recover damages for an injury resulting from the alleged negligence of the company. The defense was a denial of the negligence and a release. The case was tried at the Hudson circuit, and resulted in a direction of the verdict in favor of the defendant.

1. *Release of claim for personal injuries.* In CHICAGO & NORTHWESTERN R'Y CO. *v.* WILCOX (*U. S. Circuit Court of Appeals, Eighth Circuit, July, 1902*), 116 Fed. Rep. 913, the question of release of claim for personal injuries, was decided, on appeal from the United States Court for the Northern District of Iowa, on the following facts (stated by SANBORN, CIRCUIT JUDGE): "This is a suit in equity to rescind a release of a claim for personal injury on the ground of fraud, undue influence, and mistake. The complainant, Lucy A. Wilcox, was a widow, and she had been engaged in the occupation of nursing for ten years. She was sixty-five years of age. On December 22, 1898, as she was standing in a passenger car of the defendant, it was suddenly started, and she fell and broke the neck of the femur of her left leg. One week after her injury she compromised her claim against the railway company, and executed a written release of it for $600 and the agreement of the company to pay her doctors' bills. On March 14, 1901, she exhibited her bill in this suit to rescind this release. In this bill she alleged that her release was obtained by the fraud, undue influence, and circumvention of the agents of the defendant, in that the physician of the latter, who was attending her, and the agent of the company, informed her that her injuries were temporary, and that she would be well and able to attend to her ordinary avocation within a year, when the injuries were permanent, and she never could recover. She averred that she did not know the serious character of her injury, but relied on the statement of the physician, and was induced thereby to make the settlement and to execute the release. There were general averments of fraud on the part of the company and of incompetence to contract on the part of the complainant, but these allegations were not sustained by the evidence, and the answer denied all the equities of the bill. After a hearing the court below found that the complainant was competent to make the settlement when she signed the release, and that the agents of the

Exception was taken to this action of the trial judge, and error has been duly assigned thereon.

The plaintiff's injury happened on March, 14, 1899, in the Harsimus freight yard of the defendant, at Jersey City, while in its employ as a brakeman. A freight train of open cars, loaded with lumber, was engaged in drilling; cutting off a car at a time, and, by means of switches, locating them upon the tracks at various piers of the company on the river. The plaintiff was in charge of one of these cars just cut off from the train, and was standing at its easterly end, regulating its movements by means of a hand brake, which consisted of a wheel on top of an upright rod, with a ratchet at the foot, into which a dog would fall at each rotary movement of the brake, and hold it in place until moved again. While the car was moving eastwardly toward the dock, a switch was misplaced, whereby the car was being carried upon the wrong track, and was about to collide with an engine standing there. The plaintiff's story is that he at once applied the brake, but ineffectually, because it was out of order, and, from the force of the impact of the collision, the lumber

defendant were not guilty of any fraud, deceit, or wrongdoing in procuring it, but that the release was executed under a mistake of the probable time she would be incapacitated by her injury, and on account of this mistake it rendered a decree rescinding the contract of settlement (111 Fed. Rep. 435). The railway company has appealed from this decree."

The decision in the *Wilcox* case, *supra* (as per syllabus by the court), is as follows:

"1. In the absence of fraud or mistake an agreement of settlement and release of an unliquidated or disputed claim as conclusively estops the parties from reviving and litigating it as a final judgment. Such agreements of compromise are uniformly favored and upheld by the courts.

"2. A mere preponderance of testimony is insufficient to establish such fraud or mistake as will warrant the avoidance of a written agreement of settlement and release. The proof must be clear, unequivocal and convincing to have this effect.

"3. A mistake of a past or present fact may warrant a rescission of a contract of settlement and release. But a mistake in opinion or belief relative to the future duration or effect of a personal injury, or a mistake in prophecy or opinion as to an uncertain future event, is not a mistake of fact and is no ground for the avoidance of a release or of a contract of settlement.

"4. Complainant compromised and released a claim for a broken hip. She knew when she settled that her hip had been broken, and that it was a bad break. She was induced by the statement of her own physician, who was also the company's physician, to believe, and did believe, that she would be well within a year, and she settled upon that basis. She was mistaken, and her injury and disability turned out to be permanent. *Held*, her mistake was not a mistake of fact, but a mistake in opinion or belief as to a future event, and it furnished no ground for an avoidance of her release." Decree reversed, and case remanded to the Circuit Court, with directions to dismiss the bill.

in the car was thrown against him, causing his injuries. He says the defect in the break was that the rod was bent, causing the dog to fall below the ratchet, leaving him to hold the brake in place by main strength. It will be perceived that the charge of negligence involved, as questions in fact, the alleged defect in the brake, and the failure of the company's agents to discover it by the exercise of reasonable care, and whether the defect had existed for such a length of time as to afford the company a reasonable opportunity to discover it. The plaintiff's evidence upon these questions was traversed by that of the defendant, but, since the judge's direction was confined to the proof upon the subject of the alleged release, we will not consider, for the present, at least, the question of the failure to prove negligence, which was one of the grounds of the motion to direct the verdict. In addition to other defenses, the defendant pleaded and offered proof in support of the following facts, to wit: That the plaintiff, as an employee of the defendant, some time prior to the accident had applied for membership in the relief fund managed by the defendant company, as alleged, for the protection and benefit of such of its employees as might desire to avail themselves of its provisions; that one of the agreements in the application is that, if the applicant should be accepted as a member, the acceptance of benefits from the relief fund for injury or death should operate as a release of all claims for damages against the company arising from such injury or death, and that the plaintiff or his legal representatives would execute such further instruments as might be necessary to formally evidence such acquittance; that the application was duly approved by the defendant, and the plaintiff thereupon accepted and admitted as a member in the relief fund; that after the date of the alleged injury the plaintiff accepted from the relief fund for his said injuries, certain payments made from time to time, aggregating the sum of eighty-two dollars and gave receipts and acquittances for the same, which operated as a release of all the claims for damages alleged in the suit.

The plaintiff did not deny the facts thus alleged, but, by his pleading and proof, sought to avoid the effect of such alleged release on the ground that the agreement in question was unknown at the time of the execution of the application for membership, and that it was in fact obtained from him by fraud and deceit. The replication, setting up the fraud by general averment, was sustained on demurrer. Fivey *v.* Penn. R. R. Co. (N. J. Sup.), 9 Am. Neg. Rep. 538; 48 Atl. Rep. 553. And under the point we are now considering, the question is, was there sufficient proof of the alleged fraud and deceit before the court to send the case to the jury? In such an inquiry we must take that view of the evidence which is most favorable to the plaintiff. The case shows that the execution of the application for membership took place in the presence of the medical examiner of the defendant, in the relief department, at Jersey City, to whom the plaintiff had presented himself for the required physical examination. It occurred at the close of the examination, the results of which are found embodied in the examiner's certificate attached to and forming part of the application, which was partly printed and partly written. The plaintiff gives his version of the transaction, from which we are asked to gather the elements of the fraud alleged, as follows: Q. At the time when it was handed to you for execution, that day when you went up to the doctor's office. Confine your evidence to what was said to you when the paper was handed to you for execution. A. He simply shoved it in front of me, and told me to sign my name; that it was all a matter of form; that is all. Q. What was said to you at this time by Dr. Simpson in reference to this document just before you signed it? A. Nothing whatever. Q. The Court: You can read and write? A. Yes; there is plenty of words I didn't understand. Q. The Court: You can read? A. A little; not much. Q. You can read print? A. With the exception of some words. Q. What, if anything, did Dr. Simpson say to you at this particular time touching the nature of the paper which he asked you to sign? A. He said it was a benevolent association belonging to the employees of the railroad, and there was so much deducted from their wages every month to contribute toward the support of this fund, according to what class you would go in. Q, Did he say anything to you about the railroad companies being a part of this fund? A. Nothing whatever. Q. Did he say anything to you at this time about your releasing the railroad company in case of any accident to you? A. No, sir. * * * Q. Did he request you at any time to sign the paper? A. When he was all through he shoved it in front of me and he said: 'Sign it.' I commenced to read it. He said it was all a matter of form; it was immaterial. Q. How did you commence to read it? A. I commenced to look at the print, out of curiosity, to see what it contained, if I could possibly make it out. Q. Did you read any part of what is written in that left-hand page before he told you that it was a matter of form or immaterial? A. He would not give me time to read it. Q. Did you read it? A. No; I did not. Q. Did you read at that time anything on either side of the paper? A. No, sir." The witness further testified that the doctor did not, at or prior to the time of signing, read to him anything from the paper, nor from any book like the book of the regulations of the relief fund offered in evidence by the defendant. Are there to be found in this testimony such elements of fraud or deceit as, under the law, are sufficient to discharge a person who can read and write from the binding force of a contract in writing, otherwise valid, which has been duly executed by him? The fact that the plaintiff did not choose to read the paper, or the material parts of it, before signing, or did not know its contents at the time, cannot, in the absence of actual fraud, relieve him from its obligations. This doctrine arises from the well-settled principle that affixing a signature to a contract creates a conclusive presumption, except as against fraud, that the signer read, understood, and assented to its terms. In Lewis *v.* Great Western Ry. Co., 5 Hurl. & N. 867 (1), where a suit was brought to recover for a sack of clothes which had been shipped, but not delivered, the defense was that the package was not called for within the time required by the conditions to a receiving note signed by the shipper. The plaintiff testified: "I delivered in a paper specifying what the things were. I signed it. I did not read the paper. A person told me to sign it. He did not call my attention to the conditions or read them. I think I must have seen the word 'conditions.'" The case was heard before Pollock, C. B., and his associates; and it was held that there was nothing to rebut the presumption arising from the signature of the paper that the signer understood that the contract was subject to the conditions. In Rice *v.* Manufacturing Co., 2 Cush. 80, the principle found expression in these words: "A party who enters into a contract in writing, without any fraud or imposition being practiced upon him, is conclusively presumed to understand and assent to its terms and legal effect." Other authorities in point are In re Greenfield's Estate, 14 Pa. 491; Van Deventer *v.* Van Deventer, 46 N. J. L. 460; Upton *v.*

1. In Lewis *v.* Great Western R'y Co., 5 H. & N. 867, it appeared that plaintiff delivered to a railway company eighteen packages to be carried on their line. He filled up and signed a receiving-note, describing the goods as furniture. On the paper, under the head "conditions" were these words: "No claim for deficiency, damage or detention will be allowed, unless made within three days after the delivery of the goods, nor for loss, unless made within seven days of the time they should have been delivered, and that the company will not be answerable for the loss and detention of any goods which may be untruly or incorrectly described in the receiving-note." The plaintiff said "he was told to sign the paper, and did so. He might have seen the word 'conditions,' but he did not read them, and did not know and was not told what they were. One of the packages consisted of a sack of clothes, which was not delivered, but no claim was made until more than seven days from the time when the same should have been delivered. *Held*, that there was nothing to rebut the presumption arising from the signature of the paper by the plaintiff that he understood that the contract was subject to the conditions.

Tribilcock, 91 U. S. 45; Vickers *v.* Railroad Co. (C. C.) 71 Fed. Rep. 139; Wallace *v.* Railway Co., 67 Iowa 547, 25 N. W. Rep. 772; Chu Pawn *v.* Irwin, 82 Hun, 607, 31 N. Y. Supp. 724.

To return, then, to the question of actual fraud, the allegation is that fraud was practiced upon the plaintiff in procuring his signature, by fraudulent representations as to the nature of the paper signed, and as to the party with whom plaintiff was contracting. This averment is based upon the plaintiff's version of what the medical examiner said as to the nature of the paper about to be signed. This has already been recited. It is not a statement as to the contents of the paper, but, rather, a remark as to its nature. Whether the remark was called out by a question, does not appear. The statement is condemned as false and misleading, not because it defines the association as a benevolent one belonging to the employees of the railroad, for that was a fairly accurate description of it. The case shows that the relief fund is for the exclusive benefit of the employees who are members of it and contribute to its support, and who become disabled by sickness or accident, and of the relatives or other beneficiaries in the event of death. It is contended that the statement, though true in fact, became fraudulent and misleading, in not stating that the railroad itself was a party to the contract, and interested in the association. But the balance of the statement, to the effect that there was so much deducted from the wages of the employees every month to contribute toward the support of this fund, according to the class they should go in, would seem to indicate that the company was connected with it. But to establish a misrepresentation that will invalidate a contract, it must appear that the representations were not only false, but made with the intent to deceive, and that the party seeking relief acted upon, and was misled by, them. It is difficult to see wherein the statement of the medical examiner was false or fraudulent, within the rule here stated. Especially must this be so when we look at the other circumstances proved. It must have been in the minds of the parties that the plaintiff would be associated with fellow-employees who were members of the relief fund, who would be likely to be acquainted with the rules and regulations of the association, and who would readily give such information as plaintiff desired. It also appeared that, very shortly after signing the application, the plaintiff was furnished, according to the regular practice, with a small book, convenient for the pocket, in which was pasted a copy of the certificate of membership, and which contained all the regulations of the relief department, and an exact copy of the form of application. This book contained upon the outside cover, upon the fly leaf, and as head lines upon several pages, the words, in large print, "The Pennsylvania Railroad Voluntary Relief Department." The evidence showed, and the fact was not denied by the plaintiff, that he received the book and certificate over two months before the accident. But in this case it is contended that there are other circumstances giving color to this charge of fraud. The fact is pointed to that after this statement the medical examiner "shoved the paper" in front of the plaintiff, and "told him to sign" his name; that plaintiff "commenced to read it," and he "was told by the doctor it was all a matter of form; it was immaterial." In the case of Van Deventer *v.* Van Deventer, *supra*, the objection was that the party who had executed the obligation did not know its nature, and was told by the plaintiff that the papers were of no account, and only a formal matter. But since it was not shown that the obligor was defrauded by any representation that the documents were of a different character or import from that plainly appearing on their face, and it appearing that the obligor could read, and had liberty to examine the papers, the Supreme Court held the objection insufficient to avoid the obligation. In considering this question, it should also be observed that a charge of fraud must be clearly, and distinctly proved by the party who asserts it. The presumption is in favor of innocence, and fraud is not to be assumed on doubtful evidence. Kerr, Fraud & M. 384.

The point has been pressed, also, that because the application was a long one, and contained on the back, in small type, the rules and regulations of the association, this fact should be regarded as a badge of fraud. But in fairness it must be said that the application itself, in which was contained the agreement of release upon which the defense is based, and also the book of regulations, referred to, were printed in plain, legible type.

It was further intimated, rather than argued, that the defense should be regarded with disfavor, on the ground that the contract is a hard one, from the plaintiff's standpoint. But we see nothing in the case to justify a departure from the ordinary rules applying to the enforcement of contracts. The validity of the agreement in question was passed upon by this court, after very careful consideration, in Beck *v.* Penn. R. R. Co., 63 N. J. L. 233, 6 Am. Neg. Rep. 601, 43 Atl. Rep. 908, and it was there held that the contract was not against public policy, nor lacking in mutuality or consideration, nor *ultra vires*. The case of O'Neil *v.* Iron Co. (Mich.) 30 N. W. Rep. 688, was cited for the plaintiff as authority for the proposition that in a case like this the court should be astute to discover a fraud upon the employee in such an action; but it is not in point, because it was shown that the employee could not read, and had no knowledge of the terms or conditions of the printed matter. The other cases cited are not out of harmony with the legal rules herein expressed. There was in the present case an entire failure to show the indicia of actual fraud. Hence the determination of this point was for the court, and the result follows that the learned trial judge was justified in directing the verdict for the defendant.

There were a number of exceptions taken and sealed to the admission and rejection of evidence by the trial judge, but they are not properly before us, and cannot be considered. The questions overruled (nine or more in number) are all included in a single assignment of error. And the questions rejected (twelve or more in number) are likewise embraced in a single assignment. The objection raised by the defendant to these assignments is that they are multifarious. These assignments are framed in entire disregard of the rules of pleading and of the practice of this court, and cannot, for that reason, be considered. Associates *v.* Davison, 29 N. J. L. 418, 2 Enc. Pl. & Prac. 938, note 5; 2 Cycl. Law & Proc. 986; 3 Am. Dig. (Cent. Ed.) 3028. It may be stated, however, that the only exceptions under these last assignments pressed upon our consideration at the argument were those taken to the overruling of questions designed to elicit from the plaintiff an answer to the questions whether at any time, from the date of his application until the occasion of his signing the last receipt for benefits, he knew he would be releasing his cause of action against the railroad company by so doing. It is quite apparent from what has already been said that, in the absence of proof of fraud, the evidence to be thus elicited was entirely immaterial, and was properly overruled.

We find no error in the record, and the result is that the judgment below must be affirmed.

HAMILTON v. BORDENTOWN ELECTRIC LIGHT AND MOTOR COMPANY ET AL.

Supreme Court, New Jersey, June, 1902.

PERSON KILLED BY CONTACT WITH ELECTRIC WIRE—DUTY OF ELECTRIC LIGHT COMPANY—STATUTORY ACTION FOR DEATH. —1. It is the duty of a company maintaining in a public street an insulated electric light wire carrying a dangerous current to use reasonable care that an uninsulated telegraph wire does not come in contact therewith, and remain so long as to wear off the insulation, so that the current is diverted into the telegraph wire, and by it carried to a third wire, from which it is conducted to and against, and injures a person lawfully using the public street (1).

2. It is the duty of those maintaining an uninsulated telegraph wire in a public street to use reasonable care that it does not break and come in contact with an insulated electric light wire carrying a dangerous current, and remain so long as to wear off the insulation, and divert the current from the electric light wire through it to another wire, to the injury of a person lawfully using the public street.

3. Allegations from which it can be inferred that a suit under the death act is for the benefit of the next of kin are sufficient without a direct averment to that effect.

(Syllabus by the Court.)

1. For other actions arising out of injuries sustained by electric wires, from 1897 to date, see vols. 1-12 AM. NEG. REP., and the current numbers of that series of Reports.

See also NOTE ON ACCIDENTS CAUSED BY ELECTRIC WIRES, 8 AM. NEG. REP. 213-221.

See also the following cases arising out of accidents to employees caused by contact with electric wires:

In HART v. ALLEGHENY COUNTY LIGHT Co. (*Pennsylvania, January, 1902*), 50 Atl. Rep. 1010, an action against the defendant and another company as joint tort feasors, judgment for plaintiff against the defendant rendered in Court of Common Pleas, Allegheny county, was reversed, POTTER, J., rendering the opinion as follows: "This action was brought against two defendants as joint tort feasors. The evidence failed to show any concert of action, or any joint trespass, by the defendants, and under the principle of Wiest v. Traction Co., 200 Pa. St. 148, 40 Atl. Rep. 891, a separate recovery should not have been allowed against one defendant. The point should, however, have been brought to the attention of the court at the trial. But, aside from this question, it clearly appears from the evidence that the injury for which recovery is here sought was caused by the act of the plaintiff in placing one hand upon a telephone wire, and the other upon or in contact with an electric light wire, both wires being upon the same pole, which was the property of the electric light company. The plaintiff was an inspector, and had been employed as such by the electric light company for several years. He was an experienced man, and had been accustomed to climbing poles upon which both electric wires and telephone wires were placed. The special duty for which he was employed was to look after the lights at night, and to see that the wires were clear, and to adjust any difficulties that prevented the proper operation of the lights. It is therefore apparent that the plaintiff, above all others, was the one whose business it was to discover anything wrong with the wires. The defendant company could only be apprised of a difficulty with its wires through the report of the plaintiff, or some other inspector employed for that purpose. The plaintiff was familiar, or at least should have been with the condition of the electric light wires, and their situation upon the poles with relation to buildings, trees, and other wires. Electric light wires are, of course, always dangerous to handle. There is always a possibility of injury from them alone, or in connection with other wires. The telephone wire complained of in this instance was not, as stated in the plaintiff's declaration, a "grounded or live wire," but was an ordinary pole leading from the pole to an office near by. Of course, there was connection with the earth at some

ACTION by Annie Hamilton against the Bordentown Electric Light & Motor Company and others. *Demurrer to declaration overruled.*

ARGUED February term, 1902, before GUMMERE, C. J., and VAN SYCKEL, GARRISON and GARRETSON, JJ.

CHARLES E. ROBERTS, for plaintiff.

HOWARD FLANDERS and SAMUEL W. BELDEN, for defendant Bordentown Electric Light & Motor Co.

EDWARD A. & WILLIAM T. DAY, for defendant Delaware & A. Telegraph and Telephone Co.

J. H. GASKILL, for defendant Pennsylvania R. Co.

point on the line, but it is apparent from the testimony that the injury was caused not by any current which was carried by the telephone wire, but by reason of the fact that when the plaintiff came in contact with the light wire in one hand, and with the telephone wire in the other, his body formed a short circuit between the two wires, which resulted in his receiving a shock from the heavily charged electric light wire, causing him to fall. He had been provided with rubber gloves for the express purpose of protecting himself against an injury of this character. If he had made use of these rubber gloves upon the night in question, he would have been safe. Whether it be put upon the ground of the knowledge which the plaintiff had, or should have had, of the relative position of the two wires, or whether it be based upon his carelessness in failing to protect himself at the time of the accident by the use of the rubber gloves provided for that purpose, in either case the inference is unavoidable that, without the contributory negligence of the plaintiff, the accident could not have occurred. The first specification of error is to the refusal of the appellant's first point, which prayed for binding instructions in favor of the defendant. This assignment is sustained, and the judgment is reversed."

In BOWERS *v.* BRISTOL GAS & ELECTRIC CO., *(Virginia, September, 1902)*, 42 S. E. Rep. 296, judgment for defendant in the Corporation Court of Bristol, was affirmed, the court (per WHITTLE, J.), stating the facts as follows: "This action was brought in the Corporation Court for the city of Bristol to recover damages for the death of W. T. Bowers, the husband and intestate of plaintiff in error, alleged to have been occasioned by the negligence of the defendant company. The case made by the declaration is that deceased at the time of the accident, in September, 1900, was employed by the defendant company (a corporation owning and operating electric lights and lines in Bristol, Va., and Bristol, Tenn.) to trim with carbons the electric lights along its lines, and to replace and adjust carbons and keep the lights in proper condition. That at Anderson Park, Bristol, Tenn., Bowers, while attempting to reach a point on a pole supporting a lamp, to adjust and arrange the carbon in the lamp, "came in contact with electricity leaking or escaping from the lamp, fixture, frame, and appliances, and wire supplying the lamp with electricity, by reason of which he was shocked and thrown from the pole," receiving injuries which caused his death. That the defects complained of were known to the company, but were unknown to Bowers. The company pleaded "Not guilty," and after the testimony was closed, demurred to the evidence. Thereupon the jury returned a verdict for the plaintiff, subject to the opinion of the court on the

GARRETSON, J. — This suit is by an administratrix to recover damages for the benefit of the next of kin of the intestate, who is alleged to have been killed through the negligence of the defendants under the following circumstances: The Bordentown Electric Light & Motor Company maintained a line of poles and electric light wires carrying an intense and dangerous current in Burlington street, in the city of Bordentown. This line was crossed above it by a telegraph wire maintained by the three other defendants. This last line ran around into Carpenter street in Bordentown, and was there crossed above it by a wire of the Bordentown Telephone & Telegraph Company, not a defendant to the suit. The wire of the Postal Telegraph

demurrer to evidence, and assessed her damages at $3,500. The court sustained the demurrer and rendered judgment for the defendant. and the case is here upon writ of error to that judgment. The accident occurred and Bowers died in Tennessee. It appears that he, in company with his wife and children, was on his way to church on Sunday night, when he discovered that the arc light in question was not burning. Leaving his family at a street corner nearby, he went to the park to start the light. He was soon afterward found lying on the ground at the foot of the pole in an injured condition, and stated that he had received a shock which caused him to fall. He was carried to his home, and only survived some two hours. It is matter of conjecture as to just how the shock was occasioned. The evidence disclosed the fact that the insulation on one of the wires carrying the current of electricity to the lamp was worn off where it entered the left hood pole; and the forefinger and second finger on the right hand of the deceased were badly burned — the second finger on the inside, next to the forefinger.

"In the argument much stress was laid on the fact that the pole was in a leaning position, but that circumstance was not made a ground of complaint in the declaration, nor was it proved to what extent, if any, it contributed to the accident. The burden rested upon the plaintiff to prove by affirmative evidence that the company was negligent, and that its negligence was the proximate cause of the injury complained of. Railway Co. v. Sparrow's Adm'r, 98 Va. 640, 37 S. E. Rep. 302; Railroad Co. v. Cromer's Adm'r, 99 Va. 763, 40 S. E. Rep. 54. Conceding that it may have been negligent in failing to properly insulate its wire, it nevertheless plainly appears that that omission could not have been the primary cause of the accident. The evidence shows that contact with the wire at the hood pole, where the insulation was worn off, would not of itself have produced shock, but in order to bring about that result there must also have been connection with the carbon of the lamp, thereby shunting the electrical current from its true course and causing it to make a short circuit through the body of deceased. It is not pretended that the insulation was defective except at the one point. It must follow, therefore, that the other point of contact, necessary to form a circuit, was the carbon of the lamp. When the carbon electrodes are in contact the current is continuous, and in order to produce light they must be slightly separated. The theory of the arc light is that, by separating the carbon electrodes, some of the carbon, or the volatile constituents not expelled by previous baking, become volatilized, and the interrupted electrical current passes from one to the other in the form of a curved flame or arc. In-

& Telephone Company, Delaware & Atlantic Telegraph & Telephone Company, and Pennsylvania Railroad Company broke and came in contact with the wire of the Bordentown Electric Light & Power Company swinging against it, and wearing off the insulation of the wire, and thereby became charged with the dangerous current carried by the wire of the electric light company, The wire of the Bordentown Telephone & Telegraph Company broke, and fell into Carpenter street, and the plaintiff's intestate took hold of it to remove it from obstructing the street, when it came in contact with the highly charged telegraph wire of the three companies, which was below it, and thereby became in its turn charged with the current which had gone

tense heat is generated by the current encountering an opposing electromotive force at the arc, and energy is transformed into heat. At the same time a brilliant light is emitted by the white-hot carbon electrodes. It appears that the customary, proper, and safe way to adjust the carbons is to separate them with a dry stick — a non-conductor — a usage well known to the deceased, who had been engaged in that business for nine years. So that the necessary inference from conceded facts is that the cause of accident was the failure of Bowers to take this obvious precaution for his own safety, coupled with the defective insulation of the wire at the hood pole. In that aspect of the case, it appears that the contributory negligence of deceased was the proximate cause of the injury; and in such case, upon familiar and well-settled principles, there can be no recovery." * * *

In discussing the question of demurrer to evidence the court (per WHITTLE, J.) said: "In many of the states of the Union — possibly in all except Virginia and West Virginia — the demurrant waives all his evidence. But the rule is otherwise in this jurisdiction, and, as is well understood the demurrant is entitled to the benefit of all his unimpeached evidence not in conflict with his adversary's and to all inferences that necessarily flow therefrom.

"The fact that deceased was line inspector having been established, it follows that any injury arising from defective insulation of wires which it was his duty to inspect was a risk incident to the employment which he assumed, and cannot be made the ground of an action for damages,

"Still another question was raised and discussed, one of more than ordinary interest. As remarked, the declaration averred and the evidence showed that the alleged cause of action arose in the state of Tennessee. At common law the maxim, "*Actio personalis moritur cum persona*," prevails, and it is insisted that it was incumbent upon the plaintiff to allege and prove her right to maintain this action under some statute of Tennessee. That this court will take judicial notice of the fact that the territory of which Tennessee is composed constituted a part of the original English colonies of America, and, in the absence of evidence to the contrary, will presume that the common law obtains there. Nelson *v.* Railroad Co., 88 Va. 976, 14 S. E. Rep. 838; Stewart *v.* Conrad's Adm'r (Va.) 40 S. E. Rep. 624. Inasmuch, however, as the views already taken of the case are conclusive of it, a decision of that question is unnecessary. The judgment of the trial court in sustaining the demurrer to the evidence was plainly right and must be affirmed," into the wire of the three companies by reason of the contact with the electric light wire, and so the dangerous current of the electric light wire was transmitted to and killed the plaintiff's intestate.

The allegation of negligence and breach of duty on the part of defendants was that the wire of the Postal, Delaware & Atlantic, and Pennsylvania Companies had become cut and broken, and had been negligently and carelessly permitted by all the defendants to swing, rub, and come in contact with the electric light wire for so long a time that the insulation of the electric light wire became worn off by the rubbing, so that the electric current of great power and intensity from the electric light wire was communicated to and ran along and through the wire of the Bordentown Telephone and Telegraph Company to the plaintiff's intestate, thereby killing him. This seems to be a sufficient allegation of negligence on the part of the defendants. It is assumed that the defendants were each maintaining wires in the public highways in the exercise of a franchise; hence each was bound to take reasonable care not to injure other users of the street. It was the duty of the electric light company to use reasonable care that other uninsulated telegraph wires that crossed it should not be allowed to come in contact with its wire, which was insulated, and which carried a powerful electric current, and remain for so long a time in contact therewith as to wear away the insulation, and divert the powerful current to the telegraph wire, to the probable injury of persons who should come in contact with the telegraph wire, or in contact with other wires which might be brought in touch with the charged telegraph wire. It was the duty of the three companies maintaining the telegraph wire to use reasonable care to prevent their wire from coming in contact with the highly charged electric light wire, and remain in contact therewith in such a way and for so long a time as to wear off the insulation and divert the current to its own wire, to the danger of those who should touch it, or touch another wire with which it might come in contact. N. Y. & N. J. Telephone Co. *v.* Bennett, 62 N. J. L. 742, 5 Am. Neg. Rep. 657, 42 Atl. Rep. 759.

One cause of demurrer assigned is that there is no allegation in the declaration that the decedent left any widow, children, or next of kin. The plaintiff avers in the declaration that "the next of kin of the deceased and the said plaintiff, as administratrix, as aforesaid, by reason of the premises, were forced to pay, lay out and expend, and necessarily did lay out and expend, divers large sums of money," etc., "and that the next of kin of the deceased have, by reason of the premises, sustained and suffered great loss, injury and damage, to wit, the sum of $20,000, whereby, and by force of the statute in such case made and provided, an action hath accrued to said plaintiff, as administratrix of the goods and chattels, rights and credits of the said deceased for the exclusive benefit of said next of kin." There is a necessary inference from these allegations that there are next of kin. The action being brought for their exclusive benefit, the plaintiff cannot recover except upon showing that they exist. In McGlone *v.* Transportation Co., 37 N. J. L. 304, it was held not necessary to name the widow and next of kin, but that a general allegation that there is in existence a person or persons injured to whose benefit a recovery will inure is sufficient. This appears in the allegations set forth.

The demurrer is overruled, with costs.

HESSE v. NATIONAL CASKET COMPANY.

Court of Errors and Appeals, New Jersey, June, 1902.

MINOR EMPLOYEE INJURED BY CIRCULAR SAW — ASSUMPTION OF RISK. — An employee, although a minor, in accepting service assumes the riskof such dangers connected with his employment as are obvious to him, and cannot hold his employer responsible for injuries resulting therefrom, notwithstanding the latter has failed to point out such dangers to him (1).

DIXON, FORT, BOGERT, and VROOM, JJ., *dissenting.*

(Syllabus by the Court.) *

ERROR to Supreme Court.

Action by Ernest Hesse, against the National Casket Company. From judgment for defendant, plaintiff brings error. *Judgment affirmed.*

WELLER & LICHTENSTEIN, for plaintiff in error.

HENRY S. WHITE, for defendant in error.

GUMMERE, Ch. J. — This action was brought by the plaintiff in error, a boy of sixteen years of age, to recover damages for injuries received by him while in the service of the defendant by coming in contact with a circular saw at which he was working. The saw ran through an iron table, which was raised from the floor to such a height that it was necessary for the plaintiff, while at work, to stand upon a wooden bench in front of the saw. This bench was twenty-nine inches long, twenty-four inches wide, and four and a half inches high. The legs or cleats upon which its platform rested were set in from its ends a distance of about four inches, and it merely stood upon the floor, without being fixed to it in any way. The plaintiff

1. See NOTE ON ASSUMPTION OF RISK, in 7 AM. NEG. REP. 97-111.

was familiar with the construction of the bench, and knew it was not fastened to the floor. The accident which produced the plaintiff's injuries occurred on the fifth day after he had commenced work at the saw. It was caused by the tipping over of the bench upon which the plaintiff was working, thereby causing him to lose his balance and fall towards the saw table, thus bringing his hand in contact with the saw. Just what it was that caused the bench to tip, the testimony does not disclose. One Sullivan, who was a fellow-workman of the plaintiff, was engaged at the time of the accident in picking up scraps from the floor in close proximity to the latter's bench. No one else was in the immediate neighborhood. Immediately after the accident the plaintiff said that his fall was caused by a push which Sullivan gave him. He admitted on the witness stand that he had so stated, but his testimony then was that he did not know how the accident happened.

At the close of the plaintiff's case a nonsuit was directed. We find no error in this action of the trial court. It is manifest that the tipping of the bench must have been caused by the plaintiff's having assumed a position so near to the end of the bench as to destroy its equilibrium, and that the plaintiff assumed this position either of his own volition, or by reason of a push given intentionally or unintentionally by Sullivan to the bench or to the plaintiff himself. If Sullivan, a fellow-servant, contributed to the bringing about of the accident by pushing the plaintiff or the bench upon which he was standing, thereby causing him to lose his balance, the master is relieved from liability, upon well settled principles. If the accident resulted from the plaintiff's having of his own volition moved too near the end of the bench, the master is equally relieved from responsibility. The fact that the bench would tip over if a person standing upon it should move beyond its center of gravity, was perfectly obvious, and the plaintiff, although a minor, was chargeable with notice of that fact. He was old enough to fully appreciate the danger of having the bench tip, and the likelihood of its tipping if he stood too near to one or the other of its ends, and consequently took these risks upon himself, to the same extent as a person of more mature age. Dunn *v.* McNamee, 59 N. J. L. 498, 2 Am. Neg. Rep. 34, 37 Atl. Rep. 61.

The judgment below should be affirmed.

DIXON, FORT, BOGERT, and VROOM, JJ., dissented.

DAVIS v. CENTRAL RAILROAD COMPANY OF NEW JERSEY.

Court of Errors and Appeals, New Jersey, June, 1902.

COLLISION WITH TRAIN AT CROSSING—HORSE FRIGHTENED—PERSON RIDING IN VEHICLE INJURED—CONTRIBUTORY NEGLIGENCE.—**A light one-horse wagon, in which the plaintiff sat, had been driven by another man, over whom the plaintiff had no authority, along a public highway, in a southerly direction, over a single-track railroad crossing, when its progress was arrested by the lowering of gates that were designed to guard the crossing on that side. The horse and the wagon and its occupants were thus penned in between the gates, some six or eight feet in front of the horse and the track, the nearer rail of which was about ten feet back of the hind wheels of the wagon. The gates were operated by a man in a tower about 260 feet distant. The plaintiff and the driver shouted to the man in the tower to raise the gates. A trolley car came along the highway from the south, and stopped on the other side of the gates. The plaintiff and the driver continued to sit in the wagon. The gates were not raised. After an interval, estimated by the plaintiff at one minute and a half, a train came from the northeast at the rate of about thirty miles an hour, and the horse, becoming frightened, backed the wagon against the engine, and the plaintiff was injured.** ***Held*****, that it was for the jury to say whether the plaintiff was negligent in not alighting from the wagon (1).**

(Syllabus by the Court.)

1. *Collisions at crossings.* See vols. 11 and 12 Am. Neg. Cas., for collision and crossing accidents, from the earliest times to 1897. Subsequent actions to date are reported in vols. 1-12 AM. NEG. REP., and the current numbers of that series of Reports.

Horse frightened. See the following Pennsylvania cases:

In WEBB *v.* PHILADELPHIA & READING R'Y Co. (*Pennsylvania, May, 1902*), 52 Atl. Rep. 5, judgment of nonsuit in the Court of Common Pleas, Delaware county, was affirmed, DEAN, J., stating the case as follows; "George Webb, the husband of plaintiff, was driving his team on a country road parallel with defendant's railroad. He was approaching Bingen station, and about 400 feet from it. While Webb was opposite a deep cut on the highway above the railroad, the engineer of a locomotive, drawing a train, which had just left the station, and was about entering the cut, loudly blew the steam whistle. At the same time the locomotive emitted a considerable volume of smoke and steam. Webb's horse took fright, ran away, and he was killed. His widow brings this suit against the company, alleging her husband's death was caused by negligence of defendant, in that the engineer, 1, blew the whistle at an improper place, 2, that there was no necessity for blowing it at all; 3, that it was blown so loudly, and smoke and steam emitted in such large volume, as to make both acts unusual and extraordinary as to necessarily frighten the ordinary horse. From the evidence, it was not apparent to the court below that any negligence was shown on the part of the defendant. Consequently a compulsory nonsuit was directed.

ERROR to Supreme Court.

Action by Samuel Davis against the Central Railroad Company of New Jersey. From judgment for plaintiff, defendant brings error. *Judgment affirmed.*

which afterwards the court refused to take off, and we have this appeal by plaintiff. The facts in the case do not raise a presumption of negligence against the defendant. The blowing of a whistle by a locomotive engineer is a lawful act. The emission of steam and smoke, where steam propels machinery, is a necessary incident of the use of steam, and therefore not of itself unlawful. Both the blowing of the whistle and the escape of steam and smoke may be negligent, and therefore unlawful, according to circumstances. If the circumstances themselves do not warrant an inference of unlawful use, the mere fact that an accident was caused by either is not sufficient to convict of negligence. He who alleges negligence must go further, and prove it. He must show that, an act in itself lawful, the commission of it either at the time, at the place, or in the manner, became unlawful. This is the substance of two carefully considered decisions by this court. Railroad Co. *v.* Stinger, 78 Pa. St. 219; Farley *v.* Harris, 186 Pa. St. 440, 4 Am. Neg. Rep. 582, 40 Atl. Rep. 798. Both cases involved the question of negligence in blowing of steam whistles, and in both cases we carefully avoided any modification of the rule on the same subject laid down in Railroad Co. *v.* Barnett, 59 Pa. St. 259, followed by a long line of cases, down to Simmons *v.* Railroad Co., 199 Pa. St. 232, 48 Atl. Rep. 1070. In each of these many cases either the undisputed facts afforded some ground for an inference of negligence, or there was express affirmative evidence of negligence. As a consequence, the cases went to a jury. In the case before us a nonsuit was directed. Therefore we must take every fact as proven of which there was any evidence, yet on these facts the jury would not have been permitted to find a verdict against defendant. The train had stopped at Bingen station. Four hundred yards ahead of it was a deep cut, on a curve. The highway ran on top of the embankment, parallel with the railroad. When the locomotive was in the cut, the vehicle on the highway was not visible to the engineer; and the railroad in front of him was visible only for a short distance, because of the curve. As he approached the cut he blew the whistle, and blew it loudly. When entering and when in the cut, smoke and steam in large quantity escaped. The deceased being on the highway above, his horse took fright, either because of the whistle or the smoke, or perhaps because of both. Just what warning the engineer should give, under such circumstances, would be dictated by his carefulness and regard for the lives of others. There might be travelers on the highway approaching or even on the road above him. They ought to have warning, that they might be able to restrain their animals, either by stopping, going to their heads and holding them until the train passed, or by preparing for their sudden fright, and unexpected movements under fright. Those at some distance might prefer to wait until the train had passed before going on an embankment at the top of a deep cut. We leave out of view the question of signal posts altogether. The deep cut and curve were there as signals to the engineer, which could not, in the exercise of care, be disregarded by him. Then, what was in front of him, but out of sight on the track? Perhaps third persons having no business there, yet not to be recklessly run over, or track employees, who had a right to be there,

RICHARD V. LINDABURY, for plaintiff in error.

EDMUND WILSON, for defendant in error.

ADAMS, J. — The plaintiff, while traveling on a public highway,

and were entitled to warning of an approaching train. All the circumstances point to no conclusion of negligence in giving warning at that time and at that place. As to the allegation that the whistle was blown unusually loud, that of itself does not show negligence. How far must the sound carry, to warn those whom it was intended to reach, either on the highway or track? That would depend on the state of the atmosphere, at that time, and the knowledge of the engineer, derived from observation. No mere opinion or conjecture of those having no knowledge on the subject should be permitted to convict him of recklessness. As to emitting unusual quantities of smoke and steam, the extent of that, immediately after starting from the station, would depend on the weight of his train, and the degree of curvature of the road he must draw it over. Necessarily, it was greater with a heavy train at a curve than with a lighter train on a straight track. Giving plaintiff's testimony all the weight and significance it is entitled to, it fails to show that defendant committed a lawful act in an unlawful manner. Therefore the judgment is affirmed."

In MENDENHALL *v.* PHILADELPHIA, WILMINGTON & BALTIMORE R. R. CO. *(Pennsylvania, May, 1902)*, 51 Atl. Rep. 1028, judgment for plaintiff in the Court of Common Pleas, Chester county, was affirmed, MITCHELL, J., rendering the following opinion: "Appellant complains that this was a perfectly clear case of contributory negligence on the part of the plaintiff, which should not have been submitted to the jury. And this would be undeniable on appellant's view of the facts, and its evidence in support of them. According to this, the plaintiff, if he stopped to look and listen at all, did so, on his own admission, at a point where the coming train must have been in plain sight, and then attempted to cross in the face of manifest danger. If this were the whole case, the court would have been bound to declare plaintiff negligent as a matter of law, and to direct a verdict for defendant. But the case on plaintiff's evidence was wholly different. He testified that he had crossed the tracks, but that his horse was frightened by the escape of steam, and backed into danger again. In this view, however negligent he may have been in crossing in front of a moving train, he had in fact crossed safely, and his negligence, not having contributed to his injury, was immaterial. The accident, according to him, resulted from a new and wholly unconnected source of danger, — the escaping steam. These two accounts of the occurrence were radically different and involved different rules of law. As there was positive evidence in support of each, even if plaintiff's own testimony was ambiguous or inconsistent, it was, nevertheless, part of the whole case, which necessarily was for the jury. The steam complained of was not the usual and unavoidable escape from a locomotive, but from a heating apparatus from passenger cars situated at or near the crossing. The morning was damp and foggy, and there was testimony that the steam hung about the point of escape to a greater degree than was usual. Whether it was negligently done or not was therefore for the jury, and the rules of law as to what would be negligence on the part of defendant and also of plaintiff if he drove into manifest danger, were very fully and accurately stated to the jury in the charge. If the verdict was against the weight of the evidence, the remedy was with the trial court. Judgment affirmed."

was hurt by a railroad train. He sued the railroad company to recover compensation for his injury, and obtained a judgment, which is now to be reviewed. The single error alleged on the argument is that the trial judge submitted to the jury the question of contributory negligence. This ruling was correct. The plaintiff, without fault of his own, was suddenly and unexpectedly placed in a predicament. The danger that threatened him was known and imminent. He had a choice of several lines of conduct, and chose one of them. The jury might fairly conclude that he acted with ordinary prudence. This question was for them, and not for the trial judge.

The essential facts of the situation are these: The plaintiff was riding in a light wagon by daylight along Second avenue, in Long Branch. A Mr. Lane was driving the horse. The plaintiff had no control of Mr. Lane, and no responsibility for the management of the horse. Second avenue runs about north and south, and is crossed diagonally by a single track of the defendants' railroad, which runs northeasterly and southwesterly. Each side of this crossing is guarded by gates. The northerly gates are distant about 360 feet from the southerly gates. Other gates guard another street. All these gates are operated by a man in a tower. It does not appear whether the different pairs of gates can be operated separately. Mr. Lane was driving south along Second avenue on the right-hand or west side of the road. The northerly gates were up. He passed them, and drove at a slow trot to a point near the track, and walked his horse over the crossing. The plaintiff, who sat on the left side of the wagon, looked along the track in a northeasterly direction, and saw and heard no train. Still going at a walk, the horse approached the southerly gates, which were up. When the horse's head was eight or ten feet from the gates they were lowered. This brought the wagon to a standstill, with its hind wheels about ten feet away from the nearer rail. Up to this point no negligence is imputed to the plaintiff. Both Mr. Lane and the plaintiff shouted to the man in the tower, who was about 260 feet distant from them, and somewhat behind them, to raise the gates. A trolley car came from the south to the other side of the gates, and stopped. The man in the tower did not raise the gates. The plaintiff and Mr. Lane remained sitting in the wagon. A train came from the northeast. The testimony of the engineer as to his time schedule indicates a speed of about thirty miles an hour. The horse got frightened, and backed the wagon against the engine, and the plaintiff was injured.

The element of time is material. The plaintiff was asked: "From the time you stopped at the gate until the train came, how long was it?" He answered: "I should think it was a minute and a half." The following extracts from his testimony afford measures of time: "Q. How long had the horse been standing there before you noticed the approach of the trolley car from the south? A. It was on its way when we first stopped. Q. Did you really notice that car at all, coming from that direction? A. Yes, sir. Q. When you first stopped? A. Yes, sir. Q. How far off was it then? A. It was pretty well down, towards the West End. Q. How far do you say? A. I don't know. Q. Half a mile? A. Half a mile, perhaps. Q. Did it get to that gate before the railroad train got there? A. Just about one time, as near as I can tell. Q. It had stopped before the railroad train got there? A. Just about stopped; it hadn't any more than stopped. Q. And the gates were down? A. The gates were down. * * * Q. Did this engine ring its bell or blow its whistle? A. No, sir; if it did, I didn't hear it. Q. Did you hear the train approaching just before you were hit? A. Yes, sir; just a minute. Q. How long an interval was it between the time when you heard the roar of the train and the time when you were hit? A. Not over a second or so. Q. From the time you heard the train until you were hit? A. It was not over a second or so, and about the time I saw it we were struck. Q. After you heard the train, did you have any chance to get out of the wagon before you were hit? A. No, sir." It further appears that the plaintiff knew that he was in a place of danger, that as he sat in the wagon after its progress had been arrested he looked both ways on the railroad track; that he could see a long distance to the southwest, and that no train was approaching from that quarter; and that he could not see far to the northeast. The engineer testified that he rang the bell and blew the whistle.

It cannot be said that the length of time between the stoppage and the accident is precisely fixed. Estimates of the duration of short periods into which much experience is crowded are notoriously inexact, and are apt to be excessive. The distance traversed by the trolley car is loosely stated. There is no proof as to its rate of speed. The fair conclusion seems to be that there was an interval, short but appreciable, between the descent of the gates, and the arrival of the train. The plaintiff undoubtedly had time to alight. It is said — and this is the sole criticism of his conduct — that he was negligent in not doing so.

To one who now, at a safe distance, exercises, in the light of subsequent events, the easy function of review, it seems that several courses of action were open to the plaintiff. It is to be observed that he was in a place where injury was not inevitable. If the horse would stand still, the wagon and the occupants would be safe. The plaintiff testified that he had known the horse for several years, and that he was kind. To remain in the wagon on the chance that the horse would be steady was therefore a line of conduct which, if not wholly wise, would not have been irrational. Again, it was surely reasonable to think, at least at the outset, that the man in the tower would hear the call upon him, and to expect, or at least to hope, that, if he heard it, he would raise the gates. Again, the plaintiff might have jumped off and run away, and left Mr. Lane to get out of trouble as he best could. A man of spirits and self-respect would not be apt to do this, as long as he might be of use to his companion. Again, the plaintiff might have alighted and held the horse's head. Such an intervention, in a moment of peril, by a person with whose presence a horse is not familiar, is apt to irritate the horse and embarrass the driver, if not to injure him who intervenes. A more judicious plan would probably have been for Mr. Lane to hand the reins to the plaintiff, and to go to the horse's head himself.

It is unnecessary to pursue the subject. Enough has been said to indicate the ground of our conclusion. The exigency was sudden, the risk alarming, the best way of escape not obvious. We think that whether the plaintiff acted with common prudence was a fair question for the jury.

The judgment is affirmed.

HERBICH v. NORTH JERSEY STREET RAILWAY COMPANY.

Court of Errors and Appeals, New Jersey, June, 1902.

CHILD INJURED BY SUDDEN STARTING OF STREET CAR — INSTRUCTIONS.— 1. In the case of a plaintiff two years and nine months old, who was thrown down by the starting of a street car, which she had boarded, before she had time to be seated, and while she was for the moment out of the reach of her attendant, who was also boarding the car, it is not error for the court to refuse to charge the jury "that the starting of a car before a passenger is seated is not negligence." (1)

2. When the trial judge has stated to the jury in concrete terms the legal principles applicable to the case, it is not error for him to refuse to charge the abstract principles.

(Syllabus by the Court.)

1. *Alighting and boarding cars.* For actions relating to accidents while alighting or boarding cars, or sudden starting of cars, from the earliest times to 1897, see vols. 2–7 Am. Neg. Cas. Subsequent actions to date are reported in vols. 1–12 AM. NEG. REP., and the current numbers of that series of Reports.

ERROR to Supreme Court.

Action by Ida H. Herbich, by her next friend, against the North Jersey Street-Railway Company. Verdict for plaintiff was reversed by the Supreme Court (47 Atl. Rep. 427, 9 Am. Neg. Rep. 21*n*), and plaintiff brings error. *Judgment of Supreme Court reversed, and of Circuit Court affirmed.*

LOUIS HOOD, for plaintiff in error.

J. B. VREDENBURGH, for defendant in error.

DIXON J.—On the trial of this case in the Essex Circuit the evidence on behalf of the plaintiff was to the following effect: On the morning of July 6, 1899, the plaintiff's mother, having in charge the plaintiff, then two years and nine months old, and also carrying an umbrella and two parcels, boarded a summer street car of the defendant company at the corner of Market and Broad streets, in Newark. She first lifted the child into the car, and placed her in the aisle between the two front seats, which faced each other. She then proceeded to get into the car herself, and, before she could reach the child or be seated, the conductor, although he had both mother and child in view, gave the signal, and the car started with a jerk, which threw the child off the further side of the car, resulting in serious injury to her. The defendant's evidence substantially differed from this, in tending to prove that, before the conductor gave the signal, he saw that both mother and child were seated,—the child occupying the end seat,—and that the car made only the usual start. Upon the controversy thus indicated the defendant requested the trial judge to charge the jury that "the starting of a car before a passenger is seated is not negligence," which request the judge refused, and instructed the jury that it was for them to determine whether "the car was started at an improper time; that is, started while the plaintiff was in a position of peril,—before an opportunity had been offered to the plaintiff and her mother to reach a place of safety." The defendant duly excepted. The plaintiff having obtained a verdict and judgment, the defendant removed the record by writ of error to the Supreme Court, and there the judgment was reversed because of the refusal and charge above stated. The plaintiff has now, by a similar writ, brought the record to this court.

We regard the course pursued by the trial judge as unexceptional. As applied to the circumstances for which the defendant contended, the proposition that the starting of a car before a passenger is seated is not negligence was irrevelant, for, according to that contention, the plaintiff and her mother were both seated before the car started. As applied to the circumstances for which the plaintiff contended, the proposition was untrue, or at least it was for the jury, not the judge, to say whether it was true. While usually the proposition may be accepted as true (Ayers *v.* Rochester R'y Co., 156 N. Y. 104, 4 Am. Neg. Rep. 446, 50 N. E. Rep. 960), yet the passenger may be so infirm, by reason of infancy or old age or sickness or lameness, or other cause, that even the ordinary movement of a street car in starting before he is seated would be likely to throw him down. In such cases, if the carrier is chargeable with notice of the infirmity, it cannot be the duty of the court to instruct the jury that the starting of the car is not a breach of the carrier's obligation to exercise a high degree of care for the safety of the passenger. In the present case the infirmity of the plaintiff was evident, and must have been observed by the conductor, who, according to his own testimony, had the mother and child in view from the time when they began to board the car until the accident happened.

We have examined the other exceptions taken at the trial, and find none worthy of special mention. The case was plainly one for the jury, and the numerous requests to charge, so far as they were not complied with, were either unsound or irrelevant, or were so general as to be more likely to perplex than to assist the jury in the discharge of their functions. The legal rules applicable to the case were clearly set forth by the judge in concrete terms, and nothing further could properly be demanded.

The judgment of the Supreme Court is reversed, and that of the Circuit Court is affirmed. Let the record be remitted to the Circuit Court.

HOAG v. WILLIAMSBURGH SAVINGS BANK.

Supreme Court, New York, Appellate Division, Second Department, October, 1902.

TENANT INJURED BY SLIPPING ON ICE IN HALLWAY OF TENEMENT HOUSE—LEAKAGE—DEFECTIVE PREMISES—LIABILITY OF LANDLORD.—In an action to recover damages for injuries sustained by plaintiff, a tenant of defendant, by falling on ice, in a hallway of a tenement house, which ice had formed from leakage of a closet overhead and from the freezing temperature of the hallway, it was *held* that the primary defect being the leakage, the diligence required of the defendant was to be measured not from the time the ice had formed, but from the length of time the water had been allowed to drip upon the hallway floor from the defective closet, and judgment for plaintiff was affirmed (1).

1. *Landlord and tenant.* For actions arising out of injuries caused by defective premises, from 1897 to date, see vols. 1–12 AM. NEG. REP., and the current numbers of that series of Reports.

APPEAL from Trial term, Kings County.

Action by Jennie Hoag against the Williamsburg Savings Bank. From judgment for plaintiff, and from an order denying motion for new trial on the minutes, defendant appeals. Judgment affirmed.

Argued before GOODRICH, P. J., and BARTLETT, JENKS, WOODWARD and HIRSCHBERG, JJ.

GEO. S. ESPENSCHEID, for appellant.

EDWARD J. MCCROSSIN, for respondent.

HIRSCHBERG, J. — The plaintiff, when injured, was the tenant in possession of apartments in a double tenement house in the borough of Brooklyn, belonging to the defendant. The house was tenanted by several families, and a janitress representing the defendant was on the premises. No question is raised in denial of the legal duty resting upon the defendant to keep the halls and stairways in a reasonably safe condition, so far as that result could be effected by the exercise of reasonable care. On the 28th day of February, 1900, the plaintiff was injured by falling in one of the hallways, common to the use of all the tenants, by reason of ice which had formed upon the floor from the leakage of a water-closet overhead, and from the freezing temperature of the hallway. The appellant contends that there is no evidence of the continuance of the defective conditions for a sufficient length of time to charge the defendant with constructive notice, and that, as the ice had formed only the night before the accident, the defendant should be relieved from responsibility upon the theory of the cases which relieve municipal corporations from liability for the consequences of sudden and recent accumulations and formations of snow and ice upon public highways. The cases are not analogous. Rain and snow fall of necessity upon the public streets, and that ice should form under the conditions of our climate is inevitable. A municipal corporation is held chargeable under such circumstances, in the absence of actual notice, only for a lack of diligence during a reasonable period subsequent to the creation of the dangerous condition. Muller *v.* City of Newburgh, 32 Hun, 24 affirmed in 105 N. Y. 668. Here, however, the primary defect was in the leaky condition of the ceiling over the hall, arising from the defective condition of the closet. There was evidence from which the jury might properly conclude that this had been in existence for at least two weeks before the plaintiff's accident, and that the attention of the janitress had been called to it some days before. The diligence required of the defendant was accordingly to be measured not from the time the ice had formed, but from the length of time the water had been allowed to drip upon the floor in a hallway maintained at a temperature in which the formation of ice was reasonably to be expected.

The case contains no tenable exception; and, while other matters than the one herein considered are presented in the briefs, they relate to subjects concerning which a conflict of evidence was elicited, and upon which the verdict is conclusive. The judgment and order should be affirmed.

Judgment and order affirmed with costs. All concur.

HILL v. BALTIMORE AND NEW YORK RAILWAY COMPANY.

Supreme Court, New York, Appellate Division, Second Department, October, 1902.

INFANT — *SUI JURIS* — QUESTION FOR JURY. — Where plaintiff, a boy eleven years and nine months old, boarded a moving coal train, and, in endeavoring to dodge a piece of coal which defendant's brakeman threw at him, lost his hold of the car, fell and his leg was run over, it was error to hold that plaintiff was *sui juris* as matter of law, the question whether an infant under twelve years of age was *sui juris* being for the jury to determine.

INFANT — *NON SUI JURIS* — PRESUMPTION. — An infant under the age of twelve years is presumed to be *non sui juris*, but may be overcome by evidence to the contrary.

BOY STEALING A RIDE — MISSILE THROWN BY BRAKEMAN — PROXIMATE CAUSE. — Where defendant's brakeman threw a piece of coal at plaintiff, who was stealing a ride on a moving coal train, and the boy, in trying to dodge it, lost his hold of the car, and fell therefrom and was injured, the question whether the brakeman pursued reasonable and proper means to eject the boy from the train and whether his act was the proximate cause of plaintiff's injury, were questions for the jury to determine (1).

APPEAL from Trial Term, Richmond County.

Action by Jacob Hill, by his guardian *ad litem*, against the Baltimore & New York Railroad Company. From a judgment for defendant, and from an order denying a new trial, plaintiff appeals. *Judgment reversed.*

Argued before GOODRICH, P. J., and BARTLETT, JENKS, WOODWARD and HIRSCHBERG, JJ.

1. *Ejection from trains, etc.* For actions relating to ejection of persons from trains, etc., from the earliest times to 1897, see vol. 8 Am. Neg Cas. Subsequent actions to date are reported in vols. 1-12 AM. NEG. REP., and the current numbers of that series of Reports.

GILBERT D. LAMB, for appellant.

RICHARD REID ROGERS, for respondent.

HIRSCHBERG, J.—The plaintiff, then an infant eleven years, nine months and seven days old, was injured on the 22d day of March, 1897, while attempting to board a moving coal train of the defendant. He had caught hold of the handles of the car, and had swung his feet clear from the ground, in the attempt to board the train, when one of the defendant's brakemen threw a piece of coal at him, and in endeavoring to dodge it he lost his hold, fell under the car, and had his leg cut off. The dismissal of the complaint was before the plaintiff's case was rested, and was based by the learned trial justice upon the ground that the plaintiff was *sui juris*, and that his negligence in attempting to board the moving train barred a recovery as matter of law. The court, referring to the plaintiff, stated that, "If he was *non sui juris*, that makes another case," to which the plaintiff's counsel responded, "It is for the jury to pass upon that." After some additional evidence had been given, the court said: "The only point in the case is whether this boy is *sui juris*. I think he was. I am going to hold that he was. * * * I dismiss it upon your opening and on my own examination of the plaintiff, which has convinced me that he was *sui juris*. Mr. Lamb: I make the usual motion to set aside the direction, and to go the jury. (Motion denied. Exception by plaintiff.)" It was error to hold that the plaintiff, an infant under twelve years of age, was *sui juris* as matter of law. The question was for the jury to determine, and, if they found him to be *sui juris*, he would, of course, have been properly held liable for the consequences of his negligence, provided the jury should find that such negligence was the proximate or a contributing cause of his injury. If, however, he was not *sui juris*, he could not be lawfully made to suffer, even as a trespasser, by reason of the affirmative act of negligence on the defendant's part in throwing coal at him while he was engaged in the hazardous act of boarding the car. The fact that he had not yet secured a position of safety upon the car can make no difference in principle, provided a jury should find that he was too young to appreciate in law the negligent nature of his act, and that no negligence was chargeable to his parents or guardian. There is no case in this State to which our attention has been called which holds that an infant under twelve years of age is *sui juris* as matter of law. It is true that in Wendell *v.* N. Y. Cent., etc., R. R. Co., 91 N. Y. 420 (12 Am. Neg. Cas. 313*n*), the plaintiff's infant decedent was only seven years of age, but, as Chief Judge Ruger pointed out at page 425, "the case was tried upon the assumption by the court and both parties that the deceased was *sui* *juris*, and that his parents were not chargeable with negligence in permitting him to be in the place where he was injured." So, in the case of McCarthy *v.* Railroad Co., 37 App. Div. 187, 55 N. Y. Supp. 1013, the case was tried upon the assumption that the plaintiff was *sui juris*, and it was therefore held that the nonsuit was proper. In that case the infant plaintiff was seven years and two months old, but the court said (page 191, 37 App. Div., page 1016, 55 N. Y. Supp.): "It does not appear that any request was made to have the question of the plaintiff's responsibility submitted to the jury, nor that any express exception was taken to the decision of that question by the court." Here, however, the question was the only one considered by the court upon the trial. The plaintiff's counsel insisted explicitly that it should be submitted to the jury. Upon an adverse decision by the court, he moved for leave to go to the jury, and upon a denial of the motion filed an exception to the ruling. The question of the correctness of the ruling would, therefore, seem to be plainly presented on this appeal.

In Tucker *v.* N. Y. Cent. etc., R. R. Co., 124 N. Y. 308 (12 Am. Neg. Cas. 314*n*), 26 N. E. Rep. 916, it was held that the question at what age an infant's responsibility for negligence may be presumed to commence is not one of fact, but of law; and in analogy to the provision of section 19 of the Penal Code, to the effect that a child under the age of twelve years would be presumed to be incapable of crime, it was suggested that twelve years was the age at which the presumption of capacity to appreciate danger and to exercise caution should commence. The presumption in either case — that is, of incapacity below the age of twelve and of capacity at that age — may, of course, be overborne by evidence. But, as was said by the Court of Appeals in the recent case of Zwack *v.* N. Y., L. E. & W. R. R. Co., 160 N. Y. 362, 365, 6 Am. Neg. Rep. 669, 671, 54 N. E. Rep. 785, 786:

"The reasoning of the court in the case of Tucker *v.* N. Y. Cent., etc., R. R. Co., 124 N. Y. 308 (12 Am. Neg. Cas. 314*n*), 26 N. E. Rep. 916, is to the effect that an infant under the age of twelve years is presumed to be *non sui juris*, so that the question with respect to his capacity at that age becomes one of fact. It is true that an infant, even of more tender years, may be shown to be *sui juris*. The fact must, in such cases, depend upon the capacity and intelligence of the child; and hence becomes a question for the consideration of the jury in connection with all the facts and circumstances of the case."

In the present state of the law these two cases must be regarded as authority for the proposition that the legal presumption of *non sui juris* lasts until the infant has reached the age of twelve years, especially in view of the fact that no authoritative decision exists for the entertaining of a contrary presumption at an earlier age.

But, even if a jury should find the plaintiff in this case to be *sui juris*, and therefore chargeable with negligence, it does not necessarily follow that the defendant would be relieved from liability for the brakeman's act in throwing the coal in order to prevent him from securing a position of safety upon the car. The rule is well settled that even to a trespasser the duty exists of refraining from overt acts of violence calculated to occasion injury. It may be conceded that the brakeman, acting in the discharge of his duty to his master, would be justified in preventing the plaintiff from boarding the train by such means as would not subject the latter to extra and unnecessary hazards. As was said in a somewhat similar case (Clark *v.* N. Y., L. E. & W. R. R. Co., 40 Hun, 605, 610, 8 Am. Neg. Cas. 553, affirmed in 113 N. Y. 670, 21 N. E. Rep. 1116, where a child stealing a ride was attempting to alight from the car while in motion, and was injured in consequence of an employee of the defendant throwing water in his face for the purpose of removing him from the car:

"That the defendant's employees on the train had the right, and it was within the scope of their authority, to remove the plaintiff from the car in a lawful and proper manner, was not questioned, but was assumed at the trial; and the right of the plaintiff to recover was, by the charge, made dependent upon the use of unreasonable and improper means for that purpose. And although the act of getting upon the train while in motion was dangerous, and known to the plaintiff to be so, it cannot be said to be the proximate cause of the injury, and does not furnish imputation of contributory negligence."

See, also, Kenyon *v.* Railroad Co., 5 Hun, 479; Lang *v.* Railroad Co., 51 Hun, 603, 4 N. Y. Supp. 565, affirmed in 123 N. Y. 656, 25 N. E. Rep. 955; Meisch *v.* Railway Co., 72 Hun, 604, 25 N. Y. Supp. 244; Lang *v.* N. Y., L. E. & W. R. R. Co., 80 Hun, 275, 8 Am. Neg. Cas. 554, 30 N. Y. Supp. 137; McKeon *v.* Railway Co., 20 App. Div. 601, 47 N. Y. Supp. 374; Weitzman *v.* Railroad Co., 33 App. Div. 585, 53 N. Y. Supp. 905; Rounds *v.* D., L. & W. R. R. Co., 64 N. Y. 129, 8 Am. Neg. Cas. 536; Distler *v.* Long Island R. R. Co., 151 N. Y. 424, 1 Am. Neg. Rep. 135, 45 N. E. Rep. 937; Girvin *v.* N. Y. Cent., etc., R. R. Co., 166 N. Y. 289, 9 Am. Neg. Rep. 547, 59 N. E. Rep. 921.

In an opinion written by the learned trial justice on the denial of the motion for a new trial it is stated:

"Had the brakeman hit him [the plaintiff] with the coal, and injured him, another question would be presented; but what he did now only presents the question whether it can be deemed negligent in the brakeman to by any effective means induce the boy to desist from his foolhardy purpose. No jury could be permitted to say that such a course involved a greater risk of injury to the boy than would have done the unmolested prosecution of his dangerous purpose."

It seems to us that the questions here considered are questions of fact, and not of law. Giving the plaintiff the benefit of the favorable inferences to which he is entitled from the evidence, it is established that he had swung his feet clear from the ground in the act of stepping upon the car at the time the coal was thrown. His act, of course, was a dangerous and unlawful one, and the defendant would not be liable for any injury resulting from it. The defendant owed him no duty of care or vigilance under the circumstances, and was justified in frustrating the accomplishment of his unlawful purpose by every reasonable and proper means. Whether to throw coal at him while he was engaged in his dangerous act was a reasonable and proper means, and whether it involved greater risk of injury than the plaintiff had voluntarily incurred, are questions for the consideration and determination of the jury. If they should find that the means employed were unnecessary, improper, unreasonable, and fraught with certain and imminent peril to the plaintiff, enhanced by the very fact of the dangerous position in which he had placed himself, and that otherwise the injury inflicted could have been wholly avoided, such means might well be regarded as constituting the proximate cause of the accident; and in that view, under the authorities, a recovery might be had notwithstanding the negligence on the plaintiff's part, which would not be necessarily regarded as contributory in a legal sense. It seems to be conceded that liability would attach to the defendant if the coal had actually hit the plaintiff, and so broken his hold and caused his injuries; and it is difficult to see why any materially different principle is presented when the same effect has been accomplished by the assault, notwithstanding the fact that the brakeman missed his aim. The judgment and order should be reversed.

Judgment and order reversed and new trial granted, costs to abide the event. All concur.

NEW YORK, CHICAGO AND ST. LOUIS RAILROAD COMPANY v. KISTLER.

Supreme Court, Ohio, May, 1902.

COLLISION BETWEEN VEHICLE AND TRAIN AT CROSSING — PLEADING AND PRACTICE — SPEED OF TRAIN — LOOKING AND LISTENING — IMPUTED NEGLIGENCE.— 1. When the allegations of a pleading are so indefinite and uncertain that the precise nature of the charge or defense is not apparent, and a motion is made to require such pleading to be made definite and certain, it is error to overrule such motion.

2. In an action founded upon negligence, the petition should state the acts of commission or omission which the plaintiff claims to have caused the injury; and, that statement being made, it is sufficient to aver that such acts were carelessly or negligently done or omitted.

3. In the absence of a statute regulating the rate of speed of railroad trains, it is not negligence for a railroad company to run its trains, in the open country, at such rate of speed as those in charge of the same may deem safe to the transportation of passengers and property, unless there are facts and circumstances which, when taken in connection with a high rate of speed, would make such speed an element or factor in constituting negligence; and in such cases such facts and circumstances should be pleaded.

4. As between a person about to cross over a railroad at a crossing and a train of cars approaching such crossing, the train has the right of way. This is so because the person can stop within a few feet and the train cannot.

5. The looking required before going upon a crossing should usually be, just before going upon the track, or so near thereto as to enable the person to get across before a train within a range of his view of the track, going at the usual rate of speed of fast trains, would reach such crossings (1).

6. It is the duty of a locomotive engineer to keep a lookout on the track ahead of the train. If, while so doing, his eye takes in a person approaching the track, he may assume that such person will keep away from the track until the train passes, but when it becomes evident that such person will not keep off the track it becomes the duty of such engineer to use ordinary care to prevent injury to such person; his first and highest duty, however, being for the safety of the passengers and property in his charge for transportation.

7. As a railroad company has no control over the trees, weeds, brush, shrubbery and the like not on its right of way, it is not required to take such things into consideration when approaching a crossing.

8. While the doctrine of imputed negligence does not prevail in this State, yet, where two or more persons take an active part in a joint enterprise, the negligence of each, while so actively engaged, must be regarded as the negligence of all.

1. *Collisions and crossings.* See vols. 11 and 12 Am. Neg. Cas., for crossing-accident cases from the earliest times to 1897. Subsequent actions to date are reported in vols. 1–12 AM. NEG. REP, and the current numbers of that series of Reports.

See also NOTE ON STOP, LOOK AND LISTEN, in 9 AM. NEG. REP. 408–416.

9. **Whatever a locomotive engineer, and those with him on the engine, would see while in the proper discharge of their respective duties, they are chargeable with having seen.**

(Syllabus by the Court.)

ERROR to the Circuit Court of Sandusky County.

From judgment of the Circuit Court affirming judgment of the Court of Common Pleas in favor of the plaintiff, defendant brings error. *Judgment reversed.*

On the morning of June 2, 1892, Annie Kistler, defendant in error, and her father were driving west on the county-line road between Seneca and Sandusky counties, in a buggy drawn by two quiet farm horses, the side and rear curtains being down, the latter being loose at the bottom. Her father was very deaf, and it was his custom to take one of his children along to hear for him, and he had taken Annie along that morning for that purpose. He was aged fifty-seven years, strong and in good health. The county-line road crossed over the track of the New York, Chicago & St. Louis Railroad at grade and at an acute angle, the railroad running a little south of west and the wagon road running east and west. As the father and daughter were on the crossing they were struck by a freight train composed of an engine, four cars, and a caboose, going southwest at a speed of from twenty to forty miles an hour. The father was killed and the daughter badly injured, and this action was brought by her against the railroad company for the recovery of damages. At a distance of 216 feet east of the crossing, a road known as the "Ridge Road" crosses the county-line road and, running in a northeast direction, crosses the railroad at a point 346 feet from the crossing of the county-line road over the railroad. At a distance of eighty-nine rods east of the crossing is the west line of a tract of fifteen acres of woodland lying between the county-line road and the railroad. Just east of the ridge road, and partly on the right of way of the railroad and partly on the land adjoining on the south, there stood a wild cherry tree, which the evidence tended to show to be eight to twelve inches in diameter, thirty feet high, with a broad bushy top from twenty-five to thirty feet in diameter, and the branches coming within three to eight feet of the ground. Along the east side of the ridge road, and about twenty feet south of the cherry tree, there was a locust tree about the same size as the cherry, with some sprouts around it from four to twelve feet high. There were also some weeds three or four feet high along the ridge road, and along at that place there was a small cut two to three feet deep, and thence to the crossing where the accident occurred the county road and railroad were on a level. There were no other or further obstructions. She had often passed there, and knew the situation. The county road was sandy, and it had rained a little the previous night, and the air was clear with a slight breeze from the northeast. The father sat on the right side and drove the team, and as they passed the woods he told her that they were nearing the railroad and requested her to look and listen for trains, which she did by raising the rear curtain some three times before reaching the ridge road. After passing that road she remembered nothing, but within 100 feet of the crossing the father was seen to bend forward and look out toward the railroad. The team was going on a slow trot until it passed over the ridge road, and then it went faster, one horse trotting and the other galloping till they reached the crossing, but whether the driver was urging them ahead to get over the crossing ahead of the train, or whether he had partly lost control of them, is left in doubt by the evidence. There was no slacking of the speed of the train and the engineer did not see them before the collision, but the evidence tends to prove that the fireman and a brakeman on the engine and the conductor, brakeman, and foreman on the caboose saw them when the team was within about 100 feet of the crossing. It is conceded that a whistle for the crossing was given, but she claims that it was not given at the proper place, and that it was not given until after passing the ridge road, and that it scared the horses and caused them to increase their speed. The evidence as to the signal by whistle is conflicting. The bell seems to have been rung.

The petition avers that the railroad company negligently and carelessly approached and crossed said highway with said locomotive and train of cars at a high, immoderate and dangerous rate of speed, and negligently and carelessly omitted to give proper and sufficient signa's or warning of the approach of said locomotive and train to said crossing and of the existence of said crossing, and negligently and carelessly allowed and maintained obstructions to a proper view of its said train, locomotive, and railroad, and negligently and carelessly operated and handled its said locomotive and train of cars.

The railroad company filed a motion to compel her to make her petition definite and certain as to the acts of negligence charged, and particularly to state the facts in regard to the defendant negligently and carelessly operating and handling said locomotive and train, and to strike out the words "at a high, immoderate, and dangerous rate of speed."

The Court of Common Pleas overruled the motion, to which the defendant below excepted.

The answer was a general denial as to the negligence charged and a plea of contributory negligence on her part. She denied the contributory negligence in her reply. She recovered a judgment on the first trial, which was reversed by the Circuit Court, and upon another trial she again recovered a verdict. A motion for a new trial was overruled and judgment entered on the verdict. Proper exceptions were taken throughout the case. The Circuit Court affirmed the judgment, and thereupon the railroad company came here seeking to reverse the judgments of the court below.

C. P. & L. W. WICKHAM and JOHN H. CLARKE, for plaintiff in error.

FINCH & DEWEY and KING & GUERIN, for defendant in error.

BURKET, J.—Section 5088, Rev. St., provides that: "When the allegations of a pleading are so indefinite and uncertain that the precise nature of the charge or defense is not apparent, the court may require the pleading to be made definite and certain by amendment."

This means that the court shall in a proper case require the pleading to be made definite and certain. It is not a mere matter of discretion. It is a substantial right to a party to have the pleading against him so definite and certain as to enable him to know what he has to meet and to prepare his evidence accordingly.

The charge of negligence against the company that it "negligently and carelessly approached and crossed said highway with said locomotive and train of cars at a high, immoderate and dangerous rate of speed," and "negligently and carelessly operated and handled its said locomotive and train of cars," gave no definite or certain notice to the company as to what acts of commission or omission claimed to be negligent would be attempted to be proved or relied upon at the trial, and therefore the petition should have been required to be made definite and certain by stating the acts of commission and omission claimed to have caused the injury, so as to advise the company as to facts claimed to have been negligently done or omitted, and to enable it to meet the same. Upon the trial the evidence should be confined to the acts of negligence so specifically and definitely averred in the petition. This is in accordance with the rule of pleading laid down in Davis *v.* Guarnieri, 45 Ohio St. 470. It was there held that, the fact claimed to have caused the injury being averred, it was sufficient to state that it was negligently done. But to say that the company "negligently and carelessly operated and handled its said locomotive and train of cars" avers no fact as causing the injury, and does not aver that any fact causing the injury was carelessly done or omitted. It is a general averment at large of negligence, and the court erred in overruling the motion to make definite and certain.

The court also erred in refusing to strike out the words "at a high, immoderate and dangerous rate of speed."

As the general assembly has the power to reasonably regulate the speed of trains, not only in cities, but also in the country, and has failed to exercise that power as to speed in the country, such failure is an implied warrant to railroad companies to run their trains in the open country at such a rate of speed as those in charge of the same may deem safe to the transportation of passengers and property; such safety, however, being the paramount consideration.

As there are road crossings in the country every few miles, it is inconsistent with proper speed of transportation that trains should slack up for such crossings. Safety is secured to persons at such crossings by the observance of the statutory signals, and, such signals being given, the train is not limited as to speed.

It has sometimes been held, and correctly, that a high rate of speed, when taken in connection with other facts and the surrounding circumstances, may become an element or factor in constituting negligence, but when such is the case the facts constituting such surrounding circumstances should be pleaded, so that the court can judge from the pleadings whether the high rate of speed is a proper factor in constituting negligence, because a high rate of speed alone cannot constitute negligence as a matter of law. Elliott, R. R., § 1160, says: "In the absence of any statute or ordinance upon the subject, no rate of speed is negligence *per se*." The same doctrine is laid down in Thomp. Neg., sec. 1873.

The petition shows no fact making this crossing dangerous or other than the usual country-road crossing and no fact or circumstance which, when combined with a high rate of speed, would constitute negligence. The court should, therefore, have stricken out those words as to speed. The case of Railroad Co. *v.* Lawrence, 13 Ohio St. 66, is instructive as to the question of speed of trains. The injury in the case of Schweinfurth *v.* Railway Co., 60 Ohio St. 215, occurred at a street crossing in a city where there was an ordinance regulating the rate of speed, and it was there held that under the circumstances of that case a high rate of speed, contrary to the provisions of the ordinance, might constitute an element in determining the question of negligence; but at road crossings in the country, where there is no law regulating the rate of speed, the rule does not prevail.

At the close of the evidence, and before argument, the court, upon request of counsel for plaintiff below, gave to the jury the following charge: "The jury are instructed that the defendant railroad company had, at the time of the collision complained of, the same right to use that portion of the public highway over which its track passed at the point of collision that the public had. Its rights and those of the plaintiff were mutual and reciprocal, and the railroad company and the plaintiff were bound to have due regard each for the safety of the other."

This charge was too strongly in her favor. While in law she had the same right to use the crossing that the railroad company had, the different modes of such use constitute a difference in right. As she could stop with her team within a few feet, and the train could not stop short of many rods, it follows of necessity that, when both were approaching the crossing at the same time, the train had the right of way, and it was her duty to stop and let the train pass before attempting to cross. Thomp. Neg. 1611; Continental Improvement Co. *v.* Stead, 95 U. S. 161, 163, 12 Am. Neg. Cas. 687*n.* Such would be the conduct of all men of ordinary care under such circumstances. To rush ahead and attempt to pass, knowing the train to be close at hand, is not the conduct of ordinarily prudent persons, but is gross negligence. To drive upon a crossing without first looking for passing trains is also negligence. The looking should usually be just before going upon the crossing, or so near thereto as to enable the person to get across in safety at the speed he is going before a train within the range of his view of the track, going at the usual speed of fast trains, would reach the crossing. There should be such looking before going upon the track, even though there was a looking farther away when no train was seen approaching. A train at the usual speed will go quite a distance, while a team on a walk or trot will go a much shorter distance. The care to be taken in such cases should correspond with the danger.

The court in the special charges given at the request of plaintiff's counsel, in speaking of the duty of those in charge of the train to use care in discovering the plaintiff as she approached the crossing and using means to prevent injury to her, includes all the trainmen, without explaining the duties of any of them, but puts upon all the duty of caring for her so as to prevent injury. Three of the trainmen were in the caboose, away from the engine, and without means of immediate communication with the engineer, and yet they are included in the instruction as to trainmen, when they could do nothing to prevent the accident. The engineer also is a trainman, and the charge imposes upon him, along with the other trainmen, the duty of seeing her danger, and being careful to shield her as she approached and drove upon the crossing.

It is the duty of an engineer on a train to keep a lookout on the track ahead of him, and he is not expected to see anything on the sides of the right of way farther than his eye may take in objects within the range of vision while looking ahead along the track. Elliott R. R., secs. 1159, 1205; Thomp. Neg., sec. 1592 *et seq.* In Railroad Co. *v.* Elliott, 4 Ohio St. 474, 476, this court held that "the paramount duty of a conductor of a train is to watch over the safety of the persons and property in his charge." The same is true of an engineer. His paramount and first duty is to watch over and guard the safety of the persons and property in his charge, and that is most effectually done by keeping a strict lookout ahead along the track, so as to see any obstruction at the earliest moment, and thus be prepared to avert danger to his train. So important is this duty of the engineer to keep a lookout ahead of his train that in some of the States it is required and regulated by statute. His duty being to look ahead, it cannot be his duty to look at the same time to the sides. If, however, while so looking ahead, his eye takes in a person approaching the track at a crossing or elsewhere, he is then bound to use ordinary care to prevent injury, his first care, however, being for the safety of his passengers and property on board for transportation. He may presume that such person will keep away from the track until the train passes, but when it becomes evident that the person cannot or will not keep away from the track, then he must do all he reasonably can to prevent injury.

Upon the trial of this case it was urged by counsel for plaintiff that she was discovered by the trainmen in the act of going upon the crossing in time for the engineer to have so slowed down his train after such discovery as to have prevented the injury. The railroad company claimed that she was not seen by the engineer until the collision occurred, and that it did not become evident to the brakeman and fireman on the left-hand side of the engine that she was about to drive upon the crossing until the very moment of the collision and that it was then too late to notify the engineer. It was with reference to these different claims that the special charges were given.

It has often been held by courts that when a person suddenly finds himself in a position of imminent peril or danger he cannot be held to a strict account as to the course of conduct to be by him pursued to avoid injury. Iron R. R. Co. *v.* Mowery, 36 Ohio St. 418, 6 Am. Neg. Cas. 176; Elliott, R. R., sec. 1173; Bellefontaine & Ind. R. R. Co. *v.* Snyder, 55 Ohio St. 342, 12 Am. Neg. Cas. 491.

While engineers of locomotives are expected from their training, experience, and the nature of their duties to be equal to almost any emergency in the management of their trains, yet it must be remembered in their favor that they have mind and nerves the same as other people, and that when they are suddenly and unexpectedly confronted with imminent peril or danger to themselves or to the persons and property in their charge, by obstructions on the track or about to go thereon, they cannot be held to a strict course of conduct to prevent injury to persons or property not connected with the train, so that the action taken is in good faith and at the time believed to be the best. When a person or animal is seen approaching the track, and it becomes evident that he or it will not stop but attempt to cross, it is sometimes safer to slow down or stop the train and sometimes safer to increase the speed and get the train across first. The course to be pursued must be instantly determined by the engineer at the peril of himself and the persons and property in his charge, and the course selected by him and carried out in good faith in the face of such peril, and in view of the surrounding circumstances, cannot constitute negligence on his part, even though others might be able to suggest and point out afterwards that a different course would have been less liable to result in injury. As to the persons and property in his charge, the engineer must use the greatest care, but as to persons and property not connected with the train he must use only ordinary care. He must therefore be allowed to determine for himself in good faith, upon the spur of the moment and in view of the peril before him, the course to be pursued for the safety of the persons and property in his charge, without being called to a very strict account by those to whom he owes only ordinary care.

What was said by this court in Express Co. *v.* Smith, 33 Ohio St. 511, at page 519, is applicable to such cases: "There is an *ex post facto* wisdom which, after everything has been done without success, can suggest that something else should have been attempted, but this is a sagacity much more astute than ordinary human foresight, and can hardly furnish a fair rule by which to determine the propriety of what has been done in good faith and with judgment exercised under the best light afforded."

At the request of the plaintiff below, the court also charged the jury in different forms, before argument, to the effect that the jury must determine from the evidence under the instruction of the court whether plaintiff in approaching the crossing used such care as persons of ordinary care and prudence would use under like or similar circumstances. Sometimes the word "evidence" was left out These charges were all defective at least in this: the question was put as to approaching the crossing, instead of going onto the crossing. She may have been ever so careful in the approach, and yet extremely negligent in driving upon the crossing in the face of a rapidly approaching train. If she was negligent in going upon the crossing in front of a rapidly approaching train, thinking that she could cross in safety, and the engineer, after seeing her, was negligent in not slowing down or stopping his train, thinking that she would get across in safety, the proximate cause of the injury was the miscalculation and negligence of both, and there could be no recovery unless the engineer, after he saw her and realized her danger, had time to so slow down or stop as to prevent the injury. Or if the fireman and brakeman riding on the left side of the engine saw her, and saw and realized her danger in time to notify the engineer in time to enable him to so slow down or stop the train as to have prevented the injury, and failed to so notify the engineer, such failure would be such negligence as would sustain a recovery; but, if after it became evident to them that she was about to drive upon the crossing, there was not time to notify the engineer and then time for him to so slow down or stop the train as to prevent the injury, there could be no recovery.

When the fireman and brakeman saw her driving toward the crossing they had a right to rely that she would use due care and not go upon the crossing, and it was only when it became evident that she was going upon the crossing that the duty devolved upon them to notify the engineer, and if there was then time to save her she should have been saved, but if it was then too late to save her the injury was, as to the railroad company, an inevitable accident, and for such there can be no recovery. If, on her part, it was a race to beat the train over the crossing, the injury was her own fault and there could be no recovery. It is urged that there was a deep ditch on one side of the road and a fence on the other, and that she could not turn her team around. But no effort is shown to turn the team, and besides it is always safer to run into a fence or even a deep ditch than onto a railroad crossing in front of a fast train.

There were no facts or surroundings pleaded or proven, which when taken in connection with a high rate of speed, would make such speed an element or factor in negligence, and therefore what was said as to such high rate of speed in the charge was error.

Whatever the engineer and those on the engine with him would see while in the proper discharge of their duties they are chargeable with having seen, but they are not required to neglect their duties on the train to look outside of the right of way for approaching persons or animals not within the range of vision while looking ahead along the track.

After argument the court charged the jury as follows: "The defendant had the right to run the train at the time and place of this collision at any speed consistent with the safety which was necessary in the conduct of its business in the usual and ordinary manner, taking into consideration, however, all the circumstances, surrounding that crossing, affecting the traveling public, and having a due regard for the safety of the public using the crossing."

From what has already been said as to the speed of trains it will readily be seen that the latter part of this charge, all after the word "manner," is erroneous.

The court also charged the jury that if trees, shrubbery or weeds presented an obstruction to view, it required care and caution on part of plaintiff and defendant according to their respective rights as explained by the court. The inclusion of the defendant in this charge was error. The trees, shrubbery and weeds outside of the right of way imposed no care or caution upon the company in running its train.

The court also charged the jury as follows: "While it is true that the railroad company is not responsible for weeds or bushes growing outside of its right of way, even though they obstruct a view by travelers upon the highway, yet if you find from the evidence such weeds or bushes to have existed in such manner in this case it is a circumstance which the jury should consider in determining whether or not the railway company was guilty of negligence in approaching this crossing of the county line at the rate of speed at which it approached the same with its train upon this occasion."

This charge was clearly error, because the weeds and brush in question were not a circumstance to be considered by the jury in determining the question of negligence.

The court also, in charging as to the duty of the company and its servants after seeing her danger, included the trainmen. This was too broad, as it included those in the caboose, who could do nothing to avert the injury.

The court also charged the jury that the question of negligence was wholly for the jury to determine from the evidence. He should have added, "under the instruction of the court." The court also charged the jury that the negligence, if any, of the father, was not imputable to the daughter. While it is true that the doctrine of imputed negligence does not prevail in this State, that doctrine was not applicable to the facts as claimed to be by the defendant in this case, and as the evidence tended to prove. The father, being nearly deaf, took the daughter along to hear for him, and as they came to the west side of the piece of woods he told her to look and listen for trains, and she did so by raising the rear curtain and looking in the direction of the railroad.

If it be true that she was to do the listening and also to assist in the looking while he was doing the driving, they were engaged in a joint enterprise, and each would in such case be chargeable with the negligence of the other.

It has often been held that the negligence of a servant is imputable to the master because he is the superior. Cincinnati Street R'y Co. *v.* Wright, 54 Ohio St. 181 (12 Am. Neg. Cas. 510*n*). On principle and sound reason the rule should be applied to those who take an active part in a joint enterprise.

As to the wild cherry tree standing in the south line of the railroad right of way east of the ridge road, it is difficult to see how it could be an obstruction to her view of the train at the time of going upon the track, because the train was then far west of the cherry tree and the tree was behind the train. The time to look and listen for the last time is shortly before going upon the track, as before explained, and as the train was near enough to catch her before getting over the crossing at a fast trot or gallop, the train must have been far past the cherry tree when she should have looked the last time. If she saw the cherry tree as she drove by it, or knew of its being there, it only imposed upon her greater care and caution if she regarded it as an obstruction to her view. Penn. Co. *v.* Morel, 40 Ohio St. 338 (12 Am. Neg. Cas. 511*n*).

Judgment reversed.

MAYNE v. CHICAGO, ROCK ISLAND AND PACIFIC RAILWAY COMPANY.

Supreme Court, Oklahoma, July, 1902.

FREIGHT TRAIN BLOCKING CROSSING AT STATION — DANGEROUS APPROACH — INTENDING PASSENGER INJURED. — 1. It is negligence for a railway company to allow a freight train on a side track to block the crossing or passageway over such side track to the depot of the company at a time when a passenger train of the company is due at the station, so that persons desiring to take passage on such passenger train cannot reach the depot in time to purchase tickets and get aboard such train.

2. In case a railway company is guilty of negligence in blocking with a freight train the usual crossing to the depot, thereby compelling a person desiring to take passage on the train of the defendant company to choose some other route in order to get to the depot, and such person sustains an injury while on the way to the depot, such railway company is not liable to the

person injured, unless the negligence on the part of such railway company is the proximate cause of the injury, and the injury is the natural and probable consequence of the negligence of the company in allowing the crossing to be blocked, and the injury ought to have been foreseen in the light of the attending circumstances.

3. A railway company, having a station at a given point, by implication invites persons to come upon the premises for business, and it is the duty of the company to be reasonably sure that it is not inviting them into danger, and to that end the company must use care and prudence to render the premises safe for the visit.

4. Even though a railroad company holds out such invitation, and a person desiring to take passage on the train of the defendant company accepts such invitation, the company is not liable for an injury to such person unless it is shown that the premises were not safe for the visit, and that it ought to have been foreseen that a person attempting to reach the depot of the company was liable to be injured.

5. In an action against a railway company to recover damages for injuries received, the petition must show that the injury was the natural and probable consequence of the negligent and wrongful act of the defendant company, and that the defendant company ought to have foreseen such injury in the light of the attending circumstances; and a petition which fails to show such facts by proper averments does not state a cause of action, and an objection to the introduction of evidence on the ground that the petition does not state facts sufficient to constitute a cause of action will be sustained.

(Syllabus by the Court.)

ERROR from District Court, Grant County.

Action by Ella J. Mayne against the Chicago, Rock Island & Pacific Railway Company. From judgment for defendant, plaintiff brings error. *Judgment affirmed.*

This is an action brought in the District Court of Grant county by the plaintiff in error against the defendant in error to recover damages in the sum of $4,000, alleged to have been sustained by reason of the negligence of the defendant in error, the material facts in relation to such alleged negligence being stated in the petition as follows: "That on the morning of June 28, 1900, this plaintiff desired to take the passenger train of the defendant railway company as a passenger on the north and east-bound train, and for that purpose had her preparations made, and was ready to start to the depot of the defendant railway company to await the arrival of said train; that she was ready to go to said depot so as to arrive there a few minutes in advance of the time scheduled for the arrival of said train; that she only had a short distance to go, having stopped the night previous at a house only a short distance from said depot, on the street used as the principal business thoroughfare of said town of Renfrow; that when she was ready to start for said depot there was a freight train of the defendant railway company switching on said side track aforesaid, and running the engine and cars thereon, and plaintiff did not attempt to cross said track at that time, believing it to be dangerous, and believing that the defendant company would cause said freight train to stop switching and running said cars and engine up and down said track before the time for the arrival of the passenger train, and would clear a passageway for persons desiring to go to said depot for the purpose of taking said passenger train; that plaintiff waited for the purpose of seeing if said train would stop switching or a passageway would be cleared until the time was close for the arrival of said train, and she could see the smoke from the engine of said passenger train as it approached in the distance from the south. Thereupon plaintiff started to go over to said depot, to see if she could get to said depot, and believing that when she got near said depot that a passageway would be open up so that she could pass through, and get to said depot; that she went over toward said depot over and by the path used by persons generally going to said depot on foot, and leading to the north end of said depot; that when she came near to said freight train on said side track said train had been stopped, and said train closed up, making a solid continuous train of cars completely blocking said pathway, so that she could not get to the depot by that route; thereupon she started to go to the south to take the way or route of getting to the depot usually used by teams and wagons in going to and from said depot, as hereinbefore set out, but learned that it was also blocked by said freight train, and she could not pass that way; and plaintiff alleges the fact to be that said freight train was a solid, continuous train of cars extending a long distance each way both above and below said depot, and between her and said depot, and completely shutting off access to said depot by any of the usually traveled or used ways or routes; that the only way by which plaintiff could then get to said depot was to go around said freight train, and for this purpose she started to the north, said freight train being headed north, and the engine of said train being near the north end of said side track, and about at the south end of the stock pens of the defendant railway company at said station; that plaintiff went north and around said engine and train, and started south to go to the depot; that by this time the passenger train of the defendant railway company, and upon which the defendant desired to take passage, was rapidly approaching said station, coming north; that plaintiff hastened to get to said depot, walking rapidly down the right of way of the defendant railway company, and that by reason of the proximity of said approaching passenger train plaintiff's attention was directed to it; that between plaintiff and the depot of defendant were two mail catchers, or cranes, erected and maintained on the west side of the main track of defendant's railway; that said cranes or mail catchers were situated a few feet out from the track, and heavy beams or ties extended from the base of said cranes or catchers to said track, said beams being similar in size to the ties used in the roadbed of the railway; that said beams or ties were about six or eight inches in height from the ground, and about eight inches wide at the top; that the space in between said beams or ties was vacant, and not filled up with dirt; that, in order to get to the depot, plaintiff attempted and was compelled to pass over said beams or ties projecting between said mail cranes or catchers and the main track; that plaintiff is a large, heavy, fleshy woman, and as she went to pass over said ties or beams aforesaid in some manner she tripped, and fell heavily upon said ties or beams; that she was walking as carefully as she could under the circumstances, and that said fall was not caused by any fault or negligence upon her part; that she struck her face and nose violently upon one of said ties, on some hard substance there at the time, bruising her face badly, and causing her nose to bleed profusely; that she struck her right hand and shoulder upon said ties, or the rail of the railroad track, or some hard substance, in such a manner as to violently wrench and strain the muscles and tendons of her hand and arm, and to bruise her shoulder, and cause her hand, arm and shoulder to become inflamed and swell, and be very painful; that plaintiff struck her knee in falling upon some hard substance, badly bruising it, and causing it to swell and become greatly discolored, and injuring the kneecap; that by said fall plaintiff sustained an injury in the chest and spine, and to the muscles of the back, and she suffers almost continual pain from said injury." An answer was filed to the petition, the case came on for trial, a jury was impaneled and sworn, and a statement on behalf of the plaintiff was made to the jury. The plaintiff was called as a witness in her own behalf, and, after one or two preliminary questions had been asked, the defendant objected to the introduction of any evidence under the petition upon the ground that the petition did not state a cause of action, and also moved for judgment on the statement of counsel for plaintiff to the jury. These objections were sustained by the court, and the jury was discharged. Judgment was rendered in favor of the defendant for costs, motion for new trial was overruled, and plaintiff appealed to this court.

MACKEY & SIMONS, for plaintiff in error.

M. A LOW, W. F. EVANS, C. O. BLAKE, and E. E. BLAKE, *for* defendants in error,

PANCOAST, J. (after stating the facts). We shall consider this case in the light of the objection in the introduction of evidence unde the petition upon the ground that the same did not state a cause of action, rather than from the standpoint of the objection to the statement of counsel to the jury, as we doubt the propriety of sustaining an objection to the introduction of evidence, and rendering judgment because the statement of counsel to the jury does not make out a *prima facie* case. Elaborate briefs have been filed in this case by both parties, and numerous cases cited, yet no case is cited directly in point, or which lays down sufficient general principles upon which a decision can be based in this case. Indeed, counsel for defendant in error admit that the cases in point are few. We have been unable to find any case containing some of the material points in the case at bar, yet numerous cases are to be found which lay down principles which are applicable here. There is one grave defect in the petition in that it fails to state that the freight train occupying the side track and blocking the main crossing to the depot continued to so block the way until the passenger train arrived, or until a time so near the arrival of the passenger train that persons desiring to take passage could not have reached the depot in time to purchase tickets, check their baggage, etc. The nearest that the petition comes to a statement of that kind is that the plaintiff waited "until the time was close for the arrival of said passenger train, and she could see the smoke from the engine of said passenger train as it approached in the distance from the south. Thereupon plaintiff started to go over to said depot, to see if she could get to said depot, and believing that when she got near said depot that a passageway would be opened up so that she could pass through and get to said depot; that she went over toward said depot over and by the path used by persons generally going to said depot on foot, and leading to the north end of said depot; that when she came near to said freight train on said side track said train had been stopped, and said train closed up, making a solid continuous train of cars completely blocking said pathway, so that she could not get to the depot by that route." Thereupon she started to go south, and, learning that the south crossing was blocked, and she could not pass that way, she reversed her steps, and went north. How long a time this was before the passenger train reached the depot cannot be determined from the petition; or whether or not the freight train did open up a way for passengers to cross the side track between that time and the time of the arrival of the passenger train is not stated, and cannot be determined from the petition. This, we think, is material, in order to show negligence in the first instance upon the part of the defendant. But conceding that the defendant railway company was negligent in blocking the usual way to the depot, was such negligence the proximate cause of the injury sustained? It is not sufficient that the defendant was negligent, but such negligence must have been the proximate cause of the injury, for no negligence can furnish the foundation of an action for damages unless it was the proximate cause of the injury. 1 Thomp. Neg., sec. 44. And in order that an act of negligence shall be deemed the proximate cause of the injury, it must be such that a person of ordinary intelligence would have foreseen that the accident was liable to be produced thereby. A proximate cause is, therefore, probable cause; or, in other words, that the circumstances were such that the injuries resulting might have been foreseen as likely to result from the wrongful act, or was the natural and probable consequence of the wrongful act. Atkinson *v.* Transportation Co. (Wis.), 18 N. W. Rep. 764; Armil *v.* Railroad Co. (Iowa), 30 N. W. Rep. 42. As stated by Mr. Justice Strong in Railroad Co. *v.* Kellogg, 94 U. S. 469: "But it is generally held that, in order to warrant a finding that negligence, or an act not amounting to wanton wrong, is the proximate cause of an injury, it must appear that the injury was the natural and probable consequence of the negligence or wrongful act, and that it ought to have been foreseen in the light of the attending circumstances." Can we say that the injury in this case ought to have been foreseen by the defendant company when the company negligently blocked the usual pathway to the depot building? If not, then the injury was not the natural and probable consequence of the negligence or wrongful act. It may be conceded that it should have been foreseen that a person wishing to take passage upon the train of the defendant company, finding the usual pathway to the depot blocked by a freight train, would seek some other mode of ingress to the depot; and it may be conceded that the only other ingress to the depot in this case was that sought by the plaintiff in going around the engine and between the two tracks, but it does not appear that the route so taken was not a reasonably safe one, or that it should have been foreseen by a person using ordinary care that the accident was liable to occur. So far as can be ascertained from the averments in the petition, we think the immediate and proximate cause of the injury in this case was the tripping of the plaintiff at the point where she attempted to cross the ties which extended beyond the rails for the purpose of supporting the cranes or mail catchers. It was not negligence on the part of the defendant company to have these ties in place at that point. There must have been a considerable space between the main track and the side track. There is no statement in the petition to lead one to believe that the route taken along near the main track over these ties was the only one that could have been taken by the plaintiff. For aught that appears, except the statement that there was some brush or other obstructions near that point, the balance of the space may have been entirely open and smooth. Nor can we tell, from the allegations of the petition, how the plaintiff came to fall or trip. It does not seem that those ties, which were several feet apart, and not to exceed eight inches square, were really dangerous to a person traveling on foot in daylight, or that an injury might have been anticipated if one should attempt to reach the depot by that route. We do not think that any person using ordinary caution would have apprehended danger in traveling along that point; nor can we believe that a person using ordinary care and caution would have been injured. What is usual the law requires a person doing a wrong to anticipate and provide against, but the law does not require that even a wrongdoer shall anticipate and provide against the unusual.

Special attention is called by the defendant to the case of Bennett *v.* Louis. & Nash. R. R. Co., 102 U. S. 577, 7 Am. Neg. Cas. 349. The facts in that case, however, are so entirely different from the facts in the case at bar that the rule laid down there is not, and cannot be followed as the rule here. In that case the company negligently left open a hatchway in a building through which the passengers had to pass in order to reach the place for taking passage, and a passenger traveling along what was the usual route and the way prepared by the company to reach the point of passage in the nighttime, there being no lights provided to enable him to choose his way, coming to the open hatchway, fell into the same. Here there was not only negligence on the part of the company, but that negligence was the immediate, proximate cause of the injury, and the injured person was using due care in passing over the route prepared by the defendant company for reaching its trains and boats. It is true, in that case, as in this, the company did, by implication, invite the parties to come upon the premises for business, and it was the duty of the company to be reasonably sure that it was not inviting them into danger, and to that end the company must use care and prudence to render the premises safe for the visit. Can we say in the case at bar that the path by which the plaintiff undertook to reach the depot was not safe for a person traveling in the daytime? If it had been after dark, a different condition would have existed. The element of negligence would have been there. The plaintiff would, perhaps, have had the same right to attempt to reach the depot by the route taken, and it might be conceded that there would have been no reasonable ground to believe that there was danger; yet on account of the darkness, no light being established, it ought to have been foreseen or expected that a person would stumble over the ties which had been laid for the foundation of the crane, or that it ought to have been foreseen that the plaintiff might fall into any dangerous place, if there was one. But that would not have been this case, because there are elements entering into such a case that do not exist here. The petition does not show that the injury was the natural and probable consequence of the wrongful act of the defendant company, and that it ought to have been foreseen in the light of the attending circumstances. We therefore conclude that the petition does not state a cause of action, and that the court did not err in sustaining the objection to the introduction of evidence under it.

The judgment is affirmed, all the justices concurring, except IRWIN, J., absent.

KROEGER v. TEXAS AND PACIFIC RAILWAY COMPANY.

Court of Civil Appeals, Texas, June, 1902.

PEDESTRIAN ON TRACK STRUCK BY TRAIN — INTOXICATION — DEGREE OF CARE REQUIRED OF RAILROAD COMPANY — INSTRUCTION. — In an action to recover damages for injuries sustained by plaintiff, who, while walking along defendant's track was struck by defendant's train, it was error to charge that if plaintiff was intoxicated at the time of the accident and his condition contributed to the injury, and if defendant's servants took any steps to prevent the injury to plaintiff after they discovered his peril, the defendant would not be liable, as the defendant was required to use every reasonable means in its power, consistent with the safety of the train to prevent the injury, after discovering plaintiff's peril (1).

WALKING ON TRACK — CONTRIBUTORY NEGLIGENCE — INSTRUCTION. — Where the evidence showed that the portion of the track along which plaintiff was walking when the accident occurred was commonly used by the public, with the knowledge and consent of defendant, as a public highway, it was error to instruct the jury that plaintiff should be regarded as a trespasser, unless it was shown that he used that portion of the track which was suitable and safest for pedestrians, as this was in effect telling them that plaintiff would, as matter of law, be guilty of contributory negligence.

1. *Accidents on track.* For actions relating to accidents to persons on track, see vols. 11 and 12 Am. Neg. Cas., where the same are arranged in alphabetical order of States and chronologically grouped from the earliest times to 1897. Subsequent actions to date are reported in vols. 1-12 AM. NEG. REP. and the current numbers of that series of Reports.

CONTRIBUTORY NEGLIGENCE — BURDEN OF PROOF — INSTRUCTION. — It was error for the court, in an action for injuries sustained by a pedestrian on a railroad track, to charge the jury that the burden of proof was upon plaintiff to show by a preponderance of evidence that he was not guilty of contributory negligence.

APPEAL from Gregg County Court.

Action by John Kroeger against the Texas and Pacific Railway Company. From judgment for defendant, plaintiff appeals. *Judgment reversed.*

JUDSON H. MCHANEY, J. M. HUFFINGTON, and G. B. TURNER, for appellant.

DUNCAN & JONES, for appellee.

PLEASANTS, J. — This is a suit to recover damages for injuries alleged to have been caused by the negligence of the appellee. Appellant, while walking along appellee's track in the town of Longview, was struck by one of its engines drawing a train which was passing through said town, and thereby received the injuries complained of in his petition. The portion of appellee's track along which appellant was walking at the time he was struck was commonly used by the public as a highway, with the knowledge and consent of the appellee. Appellant's statement as to the manner in which the accident occurred is as follows: "When I was just below the trestle, just opposite the old laundry, I heard a train coming at a very rapid rate of speed, and in my fright I suddenly turned my head and saw it. I saw the light and heard the train. It was running fifteen or twenty miles an hour; not less than fifteen miles. I have run a locomotive engine as engineer, and I knew well the speed the train was making. I railroad myself. I ran a locomotive six years. The train was 250 or 300 feet from me when I first saw it. When I saw the train, I suddenly turned, and made a quick step to get out of the way of the train, and fell with my head and arms inside of the track, left side on the rail. I moved my back towards the engine, and I moved quickly, and tried to get out and off the rail to the right towards the south, and I made a quick effort to get out of the way of the engine. I was not struck by the cowcatcher, but some timber on the side of the engine, or part of the engine. If that train had been running six miles an hour, I never would have been struck and injured, as I would have had time, if the train had only given me another second or two, to have been out of the way. I do not think that the speed of the train was checked from the time I first saw it and fell until I was struck. I was listening to it all the time, and was frightened, and was doing all I could to get out of the way." The town of Longview had an ordinance in force which forbids the running of trains through said town at a greater rate of speed than six miles an hour. The evidence is conflicting as to the rate of speed at which the train was moving when it struck appellant, and there is also evidence which tends to show that appellant was intoxicated at the time of the accident, and that his fall upon the track may have been due to his being under the influence of liquor. The engineer testified that when he first saw appellant he was about 400 feet from him; that he did not know what the object was when he first saw it upon the track, and did not discover it was a man until he was within seventy feet of him, and that he then did everything in his power to stop the train. None of the other operatives of the train seem to have seen appellant before he was struck. The petition alleges that appellee's employees were negligent in not keeping a proper lookout, in not giving signals as required by law, in failing to use proper care to stop the train after they discovered appellant's peril, and in running the train at a reckless and unlawful speed through the town of Longview. Appellee's answer contains general and special exceptions, general denial, and plea of contributory negligence, in which it is averred that appellant's injury was occasioned by his own negligence in going upon appellee's track in a state of intoxication, and lying down upon the track, and failing to leave same upon the approach of the train. The trial of the cause by a jury in the court below resulted in a verdict and judgment in favor of appellee.

We shall not consider the various assignments of error categorically, nor in detail, but will in a general way point out the errors which, in our opinion, require a reversal of the judgment; and for the guidance of the court below upon another trial will state the general principles of law applicable to the case as made by the pleadings and evidence. At the request of appellee the trial court gave the jury the following instruction: "If a person go upon a railroad track in a state of intoxication, and sits down upon the track, and goes to sleep, and is struck by a train, then the railroad company would not be liable, unless, after the servants of defendant saw his peril, they took no steps to avoid the accident; but, if they did not see him in time to avoid the accident, the railroad company would not be liable." The court had in several previous paragraphs of his charge told the jury that, if appellant was intoxicated at the time of the accident, and his intoxicated condition contributed to his injury, he could not recover, unless the evidence showed that appellee's employees, after they discovered appellant's perilous position, failed to use proper care to prevent the injury. Appellee was entitled to have the issue of contributory negligence growing out of the alleged intoxication of appellant fully presented to the jury, but the court should not, by giving repeated charges upon said issue, have emphasized its importance, and given it undue prominence. The practice of repeating and reiterating in a charge the principle of law applicable to any particular issue in a case has been uniformly condemned, because it is likely to lead the jury to believe that, in the opinion of the court, the evidence in the case establishes facts which require the application of the proposition of law thus sought to be impressed upon their minds; and the spirit, if not the letter, of the statute, which forbids the court to charge upon the weight of the evidence, is thus violated. Powell *v.* Messer's Adm'r, 18 Tex. 401; Traylor *v.* Townsend, 61 Tex. 144; Hays *v.* Hays, 66 Tex. 607, 1 S.W. Rep. 895; Cross *v.* Kennedy (Tex. Civ. App.), 66 S. W. Rep. 318. The charge quoted is further erroneous in that it does not correctly state the measure of the duty of appellee's employees after they discovered appellant's danger. Under this charge, if the operatives of the train took any steps to prevent the injury after they discovered the peril of appellant, appellee would not be liable. The law required them to use every reasonable means in their power, consistent with the safety of the train, to prevent the injury, after they discovered appellee's peril, and the jury should not have been told that the appellee would only be liable in case the servants "took no steps to avoid the accident." Railway Co. *v.* Jacobson (Tex. Civ. App.), 66 S. W. Rep. 1111, Railway Co. *v.* Watkins, 88 Tex. 24, 29 S. W. Rep. 232; Railway Co. *v.* Breadow, 90 Tex. 27, 36 S. W. Rep. 410.

The court also gave the jury the following instruction: "Gentlemen of the jury, you are further charged that, although you may believe from the evidence that the defendant's road from Longview Junction to Longview was, and had been for some years, habitually used by pedestrians going to and from Longview and the junction; and if you further believe from the evidence that defendant's roadbed is wide enough so as to leave sufficient room, in good condition for walking, outside of the edge of the ties, so that pedestrians might pass trains in safety, — then you are charged that it is the duty of such pedestrians to use such space, and they would be trespassers in walking down the track and between the rails; and if you believe that the plaintiff was walking, and fell or laid down on the track, between Longview station and Longview Junction, then you are charged that the railway company's employees owed him no further duty than to use all means to stop the train after they saw his peril, and that he would not leave the track; and if you believe from the evidence that plaintiff's condition and position on the track was caused by his drinking or being drunk, then defendant would not be liable for his injuries unless the engineer and servants in charge of the engine wilfully and maliciously ran the train over him after discovering his peril." The undisputed evidence shows, and it was admitted by appellee upon the trial, that the portion of the track along which appellant was walking when the accident occurred was commonly used by the public, with the knowledge and consent of appellee, as a public highway, and it was error for the court to instruct the jury that appellant should be regarded as a trespasser unless the evidence showed that he used that portion of the track which was suitable and safest for pedestrians. The evidence and the admission of appellee as to the use of the track by the public was not restricted to any particular portion of the roadbed, and, conceding that the evidence raised the issue of negligence on appellant's part in walking between the rails, the jury should not have been told that it was appellant's duty to have walked on the outside of the rails if the roadbed was wide enough to leave sufficient room, in good condition for walking, outside the ties, for this was in effect telling them that he would, as a matter of law, be guilty of contributory negligence in walking down the center of the track between the rails. As before stated, the law required the operatives of the train to use every reasonable means in their power, consistent with the safety of the train, to prevent the injury to appellant, after they discovered his peril; and it was manifestly erroneous for the court to tell the jury in this charge, as he did in several others given at the request of the appellee, that, if appellant's "condition and position on the track was caused by his drinking and being drunk, the defendant would not be liable for his injuries unless the engineer and servants in charge of the engine wilfully and maliciously ran over him after discovering his peril." Ordinary care under circumstances of this kind would impose upon the operatives of the train the duty to make every reasonable effort to prevent the injury, while this charge only requires them to refrain from wilfully and maliciously causing the injury. Such a doctrine is unsupported by authority, and is abhorrent, and shocking to the enlightened conscience. The common-law rule that owners of premises owe no further duty to trespassers than to refrain from wilfully injuring them applies only to the duty of the owner in regard to the safe condition of the premises, and cannot be extended to protect persons who, seeing the immediate peril in which a fellow-being is placed by any act of theirs, however innocent and lawful in itself, negligently fail to make every reasonable effort to prevent the threatened injury. The court should not have instructed the jury that appellee would not be liable if the appellant went upon and voluntarily lay down on the track, and thereby contributed to his injury, because no such issue was raised by any evidence in the case.

It was manifest error for the court to charge the jury that the burden of proof was upon the appellant to show by a preponderance of the evidence that he was not guilty of contributory negligence. Gulf, Colo. & S. F. R'y Co. *v.* Sheider, 88 Tex. 152, 30 S. W. Rep. 902 (12 Am. Neg. Cas. 599*n*). If appellant was not a trespasser upon appellee's track, and was not guilty of contributory negligence in failing to leave the track when he saw the train approaching, and appellee's employees were negligent in running the train at an unlawful rate of speed, or in failing to keep a proper lookout to discover appellant, and such negligence caused the injury, appellee would be liable therefor, notwithstanding the operatives of the train may have used every reasonable effort to stop the train after they discovered appellant's peril. Galveston City R. R. Co. *v.* Hewitt, 67 Tex. 479, 3 S. W. Rep. 705 (12 Am. Neg. Cas. 623*n*); Railway Co. *v.* Matthews (Tex. Civ. App.), 66 S. W. Rep. 588. If the appellant was guilty of contributory negligence in going upon the track in a state of intoxication, and by reason of such condition he fell upon the track and was unable to leave same before he was struck by the train, appellee would not be liable for the injury unless the operatives of the train failed to use proper care to stop the train after they discovered appellant's peril. If, after the discovery of appellant's peril, the operatives of the train failed to use every reasonable means in their power, consistent with the safety of the train, to prevent the injury, appellee would be liable therefor, notwithstanding the fact that the injury would not have occurred but for the negligence of the appellant in going upon the track in an intoxicated condition. In such case the negligence of the appellant would only be regarded as remotely contributing to the injury, the direct and proximate cause of the injury being the negligence of the employees in failing to stop the train. Railway Co. *v.* Danshank (Tex. Civ. App.), 25 S. W. Rep. 297.

Upon another trial of the case these principles of law should control the court in his instruction to the jury. For errors in the charge of the court before indicated, the judgment of the court below is reversed, and this cause remanded for a new trial. Reversed and remanded.

ESKILDSEN v. CITY OF SEATTLE.

Supreme Court, Washington, September, 1902.

IMPUTED NEGLIGENCE. — In an action to recover damages for the benefit of a child, four years and three months old, who was injured on a defective railroad track, it was *held* that the negligence of the parent cannot be inputed to the child in an action brought for the benefit of the child, and not for the benefit of the parent (1).

Following Roth v. Union Depot Co., 13 Wash. 525.

INFANT — CONTRIBUTORY NEGLIGENCE. — An infant under five years of age cannot be guilty of contributory negligence (2).

CHILD INJURED ON DEFECTIVE TRACK — RUN OVER BY TRAIN — NEGLIGENCE OF PARENT — DANGEROUS PLACE — PROXIMATE CAUSE. — Where a child's foot became fastened between the planking and rail of the track which ran along a street, and the father of the child in trying to extricate the child from its position pulled the child over the rail as a train of cars was being pushed towards the child, and the cars passed over the child's leg, it was *held* that the dangerous condition of the track was the proximate cause of the accident for which the defendant city was liable, notwithstanding the act of the railroad company in passing its cars over the child and the negligence of the parent in permitting the child to be on the track.

APPEAL from Superior Court, King County.

ACTION by Edwin Eskildsen, by his guardian *ad litem*, George A. Eskildsen, against the City of Seattle. From judgment for plaintiff, defendant appeals. *Judgment affirmed.*

MITCHELL GILLIAM, WM. PARMELEE and W. E. HUMPHREY, for appellant.

E. P. EDSEN, JOHN E. HUMPHRIES and HARRISON BOSTWICK, for respondent.

DUNBAR, J. This is an action brought by Edwin Eskildsen, by his guardian *ad litem*, George A. Eskildsen, to recover for personal injuries, alleged to be due to the negligence of the city. The plaintiff at the time of the injury was four years and three months of age. He and his father were walking along Railroad avenue, in the city of Seattle, near the Northern Pacific Depot. The child desired to urinate, and was instructed by his father to go between the cars, where he did go, and where his foot got fastened between the planking and

1. See NOTE ON IMPUTED NEGLIGENCE, in 11 Am. Neg. Cas. 151–156.

See also NOTE ON THE NEW YORK RULE ON IMPUTED NEGLIGENCE, 12 Am. Neg. Cas. 293–297.

2. See NOTE ON CONTRIBUTORY NEGLIGENCE OF INFANTS, in 12 Am. Neg. Cas. 322; see also the English rule, 12 Am. Neg. Cas. 497–500.

the rail of the car track. The father was unable to extricate the child from this position, and, an engine at that time pushing one of its cars towards the child, the father pulled the child out over the rail, the cars passing over the child's leg, cutting it off above the ankle. Upon trial, judgment was rendered in favor of the plaintiff in the sum of $11,000, from which judgment this appeal is taken.

The assignments of error are: 1. The court erred in not granting defendant's motion for nonsuit. 2. In refusing to give instruction No. 1 requested by defendant. 3. In refusing to give instruction No. 6 requested by the defendant. 4. In giving instruction No. 5. 5 In giving instruction No. 15. It is insisted of the first assignment that the nonsuit should have been granted — First, because the city had no notice of the defective condition of the street; and, second, even if the city was negligent, its negligence was not the proximate cause of the injury. A perusal of the record convinces us that there was sufficient testimony for the consideration of the jury on the question of notice. It is contended that the father was the active agency in producing the injury of his child, but, outside of the great weight of authority which sustains the rule that the negligence of the parent cannot be imputed to a child, it was held by this court in Roth *v.* Union Depot Co., 13 Wash. 525, 43 Pac. 641, 44 Pac. Rep. 253 (12 Am. Neg. Cas. 638*n*), that "the negligence of the parent cannot be imputed to the child in an action brought for the benefit of the child, and not for the benefit of the parent;" and it is almost universally held that a child under five years of age cannot be guilty of contributory negligence in any event. But it is contended that, even if the negligence of the father cannot be imputed to the child, his negligence, and not that of the city, caused the child's injury, and that, assuming the father was not negligent, and that the city was negligent, yet the city would not be liable, because its negligence would not have caused the child any injury if it had not been for the intervening act of the railway company; it not being claimed that the hole in the street in itself injured the child, and that it appeared that he would have escaped injury but for the act of the railway company in passing its cars over him. We think that the great weight of authority on the subject of approximate cause is against the theory contended for by the appellant. The injury received was a reasonable and probable result of the negligence of the defendant, and it was held in Binford *v.* Johnston, 42 Am. Rep. 508, an Indiana case, that the fact that some agency intervenes between the original wrong and the injury does not necessarily bring the case within the rule, or within the maxim "*Causa proxima, et non remota spectatur.*" "On the contrary," said the court, "it is firmly settled that the intervention of a third person, or of other and new direct causes, does not preclude a recovery, if the injury was the natural or probable result of the original wrong," citing Billman *v.* Railroad Co., 76 Ind. 166; Scott *v.* Shepherd, 2 W. Bl. 892, commonly known as the "Squib Case." (1) "The rule goes so far," says the court, "as to hold that the original wrongdoer is responsible, even though the agency of a second wrongdoer intervened;" citing Clark *v.* Chambers, 7 Cent. Law. J. 11; Cooley, Torts, 70; Add. Torts, sec. 12. In that case two boys purchased of a dealer cartridges for use in a toy pistol. Another boy six years old picked up a toy pistol containing one of the cartridges, and discharged it, killing one of the boys who bought the cartridges. It was held that the dealer was liable for the death of the boy killed. It is true that it is against the statute to sell pistol cartridges to minors in that State, but the decision is bottomed on the legal doctrine announced. In City of Joliet *v.* Shufelt (Ill.) 32 N. E. Rep. 969, it was held that a city which has negligently constructed a street is liable for damages received by a person who, without negligence on his part, is thrown from a buggy on account of such defective construction, even though such accident would not have happened had not the harness broken, and the horse run away. The principle involved there is identical with the case in point, because the accident here probably would not have happened had it not been for the intervening cause, namely the approach of the car.

1. The facts in Scott *v.* Shepherd, 2 W. Bl. 892, 1 Smith's Leading Cas. (9th ed) 737, commonly called the "Squib Case," are as follows: Trespass and assault for throwing, casting and tossing a lighted squib at and against the plaintiff, and striking him therewith on the face, and so burning one of his eyes that he lost the sight of it. Plea, not guilty. Tried at Bridgewater Assizes. Verdict for plaintiff with £100 damages, subject to opinion of court on the case. On the evening of the fair day at Milbourne Port, Oct. 28, 1770, the defendant threw a lighted squib, made of gunpowder, etc., from the street into the market house, which is a covered building supported by arches and enclosed at one end, but open at the other and both the sides, where a large concourse of people were assembled; which lighted squib, so thrown by the defendant, fell upon the standing of one Yates, who sold gingerbread, etc. That one Willis instantly, and to prevent injury to himself and the said wares of the said Yates, took up the said lighted squib from off the said standing and then threw it across the said market house, when it fell upon another standing there of one Royal, who sold the same sort of wares, who instantly, and to save his own goods from being injured, took up the said lighted squib from off the said standing and then threw it to another part of the said market house, and in so throwing it struck the plaintiff, then in the said market house, in the face therewith, and the combustible matter, then bursting, put out one of the plaintiff's eyes. Held, that trespass and assault will lie for originally throwing a squib which, after having been thrown about in self-defense by other persons, at last put out the plaintiff's eye.

In that case it was said: "The general doctrine is that it is no defense in actions for negligent injuries that the negligence of third persons, or an inevitable accident, or an inanimate thing, contributed to cause the injury of the plaintiff; if the negligence of the defendant was an efficient cause, without which the injury would have occurred." Certainly, in this case, the hole in the walk was the efficient cause, without which this child would not have been run over by the car, as shown by the testimony in the case. In support of this doctrine the court cited: Wabash St. L. & Pac. R'y Co. *v.* Shacklet, 105 Ill. 364 (11 Am. Neg. Cas. 429*n*); Transit Co. *v.* Shacklet, 119 Ill. 232, 10 N. E. Rep. 896; Machine Co. *v.* Keifer, 134 Ill. 481, 25 N. E. Rep. 799; City of Peoria *v.* Simpson, 110 Ill. 301, 16 Am. & Eng. Enc. Law. 440–443, and notes; 2 Thomp. Neg. 1085. In City of Joilet *v.* Verley, 35 Ill. 58, it was held that if a plaintiff, while observing due care for his personal safety, was injured by the combined result of an accident and the negligence of a city or village, and without such negligence the injury would not have occurred, the city or village will be held liable, although the accident be the primary cause of the injury, if the consequences could, with common prudence and sagacity, have been foreseen and provided against. In that case it was stated: "If the accident would not have caused the injury but for the defect in the street, and that defect is the result of carelessness on the part of the city, and the plaintiff has used ordinary care, the city must be held liable;" citing many cases, both English and American, to sustain that announcement. In Baldwin *v.* Turnpike Co., 40 Conn. 238, it is said: "If the plaintiff is in the exercise of ordinary care and prudence, and the injury is attributable to the negligence of the defendants, combined with some accidental cause, to which the plaintiff has not negligently contributed, the defendants are liable." In Railroad Co. *v.* Dudgeon (Ill.), 56 N. E. Rep. 796, it was held that negligence in placing stones close to the track of a street-railway company, where it had piled them in making repairs, and against which a conductor struck, when thrown by the sudden starting of the car which he was attempting to board, and by which he was rolled under the car, is a concurrent cause of the injury, for which the company is liable, it being claimed in that case that the obstructions to the street were not, and could not have been, the proximate cause of the injury, and that the only efficient cause was the starting of the car, for which it is not answerable. In that case the court cited Bridge Co. *v.* Miller, 138 Ill. 465, 28 N. E. Rep. 1091, where, by reason of the want of the railing, some mules got onto the footpath, on which plaintiff was walking, and injured her;

and the court said: "In legal contemplation, the case is one where the injury was inflicted by the co-operating negligence of the bridge company and the persons in charge of the mules, and the rule is well settled 'that a person contributing to a tort, whether his fellow-contributors are men, natural or other forces or things, is responsible for the whole, the same as though he had done all without help,'" citing many cases in support of the doctrine. In the case of Terra Haute & Ind. R. R. Co. *v.* Buck, 96 Ind. 346, 3 Am. Neg. Cas. 148, it was held: "Where an injury to a passenger, caused by the negligence of the carrier, is such as to render the system of the injured man liable to take on disease, and to so enfeeble the system as to make it less likely to resist the inroads of the disease when it does set in, and death results, the death is, in legal contemplation, attributable to the negligence of the carrier." In Byrne *v.* Wilson, 15 Ir. C. L. 332 (1), a stagecoach, in which the plaintiff's intestate was a passenger, was thrown into a canal by the negligence of the driver, and the lock-keeper turned on the water, thereby causing the death, by drowning, of the passenger, and it was held that the proprietor of the coach was liable; the court saying: "The precipitation of the omnibus into the lock was certainly one cause, and, as it may be said, the primary cause, of her death, inasmuch as she would not have been drowned but for such precipitation. It is true that the subsequent letting of the water into the lock was the other and more proximate cause of her death, and that she would not have lost her life but for such subsequent act, which was not the necessary consequence of the previous precipitation, by the negligence of defendant's servants. But, in my opinion, defendant is not relieved from the liability for his primary neglect by showing that but for such subsequent act the death would not have ensued." The chief justice, in his opinion, said: "The law is clear that every party is liable, not only for the immediate consequences of his negligence, but also for the resulting consequences of his acts, whether those acts are acts of violence, or of negligence in breach of a duty which imposed the necessity of care and caution upon him." In Eaton *v.* Railroad Co., 11 Allen, 500, it was said by the court that it is no answer to an action by a passenger against a

1. In BYRNE *v.* WILSON, 15 Irish Com. Law. Rep. 332, it appeared that defendant was a carrier of persons, in whose omnibuses passengers were conveyed from one part of Dublin to another. Plaintiff's intestate was a passenger, who was by defendant's negligence precipitated into a canal and drowned. Defendant claimed that the real cause of the death was the opening of the lock by the keeper, thus letting in the water. Held, that, although the death of passenger was not immediately caused by the defendant's act, yet it was such a consequential result of defendant's act as would entitle the personal representatives of the deceased to maintain an action.

carrier that the negligence or trespass of a third party contributed to the injury. See Spooner *v.* Railroad Co., 54 N. Y. 230. A case exactly in point with the case at bar is City of Kansas *v.* Orr (Kan. Sup.), 61 Pac. Rep. 397, 8 Am. Neg. Rep. 36, where a switchman got his foot fastened between the planks and the rails of the track, and was killed by a car passing over him. It was held that the fact that it may have been the duty of the railway company, under its contract with the city, to construct and keep its tracks in a suitable and safe condition for those who have occasion to pass over the streets, does not discharge the city from its duty to the public to keep its streets in a reasonably safe condition, nor relieve it from the liability for the consequences of its negligence in that respect; citing many cases to sustain the doctrine. But, outside of the overwhelming weight of authority on this proposition, this court settled the questions involved in this cause in opposition to appellant's contention in White *v.* City of Ballard, 19 Wash. 284, 4 Am. Neg. Rep. 239, 53 Pac. Rep. 159; Howe *v.* Improvement Co., 21 Wash. 595, 59 Pac. Rep. 495, and Gray *v.* Washington Water Power Co. (Wash.), 11 Am. Neg. Rep. 561, 68 Pac. Rep. 360—where the question of the approximate cause is discussed at length, and where it was held that where a buggy attached to a runaway horse is overturned by street-car tracks negligently allowed to remain above the street level, the runaway cannot be said, as a matter of law, in an action against the car company, to be the proximate cause of an injury received by an occupant of the buggy. Upon the question of the duty of the city to keep its streets in reasonably safe condition for the use of pedestrians, see Mischke *v.* City of Seattle, 26 Wash. 616, 67 Pac. Rep. 357, and cases cited. The instruction complained of and the instruction asked for involve the point which we have just discussed, and there is no error committed by the court in giving or refusing to give the instruction when the whole instruction asked for and given is taken into consideration.

The judgment is affirmed.

REAVIS, Ch. J., and HADLEY, FULLERTON, ANDERS, MOUNT, and WHITE, JJ., concur.

ROBERTS v. PORT BLAKELY MILL CO.

Supreme Court, Washington, September, 1902.

DERAILMENT OF TRAIN; DEFECTIVE CAR WHEELS. — In an action for damages for causing the death of a conductor of a logging train in a derailment due, as alleged, to the use of defective cars that had wheels with worn flanges and that contained flaws discoverable by reasonable inspection, a nonsuit was properly denied where the evidence of plaintiff showed that the train was loaded as usual and was traveling at the usual speed, and that the track was not out of order; that the flanges on some of the car wheels were too thin to be safe, and had flaws in them, and that they broke at the time of the accident, and left marks on the rails where the cars left the track; that such a condition of the flanges made a car unsafe and dangerous, especially when rounding a curve, as the train was doing when the wreck occurred; that a reasonable and ordinary inspection would have discovered the defect; and no other cause of the accident was shown or intimated (1).

EVIDENCE. — Where a witness testified that after a derailment of a train he picked up pieces of broken flanges, and saw the car wheels with flanges broken off, and that he piled up the broken pieces that were thin and had flaws in them, and six months afterwards went to the place of the accident and picked up a piece of a broken flange there which, though he could not identify it as one he saw at the time of the accident, appeared like some he saw at the time, it was proper to admit the piece in evidence; both as illustrating the pieces the witness saw at the time of the accident, and for the jury to determine whether it was one of the pieces.

DECLARATIONS — *RES GESTÆ.* — Declarations of the general superintendent of the railroad, made while examining the wreck soon after his arrival at the scene, three hours after it occurred, that if the company used any more wheels of such make, he would not work any longer for it, and that he could not be putting new wheels under the cars all the time, were admissible against the company.

INSTRUCTION. — An instruction if you find that the plaintiff's death was not due to the negligence of the defendant, then you need consider nothing further, as your verdict in that case must be for the defendant, does not shift the burden of proof to the defendant, when the rest of the instruction clearly expressed that the burden was on the plaintiff to prove negligence.

INSTRUCTION. — An instruction defining negligence in general terms need not be given when the court specifically instructed on the negligence under consideration.

INSTRUCTION. — A refusal to instruct that negligence is never presumed is not error when there were repeated instructions that the burden was on plaintiffs to establish negligence.

1. See NOTES OF RECENT CASES OF DEFECTIVE APPLIANCES, at end of this case.

APPEAL from Superior Court, Mason County.

Action by Dora Roberts, in her own right and others, minors, by her and their guardian. From a judgment for plaintiffs, defendant appeals. *Judgment affirmed.*

S. P. RICHARDSON and PRESTON, CARR & GILMAN, for appellant.

TROY & FALKNER, for respondents.

MOUNT, J.—The respondent Dora Roberts is the widow, and Lillie Roberts and Hiram Roberts are the minor children, of Warren Roberts, deceased. In his lifetime Warren Roberts was in the employ of the appellant as a conductor on a logging railroad operated by it in Mason county, in this State. This road was a standard-gauge railroad, equipped with standard locomotive and with logging trucks, and was operated for the purpose of transporting saw logs from the forest where they were cut to tide-water. The road consisted of three sections — the first section extending from the forest where the logs were cut to a station called "Matlock;" the second, from Matlock to a station called "26;" and the third from 26 to a station called "New Kamilchie," at tide-water. On the 15th day of October, 1900, the said Roberts had charge of a train which was running from 26 to New Kamilchie. This train consisted of a locomotive and seventeen cars of logging trucks, loaded with saw logs. The train, which was running at the usual rate of speed, in rounding a curve was derailed, and Roberts was thrown from his position on the train to the ground and instantly killed. This suit was brought by his widow and minor children to recover damages for the loss of the husband and father; it being claimed that the train was derailed through the negligence of the defendant in failing to provide safe and suitable cars in this: that the flanges upon the wheels of the cars had become worn, and contained flaws which could have been discovered by reasonable inspection, and that one or more of these flanges broke, causing the train to leave the track, thereby causing the death af Warren Roberts. The cause was tried before the lower court and a jury. A verdict was rendered in favor of the plaintiffs for the sum of $4,000. From a judgment on the verdict defendant appeals. Errors of the trial court are alleged substantially as follows: 1. In denying defendant's motion for a nonsuit at the close of plaintiffs' evidence; 2, in denying plaintiffs' motion for a new trial; 3, in admitting in evidence a broken piece of flange picked up at the place of the accident several months thereafter; 4, in admitting in evidence the statement of George Tew, defendant's superintendent, made three or four hours after the accident; 5, in instructions given to the jury; and, 6, in refusing to give to the jury certain instructions requested by defendant.

1. We think the motion for a nonsuit was properly denied. The plaintiffs' evidence showed that the train was loaded as usual, and was traveling at the usual rate of speed, and that the track was not out of order. It also shows that flanges on some of the car wheels were too thin to be safe, and had flaws in them, and that they broke at the time of the accident, and left marks and indentations on the rails where the cars left the track; that such condition of the flanges make a car unsafe and dangerous, especially when rounding a curve; that a reasonable and ordinary inspection would have discovered the defect; and that the wreck occurred while rounding a curve. Here was sufficient cause for the accident. Conditions existed which rendered the operation of the train dangerous. The train was being properly operated. When the defective wheels struck the curve, they gave way and left the rail. It was the natural result. No other cause of the accident was shown or intimated by plaintiffs' evidence, nor in the subsequent evidence of appellant. This court said, in Walker *v.* McNeill, 17 Wash. 582, 30 Pac. Rep. 518: "Whenever a car or train leaves the track, it proves that either the track or machinery, or some portion thereof, is not in a proper condition, or that the machinery is not properly operated." The evidence here showed that the track was in order; that the train was properly operated; that the machinery was defective, and was liable to, and did, leave the track upon a curve; and that a reasonable inspection would have discovered the defect. There was but one cause shown for the accident, and for that cause the defendant is liable. It is argued by appellant that the entire case is one of surmises and conjectures, that the accident may have been caused by a rock or obstruction on the track or the letting off the brakes before the accident, or that there was some latent defect which no inspection could have discovered, or that a sound and sufficient wheel broke or left the rail; and the rule is invoked that "where the evidence establishes to a certainty that the accident resulted from one or two or more causes, for one or more of which the defendant would be responsible, and for one or more of which he would not be responsible, a verdict for the plaintiffs cannot be sustained." The trouble with this position is that the evidence does not show, nor is there any attempt to show, any other cause than the one above named. We think the rule laid down by the court in Walker *v.* McNeill, *supra*, is conclusive in this case. In Walker *v.* McNeill the ties of the roadbed were rotten, and when the derailed wheels struck them they broke in two. They were so decayed that they would not hold spikes, and the rails spread. In the case at bar the flanges of the car wheels were worn and danger-

ous. They contained flaws, and, when rounding a curve, were liable to, and did, leave the track. There is no distinction in principle between the two cases. The same argument used in this case for a reversal would have been applicable in that case. It does not apply to either for the same reason, viz., that there was but one cause shown for the accident, and for that cause defendant was liable.

2. The argument in support of the error assigned in denying the motion for a new trial is based upon the evidence of defendant. Defendant's witnesses testified, in substance, that the car wheels used were of approved and standard manufacture; that the cars were regularly and frequently inspected, and no defects were found; that all the flanges used were of sufficient strength; that the wheels broken in the wreck were sound and free from flaws; that the deceased conductor had full charge of the road and appliances on his run; that it was a part of his duty to look after the cars and keep them in order. The effect of this evidence was to negative the evidence of the plaintiffs, and, if true, it shows contributory negligence on the part of the deceased. This made a question of fact for the jury. After a careful reading of all the evidence, we think there was sufficient contradictory evidence on all the points named to go to the jury, and it was for the jury to weigh the same and determine the truth.

3. The court permitted plaintiffs to introduce in evidence a piece of broken flange picked up at the place of the wreck some six months after it occurred. One of the witnesses, who was a brakeman on the train at the time of the wreck, testified substantially that when the wreck occurred he was on the rear end of the train; that he jumped off, and in a few minutes thereafter went forward to the place where the wrecked cars were piled up; that he saw and examined several pieces of broken flange; that these broken pieces had flaws in them and were thin; that he saw the wheels with the flanges broken off, that he piled up the pieces; that about six months afterwards he went back to the place of the wreck with one of the plaintiff's attorneys, and near where the wreck occurred picked up the piece offered in evidence. He was not able to identify this particular piece as one which he had seen there at the time of the wreck, but said: "It was very similar to that in size and heft. * * * There were some longer, and some shorter, and some broken in different ways. * * * Q. Were there some that appeared to be like this? A. Yes, sir." We think, under this evidence, that the piece of flange was entitled to go to the jury, as the court in admitting it said, "for what it was worth;" that is, the jury had a right to determine whether it was or was not a piece of a flange which was broken from a car wheel at the time of the wreck. State *v.* Cushing, 17 Wash. 544, 558, 50 Pac.

Rep. 512; King *v.* Railroad Co., 72 N. Y. 607. Furthermore, we think the piece exhibited was competent as illustrative of the pieces which he had examined at the time of the accident, upon the principle that a drawing or model or photograph is admissible to explain oral evidence, in order that the jury may understand and apply the oral evidence in connection therewith.

4. Two of the plaintiffs' witnesses were permitted, over defendant's objection, to testify to certain statements made by George Tew, who was general superintendent and had the direction and management of the railroad. Mr. Tew arrived at the scene of the wreck about three hours after it occurred. Soon after his arrival he was examining the same. One of the witnesses testified: "I heard him say—He was looking at the flanges, and he said, if the company used any more Tacoma wheels, he would not work any longer for them." Another testified that Mr. Tew, at the same time and place, said: "This puts me in a devil of a fix, and I can't be putting new wheels under the cars all the time." We think these declarations were admissible, under the rule stated by Mr. Jones in the Law of Evidence (sec. 360), a part of which is as follows: "On the same principle reports to the general manager of a railway company concerning the circumstances and results of an accident, and also as to who was to blame therefor, made by the superintendent and conductor several days after the event, are incompetent. But, as we have already pointed out, there is a class of cases in which the rule that the declaration must be contemporaneous with the act is construed less strictly, and in which such declarations are admitted, although not technically contemporaneous, if they are spontaneous and tend to explain the transaction, and if so slight an interval of time has elapsed as to render premeditation improbable. Accordingly in numerous cases the declarations of employees and agents, made soon after an accident, have been received as part of the *res gestæ*." Mechem, Ag., sec. 715; McKelvey, Ev., p. 280; 1 Tayl. Ev., p. 519; Keyser *v.* Railway Co., 66 Mich. 390, 33 N. W. Rep. 867; Hooker *v.* Railway Co., 76 Wis. 542, 44 N. W. Rep. 1085; O'Connor *v.* Railway Co., 27 Minn. 166, 6 N. W. Rep. 481; Railway Co. *v.* Stein, 138 Ind. 254, 255, 31 N. E. Rep. 180; 32 N. E. Rep. 831; Mining Syndicate & Co. *v.* Rogers, 11 Colo. 6, 16 Pac. Rep. 719; People *v.* Vernon, 35 Cal. 49; Hall *v.* Insurance Co., 23 Wash. 610, 63 Pac. Rep. 505. The declarations of Mr. Tew were not the narration of a past event, but were the natural declarations growing out of the event, and were so nearly contemporaneous with the accident as to be held to be in the presence of it, and were made under such circumstances as necessarily to exclude the idea of design or deliberation. They were made by one having the control and management

of the road. Under these circumstances we think the declarations were admissible.

5. The court instructed the jury as follows: "The burden is upon the plaintiffs to establish that the death of the deceased was caused by the negligence of the defendant; and if you find that his death was not due to the negligence of the defendant, then you need consider nothing further, as your verdict in that case must be for the defendant. The negligence of the defendant company must be established by a preponderance of the evidence; and by a preponderance of the evidence is not meant the greatest number of witnesses, but it means the evidence which is most convincing to your minds." It is argued that the sentence, "And if you find that his death was not due to the negligence of the defendant, then you need consider nothing further, as your verdict in that case must be for the defendant," was contradictory of the rest of the instruction, and shifted the burden of proof to the defendant. But the whole instruction must be construed together. So construed, it was not error. It is true that this sentence is not technically correct; but this error is not of moment, especially when the intent of the whole is clearly expressed that the burden is upon the plaintiffs to prove negligence. This court has frequently held that where an isolated portion of an instruction, standing alone, may be technically erroneous, yet if the whole instruction, taken together, fairly states the law, it will be upheld. Seattle Gas, Electric Light & Motor Co. *v.* City of Seattle, 6 Wash. 101, 32 Pac. Rep. 1058; Duggan *v.* Boom Co., 6 Wash. 593, 34 Pac. Rep. 157; McQuillan *v.* City of Seattle, 13 Wash. 600, 43 Pac. Rep. 893; State *v.* Surry, 23 Wash. 655, 63 Pac. Rep. 557; Henry *v.* Railway Co., 24 Wash. 246, 64 Pac. Rep. 137; Miller *v.* Dumon, 24 Wash. 648, 64 Pac. Rep. 804.

6. It is alleged as error that the court refused to give instruction numbered 2, as requested by defendant. This instruction defined negligence in general terms, as "that said defendant did something or omitted to do something which an ordinarily prudent person under such circumstances would not have done or omitted to do;" but the court specifically instructed the jury as to the duty of the company to provide reasonably safe cars and wheels, and to make reasonable inspection thereof, and also that if the jury found, by a preponderance of the evidence, that the death of deceased was caused by any defects in the cars or wheels, and that such defects could have been discovered by reasonable inspection, and that defendant failed to make such inspection, it was liable. We think this was sufficient, and that it was not necessary to give a general definition of negligence, where the jury are correctly instructed upon the specific negligence under consideration.

It is also alleged as error that the court refused to give instruction No. 14 requested by defendant. This instruction is to the effect that negligence is never presumed, but must always be proven, and that it was not the duty of the defendant to explain how the accident occurred, or to show that it was not negligent. In the instructions given the court repeatedly told the jury that the burden was upon the plaintiffs to establish negligence, and, while the court did not specifically state that it was not the duty of the defendant to explain how the accident occurred, yet we think, in view of the instructions impressing it upon the minds of the jury that they must find by a preponderance of the evidence that the defendant was negligent and that this negligence caused the injury, it was not error to omit the requested instruction.

It is complained that the court refused to give an instruction requested concerning circumstantial evidence. While there was some circumstantial evidence in the case, the case, as we have seen, did not rest upon this evidence, and for that reason it was not error to refuse it.

The errors assigned as 10, 11 and 12 have reference to instructions to the effect that, if the jury find that the accident occurred by reason of a defective car wheel, still the jury must find that the defect was one which was known, or ought to have been known, to the defendant, and that if the defect was latent, or if the wheel was of standard manufacture and of a kind proven safe, even though it contained a flaw which could not have been discovered by proper carefulness, then the defendant would not be liable. Upon these questions the court told the jury: "If, therefore, you find from a preponderance of the evidence that the accident which caused the death of the deceased was due to any defect in any wheel or wheels of defendant's cars, by the flanges being worn down too thin, or to any flaw or break in the flanges, and that such defect, if any existed, could have been discovered by reasonably careful inspection of the wheels, and that defendant failed to make such inspection, then your verdict should be for the plaintiffs. * * * The company is not required to guard against defects which cannot be discovered by reasonable care, but they are required to discover defects which can be disclosed by reasonably careful inspection. * * * The master is bound to use appliances which are not defective in construction; but, as between him and his employees, he is not bound to use such as are of the best or most approved description. If they are such as are in general use, that is all that is required. The employer is bound to furnish machinery and appliances that are of ordinary character and of reasonable safety. Whatever is according to the general, usual, and ordinary course adopted by those in the same business is reasonably safe within the meaning of the law." We think these instructions as given covered the instructions requested, and were as favorable to the defendant as it was entitled to. Upon the whole, we think the instructions given fairly stated the law of the case, and that there was no substantial error in the trial.

The judgment will therefore be affirmed.

REAVIS, Ch. J., and FULLERTON, DUNBAR, HADLEY, WHITE, and ANDERS, JJ., concur.

NOTES OF RECENT CASES OF DEFECTIVE APPLIANCES.

1. **Railroad engine or car.**
   - *Brake.*
   - *Wheels.*
   - *Handhold.*
2. **Machinery.**
   - *Saw.*
   - *Knives.*
   - *Valve.*
3. **Derrick or crane.**
4. **Elevator or hoist.**
5. **Rope or cable.**
6. **Miscellaneous.**

1. Railroad car or engine.

Brake.
Handhold.
Wheels.

In BUDGE *v.* MORGAN'S LA. & TEXAS R. & S. S. CO. (La. 1902), 32 So. 535, plaintiff was a brakeman in defendant's employ, and after coupling several cars to the switch engine, and it and the first car had passed, he mounted the side of the next car to go to the next switch, and just as he reached the top of the car, the rear truck, instead of taking the turn into the switch, mounted the rail or split the switch and went off the track, causing the car to jolt and list in such a way that the plaintiff was either thrown off, or, being apprehensive that the car was about to turn over, jumped off with the result that one of his legs was caught between the derailed truck and the rail of the track and so badly crushed that it had to be amputated. The track was in perfect condition. The alleged cause of the derailment was the defective manner of fastening the truck to the car so that the truck was immobile and held on to the straight track instead of taking the curve like those that preceded it. The evidence was contradictory, but would seem to warrant the conclusion that the derailment of the car was caused by the displacement of the hanger pin and the loosening of the upper friction plate, resulting in the locking of the truck to such an extent as to prevent its taking the curve into the switch. A judgment for plaintiff was affirmed. The court said that due care required the master or some one competent and qualified to inspect and look after the condition of such appliances and see that they were kept in repair. This duty was personal to the master.

In SPRINGS *v.* SOUTHERN R'Y. CO. (N. C. 1902), 41 S. E. 100, the plaintiff was a switchman, and had been working with a regular switch engine supplied with foot boards on each end, upon which he stood when the engine was in motion. This engine getting out of order, the defendant used road engines instead for the purpose of switching the cars. The plaintiff was ordered by the man who had the right to employ and discharge him to ride on the pilots or cowcatchers of these engines while they were switching, instead of the gangway behind the engineer or behind the fireman, where he had ridden until ordered as above, and where he was comparatively safe. After riding as directed on the pilot for ten days, he was injured. It was the habit of switchmen to jump from the pilot of the moving engine in order to do the work more quickly, and no objection had been made to this course by the officers of the company. On the day of the accident the plaintiff attempted to jump from the moving engine, as he had been in the habit of doing, when his foot was caught between the ribs or slats of the pilot, and he was thrown to the ground, the engine ran over his legs, and both had to be amputated. The engine was moving slowly at the time. A judgment for plaintiff was affirmed. The court said that it was competent for the plaintiff to show that he had complained of the road engines and had been promised a safer engine on which to work.

In NORFOLK & W. R'Y. CO. *v.* PHILLIPS (Va. 1902), 41 S. E. 726, the plaintiff's intestate was a section hand in the employ of defendant company, and on the day of the accident had been ordered, with four other section hands, to go down the road on a hand car, by their foreman. At the point that they left there was located a mine where cars belonging to the railroad were left to be filled with iron ore, and when loaded were taken away by the defendant's engines, and others left to be filled. An engine had arrived just before the deceased and his fellow-laborers departed on the hand car, and two or three brakemen were allowing two of the loaded ore cars to slowly drift by gravitation to a siding, where they would be coupled to by the engine when it had got rid of the empty cars that it had brought. The front loaded ore car had defective brakes. One brake was without a panel or finger latch, which is kicked by the brakeman into the cogs of the ratchet wheel to hold the brake in its place; the brake was good in every other respect; the other brake on this car was defective in its chain being so long that it could not be wound around the brake rod and give the brake its full power. The second of the loaded cars had only one good brake, but it appeared that one good brake is usually sufficient under ordinary conditions. The brakeman who was on the front car finding he could not stop the car by holding the brake that had no panel, he went to the other brake, and finding that did not hold either, and the speed of the cars increasing, there being a down grade to the next station, he jumped off, and the cars ran wild and soon overtook the hand car with the plaintiff's intestate and the other section hands, and killed four of them. There was no fault on the part of the deceased. There was a verdict and judgment for plaintiff, which was reversed because of error in the instructions. The court said that whether the brakeman who knew of the defective brakes was acting as the *alter ego* of the defendant or the negligence was that of a fellow-servant, was for the jury.

In TEXAS & P. R. CO. *v.* ALLEN (U. S. C. C. A. 1902), 114 Fed. 177, the plaintiff's intestate was a brakeman and was killed by falling from the side of a freight car while the train was moving. The handhold was fastened to the car by lag or wood screws that were not properly screwed in the wood or the wood was rotten, thereby rendering the handhold insecure. There was also evidence that the car had been inspected within a short time prior to the death of the deceased and also the nature of the inspection. A judgment for plaintiff was affirmed.

In CHOCTAW, O. & G. R. Co. *v.* HOLLOWAY (U. S. C. C. A. 1902), 114 Fed. 458, the plaintiff was fireman on defendant's engine that was not provided with brakes, and in the night-time, while the engine was running backwards without a light and without an employee on the tender in front to give warning of danger, a collision occurred with a horse which was caught in a trestle and the plaintiff was caught between the tender and the engine when the air was applied to the brake upon the tender and seriously injured. The plaintiff knew that there was neither light nor employee on the tender in front, but he did not know of the absence of brakes on the engine. A judgment for plaintiff was affirmed. The court said that the failure to provide the engine with brakes, in the absence of evidence excusing it, was, as matter of law, evidence of the want of reasonable care to provide a reasonably safe locomotive engine. Collisions and accidents may be reasonably anticipated as the natural and probable consequence of such failure. The plaintiff knew and assumed the risk of running the engine backward, tender foremost, in the night without any light or employee on the forward end of the tender, but his contributory negligence in that regard was no defense to his action for negligence in failing to supply the engine with brakes where he did not know it.

In MEXICAN CENT. R'Y Co. *v.* TOWNSEND (U. S. C. C. A. 1902), 114 Fed. 737, the plaintiff was a brakeman and was injured by a fall from the top of a car caused by the breaking of a running board that there was evidence to warrant the jury to find to have been either rotten or sound. The brace which supported the end of the board was loose and was hanging down after the accident, but the evidence was not conclusive whether it was in that condition when the car was last inspected or when it should have been inspected. A peremptory instruction for plaintiff was given by the trial court and the judgment entered thereon was reversed, the court saying that the case should have been left to the jury.

2. Machinery.

Saw.
Knives.
Valve.

In MONTEITH *v.* KOKOMO WOOD ENAMELING Co. (Ind. 1902), 64 N. E. 610, a servant who was injured by reason of a violation of a statute requiring machinery of every description to be guarded had a right of action thereunder, and a complaint that alleged the injury and that the saw that caused the injury was unguarded was sufficient without alleging that the plaintiff did not know that the same was unguarded and the danger resulting therefrom. A judgment entered on a demurrer to the complaint was reversed. The court said that under the common law the servant would assume the risk of manifest danger, but not where a statute imposes the duty on the master of guarding machinery. A statute of the latter class imposed a specific obligation, and a violation was an unlawful act or omission.

In MULL *v.* CURTICE BROTHERS Co. (N. Y. Sup. 1902), 74 App. Div. 561, the plaintiff was employed in defendant's canning factory and it was her duty every afternoon to take apart and clean a meat-cutting machine operated by a belt which could be moved from a tight to a loose pulley and back again by means of a belt shifter. On the day of the accident, after cleaning the machine with the belt on the loose pulley, she attempted to readjust the parts, which was not a part of her duty, and while her hand was in the hopper for that purpose, the machine started and cut off her fingers. A finding was warranted that the starting of the machine was caused by the shifter failing to hold the belt in position and defective. There was evidence that the foreman had been notified of the defect and that it would be repaired by the repairer. The person whose duty it was to reassemble the parts of the machine testified that he never put his hand in the hopper when readjusting the parts. A judgment of nonsuit was affirmed. The court said that the plaintiff assumed the risk, knowing the defective condition of the machine, and that the injury was attributable in part, at least, to plaintiff's act in engaging in work not within the line of her duty and to her own negligence.

In HOES v. OCEAN STEAMSHIP CO. OF SAVANNAH (N. Y. Sup. 1900), 56 App. Div. 259, aff'd 170 N. Y. 581 (1902), the plaintiff's intestate was an oiler in the employ of the defendant on its steamship, and was in the act of turning on the throttle valve as was his duty, to let steam into the feed pump, when the bonnet and stem of the valve blew out, steam escaped and scalded him to death. There was evidence that the valve had been removed by the employees of a firm that had made extensive repairs to the machinery. The exact cause of the happening of the accident was not apparent. If the bonnet of the valve had been screwed on, as it should have been, it could not have blown out without tearing the threads, and they were not injured at all. A judgment for plaintiff was affirmed. The court said that it was the duty of the employer, after this machinery had been in the hands of the machinist, for the purpose of making the extensive repairs, which seem to have been made upon this ship on this occasion, to see that the machinery was in proper order before it was attempted to be used.

In GULF, C. & S. F. R. Co. v. HADEN (Tex. Civ. App. 1902), 68 S. W. 530, the plaintiff's intestate was an employee of the defendant in its machine shops. He worked at a lathe machine and was a skilful workman. The power to run the machine came from the main shaft overhead, and was transmitted by a belt which encircled the main shaft, and a smaller shaft attached to the machine. There were two pulleys on one of the shafts, one being loose and the other tight. When the belt was on the tight pulley the machine was in operation; when on the loose pulley the machine was at a standstill. A shifter provided, permitted the operator to shift the belt to either pulley and thus control the machine. The deceased found it necessary to change the gearing of the machine and shifted the belt to the loose pulley and brought the machine to a standstill. While changing the gearing the belt somehow got back on the tight pulley, the machine was started and the hand of the deceased was so mangled that he died from the injuries. A judgment for plaintiff was affirmed. The court said that the evidence showed that when such machine was properly constructed and in proper repair it would remain at a standstill until started by someone, and that by the use of ordinary care the machine and appliances could be kept in good condition. There was evidence that the deceased had properly shifted the belt. The machine was not started by any other person. It could have been started in motion by only two causes,— either the failure to properly shif the belt, or some defect in the machine or its appliances. The verdict of the jury excludes the first theory, and it follows that the moving cause was some defect in the machinery. The evidence warranted the finding that the injury was caused by the negligence of appellant.

In CROOKER *v.* PACIFIC LOUNGE AND MATTRESS CO. (Wash. 1902), 69 Pac. 359, the plaintiff was a minor, nineteen years of age, and employed in defendant's factory running a rip saw that had no guard, but had been assured that a guard would be placed on it. The machinery was stopped for repairs after he had been working two weeks, but no guard was put on the saw. On resuming work the next day he was given some thick pieces of wood to saw, which was more dangerous work than sawing thin pieces, but the plaintiff was not aware of it. After he had ripped some six or seven pieces a sliver or edging about an inch square caught the teeth of the saw, and was hurled forward of the saw, striking plaintiff in the right eye and injuring it. A nonsuit was granted; the judgment entered thereon was reversed. The court said that the fact that the machine in operation is in ordinary use is a material one, but it is not an absolute rule that this showing alone in all cases relieves the master from the charge of negligence. While the master is not required to procure the newest and best machines or to enter the field of experiment to provide additional safeguards, to lessen the danger of machinery in ordinary use, he must give heed to the deductions of experience. The question whether the plaintiff reasonably relied on the promise to put the guard on the rip saw at the time he was injured was for the jury.

In THE NORDFARER (U. S. Dist. Ct. N. Y. 1901), 115 Fed. 416, the libelant was a rigger on the steamship, and while taking in the slack of the line of the cargo boom, that was hoisted by means of the winch, a pin inserted in machinery of the winch proved insufficient, that caused the winch to become ineffective and the boom to fall. The accident happened so quickly that the libelant's leg was caught in the running rope and carried against the hatch covering and broken. The pin that was used was an ordinary nail that was too small to fill the aperture for which it was intended. Other nails had been used for the like purpose for eighteen months, and none had proved defective. The nails were only temporary expedients, not intended for the use to which they were put and palpably not adjusted to the machine. Provision had seemingly been made for the employment of a piece of steel that was adjusted to and would fill the place. The court said that the claimant should have observed what was required, for the mechanism was plain to see. That the nails had been used eighteen months without accident was due to good fortune. Eighteen months of negligence does not establish the fulfillment of duty. A decree for $2,650 damages for libelant was ordered.

8. Derrick or crane.

In CUNNINGHAM *v.* JOURNAL CO. (Mo. App. 1902), 68 S. W. 592, the defendant was installing a new printing press in its place of business, and the press being of great weight, machinery was required to put it together. Over the foundation for the press, about ten feet from the floor, the defendant had constructed the machinery, which consisted of two hooks or brackets, composed of cast-iron, attached to the ceiling, about twelve feet apart, which supported an iron rail on which ran a carriage moving on two wheels; a pulley was attached to this carriage, through which a chain passed which could be attached to the object sought to be lifted or carried. A man at the free end of this chain could lift a great weight. All the apparatus except the block and tackle belonged to the defendant. The company that sold the press to the defendant had an expert machinist present to superintend the work, and that company owned the block and tackle. The plaintiff was an employee of defendant, and while assisting in hoisting a casting, and being at the end of the chain, one of the said brackets broke and the block and tackle fell on plaintiff's hand. It was shown that the brackets were of a character in general use, and had proven safe and been tested in lifting a similar press when the weights had been as great. The break, it was agreed, was what was called a "clean break," there were no indications of a previous weakening. A judgment for plaintiff was reversed. The court said that the facts in the case showed that the breaking of the hanger was an accident which the experienced machinist superintending the work "could not with ordinary care have foreseen or guarded against." It was "a hazard incident to the business" which the plaintiff was engaged in and which he thereby assumed.

In MULLIGAN *v.* BALLON (N. Y. Sup. 1902), 73 App. Div. 486, plaintiff's intestate was in the employ of the defendant, with others, taking railroad ties from the hold of a boat and placing them upon a railroad car that was alongside the boat. The appliance used to take the ties from the hold of the boat resembled a derrick, and was so arranged that when the ties cleared the deck of the boat they would of their own motion swing over the car. To prevent this until such time as the signal was given a guy rope was provided, which was either held by a person having that work in charge, or else fastened to pins in the side of the boat. On the day of the accident the plaintiff's intestate and another employee were on the car receiving ties as they were hoisted from the boat, and another servant had the duty of looking after the guy rope. Immediately prior to the accident a load of ties had been raised and placed on the car, and while the intestate and his fellow-workmen were placing them another load was raised, and after it cleared the boat the employee in charge of the guy rope having either neglected to secure it, or else having carelessly let go of it, the ties swung over the car, struck the intestate, and so injured him that he died soon after. A judgment of nonsuit was affirmed. The court said that the proof did not establish negligence on the part of the defendant. The appliance was the usual one adopted for the purpose, and was in repair. The negligence was that of a fellow-servant.

In WALTERS *v.* GEORGE A. FULLER CO. (N. Y. Sup. 1902), 74 App. Div. 388, the plaintiff's intestate was employed by defendant about the construction of a building in the center of which was placed a derrick used in hoisting iron work. The derrick consisted of a mast and movable boom supported by a stiff wooden leg at the back, and also by guys which ran in different directions from the top of the mast. The boom was so long that it could not be moved past the guys without removing them, and the safety of the operation of the derrick depended upon the watchfulness of servants, whose duty it was to stop the boom when it had swung beyond a detached guy rope, until the guy rope had been replaced. The deceased and another employee were ordered by a subforeman to get on the ball or hook of the derrick, go to the street and attach to the derrick an iron column to be placed in the building. This method of operation was the usual one employed. Both men got on the ball as ordered, and after the boom was swung around and the hook had proceeded some distance, the entire derrick collapsed and the injuries were sustained that resulted in the death of the deceased. At the time of the accident all the guys had been removed except one, that with the stiff leg was supporting the entire structure. The court said that it could not be said that as matter of law the duty imposed by the statute requiring a person employing another about the construction of a building to erect safe mechanical appliances had been complied with. That the negligence of a co-servant contributing to the accident will not relieve the master from liability. That it was for the jury to say whether the deceased having full knowledge upon the subject assumed the risk of the employment. A judgment of nonsuit was reversed.

In O'Dowd v. Burnham (Pa. Superior Ct. 1902), 19 Pa. Sup. Ct. R. 464, the plaintiff was in the employ of defendants in their locomotive works, and was ordered by the foreman, who was in charge of three or four men in the boiler shop, to transfer, by means of a traveling crane, certain material from where it had been delivered to where it was to be used. The material consisted of heavy pieces of iron castings, and were made fast to the crane by slings, which consisted of short chains with either a hook or a bolt and nut at one end to be inserted in the holes in the pieces to be moved, and at the other end a ring which was placed on the hook of the chain depending from the crane. There were a number of these slings of different sizes and designs for use in moving pieces of different weight. The plaintiff directed the removal of these castings, fastened them to the slings, and gave directions to the man operating the crane where to take them. The foreman was present when one of the hooks broke, and when shown it and asked whether a man would be sent to fix it, told the plaintiff "no; go on with your work." Two hours afterwards, after the foreman had gone home, while another piece of casting was being moved, another hook used by the plaintiff and selected by him from four others broke, and the casting fell on his foot and crushed it. A judgment for plaintiff was reversed. The court said that the hook that broke in the afternoon had nothing to do with the accident. There were several chains to select from, and if the hook was, in his judgment, not strong enough to lift the casting, he was bound to take notice of an obvious danger. It is not alleged that the tools furnished were old or worn or had not been inspected, nor that they were in an unsafe condition. If another hook had been used the accident might not have happened. Employers are liable for consequences not of danger but of negligence.

4. Elevator or hoist.

In Boyle v. Columbian Fireproofing Co. (Mass. 1902), 64 N. E. 726, the plaintiff's intestate was an employee of defendant company that was one of a number of contractors engaged in constructing a building. The intestate was killed by the fall of a hoist, used to carry material, as he and two other workmen were riding down on it after the noon hour to eat their dinner. The hoist was erected by defendant, whose superintendent warned the men not to ride on it, but who rode on it himself and told the men to ride on it, as it saved time and they rode on it in the presence of the superintendent. The hoist was operated by an iron cable that had been injured by the use of a monkey wrench in hammering the cable to get it through the eye bolt attached to the hoist, but the defect was not apparent to the eye. There was also a defect in not having used a thimble in attaching the cable to the bolt. A judgment for plaintiff was affirmed. The court said that the deceased did not assume the risk, and that whether he rode on the hoist by invitation was for the jury. [There were three actions brought against the COLUMBIAN FIREPROOFING Co., for the deaths of three employees, namely, by BOYLE. MURPHY and DUNCAN, administrators, of the deceased, tried at the same time as the BOYLE case and verdicts were rendered for plaintiff in each case. See 64 N. E. 726.]

In INGRAM *v.* FOSBURGH (N. Y. Sup. 1902), 73 App. Div. 129, the plaintiff's intestate was foreman for the defendant, who was a contractor constructing a building in which were two elevators installed for the purpose of carrying brick and mortar and so constructed that when one elevator was drawn up, the other would be drawn down by means of a cable fastened to the bottom of each car by a bolt and nut, and wound around a drum operated by an engine in charge of an engineer also in the employ of the defendant. On the day of the accident the intestate stepped on one of the elevators to go to the third floor and as he was about to step off, it fell to the ground carrying him with it and causing him to sustain injuries resulting in death. The theory of plaintiff was that the nut that secured the bolt to the bottom of the elevator became loose and the bolt pulled out, causing the elevator to drop. The defendant's theory was that the nut was properly fastened and that the accident occurred through the failure of the engineer to stop the engine when the descending elevator reached the bottom of the shaft and that in consequence the bolt was stripped from the nut on that elevator, which caused it to ascend and the one on which the deceased was in to drop to the ground. There was no evidence that the nut on the elevator on which the intestate was riding was loose. A judgment for plaintiff was reversed. The court said that assuming the plaintiff's theory to be correct no recovery could be had upon the evidence presented. The elevators were for the purpose of lifting brick and mortar to the men on the different floors and not for carrying passengers. The elevator had answered the purpose and no previous accident had happened. There was nothing to indicate that the bolt or nut had been injured by use or that the elevator was less safe than when first operated. There was no occasion for employees to ride on the elevators, as ladders were provided for them, and the deceased knew it was against the rules to ride on the elevators.

5. Rope or cable.

In MOMENCE STONE CO. *v.* GROVES (Ill. 1902), 64 N. E. 335, the plaintiff was employed by defendant in its quarry, where the business of crushing stone was carried on. Cars loaded with stone were drawn up an inclined track by means of a cable attached to the cars by a hook. Plaintiff was standing beside the track when the hook broke and a loaded car started rapidly down the incline toward him. A sudden warning was given, and, plaintiff turning around, saw the car coming and tried to escape, but was overtaken by the car, that ran over his leg, which he lost. There was evidence that the track was uneven and rough and caused a strain on the hook, and also that when the pieces of the hook were picked up after the accident there was a visible flaw. A judgment for plaintiff was affirmed.

In KELLY *v.* HOGAN (N. Y. Appellate Term, 1902), 37 Misc. 761, plaintiff was employed as a longshoreman by the defendants, who were stevedores, and was injured by the breaking of a rope while engaged in putting slings on barrels of beef that were then hoisted by the rope. He and another employee had just attached two barrels to the fall and had seen them go up, and then rolled in two other barrels, and were reefing the sling to them when the two barrels that had been hooked on before fell and struck him and severely injured him. The breaking of the rope caused the barrels to fall. Great care was exercised by the defendants in selecting the ropes used, and the one that broke had been tested before put in use. The load that was being carried when the rope broke was small compared to the ordinary carrying power of such a rope. The cause of the break was unknown. The rope had been used only a short time. A judgment for plaintiff was reversed. The court said that from the evidence there was no negligence shown on the part of the defendants and the complaint should have been dismissed.

6. Miscellaneous.

In ROBERTS *v.* INDIANAPOLIS ST. R'Y CO. (Ind. 1902), 64 N. E. 217, the plaintiff was a conductor, and was required, as part of his duty, to help the motorman turn the car on a turntable at the end of the route, by shoving the car with their backs and shoulders. When the turntable was in good repair, this could be done with little exertion. At the time of the injury the table was out of repair, so that the rails scraped against the side of the turntable pit. The conductor with the assistance of some passengers had turned the car three times, but the next time he and the motorman attempted to turn the car without other assistance and the plaintiff overexerted himself and caused the injury. A judgment for defendant was affirmed. The court said that the plaintiff was under no obligation to overexert or strain himself, and was guilty of contributory negligence in so doing. That the company could not anticipate or foresee that by reason of its failure to repair the table there was any necessity to protect plaintiff against his own voluntary action, in subjecting himself to the overexertion or strain, which resulted in the injury of which he complains.

In EAST JELLICO COAL CO. *v.* STEWART (Ky. 1902), 68 S. W. 624, the plaintiff was employed as a driver of mules, that hauled the cars in and out of the defendant's mine. When the agent who employed him directed him to get the mule, he asked if it was safe, as he had heard that some of the mules kicked when he was at the mine before, and the boss answered that the mule was safe. He took the mule and during the day was kicked in the face by the mule. There was evidence that the mule was vicious. A judgment for plaintiff was affirmed. The court said that the man who employed the plaintiff made the statements, that he was the agent of the company in this matter and his statements bound the company.

In SMITH *v.* KING (N. Y. Sup. 1902), 74 App. Div. 1, the plaintiff was employed by defendant to move gravel with a horse and cart that were furnished by the defendant. The harness that the defendant furnished was not provided with a girth passing under the belly of the horse so as to prevent the cart from tipping backwards and throwing the shafts up. The plaintiff called the attention of the foreman to the defect and was told to go on with his work. The plaintiff then pulled out the tailboard, when the shafts flew up and the falling cart hit the plaintiff on the side, throwing him down upon a scow and breaking his leg. A verdict for plaintiff was set aside and a judgment entered thereon was reversed. The court said that there was no evidence that the plaintiff had any knowledge of the danger which he would incur by continuing to use the harness as it was, so as to render him chargeable with contributory negligence as matter of law.

He was a lad eighteen years of age, and although he was aware of the absence of the girth, he could hardly have been reasonably expected to refuse to obey an order of the foreman "to take his cart out of there," and the case falls within that class where it has been held not to be deemed conclusive evidence of contributory negligence that a plaintiff continues to employ unsafe appliances when he does so by express orders of the defendant, and is not fully aware of the effects to be expected from obeying such orders.

In FLET v. HUNTER ARMS CO. (N. Y. Sup. 1902), 74 App. Div. 572, the plaintiff was employed to do general work in defendant's factory, and had been there twelve years. On the day of the accident the defendant's foreman ordered the plaintiff and two other employees to move a bedplate of iron weighing about 500 pounds, that was lying on a bench about two feet from the floor. Finding the bedplate too heavy to move, they so informed the foreman, who thereupon picked up an old broom handle, placed it under the bedplate, directed plaintiff's associates to take hold of it, one at each end, and the plaintiff to take hold of the end of the bedplate behind them, and thus carry it. They did as directed, and had proceeded but a short distance when the broom handle broke, the bedplate fell to the floor, striking the plaintiff's leg and seriously injuring him. A judgment for plaintiff was reversed. The court said that it appeared that there were plenty of sticks about the shop with which the plate could have been safely carried. The work being done was of the simplest character, and the plaintiff was quite as well qualified to judge of the suitableness of the stick for the purpose, if he had examined it, as was the foreman. The broom handle was not furnished by the defendant for the purpose of moving the bedplate in question or for use in connection with work of that character. The relation of the foreman to the other workmen was that of co-employee, except as to such acts performed by him as were embraced in the duties of the defendant.

In ORR v. SOUTHERN BELL TELEPHONE, ETC., CO. (N. C. 1902), 41 S. E. 880, the plaintiff had been in the employ of the defendant for one day, when he was injured by the fall of a telephone pole that he and other employees, under the supervision of the foreman, were taking down. After digging around the pole it was found that they had no pikes to take it down, so they used their shoulders instead, the pikes being at the tool house, six miles away. The plaintiff contended that if they had pikes the pole would not have fallen. The defendant excuses itself for not having the pikes on the ground that the tool house was open in the morning and the men were told to go in and bring out the tools. The court said that was not a satisfactory answer. That the boss was there, and it would seem rather officious on the part of the plaintiff, who had just been hired, to have undertaken to supersede the boss. It was the duty of the defendant to furnish the plaintiff with proper tools and appliances, and it was not the duty of the plaintiff to furnish them.

In CHASE v. SPARTANBURG R. GAS & ELEC. CO. (S. C. 1902), 41 S. E. 899, the plaintiff was an employee of defendant, and while on the street engaged in his work, he was injured by being struck by another employee, who fell from one of the defendant's poles. The negligence charged was the furnishing to the employee who fell a defective belt and tackle to sustain him while suspended over the sidewalk, and also the careless manner in which the said employee fastened the belt. A judgment for defendant was reversed on the ground of improper instruction, which declared that the liability of the employee who fell was the correct standard by which to measure the liability of the employer and limiting the cause of the insufficient fastening to the personal negligence of the same employee. The court said that a servant as well as the master is liable in all cases when his negligent act is the direct and proximate cause of the injury sustained by a third person. The law imputes to the master the knowledge of the danger, though latent, in the use of instruments with which he provides his servants, and he cannot escape liability unless he should show that by the use of diligence he could not have discovered the danger.

STEBER v. CHICAGO AND NORTHWESTERN RAILWAY COMPANY.

Supreme Court, Wisconsin, September, 1902.

PERSON KILLED WHILE CROSSING TRACK — CONTRIBUTORY NEGLIGENCE — RULE AS TO LOOKING AND LISTENING. — The duty of a person about to step upon a railway track to look both ways and listen and to discover those dangers which can be readily discovered by the exercise of ordinary attention, and not to go upon the track in the face of such danger, is absolute, and the fact that a person may have the rights of a passenger as regards care by the railway company, and that there was no other way of reaching her destination than by going across the railway track, and in so crossing was killed, does not constitute any exception to the general rule stated (1).

Rule as to looking and listening applied, where plaintiff's wife was killed while crossing track from station at night, and her contributory negligence held to preclude recovery in action for damages for her death (2).

APPEAL from Circuit Court, Langlade County.

Action by James Steber, as administrator of the estate of Anna First, against the Chicago & Northwestern Railway Company. From a judgment for defendant, plaintiff appeals. *Judgment affirmed.*

Action for damages, caused, as alleged, to Wenzl First by the wrongful conduct of defendant in that its servants negligently operated one of its locomotive engines so as to produce his wife's death. The deceased attempted to cross defendant's railway track at the intersection thereof with one of the public streets of the city of Antigo in the night-time, while one of its switch engines was rapidly approaching such locality. She was struck by the engine and so injured that she died.

1. See NOTE on STOP, LOOK AND LISTEN, in 9 AM. NEG. REP. 408-416.

2. See vols. 11 and 12 Am. Neg. Cas., for actions arising out of accidents to persons on track, from earliest times to 1897. Subsequent actions to date are reported in vols. 1-12 AM. NEG. REP., and the current number of that series of Reports.

The particular acts of omission and commission constituting the alleged negligence are as follows: Operating the engine at an unlawful rate of speed; neglect to ring the engine bell as the approach was made to the railway crossing; failure to have a watchman or flagman at the crossing as required by the city ordinances of the city of Antigo; failure to maintain gates at the crossing as required by the city; and failure to give any notice to persons, about to use the crossing for legitimate purposes, of the approach thereto of the switch engine. All the allegations of negligence were put in issue by the answer, and contributory negligence was pleaded as a defense.

The undisputed evidence was to the following effect: The accident happened on a dark, rather stormy night. There was no street light at the crossing. The situation was such that, as a person approached the crossing from the east, as the deceased did on the occasion of the accident, there was no obstruction to prevent her seeing an engine coming from the north for a distance amply sufficient to enable her, in the exercise of ordinary care, to avoid being injured by it. The railway tracks ran north and south. The depot was just south of the street, which crossed the tracks at right angles, and upon which deceased was walking when she was injured. Prior to the injury she was at the depot with two acquaintances, a man and his mother, presumably to meet a person who was expected soon to arrive on a train from the south. She remained on the depot platform till the train arrived and such person alighted therefrom. The four then started north on the platform, walking on the easterly side of the main track till they were within the limits of the street. The engine of the passenger train was located across the sidewalk on the southerly side of the street. West of the main track was a switch track. A headlight was on the passenger engine. It threw its light across the region common to the street and the railway track. The deceased and her companions, desiring to go to a point west of the tracks, passed into the street and then somewhat northwesterly so as to avoid the passenger engine. Two of deceased's companions proceeded first. She, accompanied by the other, walked a little way behind them. The former got across the switch track, and just as the latter stepped upon it the switch engine, backing up from the north, struck her, inflicting fatal injuries.

The substance of the evidence material to be considered, in addition to such as has been referred to in a general way, is as follows: John McArthur, a witness for plaintiff, said he did not see any light on the rear end of the switch engine; that it was backing up when it struck deceased; that he could not say but that there was a light on the engine; that just before the accident he was on the depot platform near the passenger engine and heard the switch engine coming. Peter Jagla, a witness for plaintiff, said he was one of the party accompanying the deceased at the time of her injury; that he and his sister went ahead while his mother accompanied the deceased; that he hurried up to get across the track ahead of the switch engine; that the engine on the passenger train made some noise; that he saw the switch engine just as he got on the track; that he had to jump to get across; that he did not see any light on the engine, nor hear any bell; that he made a written statement of the circumstances characterizing the accident shortly after it occurred, in which he said that he heard a bell upon the engine and saw the engine coming about the time he crossed the track. The woman who was in the immediate company of the deceased at the instant of the accident said she did not see any light on the engine nor hear any engine bell; that she and deceased were about forty feet behind her son and daughter; that she saw they got across and thought she and her companion could too; that she did not see the engine. Another witness called for plaintiff said he was near the passenger engine at the time of the accident; that he heard the switch engine approaching the crossing. John Gaffney, another witness for plaintiff, said he saw the switch engine approaching the crossing, and heard it; that he was on the passenger engine; that there was a light on the switch engine and that the bell was ringing as it approached. The evidence on defendant's part fully corroborated that of the last witness. It was further to the effect that deceased and her companion, as they approached the crossing, did not pay attention to whether an engine was approaching, and that one of the trainmen who was on the footboard of the tender and had a light in his hand, grabbed hold of and tried to save them.

At the close of the evidence the court directed a verdict in defendant's favor, upon which the judgment appealed from was rendered.

MAX HOFFMAN, for appellant.

EDWARD M. HYZER, for respondent.

MARSHALL, J. (after stating the facts). — Very little can profitably be said in deciding this case. Four errors are assigned. All, so far as they relate to the issues made by the pleadings, may be properly resolved into this one proposition: Did the trial court err in deciding that the evidence disclosed, as a matter of law, contributory negligence on the part of the deceased? We are unable to see how, in the light of well-settled legal principles, the affirmative of that can be considerately urged. The duty of a person about to step upon a railway track to look both ways and listen, and to discover those dangers which can be readily discovered by the exercise of ordinary attention to that end by one so circumstanced, and not to go upon the track in the face of such dangers, is absolute. It is as firmly established as any rule of law can well be. If it were a fact, as claimed in this case, that the deceased had the rights of a passenger as regards care for her safety by the railway company, and that she had no other way of reaching her destination than by going across the railway track, that does not constitute any exception to the general rule stated. She was bound to exercise ordinary care for her own safety, and she fell below that standard in failing to use her senses to discover the approaching engine, since, from all reasonable inferences from the evidence, it was in sight and hearing and so near the crossing as to render it dangerous for her to step upon the track when she did so. As we read the evidence and the argument of counsel for appellant, there is no claim that she looked north on the track or listened for a coming train or engine before she proceeded into the region of danger. Counsel seems to think that she had the rights of a passenger, and that no other way to reach her destination than the one she pursued was open to her, hence that she was excused for proceeding as she did, regardless of the probability of danger, and was warranted in depending upon respondent to avoid injuring her. We know of no such rule of law. There is no such rule. No one is excusable for stepping upon a railway track without first using the precautions we have stated for his own protection. As has often been said, the mere presence of the track is an efficient warning of danger. That warning must be reasonably heeded by a person about to cross the track, else he will be presumed conclusively, as a matter of law, to assume the risk of doing otherwise. Lofdahl *v.* Minn., St. P. & S. S. M. R'y Co., 88 Wis. 421, 60 N. W. Rep. 795 (12 Am. Neg. Cas. 652*n*); Flynn *v.* Railroad Co., 83 Wis. 239, 53 N. W. Rep. 494; Hansen *v.* Chicago, M. & St. P. R'y Co., 83 Wis. 631, 53 N. W. Rep. 909 (12 Am. Neg. Cas. 651*n*); Schmolze *v.* Chicago, M & St. P. R'y Co., 83 Wis. 659, 53 N. W. Rep. 743, 54 N. W. Rep. 106 (12 Am. Neg. Cas. 651*n*); Schlimgen *v.* Chicago, M. & St. P. R'y Co., 90 Wis. 194, 62 N. W. Rep. 1045 (12 Am. Neg. Cas. 652*n*); Nolan *v.* Mil., L. S. & W. R'y Co., 91 Wis. 16, 64 N. W. Rep. 319 (12 Am. Neg. Cas. 652*n*); Lockwood *v.* Belle City St. R'y Co., 92 Wis. 97 (12 Am. Neg. Cas. 641), 65 N. W. Rep. 866; McCadden *v.* Abbot, 92 Wis. 551, 66 N. W. Rep. 694; Cawley *v.* Railroad Co., 101 Wis. 145, 77 N. W. Rep. 179; White *v.* Railroad Co., 102 Wis. 489, 78 N. W. Rep. 585; Walters *v.* Chicago, M. & St. P. R'y Co., 104 Wis. 257, 6 Am. Neg. Rep. 737, 80 N. W. Rep. 451; Buckmaster *v.* Railroad Co., 108 Wis. 353, 84 N. W. Rep. 845; Dummer *v.* Mil. Electric

R'y & Light Co., 108 Wis. 589, 84 N. W. Rep. 853, 9 Am. Neg. Rep. 271*n*.

The subject involved in this appeal has been so often before this court, as indicated by the cases cited and many not mentioned, and the law has been so often declared as stated herein, that there is no room in the evidence presented by the record for reasonable contention that the trial court erred in directing the verdict. The way was open for the deceased to see the approaching engine. If she had looked north on the switch track before she stepped upon it she would have observed the danger. She must either have failed to perform her duty as to looking, or have observed the engine before getting in its pathway and heedlessly attempted to rush across the track before it reached her. The legal responsibility for the consequences rests wholly upon the unfortunate woman. The damages caused to her surviving husband were in law so far produced by her that there is no way by which her fault can be so separated from that of respondent, if respondent was also at fault, as to fix upon the latter legal responsibility.

The judgment is affirmed.

EMPLOYEE INJURED BY BLASTING OPERATIONS—FELLOW-SERVANT RULE NOT APPLICABLE—IN ORMAN ET AL. *v.* SALVO (*U. S. Circuit Court of Appeals, Eighth Circuit, July, 1902*), 117 Fed. Rep. 233, an action for injuries sustained by plaintiff caused by blasting operations, judgment for plaintiff in the U. S. Circuit Court for the District of Columbia, was affirmed, the facts being stated by LOCHREN, DISTRICT JUDGE, as follows: "In the month of July, 1900, the partnership firm of Orman & Crook, defendants below, were engaged in the construction of a railroad grade between Colorado Springs and Cripple Creek in Colorado, and employed in that work a large number of men, who, to keep the work in progress, were divided into day and night shifts; the night shifts working from seven o'clock in the evening until six o'clock the next morning, and the day shifts the remainder of each day. Antonio Salvo, the plaintiff below, was, at and for some time prior to the injury complained of, a laborer in the employ of defendants, and boss of a night shift of such laborers, engaged in the excavation of a tunnel, near the opening of which other shifts of defendants' employees were excavating a cut; all such excavations being in rock, which had to be loosened by blasting. The defendants boarded and lodged the laborers working with plaintiff in tents, which they had provided and placed so near to this work of excavation that the tents were in danger from falling rocks whenever a large blast was exploded in the cut; and as the men slept in these tents during the hours when their shifts were not at work, it had been the custom for the men in charge of such blasting to cause the men sleeping in these tents to be awakened and warned of the danger, that they might seek places of safety before the explosion of such large blasts. On July 10, 1900, about three o'clock in the afternoon, and while the plaintiff and other men of his night shift were asleep in one of these tents, a blast in the work of excavating the cut, wherein about thirty-five pounds of giant powder and eight kegs of black powder had been placed in a hole eighteen or twenty feet deep, was exploded, and thereby pieces of rock were thrown upon and through the said tent, striking the plaintiff, and breaking an arm and a leg. There was contradictory testimony as to whether, before the explosion of such blast, warning had been given to the plaintiff or to the other laborers then occupying the same tent."

It was held that the question of whether warning of the coming blast was given to the plaintiff, was fairly left to the jury, with instruction that if he had such warning, and failed to go to a place of safety, he was not entitled to recover.

It was also held that the doctrine of fellow-servant did not apply, as at the time of the injury, plaintiff was not the fellow-servant of any of the defendants' employees who were at work, about which he was in no way engaged or assisting.

ST. LOUIS, IRON MOUNTAIN AND SOUTHERN RAILWAY COMPANY v. LEFTWICH.

United States Circuit Court of Appeals, Eighth Circuit, August, 1902.

PASSENGER INJURED WHILE RIDING ON PLATFORM OR STEPS OF CAR — CONTRIBUTORY NEGLIGENCE. — 1. The question whether or not a passenger who had just boarded the smoking car, and was passing through that car, over the platform, to the next coach in the rear, where he intended to ride, was guilty of contributory negligence because he turned aside, grasped the railings on both sides of the steps of the platform of the car, and stepped down upon the upper step for the purpose of expectorating and throwing the contents of his mouth clear of the train, was a question for the jury, and not for the court (1).

2. It is only when all reasonable men, in the honest exercise of a fair and impartial judgment, would draw the same conclusion from the facts which condition the issue of negligence or contributory negligence, that it is the duty of the court to withdraw that question from the jury; and it is not clear that all reasonable men would agree that there was any lack of ordinary care in the act of the plaintiff in this case.

3. A passenger who, without any reasonable cause or excuse, rides on a platform or on the steps of a railway car, or on an engine, or on a hand car, or on a freight or baggage car, or in any other place not designed for the carriage of passengers, is guilty of negligence which may bar his recovery of damages resulting from the concurring negligence of the railway company. (Syllabus by the Court.)

IN ERROR to the Circuit Court of the United States for the Eastern District of Arkansas. *Judgment for plaintiff affirmed.*

GEORGE E. DODGE and B. S. JOHNSON, for plaintiff in error.

WILLIAM G. WHIPPLE and DURAND WHIPPLE, for defendant in error.

Before SANBORN and THAYER, Circuit Judges, and LOCHREN, District Judge.

SANBORN, CIRCUIT JUDGE. — This is an action for damages for a personal injury, and it resulted in a judgment for the plaintiff.

The chief, if not the only, reason why this judgment is assailed by counsel for the railway company, is that, in their opinion, the court below should have instructed the jury as a matter of law that the plaintiff, Leftwich, was guilty of contributory negligence which

1. *Riding on Platforms and Steps of Cars, etc.* — For actions arising out of accidents to passengers on trains, etc., from the earliest period to 1897, see vols. 9 and 10 Am. Neg. Cas. Subsequent actions to date are reported in vols. 1–12 AM. NEG. REP., and the current numbers of that series of Reports.

barred his right to a recovery of the damages he claimed. At the time the injury was inflicted, Leftwich was a young man about twenty-nine years of age. He had served as a switchman and as a brakeman. On the occasion of his injury, he was a passenger on the train of the railway company, which contained two passenger coaches. The forward coach was a combination car divided by a partition into a forward and a rear compartment. The forward compartment was set apart for colored passengers, and the rear compartment was a smoking room. The next coach was a ladies' car. The plaintiff was a white man, and he had the right to ride in the smoking car or in the ladies' car as he chose. The train stopped but one or two minutes at the station where he boarded it, so that it was necessary for him to take it at once when it arrived. It was more convenient for him to ascend the steps at the front end of the smoking car when the train arrived at the station. He did so, and then passed back through this car, and out upon the platform between the two passenger coaches, on his way to the rear coach, where he intended to ride. When he was near the partition in the combination car, the train started. On his way back he coughed up some phlegm, and as he arrived upon the platform of the rear car he turned aside, grasped the railings on each side of the steps, and stepped down upon the upper step for the purpose of so expectorating that he might throw the phlegm clear of the train. As he stepped down upon this step, his foot fell upon a mass of woolen rags or waste saturated with oil, used to pack the boxes and oil the bearings of the wheels of railway cars, and commonly called "dope." As his foot struck this dope, he slipped, fell to the ground, and was injured. There was a spittoon in the coach in which he might have deposited the contents of his mouth. The facts which have been recited are undisputed, and they are all the facts material to the questions presented in this case.

The platforms and steps of railway cars propelled by steam are dangerous places for passengers to ride. They are not provided for that purpose, and passenger coaches generally carry on their doors, or in other conspicuous places, notices that the rules of railway companies forbid the passengers to occupy these places for the purpose of riding upon the trains. Moreover, it is a general rule of law that a passenger who, without any reasonable cause or excuse, rides on a platform or on the steps of a railway car, or on an engine, or on a hand car, or on a freight or baggage car, or in any other place not designed for the carriage of passengers, is guilty of negligence which, if it contributes to an injury that he sustains, will bar his recovery of damages therefor on account of the concurring negligence of the railway company. Purple *v.* Union Pac. R. R. Co., 114 Fed. Rep. 123, 129, 11 Am. Neg. Rep. 509; Memphis & Little Rock R'y Co. *v.* Salinger, 46 Ark. 528, 536, 9 Am. Neg. Cas. 34; Hickey *v.* Railroad Co., 14 Allen, 429, 9 Am. Neg. Cas. 454; Quinn *v.* Railroad Co., 51 Ill. 495, 9 Am. Neg. Cas. 246; Paterson *v.* Railroad Co., 85 Ga. 653, 657, 11 S. E. Rep. 872; Bon *v.* Railway Passenger Assurance Co., 56 Iowa, 664, 667, 668, 3 Am. Neg. Cas. 355, 10 N. W. Rep. 225; Railway Co. *v.* Roach (Va.), 5 S. E. Rep. 175; Robertson *v.* Railroad Co., 22 Barb. 91; Eaton *v.* Railroad Co., 57 N. Y. 382, 384; Penn. R. R. Co. *v.* Langdon, 92 Pa. St. 21, 10 Am. Neg. Cas. 215, 1 Am. & Eng. R. Cas. 87; Powers *v.* Railroad Co., 153 Mass. 188, 191, 192, 9 Am. Neg. Rep. 464n, 26 N. E. Rep. 446; Flower *v.* Railroad Co., 69 Pa. St. 210, 12 Am. Neg. Cas. 524; Ecliff *v.* Railway Co., 64 Mich. 196, 12 Am. Neg. Cas. 130n, 31 N. W. Rep. 180. But the platforms and steps of passenger coaches are provided for the entrance and exit of passengers, and to enable them to pass from that part of the train on which they enter to the coach where they desire and are entitled to ride. The plaintiff rightfully entered upon this train, and immediately passed back across the platform between the cars on his way to the coach where he intended, and had the right, to ride to his destination. In all this there was no misuse of train or platform, no want of ordinary and reasonable care. But, as he passed across the platform of the last car he grasped the rails on both sides of the steps, and stepped down one step, in order to free his mouth of its troublesome burden, and to throw it clear of the train. Was this an act of which a man of ordinary prudence, in the exercise of reasonable care, would not have been guilty? Was it an act of negligence? The court below submitted this issue to the jury, and the question which that ruling presents to this court is, would all reasonable men, in the exercise of a fair and impartial judgment, draw the conclusion that, under all the circumstances of this particular case, the plaintiff failed to exercise the care which a man of ordinary prudence would have exercised when he turned aside from the door of his car, and stepped down one step, to relieve his mouth and send its contents away from the train? Railroad Co. *v.* Jarvi, 3 C. C. A. 433, 53 Fed. Rep. 65; Pyle *v.* Clark, 2 Am. Neg. Rep. 100, 25 C. C. A. 190, 192, 79 Fed. Rep. 744, 746; Grand Trunk R'y Co. *v.* Ives, 144 U. S. 408, 417, 12 Am. Neg. Cas. 659, 12 Sup. Ct. Rep. 679; Railroad Co. *v.* Converse, 139 U. S. 469, 11 Sup. Ct. Rep. 569, 12 Am. Neg. Cas. 668n. This question must be answered in the negative. The situation, circumstances, and surroundings of the actor always condition the answer to the question whether or not he has exercised ordinary care. It would undoubtedly have been negligence for one without necessity or reason to have placed himself upon one of the steps of this car while the train was in motion. On the other hand, if the train had started just after one had boarded a lower step of the platform it would not have been negligence for him to have placed his feet upon the higher steps to climb upon the platform and enter the car. The case in hand is on the debatable ground between the two cases supposed, and it is by no means clear that all reasonable men would agree that plaintiff's act evidenced any want of ordinary care under the peculiar circumstances of his case. Indeed, it is by no means certain that there are not some reasonably prudent and careful men who would have been guilty of the same act under the same circumstances. The question which has been considered is the only one argued by counsel for the plaintiff in error, but at the close of their brief they state that, if it was not the duty of the court below to instruct the jury that the plaintiff was guilty of contributory negligence, still that court was in error because it failed to give to the jury ten separate instructions which they requested it to submit. These requests have been carefully read, considered, and compared with the charge of the court. So far as the rules of law which they contain were sound, pertinent, and material to the issues presented, they were fairly given in the general charge, so that there was no error in the refusal to give them in the words of the counsel for the plaintiff. Moreover, they present no question of law which is not involved in, and decided by, the conclusion that the question of contributory negligence in this case was for the jury, and not for the court.

There was no error in the trial of the case, and the judgment below is affirmed.

JOHNSON v. SOUTHERN PACIFIC COMPANY.

United States Circuit Court of Appeals, Eighth Circuit, August, 1902.

AUTOMATIC COUPLERS — FEDERAL STATUTE — CONSTRUCTION — INTERSTATE COMMERCE — BRAKEMAN INJURED COUPLING CARS — ASSUMPTION OF RISK. — 1. The act of March 2, 1893 (27 Stat., c. 196, p. 531), does not make it unlawful for common carriers to use locomotives engaged in interstate commerce which are not equipped with automatic couplers (1).

1. See Crawford *v.* N. Y. Central & H. R. R. Co. (N. Y. 1901), 10 Am. Neg. Rep. 166, for the New York ruling on the Federal statute relating to automatic couplers.

2. A statute changing the common law modifies or abrogates it no farther than the clear import of its language necessarily requires.
3. A penal statute may not be so broadened by construction as to make it cover, and authorize the punishment of, otherwise lawful acts, which are not denounced by the usual meaning of its express terms.
4. A statute which enumerates the parties, things, or acts which it denounces thereby impliedly excludes all others from its effect.
5. When the language of a statute is unambiguous, and its meaning is plain, it must be held to mean, and the legislative body must be held to have intended, what it plainly expresses, and no room is left for construction.
6. A servant assumes the ordinary risks and dangers of the employment upon which he enters, so far as they are known to him, and so far as they would have been known to one of his experience, age, and capacity by the use of ordinary care.
7. A brakeman of ordinary intelligence and experience assumes the risks and dangers of coupling cars provided with different kinds of well-known couplers, bumpers, and deadwoods, because these are the ordinary risks and dangers of his service (1).
8. The equipment, under the act of March 2, 1893, of a car with automatic couplers which will couple automatically with those of the same kind or make, is a compliance with the statute. It does not require cars used in interstate commerce to be equipped with couplers which will couple automatically with cars equipped with automatic couplers of other makes.
9. Cars loaded with articles shipped to other States, and started, whether in yards, on side tracks, or in trains, are used in moving interstate traffic. But vacant cars in yards, on side tracks, in repair shops, or in trains which are not loaded with, or in use to move articles of, interstate commerce, do not fall within the terms or meaning of the act of March 2, 1893. A dining car standing empty on a side track at an intermediate station, where it had been left by a train engaged in interstate traffic until it should be taken by another train engaged in the same traffic, going in the opposite direction, and which the owner intended to use in interstate traffic was drawn by a freight engine from the side track of the turntable, turned, and placed again upon the side track. *Held*, that the car was not used in moving interstate traffic while it was on the side track and while it was being turned.

THAYER, J., *dissenting* in part.

(Syllabus by the Court.)

IN ERROR to the Circuit Court of the United States for the District of Utah. *Judgment for defendant affirmed.*

"This is an action for damages for a personal injury, in which the court instructed the jury to return a verdict for the defendant upon this state of facts: The defendant was operating passenger trains between San Francisco, in the State of California, and Ogden, in the State of Utah. It was in the habit of drawing a dining car in these trains. Such a car formed a part of a train leaving San Francisco, and ran through to Ogden, where it was ordinarily

1. See note on THE FEDERAL RULE ON ASSUMPTION OF RISK, 11 AM. NEG. REP. 92–103.

turned and put into a train going west to San Francisco. On August 5, 1900, the east-bound train was so late that it was not practicable to get the dining car into Ogden in time to place it in the next west-bound train, and it was therefore left on a side track at Promontory, in the State of Utah, to be picked up by the west-bound train when it arrived. While it was standing on this track the conductor of a freight train which arrived there was directed to take this dining car to a turntable, turn it, and place it back upon the side track, so that it would be ready to return to San Francisco. The conductor instructed his crew to carry out this direction. The plaintiff, Johnson, was the head brakeman, and he undertook to couple the engine to the dining car for the purpose of carrying out the order of the conductor. The freight engine was equipped with a Janney coupler, which would couple automatically with another Janney coupler, and the dining car was provided with a Miller hook or Miller coupler, which would couple automatically with another Miller hook; but the Miller hook would not couple automatically with the Janney coupler, because it was on the same side, and would pass over it. Johnson knew this, and undertook to make the coupling by means of a link and pin. He knew that it was a difficult coupling to make, and that it was necessary to go between the engine and the car to accomplish it, and that it was dangerous to do so. Nevertheless he went in between the engine and the car, and tried to make the coupling three times, without objection or protest. He failed twice, and the third time his hand was caught and crushed so that it became necessary to amputate his arm above the wrist."

W. L. MAGINNIS, for plaintiff in error.

HENRY G. HERBEL (MARTIN L. CLARDY, on the brief), for defendant in error.

Before SANBORN and THAYER, Circuit Judges, and LOCHREN, District Judge.

SANBORN, CIRCUIT JUDGE (after stating the case as above), delivered the opinion of the court.

Under the common law the plaintiff assumed the risks and dangers of the coupling which he endeavored to make, and for that reason he is estopped from recovering the damages which resulted from his undertaking. He was an intelligent and experienced brakeman, familiar with the couplers he sought to join, and with their condition, and well aware of the difficulty and danger of his undertaking, so that he falls far within the familiar rules that the servant assumes the ordinary risks and dangers of the employment upon which he enters, so far as they are known to him, and so far as they would have been known to one of his age, experience, and capacity by the use of ordinary care, and that the risks and dangers of coupling cars provided with different kinds of well-known couplers, bumpers, brakeheads, and deadwoods are the ordinary risks and dangers of a brakeman's service. Manufacturing Co. *v.* Erickson, 55 Fed. Rep. 943, 946, 5 C. C. A. 341, 343; Railroad Co. *v.* Blake, 27 U. S. App. 190, 194, 11 C. C. A. 93, 95, 63 Fed. Rep. 45, 47; King *v.* Morgan, 48 C. C. A. 507, 511, 109 Fed. Rep. 446, 450; Gold Mines *v.* Hopkins, 111 Fed. Rep. 298, 304, 49 C. C. A. 347, 353; Railroad Co. *v.* McDade, 135 U. S. 554, 570, 10 Sup. Ct. Rep. 1044; Railroad Co. *v.* Seley, 152 U. S. 145, 152, 14 Sup. Ct. Rep. 530; Kohn *v.* McNulta, 147 U. S. 238, 241, 13 Sup. Ct. Rep. 298; Railroad Co. *v.* Voight, 176 U. S. 498, 20 Sup. Ct. Rep. 385; Sweeney *v.* Envelope Co., 101 N. Y. 520, 5 N. E. Rep. 358; Railway Co. *v.* Smithson, 45 Mich. 212, 7 N. W. Rep. 791; Hodges *v.* Kimball, 44 C. C. A. 193, 104 Fed. Rep. 745; Whitcomb *v.* Oil Co. (Ind. Sup.), 55 N. E. Rep. 440, 442; Boland *v.* Railroad Co. (Ala.), 18 So. Rep. 99.

This proposition is not seriously challenged, but counsel base their claim for a reversal of the judgment below upon the position that the plaintiff was relieved of this assumption of risk, and of its consequences, by the provisions of the act of Congress of March 2, 1893 (27 Stat., c. 196, p. 531). The title of that act, and the parts of it that are material to the consideration of this contention, are these:

"An act to promote the safety of employees and travelers upon railroads by compelling common carriers engaged in interstate commerce to equip their cars with automatic couplers and continuous brakes and their locomotives with driving wheel brakes and for other purposes.

"Section 1. That from and after the first day of January, 1898, it shall be unlawful for any common carrier engaged in interstate commerce by railroad to use on its line any locomotive engine in moving interstate traffic not equipped with a power driving wheel brake and appliances for operating the train brake system. * * *

"Sec. 2. That on and after the first day of January, 1898, it shall be unlawful for any such common carrier to haul or permit to be hauled or used on its line any car used in moving interstate traffic not equipped with couplers coupling automatically by impact, and which can be uncoupled without the necessity of men going between the ends of the cars."

"Sec. 6. That any such common carrier using any locomotive engine, running any train, or hauling or permitting to be hauled or used on its line any car in violation of any of the provisions of this act shall be liable to a penalty of one hundred dollars for each and every such violation. * * *"

"Sec. 8. That any employee of any such common carrier who may be injured by any locomotive, car or train in use contrary to the provisions of this act shall not be deemed thereby to have assumed the risk thereby occasioned, although continuing in the employment of such carrier after the unlawful use of such locomotive, car or train had been brought to his knowledge."

The first thought that suggests itself to the mind upon a perusal of this law, and a comparison of it with the facts of this case, is that this statute has no application here, because both the dining car and the engine were equipped as this act directs. The car was equipped with Miller couplers which would couple automatically with couplers of the same construction upon cars in the train in which it was used to carry on interstate commerce, and the engine was equipped with a power driving wheel brake such as this statute prescribes. To overcome this difficulty, counsel for the plaintiff persuasively argues that this is a remedial statute; that laws for the prevention of fraud, the suppression of a public wrong, and the bestowal of a public good are remedial in their nature, and should be liberally construed, to prevent the mischief and to advance the remedy, notwithstanding the fact that they may impose a penalty for their violation; and that this statute should be so construed as to forbid the use of a locomotive as well as a car which is not equipped with an automatic coupler. In support of this contention he cites Suth. St. Const., sec. 360; Wall *v.* Platt, 169 Mass. 398, 48 N. E. 270; Taylor *v.* U. S., 3 How. (U. S.) 197, and other cases of like character. The general propositions which counsel quote may be found in the opinions in these cases, and in some of them they were applied to the particular facts which those actions presented. But the interpolation in this act of Congress by construction of an *ex post facto* provision that it is, and ever since January 1, 1898, has been, unlawful for any common carrier to use any engine in interstate traffic that is or was not equipped with couplers coupling automatically, and that any carrier that has used or shall use an engine not so equipped has been and shall be liable to a penalty of $100 for every violation of this provision, is too abhorrent to the sense of justice and fairness, too rank and radical a piece of judicial legislation, and in violation of too many established and salutary rules of construction, to commend itself to the judicial reason or conscience. The primary rule for the interpretation of a statute or a contract is to ascertain, if possible, and enforce, the intention which the legislative body that enacted the law, or the parties who made the agreement, have expressed therein. But it is the intention expressed in the law or contract, and that only, that the courts may give effect to. They cannot lawfully assume or presume secret purposes that are not indicated or expressed by the statute itself and then enact provisions to accomplish these supposed intentions. While ambiguous terms and doubtful expressions may be interpreted to carry out the intention of a legislative body which a statute fairly evidences, a secret intention cannot be interpreted into a statute which is plain and unambiguous, and which does not express it. The legal presumption is that the legislative body expressed its intention, that it intended what it expressed, and that it intended nothing more. U. S. *v.* Wiltberger, 5 Wheat. 76; Insurance Co. *v.* Champlin (C. C. A.), 116 Fed. Rep. 858; Cold Blast Transp. Co. *v.* Kansas City Bolt & Nut Co. (C. C. A.), 114 Fed. Rep. 77, 81; Railway Co. *v.* Bagley, 60 Kan. 424, 431, 56 Pac. Rep. 759; Woolsey *v.* Ryan, 59 Kan. 601, 54 Pac. Rep. 664; Davie *v.* Mining Co., 93 Mich. 491, 53 N. W. Rep. 625; Vogel *v.* Pekoc, 157 Ill. 339, 42 N. E. Rep. 386; Campbell *v.* Lambert, 36 La. Ann. 35; Turnpike Co. *v.* Coy, 13 Ohio St. 84; Stensgaard *v.* Smith, 43 Minn. 11, 44 N. W. Rep. 669. Construction and interpretation have no place or office where the terms of a statute are clear and certain, and its meaning is plain. In such a case they serve only to create doubt and to confuse the judgment. When the language of a statute is unambiguous, and its meaning evident, it must be held to mean what it plainly expresses, and no room is left for construction. Swarts *v.* Siegel (C. C. A.), 117 Fed. Rep. 13; Knox Co. *v.* Morton, 15 C. C. A. 671, 673, 68 Fed. Rep. 787, 789; Railway Co. *v.* Sage, 17 C. C. A. 558, 565, 71 Fed. Rep. 40, 47; U. S. *v.* Fisher, 2 Cranch, 358; Railway Co. *v.* Phelps, 137 U. S. 528, 536, 11 Sup. Ct. Rep. 168.

This statute clearly prohibits the use of any engine in moving interstate commerce not equipped with a power driving wheel brake, and the use of any car not equipped with automatic couplers, under a penalty of $100 for each offense; and it just as plainly omits to forbid, under that or any penalty, the use of any car which is not equipped with a power driving wheel brake, and the use of any engine that is not equipped with automatic couplers. This striking omission to express any intention to prohibit the use of engines unequipped with automatic couplers raises the legal presumption that no such intention existed, and prohibits the courts from importing such a purpose into the act, and enacting provisions to give it effect. The familiar rule that the expression of one thing is the exclusion of others points to the same conclusion. Section 2 of the act does not declare that it shall be unlawful to use any engine or car not equipped with automatic couplers, but that it shall be unlawful only to use any car lacking this equipment. This clear and concise definition of the unlawful act is a cogent and persuasive argument against the contention that the use without couplers of locomotives, hand cars, or other means of conducting interstate traffic, was made a misdemeanor by this act. Where the statute enumerates the persons, things, or acts affected by it, there is an implied exclusion of all others. Suth. St. Const., sec. 227. And when the title of this statute and its first section are again read; when it is perceived that it was not from inattention, thoughtlessness, or forgetfulness; that it was not because locomotives were overlooked or out of mind, but that it was advisedly and after careful consideration of the equipment which they should have, that Congress forbade the use of cars alone without automatic couplers; when it is seen that the title of the act is to compel common carriers to "equip their cars with automatic couplers * * * and their locomotives with driving wheel brakes;" that the first section makes it unlawful to use locomotives not equipped with such brakes, and the second section declares it to be illegal to use cars without automatic couplers — the argument becomes unanswerable and conclusive.

Again, this act of Congress changes the common law. Before its enactment, servants coupling cars used in interstate commerce without automatic couplers assumed the risk and danger of that employment, and carriers were not liable for injuries which their employees suffered in the discharge of this duty. Since its passage the employees no longer assume this risk, and, if they are free from contributory negligence, they may recover for the damages they sustain in this work. A statute which thus changes the common law must be strictly construed. The common or the general law is not further abrogated by such a statute than the clear import of its language necessarily requires. Shaw *v.* Railroad Co., 101 U. S. 557, 565; Fitzgerald *v.* Quann, 109 N. Y. 441, 445, 17 N. E. Rep. 354; Brown *v.* Barry, 3 Dall. 365, 367. The language of this statute does not require the abrogation of the common law that the servant assumes the risk of coupling a locomotive without automatic couplers with a car which is provided with them.

Moreover, this is a penal statute, and it may not be so broadened by judicial construction as to make it cover and permit the punishment of an act which is not denounced by the fair import of its terms. The acts which this statute declares to be unlawful, and for the commission of which it imposes a penalty, were lawful before its enactment, and their performance subjected to no penalty or liability. It makes that unlawful which was lawful before its passage, and it imposes a penalty for its performance. Nor is this penalty a mere forfeiture for the benefit of the party aggrieved or injured. It is a penalty prescribed by the statute, and recoverable by the government. It is, therefore, under every definition of the term, a penal statute. The act which lies at the foundation of this suit — the use of a locomotive which was not equipped with a Miller hook to turn a car which was duly equipped with automatic couplers — was therefore unlawful or lawful as it was or was not forbidden by this statute. That act has been done. When it was done it was neither forbidden nor declared to be unlawful by the express terms of this law. There is no language in it which makes it unlawful to use in interstate commerce a locomotive engine which is not equipped with automatic couplers. The argument of counsel for the plaintiff is, however, that the statute should be construed to make this act unlawful because it falls within the mischief which Congress was seeking to remedy, and hence it should be presumed that the legislative body intended to denounce this act as much as that which it forbade by the terms of the law. An *ex post facto* statute which would make such an innocent act a crime would be violative of the basic principles of Anglo-Saxon jurisprudence. An *ex post facto* construction which has the same effect is equally abhorrent to the sense of justice and of reason. The mischief at which a statute was leveled, and the fact that other acts which it does not denounce are within the mischief, and of equal atrocity with those which it forbids, do not raise the presumption that the legislative body which enacted it had the intention, which the law does not express, to prohibit the performance of the acts which it does not forbid. Nor will they warrant a construction which imports into the statute such a prohibition. The intention of the legislature and the meaning of a penal statute must be found in the language actually used, interpreted according to its fair and usual meaning, and not in the evils which it was intended to remedy, nor in the assumed secret intention of the lawmakers to accomplish that which they did not express. U. S. *v.* Wiltberger, 5 Wheat. 76; Sarlls *v.* U. S., 152 U S. 570, 14 Sup. Ct. Rep. 720; U. S. *v.* Harris, 177 U. S. 305, 309, 20 Sup. Ct. Rep. 609; Suth. St. Const., sec. 208. The decision and opinion of the Supreme Court in U. S. *v.* Harris, 177 U. S. 305, 309, 20 Sup. Ct. Rep. 609, is persuasive — nay, it is decisive — in the case before us. The question there presented was analogous to that here in issue. It was whether Congress intended to include receivers managing a railroad among those who were prohibited from confining cattle, sheep, and other animals in cars more than twenty-eight consecutive hours without unloading them for rest, water, and feeding, under "An act to prevent cruelty to animals while in transit by railroad or other means of transportation," approved March 3, 1873, and published in the Revised Statutes as sections 4386, 4387, 4388, and 4389. This statute forbids the confinement of stock in cars by any railroad company engaged in interstate commerce more than twenty-eight consecutive hours, and prescribes a penalty of $500 for a violation of its provisions. The plain purpose of the act was to prohibit the confinement of stock while in transit for an unreasonable length of time. The confinement of cattle by receivers operating a railroad was as injurious as their confinement by a railroad company, and the argument for the United States was that, as such acts committed by receivers were plainly within the mischief Congress was seeking to remedy, the conclusion should be that it intended to prohibit receivers, as well as railroad companies, from the commission of the forbidden acts, and hence that receivers were subject to the provisions of the law. The Supreme Court conceded that the confinement of stock in transit was within the mischief that Congress sought to remedy. But it held that as the act did not, by its terms, forbid such acts when committed by receivers, it could not presume the intention of Congress to do so, and import such a provision into the plain terms of the law. Mr. Justice Shiras, who delivered the unanimous opinion of the court, said:

"Giving all proper force to the contention of the counsel for the government, that there has been some relaxation on the part of the courts in applying the rule of strict construction to such statutes, it still remains that the intention of a penal statute must be found in the language actually used, interpreted according to its fair and obvious meaning. It is not permitted to courts, in this class of cases, to attribute inadvertence or oversight to the legislature when enumerating the classes of persons who are subjected to a penal enactment, nor to depart from the settled meaning of words or phrases in order to bring persons not named or distinctly described within the supposed purpose of the statute."

He cited with approval the decision of the Supreme Court in Sarlls *v.* U. S., 152 U. S. 570, 575, 14 Sup. Ct. Rep. 720, to the effect that lager beer was not included within the meaning of the term "spirituous liquors" in the penal statute found in section 2139 of the Revised Statutes, and closed the discussion with the following quotation from the opinion of Chief Justice Marshall in U. S. *v.* Wiltberger, 5 Wheat. 76:

"The rule that penal statutes are to be construed strictly is perhaps not much less old than construction itself. It is founded on the tenderness of the law for the rights of individuals, and on the plain principle that the power of punishment is vested in the legislative, and not in the judicial, department. It is the legislature, not the court, which is to define a crime and ordain its punishment. It is said that, notwithstanding this rule, the intention of the lawmaker must govern in the construction of penal as well as other statutes. But this is not a new, independent rule, which subverts the old. It is a modification of the ancient maxim, and amounts to this: that, though penal statutes are to be construed strictly, they are not to be construed so strictly as to defeat the obvious intention of the legislature. The maxim is not to be applied so as to narrow the words of the statute, to the exclusion of cases which those words, in their ordinary acceptation, or in that sense in which the legislature ordinarily used them, would comprehend. The intention of the legislature is to be collected from the words they employ. Where there is no ambiguity in the words, there is no room for construction. The case must be a strong one, indeed, which would justify a court in departing from the plain meaning of words — especially in a penal act — in search of an intention which the words themselves did not suggest. To determine that a case is within the intention of a statute, its language must authorize us to say so. It would be dangerous, indeed, to carry the principle that a case which is within the reason or mischief of a statute is within its provisions, so far as to punish a crime not enumerated in the statute, because it is of equal atrocity or of a kindred character with those which are enumerated. If this principle has ever been recognized in expounding criminal law, it has been in cases of considerable irritation which it would be unsafe to consider as precedents forming a general rule in other cases."

The act of March 2, 1893, is a penal statute, and it changes the common law. It makes that unlawful which was innocent before its enactment, and imposes a penalty, recoverable by the government. Its terms are plain and free from doubt, and its meaning is clear. It declares that it is unlawful for a common carrier to use in interstate commerce a car which is not equipped with automatic couplers, and it omits to declare that it is illegal for a common carrier to use a locomotive that is not so equipped. As Congress expressed in this statute no intention to forbid the use of locomotives which were not provided with automatic couplers, the legal presumption is that it had no such intention, and provisions to import such an intention into the law and to effectuate it may not be lawfully enacted by judicial construction. The statute does not make it unlawful to use locomotives that are not equipped with automatic couplers in interstate commerce, and it did not modify the rule of the common law under which the plaintiff assumed the known risk of coupling such an engine to the dining car.

There are other considerations which lead to the same result. If we are in error in the conclusion already expressed, and if the word "car," in the second section of this statute, means locomotive, still this case does not fall under the law, 1, because both the locomotive and the dining car were equipped with automatic couplers; and, 2, because at the time of the accident they were not "used in moving interstate traffic."

For the reasons which have been stated, this statute may not be lawfully extended by judicial construction beyond the fair meaning of its language. There is nothing in it which requires a common carrier engaged in interstate commerce to have every car on its railroad equipped with the same kind of coupling, or which requires it to have every car equipped with a coupler which will couple automatically with every other coupler with which it may be brought into contact in the usual course of business upon a great transcontinental system of railroads. If the lawmakers had intended to require such an equipment, it would have been easy for them to have said so, and the fact that they made no such requirement raises the legal presumption that they intended to make none. Nor is the reason for their omission to do so far to seek or difficult to perceive. There are several kinds or makes of practical and efficient automatic couplers. Some railroad companies use one kind; others have adopted other kinds. Couplers of each kind will couple automatically with others of the same kind or construction. But some couplers will not couple automatically with couplers of different construction. Railroad companies engaged in interstate commerce are required to haul over their road cars equipped with all these couplers. They cannot relieve themselves from this obligation or renounce this public duty for the simple reason that their cars or locomotives are not equipped with automatic couplers which will couple with those with which the cars of other roads are provided, and which will couple with equal facility with those of their kind. These facts and this situation were patent to the Congress when it enacted this statute. It must have known the impracticability of providing every car with as many different couplers as it might meet upon a great system of railroads, and it made no such requirement. It doubtless knew the monopoly it would create by requiring every railroad company to use the same coupler, and it did not create this monopoly. The prohibition of the statute goes no farther than to bar the handling of a car "not equipped with couplers coupling automatically by impact and which can be uncoupled without the necessity of men going between the ends of the car." It does not bar the handling and use of a car which will couple automatically with couplers of its kind because it will not also couple automatically with couplers of all kinds, and it would be an unwarrantable extension of the terms of this law to import into it a provision to this effect. A car equipped with practical and efficient automatic couplers, such as the Janney couplers or the Miller hooks, which will couple automatically with those of their kind, fully and literally complies with the terms of the law, although these couplers will not couple automatically with automatic couplers of all kinds or constructions. The dining car and the locomotive were both so equipped. Each was provided with an automatic coupler which would couple with those of its kind, as provided by the statute, although they would not couple with each other. Each was accordingly equipped as the statute directs, and the defendant was guilty of no violation of it by their use.

Again, the statute declares it to be unlawful for a carrier "to haul or permit to be hauled or used on its line any car used in moving interstate traffic not equipped," etc. It is not, then, unlawful, under this statute, for a carrier to haul a car not so equipped which is either used in intrastate traffic solely, or which is not used in any traffic at all. It would be no violation of the statute for a carrier to haul an empty car not used to move any interstate traffic from one end of its railroad to the other. It would be no violation of the law for it to haul such a car in its yards, on its side track, to put it into its trains, to move it in any manner it chose. It is only when a car is "used in moving interstate traffic" that it becomes unlawful to haul it unless it is equipped as the statute prescribes. On the day of this accident the dining car in this case was standing empty on the side track. The defendant drew it to a turntable, turned it, and placed it back upon the side track. The accident occurred during the performance of this act. The car was vacant when it went to the turntable, and vacant when it returned. It moved no traffic on its way. How could it be said to have been "used in moving interstate traffic" either while it was standing on the side track, or while it was going to and returning from the turntable? If the defendant had drawn it vacant over every foot of its railroad, it would not have been engaged in moving interstate traffic, and it would not have fallen under the ban of the statute. How can it thus fall because it was moved in the same way over a small portion of the road? The argument of counsel for the plaintiff is that because it had been used in moving interstate traffic on its way from San Francisco to Promontory, and because it was the intention of the defendant to put it to the same use in a few hours, when a west-bound train arrived, it was impressed with the use of moving such traffic in the interim. But this statute must be read not only in the light of the rules of construction to which we have adverted in the earlier part of this opinion, but also in view of the limitations upon the power of Congress in this respect. It is by virtue of the power granted to Congress to "regulate commerce among the States," and by virtue of that authority alone, that this statute was enacted and has efficacy. Congress had neither the authority nor the purpose to interfere with or to touch by this act anything except commerce among the States. Is the turning of a vacant car which its owner intends to use at some future time in moving interstate traffic any part of commerce among the States? Does the intention of the owner as to a future use of an implement of transportation affect the character of the act of turning this car? If the defendant had intended to use this dining car for traffic within the State of Utah only, if it had intended to send it to the shop to be destroyed or repaired, or if, after the car was turned, it had changed its intention and concluded that it would not use it to move interstate traffic, would any of these intentions or this change of purpose have affected the act of turning the car, and have impressed it with a use in interstate commerce or intrastate commerce? The only answer to these questions is a negative one, and, if this be true, then the intention of the defendant to use this car at some future time in interstate commerce would not make the act of turning it a part of such commerce, nor bring it under the ban of the act of March 2, 1893. The opinion and decision of the Supreme Court in Coe *v.* Town of Errol, 116 U. S. 517, 525, 526, 6 Sup. Ct. Rep. 475, lend strong support to this view. In that case the owners of logs were cutting and transporting them for the purpose of exporting them from New Hampshire to Maine. The logs had been cut, drawn to and deposited in and on the banks of Clear stream, to be floated down that stream and down the Androscoggin river to the State of Maine, and the owners intended to transport them in this way to that State. They were lying in the town of Errol, awaiting water sufficient to float them down the stream. The Supreme Court held that they had not yet become subjects of interstate commerce; that they would not become such until they were "committed to the common carrier for transportation out of the State to the State of their destination, or have started on their ultimate passage to that State;" and that the fact that their owners intended to export them could not change their situation because the owners might change their intention. If commodities do not become articles of interstate commerce until they start on their final passage to another State, cars and engines cannot be "used in moving interstate traffic" until they receive articles of interstate traffic, or start to carry them from one State to another, and the act of turning a vacant car at an intermediate station cannot be the use of that car in moving such traffic. This is the effect of the decision of the Supreme Court of Appeals of Virginia in Norfolk & W. R. Co. *v.* Com., 24 S. E. Rep. 838. That court held in that case, upon the authority of Coe *v.* Errol, that a train of empty coal cars on its way to procure a load of coal which the carrier intended to transport with these cars from one State to another was not engaged in interstate commerce, and would not be until it was loaded with the articles of such commerce, to be carried to another State or started on the way. Speaking of the effect of the intention of the carrier to use the cars in moving interstate traffic, that court said:

"The common carrier has the same right to change his mind, and ship on other cars than those which he may have provided for that purpose, and the cars which were intended for that purpose may never be used. The rule fixed by the Supreme Court in the one case seems equally applicable to the other." U. S. *v* Boyer (D. C.), 85 Fed. Rep. 425, 432; Kelley *v.* Rhoads (Wyo.), 63 Pac. Rep. 935.

The power of Congress over this subject was limited to the regulation of commerce among the States. It intended to exercise that power, but not to transgress its bounds. It prohibited the hauling of cars used in moving interstate traffic unless equipped as the act directs. The intention to use cars for that purpose does not constitute such a use because that intention may change. Coe *v.* Town of Errol, 116 U. S. 526, 6 Sup. Ct. Rep. 475; Norfolk & W. R. Co. *v.* Com. (Va.), 24 S. E. Rep. 838. The fact that such cars have been or will be so used does not constitute their use in moving interstate traffic, because the prohibition is not of the hauling of cars that have been or will be used in such traffic, but only of those used in moving that traffic. Cars loaded with articles of interstate commerce, and started towards their ultimate destination, whether in trains, in yards, or on side tracks, may well be held to come within the terms of this statute and the intent of Congress. But vacant cars which are not and may never be so used cannot be held to come within the fair import of the terms of this law either because their owner intends to use them for that purpose at some future time, or because they have been or will be so used. Empty cars in repair shops, in yards, on side tracks, those in use to transport traffic within a State and for that purpose alone, are not in use to move articles of interstate commerce, and do not fall under the ban of this law. Neither the empty dining car standing upon the side track, nor the freight engine which was used to turn it at the little station in Utah, was then used in moving interstate traffic, within the meaning of this statute, and this case did not fall within the provisions of this law.

The judgment below must accordingly be affirmed, and it is so ordered.

THAYER, Circuit Judge. — I am unable to concur in the conclusion, announced by the majority of the court, that the act of Congress of March 2, 1893 (27 Stat. 531, c. 196), does not require locomotive engines to be equipped with automatic couplers; and I am equally unable to concur in the other conclusion announced by my associates that the dining car in question at the time of the accident was not engaged or being used in moving interstate traffic.

In my judgment, it is a very technical interpretation of the provisions of the act in question, and one which is neither in accord with its spirit nor with the obvious purpose of the lawmaker, to say that Congress did not intend to require engines to be equipped with automatic couplers. The statute is remedial in its nature; it was passed for the protection of human life; and there was certainly as much, if not greater, need that engines should be equipped to couple automatically, as that ordinary cars should be so equipped, since engines have occasion to make couplings more frequently. In my opinion, the true view is that engines are included by the words "any car," as used in the second section of the act. The word "car" is generic, and may well be held to comprehend a locomotive or any other similar vehicle which moves on wheels; and especially should it be so held in a case like the one now in hand, where no satisfactory reason has been assigned or can be given which would probably have influenced Congress to permit locomotives to be used without automatic coupling appliances.

I am also of opinion that, within the fair intent and import of the act, the dining car in question at the time of the accident was being hauled or used in interstate traffic. The reasoning by which a contrary conclusion is reached seems to me to be altogether too refined and unsatisfactory to be of any practical value. It was a car which at the time was employed in no other service than to furnish meals to passengers between Ogden and San Francisco. It had not been taken out of that service, even for repairs or for any other use, when the accident occurred, but was engaged therein to the same extent that it would have been if it had been hauled through to

Ogden, and if the accident had there occurred while it was being turned to make the return trip to San Francisco. The cars composing a train which is regularly employed in interstate traffic ought to be regarded as used in that traffic while the train is being made up with a view to an immediate departure on an interstate journey as well as after the journey has actually begun. I accordingly dissent from the conclusion of the majority of the court on this point.

While I dissent on the foregoing propositions, I concur in the other view which is expressed in the opinion of the majority, to the effect that the case discloses no substantial violation of the provisions of the act of Congress, because both the engine and the dining car were equipped with automatic coupling appliances. In this respect the case discloses a compliance with the law, and the ordinary rule governing the liability of the defendant company should be applied. The difficulty was that the car and engine were equipped with couplers of a different pattern, which would not couple, for that reason, without a link. Janney couplers and Miller couplers are in common use on the leading railroads of the country, and Congress did not see fit to command the use of either style of automatic coupler to the exclusion of the other, while it must have foreseen that, owing to the manner in which cars were ordinarily handled and exchanged, it would sometimes happen, as in the case at bar, that cars having different styles of automatic couplers would necessarily be brought in contact in the same train. It made no express provision for such an emergency, but declared generally that, after a certain date, cars should be provided with couplers coupling automatically. The engine and dining car were so equipped in the present instance, and there was no such violation of the provisions of the statute as should render the defendant company liable to the plaintiff by virtue of the provisions contained in the eighth section of the act. In other words, the plaintiff assumed the risk of making the coupling in the course of which he sustained the injury. On this ground I concur in the order affirming the judgment below.

COOPER v. LOS ANGELES TERMINAL RAILWAY COMPANY.

Supreme Court, California, September, 1902.

COLLISION AT STREET CROSSING — FAILURE TO SIGNAL APPROACH OF TRAIN — PROXIMATE CAUSE. — Where plaintiff, while driving across defendant's track at a street crossing, was struck and injured by defendant's train, and the evidence showed that plaintiff stopped to look and listen for the train before driving across the track, there being a curve on the track at the point of the accident, and that the defendant failed to give the usual warning on approaching the crossing, it was *held* that the jury were justified in finding that the proximate cause of the injury to plaintiff was the defendant's failure to signal the approach of the train at the crossing (1).

COMMISSIONERS' Decision. Department 1. Appeal from Superior Court, Los Angeles County.

Action by Mary Cooper against the Los Angeles Terminal Railway Company. From judgment for plaintiff, and from an order denying a new trial, defendant appeals. *Judgment affirmed.*

GIBBON, THOMAS & HALSTED, for appellant.

R. H. KNIGHT and NATHAN NEWBY, for respondent.

GRAY, C. — The plaintiff, in driving across defendant's track on a street in South Pasadena, was struck by defendant's train, and seriously injured, for which she brought this action, and obtained a verdict and judgment for $4,000. The defendant appeals from an order denying its motion for a new trial.

1. The principal contention of appellant is that the verdict is contrary to evidence, for the reason that the evidence shows that plaintiff's injury was the result of her own negligence in crossing the track without keeping a proper lookout for the train. The plaintiff testified, in substance, that before going upon the track she stopped her carriage a short distance from and at a point where she would have a clear view of the track each way, and looked and listened for a train; but, not seeing or hearing any, advanced to the track, looking all the time, as best she could, for an approaching train, and first saw the train when her horse was already on the

1. *Collisions and Crossings.* — For crossing-accident cases, from the earliest times to 1897, see vols. 11 and 12 Am. Neg. Cas., where the same are chronologically grouped and arranged in alphabetical order of States. Subsequent actions to date are reported in vols. 1–12 AM. NEG. REP., and the current numbers of that series of Reports.

track. She then struck the horse, but the locomotive caught the hind wheels of her vehicle, and wrecked it, at the same time throwing her a great distance. The evidence further tends to show that there is a curve in the track of defendant at the point of the collision, and that the train coming from the direction it did at the time of plaintiff's injury emerges from a cut between 500 and 600 feet from said point, and cannot be seen for a greater distance than that from any place on the course traveled by plaintiff as she approached defendant's track. It also appears that there is a tree and a railroad station building between where plaintiff stopped to look and listen and the railroad track, and that these objects had the effect to shut off plaintiff's view from parts of the track as she passed on towards the same. Plaintiff testified that she heard no bell or whistle, and several witnesses, who were in positions to hear, testified that no whistles, bells, or other alarms were sounded as the train approached the crossing, but that the train seemed to be coasting down a descending grade, and ran with unusual quietness at a rate of fully thirty miles an hour. The plaintiff is also corroborated by other witnesses in the matter of having stopped to look and listen for the train. In support of the verdict and the conclusion reached by the trial judge in denying a new trial, this evidence must all be taken as true. The jury seem to have concluded that the injury to plaintiff was the proximate result of defendant's failure to give the usual warnings on approaching the crossing, and was not to be attributed to any contributory negligence on the part of plaintiff. We cannot say that this was an unreasonable conclusion to draw from the facts presented, and therefore cannot say that the verdict was, as a matter of law, without support in the evidence. It was for the jury to sift the testimony, and determine which of the conflicting witnesses told the truth, and then, having ascertained the facts, it was for them to say, under proper instructions as to the law, whether the conduct of plaintiff on approaching the track was free from negligence, and accompanied with ordinary care. Of course, there are some cases where contributory negligence is so clearly and unequivocally shown that the appellate court is warranted in declaring, as a matter of law, that it should defeat the plaintiff's recovery. These are cases where but one reasonable conclusion can be drawn from the evidence. As a general rule, however, negligence is a question of fact for the jury or the trial judge to determine on the evidence presented. Here there was evidence tending to show that plaintiff exercised considerable caution in approaching the track, to ascertain if a train was in dangerous proximity to her. The jury have impliedly found on this evidence that she used all necessary caution, and, to set aside the verdict here on the ground urged, would be to interfere with the rights of parties to have their disputes as to mere questions of fact determined in the trial court; and this we may not do.

2. Nor do we think that there was any error of law upon the trial of the case. The defendant requested the court to instruct the jury that "the evidence produced upon the trial of this action fails to show that defendant's train which collided with the plaintiff's vehicle, and thereby injured her, was being, at the time of such collision, run at an unlawful or reckless rate of speed." This instruction was directed to facts not in issue under the pleadings. There was no averment in the complaint that the train was run at an unlawful rate of speed. The allegation of the complaint was to the effect that the company caused its train to approach the crossing "at a rapid and dangerous rate of speed, to wit, at about fifty miles per hour, and negligently and carelessly omitted, while so approaching said crossing, to give any warning, either by ringing the bell or blowing the whistle," etc. No ordinance or statute was put in evidence or cited to show what was a lawful or unlawful rate of speed for the city of Pasadena. Therefore, if there were no other objection to the instruction, it was properly refused, because it did not apply to the cause of action set forth in the complaint, and, so far as we can see, relied upon at the trial. The instruction was also improper because if given it would have withdrawn from the jury a question of fact that came within their province to determine. Whether the rate of speed was reckless as well as dangerous was for the jury to determine from all the evidence. Certainly, the court was not warranted in saying, as a matter of law, that thirty miles an hour was not a reckless rate of speed for a train to make within the boundaries of a city of the sixth class.

Defendant requested many instructions as to the duty of the plaintiff to maintain constant vigilance up to the point of danger before crossing the defendant's track. The court gave two or three of those instructions, containing the substance of the others, so far as the same were free from objection. The jury was fully instructed on this subject, and there was no error in refusing to further instruct the jury.

An objection is urged to a ruling of the court on the exclusion of certain evidence, but this is not deemed of sufficient importance to require special discussion.

We advise that the order appealed from be affirmed.

We concur: HAYNES, C.; COOPER, C.

PER CURIAM. — For the reasons given in the foregoing opinion, the order appealed from is affirmed.

PEDESTRIAN CROSSING STREET STRUCK BY STREET CAR — PLEADING — DEGREE OF CARE — RIGHT OF WAY. — In CONSUMERS' ELECTRIC LIGHT & STREET RAILROAD CO. *v.* PRYOR (*Florida, February, 1902*), 32 So. Rep. 797, an action by Mary E. Pryor against the Consumers', etc., R. R. Co. for damages for injuries sustained by being struck by one of defendant's street cars, judgment for plaintiff in the Circuit Court, Hillsborough County, for $775 was affirmed. The facts were as follows: "The amended declaration upon which the case was tried alleged as follows: 'That the defendant on the 5th of March, 1896, in the city of Tampa, county and State aforesaid (said city being then and there a densely populated city), was the owner of and using and operating a certain electric street railroad, then running upon a certain public highway there, to wit, Florida avenue, at a certain place in the said public highway, to wit, at the crossing of said Florida avenue by Zack street, and, so being the owner of and using and operating the said railroad as aforesaid, the defendant then and there drove a certain street car along and upon the said street railroad on said Florida avenue up to, upon, and at the crossing of the same by Zack street; and it was the duty of the said defendant to so run and operate its said street railroad as not to endanger persons or vehicles traveling upon or crossing any of the streets of said city upon which said street railroad was operated, and, when necessary for the protection of persons and vehicles traveling upon or crossing any of said streets, to stop its cars. That the plaintiff, to wit, on the date aforesaid, with divers numerous persons (the same constituting a large crowd, who had just come out of the Presbyterian Church, situated near the intersection of Florida avenue and Zack street aforesaid), was crossing Florida avenue and the track of the said defendant's street railroad, laid thereon at a regular crossing thereof (the said plaintiff being accompanied by numerous other persons as aforesaid), while one of the defendant's cars was approaching said crossing on said Florida avenue; and it was then and there the duty of the conductor and motorman running said car to so run and operate the same as to enable the plaintiff and the other persons who were with her to safely cross said track; the said conductor and motorman of said car being at such a point on said Florida avenue that they could see the crowd which was crossing the track at least 200 feet from said crossing; but therein the defendant wholly failed and made default, by not stopping said car before reaching said crossing (to enable the plaintiff, together with the crowd of people accompanying her, to cross said track in safety), by means and in consequence of which default and neglect of the defendant aforesaid (by reason of the action of its said employees) the said street car then and there ran and struck with great force and violence upon and against the plaintiff, who was then and there, with all due care and diligence, crossing the track of the said defendant's street railroad at the said regular crossing at the intersection of Florida avenue and Zack street as aforesaid, and thereby the plaintiff was then and there greatly bruised, hurt, and wounded,' etc.; further alleging injury and damage for which suit was brought. A demurrer to the declaration was overruled, and defendant filed four pleas, as follows: 1. The general issue. 2. That the injury complained of was nothing but an unavoidable accident, for which defendant was in no wise responsible. 3. That the injury complained of was caused entirely by the fault, negligence, and carelessness of plaintiff, and by no carelessness, negligence, or fault on the part of defendant. 4. That on the 5th day of March, 1896, defendant had car No. 10, with proper appliances, and operated by a motorman well skilled in operating electric cars, running from Ybor City into the city of Tampa; that immediately before crossing Zack street, at the crossing of that street and Florida avenue in the city of Tampa, the motorman on said car noticed several persons crossing the street; that immediately he began ringing the gong and to slacken the speed of the car until every one had apparently crossed the track, or stopped for the car to pass; that, when the car had run to within about ten or twenty feet of the south crossing of Zack street on Florida avenue, the plaintiff started to go across the track immediately in front of the car; that the moment the motorman saw this (he keeping a lookout in the meantime), he applied the brakes and reversed the car, but it was too late, and, though the motorman did everything that could be done to stop the car, it struck plaintiff, and thereby injured her; that the injury was caused entirely by the carelessness, negligence, and fault of plaintiff, and was not done by the fault, negligence, or carelessness of defendant. Issue was joined upon the first plea, and the others were stricken out on motion of plaintiff."

The opinion in the PRYOR case, *supra*, was rendered by Mabry, J., and the points decided are stated in the syllabus by the court as follows:

1. In actions where negligence is the basis of recovery, it is not necessary for the declaration to set out the facts constituting the negligence, but an allegation of sufficient acts causing injury, coupled with an averment that they were negligently done, will be sufficient.

2. Where the declaration is not drawn upon the theory of the rule

stated in the preceding headnote, but undertakes to set forth the acts relied on as a cause of action, without stating they were negligently done, it must appear from the direct averments of the declaration that the acts causing the injury were *per se* the result of negligence, or negligence must appear from a statement of such facts as certainly raise the presumption that the injury was the result of the defendant's negligence.

3. The act of 1891 (chapter 4071) applies to street railroads, but it does not change the rule of pleading negligence to the extent of permitting only an allegation of injury or damage by the running locomotives, cars, or other machinery of a defendant company. The statute does not fix arbitrarily liability for an injury done, but under it there is a presumption of negligence arising from injury.

4. The measure of duty under the act of 1891 is all ordinary and reasonable care and diligence, and what will constitute the amount or kind of diligence required will vary under different circumstances, as the terms "ordinary" and "reasonable" are relative, and what under some conditions would be ordinary and reasonable diligence might under other conditions amount to even gross negligence.

5. Street cars, regardless of the power by which they are impelled, have no superior rights to other vehicles or pedestrians at regular street crossings, in the absence of a specific legislative grant, but their rights are equal and in common, and impose correlative duties on the respective parties.

6. The employees of a street-car company in operating cars have the right to presume that a pedestrian will exercise ordinary and reasonable care and avoid injury from moving cars, and they are not required to stop a car until it becomes evident to a person of ordinary and reasonable care and prudence that the pedestrian has failed in his duty, and has placed or is about to place himself in a perilous situation. The duty, however, devolves upon the employees to keep a vigilant lookout for persons on or approaching the track, especially at street crossings, and, when they are discovered to be in danger or going into danger on the track, to use every effort consistent with the safety of passengers to avoid injuring such persons.

7. Additional pleas amounting only to the general issue may properly be stricken out on motion.

8. In an action against a street-car company for damages for alleged injury caused in the running of a car, an instruction to the jury is properly refused that seeks to limit the duty of the company's employees to avoid the injury to the time when they became aware of plaintiff's danger, without reference to whether they had observed

all ordinary and reasonable care before that time to discover the dangerous situation of plaintiff.

9. When the question of negligence arises upon a state of facts on which reasonable men may fairly arrive at different conclusions, the fact of negligence cannot be determined until one or the other of those conclusions has been drawn by the jury. The inferences to be drawn from the evidence must be certain and uncontrovertible, or they cannot be decided by the court.

Taylor, Ch. J., dissented from the conclusion reached on the ground of insufficiency of the testimony to support the verdict. (P. O. KNIGHT appeared for plaintiff in error; WALL & STEVENS, for defendant in error.)

WALLACE v. CENTRAL OF GEORGIA RAILWAY COMPANY.

Supreme Court, Georgia, August, 1902.

ENGINEER KILLED IN COLLISION — DIRECTING VERDICT — ERROR. — In an action to recover damages for the death of plaintiff's husband, an engineer in defendant's employ, who was killed in a collision between a passenger train and freight train, it was *held* reversible error to direct verdict for defendant, there being ample evidence to show negligence on part of defendant, and the real issue being whether or not the deceased was guilty of contributory negligence it was a question for the jury to determine (1).

[The syllabus by the Court states that "there was no material error in rejecting or in admitting testimony, but the error committed in directing a verdict requires a new trial."]

1. *Notes of recent Georgia Cases arising out of the relations of Master and Servant.*

In BINION v. GEORGIA SOUTHERN AND FLORIDA R'Y CO. *(Georgia, April, 1902)*, 41 S. E. Rep. 646, an action for injuries to plaintiff, a brakeman in defendant's employ, sustained while coupling cars, judgment on verdict directed for defendant was affirmed, the syllabus by the court stating the ruling as follows:

"1. When, as the result of the trial of a case, the judge directed a verdict for the defendant, and on a bill of exceptions sued out by the plaintiff such direction was by the Supreme Court ruled to have been error, because the evidence had on the trial was conflicting, the effect of such ruling was to declare that it was error to direct a verdict because of such conflict. Such ruling, however, does not have the effect in any way of controlling the discretion of the trial judge, exercised after a second trial of the case, when a verdict was rendered for the plaintiff, in granting a new trial on the application of the defendant, if such verdict was in the opinion of the trial judge contrary to the law or the evidence.

"2. Under the rules of law which affect the liability of the company, in view of the evidence submitted, the

ERROR from City Court of Atlanta.

Action by Josephine Wallace against the Central of Georgia Railway Company. From judgment for defendant, plaintiff brings error. *Judgment reversed.*

HOKE SMITH and H. C. PEEPLES, for plaintiff in error.

DORSEY, BREWSTER & HOWELL, for defendant in error.

LUMPKIN, P. J. — The plaintiff in error, Mrs. Josephine Wallace, brought against the Central of Georgia Railway Company an action for the homicide of her husband, which occurred on the 1st day of August, 1898.

judge did not abuse the discretion with which he is invested in granting a new trial."

In CENTRAL OF GEORGIA R'Y CO. *v.* VINING *(Georgia, August, 1902)*, 42 S. E. Rep. 492, judgment for plaintiff in action for damages for death of husband, an engineer in defendant's employ, was affirmed, the syllabus by the court stating the case as follows:

"1. A card furnished by a railroad company to its engineers, and containing a column headed 'Minimum time freight trains between stations,' but relatively to which there is no rule of the company making it an engineer's duty to regard this minimum time, is not legally binding upon the engineer, so as to forfeit the right of his widow to recover, if he, while attempting to run his train between two stations in less than the time given in the column mentioned, is killed by the negligence of his co-employees.

"2. The plaintiff having clearly showed negligence on the part of the company, it was incumbent on the latter to show that the engineer was negligent. On this point the evidence was conflicting, and the jury having determined the issue in favor of the plaintiff, and the trial judge having approved their finding, this court will not control his discretion in refusing a new trial.

"3. There was no material error in the rulings of which proper complaint is made in any of the other grounds of the motion for a new trial."

In JONES *v.* CENTRAL OF GEORGIA R'Y CO. *(Georgia, July, 1902.)*, 42 S. E. Rep. 363, judgment of nonsuit was affirmed, the syllabus by the court stating the case as follows:

"1. Although there was evidence from which the jury could have found that the plaintiff's husband, an employee of the defendant company, for whose homicide the suit was brought, was killed by the running of the defendant's train, yet, as it neither affirmatively appeared that he was without negligence, nor that the defendant was negligent, the judge of the Superior Court did not err in refusing to sanction a petition for certiorari, complaining of the grant of a nonsuit upon the trial of the case in the City Court."

In CARTER *v.* BRUNSWICK AND WESTERN R. R. CO. *(Georgia, July, 1902)*, 42 S. E. Rep. 239, an action by a railroad employee, judgment for defendant was affirmed, the point as to right of action on failure to execute release of damages being stated in the syllabus by the court as follows:

"A stipulation manifestly designed for the benefit of the company, to the effect that a beneficiary would not be paid under the relief and hospital system unless the employee first filed with the proper officers of this depart-

The undisputed facts of the case, as developed by the evidence, are substantially as follows: The deceased was an engineer in the service of the defendant, and was at the time of his death engaged in running the locomotive of an extra train which was operated between Atlanta and Hapeville. Between these points there were two main tracks, one of which was used for trains going out of the city, and the other for trains coming into it. At McPherson station, looking towards Hapeville, the right-hand main track was the one for outgoing trains, and the opposite main track was the one for incoming trains. Between these two main lines there was a middle

ment satisfactory releases, does not authorize one who has received benefits at the hands of this department, in accordance with his terms of membership therein, to prosecute his claim for damages merely because he has failed or refused to execute such a release."

In CENTRAL OF GEORGIA R'Y CO. *v.* MCWHORTER *(Georgia, April, 1902)*, 42 S. E. Rep. 82, judgment for plaintiff in the Superior Court, Clayton county, was reversed, the syllabus by the court stating the case as follows:

"1. Under the rules of the railroad company which were involved in the present case, no duty was imposed upon the conductor to examine or repair the brake, or any appliance connected with the operation of the same; such duty resting, under the rules, upon the subordinates of the conductor, and the duties of the conductor being simply those of supervision and direction.

"2. It follows from the foregoing that when the plaintiff went between the engine and the cars for the purpose of examining the air hose used in operating the air brake (the same being in a defective condition), there being no pressing emergency requiring him to perform this duty, which the rules imposed upon his subordinates, he was guilty of such fault as will preclude him from recovering damages for injuries sustained as a direct result of his having unnecessarily abandoned his position as conductor for the purpose of performing duties which, under the rules of the company, should have been performed by his subordinate.

"3. When a railway conductor, in the absence of any emergency, or of circumstances so requiring, goes outside of the line of his duties as prescribed by the rules of the company, and thus places himself in a position of danger, and is injured by the moving of a train, he is guilty of negligence, and cannot hold the company liable, even though the engineer causes such movement to be made without ringing the bell of the locomotive, and in doing so violates a rule of the company; and more especially is this true when the conductor, by reason of past experience, must be aware that the engineer, in the absence of any knowledge that the conductor is so exposing himself to danger, can, as to him, safely omit the ringing of the bell, and yet fails to inform the engineer of the intended risk which will render such omission hazardous to the conductor." (LLOYD CLEVELAND, HALL & BOYNTON, W. L. WATTERSON, W. C. BEEKS AND R. L. BERNER, appeared for plaintiff in error; HOKE SMITH AND H. C. PEEPLES, for defendant in error.) Rehearing denied.

In ATLANTA RAILWAY & POWER CO. *v.* BENNETT *(Georgia, July, 1902)*, 42 S. E. Rep. 244, judgment for plaintiff in the City Court of Atlanta was affirmed, LUMPKIN, P. J., stating the facts as track, used for switching. A spur track passed from tne middle track, and ran across the right-hand main line into McPherson barracks. Eason was the conductor of the train upon which Wallace was engineer. On the morning of the day on which the killing occurred, Eason, under the direction of the proper authority, had left a number of passenger cars to be loaded in the barracks with troops, and had gone to Hapeville, where he worked during the forenoon. His orders were to return to the barracks at one o'clock, and carry the passenger cars containing the soldiers to Atlanta. Eason's train reached McPherson on its return from Hapeville a few minutes after one o'clock. A passenger train, No. 33, was due

follows: Plaintiff's petition made a case substantially as follows: "He was an employee of the company in the capacity of motorman. On the 4th of October, 1900, while engaged in running one of its electric cars, it became necessary for him to absent himself therefrom in order to attend to a call of nature. He left the car in charge of the conductor, by whose direction another motorman of the company, who happened to be riding upon this particular car, ran it to the end of the line, and brought it back to the street at which the plaintiff had left it. As the car approached the point where he was awaiting its return, the conductor and this motorman saw him coming towards the track for the purpose of boarding the car and resuming the discharge of his duties. The car was 'slowed up' to a perfectly safe rate of speed to enable the plaintiff to get upon the same, and he undertook to do so by stepping upon the 'running board' and grasping an upright post at the front of the car; but, just as he was in the act of so doing, the motorman in charge 'negligently and carelessly put on the full current of electricity, which caused the car to bound, and jump forward very violently, and plaintiff was thrown from his position upon the running board towards the front of the car, and rolled and fell partly on the track, but was partly thrown from the track by the fender of the car, which rolled him around, and enabled the front wheels to pass him. The motorman in the meantime had shut the current off, and applied his brakes, and the car was continuing to move, but slowing up in its forward motion, when the back wheels of the car reached plaintiff, and in plaintiff's having been thrown around by the fender, and in his struggling to escape, his legs were caught by the back wheels and trucks and the apparatus which surround the same, and the car began to drag him. If the car had been stopped at this point, the plaintiff would still have been saved from the loss of his legs, but at this point the motorman, instead of continuing his hold on the brake, negligently and carelessly loosed the brake, and, the grade being descending, the car started violently forward when the brake was loosed, and ran over plaintiff's legs, cutting off entirely the right leg just below the knee, and mashing and ruining for life the left leg.' There was a verdict for the plaintiff, and the defendant company is here excepting to a judgment overruling its motion for a new trial. This motion is based upon alleged errors in charging the jury, and upon the general grounds that the verdict was contrary to law and to the evidence." * * * Held, that the evidence warranted a finding in favor of plaintiff.

to pass McPherson on the outgoing main line at fifteen minutes after one. After reaching McPherson on the incoming main line, Eason left a number of cars upon it, and then had the locomotive pulled further up this main line, and from it backed upon the middle track, and coupled to several box cars which were standing thereon. There the locomotive and these cars remained till No. 33 had passed. Eason then ordered Wallace to back the box cars attached to his locomotive across the outgoing main line, and had these cars coupled to the passenger cars which had been left in the barracks. After this coupling had been made, and the train had come to a standstill, a portion of the locomotive occupied the rails of the outgoing main line. In this situation of affairs, and while the soldiers were getting aboard the passenger cars, a freight train, known as No. 42, coming from Atlanta, collided with the locomotive of Eason's train, and, as a result, Wallace was killed.

Numerous rules of the company were introduced in evidence. Such of them as require special consideration will be hereinafter noticed. There was much conflict in the testimony as to various matters other than those mentioned above; and, after both sides had closed, the court directed a verdict for the defendant. Mrs. Wallace made a motion for a new trial, which was overruled, and she excepted. We will first dispose of the minor points, and then pass upon the main question, which is whether or not the court erred in not submitting the case to the jury.

The plaintiff's counsel offered certain testimony to which counsel for the defendant objected. The court intimated that the testimony was inadmissible, and after some discussion the counsel first mentioned remarked to the court: "I will not insist upon it at the present." This was certainly sufficient to warrant the inference that the offer to introduce this testimony was withdrawn, and the judge certifies that this was his understanding of the matter. It was on the trial below contended that the plaintiff's husband was, while engaged in switching and moving his train at McPherson, under the protection of certain rules of the company which provided for the operation of what is called the "Block System." Counsel for the company insisted that these particular rules were not applicable in such a case as the present. The plaintiff's counsel introduced testimony tending to show that, under a custom or practice which had prevailed, the block system had been relied on for the protection of train crews which engaged in switching at stations within the territory covered by the system. To meet this, the defendant's counsel were permitted to introduce, over objection, the testimony of several witnesses who had been employed by the company in the running of trains, to the effect that, so far as they knew, no such custom or practice had ever prevailed. Some of this testimony was irrelevant because it related to a period subsequent to the date of the homicide, and some of it was probably so because it related to a period long anterior to that date, when the rules of the company were not the same as those in force when Wallace was killed. The judge certifies that he ruled repeatedly and distinctly that "evidence of any custom subsequent to August, 1898, was inadmissible." With this restriction, and the further qualification that it was not permissible to show what the custom was under different rules, the testimony in question was proper. The rules pertaining to the block system were not luminously clear as to whether or not it was applicable to a situation like that involved in the case in hand. The plaintiff undertook to show that it was, by some of the company's servants, treated as being so, and the defendant was allowed to show that, by others of them, it was not so treated. As will appear before we conclude, this is not really a matter of much importance, for we will endeavor to show that the block system does not cut a substantial figure in this case. The plaintiff also excepted to other rulings made by the court in admitting and in rejecting testimony. With these we will not undertake to deal specifically, for they are, in view of what we regard as the controlling issue upon which the case should be made to turn, of but trivial moment.

The action of the court in directing a verdict for the defendant can be sustained only upon the theory that, viewing the testimony and all legitimate inferences therefrom most favorably for the plaintiff, she was not entitled to recover. As a reviewing court, we must treat as established in her behalf every contention of fact insisted upon by her which the jury would have been warranted in sustaining. There was ample evidence to show negligence on the part of the defendant, and the real issue in controversy was whether or not the deceased was guilty of contributory negligence. If he was, his widow has no right of action. If he was not, she has. If the deceased relied exclusively upon the supposed protection afforded by the block system as a justification for leaving his locomotive in its exposed condition upon the outgoing main line, he was negligent. One of the general rules of the company, No. 399, provides that "when a train stops or is delayed, under circumstances in which it may be overtaken by a following train, the flagman must go back immediately with danger signals a sufficient distance to insure full protection. When recalled, he may return to his train, first placing two torpedoes on the rail, when the conditions require it. The front of a train must be protected in the same way, when necessary, by the fireman." General rule No. 402 reads as follows: "When it is necessary for a train on double track to cross over to the opposite track, a flagman must be sent out with danger signals, as provided in rule No. 399." Rule No. 10 in the joint time table declares that: "Flagmen will not, under any circumstances, depend upon the block signals to protect their trains, but must go back with signals, as required by the general rules." It will not do to say that this rule is binding upon flagmen only. It is, under other rules introduced in evidence, but which need not be set forth, incumbent upon conductors to see to it that flagmen perform their duties; and, as has been seen, if the front of a train is exposed to danger, the fireman must act as flagman "when necessary." If, upon such a necessity arising, the fireman did not so act, and the engineer knew this to be so, he would surely be unwarranted in assuming that protection from threatened danger would come from some other source. Interpreting the special rule last quoted in the light of the others, its plain meaning is that no person connected with the running of a train has the right to rely absolutely for protection upon the block system. For this reason we have not deemed it necessary to go into further detail as to what the record discloses with regard to the nature of this system, or to discuss the particular rules relating to it; and for the same reason we now dismiss it from further consideration.

Under the rules above copied, and others in evidence regulating the duties of conductors and engineers, the contents of which are not here essential, it was the duty of Eason, before placing his train in the position it occupied when the collision took place, to send a flagman towards Atlanta to intercept train No. 42. It was the duty of Wallace, if he knew that the conductor had neglected to take this precaution, to send the fireman forward on this mission. Under such circumstances, it would have been "necessary" for the engineer to take this step. The evidence on these vital matters, taking it most favorably for the plaintiff, and giving her the benefit of the strongest legitimate inferences which could be drawn therefrom in her favor, would have warranted a finding that Eason, before causing the box cars to be backed into the barracks, did order Griggs, a flagman, to go forward and flag No. 42; that he started out as if to obey this order, and that Wallace was in a position where he could have heard and seen what occurred. In point of fact, Griggs did not flag No. 42; and he, as a witness, denied having been ordered to do so at all. Indeed, we wish to state just here in the plainest terms that we are not undertaking to say what was the truth as to any feature of the case, or to intimate what the verdict should have been. The testimony was, as already stated, conflicting at every issuable point, and we are dealing with it merely from the standpoint that it was the plaintiff's right to have the jury pass upon her contentions, and to obtain the benefit of that result which would properly ensue from their finding that the same were well founded in fact. If the truth was as above outlined, Wallace was not negligent in failing to send the fireman forward to flag No. 42. Whether, upon the assumption that he neither heard Eason order Griggs to flag that train nor saw Griggs make any movement towards doing so, he would have been negligent in not sending out the fireman, we do not now decide, but leave this question open for determination, if need be, at the next hearing. Nor did the evidence demand a finding that Wallace was negligent in not himself looking towards Atlanta, and discovering the approach of No. 42 in time to get his train out of its way. Nor were the jury by any means bound to find that Wallace was negligent in not backing far enough into the barracks to clear the main line of his locomotive at the time the box cars were coupled to the passenger cars, or that it was his duty, after this coupling had been made, to then push the entire train further back into the barracks so as to leave the main line open. On all these and many other strenuously contested questions, there was much oral testimony pro and con, and many pertinent rules of the company were introduced. We do not deem it essential to enter upon a detailed discussion of these various matters. Enough has been said, we think, to enable the clear-headed and most capable judge of the trial court to apprehend upon what lines the case should be submitted to the jury, and we are quite confident that he will do so in the able and satisfactory manner with which he usually conducts the business of his court.

Judgment reversed. All the justices concurring, except LEWIS, J., absent on account of sickness.

GEORGIA RAILROAD COMPANY v. BALDONI.

Supreme Court, Georgia, July, 1902.

EJECTION OF PASSENGER FROM TRAIN — EXPIRATION OF TICKET — NOTICE AS TO TICKETS — EVIDENCE — BAGGAGE AND MERCHANDISE — FRAUD — EXCESSIVE DAMAGES. — 1. A placard or notice posted by a railroad company at its ticket office, announcing that

tickets of a certain class must be used on the day of sale, is not admissible in evidence in favor of the company in a suit against it by a passenger for an alleged wrongful ejection from a train on the ground that the ticket had expired, unless it be shown that the passenger had read the placard or had notice of its contents (1).

2. Where such a passenger had procured his trunk to be checked two days before he undertook to use the ticket, and, when he attempted to use it, was ejected on the ground that the ticket had expired, and long subsequently it was ascertained that his trunk contained merchandise instead of baggage, it was not error for the trial judge to refuse to charge the jury that on account of this fraud the company had a right to cancel the contract, and could not be held liable for ejecting the passenger.

3. Under the evidence disclosed by the record, the verdict was so excessive as to indicate bias and prejudice on the part of the jury.

(Syllabus by the Court.)

ERROR from City Court of Macon.

Action by Peter Baldoni against the Georgia Railroad Company. From a judgment in favor of plaintiff, defendant brings error. *Judgment reversed.*

JOS. B. & BRYAN CUMMING, HARDEMAN DAVIS, and TURNER & JONES, for plaintiff in error.

M. R. FEREMAN, MINTER WIMBERLY, and ROLAND ELLIS, for defendant in error.

SIMMONS, Ch. J. — Baldoni, a peddler of balloons and confetti, bought a ticket over the Georgia Railroad from Macon to Augusta. He did not take the train on the day the ticket was purchased, but two days thereafter started on his journey. When, a few miles from Macon, Baldoni presented his ticket to the conductor, the latter informed him that the time within which the ticket could be used had expired, that the rules of the company limited the use of the ticket to the day on which it was purchased, and that therefore he could not ride upon it. Baldoni had no notice of this rule of the company, and there was no limitation expressed on the ticket. Baldoni insisted that he had paid his money and was entitled to ride. After some further conversation, the conductor informed him that they were approaching the first station outside of Macon, and that he must get off of the train. When the station was reached, Baldoni objected to leaving the train, but obeyed the orders of the conductor and alighted. The conductor seems to have called the agent at the station, and told him of putting Baldoni off, and requested him to flag the incoming train, so that Baldoni could

1. *Ejection of Persons from trains.* — See vol. 8 Am. Neg. Cas., for actions arising out of ejection of persons from trains, etc., from the earliest period to 1897. Subsequent actions to date are reported in vols. 1-12 AM. NEG. REP., and the current numbers of that series of Reports.

return to Macon. This Baldoni denied, claiming that he had to alight hurriedly in the darkness and find his way to the agent. At any rate, the incoming train was stopped, and Baldoni, paying a few cents for his fare, returned to Macon. He reached Macon before ten o'clock in the evening, having been absent therefrom but two or three hours. Baldoni then attempted, at several different boarding houses, to get lodging for the night, but was refused. He did not go to a hotel, because he was not sufficiently well dressed, and was afraid the rates would be too high. He finally slept in the city park on some straw. He became quite cold during the night, and early in the morning warmed himself in the station of another railroad company. The ejection from the train was on Saturday night. Baldoni remained in Macon all day Sunday, purchased another ticket from the Georgia Railroad Company, and, just twenty-four hours after his first attempt to make the trip, boarded a train for Augusta, which place he reached on Monday morning. He thus lost one day (Sunday) on account of the action of the conductor. At times Baldoni's business netted him as much as $100 per day, and at other times nothing. Augusta was not at that time a good place for his business. He brought suit against the company for damages, and the jury awarded him $1,250. The defendant moved for a new trial, and the motion was overruled. The defendant excepted.

1. On the trial the defendant offered in evidence a placard or notice, printed in very large type and addressed to the public, in which, among other things, it was stated that "all one-way tickets will be limited to date of sale." A copy of this placard was posted at the ticket office in the depot, and another near the entrance to the depot. The ticket sold to Baldoni had no limitation expressed upon it, and this placard was offered to show that Baldoni had notice of the regulation of the company requiring such tickets to be used on the day of sale. There was no proof that the plaintiff could read, or that he had read this notice or knew of its contents. There is nothing to show that his attention was in any way directed to this placard. We think that a placard of this character is not sufficient of itself to put a passenger on notice of the rules and regulations of the company in regard to the time limit of their tickets. In these days of hurry and bustle, passengers have little time to give to reading the notices exposed to their gaze in ticket offices and stations. Very few passengers, if any, stop to read such notices. Their usual object is to purchase their tickets, and, boarding the train, to depart upon their journeys. It would not do to charge them with notice of the rules and regulations of the company

simply because a copy of such rules or regulations was posted at the ticket office. Notice of the rule or regulation must be in some way brought home to a passenger before he can be charged with it. The court was therefore right in rejecting this evidence.

2. Pending the trial it was ascertained that the plaintiff had checked his trunks over the road of the defendant by virtue of his ticket, which he showed to the baggage master, two days before he attempted to use his ticket for passage, and that the trunks contained balloons, confetti, and other merchandise in which plaintiff dealt. The court was requested by counsel for the defendant to charge the jury that this was a fraud upon the company, and gave it the right to cancel the contract of carriage with Baldoni, and that therefore it could not be held liable for ejecting him from the train. The court refused to so charge, but charged to the contrary. In this the court did not err. The contract made with the railroad company was to transport the purchaser and his baggage. The fact that the purchaser had put merchandise as well as baggage in his trunk would not authorize the company to eject him from its train. The company could have refused to carry the trunks unless the passenger had paid the freight charges on the merchandise in them. After the trunks were checked, it might have had the right to notify the passenger that he would not be carried unless the freight was paid; this notice being accompanied by an offer to return what money was due him. After the trunks had reached their destination the company might have refused to deliver them until the proper freight charges had been paid. If the character of their contents was not discovered until after delivery, the passenger was still liable to the company in an action for the freight charges. The company did none of these things. We think that a passenger's ticket is not avoided and rendered worthless by the mere fact that he has checked in his trunk articles which are not baggage, any more than if such trunks should happen to weigh more than the company allows to be carried as baggage. Moreover, it appears from the plaintiff's evidence that the company, by its agents, did not undertake to treat the contract as canceled, but ejected plaintiff on the ground that the time limit of his ticket had expired. Having ejected him on this ground, it is doubtful if the company could set up fraud in the procurement of the contract, or a violation of the contract, as a justification of the illegal ejectment. Be this as it may, the company did not pursue any of the remedies it had, and cannot rely upon the nature of the contents of the plaintiff's trunks as a justification of his ejection.

3. One ground of the motion for new trial complains that the

verdict is excessive. We think this ground well taken. While it is true that the conductor of the train had no legal right to eject the plaintiff because of the expiration of the time limit put upon his ticket by rules of the company of which the plaintiff had no notice, the evidence of three witnesses for the defendant showed that there was no force used, but that the plaintiff obeyed the order of the conductor and alighted at the station. The plaintiff himself testified that the conductor took hold of him and got the best of him, and he surrendered, but even then it does not appear that he was in any way injured or hurt physically. He did not lose any time from the sale of his goods by reason of the delay, the day lost being Sunday. He slept in the park in Macon because, according to his testimony, the boarding-house keepers refused to entertain him, and he was not sufficiently well dressed to go to a hotel. According to his testimony, there was but one other passenger in the coach from which he was ejected. Under these facts, we think the verdict for $1,250 was so excessive as to show bias and prejudice in the minds of the jury. While railroad companies should be held to strict accountability for a violation of the rights of their passengers, we think that juries should not be allowed to run wild in the assessment of damages in cases like the present. Taking into consideration all the facts and circumstances disclosed by the evidence, we think the verdict was far in excess of what it should have been.

Judgment reversed. All the justices concurring, except LEWIS, J., absent on account of sickness.

CITY OF CHANUTE v. HIGGINS.

Supreme Court, Kansas, November, 1902.

PEDESTRIAN FALLING INTO CELLAR OPENING IN SIDEWALK — QUESTION OF LAW — DAMAGES. — 1. In an action to recover damages for personal injuries, where the facts are undisputed or sufficiently found by a jury, and but one conclusion can be drawn therefrom, whether such facts constitute negligence is a question of law.

2. A reviewing court may not set aside the verdict of a jury and a judgment rendered thereon by the trial court, on the ground that it is excessive, unless the amount so found is so clearly disproportionate to the injury sustained or so grossly excessive as to render it morally certain that such verdict could not have been the result of the calm and deliberate judgment of the triors, but was the result of passion and prejudice.

(Syllabus by the Court.)

IN BANC. Error from District Court, Neosho County.

Action by Lina Higgins against the City of Chanute. From judgment for plaintiff, defendant brings error. *Judgment affirmed.*

H. P. FARRELLY, C. A. COX, S. C. BROWN, and T. J. HUDSON, for plaintiff in error.

LAPHAM & BREWSTER and W. R. CLINE, for defendant in error.

GREENE, J. — Lina Higgins recovered judgment against the city of Chanute for injuries alleged to have been sustained by falling into the entrance of an unguarded cellarway opening upon a sidewalk of one of the principal streets of the city. It appears from the pleadings and admissions that the city of Chanute pretended to grant Jones Bros., their heirs and assigns, the right to excavate on the west side of Main street, adjoining lot No. 1, block 2, in said city, a cellarway not exceeding four feet in width or thirty feet in length, and to maintain therein a stairway to the cellar or basement of the building erected thereon, so long as the building should be maintained. This ordinance also provided that the grantees, their heirs and assigns, should construct and maintain a good and substantial railing on the east side and south end of such opening. Under this ordinance the building, which was for private purposes, was erected, and a cellarway four feet wide and thirty feet long, paralleling the sidewalk, was excavated, and steps placed therein. The outside and rear end were protected by an iron railing. The entrance was unguarded. This cellarway occupied half of the sidewalk, and was erected and maintained with the knowledge and consent of the city for a period of about two years before the accident. It appears from the evidence that on December 12, 1898, the plaintiff, a woman twenty-five years of age, left the store where she was engaged as a clerk about seven o'clock in the evening, and started down this sidewalk. The evening was dark and stormy, and there were not sufficient lights. While passing along on the sidewalk, and without fault on her part, she walked into this unguarded cellarway, and fell to the bottom, a distance of about ten feet, and sustained injuries for which she sought to recover in this action.

It is argued that the court below erred in giving the following instructions: "2. You are instructed that it was the duty of the defendant city to exercise ordinary care and prudence to keep its streets in a reasonably safe condition for travel thereon. In the light of the pleadings in this case, and such of the testimony as is undisputed, it appears that, some years prior to the time when plaintiff alleges she sustained the fall in question, the said city, by an ordinance it enacted, authorized the construction of this open cellarway upon a portion of the area of one of its streets upon which persons passing along on foot were accustomed to travel. This cellarway had a guard, or, rather, railing, on the side next to the street, and at the south end, but the north end was left open. 3. You are instructed, as a matter of law, that said city, in permitting this cellarway to be constructed on the footway portion of one of its streets, with one end of said cellarway left open, as before explained, was guilty of at least what in law is styled 'ordinary negligence.' And the fact that there may have been a portion of the area of said street, extending from the outer side of said cellarway to the street curbing, that was available for use as a sidewalk, is not, in itself, any defense to this action. The public had the right, in law, to have all of said street kept in a reasonably safe condition for travel thereon." The facts upon which these instructions were based, as expressed by the trial court, were undisputed. It is contended that whether these undisputed facts constitute negligence on the part of the city was a question of fact, and should have been submitted to the jury. Where the facts are undisputed, but of such a nature that different minds will draw different conclusions from them as to the reasonableness of the parties' conduct, it is a proper question for the determination of the jury. Railway Co. *v.* Pointer, 14 Kan. 38; Railroad *v.* Hotham, 22 Kan. 41. Where, however, the facts are undisputed or are sufficiently found by the jury, and only one conclusion can be drawn therefrom, whether such facts constitute negligence is a question of law. Railway Co. *v.* Butts, 7 Kan. 309; Railway Co. *v.* Lipprand, 5 Kan. App. 484, 47 Pac. Rep. 625; Dewald *v.* Railroad Co., 44 Kan. 586, 24 Pac. Rep. 1101. We think it impossible for fair and reasonable minds to come to different conclusions from the admitted facts in this case. The cellarway paralleled the sidewalk and occupied about one-half of its width, on one of the principal streets of the city. The entrance was unguarded. It was a dangerous excavation, and there was nothing to prevent a person, on a dark night, while walking along that street, from walking into it. Streets and sidewalks are for the exclusive use of the public, as passageways, and it is the duty of every city to keep and maintain the whole width and every part thereof free and unobstructed and in a safe condition for the uses for which they are intended. Smith *v.* City of Leavenworth, 15 Kan. 81. It was negligence for the city to allow this cellarway, with an unguarded opening, to be maintained, and to occupy a part of one of its sidewalks. The instructions complained of were as favorable as the city had any reason to expect.

It is complained that the jury was actuated by prejudice, and it is said this is evidenced by excessive separate items of damage and its general verdict. The jury allowed plaintiff $100 for medical attendance. The evidence proved that she only expended $70, and that she was required to, and did, remit $30 of said sum. It is true, the evidence only proved that she had paid $70 for such services, but there was some evidence that she had other physicians attending her, and it is silent as to what she paid or the amount incurred to them. It is contended that the item of damages for loss of time was excessive, and that this showed prejudice on the part of the jury. The difference between the amount she should have recovered, as computed by the plaintiff in error, and the amount allowed by the jury, is too small to authorize a court to say that it was the result of prejudice. It is contended that the general verdict is excessive. The total amount allowed was $4,358. There was testimony that this woman was permanently injured, both internally and externally. The extent of her injuries, as nearly as it was possible, were presented to the jury by eminent physicians, both for the plaintiff and defendant. She was required to exhibit to the jury her ankle, which she testified was so injured by the fall that she was compelled to wear a brace to enable her to walk. It was also in evidence that her internal injuries were permanent, entirely disabling or greatly impeding her in earning a livelihood. While the verdict seems to have been liberal, it is not so wanting of support in the evidence or so grossly excessive that this court can say that it was the result of passion or prejudice.

Some contention is made that on the argument to the jury one of the plaintiff's counsel made highly inflammatory and prejudicial remarks. The court, upon objection, instructed the jury not to consider these remarks; and it appears from the testimony of some of the jurors who testified on the application of the defendant below for a new trial that these remarks were not prejudicial, and did not have much effect, as they testified that "all speeches of any and all lawyers in the case was 'sweetness wasted on the desert air.'"

It is also alleged that the court erred in refusing to grant the defendant a new trial. It is said that the misconduct of the jury and the manner in which it arrived at its verdict were such that the verdict should not have been permitted to stand. It is alleged that the verdict was arrived at by each juror setting down the amount he thought the plaintiff ought to recover, adding these several sums together, and dividing the total amount by 12; the quotient being the total amount of the verdict. J. K. Harkness, one of the jurors, testified that this was the manner of arriving at the verdict. It is evident, however, that the court below did not believe the statement of Harkness, and upon this we entirely agree with that court. Every other juror who testified declared that Harkness' statement was false. There are some other alleged irregularities on the part of the jury, but nothing that appears prejudicial to the rights of plaintiff in error.

The judgment of the court below is affirmed. All the justices concurring.

MISSOURI PACIFIC RAILWAY COMPANY v. DIVINNEY.

Supreme Court, Kansas, Division No. 2, July, 1902.

PERSON ASSAULTED BY STATION AGENT — SCOPE OF EMPLOYMENT — LIABILITY. — 1. Where one not a passenger is assaulted by the station agent of a railway company, the company is not liable in damages for injuries received by reason of such assault, unless at the time of its commission the agent was engaged in the performance of some duty imposed upon him by reason of his employment as such agent, or he was acting in the exercise of some authority conferred upon him, either directly or by virtue of his employment (1).

(Syllabus by the Court.)

ERROR from District Court, Cloud County.

Action by Will Divinney against the Missouri Pacific Railway Company. From judgment for plaintiff, defendant brings error. *Judgment reversed*

Argued before DOSTER, Ch. J., and SMITH and POLLOCK, JJ.

WAGGENER, HORTON & ORR and PARK B. PULSIFER, for plaintiff in error.

G. M. CULVER and F. W. STURGES, for defendant in error.

POLLOCK, J. — Action by Divinney to recover from the railway company damages for an assault made upon him by one Taylor, station agent at the station of Ames on defendant's line of railway. There was a trial before the court and a jury. Both parties requested special findings of fact from the jury upon the evidence. These findings, in so far as material in this controversy, are as follows: Requested by plaintiff: "1. Q. Was the plaintiff a passenger

1. *Assaults.* — For actions arising out of assaults upon persons on trains, stations, etc., from the earliest period to 1897, see vol. 8 Am. Neg. Cas. Subsequent actions on the same topic are reported in vols. 1–12 AM. NEG. REP., and the current numbers of that series of Reports.

over defendant's road from Ames to Concordia on the morning of August 7, 1900? A. Yes. 2. Q. Did the agent of the defendant, Taylor, at the station at Ames, commit an assault and battery upon plaintiff by striking or beating him in or about the face? A. Yes. 3. Q. Did the plaintiff at any time, on the morning of August 7, 1900, in the station, on the platform, or elsewhere, use, towards defendant's agent, Taylor, or other employee, any language reasonably and naturally sufficient to provoke an assault and battery upon him? A. No." Requested by defendant: "1. Q. At the time the plaintiff was struck or slapped by Taylor, was he (plaintiff) attempting to purchase a ticket to ride on defendant's train? A. No. 2. Q. At the time said plaintiff was struck or slapped by Taylor, was he, said Taylor, attempting to eject or remove said plaintiff from defendant's depot or depot grounds? A. No. 3. Q. At the time mentioned in the last preceding question, was said Taylor attempting to prevent plaintiff from boarding defendant's train? A. No. 4. Q. At the time said Taylor struck or slapped said plaintiff, did he do so in the discharge of any duty imposed upon him in connection with his acting as agent of the defendant company? A. No." Upon these special findings defendant moved for judgment. This motion was overruled, judgment entered against the company, and defendant brings error.

The action of the trial court in overruling the motion of the defendant for a judgment upon the special findings of the jury notwithstanding the general verdict is the sole ground of error submitted for determination by this court. The solution of this question depends upon the extent of the company's duty to afford protection to plaintiff from the wrongful and tortious acts of its servants and agents. It is quite clear, in this case, if the assault made upon plaintiff had been the act of a third party, unassociated with the company, under the circumstances, it would not be liable. Does the fact that the assault was made by the station agent in the employ of the company change the rule as to the liability of defendant? Obviously, this must be determined by the relation plaintiff and the agent bore to the company at the time the injury to plaintiff transpired. If plaintiff had offered himself to the company, and had been received as a passenger by the company before the injury to him occurred, he would have been entitled to demand and receive from the company protection from the unlawful and violent acts of the agents and servants of the company, and third parties as well. If, at the time the injury was inflicted upon him, the agent was engaged in the performance of any duty devolving upon him by reason of his employment by the company, the act of the agent was the act of the company, and the liability of defendant would necessarily follow. The general rule heretofore announced by this court is that the company is not responsible for any act or omission of its servants which is not connected with the business in which they serve the company, and which does not happen in the course of their employment. Hudson *v.* Mo. Kan. & Tex. R'y Co., 16 Kan. 470, and authorities cited; Sachrowitz *v.* Atch., Top. & S. F. R. R. Co., 37 Kan. 212, 8 Am. Neg. Cas. 269, 15 Pac. Rep. 242. As the jury, in finding No. 4 requested by defendant, found the agent was not engaged in the discharge of any duty imposed upon him by virtue of his employment at the time of the assault made upon plaintiff, it follows the assault must be regarded as the voluntary act of the agent, and he alone liable to plaintiff for damages arising therefrom, unless plaintiff may be considered to have occupied the relation of a passenger to the company at the time of his injury, and to be entitled to the protection by law accorded to passengers from the carrier. As to this branch of the case, while the jury finds the plaintiff was a passenger upon defendant's train from the station of Ames to Concordia on the morning of his injury, yet this finding must be construed in the light of the undisputed facts found in the record. An examination of the testimony found in the record conclusively shows that the assault occurred before the arrival of the train at the station of Ames, and before plaintiff had either presented himself or been received by the company as a passenger. Hence, upon this branch of the case, it is sufficient to say plaintiff was neither a passenger at the time he received the injury of which he complains, nor does his petition allege him to have been such passenger. His cause of action, as alleged in the petition, is based upon the injury which he received from the assault made by Taylor as agent of the company in the discharge of his duty, and not upon a breach of the duty owed by a common carrier to protect its passengers from injury at the hands of its servants or third parties. It follows, from the finding made by the jury, that the agent at the time of the assault was not acting in the discharge of any duty imposed upon him by his employment. The motion for judgment upon the findings, notwithstanding the general verdict, should have been sustained.

Judgment is reversed, with instructions to sustain the motion and enter judgment in favor of defendant. All the justices concurring.

ST. LOUIS AND SAN FRANCISCO RAILWAY COMPANY ET AL. v. BRICKER.

Supreme Court, Kansas, Division No. 1, July, 1902.

EMPLOYEE INJURED BY FALLING TIMBERS — DAMAGES — LIABILITY OF RECEIVER OF RAILROAD. — 1. In an action to recover damages for personal injuries, loss of ability to earn a livelihood and permanent injuries constitute one item of damages. Where, however, the defendants in such action, in their special questions submitted to the jury, divide such item, and ask the jury: 1. "If you find for the plaintiff, how much do you allow him for the loss of ability to earn a livelihood?" 2. "If you find for the plaintiff, how much do you allow for permanent injuries, exclusive of the amount, if any, allowed for loss of ability to earn a livelihood?" — and the jury, in response to such questions, states a given amount for each, they cannot thereafter be heard to say that, because the item was thus divided, the amount allowed in answer to one of such questions includes all the plaintiff was entitled to as damages for personal injuries and loss of ability to earn a livelihood, and that the amount allowed in answer to the other question is excessive.

2. Where the property of a railway corporation is in the exclusive possession of receivers, who are operating the road, the corporation is not liable in an action for personal injuries sustained by an employee of such receivers.

3. If an action is prosecuted jointly against a railway corporation in the hands of receivers and the receivers to recover damages for personal injuries sustained by an employee, and it shall be determined that the receivers were in the exclusive possession of and operating the road at the time of the injuries, and that the corporation is not liable therefor, the action may be dismissed as to the corporation, or the judgment against the corporation set aside, without prejudice to the right of the plaintiff to have judgment against the receivers.

(Syllabus by the Court.)

ERROR from District Court, Sumner County.

Action by Ulysses Bricker against the St. Louis and San Francisco Railway Company and Aldace F. Walker and John J. McCook, receivers. From judgment for plaintiff, defendants bring error. *Judgment modified.*

Argued before JOHNSTON, CUNNINGHAM, GREENE, and ELLIS, JJ.

J. W. GLEED, J. L. HUNT, W. LITTLEFIELD (D. E. PALMER and GLEED, WARE & GLEED, of counsel), for plaintiffs in error.

J. D. HOUSTON and C. R. MITCHELL, for defendant in error.

GREENE, J. — Ulysses Bricker sued the St. Louis and San Francisco Railway Company and Aldace F. Walker and John J. McCook, as receivers of said company, to recover damages for injuries which he claims to have sustained by reason of the negligence of the employees of said company and its receivers. At the time of his injuries, plaintiff belonged to a bridge gang working under a foreman named Bowersock, repairing and reconstructing a pile bridge on a line of defendants' railroad in Ellsworth county. The bridge was situated in a southwesterly and northeasterly direction over a stream, and was about thirty-two feet long. Immediately before the plaintiff received his injuries, he was under the northeast end of the bridge, removing the nuts from the blocks which held two of the stringers of the old bridge. The bottom of the stringers was about fourteen inches from the ground at the place where he was working. While he was thus engaged the workmen on top of the bridge rolled a push car loaded with timbers onto the southwest end of the bridge, and threw one of the timbers off at that end, on the north side. Bowersock, the foreman, was standing on the bridge directly over where plaintiff was working. The push car was then rolled to the northeast end of the bridge for the purpose of throwing another timber off at that end. Just immediately preceding, or as the men were in the act of throwing this latter timber, Bowersock called to plaintiff to "Look out" or "Get out." The plaintiff, hearing this call, undertook to get out from under the bridge, and, as he did so, was caught by the falling timber, which crushed his leg, and caused the injuries of which complaint is made. It is alleged that plaintiff's injuries were sustained by the negligent acts of defendants' employees — especially that of Bowersock in directing the plaintiff to work at the time and place where the injuries occurred; in failing to instruct him of the hazard of the situation; negligently failing to look out for his safety, and to use ordinary precaution for his protection from impending danger, in failing to inform the other workmen of the position of plaintiff under the bridge; and in negligently failing to notify plaintiff in time to escape the danger which might result to him from throwing the timber.

The first contention on the part of plaintiff in error is that Bricker was guilty of contributory negligence; that he was in a place of absolute safety, had he remained at his place under the bridge; that his negligence consisted in leaving a place of safety, and unnecessarily putting himself in the way of the falling timber. It was not denied by the plaintiff that the timber could not have fallen on him had he remained under the bridge. There is considerable undisputed evidence in the record, however, that the falling timber was not the only danger against which he had to guard. There is evidence that in constructing and repairing bridges there are constantly in use many tools, such as adzes, mauls, and packing rings, which are generally kept on the top of the bridge, and the throwing of timbers will, or is likely to, jar these tools off the bridge, and there is danger of them falling on the workmen beneath. The evidence also fairly established the fact that Bowersock, the foreman, had instructed his men never to throw a timber from a bridge while men were under it at the point from which the timber is thrown. This was to guard against injury resulting from the falling of these tools. The evidence is that it was the universal custom of that gang not to throw a timber while workmen were under the bridge. This instruction and custom were known to the plaintiff, and he testified that he relied and acted upon them in this instance, and that, when Bowersock called to him to "Look out" or "Get out," he understood that Bowersock intended he should come out from under the bridge, and that the men would not throw the timber until he had time to do so. He also testified that he did not get from under the bridge because of any danger from the timber, but because the jar which the bridge would receive from the falling timber would likely dislodge the tools on the bridge, and he would thus get hurt. This testimony went to the jury uncontradicted.

Another alleged error is the exclusion of certain testimony offered by the plaintiffs in error on an application to require the plaintiff to give security for costs. On an examination of this evidence, it must be held that the court committed no error in this respect.

At the trial the defendant submitted to the jury the following special interrogatories: "No. 52. If you find for the plaintiff, how much do you allow him for the loss of ability to earn a livelihood? Ans. Three thousand dollars. No. 53. If you find for the plaintiff, how much do you allow for the permanent injuries, exclusive of the amount, if any, allowed for the loss of ability to earn a livelihood? Ans. Three thousand dollars." It is contended by plaintiffs in error that the jury having allowed the plaintiff $3,000 for permanent injuries, which generally includes the loss of ability to earn a livelihood the $3,000 allowed for loss of ability to earn a livelihood is excessive. We think it true that generally an allowance for permanent injuries includes loss of ability to earn a livelihood, but in this instance the plaintiffs in error requested the jury to divide this item into two parts, and, unless the court can say that the aggregate amount is excessive, the plaintiffs in error have no cause to complain. Another contention is made that the award of $2,000 for loss of time is grossly excessive. It was more than five years from the date of the injuries to the time of the trial. The plaintiff was earning $1.75 a day when injured. The jury, after hearing the evidence and seeing the plaintiff, was the judge as to what extent his injuries disabled him, what he could probably have earned in his disabled condition, and what he would probably have earned during this time had he not been injured. The finding was approved by the trial court, whose opportunities to arrive at a reasonably correct conclusion were equal to those of the jury. In view of these facts, this court cannot say that the award is excessive.

A contention is made by the corporation that in no event is it liable. It appears that at the time the plaintiff received his injuries, and for some time prior thereto, all the property of the corporation was in the hands of, and the road was being operated by, Aldace F. Walker and John J. McCook as receivers. The principle of *respondeat superior* has no application. The receivers were the officers of the court, and not the agents of the corporation. The corporation is not, therefore, liable for the acts of the receivers or the acts of their employees. Railway Co. *v.* McFadden, 89 Tex. 138, 33 S. W. Rep. 853; Metz *v.* Railroad Co., 58 N. Y. 61; Railroad Co. *v.* Davis, 23 Ind. 553; Gableman *v.* Railway Co. (C. C.), 82 Fed. Rep. 790; Warax *v.* Railway Co. (C. C.), 72 Fed. Rep. 637; Railroad Co. *v.* Hoechner, 14 C. C. A. 469, 67 Fed. Rep. 456; Railway Co. *v.* Smith, 59 Kan. 80, 52 Pac. Rep. 102. Again, the liability of a railroad company for injuries sustained by an employee is one created by the statute. Section 5858, Gen. St. 1901, reads: "Every railroad company organized or doing business in this State shall be liable for all damages done to any employee of such company in consequence of any negligence of its agents, or by any mismanagement of its engineers or other employees to any person sustaining such damage." It will be observed that the damages for which the corporation is made liable must arise in consequence of some negligence of the agents of the corporation or mismanagement of its engineers or other employees. The plaintiff, when injured, was not an employee of the corporation, and his injuries are not the result of the negligent act of any agent of the corporation, or of the mismanagement of any engineer or employee of the corporation.

It is argued by the receivers and the corporation that because they were sued jointly, and a joint judgment taken against both, if it should be held that the corporation is not liable the judgment cannot stand as to either. This contention cannot be sustained. This court has expressed itself upon this question in Railway Co. *v.* Smith, 59 Kan. 80, 52 Pac. Rep. 102. With the rule there stated we heartily agree.

The judgment of the court below is modified and set aside as to the corporation, and affirmed as to the receivers. The costs in this court are equally divided. All the justices concurring.

LEAVENWORTH LIGHT AND HEATING COMPANY v. WALLER.

Supreme Court, Kansas, October, 1902.

DEFECTIVE ELECTRIC WIRE INSULATION — PROPERTY BURNED — PLEADING — PROOF OF NEGLIGENCE — DEFENSE — ADMISSION — ESTOPPEL. — 1. In an action for damages upon the ground of defendant's negligence, such negligence is not admitted where the answer denies generally, and then pleads contributory negligence on the part of the plaintiff. In such case, the plaintiff is not relieved from proving negligence on the part of defendant; neither is defendant prevented from disproving it.

2. The general denial and a plea of contributory negligence are not inconsistent defenses.

3. A failure to deny under oath an allegation that a principal, through an agent, did a certain act, is not an admission that the principal did the act complained of.

4. The admission of the truth of a matter in a brief filed in a proceeding in error does not of itself estop the party making such admission from denying its truth in subsequent stages of the controversy.

(Syllabus by the Court.)

IN BANC. Error from District Court, Leavenworth County.

Action by Sophia Waller against the Leavenworth Light and Heating Company. From judgment for plaintiff, defendant brings error. *Judgment reversed.*

"Plaintiff's action was for damages done by the burning of her barn. The petition charged 'that the defendant, its officers and agents, thereunto duly authorized and empowered, entered into and contracted with said plaintiff, whereby the said defendant was to put and place lights in said barn for the use of the plaintiff;' that, in putting in the necessary wires, the same were not large enough, not properly insulated, and were placed carelessly and negligently, so that the injury of which she complains resulted. The answer was first a general denial, 'and, for a second and further ground of defense herein, defendant refers to the foregoing part of this answer as part hereof, and further avers that if plaintiff was in any wise damaged or injured as set forth in the petition, which this defendant denies, then the defendant avers that the plaintiff and her agents, by her duly appointed and authorized, so acted and conducted themselves as to contribute to the damage and injury complained of.' For reply, plaintiff filed a general denial. Upon these issues a trial was had, which resulted in a verdict and judgment for the defendant. From it error was prosecuted to the Court of Appeals, Northern Department, Eastern Division, where the same was reversed, and the case remanded for further trial. [See Waller *v.* Leavenworth Light & Heating Co., 9 Kan. App. 301, 8 Am. Neg. Rep. 82*n*, 61 Pac. Rep. 327.] A second trial was had upon the same pleadings. The defendant then sought to show by competent evidence that it was not the owner of the electric light plant operating the lights in plaintiff's barn at the time the fire occurred, but that another and separate corporation, from which plaintiff subsequently purchased, was at that time the owner. This evidence was rejected by the court upon the objection of the plaintiff, which objection was made in the following language: 'Plaintiff objects to the introduction of the deed (referring to a deed of the electric light property conveying the same to the defendant at a date subsequent to the occurrence of the fire) for the reason that it is incompetent, irrelevant, immaterial, and not within the issues in this case,' and for 'the additional reason that the defendant company in its brief, entitled: "In the Appellate Court of the State of Kansas, Northern Department, Eastern Division. Sophia Waller, Plaintiff in Error, *v.* The Leavenworth Light & Heating Company, Defendant in Error. Error from the District Court of Leavenworth County. Brief of Defendant in Error. John H. Atwood and Wm. W. Hooper, Attorneys for Defendant in Error," — admit on page 3 and otherwise in their brief that before plaintiff's fire the Leavenworth Coal Company sold out its electric lighting plant to the defendant; further, that it is a matter that has been passed upon by the Court of Appeals and decided.' The same question was presented by the defendant, by various offers, to prove by competent evidence, and by the records of the several corporations, owners of the electric lighting plant at different times, the time at which defendant in error became the owner of such plant, all of which offers upon the same objection were refused, and such evidence entirely excluded from the jury. Defendant having rested without further offer of proof, the court instructed the jury to render a verdict in behalf of the plaintiff, upon which judgment was entered in her favor, to all of which defendant excepted, and is now here for the purpose of reversing this judgment."

ATWOOD & HOOPER, for plaintiff in error.

JOHN T. O'KEEFE and DAVID KELSO, for defendant in error.

CUNNINGHAM, J. (after stating the facts). — The reasons urged for the exclusion of the evidence are: First, that the same was irrelevant and immaterial, because not within the issues in this case; second, that, when the case was in the Appellate Court, defendant's attorneys admitted in their brief filed in that proceeding in error that the defendant was the owner of the electric lighting plant at the time of the fire.

In support of the first contention it is urged first that the plea of contributory negligence contained in defendant's second defense was in effect an admission that defendant caused the damage complained of; that to deny defendant's negligence is inconsistent with the plea of contributory negligence on the part of the plaintiff; that there could be no contributory negligence on the part of the plaintiff without the antecedent negligence on the part of defendant. In the language of the defendant in error, "The plea of contributory negligence is in the nature of a plea of confession and avoidance, and, if this be true, then the defendant is estopped from denying its identity as the party properly sued." This raises a novel and important question in our practice. It will be observed that the defendant's answer contained a general denial. This, standing alone, would have put the plaintiff upon proof of all of the material allegations in her petition. One of these allegations was that the defendant's negligence was the cause of her injury. She was thereby required to establish not only negligence, but to connect the defendant with such negligence by showing its ownership of the electric light plant at the time of the injury. Railway Co. *v.* Searle, 11 Colo. 1, 16 Pac. Rep. 328; Jackson *v.* Water Co., 14 Cal. 19; Schular *v.* Railroad Co., 38 Barb. 653; Greenway *v.* James, 34 Mo. 328. This she sought to do in making her case, by introducing evidence that the defendant was the owner of the electric light plant at that time. This denial, standing alone, would not only require this proof at the hands of the plaintiff, but, *per contra*, permit the defendant to disprove this material matter. Davis *v.* McCrocklin, 34 Kan. 218, 8 Pac. Rep. 196. It will be further observed that the defendant, in its second defense, while still denying generally, says that, if plaintiff was damaged, then such damage was occasioned by the contributory negligence of the plaintiff or her agents. We do not think this claim inconsistent with the claim that the injury was not committed by the defendant, or occurred through his negligence. The defendant in error cites various authorities in support of her claim. They are strongly stated in a citation from 5 Enc. Pl. & Prac., pp. 11, 12, as follows: "The plea of contributory negligence is a plea in confession and avoidance, which admits negligence on the part of the defendant, but seeks to avoid liability therefor by alleging that plaintiff was guilty of negligence which contributed to his injury." We are not ready to grant that the authorities cited fairly support the law as thus laid down, though *obiter* remarks contained in some of them probably do. However, immediately following this quotation is the statement: "But this is not the rule in those States whose codes permit the defendant to set up as many defenses, whether of law or of fact, as he may see fit." Our statute (section 4528, Gen. St. 1901) permits the defendant to "set forth in his answer as many grounds of defense * * * as he may have, whether they be such as have been heretofore denominated as legal or equitable, or both." Notwithstanding this provision, the pleader may not rely in the same plea upon absolutely inconsistent defenses. He cannot admit and deny in the same breath. He may, however, adapt his pleadings so as to meet the possible conditions and contingencies of the case that his opponent may prove. He may say: "I was not negligent. I am wholly innocent in that matter. It is possible, however, that you may be able by your indirection or my misfortune to satisfy the jury that I am at fault. If you do, I shall assert that the injury was occasioned through your contributory negligence." Or, he may say, "If there was negligence which was the cause of your injury, I was not its author," and at the same time say, "If you were injured by the negligence of any one, you are not entitled to relief, for you contributed thereto by your negligence.' It certainly would be a very great hardship to a defendant who knows that he was not negligent, and knows that the plaintiff was, to compel him, at his peril, to elect which of these defenses, equally good, he should adopt. These defenses are not inconsistent. The truth of either by no means implies the falsity of the other. They may be availed of for the purpose of presenting the exact facts in a given case. Beyond question, a defendant might take advantage of plaintiff's contributory negligence, should such be developed in the making of plaintiff's case, even though the defendant had pleaded nothing but the general denial. It would be a queer rule that would deprive him of this, had he added to such general denial a plea of contributory negligence. The plea of contributory negligence, standing alone, would be one in avoidance, but it cannot be said to be one in confession, where accompanied by a general denial. In Railroad Co. *v.* Hall, 87 Ala. 708, 6 So. Rep. 277, on page 724, 87 Ala., and page 284, 6 So. Rep., the law is announced as follows: "A denial of the negligence charged, or plea of not guilty, although pleaded separately, repels all presumption of confession which arises from the plea of contributory negligence when pleaded alone." In Cole *v.* Woodson, 32 Kan. 272, 4 Pac. Rep. 321, which was an action for slander, where defendant had denied, and also pleaded the truth of the slanderous words, this court said (page 276,

32 Kan., and page 322, 4 Pac. Rep.): "It would certainly be a great hardship to a defendant who has been sued for slander to be required to admit that he had used the alleged slanderous words, when in fact he may never have used them, in order that he may be allowed to show that such words are true. And it would equally be a great hardship to him to be required, in effect, to admit that the words are false and slanderous, when in fact they may be true, in order to be allowed to make the defense that he never used such words. Our statutes do not tolerate any such unjust rules, but allow a defendant to set forth as many defenses as he may have, which in slander cases may be that he did not use the words charged, and also that the words are true. And it makes no difference what the common law may have been, or what may have been decided by courts in other States, where their statutes are different from the statutes of Kansas. The statutes of Kansas must govern in actions originating and instituted within the borders of Kansas. And where they are clear and explicit, we need not look any further." In Bell *v.* Brown, 22 Cal. 671, on page 678, the court, commenting upon the provisions of a statute like our own — upon a right it gives a defendant to set up all his defenses — says: "It is an absolute right given him by law, and the principle is as old as the common law itself. He may fail to prove one defense, by reason of the loss of papers, absence, death, or want of recollection of a witness, and yet he ought not thereby to be precluded from proving another equally sufficient to defeat the action." In Treadway *v.* Railroad Co., 40 Iowa, 526, the law is laid down in the syllabus: "An admission in the nature of a confession and avoidance in one count of an answer does not operate to admit matter formally denied in other counts." In Weaver *v.* Carnahan, 37 Ohio St. 363, a defendant, when sued to recover the value of services rendered, may deny that the services were rendered, and also allege that, if rendered, their value was less than the amount claimed. For cases holding analogous views, see 1 Enc. Pl. & Prac. 357.

It is further contended by the defendant in error that this evidence was not within the issues in the case, for the reason that, the allegation of the petition as to the agency of the parties who placed the wires in plaintiff's building for the defendant not being denied under oath, they must be admitted as true. This allegation was: "The defendant, its officers and agents, thereunto duly authorized and empowered, entered into and contracted with the said plaintiff, whereby the said defendant was to put and place lights in said barn for the use of the plaintiff in and about such business." This is an allegation of action, not of agency. It is nothing more than an averment that the defendant did these things. "A failure to deny under oath an allegation that a principal, through his agent, did a certain thing, is not an admission, under the statute (requiring the denial to be under oath), that the principal did the act complained of." 16 Enc. Pl. & Prac. 910, note 2, citing Railway Co. *v.* Finley, 38 Kan. 550, 16 Pac. Rep. 951.

It is further insisted that the court was right in excluding this evidence, because the defendant had estopped itself from denying that it was the owner of the lighting plant at the time the injury occurred, by its admissions in the brief referred to in the statement of facts, and because at no prior time through the progress of this litigation, which commenced in May, 1893, had it made any such claim or offer of proof. We know of no principle of law which would operate as an estoppel upon the defendant as thus claimed. The admission contained in the brief of plaintiff in error filed in the Court of Appeals was one for the purposes of that case — made, presumably, because the record in that case showed it to be so. Had it been made absolutely and as a matter of fact, without regard to what the record there showed, there is nothing about it to operate as an estoppel, nothing appearing that the plaintiff ever acted or relied upon such admission to her detriment. It would hardly do to hold that a chance or mistaken admission, accidentally made, as to facts, would forever preclude the party from showing what the facts actually were; and, beside this, the matter pending before the Appellate Court was another and different one from the matter being tried before the District Court, as it is well settled in this State that proceedings in error are independent actions, and not a continuation of the action at *nisi prius.*

Neither do we think the fact that, for the first time in the progress of the litigation, defendant then sought to show that it was not the owner of the light plant at the time of the injury, avails. It can easily be seen how such a fact might be overlooked by an attorney trying a case, or by the officers of a corporation who had newly come to their offices, and were unacquainted with the history of the corporation, or, even if fully known by either of these, we know of no rule that precludes a party from proving meritorious defense on a the second trial, even if he had neglected to do so on the first. Second trials are often sought for the purpose of introducing such proof.

We think the District Court erred in refusing to permit the proof offered, and therefore reverse its judgment and remand the case for a new trial. All the justices concurring.

RUSSELL v. ALLEN ET AL.

Supreme Court, Louisiana, June, 1901.

MINOR EMPLOYEE INJURED BY MOLDING MACHINE — WARNING OF DANGER — INSTRUCTING EMPLOYEE — EVIDENCE. — 1. In an action for damages the testimony shows that the molding machine is not considered a dangerous machine.

2. While instructions should be given to all workmen in charge of machines, the extent of the instructions and the warning to be prudent are to be gauged by the necessity because of danger.

3. The onus of proof is with the plaintiff. The foreman swore that he did not put plaintiff in charge of the machine.

4. The workman who had charge of the machine just previous to the accident, and who gave up his charge to the plaintiff, swore that before leaving this machine, he gave full instructions to the plaintiff.

5. All the witnesses, save plaintiff, testify that it was a matter of physical impossibility for the accident to have happened in the way alleged in plaintiff's petition and as he claims.

6. The witnesses swore that the wooden strip, while being worked through the molder, will never jerk back into it and throw the hand in the interior of the molder onto the blades of the lower cylinder.

(Syllabus by the Court.)

APPEAL from Judicial District Court, Parish of Caddo.

Action by G. H. Russell against Allen & Currey. From judgment for plaintiff, defendants appeal. *Judgment reversed.*

THATCHER & WELSH and WISE & HERNDON, for appellants.

ALEXANDER & WILKINSON, for appellee.

BREAUX, J. — Plaintiff, in his own right and for his minor son, sues to recover the sum of $7,610 for the loss of three fingers, while the latter (the son) was working for defendant at their planing mill in Shreveport. Plaintiff avers that his son was employed as lumber carrier and stacker; that he was ordered by the foreman to assist another young man in operating a molding machine, which was dangerous; that its appliances were not properly protected, to the end of preventing the happening of accidents; that skilled workmen only should be employed in such work; that his son knew nothing about molding machines, and had always previously engaged in work not dangerous; that he was put to work without instructions regarding the dangerous work he was to perform. Defendants answered the petition, and denied all of plaintiff's averments of negligence, and specially alleged that the injury complained of was caused by the gross carelessness of plaintiff's son. Plaintiff's son, the injured party, was in his eighteenth year. He was inexperienced, and had never worked at the molding machine until a few minutes before the accident happened. He had, for about a month and a half, worked for the defendant.

One of the employees of the defendant testifies that on the morning of the accident, and just prior to it, the foreman directed him to call on the son of the plaintiff to assist him in carrying strips to the ripsaw. After this work had been done, and the strips prepared for the molder, they were taken by him to that machine to be molded into proper shape. The molder is a machine operating mostly of itself. The workman at the molder feeds or supplies the pieces of timber. This is done by pushing the small pieces or strips between the rollers. He (the workman) stands at the head of the machine, and the feeding is done by pushing the strips between the rollers, revolving towards the instrument referred to as knives, being blades attached to heads or cylinders. The blade near the front or head of the machine trims and smooths the top of the strip, and gives it shape on one side, and the other head or cylinder is near the end of the machine and planes the lower side of the strip; that is, it cuts and makes smooth the lower or bottom surface. We are informed that usually a molding machine has four heads or cylinders — one in front and another at the tail end, as just mentioned, and one on each side. The functions of the side heads or cylinders is to trim the sides when such trimming is deemed necessary. The testimony shows that there were no blades on the side cylinders, and it follows that they were not in operation when the accident happened. Only the front and rear blades were in operation. From the time that the rollers clutch the slip, with which they are supplied or fed by the workman in front of the machine, until it passes through the machine, ordinarily, no necessity arises to touch the internal part of the machine. The molder has a board, which is known as the "pressure board," that is set or fixed, stationary, immediately above the knives, and extending beyond them. The son of the plaintiff took the place of the man at this machine, and alone, without experience, undertook the work of operating it. The strips which were being run through the molder were about fifteen feet in length. He testified that one whose place he took put one strip through the machine in his presence, and then said to him that in this work he had to run three or four strips through the machine, and then to step to the back or rear of the machine and see if they were smooth; that he complied with this instruction, and while in the rear or back of the machine, he took hold of the strip as it was being revolved out of the molder, and while he had his hand on the strip the machine jerked the strip back, and also his hand, throwing it onto the blades, by which his hand was severely cut — that is, he was holding the strip with his left hand, and the machine in some way slipped back and pulled his hand into the knives or blades before mentioned as being at the tail end of the machine.

With reference to the employment of the plaintiff's son at the molder, and as to the instruction given to avoid the accident, the testimony is contradictory. No good reason suggests itself for us to conclude that he should not have undertaken the work at the molder. A fellow-workman turned the work over to him and went elsewhere to perform other work. This was done, plaintiff's son testifies, with the knowledge of the foreman. We have before stated that the testimony regarding the instruction was conflicting. Plaintiff is flatly contradicted by the young man who left him in charge of the machine, as just stated. As this is an important point, we deem it proper to dwell at some length upon the facts, of which this is a summary: Just before the accident, Harry Bryan, a fellow-workman, said to plaintiff that he must help in getting some strips ready for the molder machine; that the foreman said that he (plaintiff) must help him (Bryan, the fellow-workman). Plaintiff says that, passing by the foreman, he inquired of him if he had given the order as stated by Bryan, and that the foreman answered, "Yes." Plaintiff swears that he and Bryan moved strips from the ripsaw station to the molding machine; that they commenced to work at the machine, and immediately after Bryan turned over the work to him of feeding the molder machine; that Bryan directed him to run three or four of the strips through the machine, and then to leave the front and step to the back of the machine, and see if the strips were of the required smoothness. It was in doing this that he was maimed as before stated. Plaintiff testifies that he did not receive any special instructions. Bryan, on the other hand, testifies that he gave him complete instructions; that he specially pointed out every part of the machinery, and warned him not to put his hands near the cylinder. This witness said: "I showed him how to start the molder, and how to stop it, and how to feed it; and I said to him, 'George, be sure to keep your fingers out of the feed rolls.' I showed him the rolls and the heads. I said to him, 'There is a head' (or cylinder). After I had shown him all about it, he started to feed the molder, and I watched him run two or three pieces through the machine, and I went to the shop to do other work." Evidently, the jury did not believe this witness, and did believe plaintiff. This is unusual. We will state here that all the witnesses agree that a skilled workman is not required to operate this machine. It is not considered a dangerous machine, and no witness recalled that any accident of a serious nature had ever happened while operating it. An experienced mechanic testified: "I have taken them younger than that, and put them to work on molders, and they have made good feeders. None of them ever lost their fingers while working on molders."

This brings us to the last point in the case. At several different times while testifying, plaintiff stated that at the moment of the accident he was standing behind the machine; that he laid his hand upon the strip of wood that was being run through the machine to see if it was smooth enough. His hand was jerked back and thrown against the knives. All the other witnesses who testified upon the subject said that this was not possible, and gave their account of why it was not possible. As this, in our view, is the most important point in the case, we insert excerpts from their testimony. L. C. Allen, one of the defendants, testified: "I do not believe that his hand could get into the cylinder from the side and be cut in that manner." W. S. Currey, the other defendant, said: "It would be impossible for that piece of molding to be jerked back into the machine. There is no force to drive it back against the self-feeding apparatus, and the hand could not slip into the space onto the knives." The foreman testified that, after an experience of some fifteen years in handling those machines, he never knew of any accident, prior to this one, happening to the feeder of the machine, and, further, standing at the tail of the machine, grabbing the strip with the left hand, it would be absolutely impossible for the strips, by being jerked back, to draw the hand into the knives. Another foreman of the defendant, in answer to the question whether such an accident was possible, as stated by plaintiff, said, "No, sir; that is impossible," and gave reasons about similar to those given by the other witnesses. Not one of the witnesses testified that it was possible for the accident to have happened in the way mentioned by plaintiff. There was no attempt made to rebut the testimony on this point. From the verdict we infer that the jury concluded that in any event the defendants were liable, and that this conclusion is based upon the theory that plaintiff was not properly instructed; that it makes no difference, in view of that fact, whether plaintiff's account of the accident is or is not correct; that it was due to a want of instructions, for which the defendants are liable. We find ourselves unable to agree with that conclusion. The fact that plaintiff is contradicted by defendants' foreman, that he is contradicted by his fellow-workman, and that he is contradicted by the facts regarding the possibility of receiving a wound in the manner he states, renders it, we think, impossible to reconcile the testimony sufficiently to support a judgment.

A close attention to the issue, and a careful review of contradicted statements at important points, results in forcing upon us the conclusion that plaintiff has not sustained his cause sufficiently to enable us to affirm the verdict. For the reasons assigned, the verdict and judgment of the District Court are annulled, avoided, and reversed, at the cost of plaintiff in both courts.

DAY v. BOSTON AND MAINE RAILROAD.

Supreme Judicial Court, Maine, February, 1902.

PERSON DRIVING WAGON KILLED IN COLLISION WITH TRAIN AT CROSSING — CONTRIBUTORY NEGLIGENCE — EVIDENCE. — 1. In an action for negligently causing the death of a person, the plaintiff has the burden of proving affirmatively due care on the part of the deceased.

2. That the witnesses who could have testified to facts showing such due care are all deceased does not change the rule that absence of evidence of due care on the part of the deceased will defeat the action.

3. A traveler upon a highway, as he approaches a railroad crossing, should use adequate means to ascertain whether a train be approaching the crossing from either direction. He should listen for the sound of trains on either hand, and look both ways along the track to see if trains be approaching. The greater the difficulties in the way of hearing or seeing approaching trains, the greater should be the effort of the traveler.

4. That the train was approaching the crossing at a much greater rate of speed than allowed by law in that locality does not lessen the duty of the traveler to use due care upon his own part to avoid collision.

5. Where the evidence only shows that a traveler with a team upon a highway, approaching a railroad crossing, stopped momentarily a few rods from the crossing and then immediately drove upon the crossing, and there is no evidence that he at that or any other time listened or looked either way for approaching trains, there is not sufficient evidence of due care upon the part of the deceased (1).

6. Evidence that such a traveler, driving toward a railroad crossing, when near the crossing was seen looking directly before him at the crossing, and was not looking in either direction along the railroad track, is not sufficient evidence of due care on his part to ascertain the approach of trains.

7. Evidence that a hand car passed over the crossing when the highway traveler with a team was some 500 feet therefrom, driving along parallel with the

1. *Crossing accidents.* — See vols. 11 and 12 Am. Neg. Cas., for crossing-accident cases, from the earliest period to 1897. Subsequent cases are reported in vols. 1–12 AM. NEG. REP., and the current numbers of that series of Reports.

railroad, and that the men on the hand car saw the traveler on the highway, does not amount to evidence that the traveler noticed the hand car. Quantitative probability as to a past event does not amount to evidence of such event.

3. Whatever the probabilities in this case, there is no evidence that the deceased traveler, as he approached the railroad crossing, observed due care to ascertain whether a train was approaching, and no evidence that any act of the railroad company or any of its servants induced him to forego such care. So far as appears, the case is the too common one where the traveler either forgot to look and listen, or, being aware of the approaching train, recklessly undertook to cross before it.

(Official.)

ACTION by Lottie I. Day, administratrix, against the Boston and Maine Railroad. Verdict for plaintiff for $4,000. *New trial granted.*

Argued before WISWELL, Ch. J., and EMERY, WHITEHOUSE, STROUT, SAVAGE, and POWERS, JJ.

E. P. SPINNEY, for plaintiff.

GEO. C. YEATON, for defendant.

EMERY, J. — The evidence for the plaintiff shows the following: The plaintiff's intestate, Edwin Day, in the forenoon of a summer day was driving alone in a hayrack drawn by one horse along a village street towards a grade crossing of the street with the railroad tracks of the defendant company in North Berwick. He was standing up next the front rail of the hayrack as he was thus driving. When first seen by any of the witnesses, he was driving along Portland street nearly parallel with the railroad tracks. He then turned from Portland street into Wells street, which led more directly to the crossing and over it at an angle of forty-three and one-half degrees with the track. The distance from the turn into Wells street to the crossing was 471 feet. He was "jogging along," as the plaintiff's witness described it, at a rate of about five miles an hour. He stopped momentarily some twenty feet from the crossing and then drove immediately upon the crossing, where he was struck and killed by a train of the defendant company, which had come along the track from the direction thus partially behind him. He was about thirty-five years of age, in the full possession of all the usual faculties, and was familiar with the crossing and the surroundings.

There is no evidence that, in approaching the railroad crossing, Mr. Day took any precautions whatever to ascertain whether a train was also then approaching the crossing from either direction. True, he stopped momentarily some twenty feet from the crossing, but it does not appear that he looked or listened or took any other measures to ascertain what might be approaching on the railroad tracks.

There is no evidence for what purpose he stopped there. He may have stopped to look at something else than railroad or trains, or his horse may have stopped of its own volition without any act or will of Day's. We can only conjecture. There is no evidence. Nor can we assume, in the absence of evidence, that he did then look and listen for trains. On the contrary, it would seem that he could not have looked and listened at that point for trains without seeing or hearing this train, which, according to the plaintiff's own theory of its speed, was then less than 300 feet away. It is also true that a witness testified that as he was going from the crossing on Wells street he met Day at a point three or four rods from the crossing, and that Day then appeared to be looking "straight ahead toward the crossing, and not off to the right" (which would be toward the railroad). This does not tend to show requisite care and precaution on the part of Day. There was then, at that distance, no occasion for him to look at the crossing itself. Nothing then on, or passing, the crossing could endanger him at that distance. Looking straight ahead at the crossing would give him no information as to what might be on the tracks at a distance from the crossing and approaching it. Looking at or toward a railroad crossing is clearly not enough precaution for any traveler who proposes to pass over. He should look both ways along the tracks, to see what is approaching the crossing as well as what is on it.

It is the firmly settled law of this State that, in approaching a railroad crossing at grade, the traveler upon the highway, to be in the exercise of ordinary prudence, must bear in mind that trains are liable to be approaching the crossing at that same time, and at any moment, from either direction; that the train cannot turn aside for him, and cannot be easily stopped to avoid him. He must, therefore, to comply with his duty to exercise ordinary care, be on the alert to ascertain by the use of his senses of sight and hearing, and by any other appropriate means, the approach of trains, and to seasonably avoid collision with them. He can usually avoid collision readily, easily, and promptly, if he be properly careful and alert while approaching the crossing. In view of the obvious peril at grade crossings and of the obvious inability of the train to turn out or stop instantly, it has further been repeatedly held that care commensurate with the peril requires the traveler upon the highway to look and listen for trains at the very time he is approaching the crossing, and that an omission to take this ordinary precaution is, if unexplained, contributory negligence *per se*, as matter of law, and will bar an action for the collision even though the railroad company was negligent in the premises. He must bear in mind, what is of common knowledge, that railroad trains move much faster than the ordinary pace of a horse drawing a vehicle along the highway, and hence must not rest content with an observation made at considerable distance from the crossing, especially if there be objects or circumstances to obstruct his vision or hearing at the more remote point. He must be mindful, must observe, look, and listen, as he approaches close to the place of peril, the crossing. Chase *v.* Maine Cent. R. R. Co., 78 Me. 346, 11 Am. Neg. Cas. 652, 5 Atl. Rep. 771; Allen *v.* Maine Cent. R. R. Co., 82 Me. 111, 19 Atl. Rep. 105; Smith *v.* Maine Cent. R. R. Co., 87 Me. 339, 32 Atl. Rep. 967 (11 Am. Neg. Cas. 653n); Romeo *v.* Railroad, 87 Me. 540, 33 Atl. Rep. 24; Giberson *v.* Bangor & A. R. R. Co., 89 Me. 337, 36 Atl. Rep. 400 (11 Am. Neg. Cas. 653n).

It is further the settled law of this State that it is incumbent upon a plaintiff, suing to recover damages alleged to have resulted from the negligence of another party, to affirmatively prove his own freedom from contributory negligence in the premises. There is no presumption that a plaintiff in such case was thus free from contributory negligence, though sometimes the circumstances may of themselves show that he was, as in the case of a passenger injured, by the negligence of a railroad company, while sitting in his seat doing nothing. In the absence of affirmative evidence tending to show that the plaintiff, himself being an actor, exercised on his part the care and effort incumbent on him to avoid the injury, he cannot maintain his suit. That the only witness who could testify to facts showing such care is dead, and the plaintiff is thus left without the evidence, does not enable the plaintiff to recover without the evidence. In support of the foregoing proposition it is only necessary to cite the late case of McLane *v.* Perkins, 92 Me. 39, 42 Atl. Rep. 255, where the proposition is fully reviewed and affirmed.

In this case the plaintiff contends that the evidence shows circumstances and conditions which made it difficult for Mr. Day to see or hear the approaching train, or to obtain any other information of its nearness to the crossing. If such was the case, it was the duty of Mr. Day to make all the more effort to ascertain the truth; but the case is barren of evidence that he made any effort whatever, great or small. The difficulty of seeing and hearing the train is therefore immaterial, since it is not claimed that it was impossible with any effort to know of the train's approach. It is the absence of evidence of any, even the smallest, effort on the part of Day, not his inability to see or hear with reasonable effort, which convicts him of contributory negligence.

The foregoing statement of the law and the evidence would seem to require a judgment for the defendant notwithstanding the verdict of the jury in favor of the plaintiff. A verdict of a jury on matters of fact, and within even their exclusive province, cannot be the basis of a judgment where there is no evidence to support it, or when they have made inferences contrary to all reason and logic. In this case Mr. Day, as he approached the crossing, had a plain duty, long and clearly defined by law, failing to perform which, he or his representative could not sustain an action. There is no evidence that he did that duty or any part of it, and such a fact must be established by evidence, and not assumed.

But the plaintiff contends in this case that some of the defendant company's servants so conducted, during Mr. Day's approach to the crossing, as to assure him that no train was approaching so near as to endanger him in attempting the crossing when he did. This assurance was given, the plaintiff says, by some of the section men propelling a hand car along the track over the crossing toward the direction from which the train was coming. The argument is that Mr. Day, seeing this hand car, and knowing that it must go nearly 1,000 feet to reach a switch or side track where it could let a train by, was thereby assured that no train from that direction would reach the crossing until that 1,000 feet had been first covered by the hand car and then by the train, which would have allowed him ample time for crossing safely; and that a jury might reasonably find that it was not negligence in Mr. Day to rely on that assurance, and cease his own personal outlook for the approach of such a train at such a time as would endanger him. Hooper *v.* Boston & Me. R. R., 81 Me. 260 (11 Am. Neg. Cas. 657n), 17 Atl. Rep. 64, and York *v.* Maine Cent. R. R. Co., 84 Me. 117, 11 Am. Neg. Cas. 650, 24 Atl. Rep. 790, are cited.

It appears in evidence that the defendant company's section men did propel a hand car along the track over the crossing in the direction named, but this was while Mr. Day was on Portland street, some fifty feet from the turn into Wells street, and while he was traveling parallel with the railroad, and not toward it. The distance from the crossing on Wells street to its junction with Portland street was 471 feet. The section men, or some of them, as they passed the crossing, noticed Mr. Day and his team at the locality named, on Portland street near Wells street.

Unfortunately for this contention, there is no evidence that Mr. Day noticed this hand car, although it was within the range of his vision. There are no circumstances tending to show that he noticed it, or, if he did notice it, that it in the least influenced his after conduct. He was on Portland street at the time, traveling parallel with the railroad, and, if he faced as he was driving, was not facing the car on the track. His momentary stop some twenty feet from the crossing does not tend to show that he noticed the car. That stop was some minute or two after the car had passed, and after the section men on the car saw him.

Of course, it is possible that he noticed the hand car. Indeed, it may be quantitatively probable that he did. Quantitative probability, however, is only the greater chance. It is not proof, nor even probative evidence, of the proposition to be proved. That in one throw of dice there is a quantitative probability, or greater chance, that a less number of spots than sixes will fall uppermost is no evidence whatever that in a given throw such was the actual result. Without something more, the actual result of the throw would still be utterly unknown. The slightest real evidence that sixes did in fact fall uppermost would outweigh all the probability otherwise. Granting, therefore, the chances to be more numerous that the plaintiff's intestate did notice the hand car than that he did not, we still have only the doctrine of chances. We are still without evidence tending to actual proof. However confidently one in his own affairs may base his judgment on mere probability as to a past event, when he assumes the burden of establishing such event as a proposition of fact as a basis for a judgment of a court he must adduce evidence other than a majority of chances.

The situation was very different from that in either of the cases cited. In each of those cases the traveler was directly at the crossing at the time of the event on the crossing. In the one case the gates were up when the traveler reached the gated crossing, and remained up. In the other case the traveler was at the crossing, halted and waiting, as the train passed directly before his face. In this case at bar the event occurred when the traveler was 500 feet distant from the crossing, traveling parallel with the railroad, and nothing appears in evidence or the situation that would force the event upon his attention as in the other cases.

For lack of evidence, even from circumstances, that Mr. Day in fact noticed the hand car as it passed along the track and was influenced by it to cease further outlook, that episode does not suffice to show that Mr. Day took the requisite precautions, or was excused from taking them by any assurance of safety from the company's conduct. The whole evidence does not show, either that he took the precaution, or that he in fact relied upon assurances of safety.

The plaintiff calls attention to evidence that this crossing was in a compact part of the town, where the speed of trains was limited by law to six miles an hour when passing the crossing, and that this train passed the crossing at a much greater rate of speed. She contends that Mr. Day could properly assume, and act upon the assumption, that the train was not moving more than the lawful rate of six miles an hour, and therefore, if he could have safely crossed the track in front of a train moving only at that rate, she has shown that he was free from contributory negligence in crossing the track when he did. Unfortunately for this contention, also, there is no evidence that Mr. Day consciously saw or heard the train at all, or reasoned about its speed as compared with his own. So far as the evidence shows, he went upon the crossing entirely unmindful of what was approaching. Had he noticed the train, it was his duty to note its actual rate of speed, and take no chances of collision with it.

The plaintiff further calls attention to evidence that no bell was rung, no whistle was blown, and no other signal of approach was given by the train. She contends that the absence of all signals of approach was an assurance of safety. As to this contention, it has been repeatedly held that the traveler upon the highway must not depend solely upon any signal from the railroad company's servants, but must, in the absence of such signals, still be on his guard, and endeavor to ascertain the actual fact whether or not a train be approaching. See cases cited above.

So far as now appears, the case is the too common one where the traveler upon the highway either took no adequate care to ascertain whether a train was approaching, or else, being aware of the approaching train, recklessly undertook to cross before it.

We find in the law and the evidence no foundation for this verdict, and it must be set aside.

Motion sustained. Verdict set aside.

WITHAM v. BANGOR AND AROOSTOOK RAILROAD COMPANY.

Supreme Judicial Court, Maine, March, 1902.

HORSE FRIGHTENED BY OBSTRUCTION ON RAILROAD RIGHT OF WAY — REPAIRS. — 1. While driving along the highway near the railroad track of the defendant, the plaintiff was thrown from her wagon and injured by her horse becoming frightened at three pieces of culvert pipe some seventeen feet outside of the highway, and upon the defendant's right of way, and which had been deposited there four days before for the purpose of repairing and improving its roadbed by substituting a culvert for a bridge at that point. The appearance of the pipe was such as was calculated to frighten horses of ordinary gentleness.

The defendant, in repairing and improving its roads, was in the exercise of a right conferred by its charter, and a duty which the law imposes upon it for the safety of the public who travel over its road.

In doing this, it must act reasonably and with a due regard for the rights and safety of persons who have occasion to use the highway. It cannot act negligently, improperly, or unreasonably. But to create a liability on its part for the resulting injury, there must be something in the time or manner or circumstances under which the act is done which charges it with a want of proper regard for the rights of others.

2. The defendant corporation was created by the public for public purposes. The public safety and convenience demand that its roadbed be kept in repair. If it exercises due care in making repairs and improvements upon its own premises, no action will lie for such inconveniences or even injurious consequences as are necessarily incident to its management and operation.

3. The appearance of the pipe being such as was calculated to frighten horses of ordinary gentleness, the defendant would not be justified in letting it remain so near the highway for an unreasonable length of time.

4. *Held*, that in view of the nature of the repairs for which the pipe was intended, the constant and regular use of the defendant's road for public travel and commerce, and the extent of its line which must be kept in repair at all times and in all places, four days was not an unreasonable length of time, under the circumstances of this case.

(Official.)

REPORT from Supreme Judicial Court, Piscataquis County.

Action by Vesta A. Witham against the Bangor and Aroostook Railroad Company. *Case reported, and judgment for defendant.*

"Action of tort to recover damages sustained by the plaintiff by being thrown from her carriage while traveling on the highway in Guilford adjoining the defendant's railroad. The cause of the accident, as the plaintiff alleged, was due to her horse taking fright at some culvert pipe placed in close proximity to the highway. There were three pieces of pipe, black in color, three feet and eight and one-half inches in diameter at one end, four feet and three inches at the other end, and twelve feet and six and one-half inches long. They weighed 6,147 pounds each.

"By agreement of the parties, the case was reported to the law court to determine whether the action was maintainable."

Argued before WISWELL, Ch. J., and EMERY, WHITEHOUSE, STROUT, SAVAGE, and POWERS, JJ.

H. HUDSON, for plaintiff.

F. H. APPLETON and H. R. CHAPIN, for defendant.

POWERS, J. — From the report we find the following facts: As the plaintiff was driving along the highway in Guilford, where it runs adjacent to and nearly parallel with the track of the defendant, her horse became suddenly frightened at three pieces of culvert pipe, and she was thrown from her wagon and injured. The pipe was lying upon the right of way of the defendant corporation, some seventeen feet outside of the limits of the highway, and had been deposited there by the defendant four days before for the purpose of repairing and improving its roadbed at Cooper brook by substituting a culvert for a bridge at that point. Each piece of pipe weighed something over three tons, and they were as near to the railroad track and the brook as it was practicable to unload and use them. The plaintiff was at the time in the exercise of due care. Her horse was kind, safe, and broken for travel upon the public roads, and the appearance of the pipe was such as was calculated to frighten horses of ordinary gentleness.

While every person is bound to use and enjoy his own property in such a manner as not to unreasonably injure another's, yet no action will lie for the reasonable exercise or use of a person's right. If a man unreasonably leaves upon his own premises an object whose appearance is such that it will frighten horses which are kind, safe, and broken for travel upon our public roads, he is liable for the injuries which result therefrom. The appearance of the object and the resulting injury alone are not sufficient to create the liability. There must be something in the time or manner or circumstances under which the act is done which charges him with a want of proper regard for the rights of others. The plaintiff in traveling along the highway was in the exercise of her lawful right. The defendant, also, in repairing and improving its road, was in the exercise of a right conferred by its charter, and a duty which the law imposes upon it for the safety of the public who travel over its road. In doing this it must act reasonably, and with a due regard for the rights and safety of persons who have occasion to use the highway. It cannot act negligently, improperly, or unreasonably. The rights of the parties are to be harmonized, but, if due care is exercised by a railroad corporation in making repairs and improvements upon its own premises, it is not responsible for the inconveniences or even injurious consequences that may arise from such acts. The public which creates these great channels of travel and commerce, and whose safety and convenience demand that they be maintained in repair, must submit to such inconveniences as are necessarily incident to their management and operation.

Each case must necessarily stand upon its own facts. Applying these principles to the case before us, we think the plaintiff has failed to show that the defendant acted negligently or unreasonably. The pipe was upon the defendant's own premises, placed there for a lawful purpose, and close to the spot where it was to be used. Its weight, 6,147 pounds to the piece, was such as precluded it from being placed on the other side of the railroad, or further away from the highway.

It is true that, in view of the fact that the appearance of the pipe was calculated to frighten horses of ordinary gentleness, the defendant would not be justified in allowing it to remain so near the highway for an unreasonable time. Under the circumstances, however, we do not think four days an unreasonable time. The nature of the repairs for which the pipe was intended, the constant and regular use of the defendant's road for public travel and commerce, the extent of its line, which must be kept in repair at all times and in all places, make it unreasonable to require that such material should not be moved to the place of its use until the very day that the use is to be made of it. Some latitude and discretion must be allowed to those intrusted with the construction and operation of great public works as to the manner in which and the means by which they will perform the duties imposed upon them. If they act in good faith, with a proper regard for the rights of others, and without carelessness or negligence, they are exempt from liability.

Judgment for defendant.

CONLEY v. PORTLAND GASLIGHT COMPANY.

Supreme Judicial Court, Maine, March, 1902.

EMPLOYEE KILLED BY GAS EXPLOSION — PLEADING — DEATH — DAMAGES — ACTION. — 1. In an action by an administrator for negligently causing the death of his intestate, there was no averment in either count that the deceased died immediately; but in the first and second counts it is alleged that he died "within twenty minutes," and in the third count that he "received injuries from which he thereafterwards died."

2. In the first count it also affirmatively appeared by express averment that he "suffered much in body and mind," and in the second count it failed to appear, either by inference or direct averment, whether he became unconscious from his injuries or endured conscious suffering while he survived. There is, therefore, no substantial ground for distinguishing the declaration in this case from that in Sawyer *v.* Perry, 88 Me. 42. It is true that in this case the decedent survived his injuries only twenty minutes, while in that

he lived about an hour. But the agonies of body and mind which "no word can speak" may in one case be suffered in twenty minutes, and much larger damages may be required as compensation in such a case than for the suffering of many hours or days from injuries of a different character.

3. *Held*, that the plaintiff in this case claims in his declaration to recover compensation for the pecuniary injuries resulting to the widow and children from the death of the decedent; but describes only a cause of action at common law in which the damages recovered must be for the benefit of the estate generally, and not for the exclusive benefit of the widow and children.

4. As construed by our court it is obvious that the statute of 1891 affords a right of action for "injuries causing death," substantially like that given to employees by the employers' liability act in Massachusetts. The third section of that act gives a right of action "where an employee is instantly killed or dies without conscious suffering."

5. Whether in the case at bar it might not reasonably be considered an immediate death within the meaning and purpose of our statute if the decedent immediately became unconscious after his injury and remained in a comatose state for twenty minutes, or even for several hours or days until life became extinct, it is unnecessary here to determine.

Sawyer *v.* Perry, 88 Me. 42, affirmed.

(Official.)

EXCEPTION from Supreme Judicial Court, Cumberland County.

Action by Henry J. Conley, administrator, against the Portland Gaslight Company. Demurrers to the declaration were overruled, and defendant excepts. *Exceptions sustained.*

"Action against the defendant company to recover damages for negligently causing the death of William John Carey, one of its employees. The declaration contained three counts; and the defendant demurred generally to the declaration and specially to each count. The presiding justice overruled the demurrers *pro forma.*

"The case appears in the opinion."

Plaintiff's declaration was as follows:

"In a plea of the case, and the plaintiff says: That on the eleventh day of August, A. D. 1900, at Portland, in said Cumberland county, the defendant, by its servants and agents, controlled and used a certain building on West Commercial street, in said Portland, for manufacturing and furnishing gas to its patrons, and that at the same time the said William John Carey, then alive, now deceased, was lawfully in and about said company's building on said West Commercial street as an employee and in the performance of his duties, and that on said eleventh day of August there was in and about said building a receptacle for gas and pipes extending around through the building through which said gas passed. That there was then and there great danger of the escape of gas from the gas pipes if they were defective or negligently kept, and that said gases, either alone or mixed with atmospheric air or ignited by fire, were dangerous explosives, all of which were known to the defendant, or, in the exercise of due care, should have been known. That said defendant owed to the said William John Carey the duty of so conducting itself and doing and acting on the premises in carrying on its business that said William John Carey should not suffer injury or damage by reason of any negligence on the part of the defendant in allowing or permitting the accumulation of dangerous gases in and about the building not properly retained and confined, and in failing to guard or inspect said pipes and tanks in which the gases were to be retained, and in failing to have, at all times, men ready and able to repair any break, defect, or leak which might occur in said tank and pipes. And the defendant well knew, through its servants and agents, or, in the exercise of due care, ought to have known, that said tanks, gas pipes, and the connections attached to them, and the means of receiving and disposing of the gases then and there manufactured, were old, broken, rotten, and improperly constructed, and not suitably arranged for the purpose of carrying on the business with safety to employees and persons then and there rightfully in and about said building in the performance of their duties. That the defendant negligently failed to guard and keep in proper repair said pipes and tanks, and negligently permitted the building to be filled with explosive gases, negligently suffered said pipes and tanks to remain out of repair, weak, defective, and dangerous, and negligently failed to inspect said pipes and tanks or properly keep them in serviceable condition and to keep a sufficient number of men properly instructed to guard against accident from explosion by the escape and accumulation of dangerous and explosive gases into said building and the accumulation thereof, and permitting fire to be where the gases would be ignited by fire and to speedily repair any breaks, defects or leaks which might occur. That, by reason of said negligent acts and omissions and negligent condition of the defendant, its servants and agents as aforesaid, the said William John Carey, on the eleventh day of August, A. D. 1900, while rightfully in and about said building and in the exercise of due care, was severely injured and killed by the explosion of gases within said space, and suffered much in body and mind, and died within twenty minutes from the result of the injuries then and there received. By reason of all which said defendant has become liable, by force of the statute in such case made and provided, to the plaintiff in his said capacity for such damages, not exceeding five thousand dollars ($5,000), as will be a fair and just compensation for the pecuniary injuries resulting from the death of said William John

Carey to Margaret Carey, widow, and Margaret Amelia Carey and Mabel Agnes Carey and William J. Carey, children of said William John Carey. And the plaintiff avers that said damages amount to the sum of five thousand dollars ($5,000).

"Also, for that the said William John Carey, at said Portland, on the eleventh day of August, A. D. 1900, then alive, was in the employ of the defendant in its gas works, so called, on West Commercial street, in said Portland, in the exercise of due care, and rightfully in and about the building where said works were then and there in operation, and whereas the said defendant was then and there, and for a long time prior thereto had been, in the possession, use, and control of said gas works, and was then and there in the possession of said works, including the tanks, pipes, machinery, and running gear of the same, and the defendant then and there, by its servants, had the government and control of said works and pipes, tanks and machinery; yet the defendant, not minding or regarding its duty in this behalf, did then and there, and for a long time prior thereto, negligently and wrongfully maintain the said gas works, machinery, pipes, tanks, and other vessels used in and about said works in a dangerous condition in carrying on the defendant's business, and that by reason of the same, and without notice to the said William John Carey, and without fault of the said William John Carey, and by the neglect of the defendant to guard the gases and avoid explosions and to have the pipes and tanks and other appliances and other things used in carrying on the business of the gas company thereat properly adjusted, that the said gases escaped and exploded, and the said pipes were torn asunder, and the said William John Carey was severely injured in his head, lacerated and cut in different parts of his person, and other bodily injuries were sustained by him, and solely from such injuries, and from no other cause, said William John Carey died within a short time, to wit, within twenty minutes after said injuries were received. And the plaintiff avers that all the injuries and damages which then and there resulted to the said William John Carey resulted solely from the negligence and want of care of the said defendant, its servants and agents, and that the said William John Carey was without fault in the premises, and suffered death as aforesaid solely through the defendant's negligence. By reason of all of which the defendant has become liable by force of the statute in such case made and provided to the plaintiff, in her said capacity, for such damages, not exceeding five thousand dollars ($5,000), as alleged a fair and just compensation for the pecuniary injuries resulting from the death of said William John Carey to Margaret Carey, widow, and

Margaret Amelia Carey and Mabel Agnes Carey and William J. Carey, children of the said William John Carey. And the plaintiff avers that said damages amount to the sum of five thousand dollars ($5,000).

"Also, for that the plaintiff says that he is the administrator of the estate of William John Carey, late of Portland, in said county of Cumberland, deceased, intestate, letters of administration having been duly issued to plaintiff by the judge of probate for the county of Cumberland; that the defendant owns and operates gas works on West Commercial street in said Portland, and was in control and management of the same on the eleventh day of August, A. D. 1900, and that on said eleventh day of August, A. D. 1900, the deceased was in the employ of the defendant in said gas works; that it was the duty of the defendant to furnish a competent and suitable superintendent, an engineer or machinist or some party understanding the business and qualified by practical knowledge to manage and control the tanks, pipes, and machinery of the gas works then and there used. That it was the duty of the defendant to furnish suitable machinery, pipes, tanks, and valves and other things in proper condition for the services required of it in said works. That it was also the duty of the defendant to protect said deceased from dangers and give proper warning and instruction to him as to the dangers attending the work in which he was engaged. That it was the duty of the defendant to see that its works and machinery and different attachments connected with the gas works were in sufficient and proper condition so that the plaintiff doing his work should not be exposed to any dangers unreasonable or unnecessary or not ordinarily incident to his employment, but that the defendant, regardless of its duties in this behalf, employed an engineer and other employees not sufficiently informed in the management of the machinery, works, and appliances of the gas works to properly manage the same so that they might be used with comparative safety, and permitted defects to exist in the machinery, gearing, pipes, tanks and connections, valves and other machinery and tools which were used in carrying on the business of the gas company, and gave no sufficient warning or caution to the deceased as to the dangers attending the business in which he was employed, and left the machinery and other portions of the works in a condition which greatly enhanced the peril of the deceased in performing his work. That the defects arose from or had not been discovered, owing to the negligence of the defendant, its servants and agents, or of that person in its service by it intrusted with the duty of seeing that its works were in proper condition. That by reason of said negligence of the said defendant in the selection of said employees, and by reason of the defective pipes, valves, connections, and other gearing and attachments and machinery used in and about the works, and on account of the negligence of the company in not giving suitable instructions to the deceased and warning him of the danger and unsafe condition of the works of the company and of the machinery, gearings, and attachments used, and from the resulting dangers owing to the escape of gases from tanks, pipes, etc., resulting from the negligence of the defendant, its servants and agents, and also from the negligence of the defendant in allowing the fires to be where the gases could come in contact with them, and from the general negligence of the defendant, its servants and agents, in not properly attending to the machinery and gearing, and in not furnishing suitable and experienced and competent managers and superintendents and employees, the deceased, while in said employment in said works and rightfully engaged in the service of the defendant, and while performing work for which he was hired by the defendant, and while in the exercise of due care, suffered personal injuries by the explosion of gases and by the flying pieces of metal, earth, and rocks and by the destruction of the different pieces of machinery, received injuries from which he thereafterwards died, by reason of all of which defects and negligence the said defendant has become liable by force of the statute in such case made and provided to the plaintiff in his said capacity for such damages, not exceeding five thousand dollars ($5,000), as will be a fair and just compensation for the pecuniary injuries resulting from the death of said William John Carey to Margaret Carey, widow, and Margaret Amelia Carey and Mabel Agnes Carey and William John Carey, children of said William John Carey. And the plaintiff avers that said damages amount to the sum of five thousand dollars ($5,000)."

Defendant's demurrer was as follows:

"And now the said defendant comes, etc., and says that the plaintiff's declaration is insufficient in law.

"And the defendant, as to the first count of the declaration, says that the said count is not sufficient in law.

"And the said defendant shows to the court here the following causes of demurrer to the said declaration as set out in said first count; that is to say:

"1. That it does not appear by the said declaration whose employee the plaintiff's intestate was, or by whom he was employed, in and about said company's building.

"2. That it does not appear by said declaration what contractual or other relations, if any, the plaintiff's intestate sustained to the defendant, or whether he was in the employ of the defendant or some other person, or was a mere licensee.

"3. That no cause is given or alleged for the explosion of gases as claimed by said plaintiff.

"4. That said declaration states no particular act or omission upon the part of said defendant which should cause the alleged injury to plaintiff's intestate.

"5. That the defendant is not informed by said declaration whether the alleged explosion occurred in said building, or about said building, nor within what space, nor where such alleged explosion is claimed to have occurred.

"6. That said declaration does not show in what particular respect, if any, the said defendant was negligent, so that such charge of negligence may be understood or answered by the said defendant; nor does it show that the alleged injury to plaintiff's intestate was caused by any of the general instances of negligence claimed.

"And the defendant, as to the second count of the said declaration, says that the said count is not sufficient in law.

"And the defendant shows to the court here the following causes of demurrer to said declaration as set out in said second count; that is to say:

"1. It does not appear by said declaration in what capacity the plaintiff's intestate is claimed to have been in the employ of said defendant, whether as laborer, independent contractor, salesman, on commission, or otherwise; nor does it appear what contractual or other relations, if any, the plaintiff's intestate sustained to the defendant.

"2. That said declaration does not state, nor does it inform said defendant of any particular act of negligence of which said defendant is claimed to be gulity; nor does it state whether the said gas works as a whole, nor whether any particular portion, nor whether all of the machinery, pipes, tanks, and other vessels used in and about said works are claimed to have been in a dangerous condition, nor in what respect any or all of them were dangerous.

"3. That said declaration does not inform said defendant of any particular place where alleged gases are claimed to have escaped and exploded, nor of any particular cause for such alleged escape and explosion, nor any particular reason for such alleged explosion, nor any particular respect in regard to which said works, machinery, and other things named were dangerous or in regard to which said defendant is claimed to have been negligent.

"4. That said declaration does not state that said explosion was in, or whether it was about, the said gas works; nor does it state that the plaintiff's intestate was at any place where such alleged explosion is claimed to have occurred; nor does it state that such alleged explosion was the cause of the injuries claimed to have been received by plaintiff's intestate; nor does it state any specific cause for such injuries.

"5. That said declaration does not show in what particular respect, if any, the said defendant was negligent, so that such charge of negligence may be understood or answered by the said defendant; nor does it show that the alleged injury to plaintiff's intestate was caused by any of the general instances of negligence claimed.

"And the defendant, as to the third count of the said declaration, says that the said count is not sufficient in law.

"And the defendant shows to the court here the following causes of demurrer to said declaration as set out in said third count; that is to say:

"1. That it does not appear by said declaration in what capacity the plaintiff's intestate is claimed to have been in the employ of said defendant, whether as laborer, independent contractor, broker, or otherwise; nor does it appear what contractual or other relations, if any, the plaintiff's intestate sustained to the defendant.

"2. That said declaration does not state any particular thing connected with the management of the machinery, works, and appliances named, concerning which it is claimed the said engineer and said other employees were not sufficiently informed, so as to properly manage the same; that it does not state any particular defect which it is alleged existed in the machinery, gearing, tools, and other things named as being used in carrying on said defendant's business; nor does it state what the condition was which it is alleged enhanced the peril of said plaintiff's intestate; and that said charges of negligence alleged against said defendant in said declaration are in all respects wholly vague and indefinite, and not sufficient to inform said defendant of any particular charge of negligence to which it can make answer.

"3. That said declaration does not state that the alleged explosion of gases was caused by said defendant, either negligently or otherwise; nor does it state that the alleged destruction of the different pieces of machinery was caused by said defendant; nor does it state that the personal injuries claimed to have been suffered by said plaintiff's intestate were caused by or due to the said defendant.

"4. That said declaration does not state or show in what particular respect, if any, the said defendant was negligent, so that such charge of negligence may be understood or answered by said defendant; nor does it show that the alleged injury to plaintiff's intestate was caused by any of the general instances of negligence claimed; nor does it state that the said alleged personal injuries were caused by any person. Wherefore it prays judgment."

Argued before WISWELL, Ch. J., and WHITEHOUSE, STROUT, FOGLER, and PEABODY, JJ.

AUG. F. MOULTON, for defendant.

WHITEHOUSE, J. — This is an action against the defendant company to recover damages for negligently causing the death of William John Carey, one of its employees. The declaration contains three counts, and the defendant demurred generally to the declaration and specially to each count. It is unnecessary to consider the numerous objections to the form of the pleadings pointed out and insisted upon as the grounds of the special demurrer, for it is the opinion of the court that each of the counts must be held insufficient for a substantial reason common to them all, not specified as a cause of special demurrer, but interposed as an objection under the general demurrer.

Each count in the declaration was manifestly designed to set out a cause of action "for injuries causing death" under the provisions of chapter 124 of the Public Laws of 1891, for it is provided in the second section of that chapter that "the amount recovered in every such action shall be for the exclusive benefit" of the widow and children, and be "a fair and just compensation, not exceeding five thousand dollars, with reference to the pecuniary injuries resulting from such death to the persons for whose benefit such action is brought;" and each count in the plaintiff's declaration concludes as follows: "By reason of all which said defendant has become liable, by force of the statute in such case made and provided, to the plaintiff in his said capacity for such damages, not exceeding five thousand dollars, as will be a fair and just compensation for the pecuniary injuries resulting from the death of said William John Carey" to his widow and children. But it is nowhere averred in either count of the declaration that William John Carey died immediately from the effect of his injuries. The first count alleges that he "was severely injured and killed by the explosion of gases * * * and suffered much in body and mind and died within twenty minutes, from the result of the injuries then and there received;" the second count represents that he "was severely injured in his head, lacerated and cut in different parts of his person, and other bodily injuries were sustained by him, and solely from such injuries, and from no other cause, said William John Carey died within a short time, to wit, within twenty minutes after said injuries were received;" and the third count simply states that he "received injuries from which he thereafterwards died." It is obvious that there is here no averment in either count equivalent to an allegation of immediate death.

A precisely similar question was presented on general demurrer in Sawyer *v.* Perry, 88 Me. 42, 33 Atl. Rep. 660, for the express purpose of obtaining from this court a judicial construction of the statute of 1891, c. 124, here in question. In that case the conclusion was that the act was intended by the legislature to apply to cases where the persons injured die immediately; and inasmuch as it was not alleged in the declaration that the injured person died immediately, but on the contrary it was averred that he lived "about an hour," it was held that the declaration described only a common-law right of action, in which the damages recovered must be for the benefit of the decedent's estate generally, and not for the exclusive benefit of the widow, and that in the form presented, declaring that the action was brought for the benefit of the widow of the deceased, the declaration was demurrable. In the opinion it is said by the court: "And when we say that the death must be immediate we do not mean to say that it must follow the injury within a period of time too brief to be perceptible. If an injury severs some of the principal blood vessels and causes the person injured to bleed to death, we think his death may be regarded as immediate, though not instantaneous. If a blow upon the head produces unconsciousness and renders the person injured incapable of intelligent thought or speech or action, and he so remains for several minutes, and then dies, we think his death may properly be considered as immediate, though not instantaneous."

In the case at bar it has been seen that there is no averment in either count that the injured person died immediately, but in the first and second counts it is alleged that he "died within twenty minutes," and in the third count that he "received injuries from which he thereafterwards died."

In the first count it also affirmatively appears by express averment that he "suffered much in body and mind;" and in the second count it fails to appear, either by inference or direct averment, whether he became unconscious from his injuries or endured conscious suffering while he survived. There is, therefore, no substantial ground for distinguishing the declaration in this case from that in Sawyer *v.* Perry, *supra.* It is true that in this case the decedent survived his injuries only twenty minutes, while in that he lived about an hour. But the agonies of body and mind which "no word can speak" may in one case be suffered in twenty minutes, and much larger damages may be required as compensation in such a case than for the suffering of many hours or days from injuries of a different character.

As construed by our court in Sawyer *v.* Perry, *supra*, it is obvious that the statute of 1891 in question affords a right of action for "injuries causing death" substantially like that given to employees by the employers' liability act in Massachusetts. The third section of that act (chapter 24, Pub. St. 1887), gives a right of action "where an employee is instantly killed, or dies without conscious suffering;" and it was held in Martin *v.* Railroad Co., 175 Mass. 502, 56 N. E. Rep. 719, that an action could not be maintained under this statute in a case where the injured person survived and endured conscious suffering less than one minute after the injury. See, also, Hodnett *v.* Railroad Co., 156 Mass. 86, 30 N. E. Rep. 224; Green *v.* Smith, 169 Mass. 485, 48 N. E. Rep. 621; Broderick *v.* Higginson (Mass.), 48 N. E. Rep. 270; Willey *v.* Boston Electric Light Co., 168 Mass. 40, 1 Am. Neg. Rep. 624, 46 N. E. Rep. 395.

Whether, in the case at bar, it might not reasonably be considered an immediate death, within the meaning and purpose of our statute, if the decedent immediately became unconscious after his injury and remained in a comatose state for twenty minutes, or even for several hours or days, until life became extinct, it is unnecessary here to determine. It is clear that the plaintiff in this case claims in his declaration to recover compensation for the pecuniary injuries resulting to the widow and children from the death of the decedent, but describes only a cause of action at common law in which the damages recovered must be for the benefit of the estate generally, and not for the exclusive benefit of the widow and children. The entry must therefore be:

Exceptions sustained. Demurrer sustained.

SNELL v. MINNEAPOLIS, ST. PAUL AND SAULT STE. MARIE RAILWAY COMPANY.

Supreme Court, Minnesota, October, 1902.

COWS TIED TO WAGON KILLED BY TRAIN WHILE CROSSING TRACK — CONTRIBUTORY NEGLIGENCE OF PERSON IN CHARGE OF CATTLE AND TEAM — SWITCHING YARD — PROXIMATE CAUSE. — 1. The plaintiff's sixteen-year-old son approached defendant's railroad crossing with a team and wagon, at the rear of which were tied two cows;

and, because they did not lead well, the boy left the team to go on without a driver, and went behind the cows to drive them along. At a point about eight rods from the track, where the view of the track was obstructed by a growth of underbrush and timber, the boy stopped and listened for signals or other indications of approaching trains, and, hearing none, he went on without further investigation. While crossing the track the cows were killed by one of defendant's trains. *Held*, the boy was guilty of contributory negligence.

2. In the village of Eden Valley defendant maintained a depot and side track for the accommodation of warehouses, lumber yard, coal shed, etc. The distance from the east to the west switch was 1,800 feet, and the space, to the extent of 200 feet west of the west switch and 350 feet east of the east switch, was left unfenced by defendant, and treated as a part of its depot grounds or switching yard. Certain stock belonging to plaintiff was killed at a point about 150 feet west of the west switch. *Held*, it was a question of fact for the jury to determine whether the proximate cause of the killing of the cattle was the absence of the fence, and whether the point where they were killed was reasonably required by the railway company as a part of its depot grounds or switching yard (1).

START, Ch. J., and BROWN J., *dissenting*.

(Syllabus by the Court.)

APPEAL from District Court, Meeker County.

Action by Robert Snell against the Minneapolis, St. Paul and Sault Ste. Marie Railway Company. Verdict for plaintiff. From an order denying a motion for a new trial, defendant appeals. *Order reversed.*

ALFRED H. BRIGHT and E. P. PETERSON, for appellant.

N. D. & C. H. MARCH, for respondent.

LEWIS, J. — First cause of action: At a point one mile from the village of Eden Valley a highway crosses defendant's railroad at an angle of about forty-five degrees. The right of way was fenced at this point, and the distance from the fence to the center of the track was fifty feet, and from the fence, running parallel to the highway, to the center of the wagon road, seventy-five feet. The space on both sides of the right of way was, for a considerable distance, covered with brush and timber, which obstructed a view of the track by a traveler on the highway until reaching the right of way fence. From the portion of the highway which crossed the right of way the view was unobstructed for a long distance, both east and west. Plaintiff's son, a lad sixteen years of age, approached this crossing with a team and wagon, at the rear of which were tied two cows. For some time before arriving at the crossing the boy had left the team to travel without a driver while he had gone back

1. See at end of this case, NOTES OF RECENT CASES ON PROXIMATE CAUSE OF INJURY.

to drive the cows, which were not leading well. According to his testimony, when he arrived within about eight rods of the railroad track he stopped the team and looked and listened for trains. At that point his view was cut off by the brush, and, not being able to hear any signals or trains, he started on again, still walking along behind the cows. When the horses were about to step upon the track, the boy noticed a gravel train close upon them, rapidly backing down from the east. The horses succeeded in getting across with the wagon, but the cows were struck and killed by the train. It is admitted that defendant was guilty of negligence in rapidly backing its train over the crossing without giving the ordinary signals. The only question is, was the boy guilty of contributory negligence? We must answer the question in the affirmative. No exception can be made on account of his age, and the evidence discloses the fact that he was a boy of average intelligence and experience. While the team was gentle, and it was not in itself an act of negligence to leave them to travel without a driver, yet it is clear that had the boy remained in the wagon, in direct control of the horses, he would have been in a position to discover the approaching train and control the team; and if he left such point of advantage, and for his own convenience walked behind the cows, he thereby placed himself and the property in a more hazardous position, because by so doing he reduced his chances of discovering approaching danger. Therefore, if his view was obstructed before reaching the right of way by reason of the disadvantage of his position at the rear, it was his duty to go forward and look for approaching trains before starting across the track; and, having failed so to do, he must be held to have contributed to the injury which followed.

2. Second cause of action: Eden Valley was an incorporated village, wherein were established defendant's depot, water tank, and coal sheds upon the main track, two elevators and a lumber yard upon the north siding track, and in addition there was a siding track running along the south side of the coal shed, and a stub track running off to the northeast. According to the record, the west switch was located at a point 1,050 feet from the depot, and 750 feet from the coal shed. The west switch was the point where the elevator and lumber-yard siding track connected with the main track, and at a point on this siding track about 150 feet east of the main west switch the stub track above mentioned branched off. The switch to the east, where the elevator and lumber siding track connected with the main track, was at a point 700 feet east of the depot and 825 feet east of the coal shed. To the east of the village the defendant had fenced its right of way to a point 350 feet east of the east

switch, and to the west the fence across the right of way was located 200 feet west of the west switch, at the end of a pile bridge which acted as a cattle guard, so that the space remaining unfenced was 2,350 feet, and the total distance between the two extreme switches was 1,800 feet. During the night some of plaintiff's cattle had broken out of the pasture, located some distance east of the village, and were huddled together upon the track at a point about 150 feet west of the west switch, and two of them were killed by defendant's train. The court instructed the jury to return a verdict for plaintiff for the value of the stock killed, upon the ground that it appeared, as a matter of law, that the cattle entered upon the railroad track by reason of the absence of a fence, and that it was the duty of the company to maintain fences at the point where the cows were killed. We are unable to agree with the court on either proposition. It was clearly for the jury to determine from the evidence, under proper instructions, whether or not the cattle entered upon the right of way at a point where the company was or was not required to fence.

The other question may be stated as follows: Was that portion of the track between the bridge and the west switch, a distance of 150 feet, reasonably necessary for the accommodation of defendant's employees in cutting off cars and in making up trains? Or does it appear, as a matter of law, that defendant should be required to maintain a fence and cattle guard at a point contiguous to the west switch, and that therefore the space between the west switch and the bridge should have been fenced? The question turns upon the effect the cattle guard would have in the vicinity. From the evidence on behalf of respondent, it appears that for the purpose of working a switch only six or eight feet of ground are necessary, and it is urged that defendant should be required to construct its cross-fence within eight or ten feet of the switch. On the other hand, the testimony on behalf of defendant tended to show that this switch was within what may be termed the depot grounds or switching yard of the village; that it was frequently used in switching cars upon the several side tracks mentioned, and, if a cross-fence was required to be maintained in that vicinity within a few feet of the switch, it would necessitate putting in a cattle guard; and that a cattle guard is a dangerous thing, increasing liability to accident by employees in charge of defendant's trains. The evidence tends to show that brakemen, in handling the switch and in cutting off cars, were required to pass back and forth over the track for the entire distance between the switch and the bridge, and that the presence of the cattle guard would unreasonably increase their liability to accident. We are of the opinion that it was a question of fact to be determined by the jury whether or not the space mentioned was reasonably required by defendant as a part of its depot grounds or yard system. It certainly does not appear, as a matter of law, from the evidence, that the defendant was required to maintain fences and a cattle guard at that point.

In the case of Greeley *v.* Railway Co., 33 Minn. 136, 22 N. W. Rep. 179, it was held that the facts in that case did not tend to bring the case within either of the implied exceptions to the statute; and those exceptions are declared in that case to exist when there is a legal duty imposed upon the company to the contrary, or when the public convenience is conserved, and a "public place" is defined as a place put into practical use by the public. We are not disposed to insist upon the term "depot grounds" as descriptive of the limitation to the implied exception to the statutory requirements We can see no distinction in principle between the necessities of a fence at a point strictly within the so-called depot grounds and a point where, by the use of switches and side tracks, the presence of cattle guards would tend to increase the hazard to employees of the railway company, although such point might be beyond the ordinary limits of the depot grounds. In other words, the implied exceptions to the terms of the statute should not be held strictly to apply to the convenience or safety of the public having business relations other than as employees. In a certain sense, the employees of a railroad company are the public, and their interests and convenience are to be considered in the application of the statute, as well as those who do not bear that relation to the company. Of course, the mere inconvenience or the mere matter of expense on the part of the railway company would not bring the case within the implied exceptions; but there may be such a condition that it is impracticable to put a fence along the yard system of a railroad, when it would materially affect the safety of those in the discharge of their duties. Although in one sense the public would not, in a direct way, be affected by such condition, yet, in another and broader sense, the public is interested in having such a condition maintained that employees may work with reasonable safety. It is better that the public dispense with the presence of the fence for the protection of persons and stock, than that a condition be maintained which would unreasonably increase the hazard of railroad employment. In Greeley *v.* Railway Co., *supra*, it does not appear from the record to what extent the yard was used for switching, and to what extent the railroad employees would be affected by the presence of the cattle guard; hence the court's attention was not called directly to the point now before us. In some of the States the legislatures have taken note of the necessity of making the exceptions applicable to such places as switching yards, and have so enacted. In our own State, in the more recent decisions, this court has recognized the necessity of extending the exceptions beyond the narrow limits understood by the term "depot grounds." In the case of Nickolson *v.* Railway Co., 80 Minn. 508, 83 N. W. Rep. 454, the court uses this language: "This implied exception has been held as to such places as depot and station grounds used for the convenience of passengers and the necessary handling of freight. This is as far as this court has gone, although there may be other and further exceptions — such, for instance, as a yard used for switching purposes, crossed at surface by streets. Fencing without cattle guards on either side of the street crossings would be of no value, and at such places guards would prove death traps to switchmen, who in such yards have to do a large part of their work on the ground." In the case of Marengo *v.* Railway Co., 84 Minn. 397, 87 N W. Rep. 1117, this language is used: "An exception would probably also apply to yards devoted distinctively to switching, and the work of receiving, distributing, or making up and sending out trains, whenever the legal duty of maintaining cattle guards at highway crossings might seriously endanger the lives of switchmen in the use of the tracks." In both those cases, however, the facts were not sufficient to bring them within the exception.

Order reversed, and a new trial granted.

BROWN, J. — I dissent. The evidence made the question of contributory negligence one for the jury. The boy did not, as said in the majority opinion, walk behind the cows "for his own convenience," but, on the contrary, for the reason that he deemed it necessary to do so. He testified — and there is nothing in the record to contradict him — that one of the cows would not lead, and because of this fact, his team being gentle and easily guided by the voice, he walked behind to drive her. If the cow would not lead, tied behind the wagon, it was clearly not necessary that the boy remain upon the seat of his wagon, and drag the animal across the track by the horns. It was for the jury to say whether he acted prudently or not. Indeed, if the evidence is conclusive either way upon this question, it is in favor of the proposition that he was not negligent. I concur in the result in other respects.

START, CH. J. — I concur in the dissenting opinion of Justice BROWN.

NOTE OF RECENT CASES ON PROXIMATE CAUSE OF INJURY.

1. **Railroads: injury to employees, trespassers and passengers.**
2. **Accidents in factories, mills.**
3. **Defects in streets or highways.**
4. **Unsafe mines.**
5. **Horse frightened or collision occurring.**
6. **Action against one who furnished defective article to plaintiff's employer.**
7. **Miscellaneous.**

1. Railroads.

Injury to employees.
Injury to trespassers.
Injury to passengers.

In DOLAN *v.* SIERRA R. Co. OF CAL. (Cal. 1902), 135 Cal. 435, 11 Am. Neg. Rep. 181, the plaintiff was a brakeman in the employ of the defendant and while on an engine it left the track by reason of a defect in the rails, and after traveling about fifteen feet upon the ties it passed upon a bridge or trestle that broke and went down with the engine, plaintiff and others. A judgment for plaintiff was affirmed. The court said that the defective construction of the trestle was the proximate cause of the injury, and it was immaterial how or when the break in the rails was occasioned.

In MISSOURI PAC. R'Y CO. *v.* COLUMBIA (Kan. 1902), 69 Pac. 338, the plaintiff's intestate was killed while employed as a fireman on one of defendant's engines that was derailed by running into some heavy grain doors that had been piled by defendant's servants upon a raised platform and had been blown upon the track by a very high wind that was unusually severe. None of the employees knew that the grain doors had been blown on the track, and it was the usual custom to pile the doors as these had been piled. A judgment for plaintiff was reversed. The court said: "Measured by authority, determined upon principle, or viewed in the light of the instructions of the court to the jury, which of the two distinct, successive causes operating independently of each other to produce the injury, — that is, the place and manner of piling and keeping the grain doors, or the severe gale, — must be held to have been the consequent, efficient, and proximate cause of this injury? Manifestly, it must be said the place and manner of piling and keeping the doors did no more than furnish the condition, afford the opportunity, for the accident which occurred. The operation of the successive, wholly independent, and unrelated cause and intervening agency, the severe gale, was the consequent, efficient, and proximate cause of the grain doors being upon the track, which resulted in the derailment of the engine and damage to plaintiff."

In WARD *v.* MAINE CENTRAL R. Co. (Me. 1902), 96 Me. 136, the plaintiff's intestate drove his horse and wagon over the defendant's tracks, upon which a freight train had recently arrived, and the cars of which were being switched. He drove to the platform of the station and backed his wagon for the evident purpose of unloading a barrel of potatoes that was in the wagon. Just then the freight train started towards where his horse was, about ten feet distant from the track, and making the usual noises caused by emitting steam and ringing the bell. He attempted to hold the frightened horse, which began to plunge and finally threw the deceased to the track a few feet in front of the locomotive that ran over and killed him. The engineer had shut off the steam of the locomotive when he discovered the situation, and the train was just "drifting along" but the bell continued to ring. The engineer tried to stop the train when the deceased was thrown to the track, but could not do so in time to avoid the accident. A verdict and judgment for plaintiff was sustained. The court said that even if it was a negligent act on the part of the deceased to go to the station platform that was so near the track when a freight was there, and with a horse that was frightened by trains, this negligence did not contribute as a proximate cause to the injury. The question for the jury was whether the engineer should have stopped his train as it was admitted he might have easily done before the horse threw the deceased on the track.

In FEZLER *v.* WILLMAR & SIOUX FALLS R. Co. (Minn. 1902), 85 Minn. 252, 11 Am. Neg. Rep. 397, the plaintiff, a boy ten years of age, went upon the defendant's right of way that was unfenced, and when a freight train came along he ran beside it trying to keep up with it, and stubbed his toe against one of the ties, fell on the track, and his foot was crushed. The court held that the absence of the fence was not the proximate cause of the injury, and a judgment for plaintiff was reversed.

In GREEN *v.* BRAINERD AND NORTHERN MINN. R. Co. (Minn. 1902), 85 Minn. 318, 11 Am. Neg. Rep. 434, plaintiff's intestate was a brakeman on one of defendant's logging trains, and was killed by a log falling upon him from the first car behind the engine as he stepped off the rear footboard of the engine as it approached the switch that connected the spur track upon which the logging train was, with the main line. The plaintiff's intestate was a rear brakeman and had been ordered by the conductor some two weeks before always to ride on the rear of the section, to be in a position to set the brake and also to see logs that might drop off the cars. The court held that the disobedience of the order of the conductor was the proximate cause of the intestate's death, and a judgment directed by the court for the defendant was affirmed.

In ILLINOIS CENTRAL R. Co. *v.* SEAMANS (Miss. 1901), 79 Miss. 106, the railroad company had constructed a house for the reception of cottonseed in a deep cut several hundred feet in length through which the main track and a side track passed. There was only one door to the house, and that was next and only a few feet from the side track. The only way that wagons loaded with seed could reach the house was to drive along the track from a crossing a short distance from the house, with one wheel, at least, on the side track. This condition of affairs had existed for a considerable time. In unloading cottonseed from the wagons, quantities had fallen on the tracks, and were permitted to remain there, and cattle that habitually wandered at large in the vicinity were enticed upon the tracks by the wasted seed which cows eat with relish. A number of cows had been killed in front of and near the seed house before the time of the accident in question. The plaintiff's son was a fireman on defendant's train that after dark struck a cow that was on the track near the seed house, and was not seen by the engineer or fireman in time to prevent the collision. The cow was run over, the engine was overturned, and the fireman, plaintiff's son, was killed. A judgment for plaintiff was affirmed. The court said that the negligence of the company in thus constructing the cottonseed house, and the kindred negligence of leaving large quantities of cottonseed lying on the railroad track, thus inviting animals addicted to the eating of them to go on the track in front of the cottonseed house to get them, were the proximate causes of the injury.

In OLNEY *v.* BOSTON & M. R. R. (N. H. 1902), 52 Atl. Rep. 1097, a locomotive engineer noticing that the cover of an armhole on the locomotive boiler was loose, called the attention of the foreman of the repair shop to it, and he promised to have it repaired. It was not repaired, and on the next trip, while the locomotive was in motion the engineer went out on the running board to fasten the cover that suddenly fell, causing him involuntarily to reach for it, when he lost his balance, fell to the ground, and was injured. A judgment entered on a verdict ordered for defendant was reversed. The court said the question of whether the negligence of defendant was the proximate cause of the injury was for the jury. As there was evidence that the plaintiff's injury was caused by the defendant's breach of duty the plaintiff had the right to have this evidence weighed by the jury unless it conclusively appeared from the evidence either that the injury arose from an assumed risk, or that the plaintiff's fault was a part of its cause. Assumption of risk is purely a matter of contract. As his contract was to run a suitable engine, he did not contract to bear the risk of injury which might come to him from the unknown defect if injured before he discovered it, or after discovery thereof before, by reasonable care, he could prevent injury to himself.

In RAILROAD *v.* KUHN (Tenn. 1901), 107 Tenn. 106, the plaintiff was a passenger in defendant's sleeping car that was derailed and thrown down an embankment, and caused his injury. Immediately after the disaster it was discovered that a brick culvert and the adjacent embankment of earth and roadbed had been so far washed away as to weaken the foundation of the track to such an extent that it gave way, and thereby derailed and overturned the sleeping coach after the preceding part of the train had passed over. The evidence of the defendant tended to show that the cause of the washout was an unprecedented rain so sudden and confined to so limited an area that the defendant's agents had been unable to anticipate or discover it before the wreck occurred, and the plaintiff's evidence tended to show that the culvert had been out of repair for some time, and that the rain, though a hard one, was not unusual in that locality. There was a judgment for plaintiff which was affirmed. The court said that if the defendant's omission of duty in respect to caring for the culvert, track and roadbed, and in the equipment and operation of the train, concurred as a proximate cause with an unprecedented rain in producing the derailment, the defendant would be guilty of actionable negligence, notwithstanding the occurrence and harmful operation of such a rain as an "act of God," in the legal sense.

In FREEMAN *v.* RAILROAD (Tenn. 1901), 107 Tenn. 340, the plaintiff's intestate was one of a bridge crew loading heavy timbers on a flat car that he and his fellow-employees stood behind, as it was easier to put the timbers on the car at the end than at the side, and while so engaged a train backed against some of the forward cars with great violence, and caused the flat car to knock down and run over the intestate, who was killed. A judgment for the plaintiff was affirmed. The court said that the members of the bridge crew were not fellow-servants of the conductor and engineer of the freight train, and that the rapid and reckless backing of the freight train on the side track without signal, and without warning, was the proximate cause of the injury, and not the mere fact of the deceased's presence on the track.

In MORRISETTE *v.* CANADIAN PACIFIC R. CO. (Vt. 1902). 52 Atl. Rep. 520, a brakeman, while going up the side of a freight car that was one of a train just leaving a siding, was struck and injured by a switch located twenty-two or twenty-three inches from the side of the car that was of ordinary size. A judgment for defendant ordered on motion for a verdict was reversed. The court said that in this class of cases the defendant's negligence is the proximate cause of the natural and probable consequences of it; and, whether the result complained of in the concrete case is the natural and probable consequence of it, is a question for the jury, unless it is plain enough to be ruled as matter of law, which it is not in this case.

In KILPATRICK *v.* GRAND TRUNK R'Y CO. (Vt. 1902), 52 Atl. Rep. 531, a brakeman, while mounting a ladder that was on the side of a freight car, contrary to the statute that provided that ladders should be on the ends of cars, was struck and knocked off by a post or standard used to uphold a bridge, and that was only twenty inches from the car and his foot was run over by the car. A judgment for plaintiff was affirmed. The court said that the position of the ladder on the side of the car was the proximate cause of the injury, and a refusal to charge as matter of law that the side ladder was not the proximate cause was no error.

2. Accidents in factories, mills.

In O'CONNOR *v.* GOLDEN GATE WOOLEN MFG. CO. (Cal. 1902), 135 Cal. 537, the plaintiff, a minor fifteen years and ten months old, was employed in a woolen factory at a machine to which the foreman assigned her, and around which he told her to sweep without warning her of the danger from the cogwheels. The machine was sometimes in motion, and sometimes still, when the sweeping was done. On the day of the accident, when she went behind the machine to sweep it was still, but while she was sweeping there the machine was started by a fellow-employee, and plaintiff's dress was caught by the unguarded cogwheels and she was drawn to the machine and injured. A judgment for plaintiff was affirmed. The court said that the act of the fellow-servant in starting the machine cannot be considered as the proximate cause of the injury; that as it was not unusual for the plaintiff to sweep behind the machine while it was in motion, if there was any negligence at all as between the two servants, it must rest with plaintiff alone; that she could not be charged with negligence as she had not been instructed as to the danger, and it could not be said, as matter of law, that from the fact that she saw the wheels and passed them daily, she must be charged with knowledge of the danger.

In HASKELL *v.* CAPE ANN ANCHOR WORKS (Mass. 1901), 178 Mass. 485, the plaintiff was an experienced workman in the defendant's employ, and was injured by the fall of a bar of steel in consequence of the breaking of a chain by which the bar was supported. He was directed to get the steel bar upon a car, and for the purpose took the only chain he saw in the neighborhood, and looked to be as good as any chain of its class, and was the kind that was always used for bars of this size. He attached the chain to the bar, and it was then hoisted by means of a crane, the plaintiff steadying the bar with his hand. While he was doing this the link next to the hook broke, and the plaintiff was hurt. The link that broke was made in the defendant's works by a fellow-servant with the plaintiff. There was evidence that it had not been used much, but was defective and crystallized because made of old instead of new iron, and that it should have been made of new. There was a judgment for plaintiff, which was affirmed. The court said whether the use of old instead of new iron was due to the indolence of the smith who made the link, or to a failure of the defendant to furnish new iron of convenient size, it is perhaps unnecessary to inquire. The chain was not worn out, but broke in consequence of inherent defects that could and should have been avoided in the manufacture, and that could not be found out later. As to permanent appliances in general, of course the fact that the proximate cause of the damage was the negligence of a fellow-servant in making them is no defense. The fact that a plaintiff was under a suspended weight which would crush him if it fell does not establish negligence, as matter of law, in all cases.

3. Defects in streets or highways.

In LINCOLN TOWNSHIP *v.* KOENIG (Kan. App. 1900), 10 Kan. App. 504, the defendant in error was driving on a highway, on a long hill slope in a deep cut. The highway was twelve feet wide, and on each side was a ditch, three to four feet wide, and from one and a half to two and a half feet deep. When the defendant in error was nearing the narrowest part of the roadway a runaway team came dashing down the hill and the wagon attached to them struck the wagon of the defendant in error, threw him out and injured him. The driver of the runaway team tried to pass without touching the wagon of the defendant in error, but the narrowness of the road prevented him. A judgment for plaintiff was affirmed. The court said that the rule applicable to the present case is thus stated in Ring *v.* City of Cohoes, 77 N. Y. 83: "When two causes combine to produce an injury to a traveler upon a highway, both of which are in their nature proximate — the one being a culpable defect in the highway, and the other some occurrence for which neither party is responsible — the municipality is liable, provided the injury would not have been sustained but for such defect."

In SUTPHEN *v.* HEDDEN (N. J. 1902), 51 Atl. Rep. 721, the defendants were contractors and had erected a high board fence along an excavation for a new building. The plaintiff was walking on the street alongside the fence when a heavy gust of wind blew the fence down and upon the plaintiff, who was thrown into the excavation and injured. A judgment for plaintiff was affirmed. The court said that, assuming that the falling of the fence was at least one of the efficient causes of the accident, it is none the less proximate in character because the wind was a concurring cause in producing that result. Such a concurrence of causes does not necessarily render either a remote cause. They may both be proximate.

In ELA *v.* POSTAL TEL. CABLE CO. (N. H. 1901), 51 Atl. Rep. 281, the defendant maintained a line of telegraph poles carrying four wires along a highway that had a curve at the place of the accident. Two of the wires were strung on the inside of the poles that were set on the outside of the curve. The highway ran through a large tract of woodland, and the growth extended to the wrought portion of the highway. A person acting independently of the defendants was clearing the wood lot, and one of the trees fell against the two wires that fell into the road, and the plaintiff, while driving along the highway, came into contact with the wires, and was injured. The person who felled the tree had placed a brace against it to prevent it falling into the highway, but a wind blew against the tree, broke the brace, and caused the tree to fall into the highway.

There was a verdict for defendants, which the court set aside on appeal. The court said that in this State it is well settled that the question of remote and proximate cause is a question of fact to be determined by the jury. The fact that the act of the person who cut down the tree caused the wires to be in the highway falls far short of exonerating the defendants from liability under the circumstances of the case. If he had felled the tree against the wires with the intention of forcing them into the highway, his act might be the proximate cause of the plaintiff's injury. But the evidence tended to show that while engaged in a lawful act he exercised due care to prevent the tree falling against the wires. To exonerate the defendants from liability, in view of this evidence, it was necessary that the jury should find that the defendants reasonably ought not to have foreseen an act of this general character.

In PINNIX v. CITY OF DURHAM (N. C. 1902), 130 N. C. 360, the defendant was paving one of its sidewalks with brick, and had a pile of bricks four feet high and about five feet square in the street near the sidewalk. The bricks had been there two or more months, and the street was lighted by an arc electric light that was within about 150 yards of the pile of bricks. An ordinance of the city required that a red light be kept on material left in the street at night, and there was no red light on the bricks this night. The plaintiff, riding a bicycle, ran into the pile of bricks and was injured. A judgment for defendant was affirmed. The court said that the plaintiff's injury was caused by his own negligence in running his bicycle into the pile of bricks, and that defendant's negligence was not the proximate cause of the injury.

In CITY OF ANTONIO v. PORTER (Tex. Civ. App. 1900), 24 Tex. Civ. App. 444, the plaintiff was driving an ordinarily gentle horse along a street exposed to a river's front, and when at a point where there was a slope from the street to the water's edge of fourteen feet the horse became frightened and backed the buggy and the occupants into the river, and caused an injury to the plaintiff. There were no railings or barriers of any kind erected or maintained to prevent such an occurrence. A judgment for plaintiff was affirmed. The court said that the negligence of the city in failing to erect barriers along the bank between it and the river was the proximate cause of appellee's injuries, and a charge that if the accident was brought about by the acts of bystanders endeavoring to assist plaintiff by taking hold of the bridle, thereby causing the horse to back the buggy into the river, the jury will find a verdict for the defendant was properly refused.

In MISCHKE v. CITY OF SEATTLE (Wash. 1901), 26 Wash. 616, the plaintiff, while walking on the sidewalk on a day when it was raining and blowing so hard that he carried his umbrella well in front of him, struck his knees against one of the iron doors of a hatchway maintained near the middle of the sidewalk for the convenience of adjoining lot owners, and with the consent of the city. The doors were raised, and he was thrown over the one he struck and against the other. A judgment of nonsuit was reversed. The court said one has the right to travel upon the street on the darkest night without a lantern, relying upon the performance of their duties by the authorities in keeping the streets in a suitable condition for travel. Certainly it does not follow that if, from a stress of weather, a person, to defend himself from torrents of rain, carries his umbrella in the only position in which he can carry it, — which is the fact shown in this case, — it can be said he has committed negligence *per se*. The court further said that it had no hesitancy in saying that the circumstances testified to by the plaintiff constituted a group of facts which it was the special prerogative of the jury to pass upon in the determination of the question whether or not they constituted contributory negligence.

In SEAVER *v.* TOWN OF UNION (Wis. 1902), 113 Wis. 322, the plaintiff was driving a span of horses drawing a bob sled, upon which was loaded a heavy saw frame and some pieces of machinery, making a top-heavy load, when he met a team of horses drawing also a bob sled, also loaded. The latter team was turned by its driver to the right so as to surrender as much as he could of the traveled part of the highway, that at this point, and for several hundred feet in both directions, was a narrow channel from ten to twenty inches below the banks on each side, made so by travel and the washing of surface water. There was not sufficient room for the teams to pass, which compelled the plaintiff to turn his team on to the bank, which was thirteen inches above the narrow traveled part of the road, and after passing the team, and while attempting to regain the traveled part at a place sixteen inches above it, the sled was overturned and the load fell in such a manner as to crush the plaintiff's arm. A judgment for plaintiff was reversed. The court said: "It is not often that a case is presented which so perfectly illustrates the doctrine of proximate cause in the law of negligence, the importance of it, and its applicability to an action to recover compensation for an injury alleged to have been caused by the insufficiency of a highway, the same as to every action grounded on negligence of the defendant. The immediate cause of plaintiff's injury was the condition of the highway, in that it was in a narrow cut at the place where the injury occurred, but the proximate cause thereof was the negligence of the respondent in going into the cut as he did, and paying no attention to whether a team was already in there, till he had passed by the last place where he could have safely turned out. That first act of negligence set all the other events in motion, each being started by the one which preceded it down to the instant of the injury."

4. Unsafe Mines.

In EWELL *v.* JOE BOWERS MINING CO. (Utah, 1901), 23 Utah, 192, 9 Am. Neg. Rep. 639, the plaintiff was a miner in defendant's mine, and was injured by being struck by a fall of rock, while he was sorting ore as directed on a platform under a hole through which ore was shoveled from above. There was evidence that the walls of the mine above the hole and immediately surrounding it were unsafe and parts would drop off unless properly timbered, and that before the accident the foreman informed the superintendent of the mine that more stulls were needed to hold the walls, and asked him if he would put in a chute as the walls were unsafe and that there was caving around the stulls. It also appeared that to make the ground safe it was necessary to put in square sets or chutes. There was no evidence where the rock that struck the plaintiff came from, but there was evidence that it was the same looking stuff as the hanging walls from the hole above. A judgment for plaintiff was affirmed. The court said where the evidence is conflicting or consists of circumstances from which fair and reasonable inferences may be drawn, for or against it, it is within the province of the jury to determine under proper instructions from the court, whether or not the evidence establishes it as the proximate cause of the injury complained of.

5. Horse frightened or collision occurring.

In COLEMAN *v.* WRIGHTSVILLE & TENNILLE R. CO. (Ga. 1901), 114 Ga. 386, it was said by the court that while under some circumstances a railroad company may be under a duty to warn a person, who is near its track by its permission, of the approach of a train, the failure to do so in the present case did not authorize a recovery because it is manifest from the evidence that the omission to give such warning was not the proximate cause of the plaintiff's injuries; where the proximate cause of an injury received by a person from a plunging horse which took fright at an approaching train, was the noise made by the emission of steam by the engine of the train, the railroad company will not be liable in damages, to the person so injured, unless it appears that the noise was "unusual and unnecessary" at the time when and the place where it was made, and while the plaintiff introduced evidence tending to show that it was unusual to emit steam from the engine at the time when and the place where it was emitted, there was no evidence from which a jury could have inferred that the noise so made was unnecessary; and this being the only theory presented by the declaration upon which a recovery would have been warranted there was no error in granting a nonsuit.

In CENTRAL OF GEORGIA R. CO. *v.* BLACK (Ga. 1901), 114 Ga. 389, the court said that it plainly appearing from the evidence that the proximate cause of the plaintiff's injury, which resulted to her from being thrown from a wagon, the horse hitched to which became frightened and ran away, was a noise made from falling timbers with which a car on the defendant's track was being loaded, and it not appearing that the noise so made was "unusual and unnecessary," a recovery against the defendant was unwarranted, irrespective of the question whether or not the persons loading the car were to be properly regarded as the agents of the defendant.

In OATES *v.* METROPOLITAN ST. R'Y CO. (Mo. 1902), 168 Mo. 535, the plaintiff's horse became frightened at an approaching street car, and began backing until the buggy was on the track in front of the car that continued to approach, and the men in charge continued violently ringing the bell until the car was only a few feet distant, when the horse wheeled around and almost upset the buggy, threw the plaintiff out, and ran away. There was a judgment for defendant, which was reversed. The court said that it was the duty of the operator when he saw that the horse was frightened to cease sounding the bell, and to stop the car. The court also said that it is only where plaintiff's negligence contributes directly to his injury that it precludes his recovery therefor, and the plaintiff's contributory negligence must mingle with the defendant's negligence as a direct and proximate cause in order to bar a recovery. Therefore, it was error to instruct that the defendant was not liable unless its negligence was the direct cause of the injury, while plaintiff was not entitled to recover if his negligence "but contributes to the injury."

In RIDER *v.* SYRACUSE RAPID TR. R'Y CO. (N. Y. 1902), 171 N. Y. 139, a covered delivery wagon, while crossing defendant's tracks at the intersection of two streets, was struck by one of defendant's electric cars, which caused the driver to be thrown to the pavement in such a violent manner as to subsequently cause his death. The wagon was not immediately overturned when struck, but was carried along the track from twenty-five to forty feet before it was overturned and the driver injured. This action was for damages for his death.

There was conflicting evidence as to whether the car at the time the driver drove the wagon on the track was twenty or eighty feet away, or some distance between. The car was traveling at the rate of from six to nine miles an hour. By the judge's charge and rulings the jury were permitted to find a verdict against the defendant, notwithstanding any negligence on the part of the deceased in driving upon the tracks, provided that they could find that the motorman could have stopped the car before it upset the carriage in which the deceased was riding. A judgment was rendered for plaintiff which was reversed on appeal. The court said that upon the rule that there must be an absence of contributory negligence on the part of the injured party there has been grafted an important exception, which the learned trial judge sought to apply to the facts in this case, and that is that the contributory negligence of the injured party, which will bar an action in his behalf, must be the proximate and not a remote contributory cause of the injury. It is impossible to separate that part of the transaction which took place after the first contact of the car with the vehicle from what took place before. It was all one transaction. It does not seem to us that the exception to the general rule in cases of this character was properly applied to the facts in this case. (This case was decided by a divided court, four judges to three; there was a dissenting opinion.)

In McKinney *v.* United Traction Co. (Pa. 1902), 19 Pa. Super. Ct. 362, the plaintiff was riding a young horse bareback, and used a carriage bridle with blinders. He was between the track and the curb, when for some reason the horse became frightened, and went upon the tracks, moving sideways, rearing and plunging. The plaintiff turned the horse off the track and the defendant's car that had approached passed him. The horse then became unmanageable, rearing, backing, and plunging abreast of and ahead of the car, when he suddenly wheeled, faced the car, stumbled and threw the plaintiff off in front of the car, which was then a short distance off, but stopped before it reached him. The car was under the control of the motorman all the time, and was promptly brought to a standstill when the plaintiff was thrown upon the street. The gong was sounded several times. The uncontradicted evidence shows that the horse was nervous, excited, and frightened before the car appeared, and it cannot be more than a guess to hold that the movement and management of the defendant's car was the proximate cause of the accident. It is just as probable that the insufficient bridle and lack of a saddle were inciting causes of the nervous condition. But, assuming that the horse took fright at the car, the car was in its proper place, and in determining what is proximate cause, the true rule is that the injury must be the natural and probable consequence of the negligence, such a consequence as under the surrounding circumstances of the case might and ought to have been seen by the wrongdoer as likely to flow from his act. The company had a right to ring the gong, but was not required to hold its car at a standstill until the horse and rider were off the street. A judgment for plaintiff was reversed.

6. Action against one who furnished defective article to plaintiff's employer.

In Boston Woven Hose and Rubber Co. *v.* Kendall (Mass. 1901), 178 Mass. 232, 9 Am. Neg. Rep. 496, the plaintiff was a manufacturer of rubber goods, and the defendants were manufacturers of boilers. The plaintiff ordered from defendants a boiler to withstand a specified pressure, and when the boiler was used it failed to withstand the pressure because of a defect that was patent, and might have been discovered by inspection and several of plaintiff's employees were injured, and were paid their damages by plaintiff, who in this action seeks to recover the amount so paid from defendants. A judgment for plaintiff was affirmed. The court said that a verdict for the plaintiff could be sustained on the ground that the plaintiff's failure to inspect the boiler before using it was due to the warranty or representations of the defendant, the consequences of the false warranty being not too remote.

In WATERS PIERCE OIL CO. v. DAVIS (Tex. Civ. App. 1900), 24 Tex. Civ. App. 508, the defendant oil company, through its agent, sold to the proprietor of a laundry a drum of eighty-seven-degree gasoline, and the agent told the proprietor of the laundry that it would be safe to store the gasoline in a shed that was thirty feet distant from the furnace. The plaintiff's intestate was the engineer employed in the laundry, and it was his duty to draw some of the gasoline every day, as it was used to heat the ironing machinery. On the day of the accident, while he was drawing some of the gasoline from the drum, the gas which had generated in the drum escaped, and permeated the atmosphere, and came in contact with the furnace fire, which caused it to explode and seriously injured the intestate, and caused his death in two days. The dangerous character of the gasoline was known to the defendant company, but was not known to the agent or to the laundry proprietor, or to any of his employees. A judgment for plaintiff was affirmed. The court said that, although the proximity of the furnace fire and the heat thereof was the immediate cause of the explosion, the failure to inform the purchaser of the dangerous character of the gas was the proximate cause of the injury.

7. Miscellaneous.

In ANDREWS v. KINSEL (Ga. 1901), 114 Ga. 390, the plaintiffs rented from defendant a storehouse which adjoined another storehouse of defendant, who, while making repairs to the latter storehouse, took down a part of the partition wall separating the two stores, and upon leaving the place at night the defendant's servants negligently and carelessly left open two rear windows in the store next plaintiff's, and through which windows burglars entered, gained access to plaintiff's store through the opening left in the partition, and stole the plaintiff's merchandise. No notice was given to plaintiffs that the partition had been removed, or that the windows had been left open. The court said: "It is unnecessary to argue or to cite authorities to sustain the well-settled legal principle that, to enable one to recover for damages resulting from the negligent conduct of another, it must appear that the negligence of the defendant was the proximate cause of the injury sustained. It is also a well-recognized principle that where there has intervened between the defendant's negligent act and the injury an independent illegal act of a third person producing the injury, and without which it would not have happened, the latter is properly held the proximate cause of the injury, and the defendant is excused. * * * Applying these principles to the case now before us, it is manifest that the plaintiffs did not make out a cause of action by their petition. Granting as true all of their allegations as to the negligence of the defendant, it is also true, upon the face of their pleadings, that there intervened, as a direct cause between the negligence of the defendant and the damage sustained by themselves, the independent criminal act of a responsible human agency. The demurrer should have been sustained."

In WINDELER *v.* THE RUSH COUNTY FAIR ASS'N (Ind. App. 1901), 27 Ind. App. 92, the plaintiff was a visitor at the annual fair of the defendant, having paid the regular admission fee, and while she was viewing a horse race an accident happened on the track that caused one of the horses to run away through an opening in the fence surrounding the track, and towards the benches where the plaintiff was sitting. In endeavoring to escape from the approaching horse the plaintiff fell over a bench and was injured. A judgment for defendant was reversed. The court said that the defendant negligently made an opening in the fence surrounding the track, and through this opening a horse ran from the track and among the people, and causing plaintiff's injury. It is earnestly contended that the proximate cause of the injury was the running away of the horse, and not the failure properly to inclose the track. The proximate cause, which happened to be nearest in point of time in this case is the one for which defendant is responsible; had it done its duty plaintiff could not have suffered from the running of the horse.

In JOHNSON *v.* WESTERN UNION TEL. CO. (Miss. 1901), 79 Miss. 58, the telegraph company failed to deliver a telegram that contained information that the plaintiff would have an opportunity to make a contract for the construction of a railroad that the plaintiff alleged would, if made, have yielded him large profits, and he brought this suit to recover them. The court said that the damages claimed were not the direct result of the breach of duty complained of and that the judgment for defendant should be affirmed.

In NEWBURY *v.* LUKE (N. J. 1902), 52 Atl. Rep. 625, the defendant hired the plaintiff's horse on Sunday, and so overdrove him and abused him that he died. A judgment for plaintiff for the damages was affirmed. The court said: "The defendant argues that the plaintiff's right of action rests upon a contract of bailment made on Sunday, and as that contract is void the action must fail. The fallacy is exposed by reference to the fundamental maxim, "*Causa proxima, non remota, spectatur.*" The Sunday hiring and the Sunday driving happened to furnish the conditions under which the death of the horse was occasioned. But its death was the direct and natural result of the overdriving and abuse, and of these alone. The contract fails because made on Sunday. That destroys the defendant's right to drive the horse, but it certainly does not confer the right to overdrive it. It vitiates the temporary right of use, but it does not pass the permanent right of property. In short, it leaves the defendant's liability upon the same basis as if the horse had been taken without the leave or license of the plaintiff." As the plaintiff can make out his case without reference to the illegal contract, the maxim, "*In pari delicto potior est conditio defendentis*" has no applicancy.

In GALVESTON, HARRISBURG & S. A. R. CO. *v.* NASS (Tex. 1900), 94 Tex. 255, a brakeman injured by a fall from a car caused by the giving way of a "handhold" that broke loose from the wood that was rotten, sued his employer for damages for the injury, and the latter sought to obtain a judgment against the connecting line that owned the car and furnished it for use, for the amount paid. The court held that the employer of the brakeman could only be liable for its own negligence in failing to make a proper inspection of the car, and this being a proximate cause of the injury, there could be no recovery against the owner of the car.

In BIRKEL *v.* CHANDLER (Wash. 1901), 26 Wash. 241, the defendant was a professional safe mover and was employed by one Heath, who had contracted to move office furniture into a building, to move the safe that was part of the furniture. The safe had been safely placed in the office and an effort was made to lower some heavy planks that had been used to roll the safe from the window when it was taken into the building. A rope was tied around the planks and was also attached to a windlass situated on a wagon below. The planks thus held were being lowered by unwinding the rope from the windlass below. The defendant was at the time standing upon the wagon and was giving general directions to those engaged in lowering the planks. A guide rope was attached to the larger rope for the purpose of swinging the planks clear of the windows and other obstructions in the way of their descent. The planks became lodged against some telegraph wires, and while all were endeavoring to free them from the wires, they slipped through the noose and fell to the street, where the plaintiff's son happened to be passing, and the planks struck him and injured him. A judgment for plaintiff was affirmed. The court said that it claimed that the evidence shows the accident due entirely to the careless manner in which the knot was tied around the planks; that the knot was tied by Heath, or under his immediate direction; and that the defendant, who was down in the street, in no way assisted in tying the knot. There was evidence introduced by respondent, however, to the effect that the noose which held the planks was loosened by the manner in which the planks were permitted to strike the wires, and that if the planks had been kept clear of obstructions, the noose would have held them securely until they reached the ground. It was under this testimony proper to submit to the jury the question whether the defendant was guilty of negligence, inasmuch as it clearly appeared that he was assisting in lowering the planks.

KLAGES v. GILLETTE-HERZOG MANUFACTURING COMPANY.

Supreme Court, Minnesota, June, 1902.

EMPLOYEE KILLED BY ELECTRIC SHOCK — CONTACT OF ELECTRIC WIRES WITH DERRICK CABLES — *RESPONDEAT SUPERIOR.* —

1. Whether the doctrine of *respondeat superior* applies to any particular case between the original contractor and a subcontractor is determined by the contract between the parties with reference to the right of the former to control or direct the latter as to the time, place, and manner of performing the work.
2. The true relation of the parties in this respect is *prima facie* as expressed by the terms of the written contract, if there be one. But such contract is to be considered in view of the circumstances under which it was made and the manner in which the work was performed. If it appears that the writing was not executed in good faith to express the real relation of the parties, or if it appears that, notwithstanding such contract, supervision or control of the work was assumed by the original contractor, then the application of the rule is to be determined by the conduct of the parties.
3. Test applied in an action where appellant's husband was killed by an electric shock, caused by the cables of a derrick coming in contact with electric

wires in the public street, and *held*, the evidence was not conclusive that the derrick was placed in position and operated by independent contractors.

4. *Held*, the evidence was not conclusive that deceased was guilty of contributory negligence in attempting to push the loose part of a derrick cable, charged with electricity, from the open street into the gutter (1).

COLLINS, J., *dissenting*.

(Syllabus by the Court.)

APPEAL from District Court, Hennepin County.

Action by Susanna Klages, administratrix of Herman Klages, against the Gillette-Herzog Manufacturing Company. Verdict for defendant. From an order denying a new trial, plaintiff appeals. *Order reversed.*

YOUNG & WAITE, for appellant.

JAMES D. ARMSTRONG, for respondent.

LEWIS, J. — The Gluek Brewing Company's buildings are situated on Marshall street, in Minneapolis, and the company entered into contracts for the construction of an addition to their refrigerator building. The dimensions of this new building were 100x100, varying in height from one story to eighty-six feet. Directly north of the space to be occupied by this building ran an alley fifty feet in width, which the company used in driving in and out in the conduct of its business; and immediately north of it was an ice house. The old and new buildings, as well as the ice house, faced east, flush with Marshall street; and to the west of the excavation, and between that and the river, was an open space of about seventy-five feet. On January 16, 1900, the brewing company entered into contracts with one Johnson for the masonry work, and with respondent for the structural and ornamental iron work, by the terms of which respondent agreed to furnish the material, and within six months to erect and complete its work, according to certain plans and specifications, for the consideration of $20,009.73. On June 4. 1900, respondent entered into the following contract with Winblad & Bruce: "Gentlemen: We will pay you $3.60 per ton for the erection of the structural ironwork, not including stairs, on our order No. 131 for Gluek Brewing Company, you to erect same in a satisfactory manner, according to plans, to bolt all lintels together as required, and paint all material one coat when not already painted. It is understood that you are to take this material from the place where it is now piled. You are to make out your pay rolls, and we will

1. *Accidents from Electricity.* — For actions arising out of injuries sustained by contact with electric wires, from 1897 to date, see vols. 1-12 AM. NEG. REP., and the current numbers of that series of Reports.

See also NOTE ON LIABILITY FOR PERSONAL INJURIES CAUSED BY ELECTRIC WIRES, 8 AM. NEG. REP. 213-221.

pay the same on regular pay days at this office. If you want to discharge a man, we will pay him on presentation of regular discharge slip signed by you. It is understood that we are to furnish all tools and paint. Yours truly, Gillette-Herzog Manfg. Co., by Peter Lees, Supt." The brewing company obtained from the mayor a license or permit to occupy for three months one-third of the street in front of the building to be erected for the disposition of building material, which stated that care be taken to incommode the public as little as may be during the construction of the building, and that the permit was granted upon the condition that proper guards would be placed around the material, and a suitable number of red lights kept burning through the nights to warn the public of danger, and that it was revocable at the mayor's pleasure. On June 7, 1900, Winblad & Bruce began operations under their contract, selected their tools and derrick from respondent's supply, and respondent hauled the derrick to its indicated location near the southerly corner of the excavation, and not very far from the side of the street. A few feet to the southwest from it stood an electric pole, strung with wires belonging to the Minneapolis General Electric Company. Near the top of this pole were two cross-bars, one a little above the other; and the upper one, slightly lower than the top of the derrick, carried two "primary" and the lower one two "secondary" wires. On the day in question these primary wires were each charged with 1,000 volts of electricity, and the secondary wires carried about 108 volts. On the pole north, next to the one above described, was a "transformer," and one of the secondary wires went from this pole into the brewery for lighting purposes. The derrick was maintained in an upright position by four wire cables running north, south, east, and west, respectively, and these were fastened to an iron band at the top of the derrick mast by means of iron hooks. The north cable was fastened to the upper end of the ice house, about 175 feet from the derrick mast; the one to the east was made fast to a post in a vacant lot about seventy-five or eighty feet back from the street. The southern guy rope was fastened to a post directly in front of the south corner of the office, and a loose end extended northerly in the gutter some fifteen or twenty feet, and then curved back. The western cable had been pulled over the sidewalk primary wire and fastened to the window of the old malt kiln, and in operating the derrick it had come in contact with the primary wire, worn the insulator, and, as a consequence, that wire had become broken or burned off. The electric company were notified of the fact, and had repaired the break and restrung the wire, raising it about six inches above the guy line, so as to remove the danger of further contact. But afterwards, in operating the derrick, this cable, which the testimony shows was very slack when the burned wire was repaired, had become taut, and again in contact with the primary wire, lifting it some five or six inches from its natural position. Such contact transmitted to all the cables of the derrick an electrical current, which rendered it unsafe and impossible to work with, and the electric company was informed of the situation, and requested to adjust the difficulty. But before imminent danger was apprehended, and about three o'clock in the afternoon on June 8th, Johnson, one of the contractors, received a slight shock upon touching some part of the derrick, and from then on until about 5:30, when the accident here involved occurred, different persons received shocks upon contact with the derrick and certain charged portions of the ground near it. Herman Klages was an engineer in the employ of the brewing company, and had charge of their electric lighting plant. About 5:30 o'clock he came out of the engine room, and joined the other men, and asked them what the matter was. One Proehl, who had just received a shock from the ground which threw him backwards into the street, told him the ground and derrick were charged with electricity. The men then dared him to take hold of the cable, but he looked at the soles of his shoes, and said: "No, my feet are wet. It wouldn't be dangerous. It is only 108 or 110 volts." He asked Proehl to show him the spot where he had received the shock, and when pointed out to him, warned Proehl, and a man standing with him, away from the place, saying: "It is kind of dangerous. You better step back." At this time Klages was informed that the electric company had been notified of the condition. He then went across the street, and returned with a stick or dry board some two and a half feet long and four inches wide, one end narrower than the other, with which he began to poke the loose part of the cable towards the sidewalk. By the "fooling" of the men it had been pushed some four or five feet into the street, and the end of it had come in contact with an iron catch-basin cover in the gutter, thus causing occasional sparks. While he was thus pushing the loose part of the cable towards the gutter, the men watching him saw him suddenly make a movement as if he had slipped, and in flinging his arms out as if catching at something for support his left hand came in contact with the cable, to which, a witness says, "he held on, gave a groan, and swung around so that his neck or jaw came right across the guy." With some difficulty the men removed contact of the body with the cable, but death was conceded to have been instantaneous, and the result of an electric shock. This action was brought for the purpose of recovering damages, on the theory that respondent was negligent in erecting and operating the derrick in a public street at a place contiguous to electric wires where persons having occasion to use the highway might come in contact with it. Respondent interposed the defense that it was not in charge of the derrick at the time of the accident, and that it was erected and operated by a firm of independent contractors, and that the deceased was guilty of contributory negligence. At the close of the evidence the court directed a verdict for respondent, and from an order denying plaintiff's motion for a new trial plaintiff appealed.

The order must be reversed, unless it conclusively appears that the work was done by independent contractors, and the relation of *respondeat superior* did not exist, or that deceased was guilty of contributory negligence. It was gross negligence to place the derrick in the public street with its metal cables contiguous to the electric wires, and to operate the same in lifting and swinging heavy iron beams so that contact was made in the manner stated. The inquiry is whether respondent was itself in charge of the work, or whether it had been unrestrictedly delegated to Winblad & Bruce. In the case of Rait *v.* Carpet Co., 66 Minn. 76, 68 N. W. Rep. 729, the following language is used: "In every case the decisive question in determining whether the doctrine of *respondeat superior* applies is, had the defendant the right to control in the given particular the conduct of the person doing the wrong? If he had, he is liable. On this question the contract under which the work was done must speak conclusively; in every case reference being had, of course, to surrounding circumstances." And under the circumstances of the case it was left to the jury to determine whether the defendant surrendered all control over the manner of performing the work there under consideration. In Barg *v.* Bousfield, 65 Minn. 355, 68 N. W. Rep. 45, the rule was declared as follows: "Where one who performs work for another represents the will of that other, not only as to the result, but also as to the means by which that result is accomplished, he is not an independent contractor, but the agent of that other, who is responsible for his acts and omissions within the scope of his authority." In the case of Whitson *v.* Ames, 68 Minn. 23, 2 Am. Neg. Rep. 178, 70 N. W. Rep. 793, it was said: "The decisive test in determining whether the doctrine of *respondeat superior* applies is whether the defendant had, under the contract of employment, the right to control in the given particular the conduct of the person doing the wrong." In Vosbeck *v.* Kellogg, 78 Minn. 176, 7 Am. Neg. Rep. 86, 80 N. W. Rep. 957, a written contract was construed, and held to show conclusively that the person in charge of the work was an independent contractor; but in that case that entire question was submitted upon the terms of the contract itself. In Aldritt *v.* Gillette-Herzog Mfg. Co. (Minn.), 11 Am. Neg. Rep. 268n, 88 N. W. Rep. 741, the rule is affirmed as stated in Rait *v.* Carpet Co., *supra*, in the following language: "The question whether the doctrine of *respondeat superior* applies to any particular case depends upon the question whether the original contractor had control of and the right to direct the subcontractor as to time, place, and manner of performing the work, and this question must be determined from the contract between the parties in the light of surrounding circumstances." We think the contract, on its face, clearly indicates that respondent did not, in any respect, retain control of the work as to the method, time, or place of its execution, but only as to the result accomplished, viz., that it should be in accordance with the specifications. But from a consideration of all the evidence surrounding the making of the contract we are of the opinion that it does not conclusively appear that the true relations of the parties were defined by the writing. At the time this contract was entered into, the ironwork to be put in place by Winblad & Bruce was lying in a vacant lot on the other side of the street opposite the building in which it was to be placed. For several reasons the best location for the derrick seemed to be in the street in front of the building, because the ironwork was nearer to that point than any other, the street was higher than the ground at the rear of the building, and the alley was hardly wide enough for the required purposes, and, besides, it was used by the brewing company in the daily conduct of its business. It was known to respondent that the street could not be occupied without securing a permit, and Winblad consulted respondent's superintendent in reference thereto. The contract provided that the men employed by Winblad & Bruce should be placed on the pay rolls of the respondent company, and that all tools and appliances were to be furnished by it, and the derrick was delivered in the street by respondent. The construction of the ornamental ironwork respondent reserved to itself, and on one occasion superintended and put in place certain iron plates, which was part of the work of Winblad & Bruce. It appears that Mr. Winblad had been a regular employee of respondent for about sixteen years, that he was accustomed to act as foreman of this kind of work, and had on several occasions during that period taken similar contracts to the one under consideration. Under all of these circumstances we do not think it appears conclusively, as a matter of law, that respondent did not reserve the right of supervision as to time, place, and method of putting up the structural iron, and whether it did not in fact exercise supervision, to some extent, as to the use of the derrick, and its location with reference to the electric wires. If respondent did exercise such supervision, or if the contract was not intended to express the true relation between the parties in respect to the control or superintendence of the work, then Winblad & Bruce were not independent contractors as defined by the decisions of this court. The case of Aldritt *v.* Gillette-Herzog Mfg. Co., *supra,* involved a similar contract to the one under consideration, but the facts in that case were essentially different, and the decision rested upon the ground that the legal status of the parties was determined by the contract itself.

But respondent contends that the record conclusively shows that the deceased came to his death by reason of his own carelessness. The argument to this effect is based upon the fact that he had some experience as an electrician; that he knew contact existed between the derrick cable and the electric wire; that other people had received shocks by touching the cables, and that he was fully warned of the danger, so that his attempt to push the cable back towards the gutter was in a spirit of bravado or criminal carelessness, and not in the exercise of any duty devolving upon him. A close examination of the evidence makes it by no means certain that the deceased was not in the exercise of reasonable care, or that he was not acting in a commendable manner in attempting to move the cable to a less dangerous location. In the first place, his experience as an electrician was limited to the running of an ordinary dynamo. For some reason he assumed that it was one of the secondary wires, charged with 108 or 110 volts, which was in contact with the derrick. It does not appear conclusively that he was negligent in not knowing that it was the primary wire instead of the secondary. If he had been thoroughly familiar with the construction of the electric system, he would have known that the cable was in contact with the primary wire, and that the danger was greater; but he assumed that conditions were different, and that the cables were charged with 108 or 110 volts, which, it appears from the evidence, could not be fatal. When some one dared him to touch the cable, he refused upon the ground that his shoes were wet, but remarked that it would not be dangerous, which tended to show precaution upon his part. It is true he had been informed that the electric company had been notified of the condition, but there is no evidence as to what time they were expected to make the repairs, and that fact alone is not sufficient to warrant the conclusion that the deceased was simply playing with an instrument of death. It is urged that there was no duty resting upon him to go into the street and interfere with the cable, and that by so doing he assumed the risk, and was alone responsible for the result. True, he was not, in the ordinary sense, a traveler along the public highway at that time, for it may be said that he was attracted to the place by the fact that the derrick had become charged with electricity; but he had a right to be in the street, not only as a public traveler, but also for the purpose of observing what was going on; and, if a traveler would have the right to stop and remove from the highway a nuisance which he conceived to be dangerous to other travelers, then the deceased had a similar right to remove a dangerous instrument which came under his observation, although he was attracted to the place by the very fact of its existence. In the case of Dillon *v.* Allegheny County Light Co., 179 Pa. St. 482, 1 Am. Neg. Rep. 174, 36 Atl. Rep. 164, it was held that a police officer was justified in attempting to remove a live electric wire from the public street with his mace. The decision does not necessarily rest upon the fact that he was a public officer whose particular business it was to remove such dangerous appliances. If a patrolman would be justified in so doing, then any person, with reasonable care and caution, may do the same thing. In the case of Bourget *v.* City of Cambridge, 156 Mass. 391, 31 N. E. Rep. 390, it was held that one who was traveling in the highway was justified in attempting to remove a loose telephone wire; and, while the opinion in that case discusses the question from the standpoint of a traveler, it is clearly stated that the attempt to remove the wire was justified, in that it did not appear to be an intermeddling by a volunteer. In Light Co. *v.* Orr, 59 Ark. 215, 27 S. W. Rep. 66, it was held to be a question for the jury whether a boy, who had been warned, was guilty of contributory negligence in picking up a live wire that was lying across the street. The case should have been submitted to the jury.

Order reversed, and a new trial directed.

COLLINS, J. — I cannot concur in the conclusion that Mr. Klages was not guilty of contributory negligence which caused his death. He left his work out of curiosity, went into the street, was told of the danger, fully realized it, decided to let the wire cable alone, went away, then returned, and, without having any duty to perform, attempted to move it to one side, simply, in my judgment, because he had previously been dared to handle it by his fellow-workmen, who were standing by in sufficient numbers to warn and protect travelers on the street, if there were any — of which there was no proof, and no presumption, because of the torn-up condition of both wagon track and sidewalk. If this was not gross carelessness and negligence, I cannot imagine what is, and therefore dissent.

BOYER v. EASTERN RAILWAY COMPANY OF MINNESOTA.

Supreme Court, Minnesota, November, 1902.

EMPLOYEE INJURED WHILE UNLOADING LOGS — ASSUMPTION OF RISK — RULES — FELLOW-SERVANT. — 1. The ordinary labor of unloading logs from flat cars is not attended with extra hazards or involved in such complicated and obscure conditions as to require, by the corporation engaged therein, the formulation of rules for the conduct of the business of its employees.

2. Where a servant is ordered, with other employees, to unload logs from flat cars, where the risk arising from the incidental performance of the work is open and apparent to observation he assumes the dangers caused by the negligence of fellow-servants (1).

3. Allegations of the complaint in this case considered, and *held*, that the work described therein was of a usual and customary character, and the dangers thereof open to observation, and that an injury resulting in the performance of the work by a fellow-servant was incident to the common employment and remediless.

(Syllabus by the Court.)

APPEAL from District Court, Hennepin County.

Action by Peter Boyer against the Eastern Railway Company of Minnesota. From an order overruling a demurrer, defendant appeals. *Order reversed.*

W. E. DODGE, ROME G. BROWN, and CHARLES S. ALBERT, for appellant.

FRANK D. LARRABEE, for respondent.

LOVELY, J. — Appeal from an order overruling a demurrer.

The material facts in the complaint may be summarized as follows: Plaintiff, a bridge carpenter, was employed to work in defendant's yards at Superior, Wis. Flat cars loaded with poles were placed upon a side track to be unloaded. These cars were thirty-eight feet in length, while the poles placed thereon were seventy feet long, each being two feet in diameter at the large, and eight inches at the smaller, end. The poles were placed upon the floor of the cars lengthwise; five of each being laid side by side, in four tiers, with crosspieces between the tiers, two poles being laid on top, making the fifth tier. The poles were held in place by stakes fastened by three braces on each side of the cars, extending above the top tier of the poles. At the time of the injury plaintiff was ordered from

1. See NOTE ON ASSUMPTION OF RISK, 7 AM. NEG. REP. 97-111.

his work as bridge carpenter, to assist in unloading the cars. In this work he had no experience, the details were unknown to him, and he was under the direction of a general foreman, who had the right to discharge him and to give orders as to how he should perform his work. Under the instructions of the foreman and others, a skidway was constructed from the floor of the car to another skidway nearer the ground. The stakes on one side of the car were taken out, and logs were rolled off the cars, by plaintiff and others, down the skidways. It is alleged that the only proper way to have unloaded the logs was to have sawed off stakes as each layer of logs was to be removed, and to roll off each tier consecutively, but that defendant negligently, through its foreman, removed logs from the side of the car after the stakes were displaced, so as to permit the logs to spread when one of them which was very crooked in the middle slipped into a space, made by the spreading of the logs, and swung around, knocking plaintiff from the car.

It is specifically alleged that defendant failed to provide rules and regulations for the conduct of the work, for plaintiff's benefit. Upon this complaint, we are not authorized to inquire into any peculiar statute of Wisconsin involving the duties of master and servant. It was not pleaded, and undoubtedly could not be considered. Myers *v.* Railway Co., 69 Minn. 476, 72 N. W. Rep. 694. Hence the liability arises upon the common-law obligation of master and servant, as is conceded by plaintiff, and the case is simply one where a foreman, with other servants, engaged in a common employment with plaintiff, and by the alleged negligent manner of their performance of the work occasioned the injury to him. In this respect he must be held to have assumed the risk under the principle announced in O'Niel *v.* Railway Co., 80 Minn. 27, 82 N. W. Rep. 1086, unless the allegation with reference to the inexperience of the plaintiff and the failure to furnish proper rules distinguish it from the established rule recognized in that case; and it does not appear to the court that it does. It is alleged in the complaint that there was a proper method of doing the work. This, so far as such allegation goes, is nothing more than an opinion of the pleader; as there is no further statement that the sawing off of the stakes is a usual and customary method of unloading logs from cars in the railroad service, and we cannot assume it to be so. The allegation that the hazards of this service were unknown to plaintiff, even though he was inexperienced, is not sufficient, when the nature of the business itself is considered, to require the establishment of rules and regulations, or so obscure as to demand specific warnings of the danger; for it is only where the business is complicated, as well as dangerous, that it is the absolute duty of the master to provide rules (Vogt *v.* Honstain, 81 Minn. 174, 8 Am. Neg. Rep. 443, 83 N. W. Rep. 533; Reberk *v.* Horn & Danz Co., 85 Minn. 326, 11 Am. Neg. Rep. 271, 88 N. W. Rep. 1003), or not observable, that notice of danger is required (Gray *v.* Commutator Co., 85 Minn. 463, 11 Am. Neg. Rep. 267, 89 N. W. Rep. 322).

But in this case the work was of the most ordinary character, where, from the description of the manner of performing it as set out in the complaint, the dangers incurred thereby were patent and open to observation, requiring no peculiar skill; and it has never been required that rules and regulations for the conduct of the business should be provided in such cases. Such hazards between the master and servant are necessarily assumed, and where an injury arises the master cannot be held liable therefor unless he is made an insurer, and responsible for every accident that occurs to his employees.

Order reversed.

BERRY v. DOLE ET AL.

Supreme Court, Minnesota, November, 1902.

PERSONAL INJURIES — PLEADING — COMPLAINT — DEMURRER. — 1. The complaint in a personal injury action *held* not to allege facts constituting a cause of action, for the reason that it contains no direct allegations that the plaintiff's injuries were caused by any act or omission of the defendants.

(Syllabus by the Court.)

APPEAL from District Court, Hennepin County. Action by Andrew J. Berry against George A. Dole and another. From an order sustaining a demurrer to the complaint, plaintiff appeals. *Order affirmed.*

J. M. MURRAY, for appellant.

WOODS, KINGMAN & WALLACE, for respondents.

START, Ch. J. — Appeal by the plaintiff from an order of the District Court of the county of Hennepin sustaining a general demurrer to his complaint. The here material allegations of the complaint are to the effect following: That on and for a long time prior to June 29, 1900, the defendants maintained in a public street of the city of Minneapolis a wooden structure or bridge over the gutter therein to facilitate passage of teams and wagons of their tenants and their customers into an alley upon their premises, and invited the public and the plaintiff to use the same; that on that day the wooden structure or bridge was, and for a long time prior thereto had been, in a defective, rotten, and unsafe condition, which condition was well known to defendants, although plaintiff had no notice or knowledge thereof; that on that day plaintiff, in the course of his employment as a servant of a customer of one of defendants' tenants, was lawfully and with due care, and by invitation of the defendants, driving over the bridge, from the alley to the street, a loaded wagon, upon which he was seated, when the bridge suddenly, and without fault of plaintiff, broke down and gave way under the wagon, and thereby caused it to lurch suddenly to one side, and throw plaintiff therefrom, head foremost, violently to the pavement of the street, whereby he sustained serious personal injuries. As against a demurrer, the facts essential to a cause of action must be directly alleged, and not by way of recital, argument, or inference. Tested by this rule, the complaint does not state a cause of action, in that it contains no allegation that the plaintiff was injured by reason of any negligent act on the part of the defendants. It is true that it alleges the disrepair and unsafe condition of the bridge, but it does not allege the fact that it was the defendants' duty to keep it in repair, nor that the bridge broke down and gave way under the wagon by reason of any act or omission of the defendants, or its alleged condition. Such ultimate facts may possibly be inferred from the facts alleged, and probably would be in support of a pleading if the question of its sufficiency was raised for the first time in this court, or after verdict, but will not be as against a demurrer.

Order affirmed.

ANNA v. MISSOURI PACIFIC RAILWAY COMPANY.

Court of Appeals, St. Louis, Missouri, November, 1902.

CHILD COASTING RUN OVER ON TRACK — CONTRIBUTORY NEGLIGENCE. — 1. Plaintiff, a child, being caught under a train of the defendant railway company, while coasting in a toy wagon lodged in a ditch, so that some cars passed over without hurting him; but the boy crawled out of the ditch, and had his foot mashed in trying to get from under the train. *Held*, it was for the jury to decide whether, taking into account the child's age, his alarming situation, and all the circumstances, he was guilty of contributory negligence in crawling out of the depression where he was

safe, there being no showing that the railway company was to blame for his being caught under the train in the first place (1).

(Syllabus by the Court.)

APPEAL from St. Louis Circuit Court.

Action by Martin Anna, by a next friend, against the Missouri Pacific Railway. Verdict for plaintiff. From an order granting a new trial, plaintiff appeals. *Order affirmed.*

"Martin Anna was a lad between ten and eleven years of age at the time his left foot was crushed on a switch track of the Missouri Pacific Railway Company in the city of St. Louis by some freight cars passing over it. The accident occurred at the foot of Cherokee street, an east and west thoroughfare, which intersects some of the defendant's tracks running north and south near the west bank of the Mississippi river. The testimony is that the improved portion of the street ended at the west side of the railway tracks, no crossing having been made, although wagons and teams belonging to the Anheuser-Busch Brewing Association were driven across the tracks at that place, and then north along the east side of the tracks to an icehouse some distance above, and that people and wagons crossed in going to and from shanties built on the river bank. On the north side of Cherokee street there was a sidewalk coming down to the switches, and at the northwest corner stood a building (perhaps the icehouse mentioned above) that obstructed the view of the tracks to the north, so that a person going down the sidewalk towards the river could not see cars approaching from that direction until he emerged beyond the line of the building, which would carry him within three feet of the first switch. Martin Anna and his younger brother were coasting down the sidewalk on a Sunday afternoon in a toy express wagon, such as boys play with. At the same time an engine pushing some cars was backing along the west switch from the north, and the wagon, with Martin Anna in it, either ran onto said switch, and was struck by the rear car, as some witnesses said, or ran between the trucks of the car, as others said. At that spot there was a ditch or depression of uncertain depth in defendant's roadbed between its tracks, in which Martin lodged and lay unhurt until two or more cars had passed over him, when, in the excitement and confusion of the moment, which was increased by by-standers shouting to him to get out, he raised himself from the ditch and attempted to crawl from under the train, with the

1. *Accidents to children on track.* — See numerous cases relating to accidents to children on track, from the earliest period to 1897, reported in vols. 9-12 Am. Neg. Cas. Subsequent actions to date appear in vols. 1-12 AM. NEG. REP., and the current numbers of that series of Reports.

result that the wheels caught his left foot on the rail and crushed it. The petition charges the defendant's employees with several careless acts and omissions of duty, to wit, failure to ring the bell or blow the whistle while the train was backing; having no watchman at the crossing to notify persons of the approach of the train and no man on the rear car to keep a lookout while the train backed, as an ordinance of the city of St. Louis required; and neglect of the servants operating the train to stop its movement as soon as possible after discovering, or being able, by ordinary care to discover, the danger of the plaintiff. The defenses pleaded were a general denial and a plea of contributory negligence, which charged the plaintiff with running the wagon he was in so rapidly that he was unable to control its movements, although he knew there was danger ahead; failing to look or listen for the approach of trains or heed warnings given by persons near the track, or the noise of the train and the engine bell; with neglecting to lie still after he was in a safe place under the train, and to otherwise exercise such care as a boy of his age would have exercised under similar circumstances. At the instance of the defendant the court gave the following instruction: "7. The jury are instructed to disregard all the evidence taken in this cause, except that which relates to the allegation in the petition that the servants of defendant in charge of the train discovered, or could, by the exercise of ordinary care, have discovered, the peril of plaintiff in time, by the exercise of ordinary care, to have avoided injury to plaintiff; and in respect to that allegation the jury are instructed that, unless they believe from the evidence that the employees of defendant in charge of the train which injured the plaintiff knew that he was under the cars while the same were moving, or that by the exercise of ordinary care they might have known, after he had been thrown under them, that he was there, and failed to stop the train as soon as they could stop it, the verdict must be for the defendant." This instruction was likewise given by the court of its own motion: "No. 10. The jurors are instructed that, if you believe and find from the evidence in this case that on the 26th day of August, 1900, Cherokee street was an open public street in the city of St. Louis, and that the railway switch track mentioned in evidence was laid upon and across said street; and if you further believe and find from the evidence that on said day the defendant, St. Louis, Iron Mountain & Southern Railway Company, was running and operating its cars upon and over said track, and that the plaintiff, Martin Anna, while riding in a small wagon in an eastwardly direction on the north side of said Cherokee street, ran into, or was struck by, the wheel or wheels of one of the cars of a train of cars of said defendant moving in a southwardly direction on said track at said time, and was thereby thrown under said train of cars; and if you further believe and find from the evidence that the servants and employees of defendant in charge of and operating the engine and said train of cars discovered, or by the exercise of ordinary care might have discovered, the peril and danger of plaintiff near or on said track, if you believe and find from the evidence he was in a position of danger, in time to have stopped said train of cars and averted the injury to plaintiff and that they failed to do so, — then you should find a verdict for the plaintiff." This instruction, requested by the defendant, was refused: "No. 2. The jury are instructed that, if they find from the evidence that both plaintiff and defendant were guilty of negligence which directly contributed to plaintiff's injury, plaintiff cannot recover." The jury returned a verdict for the plaintiff, and defendant filed a motion for a new trial, which the court sustained on two grounds: First, that error was committed in refusing said instruction No. 2; second, that error was committed in failing to embody in instruction No. 10 the defense of contributory negligence, specially pleaded, that plaintiff failed to lie still after he got upon the railroad track under the train. This appeal was taken by plaintiff from the order sustaining the motion for new trial."

WEBB & WEBB and JOHN A. BLEVINS, for appellant.

CLARDY & HERBEL, for respondent.

GOODE, J. — The trial court excluded from the consideration of the jury all evidence tending to establish any act of negligence on the part of the defendant except that its servants in charge of the train omitted to stop the train as soon as possible after they knew of the perilous position of the plaintiff, and, as no question has been raised concerning the correctness of that ruling, we will assume it was correct in disposing of the appeal. The court must have thought the defendant's servants were innocent of blame in other respects, or that the plaintiff's own carelessness so contributed to his being caught under the train as to shut him off from relief because of any negligent act of which the defendant's employees may have been guilty, except neglect to use proper measures to save him after they knew he was there. The case stands before us, then, for decision on the conduct of the parties after the boy had lodged in the ditch or depression between the rails, and the efforts made by the trainmen and himself to obviate a harmful result. Did the court fairly present the behavior of both sides in the instruction given, so as to enlighten the jury about the issue, and enable them to intelligently decide whether the plaintiff or the defendant's servants, or both, did what was incumbent on them to do to prevent the plaintiff from being crushed? The only negligent act of which the plaintiff is accused in that emergency is that, instead of lying still where the cars could not hurt him, he left that position of safety, crept onto a rail of the track, and, in consequence, got his foot mashed. His counsel admits he did this, but contends that in law it was not a negligent act which will bar his recovery, considering the fright and confusion then affecting him, and that, therefore, the court was not bound to leave it to the jury to say whether it constituted a defense. We agree that the youth of the boy and his dismay and confusion in his terrible danger place the degree of care he was bound to exercise below what is required of a person of mature years in a position of safety; but cannot agree either that the law excuses him for not exercising any prudence whatever, or that evidence tending to show his behavior was negligent is lacking. As to the latter part, the fact that one or more cars passed over him while he lay where he originally fell without hurting him is evidence tending to prove he was negligent in moving while the cars were still passing. The rule of law by which responsibility for injury to a person in a situation of danger like the one plaintiff was in is measured is that the individual thus exposed must use the care that an ordinarily prudent person of his years and capacity may be expected to use in a like situation. Klieber *v.* Railway Co., 107 Mo. 240, 17 S. W. Rep. 946; Twomley *v.* Railway Co., 69 N. Y. 158; Railway Co. *v.* Farmer, 97 Ala. 141, 12 So. Rep. 86; Transit Co. *v.* Nichols, 37 Neb. 332, 55 N. W. Rep. 872; Beach, Contrib. Neg. (3d ed.), sec. 40. The above rule is applied in most jurisdictions, even when the plaintiff's danger was due to the defendant's negligence, and is certainly applicable to this case, in which the plaintiff's danger was not thus produced, according to the theory on which the lower court submitted the case to the jury and as it is presented to us. We agree with the learned trial judge that it is immaterial whether the first instruction on contributory negligence was too general or not, because the instruction given by the court of its own motion attempted to cover the entire case, and erroneously omitted the defense of plaintiff's contributory negligence in moving from a place of safety to one of danger.

We approve of the order granting defendant a new trial, and remand the cause.

BLAND, P. J., and BARCLAY, J., concur.

HIRST v. RINGEN REAL ESTATE COMPANY.

Supreme Court, Missouri, Division No. 1, June, 1902.

CHILD OF TENDER YEARS FATALLY INJURED BY FALLING INTO HATCHWAY — PLEADING — ORDINANCE. — 1. In an action for damages by plaintiff, the mother of infant child, who was fatally injured by falling into hatchway on defendant's premises, it was *held* that where the right to recover was predicated solely on the ground of violation of a city ordinance, recovery could not be had on the ground of common-law negligence (1).

PLEADING — DEMURRER. — 2. Where the petition alleged "that this hatchway, areaway and entrance, at the time of the injury to plaintiff's child, was not barred, inclosed by railing, gates or other contrivances to prevent accidents or injuries to persons therefrom, as required by section 749, art. 3, chap. 16, of the Revised Ordinances of the city of St. Louis," it was *held* that such allegation was sufficient to withstand attack by a general demurrer, and it was error for the Circuit Court to sustain the demurrer to the petition.

[MARSHALL, J., dissented from the ruling announced in paragraph 2 of the syllabus.]

APPEAL from St. Louis Circuit Court.

Action by Mary Hirst against the Ringen Real Estate Company. From a judgment for defendant, plaintiff appeals. *Judgment reversed.*

"This is an action for damages by the mother of an infant child who was killed by falling into a hatchway on premises owned by the defendant. The defendant demurred generally to the petition. The court sustained the demurrer. The plaintiff stood upon the ruling, final judgment on demurrer was entered for the defendant, and the plaintiff appealed. The sufficiency of the petition is, therefore, the sole question involved herein. The petition is as follows: 'Plaintiff, for her amended petition, leave of court first had and obtained, states that the defendant, the Ringen Real Estate Company, is now, and was at all times hereinafter mentioned, a corporation duly incorporated under the laws of Missouri. That the plaintiff is a widow, and the mother of Albert Robert Hirst, now deceased, the father having died prior to any time hereinafter mentioned. That she was the tenant of the said defendant at No. 1435 Old Manchester Road, located in city block No. 3991, in the said

1. See at end of this case, NOTES OF RECENT CASES RELATING TO LIABILITY FOR INJURIES TO CHILDREN WHILE ON DANGEROUS AND DEFECTIVE PREMISES.

City of St. Louis, State of Missouri, on the 1st day of September, 1899, and for several months prior thereto, and as such did occupy the store room and two rooms in the rear, on the first floor at said number, also the front half of the cellar under said store room and rooms, the entrance to this portion being inside the store room. That there was a partition wall between this half occupied by the plaintiff and the rear half of the cellar. That there was a rear door from the rooms so occupied by the plaintiff into a court yard, which yard was under the control of the said defendant, but was used in common by all of defendant's tenants occupying its flats opening out into said yard, for drying clothes and various other purposes of like kind. That the said flats of said defendant were two stories. The one so occupied by the plaintiff was, at the time plaintiff first went to live there, occupied by a tenant on the second floor, who had the exclusive use and control of the rear portion of said cellar and the entrance thereto, but had vacated said second story and cellar; both of these were in the exclusive possession of the defendant at the time of the injury to plaintiff's child. That the hatchway, area, and entrance was from the yard near to plaintiff's said rear entrance, and on the surface presented a square frame of wood about four feet by five feet and about six feet deep, the frame being on a level with said yard. That this hatchway, areaway, and entrance, at the time of the injury to plaintiff's child, was not barred, inclosed by railings, gates, or other contrivances to prevent accidents or injuries to persons therefrom, as required by section 749, art. 3, c. 16, of the Revised Ordinances of the City of St. Louis, approved April 7, 1893. That it was the duty of said defendant to have said hatchway, areaway, and entrance to said rear cellar protected as required by said ordinance. Plaintiff further states that on or about the 1st day of September, 1899, the said Albert Robert Hirst, the infant child of plaintiff, aged two years and eight months, fell into said hatchway, areaway, and entrance, and was thereby seriously and fatally injured on the head and spine, from the results of which he died on or about the 24th day of October, 1899. Plaintiff further avers that said hatchway into which her said child fell was never used by her or any other of the tenants opening into or using said yard, from the time it became vacant or before; only the tenant who occupied the second story of said flat. Plaintiff avers and charges the fact to be that the neglect and failure of the defendant to perform the duty imposed upon it by said ordinance to protect said hatchway, areaway, and entrance to said cellar, and the neglect to perform his duty to all who entered into said yard, were culpable carelessness and negligence; that said neglect of duty, culpable carelessness, and negligence on the part of the defendant were the cause of the death of her said child, Albert Robert Hirst; that she was put to great expense in nursing said child, and paying doctors' bills and medicine for said child, from the time of said injury to said child up to the time of said child's death; that she has been damaged by the care given said child and its death in the sum of five thousand dollars, for which she prays judgment and her costs."

McKEAG & CUMMINGS, for appellant.

KORTJOHN & KORTJOHN, for respondent.

MARSHALL, J. (after stating the facts). — The plaintiff contends that the decision of this court in McGinley *v.* Alliance Trust Co. [Mo. 1901], 11 Am. Neg. Rep. 316, 66 S. W. Rep. 153, is decisive of this case in her favor. The McGinley case was predicated entirely upon the common-law negligence of the defendant in not keeping the part of his premises that was intended for the common use of all the tenants on the premises, but which was not rented to any one of them, in a safe condition, and no city ordinance whatever was in the case; whereas this case is bottomed solely upon an ordinance of the city of St. Louis. Therefore the McGinley case is not decisive of this case, nor even applicable to it (1).

Parties cannot declare on one cause of action and recover upon another, even though they might have had a right to recover upon such other cause of action if it had been pleaded. Cole *v.* Armour, 154 Mo. 333, 55 S. W. Rep. 476. This case is more nearly akin to the case of Wendler *v.* Furnishing Co. (Mo. Sup.), 65 S. W. Rep. 737, for that was an action for common-law negligence, and upon an ordinance of the City of St. Louis. The author hereof did not agree to that decision, because he has never been able to understand how an ordinance of a city, passed in pursuance of the police power of the city, and carrying its own punishment, as for a misdemeanor, for its violation, can afford the basis of a civil liability from one third person to another; nor has he ever believed that when the action is for common-law negligence, and not predicated upon the ordinance, such ordinance is admissible in evidence at all, as is frequently allowed in such cases. It cannot be true that the ordinance affords the basis of a civil liability between third persons and be also true that it is evidence of negligence in an action for common-law negligence. It cannot be that such an ordinance is evidence of anything. It is either a rule of action or it is nothing. However, a majority of this court held otherwise as to its affording

1. See McGinley *v.* Alliance Trust Co. (Mo. 1901), 11 AM. NEG. REP. 316, together with NOTE ON LIABILITY OF LANDLORD FOR DAMAGE TO PROPERTY OF TENANT CAUSED BY DEFECTIVE PREMISES, 11 AM. NEG. REP. 315–322.

a basis for a civil action in the Wendler case, and the dissent of the author hereof was unavailing.

Under the rules laid down in that case, it is not discernible how it can be said that this petition does not state a cause of action. The allegation of the petition is "that this hatchway, areaway, and entrance, at the time of the injury to plaintiff's child, was not barred, inclosed by railing, gates, or other contrivances to prevent accidents or injuries to persons therefrom, as required by sec. 749, art. 3, c. 16, of the Revised Ordinances of the City of St. Louis., approved April 7th, 1893." This is an averment that sec. 749 of the city ordinance required this hatchway, areaway, and entrance to be barred or inclosed by a railing, gate, or other contrivance to prevent accidents or injuries to persons therefrom. This statement of the substance, general tenor, and legal effect of the ordinance is sufficient to withstand attack by a general demurrer. City of Moberly *v.* Hogan, 131 Mo. loc. cit. 25, 32 S. W. Rep. 1014. If such ordinances are admissible in evidence without being pleaded at all when not relied on as a rule of conduct, it is hard to see why they are not sufficiently pleaded when their substance, general tenor, and legal effect are set out, with a specific reference to the section, article, and chapter of the revised ordinance wherein the particular provision can be found. Speaking for myself alone, my views have not changed in the least, and I am still of opinion that such ordinances do not constitute a rule of conduct binding third persons *inter se*, but are mere police regulations, carrying their own punishment for their violation, and that punishment a fine, and that they are not admissible in evidence at all in an action based upon common-law negligence; for no utterance of a municipal assembly can be evidence of common-law negligence. But as the majority of this court, in banc, holds otherwise as to such ordinance affording the basis for a civil action, the proper administration of the law requires that such decision shall be obeyed and followed by all the members of the court until the court otherwise rules. Therefore, in deference to duty, but contrary to my convictions of the true law, it must be held in this case that the petition stated a good cause of action, and that the Circuit Court erred in sustaining the demurrer thereto. The subcontention of the defendant that, even if this be true as a general proposition, it is not true in this case, because the ordinance pleaded only applies to hatchways, etc., that are in the inside of a house, and not to hatchways that are outside of the house, but in a yard used in common by all the tenants occupying the several parts of the house separately, is untenable, for the reason that the petition alleges that the ordinance applies to such hatchways as are described in the petition, and the demurrer admits this fact so pleaded. It may not be true in fact, and when offered in evidence the ordinance may not so provide, but in this state of the pleadings it must be treated as if the ordinance applied to hatchways of the character of this one.

For these reasons, the judgment of the Circuit Court is reversed, and the cause remanded, to be proceeded with in conformity herewith. All concur.

NOTES OF RECENT CASES RELATING TO LIABILITY FOR INJURIES TO CHILDREN WHILE ON DANGEROUS AND DEFECTIVE PREMISES.

Boy stepping into pool of hot water — Owner of premises not liable.

In BRINKLEY CAR WORKS & MANUFACTURING CO. *v.* COOPER *(Arkansas, April, 1902)*, 67 S. W. Rep. 752, judgment for plaintiff in Circuit Court, Monroe county, was reversed, RIDDICK, J., stating the facts as follows: "The Brinkley Car Works & Manufacturing Company, a corporation organized under the laws of this State, has its plant located at Brinkley, Ark. It was the custom of the company to let the water out of its boiler once every two weeks to cleanse the boiler. When the water was thus let out, it flowed into a depression on the premises of the company, and formed a shallow pool of hot water, but in about an hour it sank into the earth. The water was usually let out on Sunday so that the boiler could be cleansed out on Monday following. On a Sunday, shortly after the boiler was emptied, Fred Cooper, a boy six years and two months old, who was playing on the premises of the company, walked into the pool of hot water, and was severely scalded on his feet, legs, and hands. He brought this action against the company to recover damages for the injury. In explanation of the accident, he testified that he and another boy were on the side of the mill where the water came out of the box, and went into the pool. "We were," he said, "throwing barks and chips into the water in the mouth of the pit, and watching the steam rise. The pool was covered with bark, except when the force of the water had pushed it back at the mouth of the pool. The rest of the pool was covered up with trash and bark, so that the water could not be seen, and when I stepped in I thought it was ground, and did not see the water." The court in its instruction No. 1 instructed the jury as follows: "If the jury believe from the evidence that the agent or agents of the defendant had knowledge, or ought reasonably to have known, that the plaintiff, and boys about the age of plaintiff, were in the habit of playing at the pool of water where the plaintiff was injured, and on and about its premises around and near said pool, and thereafter made no effort to protect said pool from exposure as would prevent the plaintiff and other children of his age from going into it and receiving said injury, the defendant would be guilty of negligence, and you will find for the plaintiff." Defendant duly objected, and saved exceptions to the giving of this instruction. The plaintiff recovered judgment for $1,800, from which judgment the company appealed. This is the second time the case has been before this court, and a fuller statement of the facts can be found reported with former opinion, in 60 Ark. 545, 31 S. W. Rep. 154. * * *

The court (per RIDDICK, J.), said: "An owner of land has the right to use it for any lawful purpose, and this company had the right to operate its manufacturing plant and empty the hot water from its boilers on its own premises when it became necessary to do so, and before it can be made liable for an unintentional injury caused to a boy of six years of age by such hot water two things are necessary: First, it must be shown that the company had notice that this boy or other children were likely to come upon its premises; and, second, that by reason of the concealed nature of the pool of water, or the want of notice on the part of the children of the condition of the water, injury to them ought reasonably to have been foreseen on the part of the company as a consequence of leaving the pool of water in that condition. Wats. Dam., p. 291, sec. 234. If the pool of water was open, and not concealed, and the boy had notice that it was hot, we think the company could reasonably suppose that a boy six years of age would not intentionally or carelessly put his foot into water known by him to be hot, and if he did so, and injury resulted, we do not think the company is responsible. The law on this point was correctly stated in the sixth instruction given at the request of the defendant, and other instructions given at the trial were correct, but others were not so clear, and instruction No. 1, given at the request of the plaintiff, seems in conflict with some of those given for the defendant." * * * Judgment reversed. (N. W. NORTON and C. F. GREENLEE, appeared for appellant; M. J. MANNING, J. P. LEE, and GRANT GREEN, JR., for appellee.)

Boy injured by explosion of dynamite cap — Trespassing in building — Owner of premises not liable.

In BALL *v.* MIDDLESBORO TOWN & LANDS CO. *(Kentucky, May, 1902)*, 68 S. W. Rep. 6, judgment for defendant in the Circuit Court, Bell county, was affirmed, the case being stated in the opinion by HOBSON, J., as follows:

"Timothy Ball, a little boy six years old, was painfully injured by the explosion of a dynamite cap, and one of his eyes was put out. He filed this suit by his next friend to recover damages for his injury from the appellee, the Middlesboro Town & Lands Company, charging that the injury was due to its negligence. At the conclusion of the testimony offered for him the court instructed the jury peremptorily to find for the defendant, and he appeals. The facts shown by the proof on the trial are as follows: About the year 1890 Chapman, Warren, and Farquahar were constructing a canal in Middlesboro, and used a building which had been built some time before to store away their tools and implements. They used dynamite in their work. Afterwards, just when it does not appear, the Middlesboro Town & Lands Company became the owner of the building. It was situated on an alley, and was securely locked. Slats were nailed across the windows, but in the process of time one of these slats across the upper part of one of the windows, and about six feet from the ground, was removed in some way. The building was unused and about April, 1898, the lands company sold a partition out of the building to another, who had it removed. There was a shelf on this partition, and on this shelf were some wires with dynamite caps attached to them. The workman who tore down the partition threw these wires down on the floor of the room without apparently noticing what they were. After this, in June, 1898, the little boy, Timothy Ball, and two other little boys, climbed into the house at the hole in the window where the slats were knocked off, six feet above the ground, and in playing around there Ball exploded one of the caps, and thus received the injuries sued for. He says he picked up the wires and then threw them down, and that when they fell the explosion occurred. But there is other proof that the caps could not be exploded in this way, and that they showed signs of being beaten. But, however this may be, there was no proof of negligence on the part of the lands company. It did not place the dynamite in the building, and, so far as appears, did not know it was there. It had evidently been upon this old shelf for a number of years before it was thrown down on the floor by the carpenter. The lands company did not know of his act, and he was not its agent. The house was locked, there was no invitation for any one to enter it, and the circumstances did not impose upon the lands company the duty of keeping the premises safe as against trespassers or charge it with negligence under the facts shown by the evidence. It is shown by the proof that the school children for some months had at times climbed into this old building and hid there for the purpose of playing hooky. Appellee's agent found this out, and stopped it, or tried to do so. It is also shown that appellant had been in the house on the day before he was injured.

"As to how far the owner of property is liable for injuries to children trespassing upon it there is a decided conflict of authority. See 1 Thomp. Neg., secs. 1024–1037. The rule adopted by this learned author is that where the owner of the premises creates or brings thereon any dangerous thing which, from its nature, has a tendency to attract the childish instincts of children to play with it, he is bound, as a matter of social duty, to take such reasonable precautions as the circumstances admit of to protect them from injury while playing with it or in its vicinity. This rule was adopted by this court in Bransom's Adm'r *v.* Labrot, 81 Ky. 638; but it cannot apply to this case, for the reason that the lands company did not place the dynamite in the house or even know it was there, and the house being locked, and the only way to enter it being through a missing slat six feet from the ground, there seems to be no proof of negligence on its part. The ground of liability in this class of cases is that the defendant failed to exercise such care as might reasonably be expected of a person of ordinary prudence under the circumstances. The appellee, under the proof, exercised ordinary care. If it had stored a quantity of dynamite in the house with the knowledge that boys were using it as a hiding place and without closing the hole at which it knew they entered, a different question would be presented. Judgment affirmed. (T. G. ANDERSON, appeared for appellant; J. R. SAMPSON, for appellee.)

Boy trespassing on track — Finding torpedo — Explosion — Railroad company not liable.

In HUGHES *v.* BOSTON & MAINE R. R. *(New Hampshire, April, 1902)*, 51 Atl. Rep. 1070, where a boy, nine years old, was injured by the explosion of a torpedo, which he had found on defendant's track, some distance from its station, and which he struck with a rock, judgment of nonsuit was affirmed, and plaintiff's exceptions overruled, PARSONS, J., in rendering the opinion, stating the case as follows: "If the unexploded torpedo lying beside the track rendered the defendants' premises unsafe for the use which the plaintiff, a boy nine years old, was attempting to make of them, that fact does not establish that the defendants were guilty of negligence. Actionable negligence is the breach of a duty owed by the defendant to the plaintiff. Where there is no duty there is no negligence." * * * "At the close of the opening, counsel was asked what the evidence would be to prove the defendants' fault. The

ruling granting the nonsuit was, in effect, that the facts stated were insufficient to authorize the inference that the plaintiff's
tionally or wantonly inflicted by the defendants. The ruling was correct. The only facts suggested were the finding of the torpedo upon the defendants' right of way beside the track, at a point one-fourth of a mile from a crossing or station; that the torpedo was of a kind used only by the railroad; and the inference which could be made from the rules of the road, by which the trainmen were required to be supplied with torpedoes, and were directed how to use them as signals. These facts furnish no evidence of intentional or wanton injury. In the absence of evidence, it cannot be inferred from the rules requireing the use of torpedoes by trainmen that such use was unnecessary or improper." * * * "The action of the plaintiff, though only nine years of age, in placing the torpedo upon the rail and striking it with a stone, might be thought to indicate he had some knowledge of its properties. Doubtless he did not know of the danger from an explosion so made. His injury is to be ascribed, upon the facts stated, to accident or misfortune attributable to his childish ignorance and inexperience, and not to any actionable fault of the defendants. 1 Thomp. Neg., sec. 1051." (Numerous authorities were cited by PARSONS, J., in support of the propositions laid down in his opinion.)

Boy playing along railroad path scalded by steam and hot water discharged from adjoining premises.

In WILSON v. AMERICAN BRIDGE CO. *(N. Y. Sup. Ct., App. Div., Fourth Dept., July, 1902)*, 77 N. Y. Supp. 820, where a boy, nine years old, was scalded by steam and hot water discharged from defendant's manufacturing plant, from a pipe which projected onto a railroad path or embankment much used by persons, judgment for plaintiff for $7,647.97 was affirmed, it being held that defendant could not escape liability on the ground that the railroad path was used by persons without permission of the railroad company. It appeared that plaintiff was playing with a companion on the railroad path when the water and steam were expelled from defendant's pipe severely scalding his left leg and injuring him permanently. SPRING, J., in the course of his opinion, said: "The slightest care on the part of defendant's servants would have obviated any danger. To look out along the course of the projected stream and ascertain if the way was clear required but a moment's time. The deflection of the pipe downward, or to protect it by a hood, could have easily been done, and removed the peril." * * * "At best, the use of this steam and hot water with the terrific force in its emission was perilous to people passing along this pathway. At any point between the defendant's premises and the footpath was in close proximity to the latter, there was no fence or guard separating the embankment from the footpath; children were accustomed to pass along there and deflect from the beaten path, — all of which are circumstances bearing upon the defendant's negligence. The plaintiff may not be said to have been careless, and it is not so contended. He had never seen the pipe, had no notice he was in any peril, and was playing in the same locality which he had frequented." * * * (MCLENNAN and WILLIAMS, JJ., concurred with SPRING, J.; HISCOCK and ADAMS, P. J., dissented.)

Child struck by fall of pipes from building material standing on sidewalk.

In WALSH v. MCGARRY ET AL. *(N. Y. Sup. Ct., App. Div., Second Dept., April, 1902)*, 75 N. Y. Supp. 906, judgment for plaintiff for $500 in the Municipal

Court, Borough of Brooklyn, was affirmed, the facts, as stated by WILLARD BARTLETT, J., being as follows: "The plaintiff, an infant, was injured while walking on a public street in the Borough of Brooklyn, by the fall of several flue pipes from a pile of building material which had been placed upon the sidewalk by the defendant Cooper, and was maintained there by the defendant McGarry. Upon the trial the complaint was dismissed as against the defendant Cooper, but the defendant McGarry was held liable in damages to the extent of $500. At the time of the accident the child was walking in company with an adult, who testifies that as they passed the pile the flue pipe fell, without being touched by either of them. This witness, when asked whether there was any apparent reason why the flue pipe fell down, answered: "They were roughly put up there. They were hanging over." As the witness was leading the child by the hand, and saw that the pipe was badly piled and overhanging, it is contended that the witness was guilty of contributory negligence, which is imputable to the child, inasmuch as there was a clear space of ten or eleven feet of sidewalk, which would have enabled them to avoid the danger entirely. It does not follow, however, as matter of law, that there was any contributory negligence in the case. The evidence does not indicate that the condition of the pile was perceived until after the pipe fell, and negligence is not necessarily to be inferred on the part of a traveler upon a public street because he assumes that building material thereon has been placed in such a manner that it will not fall upon the passer-by." * * * Judgment affirmed.

Boy injured by explosives found on vacant lot adjacent to factory.

In TRAVELL *v.* BANNERMAN *(N. Y. Sup. Ct., App. Div., Second Dept., April, 1902)*, 75 N. Y. Supp. 866, boy injured by explosives found on vacant lot used as a dumping ground by defendant's ammunition factory, judgment for plaintiff for $600 was affirmed, the facts, as stated by WOODWARD, J., being as follows: "The evidence tends to establish the following facts: At the time of and before the injuries in question the defendant was the owner and in possession of a gun and ammunition factory in the block bounded by Bergen street, Utica, St. Marks, and Schenectady avenues, in the Borough of Brooklyn. The factory premises were inclosed by a fence, but the adjoining lot, also owned by the defendant, and casually used as a temporary dumping place for ashes and other refuse material from the factory, was unfenced, and criss-crossed by paths worn by people of the neighborhood. For a long time the plaintiff, fourteen years of age, and other boys, had used this open lot as a playground. On September 14, 1900, the plaintiff was standing in St. Marks avenue, just outside this vacant lot, when two younger boys approached him with a mass of black, asphalt-like material, composed of caked gunpowder and old cannon primers. This mass, which was about a foot long, the boys had found among the rubbish on the vacant lot, and, after joining the plaintiff, they proceeded to extract the pieces of brass which it contained. In doing so, one of the boys (not the plaintiff) pounded the lump with a rock, and an explosion resulted, in which the plaintiff received the injuries which form the basis of this action." * * * After discussing numerous authorities the court said: "We think there was at least enough evidence to go to the jury upon the question whether proper care had been taken by the defendant in dumping material upon the lot in question; and the action may be maintained on the principle that the consequences complained of naturally and directly resulted from the careless and improper conduct of the defendant's servants." * * * (GOODRICH, J., dissented.)

Girl falling into excavation in street.

In MURPHY *v.* PERLSTEIN *(N. Y. Sup. Ct., App. Div., First Dept., June, 1902)*, 76 N. Y. Supp. 657, where plaintiff, a girl fourteen years of age, was injured by falling into an excavation in the street, judgment for plaintiff was reversed, for error of the trial court in refusing defendant's request to charge that plaintiff was *sui juris*, and chargeable with contributory negligence. The facts, as stated by HATCH, J., were as follows: "It appeared from the evidence in the case that the defendant was the owner of certain premises situate at the corner of Oak and Oliver streets in the Borough of Manhattan, in the city of New York, and for the purpose of building thereon had caused to be made a deep excavation next to the line of the street, and had left it in an unsafe and unguarded condition, constituting the same dangerous to the traveling public; that without fault or negligence upon the part of the plaintiff, and by reason of the unguarded state of the excavation, she slipped upon the walk, fell into the same, and received serious injuries. The plaintiff at the time of the accident was an infant fourteen years of age, was living with her parents on the opposite side of the street from the place of the excavation, and on the day in question had been attending school, had come home at noon for lunch, and was returning to school when she met with the accident. It appeared that the sidewalk opposite the excavation had been torn up while the building was in process of construction, and the ground opposite the same was rough and uneven. Prior to the day in question it had snowed, then thawed, and at the time of the accident the walk in front of the premises was covered with slush and water, the depth of which could not be determined by the eye. Immediately adjacent to the excavation was a strip about a foot wide, which was above the slush and water, and the plaintiff attempted to make passage thereon. It was somewhat rough, with little mounds, and in passing over it she slipped, and, the excavation being unguarded, fell therein. The plaintiff could have proceeded upon the sidewalk along the opposite side of the street without danger, but the route which carried her past these premises was the nearest route to the school, which was the reason why she went that way. It is not necessary that we set out the evidence in detail, nor is it necessary for the proper disposition of the case, so far as the present appeal is concerned. It is sufficient now to say that an obligation rested upon the defendant, when he made or caused to be made the excavation in question, to take proper precautions in protecting persons traveling upon the street, and to guard the excavation in such manner as to reasonably insure the safety of pedestrians having occasion to make use of the walk. The evidence was sufficient from which we think the jury were authorized to find that the duty which rested upon the defendant in this regard was not properly performed, and therefore predicates negligence thereon. Nor do we think that it was contributory negligence, as matter of law, for the plaintiff to attempt passage along the street. Its dangerous condition was not so apparent as to authorize the court to say that it was negligence for a person to pass over it; on the contrary, the jury were authorized to find that a person exercising reasonable care might pass over this place with safety. Consequently the plaintiff could not be charged as matter of law with contributory negligence in making use of this walk under its existing conditions. The questions of negligence and of contributory negligence, therefore, became proper questions to be submitted to the jury for their determination, and no error could be predicated thereon." * * *

FREMONT BREWING COMPANY v. HANSEN.

Supreme Court, Nebraska, July, 1902.

EMPLOYEE INJURED WHILE MOVING TANK IN BREWERY — ASSUMPTION OF RISK. — 1. A servant assumes the ordinary risks and dangers of the employment upon which he enters, so far as they are known to him, and so far as they would have been known to one of his age, experience, and capacity by the use of ordinary care; and he is bound to take notice of the ordinary operation of familiar laws of gravitation, and he assumes the risks necessarily incident thereto.

2. When the evidence introduced by the plaintiff is insufficient to prove a cause of action, it is the duty of the court, upon the request of the defendant, to instruct a verdict in his behalf.

(Syllabus by the Court.)

COMMISSIONERS' OPINION. Department No. 3. Error to District Court, Dodge County.

Action by Broder Hansen against the Fremont Brewing Company. From judgment for plaintiff, defendant brings error. *Judgment reversed.*

COURTRIGHT & SIDNER, for plaintiff in error.

F. DOLEZAL, for defendant in error.

AMES, C. — The defendant in error, who will hereafter be called the "plaintiff," was employed by the defendant brewing company in the capacity of a general workman in and about its establishment. He was strong, healthy, mature, and intelligent, and capable of handling heavy weights, in the doing of which the duties of his employment, to a considerable extent, consisted. In one of the rooms of the brewery was an iron tank, of dimensions, when in position for use, of about ten feet in length by nine and one-half feet in width, and six feet in height. It had been lifted up for repairs, and was resting upon one of its sides or edges. Along the sides were three so-called flanges, extending several inches from its body, — one at the bottom, one at the top, and one midway between.

The weight of the structure was between one and two thousand pounds, — probably about twelve to fifteen hundred pounds. The plaintiff, together with some fifteen or sixteen other employees of the company, was called upon to tip the tank over from its side, so that its bottom would rest upon the floor, in position for use. This was done by the foreman and several of the men lifting upon the upper flange, then resting upon the floor, so as to throw the tank forward towards the east, while the remainder of the force ranged themselves on the other three sides, and grasped the middle flanges, for the purpose of steadying the motion and breaking the fall of the structure. The plaintiff came into the room after the operation had been begun, and, in obedience to a direction by the foreman, took his place at what was then the upper, and, after the task had been accomplished, the eastern, side of the tank. After the tank had moved so far over as to shift its line or center of gravitation, its motion was, as was natural, considerably accelerated, and when it reached the floor it caught underneath it one of the plaintiff's feet: inflicting an injury, to recover damages for which this action was brought. The evidence adduced at the trial was that of the plaintiff alone. The jury found a general verdict for the plaintiff, and, in response to special inquiries, found that he was not guilty of negligence, but that the defendant was guilty of negligence, through or by its foreman, which "consisted in his neglect to properly direct and superintend the men ordered by him to turn over the tank." We are unable to find in the record any sufficient evidence of such negligence. The only evidence touching this matter to which counsel have called our attention is the following testimony by one of the men, a boiler maker by trade, who was engaged in the operation, and who was called and examined by counsel for the plaintiff, in part as follows: "Q. Do you know what the proper and ordinary way of turning such a tank as this was would be? A. I guess I do in my own way, while other men may have different ways. Q. You have worked at this kind of work, you say, for the past sixteen years, — this kind of work; that is, in the turning of large bodies of this kind, while you would be conducting the repair of the same? A. Yes, sir. Q. You may go on and state what would have been the proper and ordinary manner, method, and way for men handling such tanks, in such a position as this tank was in, to have turned it over? A. Well, in the position the tank was in, it would be just the way I would do it. Q. That is, you mean you would turn it over to the west? A. Yes, sir. Q. But in the manner of doing it and as to the method of doing it, — how as to that? A. Well, that would be a proper method. Of course, it all would depend, and that altogether, whether you desired to let it fall, or whether you intended holding it. It would be just as you wished in the turning of it. Q. Would you have that understood before you attempted to turn the tank? A. Yes, sir. Q. In that manner and in that regard would there be any orders given to the men previously? A. Yes, sir. Q. Orders to the men what to do? (Objected to as immaterial, irrelevant, and incompetent. Sustained.) Q. Now, Mr. Sands, if plank had been put upon the floor to the west of the tank, and where it was to have fallen (say, plank of six inches in thickness, so as the tank would rest upon them, — such plank as that), would that have been a fair device to prevent the people from getting hurt under the tank in the process of turning? A. Well, perhaps that would have been all right, if a person wanted to lower it over in that way; but, for my part, I would not have anything there, or anything under it, for the simple reason that it would not hurt the tank to let it fall, because it was all iron." An attempt was also made to show that other appliances, such as "block and tackle," should have been used; but, as the foregoing testimony indicates, it utterly failed, although the witness says such means might have been used as would "let the tank down easily," — a fact which is manifest without evidence, — but it was proved that there were men enough, present and engaged, to have taken the structure up and carried it away. From the foregoing it is plain, beyond dispute, that the employment of appliances would not have been in accordance with usage in such cases, and was not required by ordinary prudence, and that the manner in which the tank was pushed forward and allowed to fall to the floor was such as was customary and proper under such circumstances. In what respect the management was at fault in failing to give previous directions for an ordinary, usual, and prudent way of doing an act in an instance in which, by the plaintiff's own showing, the act was in fact done in that manner, we are unable to understand. The plaintiff, being a strong, healthy, and intelligent man, of mature years, and accustomed to the handling of heavy bodies, must have known that, as the upper side of the tank should approach the floor, its motion would tend to become accelerated, and the ability of the men to restrain or control it would be diminished. In other words, he knew as well as any other person present the danger to be apprehended from a falling body of great weight, and the risk therefrom to those engaged in the operation. This risk he deliberately incurred, as incident to his employment. The jury found, no doubt correctly, that he was not guilty of negligence; but they seem to have thought that without negligence the injury would not have been inflicted, and thereupon convicted the defendant of having been guilty thereof. Accidents of the most grievous character are continually happening without assignable fault or negligence by anybody, and this case, so far as the record discloses, was an instance of that kind. Authorities are numerous and familiar to every lawyer that to quote from Motey v. Granite Co., 20 C. C. A. 366, 74 Fed. Rep. 155, "a servant assumes the ordinary risks and dangers of the employment upon which he enters, so far as they are known to him, and so far as they would have been known to one of his age, experience, and capacity by the use of ordinary care;" and from Walsh *v.* Railroad Co. (Minn.), 8 N. W. Rep. 145: "In performing the duties of his place, a servant is bound to take notice of the ordinary operation of familiar laws of gravitation, and to govern himself accordingly. If he fails to do so, the risk is his own. If the instrumentalities furnished by the master for the performance of the servant's duties are defective, and the servant is aware of this, though not aware of the degree of defectiveness, he is bound to use his eyes to see that which is open and apparent to any person using his eyes; and, if he fails to do so, he cannot charge the consequences upon his master." See also Sullivan *v.* File Co. (R. I.), 45 Atl. Rep. 549; Sugar Co. *v.* Hight, 56 Neb. 162, 76 N. W. Rep. 566. It may be assumed that there was no other evidence in support of alleged negligence than that mentioned in the special finding of the jury, and none other has been brought to our attention by counsel, or, so far as we can ascertain, is disclosed by the record. Some complaint was made in the argument that the foreman assisted the men in lifting the tank from its position, and the assertion is made that perhaps more force was used than was requisite, and that by this means the structure was thrown forward with unnecessary violence; but the evidence, if any, to this effect, was so slight that the jury did not regard it as sufficient proof of negligence, and in this regard we agree with them.

The conclusion from the foregoing is that the evidence is insufficient to sustain the verdict, and that the defendant was entitled to the peremptory instruction, which it asked, for a verdict in its favor. It is therefore recommended that the judgment of the District Court be reversed, and a new trial granted.

ALBERT and DUFFIE, CC., concur.

PER CURIAM. — For reasons stated in the foregoing opinion, it is ordered that the judgment of the District Court be reversed, and a new trial granted.

CENTRAL CITY v. ENGLE.

Supreme Court, Nebraska, October, 1902.

PEDESTRIAN INJURED ON DEFECTIVE SIDEWALK — MARRIED WOMAN — DAMAGES. — 1. A petition by a married woman, in an action for damages for a personal injury, which does not allege that she is, or has been, or anticipated being, the owner of any separate estate or property, or engaged in any trade, business, or service, or the performance of any duties, except those pertaining to her husband's household, does not entitle her to recover damages on account either of loss of earnings already incurred, or of her diminished capacity to earn money as a result of the injury.

a.* Where it is shown that a person is affected by a serious constitutional disease or a tendency thereto, it is error to submit to the jury the question of his expectancy of life, in the absence of any evidence bearing upon that question.

(Syllabus by the Court.)

COMMISSIONERS' OPINION. Department No. 3. Error to District Court, Merrick county.

Action by Mamie Engle against the City of Central City. From judgment for plaintiff, defendant brings error. *Judgment reversed.*

W. T. THOMPSON and JOHN C. MARTIN, for plaintiff in error.

J. E. DORSHEIMER, for defendant in error.

AMES, C. — The defendant in error, plaintiff below, who is a married woman living with her husband, prosecuted this action to recover damages for personal injuries suffered while walking upon one of the sidewalks of the defendant city, alleged to have been defectively constructed, and to have negligently been permitted to become and to remain out of repair so as to be a source of danger to persons making use of it. The plaintiff alleged that by reason of her injury she "has suffered constant and severe pain, and has been continuously, and is now at the time of verifying this petition, wholly unable to perform her household duties, and by reason of the aforesaid injury is, and has become, a cripple for life" It is not alleged that the plaintiff, who was about forty-one years of age, was or had been, or anticipated being, the owner of any separate estate or property, or engaged in any trade, business, or service separate from her husband, or in the performance of any duties except those pertaining to her husband's household. The answer was, in substance, a general denial. On the trial the plaintiff was permitted to testify, over objection by counsel for the defendant, that her "earning capacity," at and before the time of the happening of the accident, was seven dollars per week, and at the time of the trial was "nothing at all," and that shortly prior to suffering the injury she had received that wage. At the conclusion of the trial the court, of its own motion, gave the following instruction:

"If, under the evidence and the law, you find for the plaintiff, it will be your duty to fix the amount of her damages. In doing so you should carefully consider the nature, extent, and character of the injury sustained, whether the disability, if any, is temporary or permanent, partial or total, and what degree of disability. The age of the plaintiff and her reasonable expectancy of life must be important, for you should allow not only for damages already past, but for all damages which would naturally and reasonably result from the injury, whether in the past or future. You should find from the evidence how much money plaintiff would have been reasonably expected to earn if she had not been injured as alleged, and how much she was and is and will be able to earn with her reduced capacity resulting from said injury, and the difference between these two amounts will be the measure of this element of her damages. You should also allow such damages for pain and suffering as under the evidence you believe the plaintiff is entitled to. The law fixes no rule by which to estimate or fix a price upon pain, suffering, and agony, and leaves it to you to allow to her such reasonable sum for this element as may be just and reasonable under the circumstances, not exceeding $7,000 in all."

Complaint is made both of the foregoing instruction and of the above-mentioned testimony, and we think justly so. The plaintiff was not entitled to recover for her decreased earning capacity in relation to her ability to perform satisfactorily her household duties. Such damages accrued, if at all, to her husband, who was charged with the duty of her care and maintenance, and the petition by no fair construction can be said to have apprised the defendant that she claimed to have suffered any pecuniary loss except such as was the direct result of the pain and mutilation inflicted on her person, and for which there is no accurate pecuniary measure. There is nothing in the pleading to indicate that she had suffered, or would probably suffer, any pecuniary loss to her separate or individual estate or property by reason of the alleged diminution of her ability to earn money in any service or employment. All such matters were outside the issues, and were erroneously submitted to the jury. The instruction was erroneous for another reason. It was in evidence that the plaintiff had, previous to the happening of the injury complained of, suffered the loss of one of her arms, in consequence of a disease known as "periostitis," which a physician, produced as a witness by the plaintiff, had testified was tubercular and constitutional in character, predisposing the patient to a recurrence of its acute stage on the happening of any injury such as she had lately suffered. Now, without deciding the question whether alleged damages resulting from the aggravation of this tendency, being consequential and not direct in their nature, should have been pleaded, it appears to us that it was error to submit to the jury any question touching the plaintiff's expectancy of life in the absence of any evidence bearing upon the inquiry. If it should be conceded — which we do not determine — that a jury may speculate upon the probable duration of the life of a healthy person, in the absence of any evidence with respect thereto, it appears to us that they are incompeent to decide that question in the case of a person suffering from a constitutional tubercular disease which, in the absence of testimony, may be fairly presumed to have a tendency to abbreviate her physical existence. We are, however, strongly of the opinion that, in these days when tables of expectancy and expert testimony concerning that subject are readily procurable, it is error in any case to submit that question to a jury without the production of some of them.

There are a large number of other errors assigned in the record, some of which present questions of a very serious character, but, inasmuch as the foregoing disposes of the case for the present hearing, we refrain from discussing them, and recommend that the judgment of the District Court be reversed, and a new trial awarded.

ALBERT and DUFFIE, CC., concur.

PER CURIAM. — For reasons stated in the foregoing opinion, it is ordered that the judgment of the District Court be reversed, and a new trial awarded.

DAME v. LACONIA CAR COMPANY WORKS.

Supreme Court, New Hampshire, June, 1902.

FALLING OBJECT — LADDER BLOWN DOWN — PERSON FOUND DEAD — CAUSE OF DEATH — PRESUMPTION. — In an action to recover damages for the death of plaintiff's intestate, alleged to have been caused by the blowing down of a ladder belonging to defendant, it was *held* that the fact that plaintiff's intestate was found dead in proximity to the ladder was not to be inferred as a conclusion of fact or as a presumption of law that the ladder caused his death by blowing down upon him or in any other way, in the absence of any evidence of physical injury or condition of his health.

EXCEPTIONS from Superior Court.

Action on the case by Rosa J. Dame, administratrix, against the Laconia Car Company Works for negligently causing the death of her decedent. From a verdict for defendants, plaintiff excepts. Transferred from the November term, 1901, of the Superior Court, by PEASLEE, J. *Exceptions overruled.*

SHANNON & YOUNG and E. A. & C. B. HIBBARD, for plaintiff.

JEWELL, OWEN & VEAZEY and FRANK S. STREETER, for defendants.

BLODGETT, Ch. J. — The facts appearing in the case disclose no error in the direction of a verdict for the defendants. In any permissible view of the evidence, the plaintiff leaves the cause of her intestate's death wholly conjectural. Upon this vital point it is simply shown that he was found lying dead in a passway between the defendants' office and one of their shops; that a heavy ladder, which had been put up against the shop some hours before and left unfastened, with its foot projecting into the passway some seven or eight feet, was lying on the ground near his body; that when he was so discovered "it was windy and gusty," and had been for an hour or so preceding, so that the ladder might have blown down upon him and caused his death; and "that it is dangerous to leave ladders as this one was, because of their likelihood of being blown down." This evidence manifestly does not afford the legitimate medium of proof recognized by the law, and which the plaintiff has the burden of establishing. U. S. *v.* Ross, 92 U. S. 281, 283, 284. "The law demands proof, and not mere surmises." Bond *v.* Smith, 113 N. Y. 378, 385, 21 N. E. Rep. 128. Merely because the intestate was found lying dead in proximity to the ladder, it is not to be inferred as a conclusion of fact or as a presumption of law that the ladder caused his death by blowing down upon him or in any other way; and, *a fortiori*, in the absence of any evidence of physical injury, or as to the condition of his health, and when his death may have resulted from any one of several well-recognized and not infrequent natural causes. U. S. *v.* Ross, and Bond *v.* Smith, *supra;* Deschenes *v.* Railroad, 69 N. H. 285, 288, 46 Atl. Rep. 467; Horan *v.* Byrnes, 70 N. H. 531, 533, 49 Atl. Rep. 569; White *v.* Dakin, 70 N. H. 632, 47 Atl. Rep. 611. There is consequently no occasion to now consider the relation in which the deceased stood to the defendants, or whether he was killed by the negligence of a fellow-servant, and it would be contrary to the established practice of the court to do so. See State *v.* Morin, 65 N. H. 667, 668, 23 Atl. Rep. 529, and cases cited; Manufacturing Co. *v.* Gilford, 66 N. H. 621, 34 Atl. Rep. 154; State *v.* Lewis, 66 N. H. 623, 32 Atl. Rep. 151.

If the plaintiff can supply the requisite proof as to the cause of her intestate's death, and if justice requires it should be done, she is afforded an adequate remedy by a petition for a new trial. Pub. St., c. 230, sec. 1.

Exception overruled. All concurred.

SCHUTTE ET AL. v. UNITED ELECTRIC COMPANY OF NEW JERSEY.

Supreme Court, New Jersey, November, 1902.

BUILDING DAMAGED BY FIRE — DEFECTIVE ELECTRICAL WORK — SUB-CONTRACTOR'S NEGLIGENCE — CONTRACTOR'S LIABILITY. — A contracted with B to put in a meter to measure the electricity used by him in his house. B sub-contracted the work to C, who exercised an independent employment. *Held,*

1. That B, by force of the contract with A, is liable to A for damages resulting to him from the negligence of C in doing the work.
2. That, if B himself had done the work negligently, other persons injured thereby could maintain an action of tort against B for his negligence, although they could not base their action upon the contract, to which they were not a party.
3. As between B and C, the latter exercised an independent employment, and that gave B the same immunity against an action by others than A for the negligence of C that A would have if sued for the negligence of B or C.

(Syllabus by the Court)

ACTION by Anna Schutte and another against the United Electric Company of New Jersey. The complaint was amended by substituting the Hoboken Land & Improvement Company as plaintiff. Verdict for plaintiff. Rule to show cause why new trial should not be granted. *Rule entered.*

Argued June term, 1902, before VAN SYCKEL and FORT, JJ.

EDWARD A. & WM. T. DAY, for plaintiff.

BEDLE, EDWARDS & LAWRENCE, for defendant.

VAN SYCKEL, J. — This is an action to recover damages for injury by fire to six buildings owned by plaintiffs. The real plaintiff is an insurance company, which claims to be subrogated to the rights of the insured. It is claimed that the fire was caused by electrical work carelessly done by the O. K. Electric Company. On the trial of the cause, motion was made and denied for the direction of a nonsuit, and for the direction of a verdict, on the ground that the work done was the act of an independent contractor duly qualified for the work, for whose negligence the defendant could not be held responsible. Six buildings were injured by the fire, which appears to have originated at the top of an electric switch box through which the electric wires passed in entering building No. 51, in which a liquor saloon was kept by William Verdon. This switch box had been installed about April, 1899, by the Hudson Electric Light Company, a corporation with which the defendant was not connected, so far as appears. In the spring of 1900 the North Hudson Light, Heat & Power Company, a corporation subsequently merged into the defendant company, and which was then furnishing electricity to Verdon, required him to install a meter for the purpose of measuring the electricity used in the building. Thereupon Verdon signed an application, dated May 21, 1900, directed to the company, as follows: "I hereby make application for connections for electric current for two A. C. arcs and seven incandescent lights, of sixteen-candle power, or the equivalent, for twelve months, at No. 51 Fourteenth street, Hoboken, N. J. I agree to pay for the same at the rate of twelve cents per kilo-watt hour, as the same shall be measured by the meter or meters furnished by you, during the above-mentioned period, and thereafter as long as used." On or about June 8, 1900, the North Hudson Light, Heat & Power Company installed in Verdon's saloon a meter, connecting the same with the wires and apparatus which had been put in a year or more before. The plaintiffs claimed that the fire occurred by reason of the defective manner in which this meter was installed. It is not denied that, when the meter was installed, some of the wires of the switch were disconnected in the course of doing the work.

The North Hudson Light, Heat & Power Company made a contract with the O. K. Electric Company, an independent electric contractor, to make the alterations of the wires in the switch box which was necessitated by the installation of the meter. It is insisted by the defendant that, if there was any negligence in altering the wiring in the switch box, it was the negligence of an independent contractor, who had exclusive charge of the work, and which cannot be imputed to the defendant. The contract of Verdon was with the North Hudson Light, Heat & Power Company, under which said company was bound to use reasonable care in the work necessary to complete the installation of the meter, — a care commensurate with the risk which attends the use of an agency so highly dangerous. As to Verdon the said company was an independent contractor, for whose negligence Verdon was not liable. There was no privity between Verdon and the O. K. Electric Company, and the North Hudson Light, Heat & Power Company could not escape liability to Verdon under its contract with him by employing another company to do the work, and thereby turn him over, without his consent, to a party which might be irresponsible for the damages he might sustain by breach of the contract he made with the North Hudson company. The rule applicable to negligence of an independent contractor is not involved in this controversy, so far as Verdon is concerned. If the owners of the buildings had sued Verdon for their loss, he was in a position to invoke that rule, but it constitutes no defense in an action by Verdon against the party with which he contracted.

The right of action of the owners of the houses rests upon a different principle. It cannot be based upon the contract of Verdon. It is the recognized law of this State that one who is not a party to a contract cannot sue in respect of a breach of duty arising out of the contract. Appleby *v.* State, 45 N. J. L. 165; Styles *v.* Railroad Co. (N. J. Sup.), 51 Atl. Rep. 710; Marvin Safe Co. *v.* Ward, 46 N. J. L. 19. But Mr. Justice Depue, in his able review of the cases on that subject, was careful to limit the application of the rule as follows: "There is a class of cases in which a person performing services or doing work under a contract may be held in damages for injuries to third parties occasioned by negligence or misconduct in the execution of the contract; but these are cases where the duty or liability arises independent of the contract, and in such cases the plaintiff must count upon a wrongful act or negligence, — a tort as distinguished from a mere breach of contract. The same distinction is observed by Chief Justice Beasley, in delivering the opinion of the Supreme Court in Van Winkle *v.* Steam-Boiler Co., 52 N. J. L. 247, 19 Atl. Rep. 475, where he says: "And it would seem that there is a broader ground than the one above defined on which the present case can be based. It is this: That in all cases in which a person undertakes the performance of an act which, if not done with care and skill, will be highly dangerous to the persons, or lives of one or more persons, known or unknown, the law, *ipso facto*, imposes as a public duty the obligation to exercise such care and skill." This declaration must be accepted as the law of this court, and we agree that it is correct in principle and in accordance with the cases. If the negligent work had been done by the North Hudson company, the landowners, who are not parties to the contract of Verdon, could, under the cases last cited, have maintained their action of tort against the North Hudson company, and not upon the contract. But there is another factor in the case before us, which, under the case of Cuff *v.* Railroad Co., 35 N. J. L. 17, we feel constrained to hold, furnishes immunity to the North Hudson company against such action for tort. In that case Mr. Justice Depue says: "The principle upon which the superior, who has contracted with another, exercising an independent employment, for the doing of the work, is exempt from liability for the negligence of the latter in the execution of it, applies as between the contractor and the subcontractor." In that case although the work was of a highly dangerous character, it was held that, because the subcontractor was exercising an independent employment, an action would not lie either against the railroad company, or against the persons with whom it made the contract for the negligence of the subcontractor. As between the North Hudson company and the O. K. Electric company, the latter was an independent contractor, for whose negligence the former company cannot be held except as before stated.

We are of opinion that, while there may be sufficient evidence of negligence to sustain a verdict in favor of Verdon, the action will not lie in favor of the owners of the other houses. Let a rule be entered accordingly.

MINNUCI v. PHILADELPHIA AND READING RAILWAY COMPANY.

Supreme Court, New Jersey, November, 1902.

EMPLOYEE INJURED WHILE UNLOADING COAL CARS — PLEADING — DECLARATION — DEMURRER. — 1. In an action for personal injuries, allegations of negligence on the part of the defendant, contained in the declaration, but which are not connected by proper averments with the injuries complained of, cannot be considered in determining whether or not the declaration shows a cause of action.

2. An averment in a declaration in such an action that the plaintiff's injuries were caused solely by the negligence of the defendant, without more, does not fulfill the requirement of the rule of pleading that the certainty of statement of the plaintiff's case must be such that, in a reasonable measure, it apprises the defendant of the case to be made against him. Such lack of certainty, however, although affording sufficient ground for striking out the declaration on motion, cannot be taken advantage of on general demurrer.

(Syllabus by the Court.)

ACTION by Francesco Minnuci against the Philadelphia & Reading Railroad Company. *Demurrer to declaration overruled.*

Argued June Term, 1902, before GUMMERE, Ch. J. and VAN SYCKEL, FORT, and GARRETSON, JJ.

MCEWAN & MCEWAN, for plaintiff.

JAMES J. BERGEN, for defendant.

GUMMERE, Ch. J. — The plaintiff, in his declaration, alleges that while he was engaged, as an employee of the defendant company, in assisting to unload certain coal cars at the company's chutes at Port

Reading, he had his hand run over and crushed by one of its cars. He then avers that the defendant company negligently failed to provide him with a safe place in which to work; that it negligently permitted the place where he was working to become unsafe and dangerous; that it negligently failed to provide and force a safe system for doing the work about which he was employed; that it failed to provide and enforce proper rules for maintaining and operating its railroad, and for maintaining and operating its cars during the transferring of coal therefrom to the chutes; that it failed to provide and enforce a proper method of signaling for the purpose of warning persons at work about the chutes; that it negligently failed to employ a sufficient number of workmen to perform the work required to be done with sufficient safety; and that it negligently failed to employ competent and careful persons for the work of unloading cars at its chutes, but, on the contrary, employed incompetent, unfit, careless, drunken, and incapable persons to do this work, and especially employed a careless, drunken, and incompetent foreman to superintend it. He then avers that the injury to his hand "was caused solely by the negligence of the defendant," and without any negligence on his part. Then follows a description of the suffering caused by the injury, its effect upon his earning power, and the pecuniary loss which it has entailed upon him.

From the foregoing recital, it will be seen that, although the plaintiff avers that the injury which he received was caused solely by the negligence of the defendant, and also sets out in his declaration numerous specific acts of negligence by it, he fails to state that any one or more of those specific acts was the negligence which produced the injury. For aught that appears in the pleading, they may have played no part whatever in bringing about the accident. Indeed, in passing upon the sufficiency of the declaration, we must assume that they did not, for it is a familiar rule of pleading that everything shall be taken most strongly against the pleader, and that a vital fact not set out is not to be added by the court by conjecture. Eliminating these specific acts of negligence, all that is left of the declaration is that the plaintiff was an employee of the defendant, that the injury from which he suffers was received by him while engaged in the work of his master, and that it was caused solely by the negligence of the latter. So vague an allegation affords little information to the defendant of the case to be set up against it. As was said by this court in Van Horn *v.* Central R. R. Co., 38 N. J. L. 139, 5 Am. Neg. Cas. 13: "The field covered by it is immense, for it embraces everything involved in the construction of the road and its equipment, or in any wise connected with its method of running. A railroad company must of necessity transact its business by means of innumerable agents, and hence to allege that, by some act done or omitted by some one of such agents, an accident has occurred, is to convey very little practical intelligence. * * * The certainty in the statement of the plaintiff's case must be such that it is intelligible, and that, in a reasonable measure, it apprises the defendant of the substantial case to be made against him." This lack of certainty, however, although affording a sufficient ground for striking out the declaration on motion, cannot be taken advantage of on general demurrer. Van Horn *v.* Railroad Co., *supra.*

The demurrer is overruled, with costs, but without prejudice to the right of the defendant to move to strike out the declaration.

ECKMAN v. ATLANTIC LODGE, No. 276, B. P. O. E.

Supreme Court, New Jersey, June, 1902.

COLLAPSE OF FLOOR IN BUILDING USED FOR PUBLIC MEETING PURPOSES — TEMPORARY LESSEE — LIABILITY — INSPECTION. — In an action to recover damages for personal injuries sustained by plaintiff by the collapse of the floor of a building in which a meeting of defendant association was being held, and at which plaintiff was a member of a band engaged by defendant association to take part in the same, it was held that if any liability of defendant, as temporary lessee of the building, existed, for injuries resulting from defective construction, it must be limited to such defects as an inspection would disclose, and not for an accident produced by a latent defect (1).

ACTION by J. L. Prescott Eckman against the Atlantic Lodge, No. 276, of the Benevolent Protective Order of Elks. There was judgment for plaintiff. On rule to show cause. *Rule to show cause made absolute.*

Argued February term, 1902, before GUMMERE, Ch. J., and VAN SYCKEL, GARRISON and GARRETSON, JJ.

SAMUEL A. ATKINSON, for plaintiff.

JOHN W. WESCOTT, for defendant.

GUMMERE, Ch. J. — This is an action to recover damages for personal injuries. The plaintiff was a member of a band employed by the defendant association to play at their annual meeting of 1895,

1. See notes of recent cases, at end of the case at bar, arising out of liability for personal injuries sustained by reason of defective premises.

which was held at the Baltic Avenue Casino at Atlantic City. During one of the sessions of the association the floor of the building where the meeting was held collapsed, and the plaintiff, together with a large number of other people, was precipitated to the floor below, receiving the injuries for which he sues. It is sought to hold the defendant liable upon the ground that the accident happened by reason of its failure to properly perform the duty which it owed the plaintiff of using reasonable care to see that the building in which its meeting was held was in a safe condition. A suit for injuries received through the same disaster was previously brought in this court by one Klapproth against the Baltic Pier & Pavilion Company, the owners of the building, and others, and a verdict in favor of the plaintiff was sustained. Klapproth *v.* Baltic Pier & Pavilion Co. (N. J. Sup.), 43 Atl. Rep. 981. The law seems to be settled that the owner of a building which has been constructed for public purposes holds out to the public, by letting it for such purposes, that it is safe; and, further, that the owner is bound to use reasonable care to see that it has been properly constructed, and is maintained in a fit condition for the purposes for which it is used; and that he is responsible for injuries resulting from his failure in that regard which are received by persons who are present on public occasions, whether as spectators or as employees. Francis *v.* Cockrell, L. R. 5 Q. B. 501 (1); Camp *v.* Wood, 76 N. Y. 92. And it has been held that the liability of the owner extends to injuries received at public functions held under the auspices of one to whom he has temporarily

1. In Francis *v.* Cockrell, L. R. 5 Q. B. 501, affirming Id. 184, it was held that a man, who causes a building to be erected for viewing a public exhibition and admits persons on payment of money to a seat in the building, impliedly undertakes that due care has been exercised in the erection, and that the building is reasonably fit for the purpose; and it is immaterial whether the money is to be appropriated to his own use or not.

In Francis *v.* Cockrell, L. R. 5 Q. B. 184, it appeared that the defendant, acting on behalf of a committee of which he was a member, employed certain persons to erect and let to them a temporary stand for the use of persons desirous of seeing a steeple-chase. The stand having been erected, the defendant, on behalf of himself and his colleagues, received money from the plaintiff and other visitors for the use of places on the stand. The contractors were competent and proper persons to be employed to erect the stand, but it was in fact so negligently erected that it fell, and caused injury to the plaintiff, while he was upon it, looking at the races. Neither the plaintiff nor the defendant knew of the improper construction of the stand. Held, that the contract by the defendant, to be implied from the relation which existed between him and the plaintiff, was that due care had been used not only by the defendant and his servants, but by the persons whom he had employed to erect the stand, and that consequently he was liable for the injury to the plaintiff. (Affirmed in L. R. 5 Q. B. 501.)

let the building. Fox *v.* Buffalo Park, 21 App. Div. 321, 47 N. Y. Supp. 788, on error, 163 N. Y. 559, 57 N. E. Rep. 1109. It has been assumed in the present case that the duty of inspecting such a building for the purpose of seeing that it is safe rests as well upon a person who hires it for the purpose of holding a public ceremony in it. Whether such a duty rests upon the temporary lessee of a building constructed and used for public purposes may be doubted, and the determination of this case does not require a decision of that question. Conceding that such duty exists, the liability of the temporary lessee to answer for injuries resulting from defective construction or maintenance must be limited to such defects as an inspection would disclose, and does not charge him with responsibility for an accident which is produced by a defect entirely latent; and the evidence submitted in this case strongly tends to the conclusion that the accident which caused the plaintiff's injury was due to a defect in one of the pilings upon which the building rested, which would not have been discovered even if the defendant had made an inspection. In the Klapproth case (*supra*), we refused, although with some hesitation, to set aside the verdict, considering that, upon the evidence then produced, it might fairly be concluded that a proper inspection would have shown the unsafe condition of the building. The evidence now submitted is much more persuasive than it was in the earlier case that an inspection would not have had that effect. In fact, the weight of the evidence is against such a conclusion.

The rule to show cause should be made absolute.

NOTES OF RECENT CASES ARISING OUT OF LIABILITY FOR PERSONAL INJURIES SUSTAINED ON DEFECTIVE PREMISES.

Falling over step leading to public hall.

In JORDAN *v.* SULLIVAN *(Massachusetts, May, 1902)*, 63 N. E. Rep. 909, plaintiff's exceptions to verdict rendered for defendant (Sullivan) were overruled, LORING, J., stating the case as follows: "This is an action for damages caused by falling over a step at the entrance of a flight of stairs leading to a public hall owned by the defendant. The hall had been let for the installation of a new lodge of the New England Order of Protection. Whether the plaintiff came to the hall for her own curiosity or convenience, as the plaintiffs did in Plummer *v.* Dill, 156 Mass. 426, 31 N. E. Rep. 128, and Coupe *v.* Platt, 172 Mass. 458, 52 N. E. Rep. 526, or as an invited guest, is not plain; but, in our opinion, that is not material. The hall was up one flight of stairs, and was reached from the street by going through a vestibule to a landing, called in the bill of exceptions an 'inner hall,' and then up a flight of stairs. The floor of the landing was one step higher than the floor of the vestibule. The inner door of the vestibule was on the outer edge of the floor of the landing, and opened out into the vestibule. The outside door of the vestibule also opened outward.

The plaintiff got to the hall between seven and eight o'clock on the evening of January 31st. It was a stormy night, and snowing heavily. There were no lights outside the outer door. It appeared that two persons went through the two doors before the plaintiff, and that the doors closed, or were closed, after them. The plaintiff opened the outer door, and found herself in the vestibule, which was entirely dark. She found the knob of the inner door by feeling for it, opened it, and, without looking to see if there was a step-up, went straight along, fell over the step-up, and broke her arm. She testified that she never had been to the hall before; that she did not know that the hall was upstairs, but 'thought she was going into an entry, and then into the hall.' She did not look to see whether there was a step, because it was so dark she could not see, and 'because she thought this hall was built like the hall of her own lodge.' On the evidence it could have been found that it was really dark at the landing at the time in question, even after the inner door had been opened. The only means provided for lighting the landing at the foot of the stairs came from one gas jet at the head of the stairs behind a portiere. The rod of the portiere was three and one-half feet from the ceiling and when it was drawn across the head of the stairs the only light coming to the landing was that which came through this three and one-half foot space. This gas jet was lighted on the night in question, and there was evidence at the time of the accident the portiere was drawn wholly, or nearly wholly, across the head of the stairs. It appeared by the agreement of hiring that the hall was to be heated and lighted by the defendant. It also appeared that the janitor of the building was present on the premises when the first member of the new lodge arrived there on the night in question. There was no other evidence on the question whether the entrance was in the control of the defendant or not. It is plain that the defendant was not in control of the curtain. The curtain was manifestly put where it was to shut off the stairs from an anteroom at the head of the stairs on the left from the main entrance to the hall, which was across the entry at the head of the stairs on the right.

"We are of the opinion that Roche *v.* Sawyer, 176 Mass. 71, 57 N. E. Rep. 216 (8 Am. Neg. Rep. 6n), is decisive of the matter. If the plaintiff was invited to the hall at all, it was as a guest of the lodge which was to be installed. It is plain that the members of the lodge who hired the premises cannot be heard to say that the entrance was not a better one, and that the construction should have been changed by putting up a gas jet to light the landing at the foot of the stairs. Woods *v.* Cotton Co., 134 Mass. 357; Lindsey *v.* Leighton, 150 Mass. 285, 22 N. E. Rep. 901. And it was settled in Roche *v.* Sawyer, *supra*, that one who comes on the premises as an invited guest of the tenant comes in under the tenant, and has no greater rights than he has. The plaintiff in Learoyd *v.* Godfrey, 138 Mass. 315, did not enter on the common passageway on the invitation of the tenant alone, but he came there as a public officer in the discharge of his duty. As the passageway was one within control of the defendant, and was the way provided by him for access to the tenement let by him, to which the plaintiff's duty called him, the defendant was under the duty of using due care to make the way safe as against the plaintiff, even if it were necessary to change the construction, although he was not under such an obligation as against a tenant and those coming under a tenant's rights. The plaintiff is not helped by Oxford *v.* Leathe, 165 Mass. 254, 43 N. E. Rep. 92. In that case the landlord was held liable for a defect which was on the premises when they were let, on the ground on which a landlord is liable for a nuisance which is on the premises when a lease is made, namely, on the ground that he has been paid for the very use of the property which has been made of it, and, having been paid for that, he is liable if it was defective when put to that use. The principle of that case is that the landlord is liable as well as the tenant. Whether the plaintiff would have a remedy against the lodge if she was invited by them is an open question. Coupe *v.* Platt, 172 Mass. 458, 52 N. E. Rep. 526; Plummer *v.* Dill, 156 Mass. 426, 31 N. E. Rep. 128. But it was held in Roche *v.* Sawyer, *supra*, that, however it may be with a tenant, a landlord is under no greater liability to the guests of a tenant than he is to the tenant. And there is nothing to show that the landlord contemplated the use of the hall by guests, within the meaning of that word in cases like Oxford *v.* Leathe, *supra*. Exceptions overruled."

Falling in hallway leading to room in public building.

In WARE *v.* EVANGELICAL BAPTIST BENEVOLENT & MISSIONARY SOCIETY OF BOSTON *(Massachusetts, May, 1902)*, 63 N. E. Rep. 885, judgment was ordered entered for defendant, on report from the Superior Court, Norfolk county, after verdict for plaintiff. The opinion by MORTON, J., states the case as follows: "This is an action of tort to recover for personal injuries sustained by the plaintiff through the alleged negligence of the defendant. At the conclusion of the plaintiff's evidence the defendant asked the court to rule that the plaintiff could not recover, and to direct a verdict for the defendant. The court did not rule as thus requested, though expressing the opinion that the action could not be maintained. But it was agreed instead by the parties, after conference with the court, that the case should be submitted to the jury, and if the jury returned a verdict for the plaintiff the case should be reported to the Supreme Judicial Court, and, if that court was of opinion that a verdict ought to have been directed for the defendant, judgment was to be so entered. The jury returned a verdict for the plaintiff, and the case is here as thus stipulated.

"The injury complained of was due to a fall received by the plaintiff while passing from one of the rooms in the Tremont Temple Building, so called, in Boston, belonging to the defendant, to the hallway or corridor on which the room opened. The floor of the room was four and seven-eighths inches above the floor of the hallway, and it was this difference in height which caused the plaintiff, as she stepped forward out of the room, to fall. She had entered the room a few minutes before through the same door. She had never been in the building previously, if that is material. It is contended that this construction was defective, and this is the negligence alleged. It is matter of common observation that in entering and leaving stores, halls, railway-car stations and platforms, office buildings, and other buildings and places, and private houses, adjoining surfaces are frequently at different levels; and the difference in level has to be overcome by one or more steps, of greater or less height, or by some other device. The same thing happens in the interior of buildings and structures. We cannot think that such a construction is of itself defective or negligent. There is nothing in the nature of things which requires that the floor of a room which is entered from a hall or corridor, especially in a building like the Tremont Temple Building, should be on the same level as that of the hall or corridor. Such may be the more usual and common construction, but there is nothing, we think, which requires it to be so, at the peril of being regarded as defective or negligent if it is not, and if suitable safeguards are not adopted to warn and protect those invited there. Moreover, the plaintiff had gone into the room, without stumbling, over the same step where she fell when coming out. It would seem that the accident was due, to say the least, quite as much to her own inattention, as to the presence of the step. It may be, as the plaintiff contends, — though we do not mean to make any intimation to that effect, — that, if the accident was due to a defect in the original construction or plan of the building, the defendant would be liable, notwithstanding it had leased that part of the building to the Tremont Temple Baptist Church; but it is not necessary, in the view which we have taken of the question whether there was a defect, to consider that matter, since we are of opinion, as already observed, that the construction cannot be regarded as defective or negligent. The result is that, according to the report, judgment is to be entered for the defendant. So ordered."

Tenant injured by fall of ceiling.

In GOLOB *v.* PASINSKY *(N. Y. Sup. Ct., App. Div., First Dept., May, 1902)*, 76 N. Y. Supp. 388, tenant injured by fall of ceiling, the case is stated in the opinion by PATTERSON J., as follows: " The defendant appeals from an interlocutory judgment overruling a demurrer to the complaint in an action brought to recover damages for injuries sustained by the plaintiff in consequence of the falling of a part of a ceiling of a room in an apartment which she hired from the defendant, in premises owned by him. The allegations of the complaint are that the defendant owned a tenement house in Henry street, in the city of New York, which was divided or separated into apartments for the use and occupation of different tenants; that the plaintiff and her husband occupied an apartment on the top or fifth floor of the defendant's building; that the defendant had reserved to himself control of the roof and ceilings in the said building as well as other parts and portions thereof; that the defendant negligently and carelessly permitted the roof of said building and ceilings in the apartment occupied by the plaintiff to be, become, and remain in a defective and dangerous condition, and in such a condition as to become and remain out of repair, and dangerous to the health, life, and limb of persons occupying said apartment; that on the 5th day of July, 1901, while the plaintiff was lawfully in the apartment, without any negligence or fault on her part, and by reason of the carelessness and negligence on the part of the defendant in permitting the roof of said building and the ceilings of said apartment to be and remain in a dangerous condition, a large piece of plaster or other substance from the ceiling in one of the rooms in said apartment occupied by plaintiff fell and struck her on the head and back, from which she sustained injuries, and that for a long time prior to the happening of the accident the defendant had notice or knowledge of the dangerous condition of the premises. The demurrer is interposed on the ground that the complaint does not state facts sufficient to constitute a cause of action. It was overruled, the learned judge below being of the opinion that while, under the allegations of the complaint, no connection was shown between the alleged condition of the roof and the fall of the ceiling, nevertheless the allegation that the defendant reserved the control of the ceilings of the building brings the case within the doctrine of Dollard *v.* Roberts, 130 N. Y. 269, 29 N. E. Rep. 104, and cognate cases. The respondent does not question the ordinary rule that, in the absence of contract, the landlord was not bound to make repairs, nor the proposition that the breach by the landlord of a contract to make repairs would not create a liability for personal injuries sustained by that breach and the consequent falling of the ceiling. Schick *v.*

Fleischhauer, 26 App. Div. 210, 49 N. Y. Supp. 962. The contention, however, is that a duty devolved upon the landlord to keep the ceiling of the plaintiff's apartment safe, and that for negligence in failing to perform that duty a liability arises analogous to that recognized in the Dollard case, and in those cited by Judge Bradley in his opinion in that case. The question here is whether this complaint contains sufficient allegations to bring this action within the rule invoked by the plaintiff. It appears that she and her husband were in the occupation of this apartment as tenants; that relation necessarily gave to them the possession of the whole apartment. The ceilings of the rooms were as much parts of the demised premises in their possession as were the walls and floors of the apartment. The rule imposing liability upon landlords for negligence in maintaining stairways and hallways and the ceilings of hallways and the appurtenances of demised premises in good order over which they retain control applies to those parts of the premises which are in common use by tenants and those invited upon the premises. The complaint in this action fails to state any fact which indicates negligence of the landlord in his failure to perform a duty imposed by law upon him. The allegation that he reserved control of the roof and the ceilings of the apartments does not necessarily convey the idea of a legal duty to keep the ceiling of the plaintiff's or any other apartment in the house in safe condition, or that there was any more than a contract obligation on his part to keep the ceiling of the plaintiff's apartment in repair. It is alleged that the defendant carelessly and negligently permitted the roof of the building and the ceilings in the apartment occupied by the plaintiff to become and remain in a defective and dangerous condition, but the dangerous condition of the ceiling is not by any allegation connected with any defect in the roof, nor is it alleged that the falling of the ceiling was caused by leakage of water through the roof, or as a consequence of any other fact connected with the condition of the roof. It does not result from the allegation that the defendant retained control of the ceiling of the apartment that such reserved control was otherwise than by contract, and, if that inference may be drawn, the case falls within Schick *v.* Fleischhauer, *supra.* The difficulty with this complaint is that the phrase 'reserved control' of the ceilings does not, in the absence of other allegations, necessarily import a legal duty for the negligent failure to perform which an action would lie." The interlocutory judgment overruling the demurrer reversed, and demurrer sustained, but with leave to plaintiff to amend complaint.

PAYNTER v. BRIDGETON AND MILLVILLE TRACTION COMPANY.

Court of Errors and Appeals, New Jersey, June, 1902.

PASSENGER FALLING FROM STREET CAR — PRESUMPTION — *RES IPSA LOQUITUR.* — 1. A mere fall from a street car, without any evidence to show how the fall was occasioned, raises no presumption of negligence on the part of the operators of the car (1).

1. For Alighting and Boarding Cases, from the earliest period to 1897, see vols. 2-7, Am. Neg. Cas. Subsequent cases to date are reported in vols. 1-12 Am. Neg. Rep., and the current numbers of that series of Reports.

2. The doctrine of *res ipsa loquitur* is applicable only when the thing shown speaks of the negligence of the defendant, not merely of the happening of the accident (1).

(Syllabus by the Court.)

ERROR to Supreme Court.

Action by Belle Paynter against the Bridgeton & Millville Traction Company. From judgment for plaintiff, defendant brings error. *Judgment reversed.*

J. H. GASKILL, for plaintiff in error.

WALTER H. BACON, for defendant in error.

GARRETSON, J. — The plaintiff brought suit against the defendant to recover damages for personal injuries alleged to have been caused by the negligence of the defendant. A verdict was rendered for the plaintiff.

The plaintiff was a passenger upon the defendant's trolley car. She testifies: That, as she neared her destination, she heard the bell ring for the car to stop. She looked up to see if the conductor rang for her, and he bowed to indicate that he did, and she arose to leave the car. She waited a moment for the car to stop. She waited a moment, when she arose, and then stood on the threshold of the car until it had fully stopped; that is, as she says, in the doorway, inside, in the body of the car. Before she stepped on the platform, while she stood there, she turned and smiled good night to two ladies in the car, and after that she stepped on the platform and was about to alight; and while she was in the act of alighting she was thrown to the ground. That she did not reach the ground standing upright on both her feet. That the first she knew she was on her feet, and some one was holding her up. That she did not know who picked her up. It must have been either Mr. Laning (a passenger and witness in the case) or the conductor. Both were beside her when she regained consciousness. That she did not get off the car in safety and then fall down. That she did not get off the car in safety and her ankle turn under her. In response to a question, "What was it that caused you to become separated from the car?" she answers, "I thought the car—" when she was stopped from further answering by objection. On cross-examination she testifies that she remembered the car stopping while she was on her feet after she arose from her seat, and it came to a full stop before she went on the platform; and her cross-examination then proceeds as follows: "Q. There was nothing in the motion of the car at the time you got up out of your seat, or the time you

1. See NOTE ON THE DOCTRINE OF RES IPSA LOQUITUR, 3 AM. NEG. REP. 488–496.

reached the back door and stepped on the platform, that attracted your attention? A. Anything that attracted my attention? Q. Yes; in the motion of the car? A. I can't say that there was particularly. Q. Now the car did not start again until after you had fallen, did it? A. I am not allowed to say what I think? Q. No; you are not allowed to say what you think; but only what you remember, — what you know. A. I remember stepping out on the platform. Q. Yes; but pardon me. (Former question repeated.) A. I think it did. Q. Are you positive? A. Well, I was so soon unconscious. Q. Before you became unconscious, can you say that the car started from the time you got up out of your seat up to the time that you found yourself on the ground? A. I believe it did. Q. I didn't ask you what you believed. I asked you if you say that the car started? A. Well, I can only answer you what I have already said. Q. Well, you are unable to say that the car started, are you not? You can't say that the car started? A. I think the car started. Q. But you can't say that it did start? A. I can only answer you as I have. Q. You don't remember it starting? Put it that way. A. I am afraid I don't remember much that occurred just then. Q. You don't remember the car starting at any time after you left your seat and at once come to a stop, do you? I am asking for your recollection now. A. Well, whether it is recollection or whether it is feeling, it seems to me the car started. Q. Do you say that you distinctly recollect the car starting after you had left your seat and before you found yourself on the ground? A. I don't know. I really don't positively know. I had a feeling. Something threw me. I don't know what. Q. You don't remember any sudden jar or jolt of the car, do you? A. Just at that time? Q. Yes; after you had left your seat and before you found yourself on the ground? A. I didn't find myself on the ground. I was so quickly removed, my memory was so quickly taken from me, that I can't answer that. Q. Well, to the time you fell on the ground? A. I can't answer to the time I fell on the ground. Q. I say you can't remember any sudden jolt or jar, or sudden motion of the car, from the time you left your seat up to the time you became unconscious, you say? A. I have no recollection of anything, except that I was in the act of alighting from the car, and the next I knew is some one had picked me up. Q. And as you were in the act of alighting from the car, which you distinctly remember, you don't associate with it any recollection of any motion or jar or jolt of the car? A. I have no distinct associations. Q. Did you fall on your back? A. I don't know, sir. I have been told that I fell on my back."

Isaac Laning, who was a passenger in the car and was called as a witness on the part of the plaintiff, testifies that he saw the plaintiff when she arose to leave the car; that he arose and followed right after her; that she went out of the car on the platform; that he was only a few steps behind her; that he saw her after she had left the car, and she was then on the ground, lying flat on her back, with her head in the direction toward the front of the car, and the car slightly past her; that when he left his seat in the car, and started toward the exit, the car was then in motion; that when he got to the platform he don't know whether it had stopped; that the car, as a matter of course, started after he left, and it was moving as he approached the door, but when it stopped he could not tell. He says, on cross-examination, that so far as he recollects the plaintiff, from the time she got up, kept in motion, walking, until he saw her on the ground; that he does not know whether the car stopped before she attempted to get off; that he has no recollection of the car coming to a standstill before she got off; that he was not conscious of any act, excepting walking and coming to the front of the door, seeing the plaintiff on the ground, and jumping to pick her up; that he had no recollection whatever of any starting of the car which caused the fall; that when he saw her on the ground she was lying flat upon her back, with her head toward the front of the car; that the rear platform, when the car stopped, had passed her head slightly as she lay on the ground on her back; that there was only one stopping of the car, and one starting; after it stopped, it did not start again until after the plaintiff was picked up and the conductor got back again in the car, and then they resumed their journey; that he was not conscious, when the car stopped, of its stopping with any unusual or peculiar jolt or jar or lurch.

Mrs. Carpenter, a passenger and witness for the plaintiff, testifies that after the plaintiff got up, and as she was going toward the door, the car stopped; that she thought, when the plaintiff passed out on the platform, the car had stopped; that the car stopped quite a long time, and she heard them ask if some one was hurt. On cross-examination she says that when the plaintiff arose the car was in motion, but she stopped a second in front of the witness, and then started toward the door, but it had stopped by that time; that after the plaintiff got up and started to go out she does not remember whether the car started again until after she heard some one say, "Are you hurt?" that she had no recollection of the car starting again until it started to move again on to where she was going; that she is sure the car stopped before the plaintiff got on the platform; that she only remembers of the car stopping once; that she don't remember whether, when it stopped, it stopped smoothly and quickly; that she don't recall any jerk or lurch or jar, or remember any unusual movement or motion of any kind there, that evening, at all like a jerk or jar, or a sudden start or sudden stop.

The mere happening of the accident is not sufficient to place legal responsibility for its effects upon the defendant. There is no evidence on the part of the plaintiff showing how the accident happened. She herself says that she has no recollection of anything, except that she was in the act of alighting from the car, and the next she knew was some one picked her up. There is nothing in her testimony, nor in that of her witnesses, nor in the attendant circumstances, to show how it happened that she fell. She merely has a belief, a thought, a feeling, a seeming to her that the car started; but, when pressed to say whether she remembers any sudden jolt or jar, or sudden motion of the car, she says, "I have no recollection of anything, except that I was in the act of alighting from the car, and the next I knew some one picked me up." Surely there is no proof in this testimony that the fall was occasioned by the sudden, or any other, starting of the car from a state of rest, or by any unusual motion, jerk, jar, or jolt of the car which the defendant was called upon to explain. In Hansen *v.* North Jersey St. R'y Co., 64 N. J. L. 686, 8 Am. Neg. Rep. 276, 46 Atl. Rep. 718, the court reversed a judgment on a verdict directed for the defendant on the ground that the facts proved might justify a jury in inferring negligence on the part of the defendant. In Whalen *v.* Consolidated Traction Co., 61 N. J. L. 606, 4 Am. Neg. Rep. 422, 40 Atl. Rep. 645, it was testified that the plaintiff was pulled off the running board of the car by the conductor. In Fielders *v.* North Jersey St. R'y Co. (N. J. Sup.), 11 Am. Neg. Rep. 52, 50 Atl. Rep. 533, the plaintiff was injured by stepping into a hole in the street, which it was claimed the defendant should have repaired. In Consolidated Traction Co. *v.* Thalheimer, 59 N. J. L. 474, 9 Am. Neg. Cas. 566, 37 Atl. Rep. 132, the evidence was that the plaintiff was thrown from the platform of the car by a sudden lurch or jerk. In Scott *v.* Traction Co., 63 N. J. L. 407, 43 Atl. Rep. 1060, affirmed in 64 N. J. L. 362, 48 Atl. Rep. 1118, a lurch forward of the car while the plaintiff was alighting was proved. In Bliss *v.* Traction Co., 64 N. J. L. 601, 46 Atl. Rep. 624, injury was caused to an employee by wrong signals. In Fenig *v.* Railway Co., 64 N. J. L. 715, 46 Atl. Rep. 602, the car was started when the plaintiff had one foot on the ground and the other on the car. In Railroad Co. *v.* Williams, 61 N. J. L. 646, 40 Atl. Rep. 634, the car was started suddenly while the deceased was alighting at a crossing where a stop had been made. In Foley *v.* Brunswick Traction Co. (N. J. Err. and App.), 50 Atl. Rep. 340, 11 Am. Neg. Rep. 568*n*, the case turned upon the question of the liability of the company for the condition of the street where the car stopped for a passenger to alight. In all these cases facts were proved of acts by the employees of the company, or of movements of the cars or appliances of the company, from which the jury might infer negligence; but in this case no such facts appear in the evidence. The mere happening of the accident raised no presumption of the negligence of the defendant. It was necessary to show by direct evidence that the defendant was responsible for the accident, or to show the existence of such circumstances as would justify the inference that the injury was caused by the wrongful act of the defendant, and would exclude the idea that it was due to a cause with which the defendant was unconnected. Electric Co. *v.* Nugent, 58 N. J. L. 658, 34 Atl. Rep. 1069; Houston *v.* Traphagen, 47 N. J. L. 23; Benedick *v.* Potts (Md.), 4 Am. Neg. Rep. 484, 40 Atl. Rep. 1067.

A fall while alighting from a street car is not such a fact, standing alone, as to authorize the application of the doctrine of *res ipsa loquitur*. The thing that happened in no way can be said to prove that the defendant was negligent. The only thing proved was the fall. Nothing was proved causing the fall, or any circumstances which could be in any way said to show that the defendant was negligent. If it had been proved that a jerk or jolt of the car had produced the fall, that fact, unexplained, might be said to prove the defendant's negligence, although the defendant might furnish an explanation of it which would relieve from responsibility. These principles are very fully discussed in the case of Benedick *v.* Potts, *supra*, by Chief Justice McSherry, of the Maryland Court of Appeals

The application for a nonsuit at the close of the plaintiff's case should have been granted. This determination renders it unnecessary to consider other errors assigned upon exception taken to the refusal to direct a verdict for the defendant, to portions of the charge of the court, and to the refusal of the court to charge the several requests of the defendant.

The judgment below will be reversed.

KNEELAND v. BEARE.

Supreme Court, North Dakota, June, 1902.

TENANT'S GOODS DAMAGED BY WATER FROM ROOF OF BUILDING — DEFECTIVE PREMISES — LIABILITY OF LANDLORD. — 1. Where portions of a tenement building are let to tenants, and the landlord retains the exclusive possession and control of other portions, he is bound to exercise common care and prudence in the management and oversight of the portion of the building retained; and, if damages are sustained by a tenant, by reason of his failure to do so, the landlord is liable therefor (1).

2. It is *held*, in an action for damages by a tenant against his landlord, and upon a review of the entire case in this court, that the trial court properly found that the defendant was negligent in caring for the portion of the rented building which was under his control, and that the damages sustained by the plaintiff were properly assessed by the trial court.

(Syllabus by the Court.)

APPEAL from District Court, Grand Forks County.

Action by E. W. Kneeland against Thomas Beare. From judgment for plaintiff, defendant appeals. *Judgment affirmed.*

TRACEY R. BANGS, for appellant.

COCHRANE & CORLISS, for respondent.

YOUNG, J. — The plaintiff brought this action to recover damages for a partial destruction of certain household goods, which he claims was occasioned by defendant's negligence. The damage for which compensation is sought occurred on September 27, 1899, during a heavy rain storm, and was caused by water flowing through a hatchway in the roof of the Phillips Block, a tenement building situated in the city of Grand Forks, owned by the defendant, and into the apartments then occupied by the plaintiff and his family as tenants. The action is based upon the alleged negligence of the defendant in caring for the roof of said building. There is no claim that the roof was not properly constructed, or that the provision made for conveying the water therefrom was not adequate for that purpose. The plaintiff's contention is that the defendant negligently suffered the conductor pipe, which was provided for carrying the water from the roof, and which furnished the only means for its escape, to become obstructed, with the result that the water backed up and flowed through a hatchway on the roof, and down into plaintiff's apartments, causing the damage of which he complains. The case was tried to the court without a jury. The

1. See NOTE ON LIABILITY OF LANDLORD FOR DAMAGE TO PROPERTY CAUSED BY DEFECTIVE PREMISES, 11 AM. NEG. REP. 315-322.

trial court found for the plaintiff, and assessed his damages at the sum of $60. The defendant has appealed from the judgment and demands a review of the entire case in this court.

The building in question is described as a two-story brick structure, with a flat tin roof, which slopes from the front to the rear of the building. The walls of the building extend several feet above the roof, thus inclosing the roof by a continuous wall, without openings. The water which accumulates on the roof is carried off by means of a conductor pipe six inches in diameter, which enters the roof at the lowest part thereof, and at the southeast corner. From the opening in the roof the pipe descends perpendicularly six inches, then slopes for seven inches at an angle of about forty-five degrees, and then descends perpendicularly on the inside of and in the corner of the building, through the two stories, until it connects with the sewer. The hatchway referred to is about thirteen feet from the rear end of the roof, and is about twelve inches higher than the lowest part of the roof. The first story of the building was rented as a store. The second story is divided into four flats, which were occupied by the plaintiff and three other tenants. The trial court found (and this finding is not disputed) that the roof of the building was not leased to the plaintiff or to any of the tenants, but that the same remained in the possession and under the control of the defendant, and that the defendant exercised control thereover by himself and the janitor of the building, who was employed by the defendant for the purpose of looking after said building. The trial court also found "that prior to the 27th day of September, 1899, the defendant negligently suffered and caused the pipe or conductor constructed for the purpose of carrying off from said roof into the sewer the water accumulating thereon during times of rain to be choked and stopped up with rags and other material, and that defendant negligently failed to clean out the said pipe; * * * that the defendant did not actually know of the condition of the conductor referred to, but that he was chargeable with knowledge of said condition because of the fact that the same had existed for a long time prior to the 27th of September, 1899, and could have been easily ascertained by the exercise of due care in looking after the said conductor to see that the same was not stopped up; and the court finds that the defendant was negligent in failing to exercise due care in keeping the said conductor clean; that he failed to insert therein any screen or other device to prevent matter accumulating in said conductor, although such devices were in common use for such purpose, and that by reason of the fact that said roof was surrounded by a wall on all sides, rising above the same to the height of at least two feet, the risk of damage to the plaintiff and other tenants of said building from the stoppage of said conductor, causing water to accumulate on said roof, was greater than if there had been no such walls to prevent the flow of water from the roof down the outside of the building, and that the scuttle on said roof and the flashing were so constructed that the water could accumulate on said roof to sufficient depth to flow through said scuttle and back up under said flashing, and flow down upon the tenants below, and that, as a matter of fact, rain which fell upon the roof of said building on or about the 27th of September, 1899, was prevented from escaping from said roof through said pipe by reason of the same being stopped up through the negligence of defendant; that, in consequence thereof, water accumulated upon said roof to such an extent that the same backed up and flowed through the said scuttle and under said flashing, and flowed down into the rooms so occupied by the plaintiff, in large volumes, wetting and damaging the plaintiff's carpets, furniture, curtains, shades, pictures, and other household goods, the property of the plaintiff, to his damage in the sum of $60.

It will be noted that this case does not present the mooted question as to whether the landlord or the tenant is responsible for injuries resulting from a defective condition of leased premises which arises during the tenancy. In this case, as has been stated, the roof was in the exclusive possession and control of the defendant, and was not leased to the plaintiff or any of the tenants. The obligation rested upon the defendant to keep the roof, the possession of which was retained by him, in proper repair and condition, so that his tenants would not, through his fault or neglect, be damaged or injured in their persons or goods. In this case, as in Toole *v.* Beckett, 67 Me. 545, a case very similar to the case at bar, — the tenants had no right to interfere with the roof, or control of it. "The defendant had such care and control for the benefit of himself and all his tenants," and, as said by the court in that case, by implication he undertook so to exercise his control as to inflict no injury upon his tenants. "If the landlord does not exercise common care and prudence in the management and oversight of that portion of the building which belongs to his special supervision and care, and damages are sustained by a tenant on that account, he becomes liable for them. He is responsible for his negligence. Priest *v.* Nichols, 116 Mass. 401; Kirby *v.* Association, 14 Gray, 249; Gray *v.* Gaslight Co., 114 Mass. 149; Norcross *v.* Thoms, 51 Me. 503." (1) In support of the foregoing rule of liability, see

1. See notes of these cases in 11 AM. NEG. REP. 315-322.

Glickauf *v.* Maurer, 75 Ill. 289; Inhabitants of Milford *v.* Holbrook, 9 Allen, 17; Shipley *v.* Fifty Associates, 106 Mass. 194. As to portions of the building of which the landlord has control, he retains all of the responsibilities of a general owner to all persons, including the tenants of the building. Looney *v.* McLean, 129 Mass. 33. See also, to the same effect, Freidenburg *v.* Jones, 63 Ga. 612; Jones *v.* Freidenburg, 66 Ga. 505; 2 Wood, Landl. & Ten. 843; 2 McAdam, Landl. & Ten. 1234; 2 Shear. & R. Neg., sec. 710.

The question which is decisive of defendant's liability to respond in damages in this case is purely a question of fact. He was, as we have seen, under obligation to exercise reasonable care and prudence in looking after the portion of the building in his possession and under his control, with a view to preventing injuries to his tenants and others. The question is, did he use such care in reference to the conductor pipe? The trial court found that he did not, and that he was negligent in suffering it to become obstructed. After a careful examination of the evidence, we have reached the conclusion that this finding of the trial court is fully sustained. It is true, there is no evidence in the record from which it can be ascertained with certainty just when the pipe first became obstructed. It is evident, however, that it had been obstructed for some time. The first discovery of the fact appears to have been made during the storm. Only one witness testified as to the character of the obstruction. As soon as it was known that the pipe was stopped up, the tenants summoned one C. W. Barnes, a hardware merchant, to remove the obstruction. He testified as follows: "I discovered that at the rear of the building there was water standing within six inches from the top of the rear wall. Water was then coming down in the store. * * * I didn't know where the outlet was. * * * I knew it was some place in the back of the roof. * * * I located it in the corner, and tried to get it clear, but was unable to do it. I took some substance out of the pipe. How many times I don't know. I put my hand down in there, and got hold of what I could, and pulled it out. The stuff I pulled out seemed to pull pretty tough. Just what it was, I do not know. I don't know whether it was paper or cloth. It was something that pulled out in chunks or handfuls. I took out what I could with my hand each time. I got a stick and pounded in the hole, and after pounding some time the obstruction that was there went away. It was down three or four or five inches. I used all kinds of movements with the stick, and I pounded until I got some of the water to leave. The stuff that was in the pipe did not respond to the first stroke of the stick. I took both hands to it and pounded. Whatever I struck must have been solid, or it would have gone. I pounded there some little time before the obstruction was removed." It is hardly reasonable to believe that an obstruction such as this witness describes could have been formed during the storm, and just before it was removed by him. We think that a fair and natural inference from the description given by the witness is that the substance he removed had been in the pipe for some time, and there is no evidence to repel this inference. On the contrary, such evidence as there is sustains the view that the substance which obstructed the pipe was not washed into it by the rainfall of September 27th. The defendant and two other witnesses testified that the roof was entirely free from rubbish of any kind a few days prior to the storm, and there is no evidence that any opportunity existed for a subsequent accumulation of rubbish on the roof. We are therefore led to the conclusion that the obstruction was not formed during the storm in question, but that it had existed for some time prior thereto. The question, then, is this: Was the defendant negligent in not knowing of the condition of the conductor pipe? We are agreed that he was. The defendant testified that he was upon the roof a great many times prior to September 27th, in connection with the painting of the roof. While he testified that he swept the roof diligently and on numerous occasions, he does not state that at any time or on any occasion he inspected the pipe to see that it was open and in a fit condition to carry off the water. He knew that, if it was not open, water accumulating on the roof could not escape except through the hatchway. The obstruction in the pipe was near the top, and could have been seen by a mere casual inspection. It was not enough for defendant to show that at different times he removed the rubbish which had accumulated on the roof. Common prudence and a proper regard for the rights of his tenants required that he should exercise reasonable care in seeing that the pipe was open and unobstructed. This he failed to do, and in this we find he was negligent. In opposition to our conclusion that the pipe was obstructed prior to September 27th, it is shown that the storm of that date was accompanied by a strong wind, and it is suggested by defendant's counsel that newspapers might have been blown upon the roof and washed into the pipe during the storm. We think the possibility is too remote to be seriously considered, in view of the fact that the evidence shows that the conductor pipe was adequate to carry off newspapers without difficulty. Further, the character of the obstruction, as described by the witness Barnes, emphatically negatives this theory of its origin. We base our conclusion as to defendant's negligence upon his failure to inspect the pipe to see whether it was or was not obstructed. Whether he was negligent in not protecting the opening of the pipe with a screen or other device is perhaps a debatable question. Upon this we express no opinion.

The conclusion of the trial court meets our approval, and we find that the damages awarded the plaintiff were properly assessed. Judgment affirmed. All concur.

THE BALTIMORE AND OHIO SOUTHWESTERN RAILWAY COMPANY v. COX, ADM'X.

Supreme Court, Ohio, May, 1902.

PERSON RIDING IN CABOOSE OF FREIGHT TRAIN BY CONDUCTOR'S PERMISSION KILLED IN COLLISION — ACT OF CONDUCTOR NOT BINDING ON RAILROAD COMPANY — RULES AND REGULATIONS. — 1. An action to recover for an injury occasioned by negligence, the element of wilfulness being absent, will not lie unless there exists between the defendant and the person injured a relation out of which there arises a duty of the former to exercise care toward the latter.

2. A conductor in charge of a train designed exclusively for the carriage of freight, and operating under rules which forbid the carriage of passengers thereon, cannot, by consenting that a person may ride on such train, impose upon the company the duty of exercising toward him the care which it owes to a passenger.

(Syllabus by the Court.)

ERROR to the Circuit Court of Ross County.

"Mrs. Cox, as administratrix, brought suit in the Court of Common Pleas to recover from the railway company damages for the death of her intestate, which was alleged to have been caused by the negligence of the company. In her petition she alleged that on January 4, 1896, her intestate was employed by the company as a locomotive fireman and was riding by its order on one of its freight trains from Mineral City, where he had been employed prior to that time, to Chillicothe; that the train, having reached Schooley's Station, stopped on the siding to permit the passage in the opposite direction of a passenger train, when he left the caboose in which he had been riding and went forward to the engine to talk to the engineer about the employment of the decedent and, at the request of the engineer, climbed upon the engine; that while he was so upon the engine engaged in conversation with the engineer, the said passenger train approaching at a high rate of speed was, by the negligence of the company, run upon said siding, colliding with said engine and causing the instant death of said John H. Cox. The petition also sets out the names of the next of kin of said Cox for whose benefit the recovery was sought.

"In its answer the company admitted that the deceased was killed while upon its locomotive which was standing upon a side track at Schooley's, by a collision with a passenger train which was run upon the siding in consequence of the fact that one of its employees, a brakeman who was acting as a switchman, had failed to disconnect the side track on which said freight train stood from the main track on which said passenger train was approaching, of which neglect the company had no knowledge. It denied all other allegations of the petition and alleged that decedent was upon said freight train and the locomotive connected therewith without the knowledge or permission of the company, and was not there upon any business of or connected with it and was wholly without right to be there.

"Upon the trial the plaintiff, while introducing a mass of evidence having no relation to any issue in the case, also introduced evidence tending to establish the following facts: The accident was due to the negligence of a brakeman who opened the switch to permit an engine to pass from the siding on to the main track, and did not close it. The decedent had been occasionally employed by the company as a fireman for several years, but had not been in its service after the 27th day of the month preceding the accident. In the meantime he had been visiting friends at Mineral City, and on the day of the accident he boarded the freight train, whose conductor was his friend, his purpose being to ride to Chillicothe to look for further employment with the company; and that was the purpose of his interview with the engineer. He had no pass, did not pay fare, and did not intend to. The rules of the company were introduced showing that freight trains, unless running as accommodation trains, were not permitted to carry passengers except upon special order. This train was not running as an accommodation train, and there was no special order. Another rule forbade engineers to permit any but employees to ride on their locomotives. The train on which the decedent was riding was composed wholly of freight cars with a caboose attached.

At the conclusion of the plaintiff's evidence the trial judge directed a verdict for the company. In the Circuit Court a judgment which had been rendered in the Common Pleas upon the verdict so directed was reversed and the cause was remanded to the Court of Common Pleas for a new trial." *Judgment of Circuit Court reversed and that of the Common Pleas affirmed.*

ROBERT E. HAMILL, EDWARD BARTON and WILLIS H. WIGGINS, for plaintiff in error.

JOHN C. ENTREKIN, for defendant in error.

SHAUCK, J. — It is elementary that actionable negligence exists only when one negligently injures another to whom he owes the duty, created by contract or operation of law, of exercising care. Burdick *v.* Cheadle, 26 Ohio St. 393; Railway Co. *v.* Bingham, 29 Ohio St. 364; Elster *v.* Springfield, 49 Ohio St. 82. There being in the present case neither allegation nor evidence that the fatal injuries were inflicted wilfully or intentionally, there can be no recovery unless there existed between the decedent and the company a relation which imposed upon it the duty of exercising care toward him. Although it was alleged in the petition that he was at the time of the accident in the service of the company and traveling on a freight train in obedience to its orders, the allegation was denied in the answer and refuted by the testimony of the plaintiff herself.

The view of counsel for the defendant in error appears to be that the duty of the company to exercise care toward the decedent arose out of the fact that he was riding on the freight train with the express or implied assent of the conductor; and this view is said to have been taken in the Circuit Court. It invokes the doctrine of the law of agency; and, since the company did not authorize the transportation of passengers on its freight trains, it relies upon the implied or apparent authority of the conductor to bind the company to a relation which its rules forbade.

It assumes that the company had given to the conductor an apparent authority which its operating rules had expressly denied him. But the apparent authority of the conductor was to represent the company in the conduct of that portion of its business to which the train in his charge was appropriate. It did not, therefore, exceed his actual authority. The difference between trains intended exclusively for the carriage of freight and those intended for the carriage of passengers are so obvious and familiar as to forbid the view suggested. The cases in which a recovery has been denied upon such facts as are here presented are so numerous that it is not practicable to cite them fully. Among them are Eaton *v.* Railroad Co., 57 N. Y. 382; McVeety *v.* Railroad Co., 45 Minn. 268; Railroad Co. *v.* Roach, 83 Va. 375; Files *v.* Railroad Co., 21 N. E. Rep. 311; Smith *v.* Railroad Co., 124 Ind. 394; Railroad Co. *v.* White, 34 S. W. Rep. 1042; Railroad Co. *v.* Hailey, 94 Tenn. 383; Railway Co. *v.* Black, 87 Tex. 160.

The adjectives used to characterize the negligence of the brakeman in leaving the switch open should not be permitted to excuse the obvious failure of the plaintiff below to place her intestate in the position of one to whom the company owed care. In directing a verdict for the defendant the trial judge correctly applied to the evidence the pertinent principles of the law as they are illustrated in the decided cases.

Judgment of the Circuit Court reversed and that of the Common Pleas affirmed.

BURKET, DAVIS and PRICE, JJ., concur.

THE BALTIMORE AND OHIO RAILROAD COMPANY v. GLENN.

Supreme Court, Ohio, June, 1902.

RIGHT OF ACTION BY HUSBAND FOR INJURIES TO WIFE — DAMAGES. — **At common law, a husband has a right of action against one who wrongfully, or through negligence injures his wife, to recover for the resulting loss of her services, and for his necessary medical, surgical and other expenses in healing her injuries; and this right of action is not abridged or affected by the legislation embraced in sections 3108 to 3117, inclusive, of the Revised Statutes.**

(Syllabus by the Court.)

ERROR to the Circuit Court of Licking County.

"This case was heard and submitted with No. 7196, The Baltimore & Ohio R. R. Co. *v.* Melissa Glenn. In that case Mrs. Glenn recovered a judgment in the lower court against the plaintiff in error, for damages sustained through the alleged negligence of the servants of the railroad company in so operating and running an engine in its yards over a public street in the city of Newark, as to strike her and crush her left foot in such a manner as to require amputation above the ankle. The injuries alleged in her case were the loss of the foot as a permanent injury, and the pain and suffering incident thereto. This court has recently affirmed the judgment in her favor in that case.

"The defendant in error in this case, James P. Glenn, is the husband of Melissa Glenn, and he brought his action against the railroad company, charging in his petition the same acts of negligence on the part of the company, and the same injuries to the wife which were contained in her petition. The recovery sought by the husband in this case is for the loss of the services of the wife which resulted from her injuries, and also for money expended by him in her surgical and medical treatment in the endeavor to cure and heal them.

"The railroad company filed a general demurrer to the petition of the husband in this case which was overruled by the trial court. An answer filed denied all allegations of negligence made against it, and charged contributory negligence upon the wife, Melissa. This charge was denied by a reply.

"On the issues joined, the jury found for the plaintiff and assessed his damages. Thereupon the company moved the court for judgment on the pleadings notwithstanding the verdict. This motion was overruled, and also a motion for a new trial, and judgment was entered on the verdict. The Circuit Court affirmed this judgment, and error is prosecuted in this court to reverse both judgments.

"The same grounds of error assigned for the reversal of the judgment of the wife, Melissa Glenn, are assigned in this case, with the additional claim that since the passage of the law found in secs. 3108 to 3117, inclusive, of the Revised Statutes, the husband has no right of action for the loss of the services of his wife occasioned by the negligence of another, nor for her necessary surgical and medical attention; and this question is preserved in the record by the demurrer to the petition, the motion for judgment on the pleadings and by exceptions to the charge of the court."

J. H. COLLINS and KIBLER & KIBLER, for plaintiff in error.

B. G. SMYTHE and S. M. HUNTER, for defendant in error.

BY THE COURT. — In the case of the plaintiff in error against Melissa Glenn, recently affirmed, this court has decided all the questions of error which are common to both cases, and they will not be further considered in this opinion. Here, however, it is asserted by the plaintiff in error that the wife, Melissa, having recovered for the injuries she sustained through the negligence of the railroad company, the husband, defendant in error, is without a right of action for his loss of her services while disabled by such injuries, or for expenses necessarily incurred by him in caring for her and healing her of the same. This assertion is connected with the proposition that if there once existed at common law in this State a right of action in the husband to recover on such grounds, it has been superseded or taken away by statute. It is not seriously questioned by counsel that, at common law, the husband is entitled to the society and services of his wife, and that for the invasion of such right to his damage he could maintain an action. And this right of the husband is not affected by the fact that the wife has sued and recovered for the damages she has sustained.

It is not averred in the answer in this case, nor claimed in argument, that Mrs. Glenn, in her petition against the railroad company, made any demand for the expenses of her care, or medical or surgical treatment; and, of course, the loss of her services to the husband, while she was disabled by reason of her injuries, could have formed no part or element of her suit. Hence, it is still the law that for such expenses and loss of services the husband has a right of action against one whose negligence or wrong inflicted the injuries, unless the right is taken away by legislation. It is said this change has occurred by reason of Revised Statutes, secs. 3108 to 3117, inclusive. These sections are found under the title "Husband and wife," and they make some brief provisions regarding the marriage relation, some of which are not new to, or an improvement upon the common law. For example, sec. 3108 states that "husband and wife contract toward each other obligations of mutual respect, fidelity and support;" and sec. 3110 makes it the duty of the husband to support himself, wife and minor children. If he is unable to do so, the wife must assist him so far as she is able. There is nothing new or novel in this statement of duty. The only other section which makes any approach to our subject is 3111, which provides that "neither husband nor wife has any interest in the property of the other, except" dower in real estate. This section does not abridge the common-law right of the husband in this case. He is not asking for any interest in the property of the wife. She never had any interest in his cause of action. For her personal injuries and suffering incident thereto, she has exercised her separate right of action, but she has not and could not assert in her action the grounds for recovery which exist only in the husband.

In brief, there is nothing in these sections, or any of them, which abridges the right of the husband to recover as he has done in this case. The holdings of the lower court being in harmony with these views, its judgment is affirmed.

Judgment affirmed.

BURKET, SPEAR, DAVIS, SHAUCK and PRICE, JJ., concur.

PAOLINO v. McKENDALL.

Supreme Court, Rhode Island, October, 1902.

TRESPASSERS — CHILD ATTRACTED TO FIRE AND BURNED. — **One who set a fire on his premises where he knew that children were accustomed to play is not liable for injuries to a child that was attracted by the fire and burned though he took no means to prevent the children approaching the fire (1).**

Action by Angelo Paolino against Frank McKendall. *Demurrer to declaration sustained.*

Argued before STINESS, Ch. J., and TILLINGHAST and ROGERS, JJ.

D. J. HOLLAND, for plaintiff.

MILLER & CARROLL, for defendant.

ROGERS, J. — This is a demurrer to both counts of the plaintiff's declaration in an action of trespass on the case for negligence. The first count is as follows: "For that the said defendant on, to wit, the 8th day of July, A. D. 1901, by his agents and servants, was engaged in erecting a building on Swiss street, near Knight street, public highways in the city of Providence; that near to and adjoining the lot upon which said building was erected was a vacant lot, which for a long time theretofore had been used by the occupiers of the premises in the vicinity and neighborhood thereof as a common resort for pleasure of said occupiers, and as a playground for their children, and in which the plaintiff's intestate, a child of one of said occupiers, and other children, the children of said occupiers, with the knowledge and consent and by the invitation of the owner of said premises, were accustomed to play, to the knowledge of said defendant; and that on, to wit, the 8th day of July, A. D. 1901, the said defendant, by his agents and servants, lighted a large fire upon said lot for the purpose of burning waste materials used in the building of said house. And the plaintiff avers that it was the duty of the defendant to take and use reasonable and proper means and precautions to prevent accident or injury happening to the plaintiff's intestate while using said parcel of land as a playground aforesaid, and to keep and maintain said fire so started by him as aforesaid properly guarded and protected against damage to the lives of children of tender years who might go, wander, or be allowed or attracted thereto by their childish instincts, yet the

1. See at end of this case. NOTE OF RECENT CASES ARISING FROM INJURIES TO TRESPASSERS.

defendant, well knowing the premises, but not regarding his duty therein as aforesaid, neglected, failed, and refused to take and use reasonable and proper means to prevent accident or injury to the plaintiff's intestate while using said parcel of land as a playground as aforesaid, and did not keep and maintain said fire so started as aforesaid properly protected and guarded. And the plaintiff avers that on, to wit, the 8th day of July, A. D. 1901, at Providence, the plaintiff's intestate, who was then and there a child of tender years, to wit, of the age of five years, being a child of one of the occupiers of the premises in the vicinity and neighborhood of said parcel of land, while using said parcel of land as a playground aforesaid, with the knowledge and consent and by the invitation of the defendant, and while in the exercise of due care, and allured and induced by her childish instincts to approach said fire, her dress suddenly caught fire from said flame, and she was so seriously burned that in consequence thereof she died." The second count is substantially like the first, except that it is alleged that the defendant was building the house as a contractor, and it is not alleged that the plaintiff's intestate went upon the lot by reason of any invitation of the defendant or the owner of said lot. The grounds of demurrer to the first count are: 1. Because it does not state facts sufficient to constitute a cause of action; 2, because it does not set forth with sufficient certainty wherein said defendant's negligence consists; and, 3, because it appears therein that the injury to the plaintiff's intestate was caused by her own negligent act in approaching said fire. The grounds of demurrer to the second count are the same as those to the first count, with two additional grounds, but the third ground to the first count constitutes the fifth ground to the second count. The third and fourth grounds of demurrer to the second count are: 3. Because there is no averment therein that plaintiff's intestate was upon said lot upon the invitation or with the knowledge or consent of said defendant, or upon the invitation or with the knowledge or consent of the owner of said lot, if said defendant was not the owner thereof, nor is there set forth in said count any fact showing such invitation, knowledge, or consent; 4, because, according to the allegations in said second count, the defendant owed no duty to the plaintiff's intestate to keep her from being injured as set forth in said count while on said premises.

In the words of the plaintiff's brief: "The plaintiff bases his case solely upon the theory that an occupier of land, having thereon dangerous agencies, to which children of tender years, too untrained and inexperienced to appreciate the dangers and resist the temptations placed before them, are likely to be allured or attracted, is under the duty of exercising the care which an ordinary person would exercise in the premises to prevent injury therefrom, to such children, either by guarding or inclosing the dangerous agency, or by giving warning to parents of the existence of the danger." The words "by the invitation of," referring to the owner or occupier of the premises, in connection with the use of said lot as a common resort as a playground for the children of the neighborhood, including the plaintiff's intestate, are more than once used in the first count of the declaration, yet an express invitation is nowhere alleged, and those words are always preceded by the words "with the knowledge and consent and." With such a use of words, coupled with the theory upon which the plaintiff bases his claim, as shown in the above quotation from his brief, we understand that the only invitation to use said lot as a playground for children, intended to be alleged, was only a constructive invitation, or such, if any, as could be implied from the owner's or defendant's knowing said lot was so used without objection made, and that, as to the fire, there was no invitation to approach it, other than the fact of the fire being there, whereby the plaintiff's intestate was "allured and induced by her childish instincts to approach said fire." We are further led to this understanding by the fact that some of the cases cited on the plaintiff's brief proceed upon the doctrine of constructive invitation; that is, that if, by way of illustration, a person is allured, or, more properly, tempted, by some act of a railroad company to enter upon its land, he is not a trespasser; and it has been held that leaving a turntable unguarded is such an act. We have been thus particular in defining our understanding of the use of the word "invitation," in the first count of the declaration, because if the invitation to the plaintiff's intestate to use said vacant lot as a playground was express, or by implication making it equal in significance to an express invitation, the rule as to liability would be very different from what it would be if the invitation was only constructive, consisting of the kind of allurement or mere license we have referred to.

The basis of a cause of action for injury to a person by reason of negligence or want of due care is the breach of some duty or the nonobservance of some obligation that the defendant is under to the plaintiff. As said by the New Jersey Court of Errors and Appeals, in Del., L. & W. R. R. Co. *v.* Reich, 61 N. J. L. 635, 637, 4 Am. Neg. Rep. 522, 40 Atl. Rep. 682, "There cannot be such a thing as the negligent performance of a nonexistent duty." The very first step in attempting to fasten a liability upon a defendant is to show a duty he is under, either by commission or omission, to the plaintiff.

Having done that, the next step is to show the breach or neglect of such duty. "There is a clear distinction," said the court in Beehler *v.* Daniels, 18 R. I. 563, 565, 29 Atl. Rep. 6, "between a license and an invitation to enter premises, and an equally clear distinction as to the duty of an owner in the two cases. An owner owes to a licensee no duty as to the condition of premises, unless imposed by statute, save that he should not knowingly let him run upon a hidden peril or wilfully cause him harm, while to one invited he is under obligation for reasonable security for the purposes of the invitation." In speaking of this class of cases, Bigelow, Ch. J., in Sweeny *v.* Old Colony & Newport R. R. Co., 10 Allen, 368, 373 (12 Am. Neg. Cas. 75n), after referring to keepers of inns and of shops, said: "The general rule or principle applicable to this class of cases is that an owner or occupant is bound to keep his premises in a safe and suitable condition for those who come upon and pass over them, using due care, if he has held out any invitation, allurement, or inducement, either express or implied, by which they have been led to enter thereon. A mere naked license or permission to enter or pass over an estate will not create a duty or impose an obligation on the part of the owner or person in possession to provide against the danger of accident. The gist of the liability consists in the fact that the person injured did not act merely for his own convenience and pleasure, and from motives to which no act or sign of the owner or occupant contributed, but that he entered the premises because he was led to believe that they were intended to be used by visitors or passengers, and that such use was not only acquiesced in by the owner or person in possession and control of the premises, but that it was in accordance with the intention and design with which the way or place was adapted and prepared or allowed to be so used. The true distinction is this: A mere passive acquiescence by an owner or occupier in a certain use of his land by others involves no liability; but, if he directly or by implication induces persons to enter on and pass over his premises, he thereby assumes an obligation that they are in a safe condition, suitable for such use, and for a breach of this obligation he is liable in damages to a person injured thereby." As to what such an inducement or allurement is, will be considered later. "The rule is," said the Supreme Court of New Jersey, in Vanderbeck *v.* Hendry, 34 N. J. L. 467, 472, "that he who enjoys the permission or passive license is only relieved from the responsibility of being a trespasser, and must assume all the ordinary risk attached to the nature of the place or the business carried on."

In the case at bar the defendant is sought to be made liable upon the doctrine of a series of cases called the "Turntable Cases," consisting of Sioux City & Pac. R. R. Co. *v.* Stout, 17 Wall. 657, 9 Am. Neg. Rep. 614, decided in 1873, and reviewed and adhered to in Railroad Co. *v.* McDonald, 152 U. S. 262, 14 Sup. Ct. Rep. 619, decided in 1894, and of other cases following it. In the Stout case, a boy six years old was injured while playing on a railroad company's land on a railroad turntable that was not attended or guarded by any servant of the company, was not fastened or locked, and revolved easily on its axis. The propositions laid down in that case by Hunt, J., delivering the opinion, are that: "While it is the general rule in regard to an adult that, to entitle him to recover damages for an injury resulting from the fault or negligence of another, he must himself have been free from fault, such is not the rule in regard to an infant of tender years. The care and caution required of a child is according to his maturity and capacity only, and this is to be determined in each case by the circumstances of that case." Further, that, "while a railway company is not bound to the same degree of care in regard to mere strangers who are unlawfully upon its premises that it owes to passengers conveyed by it, it is not exempt from responsibility to such strangers for injuries arising from its negligence or from its tortious acts." The doctrine of that series of cases is thus clearly and comprehensively stated in 7 Am. & Eng. Enc. Law (2d ed.), 403, 404: "When a child of tender years commits a mere technical trespass, and is injured by agencies that to an adult would be open and obvious warnings of danger, but not so to a child, he is not debarred from recovering, if the things instrumental in his injury were left exposed and unguarded, and were of such a character as to be likely to attract children, excite their curiosity, and lead to their injury, while they were pursuing their childish instincts. Such dangerous and attractive instrumentalities become an invitation by implication (1)."

The facts alleged in both counts of the declaration in the case at bar are so analogous to those in the Turntable cases as to make the principle of law properly applicable to one also applicable to the other; and inasmuch as the rule of the so-called Turntable cases has been adopted by many courts, thus affording ample authority, yet whether we shall follow that rule depends upon the weight of the reason on which it rests, for some of the courts which have recognized the rule have limited its operation strictly to turntables and other dangerous and attractive machinery, and it has been utterly rejected by the courts of last resort of New Hampshire in 1886,

1. See NOTE ON LIABILITY OF RAILROAD COMPANIES FOR ACCIDENTS TO CHILDREN ON TURNTABLES, 9 AM. NEG. REP. 611–616.

Massachusetts in 1891, New York in 1895, Texas in 1897, New Jersey in 1898, West Virginia in 1898, and again in 1901, Michigan in 1901, and Georgia in 1901. See Frost *v.* Eastern R. R., 64 N. H. 220, 9 Am. Neg. Rep. 615n, 9 Atl. Rep. 790; Daniels *v.* N. Y. & N. E. R. R. Co., 154 Mass. 349, 28 N. E. Rep. 283, 9 Am. Neg. Rep. 616n; Walsh *v.* Fitchburg R. R. Co., 145 N. Y. 301, 39 N. E. Rep. 1068; Dobbins *v.* Railway Co., 91 Tex. 60, 41 S. W. Rep. 62; Del., L. & W. R. R. Co. *v.* Reich, 61 N. J. L. 635, 4 Am. Neg. Rep. 522, 40 Atl. Rep. 682; Ritz *v.* City of Wheeling, 45 W. Va. 262, 31 S. E. Rep. 993; Uthermohlen *v.* Bogg's Run Co., 50 W. Va. 457, 40 S. E. Rep. 410; Ryan *v.* Towar (Mich.), 87 N. W. Rep. 644; Savannah, Fla. & W. R. Co. *v.* Beavers, 113 Ga. 398, 10 Am. Neg. Rep. 8, 39 S. E. Rep. 82.

The disapproval of Railroad Co. *v.* Stout, *supra*, in the cases just cited is very emphatic, and the president of the Supreme Court of Appeals of West Virginia, in Ritz *v.* City of Wheeling, *supra*, concludes his stricture upon it in this wise (page 270, 45 W. Va., and page 996, 31 S. E. Rep.): "I am guilty of no undue assumption in condemning the Stout case, as it has received in some courts — the most eminent in the land — open condemnation, and in others criticism tantamount to condemnation, and some which followed it limit its application to its facts, or desire to recant."

It is apparent, as stated in the New Jersey case of Railroad Co. *v.* Reich, *supra*, and in the West Virginia case of Uthermohlen *v.* Bogg's Run Co., *supra*, that the principle on which the doctrine of liability rests in the Turntable cases, if sound, must be applicable more widely than to railroad companies and their turntables, and that it would require a similar rule to be applied to all owners and occupiers of land, in respect to any structure, machinery, or implement maintained by them which presents a like attractiveness and furnishes a like temptation to children.

The Stout case was decided in October, 1873, and since then has been referred to at least twice in the court of last resort in this State. Bishop *v.* Union R. R. Co., 14 R. I. 314, 6 Am. Neg. Cas. 394, decided in January, 1884, was a case of negligence, where two empty horse cars of the defendant, fastened together, one behind the other, and drawn by a single horse, were driven slowly over the company's tracks in a public highway in the city of Providence, by a driver occupying the platform in front of the forward car, from the stable, in Elmwood, to the repair shop, on Thurber's avenue. The plaintiff, a boy six years old, to outstrip a playmate with whom he was racing, jumped on the rear platform of the leading car, and soon afterwards fell off or jumped off, and was seriously injured.

After nonsuit, the plaintiff petitioned for a new trial, which was denied; and Durfee, Ch. J., delivering the opinion, in referring to a dangerous object left exposed, without guard or attendant, in a place of common resort for children, said: "An object so left is a standing temptation to the natural curiosity of a child to examine it, or to his instinctive propensity to meddle and play with it. In Keffe *v.* Minn. & St. P. R'y Co., 21 Minn. 207, 9 Am. Neg. Rep. 613n, which was precisely like Stout *v.* Railroad Co. (the name of the Stout case in the court below), this peculiarity was specifically stated, and commented on as the ground of liability. 'The defendant knew,' say the court, 'that, by leaving this turntable unfastened and unguarded, it was not merely inviting young children to come upon the turntable, but was holding out an allurement, which, acting upon the natural instincts by which children are controlled, drew them by those instincts into hidden danger.' These cases seem to reach the limit of liability. They go beyond what was thought to be the limit in Mangan *v.* Atterton, L. R. 1 Exch. 239 (1)." The court then proceeds to distinguish the case from the Turntable cases. In Goodwin *v.* Nickerson & Dugan (R. I.), an unreported case, being decision No. 3,834, in this court, October term, 1891, the declaration set out that the defendants, being in the business of moving buildings, in the course thereof used their own lot, situated on South Bend street, in Pawtucket, a public highway, and surrounded by many houses, and entirely open and unfenced, and commonly used by children of tender age as a playground, for storing and placing thereon large quantities of timber and blocking, and were in the habit of piling such blocking and timber in such manner that certain long timbers, by being placed upon a pier of said blocking, were easily tilted or balanced, and formed what is commonly known as a "seesaw," thus rendering said timber upon said piles of blocking not only dangerous, from its liability to fall, but also attractive to children, etc., whereby the duty devolved upon the defendants to take such care in the piling of such timbers and blocking so to place them that they should not attract children

1. In Mangan *v.* Atterton (or Atherton), 4 H. & C. 388, L. R. 1 Exch. 239, it appeared that the defendant exposed in a market-place a machine for crushing oil cake, without the handle being fastened or its being thrown out of gear or in the care of any person. The plaintiff, a boy four years old, on returning from school under the care of his brother, who was seven years old, stopped with other boys at the machine, and while one of them was turning the handle, put his fingers in the cogs of the wheels, on being told by his brother to do so, and three of his fingers were crushed. Held, that the defendant was not liable, as there was no negligence on his part, and the injury was caused by the act of the plaintiff and the boy who turned the handle.

thereto, and that the same should not be in danger of falling upon and crushing said children, and so to fence and otherwise to protect said lot and said pile of timber and blocking that children should be prevented from coming thereupon, or in such proximity thereto as to cause peril to life, and alleging defendants' neglect of said duty, whereby a large beam fell upon the plaintiff's son, less than four years old, who had been attracted to said lot by said timbers, and so grievously injured him as to cause death. The defendants demurred, and the court overruled the demurrer in a short rescript, in this wise: "The court is of the opinion that the plaintiff's case, as set forth in the declaration, falls within the class of cases represented by Railroad Co. *v.* Stout, 17 Wall. 657." The recognition of the authority of the Stout case, *supra*, accorded in the Bishop case, *supra*, is altogether too dubious, and that in the Goodwin case, *supra*, is too little considered, to establish a rule of law by which we are willing to abide in the case at bar and in future cases. In the Bishop case, *supra*, the court not only does not follow the Stout case, *supra*, but attempts to distinguish it, and characterizes it as "seeming to reach the limit of liability," if not, indeed, intimating that it has exceeded it, by the reference to Mangan *v.* Atterton, L. R. 1 Exch. 239, *supra*. In the Goodwin case, *supra*, the Stout case, *supra*, seems to have been accepted as authority, as a matter of course, apparently without mature consideration, notwithstanding the very equivocal treatment of it in the Bishop case, *supra*, and the fact that our neighboring State of New Hampshire, in Frost *v.* Railroad, *supra*, decided in 1886, four years before the Goodwin case, declined to follow the Stout case, in the following unambiguous terms: "We are not prepared to adopt the doctrine of Railroad Co. *v.* Stout, 17 Wall. 657, and cases following it, that the owner of machinery or other property attractive to children is liable for injuries happening to children wrongfully interfering with it on his own premises. The owner is not an insurer of the safety of infant trespassers."

The reasoning of the Stout case, *supra*, is so unsatisfactory that we cannot give it our approval, and it is evident from the trend of decisions during the last seven years that disapproval of the doctrine of that case has been greatly on the increase. The Supreme Court of Michigan, speaking as late as October 22, 1901, in Ryan *v.* Towar, *supra*, said: "The rule laid down in Railroad Co. *v.* Stout, *supra*, must be a general one, applicable to every one; and, aside from the impropriety of judicial legislation, a wise public policy should forbid such a sweeping innovation by judicial main strength. In innumerable cases the courts have applied and continue to apply the general rule that a landowner need not protect a trespasser, every case being an assertion of the principle which is disregarded in the cases relied on by the plaintiff. We have cited a few of them, — enough, we think, to show that the great weight of authority does not sustain the principle of the Turntable cases. While some of the courts have followed the rule of Railroad Co. *v.* Stout, *supra*, both the courts and profession have evinced a tendency to allow this innovation to go no further, and refuse to consider it applicable to other cases every way analogous. They speak of the cases generically, as the 'Turntable cases,' and treat such cases as exceptional. We are of the opinion that they are exceptional, and that they are not based upon principle, but contravene one of the old and established rules of the law; and we therefore decline to recognize them as authority, preferring to adhere to the better doctrine of the other cases cited. The defendant owed no duty to these children, who were trespassers."

We find no satisfactory ground for the distinction sought to be made between infants and adults in the duty of the owner or occupier of land to a mere trespasser to keep his premises safe. Clark, J., in Frost *v.* Railroad, *supra*, states the law very clearly in this wise: "A landowner is not required to take active measures to insure the safety of intruders, nor is he liable for an injury resulting from the lawful use of his premises to one entering upon them without right. A trespasser ordinarily assumes all risk of danger from the condition of the premises; and, to recover for an injury happening to him, he must show that it was wantonly inflicted, or that the owner or occupant, being present and acting, might have prevented the injury by the exercise of reasonable care after discovering the danger. * * * The maxim that a man must use his property so as not to incommode his neighbor only applies to neighbors who do not interfere with or enter upon it. * * * To hold the owner liable for consequential damages happening to trespassers from the lawful and beneficial use of his own land would be an unreasonable restriction of his enjoyment of it. * * * One having in his possession agricultural or mechanical tools is not responsible for injuries caused to trespassers by careless handling; nor is the owner of a fruit tree bound to cut it down or inclose it, or to exercise care in securing the staple and lock with which his ladder is fastened, for the protection of trespassing boys who may be attracted by the fruit. Neither is the owner or occupant of premises upon which there is a natural or artificial pond or a blueberry pasture legally required to exercise care in securing the gates and bars to guard against accidents to straying and trespassing children. The owner is under no duty to a mere trespasser to keep his premises safe, and the fact that the trespasser is an infant cannot have the effect to raise a duty where none otherwise exists. 'The supposed duty has regard to the public at large and cannot well exist as to one portion of the public and not to another, under the same circumstances. In this respect, children, women, and men are upon the same footing. In cases where certain duties exist infants may require greater care than adults, or a different kind of care; but precautionary measures, having for their object the protection of the public, must, as a rule, have reference to all classes alike.' Nolan *v.* Railroad Co., 53 Conn. 461, 4 Atl. Rep. 106."

Again, the Stout case, *supra*, it seems to us, errs in construing a mere temptation as an allurement sufficient to legally constitute an invitation to enter the premises of another. "Temptation," says Holmes, J., in delivering the opinion in Holbrook *v.* Aldrich, 168 Mass. 15, 1 Am. Neg. Rep. 451, 46 N. E. Rep. 115, "is not always invitation. As the common law is understood by the most competent authorities, it does not excuse a trespass because there is a temptation to commit it, or hold property owners bound to contemplate the infraction of property rights because the temptation to untrained minds to infringe them might have been foreseen." It is not easy to give an exhaustive definition, within reasonable limits, of exactly what is meant by the words "allurement or inducement" that legally operate to constitute an invitation to enter the premises of another; but, as we have seen that mere temptation does not form such an inducement, a single illustration of what would form such an inducement will be sufficient for our purpose. Sweeny *v.* Old Colony & Newport R. R. Co., 10 Allen, 368 (12 Am. Neg. Cas. 75n), from which we have already quoted as to the difference in the duty of an owner or occupier of land to one who enters upon his land by invitation, express or implied, and to one who enters without such invitation, even if he has a mere naked license or permission to enter or pass over the land, affords us that illustration. In that case a railroad company that had made a private crossing over its track, at grade, in a city, and allowed the public to use it as a highway, and stationed a flagman there to prevent persons from undertaking to cross when there was danger, was held liable to damages to one who, using due care, was induced to cross by a signal from the flagman that it was safe, and was injured by a collision which occurred through the flagman's carelessness.

We see no good purpose to be served by our further considering the general principles upon which the case at bar rests. Suffice it to say that we approve the cases hereinbefore cited as disapproving the doctrine in the Stout case, *supra*, as well as a masterly monograph entitled "Liability of Landowners to Children Entering without Permission," in 11 Harv. Law Rev. 349–373, 434–448, by Hon. Jeremiah Smith, formerly one of the justices of the Supreme Court of New Hampshire, all of which have learnedly, and some of which have exhaustively, considered those principles, and afford ample support for the views we entertain.

The plaintiff urges upon our attention the unreported case in this court of Lemieux *v.* Darling *et al.*, Ex. No. 2,688 of 1900 [R. I.], wherein the plaintiff recovered, as one exactly analogous to the case at bar. In that case the plaintiff's intestate, a child five years old, while attracted to the unfenced lot of the defendants abutting on two public highways in Woonsocket, by an apple tree thereon, the branches whereof hung over an insecurely guarded well, situated 241 feet from one highway, and ninety-five feet from the other, fell into said well and was drowned. The court, in a brief rescript, said: "The principal question argued, namely, the liability of a landowner for injuries received by trespassing children from some dangerous object, agency, or condition negligently permitted by such landowner to exist on the land trespassed upon, is not before us. No ruling of the court denying such liability was asked for by the defendants." After a brief recital of the instructions given by the trial justice to the jury, followed by the words, "and no exception was taken by the defendants to such instructions," the rescript concludes as follows: "There is no evidence that the plaintiff knew that the well was not securely covered so that it would be safe, and therefore the jury were warranted in finding that he was not negligent." That case seems to us to furnish no authority for the case at bar, for in the Lemieux case, *supra*, the defendants, by not raising any question of the defendant's liability to the trespassing child, practically admitted that they had been guilty of a neglected duty, and defended against their liability thereon, on the ground that the child had been guilty of contributory negligence, whereas the question in the case at bar is simply whether, on the facts alleged in the declaration, — construing the word "invited," contained therein, as referring only to a constructive invitation, as explained in the quotation from the plaintiff's brief hereinbefore set forth, — the defendant was liable on any neglect of duty he owed to the plaintiff's intestate. With such a construction of the word "invited," used in the first count, as intended by the plaintiff's counsel, already explained, leaving both counts without an allegation of invitation to the infant, express or implied, other than a constructive one, amounting at most to a mere license to enter upon the land, we are of the opinion that neither count of the declaration states facts sufficient to constitute a cause of action, because there is no breach alleged of any legal duty the defendant owed the infant; and, of course, if there was no duty owed, there could be no neglect of duty, and the infant's injury was caused by his own negligent act, solely, in approaching the fire. We have already decided that the constructive invitation set out, or intended to be set out, and hence treated by us as such, is not a sufficient invitation to cast a legal duty upon the defendant in regard to said infant, other than not wilfully subjecting him to injury; and, as no such wilful injury has been alleged, we fail to see how the suit can be sustained without allegation and proof of an invitation to the infant, express or implied, to enter upon said premises.

The plaintiff raises the point whether the question of what is an attraction for children is not one for the jury. In our view of the law, the question in this case is not whether a fire is or is not attractive to a child, but whether, on the undisputed facts alleged in this case, — for the demurrer admits them to be true, — there was any duty on the owner or occupier of the land on which this fire was located to guard the child against it. Whether the facts alleged, not being questioned, raised a duty on the defendant in favor of the child, it seems to us, is a question of law for the court, that can properly be decided on demurrer. In Ritz *v.* City of Wheeling, *supra*, Brannon, president of the West Virginia Court of Appeals, on page 263, 45 W. Va., and page 994, 31 S. E. Rep., says: "The case is not one involving credibility of witnesses, or weight of evidence, or the proper inferences and deductions from evidence, which are matters proper for the consideration of a jury; for the material facts of the case are undisputed, and the case presents simply the question of law, whether upon the facts a liability rests on the city. * * * Where the case turns on the weight and effect of the evidence in proving or not proving facts necessary to support the action, and the evidence appreciably goes to prove such facts, it ought to go to the jury, as a verdict upon such evidence gives it a force which it might not have with the judge before verdict, and fortifies the case more against the action of the court, as the court cannot set the verdict aside unless plainly and decidedly contrary to or without evidence; but where the case is not such, but one of undisputed or indisputable facts, leaving it only a matter of law whether the facts show a liability on the defendant, the court should take the case from the jury, and direct a verdict, if the evidence shows no case for the plaintiff, because, if there were a verdict for him, it would be a finding against law, and the court always annuls a verdict against law upon conceded or indisputable facts."

For the reasons hereinbefore set forth, we think the demurrers to both counts of the declaration must be sustained. Demurrers sustained, and case remitted to the Common Pleas Division for further proceedings.

NOTE OF RECENT CASES ARISING FROM INJURIES TO TRESPASSERS.

1. **Persons walking on right of way, track, trestle or bridge.**
2. **Jumping from moving car.**
3. **Ejection by act of train hand.**
4. **Children attracted.**
   By turntables.
   By fire on owner's lot.
   By mill wheel, etc.
5. **Licensee.**
6. **Injury from collision.**
7. **Shot by watchman.**
8. **Other cases.**

1. Persons walking on right of way, track, trestle or bridge.

In CHICAGO TERMINAL TRANSFER R. R. Co. v. GRUSS (Ill. App. 1902), 102 Ill. App. 439, the appellee was one of an excursion party that had been passengers, and had crossed a trestle railroad bridge in the morning to go to a grove, and when returning to the station in the afternoon about five o'clock to take the return train that had arrived at the station, the train began to back over the trestle bridge while some of the excursionists were on it, the appellee among them, and she moving to the side of the bridge, was knocked off to the creek below by the train, and injured. A judgment for appellee was affirmed. The court said that even on the hypothesis that the appellee was not a passenger but a trespasser on appellant's right of way, the evidence was sufficient to sustain the verdict. The brakeman stationed on the rear of the train must have seen the people crossing the bridge, and must have known that they were coming to take the train for the return trip, that no bell was rung nor whistle sounded as the train backed, nor was any signal given to stop the train, although appliances for that purpose were conveniently near to the brakeman.

In JAMES v. ILLINOIS CENT. R. Co. (Ill. 1902), 63 N. E. Rep. 153, the plaintiff, wanting to send a telegram, and it being too early for the operator to be at the defendant's station, walked on the tracks in the hope of meeting the operator, and was struck by a freight-train locomotive moving at the rate of about five miles an hour, and injured. A judgment for defendant was affirmed. The court said that the railroad tracks adjacent to a railroad station are not public places, or such places as the public are invited upon or can go, unless it be shown that it is for some purpose connected with the business of the railroad company. That the plaintiff was as much a trespasser at the place where she was as if there had been no railroad station there.

In THOMAS v. CHICAGO, M. & ST. P. R. Co. (Iowa, 1901), 114 Iowa, 169, a minor son of the plaintiff, less than four years of age, was with another child, younger than himself, on an open uncovered bridge that spanned a private farm crossing when he was run over by defendant's train, and his foot so crushed that it had to be amputated. The bridge where the accident occurred was between a railroad station and another bridge that crossed a highway, access from which to the latter bridge being obtained by means of a ladder left there for the use of the railroad employees to inspect the bridge, but was used by those who were traveling to the station. There were well-worn paths leading from the station to the ladder. The defendant fenced its right of way at the place, but the fence was often torn down. The fence consisted of four or five wires. This is the third time the case has been to the Supreme Court. On the last trial a judgment was entered on a verdict for defendant and was affirmed. The court said that the instructions presented two theories of the case to the jury — one bottomed on the fact that the children were licensees or went on the track by reason of an implied invitation; and the other on the proposition that they were trespassers. After fully instructing on the first theory, the court took up the second, and on this instructed that it was not what defendant's employees could have seen, but what they did in fact see, of the children, and what they did after they saw the children on the track. These instructions are said to be erroneous, because they eliminate the question of what by ordinary care the employees might have seen. This claim is without merit. If the children were trespassers, the defendant owed them no duty until it saw them on the track, and in a place of danger.

In SCOTT *v.* ST. LOUIS, KANSAS & N. W. R. Co. (Iowa, 1900), 112 Iowa, 54, 8 Am. Neg. Rep. 391, the plaintiff, going to the defendant's freight house on business, used a path generally used by pedestrians in going to that place, and owing to the path being blocked by a freight train, he deviated from the path in order to get to the end of the car which barred his way. The court said that that fact did not, as a matter of law, make him a trespasser, and where it appeared that he was injured while climbing through the freight train after assurance of the brakeman that he had plenty of time, the fact that he was a trespasser did not relieve the company.

In PURCELL *v.* CHICAGO & N. W. R. Co. (Iowa, 1902), 91 N. W. Rep. 933, the plaintiff's intestate was walking on a railroad bridge when he was struck by a train and killed. There was evidence from which the jury could have concluded that the engineer saw the deceased on the bridge and in a place of peril in time to have stopped the train and avoided the injury. A judgment for plaintiff was affirmed.

In BYRNES *v.* BOSTON & M. R. R. (Mass. 1902), 63 N. E. Rep. 897, the plaintiff, a boy eight years of age, with some other boys, for the purpose of making a short cut, entered defendant's freight yard that was unfenced, and while crossing some tracks beyond the freight yard, stumbled and fell and his foot was run over by a train that he did not see until it struck him. There was no fence between the freight yard and the tracks. There was a judgment for defendant. The court said there was nothing in the case to show that the defendant maintained or constructed a way across its freight yard which the public was invited to use. The most that can be said on the evidence is that people were in the habit of crossing the yard in order to make a short cut. All doing so were, at the most, mere licensees, to whom the defendant owed no duty except not to injure them wilfully or recklessly.

In TRUDELL *v.* GRAND TRUNK R. Co. (Mich. 1901), 126 Mich. 73, 10 Am. Neg.

Rep. 426, a boy seven years of age, while on a track, was struck by a train and fatally injured, while he was watching a train coming on another track. A judgment for plaintiff was reversed. The court said that a boy seven years of age playing on a railroad right of way is a trespasser, as matter of law, and that the company was not chargeable with gross negligence from the fact that the boy stood on the track in full view of those in charge of the train for full two minutes before he was struck, since if they saw the boy they were justified in believing that he would step off the track in time to avoid being struck.

In BLEDSOE *v.* GRAND TRUNK R'Y CO. (Mich. 1901), 126 Mich. 312, 10 Am. Neg. Rep. 407, where the plaintiff's decedent, a boy ten and one-half years of age, went uninvited, and contrary to notices posted, into the defendant's railroad yard where there were eighteen tracks, crossed the tracks, went to the slip where the car ferries landed, crawled under a fence and was struck by a lever used in lowering and hoisting the apron to the slip and killed, the defendant was not liable for the death of the boy.

In DAVIS *v.* BOSTON & MAINE R. CO. (N. H. 1900), 70 N. H. 519, the plaintiff, while walking on defendant's track towards the roundhouse on his own business, was struck and injured by an engine that approached him from behind, and gave no signal. There was a judgment for defendant, and plaintiff's exceptions thereto were overruled. The court said that if there had been any evidence that the defendants knew of the plaintiff's danger before the accident happened, it would have been for the jury to say whether, after they knew of it, they could have prevented the accident by the exercise of ordinary care. All the evidence tends to prove that the slightest care on the part of either plaintiff or defendant would have prevented the accident, or, in other words, that their wrongful acts concurred to produce it.

In WEEKS *v.* WILMINGTON & W. R. CO. (N. C. 1902), 42 S. E. Rep. 541, plaintiff and two other ladies walked along defendant's railroad track and out upon a trestle 120 feet when, looking back, they saw a train coming and turned back, and when about twenty-four feet from the end of the trestle the plaintiff jumped off to the ground, a distance of fourteen feet, and was injured. The train was not intended to cross the trestle, though plaintiff did not know that, and it was stopped between twelve and sixteen feet from the trestle. The trestle was constructed solely for the use of the defendant company, and no invitation was extended to the public to go upon it, so no place of safety was provided against the passing of trains. A judgment for plaintiff was reversed. The court said that the plaintiff was a trespasser and had voluntarily put herself in a dangerous and perilous position, and it was her own act of jumping that caused her injury, and as the train was stopped before the trestle was reached, the doctrine of discovered peril did not apply.

In CEDERSON *v.* OREGON NAVIGATION CO. (Oregon, 1900), 38 Ore. 343, plaintiff's decedent was killed by the derailment of defendant's train while he was walking on a wagon road constructed by his employers on defendant's right of way, between the track and a rocky bluff, in which a cut had been made when the road was built. The wagon road had been made by widening the cut while defendant and its predecessor in interest were operating the railroad. At the point of the accident, which was near a junction of a siding used by defendant, the wagon road had been in frequent and constant use by decedent's employers for their men and teams for about ten years, and it was also used more or less by the public. There was a judgment for plaintiff which was affirmed. The court said that there was sufficient evidence to go to the jury on the question whether the decedent was a licensee by invitation to whom the defendant owed the duty of active vigilance to avoid injuring him while using the wagon road for the purpose for which it was built.

2. Jumping from moving car.

In INDIANAPOLIS ST. R'Y CO. v. HOCKETT (Ind. App. 1902), 64 N. E. Rep. 633, the plaintiff was a newsboy and got on defendant's open car to sell papers to the passengers. The car was standing when he boarded it, and before it started, or just as it was starting, the conductor told him to "get off." Instead of immediately obeying, the plaintiff moved along the running board towards the front of the car, and after it had attained a speed of four or five miles an hour he jumped off, fell under the car, and his leg was run over. A judgment for plaintiff was reversed. The court said: "If it be conceded that he was on the car by the permission of the appellant, that permission was withdrawn when he was ordered to get off, when he could have done so with safety, and thereafter remaining on the car he became a trespasser. The law protects a trespasser from wilful injury only, and wilful injury is not claimed or shown in the case at bar."

In CARTER v. CHARLESTON & W. C. R. CO. (S. C. 1902), 43 S. E. Rep. 161, plaintiff boarded a train standing at a crossing, for the purpose of buying oranges from the train boy, and after the train started the plaintiff jumped off and broke his leg. The negligence charged was the starting of the train without giving the statutory signals and the shortness of the time that the train stopped. There was a judgment of nonsuit, which was affirmed. The court said that the statutory signals were intended for the protection of the public from collisions at railroad crossings and had no reference to bystanders, and the length of a stop at a station referred to railroads and their passengers.

3. Ejection by act of train hand.

In O'BANION v. MISSOURI PAC. R. CO. (Kan. 1902), 69 Pac. Rep. 353, the plaintiff was a trespasser on a freight train and was ejected by a brakeman who he alleged wanted to extort money for the privilege of riding. The brakeman pushed the plaintiff, who fell under a car and was run over. A judgment for defendant, entered on a demurrer to the evidence of the plaintiff, was reversed. The court said that it is within the scope of the implied authority of a brakeman in charge of a freight train to eject trespassers therefrom, and whether the plaintiff was ejected in the discharge of the brakeman's duty that he owed the company, or for the purpose of extorting money from the plaintiff, or out of resentment for failing to meet the demands of the brakeman, should have been left to the jury.

In GALVESTON, H. & S. A. R. CO. v. ZAUTZINGER (Tex. 1899), 93 Tex. 64, the plaintiff, a minor seventeen years of age, without the consent or permission of any one, and contrary to the rules of the railroad company, jumped upon the footboard of an engine that was drawing a slowly-moving freight train. After he had ridden a short distance, the engineer opened the cylinder cock of the engine, whereby hot water and steam were thrown upon his legs and feet, whereupon he sprang from the footboard towards the flat car that was next to the engine, intending to get on it, but he missed it and fell to the track, where he was run over, and lost the use of one of his legs. The evidence showed that the engineer intended to throw the hot water and steam on the boy to make him get off the engine, but not to injure him as the boy was injured. The engineer had authority to eject persons wrongfully riding on the engine. There was evidence tending to show that the engineer saw the boy fall between the cars, and could have stopped the train in time to have avoided the injury. The evidence shows the boy was a trespasser. A judgment for plaintiff was affirmed.

4. Children attracted.

By turntables.
By fire on owner's lot.
By mill wheel.

In SAVANNAH, FLORIDA & W. R. Co. *v.* BEAVERS (Ga. 1901), 113 Ga. 398, 10 Am. Neg. Rep. 8, a child five years old, in company of two other children, went on defendant's land to an excavation that was partly filled with water, and while playing there fell in and was drowned. A judgment for plaintiff was reversed.

In EDGINGTON *v.* BURLINGTON C. R. & N. R. Co. (Iowa, 1902), 12 Am. Neg. Rep. 27, a child seven years and eight months old, was injured while playing on a turntable on an unfenced lot near a public alley, and that had been unfastened by one of the other children with plaintiff. A judgment for plaintiff was affirmed. The court said that the child could not be considered as a matter of law of sufficient age and intelligence to appreciate the danger to which she exposed herself, and the question of contributory negligence was properly left to the jury.

In RYAN *v.* TOWAR (Mich. 1901), 87 N. W. Rep. 644, a corporation was the owner of an unused pump house that contained a small overshot waterwheel. The plaintiff and other children were in the habit of crossing the company's land and passing this pump house on the way to school. There was a hole in the stone wall of the house enclosing the wheel, made by the children to enable them to reach the wheel. On the day of the injury the plaintiff's brothers went through the hole to the wheel, which they mounted, and by their weight were enabled to move back and forth, when a younger sister was caught between the wheel and the wheel pit, and hearing her scream, the plaintiff went to her assistance through the hole, and while aiding her sister was herself injured. A judgment entered on a directed verdict for defendant was affirmed. The court said that though the water wheel may have been attractive and accessible to children, they were trespassers, and so was the plaintiff, to whom the corporation did not owe the duty of warning or protection.

In PENINSULAR TRUST CO. *v.* CITY OF GRAND RAPIDS (Mich. 1902), 92 N. W. Rep. 38, a child being out in the street to play, left the traveled part of the street, and went under a fence that surrounded a reservoir, and in attempting to wade in the water was drowned. The fence was a tight board fence, eight feet high, extending all around the reservoir, except at the place where the child had gone under. There the earth had been either dug out or washed out. There was a judgment for the plaintiff, that sued as administrator, which was reversed, and no new trial was ordered. The court cited the recent case of Ryan *v.* Towar (1901), 87 N. W. Rep. 644, as controlling the case at bar.

In TUCKER *v.* DRAPER (Neb. 1901), 62 Neb. 66, 10 Am. Neg. Rep. 307, a boy ten years of age went upon some open lots upon which there was an unguarded well and fell in and was drowned. The public used the lots for hitching teams and for playing games, and there was a path leading through the lots close to the well. A judgment for the plaintiff was reversed on the ground of the error of the trial judge in excluding evidence of the contributory negligence of the father of the boy, the plaintiff in the action.

In CHICAGO, B. & Q. R. Co. *v.* KRAYENBUHL (Neb. 1902), 91 N. W. Rep. 880, the plaintiff was a child four years of age and was injured by having his foot crushed while playing with other children on defendant's turntable that was often left unlocked, and that defendant's servants knew was used as a playground by children. The turntable was near a station, and a pathway was within seventy feet of it. A judgment for plaintiff was reversed because of improper instructions relative to the damages to be awarded. The court said: "When the owner of dangerous premises knows or has good reason to believe, that children, so young as to be ignorant of the danger, will resort to such premises, he is bound to take such precautions to keep them from such premises, or to protect them from injuries likely to result from the dangerous condition of the premises while there, as a man of ordinary care and prudence, under like circumstances, would take.

In UTHERMOHLEN *v.* BOGG'S RUN CO. (W. Va. 1901), 50 W. Va. 457, the defendant was engaged in the business of mining coal, and in its operations used a cable for hauling its coal cars from its mine to the tipple at the railroad and back to the mine. This cable ran over some pulleys necessary for its operation. The plaintiff, a boy between seven and eight years of age, was playing with two other small boys on the premises of the company, and in some way he was caught by the cable and his leg fastened between the cable and one of these pulleys, and badly injured. A judgment entered on a verdict directed for the defendant was affirmed. The court said that the little boy, as well as others, were uniformly before this accident warned off the premises. Thus it can be said that the company did not tolerate their presence on the premises. The plaintiff's case must rest, in the absence of negligence, upon the theory, and only upon the theory, that the pulleys and cable were things dangerous and attractive to children, and that merely for that cause the plaintiff is entitled to recover. If so, what machinery would not be likewise? We think that the court committed no error in directing a verdict for defendant.

5. Licensee.

In MANLOVE *v.* CLEVELAND, ETC., R. Co. (Ind. App. 1902), 65 N. E. 212, plaintiff's intestate was walking on the defendant's track that had been used by the general public as a footway with the consent and license of the defendant, holding an umbrella in front of her, as it was raining, when she was struck by a train, one of the windows of the locomotive of which was obstructed, and of the approach of which no signal was given. There was no evidence that the deceased was seen, or where she came on the track, nor did it appear that the speed of the train was greater than usual. A judgment for defendant was affirmed.

In DE TARR *v.* THE FERD. HEIM BREWING CO. (Kan. 1900), 62 Kan. 188, 8 Am. Neg. Rep. 8, the defendant was the owner of a lot that had been used by the public as a passageway between two lines of railroads, but had been partly occupied by a tenant whom the owner tried to remove, to put up a building, and did remove so far as to take down the tenant's structures, including a watercloset. Litigation followed, and the owner was restrained from proceeding with the improvements. The owner then boarded over the vault of the watercloset and left it. The plaintiff herein was hurrying over the lot along the path made by the public, when she fell into the vault that was close to the path from which she had deviated in her hurry to catch an approaching car. A judgment entered on a verdict for defendant was affirmed. The court said that the path across the lot had been used by the public for a long time — so long that permission by the occupant and owner must be presumed. The plaintiff, therefore, was not to be regarded as a trespasser or as a mere licensee, as she used the way with the implied permission of those in control of the premises. If the defendant had the possession and control of the lot, it owed a duty to the public to cover or fill up the hole, but the jury were warranted in finding that the defendant had not the possession or control of the lot at the time of the injury, and had no notice that a board of the covering had been removed, and was not liable for the negligence of the tenant.

In THORNTON *v.* LOUISVILLE & N. R. Co. (Ky. 1902), 70 S. W. Rep. 53, plaintiff, in company of other boys, with permission of the fireman, boarded a slow freight train, and after riding a short distance, attempted to get off. The other boys safely alighted, but the plaintiff's foot got caught in the stirrup, and when he let go with his hands of the ladder his leg was run over. A judgment entered on a peremptory instruction to find for defendant was affirmed. The court said that because the plaintiff was on the train by invitation of the fireman the defendant did not owe him any duty to stop the train to permit him to get off, or to prevent him from jumping therefrom. It is clear that the plaintiff was a mere licensee, if not a trespasser, and defendant owed him no duty unless his danger was discovered in time to have prevented an injury by some agent of defendant.

In SCHREINER *v.* GREAT NORTHERN R. Co. (Minn. 1902), 90 N. W. Rep. 400, the plaintiff, using the defendant's track to walk on, was approached by a train when he stepped to one side to allow it to pass, and was run against by a cow that was pasturing on defendant's unfenced right of way, and was thrown down with his arm on the track and was injured. A judgment sustaining a demurrer to the complaint was affirmed. The court said that, admitting that the plaintiff had defendant's permission to use the track, resting upon the usage by the public, he was at best a licensee. His presence there was not invited. Where a licensee, for his own benefit, is upon the property of another, without objection from the owner, such owner owes no duty to guard such licensee against the obvious risks and dangers which exist thereon.

In GULF, C. & S. F. R. Co. *v.* MILLER (Tex. Civ. App. 1902), 70 S. W. Rep. 25, the plaintiff, while walking on the defendant's tracks that, at the place of the accident, had been for several years used as a passway, was struck by a train that approached him behind without giving any signal. There was nothing to prevent a view of the track upon which he was walking. A judgment for plaintiff was reversed. The court said that it may be conceded that plaintiff was not a trespasser, and that after going on the track he was guilty of no such negligence as will relieve defendant from its negligence in failing to keep a proper lookout, and to give the required signals of warning; yet plaintiff's right to the use of the track as licensee was not greater than that of the defendant. On the contrary, it was subordinate; and for the preservation of human life and property generally, as well as for his own protection, it was plaintiff's duty, before going into and upon dangerous ground, to use his senses of sight and hearing. The consequences of a failure to do so is not relieved by the fact of concurring negligence on the part of another.

In WENCKER *v.* MISSOURI, K. & T. R. Co. (Mo. 1902), 70 S. W. Rep. 145, plaintiff's intestate, a child eleven years of age, went upon a caboose of a freight train immediately upon its stopping, to leave lunches there for the trainmen, as he had often done, and had been directed by them to do. When on the steps of the caboose, a sudden movement of the car backward threw him under the car immediately in front of the caboose, and he received injuries from which he died. The sudden movement of the train was caused by the "running out of the slack" of the train, a movement of constant occurrence in freight trains after the engine comes to a standstill. A directed judgment for defendant was affirmed. The court said that the boy was at most a mere licensee, and that the defendant owed him no duty other than not to negligently or wantonly injure him. The boy's business was with the trainmen, including the conductor, not with the defendant, and it was under no obligation to notify him as he approached the car of the danger to be apprehended by him "by the running out of the slack of the train," and the fact of his being only eleven years of age is of no significance.

6. Injury from Collision.

In FEEBACK *v.* MISSOURI PAC. R'Y CO. (Mo. 1902), 167 Mo. 206, two freight trains were to meet at a small station, and the one that first arrived took the switch but continued to move slowly, the engineer getting off and going in for orders without notifying the fireman, who did not know of his absence, and who did not try to stop the engine, that continued to move and had got within three rods of the main track before the engineer started to get on it, and before he got to it, the engine had reached the main track, and the other train, a through freight, had crashed into it, and the plaintiff's husband was killed. He had asked permission at the previous station to ride on the through freight, and being refused had crawled up between two cars unknown to the trainmen, who did not know he was there until after the accident. At the trial the plaintiff attempted to show that the conduct of the engineer in fault was so grossly negligent that the defendant was liable, although deceased was a mere trespasser. A judgment for defendant was affirmed. The court said that the deceased, being a mere trespasser, the defendant owed him no duty except to avoid wantonly to injure him.

In BURNS *v.* SOUTHERN R'Y (S. C. 1901), 63 S. C. 46, the complaint alleged that the plaintiff, a boy, being invited by the engineer and conductor of a construction train went into the cab to ride, and while there the train was run out upon the bridge that was being constructed and anchored on the track so high from the ground that the boy could not get out, and while so situated a freight train that usually stopped when approaching the work, ran into the cab without stopping, and injured the boy. The court said that as there was no allegation of wanton or wilful injury, there was no cause of action stated as the boy was a trespasser on the train.

7. Shot by watchman.

In BELT RAILWAY CO. *v.* BARRICKI (Ill. App. 1902), 102 Ill. App. 642, the appellee was on appellant's right of way in the freight yard and while obeying an order of the appellant's watchman to leave the premises, was shot by him. A judgment for the appellee was reversed. The court said that, according to all the evidence, appellee was, when injured, a trespasser, and appellant owed to him no duty except not to wantonly or wilfully inflict injury on him. That the mere employment of a watchman to guard property and keep away trespassers does not involve an authority to shoot trespassers; and authority for such shooting cannot be presumed. In the present case there was no evidence either of authority to shoot, or that the defendant knew that the watchman carried firearms. The shooting of a trespasser who is actually leaving the premises is not within the general or implied authority of a mere watchman.

In MAGAR v. HAMMOND (N. Y. 1902), 171 N. Y. 377, the defendant owned a large tract of land with a lake that he stocked with trout, and where he kept a watchman, whose duty it was at night to be on the lake to protect the fish from poachers and wild animals that frequently came to the place to take the fish. The owner had two guns, one a shotgun and the other a rifle, and the watchman carried one or the other when on the lake in a boat, for the purpose of killing muskrats and mink, and he sometimes fired in the air to frighten off poachers. The place was posted with notices to warn off trespassers, as prescribed by the state statute. The plaintiff, with two companions, visited the lake one night to take fish, and after doing some fishing, they retired to the woods on the shore, where the crackling of the brush indicated to the watchman that some one was there. The watchman had the rifle, and, on hearing the noise, he fired at least three shots in the direction, and one of the bullets struck the plaintiff in the hip, inflicting a severe injury. A judgment for plaintiff was reversed, because of the refusal of the trial judge to instruct that if the plaintiff knew that the watchman on the lake was in the habit of discharging a gun, and went there after receiving such information, he cannot recover, even if the defendant or the watchman was negligent, and that if the plaintiff knew or had heard that the lake was generally protected by a watchman who had and discharged a gun, there could be no recovery; since the request embodied the rule that the contributory negligence of the injured party prevented his right to recover for the injury though the defendant was negligent.

8. Other Cases.

In SIAS v. LOWELL, L. & H. ST. R. CO. (Mass. 1901), 179 Mass. 343, the defendant furnished the electric power to operate the cars of another company that owned the wires and poles. The poles were also used by a telephone company, who employed the plaintiff as a lineman. A telephone of a customer had burned out, and the plaintiff located the cause at a span wire of the railroad company. He mounted a pole and while tightening the span he received a shock and fell to the ground. Exceptions to a verdict for defendant directed by the court were overruled. The court said that the plaintiff was injured while at work upon a wire of the railway company, and it did not appear that this was at the request or solicitation of the company. It did not appear that the telephone company was expected to repair or meddle with the wires of the railway company. The plaintiff at the time of his injury was at work, not upon a telephone wire, but upon a wire of the railway company, without its permission, express or implied. While he was thus at work the highest duty the railway company owed him was that of not wilfully or wantonly injuring him. The defendant owned neither poles nor wires, and though it was shown that the wires belonging to it were not perfectly insulated, the imperfect insulation was at a point several hundred feet away from the place of the accident, which was caused, as claimed by the plaintiff, by the sagging wire at the place where he climbed the pole.

In DYCHE *v.* VICKSBURG, S. & P. R. Co. (Miss. 1901), 79 Miss. 361, the plaintiff's intestate, after attempting in vain to obtain a free ride on a freight train, went into a caboose standing on a spur track, and shortly afterwards he left the caboose, and while standing behind it several cars were kicked down the track against the caboose which ran over him and crushed his leg. Defendant's employees took him from under the car, and he was sent on a freight train eighteen miles to a station, where a physician attended him, bandaged his leg, and advised that he be sent to a hospital. He was carried on a freight train the next day back to where the accident occurred, and placed on a ferry boat, where he was ferried back and forth until the afternoon, when he was taken to the hospital, and his leg was amputated, about twenty-four hours after he had been injured. He died on the following day. A judgment entered on a directed verdict for defendant was reversed. The court said that though the plaintiff's intestate was a trespasser when he was injured, the company, in assuming charge of the intestate as it did, was charged with the duty of common humanity, and the jury should have been allowed to pass upon whether or not it performed this duty.

SESLER v. ROLFE COAL AND COKE COMPANY.

Supreme Court of Appeals, West Virginia, March, 1902.

DANGEROUS PREMISES — COAL TIPPLE — DUTY OF OWNER — INDEPENDENT CONTRACTOR — PERSONAL INJURY — EVIDENCE. —

1. To one going upon another's premises, not as a trespasser or mere licensee, but by invitation in legal sense, — as, for instance, independent contractor going upon such premises to do a work under contract with the owner, — the owner owes the duty of reasonable care to have and keep his premises in safe condition for such person's work, unless defects be known to such person.
2. If a contractor goes upon premises of another to perform a contract to do work for the owner, and is injured from defect in the premises known, or which by fair care ought to be known, to the owner, and unknown, or which by fair care cannot be known, to such contractor, the owner is liable; but, under the reverse of these circumstances, he is not liable.
3. In an action for personal injury, evidence that the plaintiff is a married man, with young children, is irrelevant and incompetent, and it is error to admit it.
4. Jury trials should be strictly confined to the issues made and the legitimate facts bearing on them, and the practice of dragging in extraneous matters to influence a jury cannot be too strongly condemned. Nothing outside of the legitimate facts should be introduced to affect the minds of those who are to decide the case.

5. When a question is put to a witness, and the court refuses to allow it to be answered, if the question does not plainly itself import that the answer will prove a fact material, it must appear by a bill of exceptions what was proposed and expected to be proven, else there is no error apparent. If a question objected to is answered, the answer must be shown, else there is no error apparent.

6. If the owner of a coal tipple promises a contractor executing a contract for masonry work in repairing the tipple not to have carpenters throw down old timbers of the tipple from any section of the tipple while the contractor is working at the masonry at a particular section of the tipple, and the contractor goes to another section of the tipple in work connected with his contract, relying upon such promise, and being ignorant that carpenters of the owner of the tipple are still engaged in removing old timbers, and the contractor is injured by a piece of timber being thrown upon him in the work of removal by the carpenters, the owner of the tipple is liable. But in the absence of such promise the owner would not be liable if the contractor knew that carpentry work was going on above such other section, though he did not know that the particular work of removing old timbers was being done, if he took no precaution to learn the character of the work being done.

(Syllabus by the Court.)

ERROR to Circuit Court, McDowell County.

Action by Louis Sesler against the Rolfe Coal & Coke Company. From judgment for plaintiff, defendant brings error. *Judgment reversed.*

RUCKER & ANDERSON, R. C. MCCLAUGHERTY, and BERNARD MCCLAUGHERTY, for plaintiff in error.

T. L. HENRITZE and W. L. TAYLOR, for defendant in error.

BRANNON, J. — Louis Sesler, in an action in the Circuit Court of McDowell county, recovered a verdict and judgment against the Rolfe Coal & Coke Company for $7,000, and the company has brought the case here.

The first complaint against the judgment is the overruling of a demurrer to the declaration. The declaration contains two counts. The first count alleges that the defendant owned and operated a coal mine and tipple, the tipple being used in unloading mine cars of coal into railroad cars for shipment to market, and that the plaintiff was the servant and employee for hire of the defendant, engaged in repairing the stone foundation of the tipple, and that while so engaged it was necessary for him to go under the tipple for the purpose of repairing and building the foundation of the tipple; and that it was the duty of the defendant to furnish the plaintiff a safe place for him to work, yet the defendant did not use proper care in providing such safe place, and that the defendant placed the plaintiff under the woodwork of the tipple and negligently caused the woodwork to be knocked down while the plaintiff was at work in his place of duty as such servant, and negligently caused a large piece of timber of the tipple to fall upon the plaintiff, whereby he was permanently injured, as further specified in the declaration. To this count, as a plain count based on the relation of master and servant, there is no objection made by counsel. The objection goes to the second count. This second count states that the plaintiff entered into a contract with the defendant, by which it was agreed that for a certain sum of money the plaintiff was to erect, construct, and repair the foundation of the tipple, and then alleges that the plaintiff "thereby became the servant and employee of the defendant for hire and reward, and then and there engaged in the work of the defendant in erecting, constructing, and repairing the foundation of the tipple, and while so engaged in the discharge of his duty it became necessary for the plaintiff to go under, upon, and about the tipple." The count then avers that "it became and was the duty of the defendant to furnish for the plaintiff, while he was so in its employ, a good, proper, safe, and suitable place for him to work, so that he might be secure and safe in all respects from injury against which ordinary care and foresight could avail." The count then avers that the defendant did not use proper care in providing a safe place for the plaintiff to work, but that, on the contrary, the defendant put the plaintiff to work under the woodwork of the tipple, and negligently caused the woodwork to be knocked down, and negligently and carelessly caused a large piece of the timber of the tipple to fall on the plaintiff, thereby inflicting great injury upon him. It is urged before us that, as this second count states a contract to do work, it created no relation of master and servant, and did not place the defendant under that duty resting on a master for the safety of his servant, namely, the duty to give him a safe place in which to work. What duty, by law, is due from an employer to one who is an independent contractor to do a specific work? It is not that of a master to a servant. 1 Thomp. Neg., sec. 680. But though this is so, the averment of the declaration that a duty of master to servant rested on the defendant is merely an averment of matter of law, not of fact, and as a declaration need not, and should not, aver matter of law, we treat such averment as harmless surplusage. Hogg. Pl. & Prac. 59. This is not the case of a mere trespasser or licensee going upon the premises of another and receiving hurt, as discussed plainly by Judge English in Woolwine's Adm'r *v.* Chesapeake & Ohio R'y Co., 36 W. Va. 329, 15 S. E. Rep. 81, 10 Am. Neg. Cas. 414n. Rather does the case fall in that class of cases where one goes upon the premises of another by invitation of that other, and receives hurt. We do not mean one invited merely by courtesy to visit. Such a person takes the premises as he finds them. 2 Jagg. Torts, sec. 258. By one going upon premises under invitation I mean invitation in a legal sense. "To come under an implied invitation, as distinguished from the mere license, the visitor must come for a purpose connected with the business in which the occupant is engaged, or which he permits to be carried on there. There must be some mutuality of interests in the subject to which the visitor's business relates, although the particular thing which is the subject of the visit may not be for the benefit of the occupant." 3 Elliott, R. R., sec. 1249; Plummer v. Dill (Mass.), 31 N. E. Rep. 128; 2 Bailey, Pers. Inj., sec. 3183. The plaintiff was upon the premises of the defendant at the call of business, and was there under legal invitation, and not a trespasser or licensee. So, treating him as an invitee, the question arises, what duty did the company owe him? That very late great work, Thompson's Commentaries on Negligence (2d ed., vol. 1, sec. 979), says: "It is not necessary to suggest that, where a proprietor engages an independent contractor to do work upon his premises, the contractor, while executing the work, will be there in pursuance of the invitation of the proprietor, and the proprietor will, under the principles discussed in this chapter, be under the duty of exercising ordinary or reasonable care to the end of promoting his safety." In Bennett v. Louis. & Nash. R. R. Co., 102 U. S. 577, 7 Am. Neg. Cas. 349, the syllabus is as follows: "The owner or occupant of land who induces or leads others to come upon it for a lawful purpose is liable in damages to them (they using due care) for injuries occasioned by the unsafe condition of the land or its approaches, if such condition was known to him and not to them, and he negligently suffered it to exist, without giving timely notice thereof to them or the public." In Samuelson v. Mining Co., 43 Am. Rep. 456, Judge Cooley uses this language, which seems applicable to this case in the view considered: "If the mine were in an unsafe condition when it was handed over to the contractors, and this was known to the defendant, or by the exercise of proper care ought to have been known, and if, in consequence, a miner, who was brought there in ignorance of the danger, was killed, the defendant should be held responsible. Every man who, expressly or by implication, invites others to come upon his premises, assumes to all who accept the invitation so to do the duty to warn them of any danger in coming which he knows of, or ought to know of, and of which they are not aware. This is a very just and very familiar principle." In Bright v. Barnett & Record Co. (Wis.), 26 L. R. A. 524, note (s. c., 60 N. W. Rep. 418), the law is, I think, correctly stated as follows: "With few exceptions, the cases agree in holding that the premises upon which an independent contractor is required to labor for the benefit of the owner must be reasonably safe for the purposes of such labor, so far as freedom from concealed danger is concerned." We may thus say that, if the decision of this case does in fact rest on any duty arising merely from the relation of the parties because of the contract between them, the unsafety of the premises must be such as was known, or by fair care could have been known, to the defendant, and was unknown, and by fair care could not have been known, to the contractor; for it is very clear that if the plaintiff knew, or by fair care could have known, of the work which injured him, he cannot recover." Whart. Neg., sec. 833. It is well established that if one knows, or by fair care could know, of danger threatening him, he cannot encounter that danger, and charge his injury upon the owner of the premises, even though that owner be in fault. Such would be even the law between master and servant. Davis' Adm'r *v.* Coke Co., 34 W. Va. 500, 12 S. E. Rep. 539; Knight *v.* Cooper, 36 W. Va. 232, 14 S. E. Rep. 999. Such being the duty of the owner to one upon his premises under legal invitation, it would seem that the second count ought to have gone beyond the mere averment of a contract between the parties, and averred an unsafety and danger in the premises known or knowable to the defendant, and not known or knowable to the plaintiff; in other words, that the work being done by the carpenters in the removal of the woodwork of the tipple was not known, or could not have been by fair care known, to the plaintiff. If we base the count on any peculiar duty growing out of that contract relation, the count is bad. But treating the averment of this contract merely as matter to show that the plaintiff was upon the defendant's premises, not as a trespasser or mere licensee, but by invitation of a business engagement, as the count avers that the defendant carelessly and negligently caused the woodwork of the tipple to be knocked down, and a piece of timber to be thrown upon him, the count is good without such additional averment. We have a liberal rule in this respect, under which a general charge of negligence is sufficient. Hawker *v.* Railroad Co., 15 W. Va. 628. This count avers no defect in the premises whatever. It does not proceed upon the idea of unsafety inherent in the premises, known or knowable to the defendant, and unknown and unknowable to the plaintiff. It does not state any facts showing any peculiar duty, save ordinary care arising out of that contract or the particulars wherein the duty was broken. It simply states that the plaintiff was lawfully upon the premises, and that the defendant, while the plaintiff was executing his contract in masonry work, by negligence threw down a piece of timber upon the plaintiff. Really that is the test of this case as made by that count, and in fact as made by the plaintiff's evidence. I do not see that the existence of that contract made any peculiar relation carrying with it any peculiar duty between the parties. As both the plaintiff and the defendant were lawfully engaged each in his separate work, the question is, simply, did the defendant so negligently conduct its carpenter work as to endanger the plaintiff? If so, did the plaintiff, knowing that this work was going on, and that it was dangerous, so knowing, did the plaintiff, nevertheless, go on with his work or do any act disregarding the dangers from the defendant's work, and thus assume the risk of danger? If so, the company is not liable. Under these views the second count is good.

The defendant offered to prove that it was a rule of the company to have the carpenter's work proceed on one part of the tipple and the masonry work on another part, so as to save those engaged in the masonry work from injury from timbers falling from above in the process of their removal; but this evidence was rejected by the court. If such a rule existed, known to the plaintiff, and he violated it, the evidence was admissible. Davis' Adm'r *v.* Coke Co., *supra;* Gregory's Adm'r *v.* Railroad Co., 37 W. Va. 606, 16 S. E. Rep. 819.

The plaintiff was permitted to prove that a man hauled stone under that part of the tipple where the carpenters were engaged in work. It seems they were engaged on one part of the tipple and the plaintiff on another part. Was this evidence introduced to show negligence in other respects than as to the plaintiff, — to show negligence generally? The evidence was not admissible. It was not shown to be the master's act. But the driver of the wagon is not suing. Suppose the company was negligent in exposing that wagoner, does that show that it was negligent to the plaintiff in any respect? The plaintiff did not receive his injury from hauling stone under that tipple. What had it to do with the plaintiff?

The court erred in admitting a deposition of Sagoda, because there was no evidence to show his death, absence, or other circumstance to warrant the admission of the deposition. Code, c. 130, sec. 36; Bart. Law Prac. 449.

The court refused questions as to whether the plaintiff, in other jobs of work for the company, worked at masonry when the carpenters worked on the tipple above. It seems they ought to be admitted as tending to show that the plaintiff knew of the dangers of so doing, and assumed their risk on this occasion. However, the court committed no error herein, for the reason that the questions did not import that certain answers favorable to the plaintiff must be given, and we cannot say whether the defendant was prejudiced from refusal of the questions. Where a question is refused by the court, it ought to be shown what was proposed to be proven, unless the question necessarily imports a particular answer; and, if the question is answered against objection, the answer ought to be given, otherwise no reversible error exists. Insurance Co. *v.* Pollard, 94 Va. 146, 26 S. E. Rep. 421; Jackson *v.* Hough, 38 W. Va. 236, 18 S. E. Rep. 575; Kay *v.* Glade Creek & Raleigh R. R. Co., 47 W. Va. 467, 8 Am. Neg. Rep. 636, 35 S. E. Rep. 973. The plaintiff was a witness in his own behalf, and the case turned most materially upon his evidence. He claimed that the defendant's superintendent, Jones, requested him to do the masonry work under that part of the tipple specified in the case as bent No. 5 in the forenoon, and that he declined to do so, saying that the carpenters were working in removing the old woodwork over that part of the tipple, and that Jones then said that he would by noon have all the timbers down which he intended then to take down, and if he should not be able to do so by noon he would keep his hands working at the noon hour so as to finish taking down such timbers, and thus it would be safe for the plaintiff to proceed with the masonry. The plaintiff claimed that, relying upon such promise, he went to work after dinner, and that, needing some plank for scaffolding, he went over from bent No. 5 to bents specified in the case as Nos. 6 and 7 to get plank for scaffolding, and while there the carpenters knocked down an old timber upon the plaintiff. He claimed that the promise of Jones was that no more timber would be knocked down so as to endanger him and his hands while at work in the afternoon. On the other hand, the defendant claimed that Jones promised the plaintiff to take down before the afternoon all the timbers of bent 5, and that he requested the plaintiff to build the wall for bent 5, and that it was agreed that the masonry should be built that afternoon only there, and the defendant denied that Jones had made any promise to cease from taking down timber elsewhere in the tipple. The defendant claimed that Jones left bent No. 5, where he was entirely safe, as all the timbers had been taken down before dinner from that section of the tipple, and that the plaintiff negligently went from bent No. 5 to a point between 6 and 7, and there remained, taking nails out of some old planks, and there received his injury through his own negligence. The defendant claimed that it was distinctly understood between the plaintiff and Jones that the plaintiff was to do masonry work that afternoon only under bent 5. The defendant claimed that whilst its carpenters were at work at bents 6 and 7 the plaintiff well knew the fact, knew that the men were working over those bents, heard their hammers and axes, and saw the chips falling from their work, and that, notwithstanding all this, he took the risk of danger, and thereby received his injury. The defendant claimed that it was not necessary for the plaintiff to go there for planks, as he could have gotten them elsewhere. The defendant also claimed that the plaintiff, even after he went from bent 5, did not take the precaution to look up to see what the carpenters were doing, and that, if he had used this prudence, he would have known that they were removing the timbers. The plaintiff admitted that he did not look up. In short, the defendant placed its reliance upon the negligence of the plaintiff. Under these circumstances counsel for the defendant proposed to ask the plaintiff these questions: "Did you not, a few days after the accident, and before you went to the hospital, in your house tell W. H. Walters, at Rolfe, that the injury was caused by your own negligence or carelessness, and that, if you had stayed where your work was, and where you ought to have been, that you would not have been injured, or words to that effect? Did you not, in the same conversation, at the same place, say to Mr. Walters that your injury was the result of an accident, for which no one was to blame, and, if you had stayed where your work required you to be, you wouldn't have been hurt, or words to that effect?" The court refused to allow these questions to be answered, but proposed to allow the defendant's counsel to ask Walters whether he did not say that, if he had remained where his work required him to be, he would not have been hurt. It seems that these questions should have been answered as put. They asked for yes or no. Was it not admissible for the defendant to show the plaintiff's admission that no one was to blame for his injury but himself and that it was due to his own negligence? Would not such admission repel the idea that he was misled by the superintendent's promise to take no more timber down after one o'clock? Would it not be an admission that he knew the danger before risking it? Would it not be an admission by him, he peculiarly knowing all the facts of the situation, that his injury was an accident, for which the company was not responsible, and chargeable to his own imprudence? Would it not show that he acted negligently in leaving bent 5, and working elsewhere, and sustain defendant's claim that the plaintiff was only to work at bent 5? The questions were admissible for the double purpose of contradicting the plaintiff and to show admission by the plaintiff himself, and admissible as independent, original evidence. It is said that the court rejected these questions on the ground that they called for mere expression of opinion. But they did not. They called for statement of fact. They called for self-disserving statement of fact. The offer of the court to allow a question covering part of the ground covered by the questions propounded did not cover the ground which the defendant was entitled to cover by such proposed questions, which went to the very gist of the case, — that of contributory negligence. I think these questions were improperly refused. They were very material questions.

The court erred in allowing plaintiff to prove that he was a married man, with three young children. The United States Supreme Court, in Penn. Co. *v.* Roy, 102 U. S. 451, 10 Am. Neg. Cas. 593, held: "In such a case, the injured passenger being entitled only to compensatory damages, evidence of his poverty, or the number and ages of his children, is irrelevant." This court has held such evidence improper, and its admission erroneous, in Moore *v.* City of Huntington, 31 W. Va. 842, 8 S. E. Rep. 512. It is very readily perceptible that this evidence appealed to human sympathy, and tended both to induce a verdict for the plaintiff and to aggravate damages. Where improper evidence is given, it is presumed to work injury, unless it very plainly appears not to have done so. Taylor *v.* Railroad Co., 33 W. Va. 39, 10 S. E. Rep. 29. In O'Hagan *v.* Dillon, 76 N. Y. 170, the court well said what ought to be impressed upon trial courts with emphasis: "Jury trials should be strictly confined to the issues made and to the legitimate facts bearing on them, and the practice of dragging in extraneous matters to influence a jury cannot be too strongly condemned. Upon a closely contested question of fact slight influences may turn the scale, and every rule of propriety and justice demands that nothing outside of the legitimate facts should be introduced to affect the minds of those who are to decide the question."

We will not pass upon the evidence under the motion for a new trial, but will let the case go back to the Circuit Court, to be tried upon the evidence, without decision as to its effect by us; but as matters of law pertinent to the case we will say that, if in fact the defendant's superintendent did promise the plaintiff that he would, before one o'clock, take down all the old timbers that were to be taken down that day, and that the plaintiff, being misled by that promise, went from bent 5 to get those planks for the purposes oi his work, and relying upon that promise, and not knowing or having reason to believe that the carpenters were engaged in knocking down old timbers, he would be entitled to recover. If, however, the defendant's superintendent did not make such promise not to take down timbers that afternoon, and did not thus mislead the plaintiff, and the plaintiff, knowing that the carpenter's work was going on, left his proper place of work, and went under where the carpenters were at work, and failed to look so as to see what they were doing, he was guilty of contributory negligence, and assumed the risk of danger, and under well-known principles cannot recover. Though such promise was made, and though calculated to mislead, yet if the plaintiff knew of the dangerous situation, and exercised no such precaution as a prudent man should do to save his own life and limb, he could not recover; but if lulled and misled by such promise, relying upon it, he received injury without culpable negligence, he would not be precluded from recovery. Graham *v.* Coke Co., 38 W. Va. 273, 18 S. E. Rep. 584.

For reasons above stated, we reverse the judgment, set aside the verdict, and remand the case for a new trial.

BARKER v. OHIO RIVER RAILROAD COMPANY.

Supreme Court of Appeals, West Virginia, April, 1902.

PASSENGER INJURED BY STEPPING INTO HOLE IN STATION PLATFORM — DUTIES OF CARRIER AND PASSENGER. — 1. It is the duty of a railroad company to keep its depots and platforms in safe condition, and free from dangerous defects, for the safety of its passengers.

2. A person going to a depot to become a passenger has the right to presume that the company has discharged such duty, and is not bound to keep a lookout for defects occasioned by the company's negligence, other than such as ordinary prudence might require for self-protection.

3. If a passenger, while trying to get her children onto the platform of a railroad station, unconsciously steps back into a hole in the platform, of which she had no previous knowledge, she is not guilty of contributory negligence, although if she had been walking face forwards, in the direction of such hole, she could have easily seen the same. Her walking backwards, or failure to look backwards, is not negligence, when there is nothing to warn her of the company's negligence; and it is not her duty to presume it or look for it (1).

4. A railroad company cannot be excused from gross negligence on its part, although the act of the injured person contributed thereto, unless it be

1. *Accidents at Stations and on Platforms.* — See vols. 9 and 10 Am. Neg. Cas., for cases relating to accidents to persons at stations, etc., from the earliest period to 1897. Subsequent cases on the same topics to date, are reported in vols. 1–12 AM. NEG. REP., and the current numbers of that series of Reports.

shown in evidence that such person was guilty of legal negligence; that is, some act of negligence that an ordinarily prudent person would not have been guilty of under the same circumstances.

5. It is not reversible error to admit in evidence the fact that the plaintiff's two children, who were with her at the time of her injury, were still living.

6. It is not reversible error to permit a physician to give his opinion as to the cause of a diseased condition of the human body.

(Syllabus by the Court.)

ERROR to Circuit Court, Mason County.

Action by Myrtle L. Barker against the Ohio River Railroad Company. From judgment for plaintiff, defendant brings error. *Judgment affirmed.*

W. R. GUNN, C. E. HOGG and SOMMERVILLE & SOMMERVILLE, for appellant.

H. P. CAMDEN and RANKIN WILEY, for appellee.

DENT, P. J. — The Ohio River Railroad Company complains of a judgment of the Circuit Court of Mason county rendered against it on the 21st day of May, 1900, for the sum of $6,500, in favor of Myrtle L. Barker, plaintiff. The facts necessary to a determination of this controversy are as follows: On the 2d day of July, 1898, the plaintiff, in the daytime, went to the depot at Clifton of the defendant, for the purpose of taking a south-bound train. She had with her two children, one a nursing babe in a baby carriage; the other four years old, was following behind her. She stepped upon the rear platform of the depot, and she and her sister lifted the baby carriage up. She called her other child, with the intention of lifting him upon the platform, took a step backwards, and fell into a hole twelve inches wide, and extending clear across the platform in front of the entrance door; it being occasioned by a plank becoming loose and having been washed out by the March flood. The station agent's attention had been especially called to it, but no pretense had been made to repair it. The company's negligence, under the circumstances, was as gross as it possibly could be, and the only possible avenue of escape is the customary *dernier ressort* of alleged contributory negligence, and yet numerous errors are assigned for the consideration of the court. They are classified under the following four classes by defendant's attorneys: 1. Does the declaration aver, and does the evidence prove, that the defendant was a common carrier of passengers, so as to charge it with the high duty imposed by the common law upon common carriers of passengers? 2. Was the plaintiff guilty of contributory negligence? 3. Did the court err in refusing to enter judgment for defendant on the special findings of the jury? 4. Did the court err in refusing to grant a new trial?

It is useless to dwell on the first. The objection is that the declaration does not allege in express terms that the defendant is a common carrier. It does allege that it is a railroad corporation operating a railroad from the city of Wheeling to the town of Kenova. All railroads in this State are common carriers. Section 9, art. 11, Const.; Laurel Fork & Sand Hill R. Co. *v.* West Virginia Transp. Co., 25 W. Va. 324.

On the question of contributory negligence the facts are undisputed, and it depends entirely on the degree of care required of passengers entering upon a railroad platform or depot. Are they in duty bound to keep a lookout for pitfalls or deathtraps, or have they a right to assume that the depot is in safe repair, and, without knowledge of a defect, are they only required to use such ordinary care as is required of a person in case such depot is in safe repair? If the defect is apparent, and they carelessly walk into it, they are guilty of contributory negligence, on the theory that he who is aware of another's negligence must avoid it if possible. The plaintiff had the right to assume that the platform was reasonably safe for travel, and she was not in duty bound to keep a lookout for defects. The portion on which she had momentarily entered was safe, and nothing had suggested to her that any portion was unsafe. She was busily engaged in getting her children onto the platform when she stepped backward into the hole. Had she looked, she could have seen it, yet she did not know it, and there was nothing other than the fact it was there to call her attention to it. In Elliott, Roads & S., sec. 638, it is said that "where the plaintiff, assuming that a sidewalk was safe, and knowing nothing to the contrary, permitted her attention to be momentarily attracted to some children playing in the street, and fell into a hole in the sidewalk from which the cover had been removed, she was held not guilty of contributory negligence." In the case of Barry *v.* Ferkildsen, 72 Cal. 256, 13 Pac. Rep. 658, the court says: "The fact that her attention was momentarily attracted in another direction — a thing of the most common occurrence to travelers along a street — falls far short of that contributory negligence which in law defeats an action of damages." In the case of Jennings *v.* Van Schaick, 108 N. Y. 531, 15 N. E. Rep. 424, the court says in speaking of a plaintiff who fell in a coal hole in the sidewalk: "She had the right to assume the safety of the sidewalk, and so was not called upon to give attention to her steps until in some manner warned of danger." In the case of Lighting Co. *v.* Kelley, 126 Ind. 221, 25 N. E. Rep. 812, the court, in approving the quotation above from Elliott on Roads and Streets, says: "She had the right to presume that the sidewalk was free from obstructions until her attention was in some way called thereto, and to act upon such presumption." And further on: "We can imagine many circumstances whereby the attention of the pedestrian might be attracted from the sidewalk, which would be sufficient to divert the attention of any reasonable person." Improvement Co. *v.* Loehr, 124 Ind. 79, 24 N. E. Rep. 579. Plaintiff had the right to assume that the platform was in a safe condition, and act on such assumption, until her attention was in some way called to the defect; and her attention to her children was such as any reasonable person might be expected to give. In fact, there was no imprudence on her part. If before she stepped backward she had looked, she would have seen the hole; but she was resting under the justifiable assumption that no such hole existed, and therefore there was nothing calling upon her to look backward. She had the right to assume that the company had discharged its duty, and that she could give the necessary attention to her children without danger of injury from its culpable negligence. In short, she acted as any other prudent person would have done under the same circumstances and with the same knowledge. 1 Fet. Carr. 130. Because she innocently confided in the company's faithful discharge of its duties towards its passengers, she cannot be held guilty of contributory negligence. Trust and confidence is not contributory negligence, although it may be unworthily bestowed. She will not be so confiding hereafter. Her knowledge and experience have increased, but her confidence is shattered and her health destroyed. It is impossible to say that she acted differently under the circumstances from what any other person of ordinary caution and prudence would have acted. Of course, there are persons naturally highly cautious, and others who have had large experience with the manner in which railroad stations and depots are usually managed, and who are continually on the alert for such defects. Such persons cannot be classed as ordinarily prudent. The law requires an engineer to keep a lookout for helpless trespassers on the track, qualified by consistency with the proper discharge of his other duties. So any lookout for open defects the law may require of passengers must be qualified not only by consistency with the discharge of other duties to other persons, but also with the just assumption of duty discharged on the part of the company. A mother who goes to a depot to take a train with her helpless children cannot be required to neglect proper attention to such children, and keep an active lookout for dangerous pitfalls in her way by the negligence of the company, for she has the right to assume there are none until she is in some manner warned of their existence.

Her first warning and knowledge of the company's negligence came to her when she fell backwards therein, and was too late for her to avoid it. If greater prudence is required of passengers than was exercised by her on this occasion, railroad companies should be required to put up a general warning to the traveling public not to go to their depots, except at personal risk, and thus avoid being guilty of contributory negligence in case of accident. A little care and a few nails at the proper time and place would save an immense amount of trouble. "The plaintiff, as a passenger of the appellant, was entitled to demand that the station's approaches and accessories used by it should be kept in a safe condition." Louis., N. A. & Chicago R'y Co. *v.* Lucas, 119 Ind. 589, 3 Am. Neg. Cas. 240, 21 N. E. Rep. 968. "Though the conduct of the passenger has contributed to the injury sustained, yet if such conduct has not been, in a legal sense, imprudent or negligent, he may recover, provided the carrier is in fault." 5 Am. & Eng. Enc. Law (12th ed.), 645. "To exonerate defendant from liability for its negligence, which also caused plaintiff's injury, it is not sufficient that plaintiff by his act contributed thereto, but it must further appear that in doing that act he was at fault, and guilty of what the law calls negligence." Railroad Co. *v.* Ball, 53 N. J. L. 289, 21 Atl. Rep. 1052 (9 Am. Neg. Cas. 575n, and 5 Am. Neg. Cas. 36n). The only alleged act of negligence that defendant can find in plaintiff's conduct was that she was not on the lookout for and did not discover defendant's negligence in time to avoid it. This is not legal negligence, for she had the right to confide in defendant to some extent. Contributory confidence is not contributory negligence. A person guilty of negligence should not be permitted to escape the results thereof by setting up misplaced confidence as contributory negligence. Facts sufficient to establish contributory negligence not appearing determine the various other questions presented in favor of the plaintiff.

Defendant insists that the court erred in giving the following instruction: "The court instructs the jury that if they believe from the evidence that the plaintiff, Myrtle L. Barker, went to the defendant's depot in the town of Clifton on the second day of July, 1898, with the intention and for the purpose of becoming a passenger on one of the defendant's passenger trains; and if they further believe from the evidence that the said Myrtle L. Barker, after reaching the platform of the said depot, and while on the said platform, still intending so to become a passenger, not being at the time guilty of contributory negligence on her part, fell into a hole in the said platform, whereby she was injured, as in her declaration is alleged; and if they further believe from the evidence that the hole in the said platform was there in consequence of the negligence of the defendant, — then the jury should find for the plaintiff, and assess her damages at such an amount as the jury, under all the evidence in the case, believe her entitled to recover, not exceeding, however, the sum of $10,000." The objection to this instruction is that it leaves out the question of contributory negligence. A bare reading of the instruction shows this contention is unfounded.

Defendant also objects to the following instruction: "The jury are further instructed that if they believe from the evidence that there was a hole in the platform of the defendant's depot, into which the plaintiff fell and was injured, and that she was there, at the time of her injury, intending to become a passenger on one of the defendant's passenger trains, and that the hole was there by reason of the defendant's negligence, then the court further instructs the jury that, before the defendant can avoid the consequences of such negligence on its part, it has the burden of proof upon it to show the contributory negligence of the plaintiff, and that such contributory negligence was the proximate, and not the remote, cause of the plaintiff's injury. And the court here instructs the jury that contributory negligence is the absence of that degree of care which an ordinarily prudent person of similar intelligence, and of the same class, would exercise under like circumstances." This instruction is not open to serious objection in this case. While it puts the burden of proof on the defendant to prove contributory negligence, yet it does not deny the right of defendant to show such negligence by the plaintiff's evidence, but is only to the effect that contributory negligence cannot be sustained except by a preponderance of the evidence. "Similar intelligence," used in this instruction, means ordinary intelligence and "the same class" is a distinction between passengers and employees, trespassers and licensees. Employees are charged with a much higher degree of care to avoid accidents than passengers, and such an accident as this to an employee would be completely covered over with the flexible and expanding blanket of fellow-servantcy. The defendant was not injured by this instruction.

Defendant objects to the following instruction: "The court further instructs the jury that the defendant, as a carrier of passengers, owes to those approaching or leaving its trains the duty of keeping its stations, and platforms thereof, in a reasonably safe condition for convenient use; and therefore the court instructs the jury that if they believe from the evidence that the plaintiff, Myrtle L. Barker, went to the defendant's depot in the town of

Clifton on the second day of July, 1898, with the intention and for the purpose of becoming a passenger on one of defendant's passenger trains, she had the right, upon reaching the platform of said depot, to assume, in the absence of information to the contrary, that such platform was then in a reasonably safe condition for her convenient use as such intended passenger, and, relying upon this assumption, she could neglect precautions that are ordinarily imposed upon persons, under such circumstances, not holding the relation to each other of that of passenger and carrier." This is simply no more than saying that the defendant owed her a higher degree of care than if she were not a passenger, and that therefore she was not required to take the same precautions as a trespasser, licensee, or employee. Because defendant succeeded in getting instructions in terms stronger than it was entitled to does not justify the reversal of the judgment, although such instructions apparently conflict with defendant's instructions. Defendant, in its management of this case, by instructions and otherwise, was endeavoring to show that it was the duty of plaintiff not to confide in its discharge of duty, but to keep a lookout for its negligence, so as to avoid the same. If the plaintiff acted prudently, that was all she was required to do. There is no act of imprudence charged to her, except that the defendant would make the fact that she did not keep a lookout for its negligence an act of imprudence. This may be true in fact, but it is not in law.

The defendant objects to the following instruction: "The court instructs the jury that to become a passenger, and entitled to protection as such, it is not necessary that a person shall have entered a train or paid his fare; but he is a passenger as soon as he comes within the control of the carrier at the station, through any of the usual approaches, with the intent to become a passenger. And the court therefore further instructs the jury that if they believe from the evidence that the plaintiff, Myrtle L. Barker, on the second day of July, 1898, went to the defendant's depot at the town of Clifton, by one of the usual routes thereto, for the purpose and with the intention of taking the next train, and stepped upon the platform of said depot with the intention and purpose of becoming such passenger, the plaintiff then became, in contemplation of law, a passenger of the defendant, provided she came to said depot and platform within a reasonable time before the time for the departure of said train, whether or not she had purchased a ticket from the defendant or its agent." It states the law correctly, as the plaintiff was entitled to the rights and protection of a passenger even before she purchased her ticket. 5 Am. & Eng. Enc. Law (2d ed.) 489.

Defendant insists the court should have given the following instruction: "The court instructs the jury that a person who uses a platform of a railroad station, which his observation, exercised with an ordinary degree of care, would have informed him was dangerous, takes the risk of injury from such open and apparent defects therein that such ordinary observation would have detected. Therefore, if the jury believe from the evidence that the defect in the platform complained of as the cause of the injury in this case was at the time of the alleged injury open and apparent to ordinary observation; and if they further believe from the evidence that such observation, exercised with an ordinary degree of care, would have informed the plaintiff that the platform was dangerous; and if the jury further believe from the evidence that the plaintiff, under these circumstances, attempted to use the platform, — then the court instructs the jury that she took upon herself the risk of all injuries resulting to her from such open and apparent defect, and that she cannot recover for injuries resulting therefrom." This instruction destroys the right of a passenger to assume that the company has done its duty, and requires him to keep a lookout for the company's negligence. If a passenger knows of, or is in any manner put on his guard against, the company's negligence, he is bound to avoid it; but he is not bound to be in continual fear thereof, or keep up a ceaseless observation to detect the same.

Defendant insists that the following instruction should have been given: "The court instructs the jury that there is no situation which will excuse a person from exercising that ordinary degree of care that would be exercised by an ordinarily prudent person under the same circumstances, and the court therefore instructs the jury that the plaintiff cannot excuse herself for failure to exercise such ordinary degree of care by showing that her attention was diverted from her own footsteps by solicitude for her child." This instruction wrongfully assumes that plaintiff did not exercise an ordinary degree of care under the circumstances, and tried to excuse herself therefrom by showing that solicitude for her children diverted her attention. This is a false assumption. Her children, however, were a part of the circumstances; and, in determining the degree of care she must use under the circumstances, they must be taken into consideration. For a person with the care of children on her hands is not as free to devote her attention to her own safety as she would otherwise be. She owed the duty of protection to them as well as to herself. If they had been injured, the company would have been very anxious to impute her negligence to them.

Defendant also insists the following instructions should have been given: "The court instructs the jury that if they believe from the evidence that there was a hole in the platform of defendant's depot, and that the plaintiff, in approaching and getting on the platform, could, by exercising ordinary care, have seen the said hole, and could by so seeing it have avoided the injuries complained of, then her failure to exercise such ordinary care to discover such hole is contributory negligence, and the jury must find for the defendant." This casts on the plaintiff the duty of keeping a lookout for the defendant's negligence, instead of having the right of assuming its faithful discharge of its duties.

Defendant excepts to the evidence that the plaintiff had children living. This evidence is not objectionable, although it may be immaterial and irrelevant. It is shown she had two children with her at the time of the accident. The additional evidence only showed that they were still living. Defendant asked no instruction in relation thereto, and its objection appears to be purely technical. Moore *v.* City of Huntington, 31 W. Va. 842, 8 S. E. Rep. 512; Johns *v.* Charlotte, C. & A. R. R. Co., 39 S. C. 162, 10 Am. Neg. Cas. 243, 17 S. E. Rep. 698; Alberti *v.* Railroad Co., 43 Hun, 421.

Defendant excepts to the physician's evidence, because he was permitted to give his opinion that the plaintiff's condition might have been caused by a shock, a fall, or anything that produces a shock to the spinal column. By other evidence this condition was connected with the accident. It is expert evidence, and not objectionable. 12 Am. & Eng. Enc. Law (2d ed.), 447; Bowen *v.* City of Huntington, 35 W. Va. 682, 14 S. E. Rep. 217; Turner *v.* City of Newburg, 109 N. Y. 301, 16 N. E. Rep. 344; Keane *v.* Village of Waterford, 130 N. Y. 188, 29 N. E. Rep. 130.

Defendant excepts because of evidence admitted showing what a competent nurse would have cost, she having been nursed by her mother and sister. The evidence was it would cost from five dollars to six dollars per week. She was in bed three months. A nurse at this rate would have cost less than $100, — being beneath the jurisdiction of the court, — and could only affect the verdict to this extent, if at all. Some authorities hold that such evidence is incompetent if the services were gratuitously given to her. Goodhart *v.* Railroad Co., 177 Pa. St. 1, 35 Atl. Rep. 191. In that case it is said: "Such services involve no liability on the part of the plaintiff, and therefore afford no basis for a claim against the defendant as for expenses incurred." The services referred to were those of wife and children to husband and father. In such a case no legal responsibility could accrue. For neither could a wife charge a husband for such services, nor a child, in the absence of a contract, its father.

Their services are provided for in the other damages allowed for the injury. A different rule prevails where the services are rendered by one who has the legal right to charge for them; for such a one donates them to the injured party, and not to the injurer. Pennsylvania Co. *v.* Marion, 104 Ind. 239, 3 Am. Neg. Cas. 175, 3 N. E. Rep. 874; Klein *v.* Thompson, 19 Ohio St. 569. In the latter case it was held that although the plaintiff was under no legal obligation to pay for services gratuitously rendered, or paid for by others out of charity, yet he was entitled to be placed in a position to pay for such services voluntarily, if in good conscience he should see proper to do so. The plaintiff in this case is a widowed woman, compelled to rely on her own efforts for support. She was nursed and taken care of by her mother and sister, who were under no legal obligation to do so, and who have the right to charge her for such services, if she is able to pay them or return them in kind. It is not shown in the evidence whether such services were rendered gratuitously or not. Certainly they were not rendered gratuitously to the defendant, but, in so far as defendant is concerned, they may reasonably have expected to be compensated. At least, the plaintiff should be put in a condition to compensate them. This is a matter of love and affection between themselves, and is not a matter of contributory negligence, that should diminish the amount of damages occasioned by the defendant's negligence. They have the right to say to her: "If you recover for our services from the defendant, we will expect you to pay us; otherwise we give them to you freely, through love and affection, and expect only a return in kind." In view of what has been said, it is unnecessary to copy herein, and comment on, the special findings of the jury. They amount to this: that if the plaintiff had been in position to do so, and had been looking toward the hole, she could have seen it, but that the necessary attention to her children prevented her from looking in the direction of the hole. All the rest of the platform was in good order, so that the portion that plaintiff did see and occupy led her to believe that the residue thereof was in a like condition; and when she raised her baby buggy upon the platform, with her back to the hole, there was nothing to indicate to her, within the range of her then vision, that the platform behind her was not in like condition as the portion on which she was then standing; and assuming it was, under the circumstances, it was not negligence in her to step backwards without looking, as, not knowing, she could not foresee that the company would permit such a dangerous trap in the platform. It might well be held that the company, in permitting this dangerous trap in its platform for three months, was guilty of such wanton and wilful recklessness and disregard of the limbs and lives of its passengers as to make it liable for criminal negligence, and for punitive or vindictive damages. Gross negligence warrants punitive damages whenever there is such want of care as raises the presumption of a conscious indifference on the part of the company to the safety of its passengers. 5 Am. & Eng. Enc. Law (2d ed.), 711. To leave a dangerous trap, such as is shown in this case, in front of a depot door, undoubtedly shows on the part of the company a conscious indifference to the safety of those invited to take passage on its trains. Railroad Co. *v.* Arnold, 80 Ala. 600, 2 So. Rep. 337; Mil. & St. P. R'y Co. *v.* Arms, 91 U. S. 489, 12 Am. Neg. Cas. 686. This question, however, is not raised in this case.

There is no error that will justify the setting aside the verdict and granting a new trial. Already two trials have been had, resulting in substantially the same verdict. Under the law as propounded, a new trial might be more disastrous to the defendant. Sometimes Providence takes care of railroad companies as well as infants. The judgment is affirmed.

HIVELY v. WEBSTER COUNTY.

Supreme Court, Iowa, October, 1902.

CHILD OF TENDER AGE KILLED ON HIGHWAY — EXCESSIVE DAMAGES. — In an action to recover damages for the death of a child, a boy four years and four months old, healthy and ordinarily bright and active, the death being caused by a horse attached to a wagon, in which deceased was riding with his mother and other children, becoming frightened and backing off bridge on highway, falling on the child, it was held that a verdict for $6,000 was excessive, the sum of $3,000 being considered sufficient damages (1).

APPEAL from District Court, Wright County.

"On the 31st of August, 1898, Mrs. A. W. Hively was on her way with a neighbor (Mrs. Newson) to visit a brother. They sat with their babies in the back seat of a platform spring wagon, while her son Willie, twelve years old, occupied the front seat and drove the

1. *Damages.* — See the title "DAMAGES," in American Negligence Digest, pages 258–285, where numerous cases of excessive damages reported in vols. 1–11 Am. Neg. Cas., and vols. 1–9 AM. NEG. REP., are cited. See also the indices in the series of AMERICAN NEGLIGENCE CASES and AMERICAN NEGLIGENCE REPORTS.

team. With him sat John Hively, a child of four years. As the horses were passing over the bridge, they noticed some iron tiles, four of which, from twenty-four to thirty inches in diameter and ten or twelve feet in length, had been placed by the county at the right side and near the traveled part of the road, about two rods west of the bridge. Becoming frightened, the team immediately backed off from the bridge or approach into a deep ravine, where one horse fell on John Hively, causing his death. The plaintiff, as the administrator of the estate of deceased, was allowed damages resulting from his death, and defendant appeals." *Conditionally affirmed.*

HACKLER, DUNCOMBE & WRIGHT, for appellant.

MAURICE O'CONNOR, A. N. BOTSFORD and HEALY & HEALY, for appellee.

LADD, Ch. J. — A careful examination of the record has convinced us that but one of the errors assigned demands discussion. The others relate to rulings so manifestly correct or free from prejudice as to require no vindication. The verdict returned was for $8,000. Of this, $2,000 was remitted, and judgment entered for the remainder. The child, when killed, was four years and four months old, healthy, and ordinarily bright and active. His father was a farmer, owning 160 acres of land; and there is, of course, some ground for thinking the son would possibly have followed the same vocation. His habits were unformed, and his probable ability to earn money a matter of conjecture. His expectancy of life was 50.76 years, or thirty-four years after attaining majority. The measure of damages in such a case is the present worth of decedent's life to his estate (Wheelan *v.* Railway Co., 85 Iowa, 167, 52 N. W. Rep. 119); and, as nothing would have accrued thereto before he reached the age of twenty-one years, the estimate was made nearly seventeen years before the estate would have derived any advantage from his life. Recovery ought not, then, to exceed the present worth of the damages which would be allowed for the wrongful death of a person of similar prospects in life at majority. Some help in fixing the proper amount of the damages which should be allowed may be gained from examining authorities determining whether verdicts for the death of adults were excessive. In Rose *v.* Des Moines Valley R. R. Co., 39 Iowa, 246, 9 Am. Neg. Cas. 332n, a verdict of $10,000 for the wrongful killing of a passenger twenty-four years old, whose expectancy was thirty-eight years, and net earnings $263 per annum, was held excessive, and the judgment affirmed on condition that all above $5,000 be remitted. In Haas *v.* Railway Co., 90 Iowa, 259, 57 N. W. Rep. 894, the deceased was a fireman earning $2.20 per day, and had an expectancy of over forty years, and an award of $8,000 damages for causing his death was upheld. In Locke *v.* Railroad Co., 46 Iowa, 109, a verdict of $7,000 for the death of a conductor receiving $75 per month, with an expense of $35, and an expectancy of thirty-six years, was held not excessive. In Moore *v.* Railway Co., 89 Iowa, 223, 56 N. W. Rep. 430, $600 was allowed for the death of a man seventy-one years of age. The same ruling was made in Lowe *v.* Railway Co., 89 Iowa, 420, 56 N. W. Rep. 519, where a brakeman of twenty-five years, earning $55 per month, was killed, and the verdict was $5,000. In Walter *v.* Railroad Co., 39 Iowa, 33, deceased was between fifty-seven and sixty-five years of age, and had some property. A verdict of $4,500 was upheld. In Berry *v.* Railway Co., 40 Iowa, 564, deceased was a foreman of car repairers, receiving $2.50 per day. He was thirty-two years old, and had an expectancy of thirty-three years. A verdict of $5,000 was held not to be excessive. In Cooper *v.* Mills Co., 69 Iowa, 350, 28 N. W. Rep. 633, action was brought by the injured party before death, and therefore damages were included for pain and suffering. In no case has a verdict of more than $8,000 been sustained. In several of the States $5,000 is fixed by statute as the maximum of recovery for causing the death of a human being, but the statutes authorizing such actions differ so widely that little aid can be had from examining authorities elsewhere. See cases collected in 8 Am. & Eng. Enc. Law, 933. Larger sums are allowed persons who have been permanently injured, because of the consideration of other elements, such as pain and suffering, in measuring the damages. These are not to be taken account of in an action begun by the administrator. Dwyer *v.* Railway Co., 84 Iowa, 479, 51 N. W. Rep. 244. Compensation for the life that is lost is impossible, and the law will not undertake to estimate the sorrow occasioned by the untimely death. Merely compensation for the pecuniary loss to the estate is the only remedy available in the courts. In each of the cases cited the earning capacity of the persons killed was shown, but in this we are left to deal entirely with the uncertainties, though possibilities, of life. It is fair to assume, however, that this boy would have developed into an average man, and that he would have earned an average net income. What that would have been, so remote in the future, is difficult of ascertainment. Under the circumstances as disclosed, we think that the damages should not be fixed at a sum exceeding $3,000. This would be equivalent to $6,000 at majority, without compounding interest; affording, in addition to the principal, a net annual income of $360, computing interest at the statutory rate of six per cent. per annum. It may well be doubted whether the accumulations of the average person, independent of inheritance, etc., will equal that sum. Even this estimate rests largely on conjecture and the probabilities of an unfathomed future. Rein is not to be given to the imagination in such cases, and account taken, as suggested by appellee, of the possibility that deceased would have married, and absorbed into his estate the earnings of wife and a numerous progeny of children. Both the probability of the future marriage of a minor of tender years, and of the financial benefit to be derived therefrom, is mere speculation. Even if these were probable, other distributees than those now interested might take their estate. Family and social relations likely to be formed in the future are contingencies too remote and conjectural to be taken into account as elements in estimating the amount of damages to be allowed. Railroad Co. *v.* Herndon, 100 Ala. 451, 14 So. Rep. 287; Seaman *v.* Trust Co., 15 Wis. 578. In Railroad Co. *v.* Wright, 134 Ind. 509, 34 N. E. Rep. 314, the court held that no presumption would be indulged against future marriage. See also Burk *v.* Railroad Co., 125 Cal. 364, 57 Pac. Rep. 1065. Evidence that an injured party was in the line of promotion was rejected in Chase *v.* Railway Co., 76 Iowa, 675, 39 N. W. Rep. 196; Brown *v.* Railway Co., 64 Iowa, 652, 21 N. W. Rep. 193. All held in Walters *v.* Railroad Co., 41 Iowa, 71, was that substantial damages might be allowed. No claim was made that the verdict was excessive, save in that more than nominal damages were included. In Eginoire *v.* Union Co., 112 Iowa, 558, 84 N. W. Rep. 758, the child for whose death damages were allowed was eight years old, and hence with a greater expectancy; exceptionally bright for her years. Judgment for $2,500 was upheld. What was there said sufficiently answers the contention that a wider difference should be recognized as existing between the earning capacities of the sexes.

If plaintiff shall file a remittitur of all in excess of $3,000, and interest thereon, within thirty days from the filing of this opinion, the judgment will stand affirmed; otherwise it will be reversed.

WEAVER, J, took no part.

COFFEYVILLE MINING AND GAS COMPANY v. CARTER.

Supreme Court, Kansas, November, 1902.

PRACTICE — JUDGMENT — DEATH BY WRONGFUL ACT — EVIDENCE — DAMAGES — FINDINGS. — 1. It is not error to deny a motion for judgment based upon the opening statement of plaintiff's case to the court and jury, unless such statement admits the existence of facts which absolutely preclude a recovery by plaintiff.

2. In an action of damages for death by wrongful act it is proper to receive evidence of whatever facts made the life of the deceased of pecuniary value to the survivors entitled to sue and recover damages for the death, including the ability of deceased to earn money or accumulate property, his disposition to contribute support, his condition of health, the probable duration of his life, and also the number, age, sex, health, or condition in life of his surviving children dependent upon him for care, support, education, and maintenance.

3. Findings of jury examined, and *held* to authorize neither a judgment in favor of defendant as against the general verdict nor the granting of a new trial. (Syllabus by the Court.)

IN BANC. Error from District Court, Montgomery County.

Action by Lulu Carter against the Coffeyville Mining & Gas Company. From judgment for plaintiff, defendant brings error. *Judgment affirmed.*

H. C. DOOLEY (W. V. MOORE and A. M. ETCHEN, of counsel), for plaintiff in error.

A. B. CLARK and J. D. BROWN, for defendant in error.

POLLOCK, J. — This action was brought by Lulu Carter, daughter and administratrix of the estate of David Carter, a widower, deceased, against the Coffeyville Mining & Gas Company, to recover damages for the death of deceased by wrongful act. The facts necessary to a determination of this controversy are: Defendant put down and was the owner of a natural gas well on lot 14, block 62, in the city of Coffeyville. East of this gas well about fifty feet there was erected a two-story brick building. Immediately south of this building, and adjacent thereto, stood a small frame building, used as a blacksmith shop. David Carter was a blacksmith, and on the 21st day of May, 1896, was working at his trade in this shop. By reason of defects in the materials used or the manner of construction of the gas well, gas escaped therefrom through crevices in the earth to a cellar or basement underneath the brick building. This accumulated gas, from some cause unknown, was exploded, which explosion demolished the brick building, and threw the south wall thereof upon the frame blacksmith shop, instantly killing Carter. There is much testimony in the record tending to show that at the time the brick building was constructed, and thereafter, gas from the well escaped through crevices in the earth into the bottom of the cellar; that the water in drinking wells in the vicinity of this gas well, free from gas before the boring of the well, afterwards became contaminated by gas, and unfit for use. The cellar or basement under the brick building was rented by one Irwin, and had been closed for about ten days prior to the death. Matches had been lighted therein the day preceding the accident without harm. At the time of the explosion Irwin had gone to the cellar with some colored help to carry out water therefrom. The explosion followed upon opening the cellar door. At the trial there was a verdict and judgment for plaintiff. The jury, at request of defendant, also made special findings of fact. Defendant brings error.

Many assignments of error are urged upon our attention. We shall examine separately only such as we deem of sufficient importance to merit special attention. It is first contended there was error in denying the motion of defendant for judgment upon the statement of the case to the court and jury made by counsel for plaintiff. This court has held, where the opening statement of counsel for plaintiff, made to the court and jury, contains an admission of facts, which absolutely precludes a recovery by plaintiff, the court is warranted in acting upon such admissions, and entering judgment against plaintiff. Lindley *v.* Railroad Co., 47 Kan. 432, 28 Pac. Rep. 201. Is the rule applicable in this case? The contention of counsel for plaintiff in error is based upon two grounds: 1. Counsel for plaintiff, in his opening statement, admitted the manner in which the gas in the cellar of the brick building became ignited was unknown to plaintiff. 2. The acts of negligence relied upon for recovery are set forth in an amended petition, filed more than two years after the death of Carter; and it is claimed the cause of action for such negligence was barred by the statute of limitation. As to the second ground, little need be said. Defendant did not raise the question of the statute of limitation, either by demurrer or answer to the amended petition. The cause of action set forth in the amended petition is merely an enlargement upon that stated in the original petition. It is the same cause of action, and was not barred by the two-years' limitation found in sec. 422 of the Code. Railway Co. *v.* Ludlum, 63 Kan. 719, 66 Pac. Rep. 1045. As to the first ground, it is argued by counsel for plaintiff in error that the proximate cause of the death of Carter was the ignition of the accumulated gas in the cellar, and not in permitting the gas to escape from the well and accumulate in the cellar. And, in consequence, the admission made by counsel for plaintiff in the opening statement of her case to the court and jury is an admission of want of knowledge and lack of proof upon a vital issue of fact fatal to a recovery, and warranted the court in entering judgment thereon. With this contention we do not agree. Defendant was employing for its profit a subtle and highly explosive agency. The rule at common law is, where an agent so introduced is controllable by care, attention, or science, he who receives the benefit must assume the responsibility. It is neither pleaded, nor was an attempt made to show, contributory negligence on the part of deceased. In this condition of the record it was wholly immaterial how the gas became ignited. In Koelsch *v.* Philadelphia Co., 152 Pa. St. 355, 25 Atl. Rep. 522, it is held: "The fact that an explosion of gas, which has accumulated in a cellar by negligence of a gas company, was caused by the act of a third person in lighting a match, will not relieve the gas company from liability." City of Kansas City *v.* Gilbert (No. 12,651, Oct., 1902), 70 Pac. Rep. 350 (1). The motion for judgment was properly overruled.

The next claim of error arises upon the reception of testimony, and especially that of plaintiff, a witness in her own behalf, wherein she was permitted to state she was, and for years had been, in bad health, and that her father was kind and affectionate toward her and his other children. It is insisted this is error, and many cases are cited in support of the contention made. In an action for personal injuries not resulting in death — and of such nature are the cases cited — the character of evidence offered and received is inadmissible. Pennsylvania Co. *v.* Roy, 102 U. S. 451, 10 Am. Neg. Cas. 593; City of Galion *v.* Lauer, 55 Ohio St. 392, 45 N. E. Rep. 1044; Dayharsh *v.* Railway Co., 103 Mo. 570, 15 S. W. Rep. 554. The case at bar is an action to recover damages for death by wrongful act. The rule here is different. Here plaintiff, in her representative capacity, is seeking recovery of damages for the death for the benefit of herself and the other children of deceased. In such case regard is had alone to the necessities and wants of the surviving children. While, as has been held by this court, no inflexible rule can be laid down governing all cases, as each case must be ruled by its peculiar circumstances, yet from the authorities it is

1. See this case reported in this volume of AM. NEG. REP., viz., KANSAS CITY *v.* GILBERT (*Kansas Supreme Court, October, 1902*), 12 AM. NEG. REP. 272, *ante*.

safe to say, while the statute limits the amount of recovery in any given case to $10,000, within this limit just compensation for the loss sustained by the wrongful death is not by law meted out with miser hand. Whatever made the life of the deceased of pecuniary value to his surviving children, whether arising, on the one hand, from the ability and disposition of the deceased to contribute to the survivors, as evidenced by his capacity to earn money and accumulate property, his inclination to provide support, the condition of his health, the probable duration of his life, or, on the other hand, from the necessity that the survivors receive assistance as measured by the number, age, sex, health, or condition in life of the surviving children who are left dependent upon the life for care, support, maintenance, and education, may be shown in estimating the pecuniary and just measure of value of such life. Hence it was competent in this case to show the ill health of plaintiff, and the strength of the attachment of the father for his children, as revealed in his treatment of them, as tending to show the extent of the dependency of the children upon the father, and the probability of his continuing to contribute to their support. This court, in Railway Co *v.* Cutter, 19 Kan. 83, said: "In determining the amount of such compensation, much must be left to the good sense and sound judgment of the jury upon all the facts and circumstances of the case. No uniform and precise rule can be laid down for estimating the value to the survivors of the life of the deceased, for the elements which go to make up such value are personal to each case." In the opinion, Mr. Justice Brewer said: "In the very nature of things, it seems to us an exact and uniform rule for measuring the value of the life taken away to the survivors is impossible. The elements which go to make up the value are personal to each case. All that can well be done is to say that the jury may take into consideration all the matters which go to make the life taken away of pecuniary value to the survivors, and, limited by the amount named in the statute, award compensation therefor." See also Railroad Co. *v.* Brown, 26 Kan. 443; McKeigue *v.* City of Janesville, 68 Wis. 50, 31 N. W. Rep. 298; Hetherington *v.* Railway Co., 9 Q. B. Div. 160 (1); Railway Co. *v.* Glover, 92 Ga. 132, 18 S. E. Rep. 406; Hall *v.* Railway Co. (C. C.), 39 Fed. Rep. 18; Felton *v.* Spiro, 24 C. C. A. 321, 78 Fed. Rep. 576, 47 U. S. App. 402; Tetherow *v.*

1. In Hetherington *v.* Northeastern R'y Co., L. R. 9 Q. B. Div. 160, an action under 9 & 10 Vict., c. 93. for the benefit of the father of the deceased, evidence was given that the father, who was fifty-nine years of age, was nearly blind and injured in his leg and hands, and was not so able to work as he had been, but worked when he could; that the son used to contribute

Railway Co., 98 Mo. 74, 12 Am. Neg. Cas. 195n, 11 S. W. Rep. 310; Abbot *v.* McCadden, 81 Wis. 593, 51 N. W. Rep. 1079.

The remaining questions arise upon the special interrogatories requested and submitted to the jury. In this regard it is insisted the court erred in refusing to submit special questions Nos. 34, 36, and 37 requested by defendant. In these questions the jury is asked to find the amount awarded plaintiff by way of punitive damages for loss of companionship and loss of love and affection. As the court, in its instructions, limited the amount of plaintiff's recovery to the pecuniary loss suffered by his surviving children, the general verdict being for compensatory damages only, and as the jury in answer to special question No. 35 fixed the actual damages sustained at the sum of $3,000, the amount of the judgment rendered, no error was committed.

Again, it is urged defendant was entitled to judgment upon the special findings made by the jury. In answer to special questions 29 and 38, the jury find the death of Carter was not accidental. In answer to special question 39, it is found the negligence of the defendant was the cause of the death. And in answer to special questions 40 and 45, it is found the gas well was not constructed in a safe, careful, and prudent manner, but that the officers of the company were negligent in the construction of the well, and in laying pipes therein in such manner as to permit the escape of gas therefrom. As the findings made are neither contradictory nor destructive of plaintiff's right of recovery, the motion for judgment upon the findings was properly denied. Anderson *v.* Pierce, 62 Kan. 756, 64 Pac. Rep. 633.

The final contention made is that the answers returned to special questions are so inconsistent, and evince such bias and prejudice of mind on the part of the jury, as to entitle defendant to a new trial of the action. An examination of the record discloses the fact that a portion of the special questions submitted at the request of defendant remain unanswered; that answers returned to others are not complete or responsive to the questions asked. But as defendant at the trial neither insisted upon answers to the questions unanswered nor to more direct and specific answers where the answers are incomplete, but remained content therewith, such error, if any, is waived. As the answers returned are neither

to his support; that five or six years previously, the father being out of work for six months, the son had assisted him pecuniarily out of his earnings, but had not done so since. *Held*, that there was evidence for the jury of pecuniary injury to the father from the son's death.

contradictory of nor inconsistent with one another or the general verdict, the verdict must stand, and judgment thereon be affirmed. All the justices concurring.

METROPOLITAN STREET RAILWAY COMPANY v. AGNEW ET AL.

Supreme Court, Kansas, October, 1902.

DRIVING ACROSS TRACK AT STREET CROSSING — COLLISION — LOOKING AND LISTENING — INSTRUCTION. — **In an action against an electric street railway company, by a party who was struck by a car and injured while attempting to drive over its tracks in a walk at a street crossing, the company introduced testimony that an approaching car could be seen for a distance of 277 feet by a person standing within fifteen feet of the railway tracks. This contradicted the plaintiff, who testified that by reason of obstructions to her view she could see in the direction the car came eighty or ninety feet only, when she was fifteen feet from the crossing. *Held*, that it was error to refuse an instruction tendered by the railway company to the effect that, if an approaching car was within the range of vision of the person injured, she was chargeable with knowledge of its coming, notwithstanding the fact that she testified that she did not see it (1).**

(Syllabus by the Court.)

IN BANC. Error from District Court, Wyandotte County.

Action by Marie M. Agnew and others against the Metropolitan Street Railway Company. From judgment for plaintiffs, defendant brings error. *Judgment reversed.*

MILLER, BUCHAN & MORRIS, for plaintiff in error.

ANDERSON & ROBINETT, for defendant in error.

SMITH, J. — Defendant in error recovered a judgment against the Metropolitan Street Railway Company for personal injuries sustained at a place where Parallel avenue, in Kansas City, Kan., crosses the tracks of said company. She was driving a horse hitched to a surrey, and in attempting to go over the railway tracks the vehicle was struck by a car. She testified that the horse was going in a walk, and that at a distance of fifteen feet from the crossing she could see up the track, from which direction the car came that caused her injuries, no further than eighty or ninety feet, by reason of obstructions to her view caused by houses and trees. She

1. *Accidents at crossings.* — See vols. 11 and 12 Am. Neg. Cas., for crossing-accident cases, from earliest period to 1897. Subsequent actions to date are reported in vols. 1-12 AM. NEG. REP., and the current numbers of that series of Reports.

also testified that when within six or eight feet from the track she looked up north, and saw no car approaching. The defendant below introduced a witness who testified that he had made measurements and taken observations at the place where the accident occurred, showing that at a distance of fifteen feet west of the street-railway track a car could be seen approaching from the north at a distance of 277 feet. Plaintiff below was familiar with the crossing, and knew that cars were constantly passing over it. The negligence alleged and sought to be proved by the plaintiff below was that the street car was recklessly run at a speed of eighteen miles per hour, and that it approached the street crossing without ringing the bell or giving other warning. Plaintiff below did not deny that the car could be seen at a distance of about eighty or ninety feet from the crossing when she was within six or eight feet from the track.

Counsel for the street-railway company requested the court to give the following instruction to the jury, which request was denied: "If you find from the evidence that plaintiff looked to the north for an approaching car before going upon the track, and you further find that at the time she so looked the said car was there approaching and within view of her, then you are instructed that plaintiff is chargeable with knowledge of its approach, although plaintiff claims that she did not see said car approaching." No instruction was given covering the same point, nor was the attention of the jury called to the legal effect of a failure on the part of the plaintiff below to observe the car if it was within the range of her vision. If the jury believed the testimony of the witness above referred to, who measured the distances and made the observations, they must have concluded that, if the plaintiff looked up the track with an unobstructed view for 277 feet, she could have seen the approaching car in time to have avoided the accident. In view of this, it was proper that they should have been directed to consider the effect of her negligence in attempting to cross in the face of visible danger. It seems probable, also, that she might have escaped injury, at the gait the horse was going, had she seen the car coming, from a distance of eighty or ninety feet, when she was six or eight feet distant from the crossing. She either saw the car, or else her testimony was untrue, if the testimony introduced by defendant below was given credence. Young *v.* Railway Co., 57 Kan. 144, 45 Pac. Rep. 583. In the case cited the court quoted approvingly from the case of Railway Co. *v.* Elliott, 28 Ohio St. 340-355 (12 Am. Neg. Cas. 485n), where it is said: "It is nothing to the purpose that he should say he looked this way and that, when the object he seeks to discover is plainly and palpably before him, and he fails to see it. Either his statement is not true, or his exercise of vision was such as to be not only negligent, but culpable. The instruction asked should have been given.

The judgment of the court will be reversed, and a new trial ordered. All the justices concurring.

ATCHISON, TOPEKA AND SANTE FE RAILWAY COMPANY v. JUDAH.

Supreme Court, Kansas, October, 1902.

DRIVING ACROSS TRACK — NEGLIGENCE OF DRIVER — PERSON RIDING INJURED — WARNING — SPEED OF TRAIN — COUNTRY CROSSING — IMPUTED NEGLIGENCE. — 1. A traveler on the highway, who is about to cross a railroad track, and who is already warned of the approach of a train in time to escape injury, cannot complain of the negligence of the railway company for its failure to give signals of danger.

2. In an open country, where the view of a traveler on the highway is unobstructed, a railway company is not chargeable with negligence in running its passenger trains over a road crossing at a speed of from forty to fifty miles per hour.

3. Whether the carelessness of the driver of a wagon can be imputed to another riding with him, who is injured at a road crossing in a collision between the vehicle and a railway train, becomes immaterial when it is found that the railway company was guilty of no acts of negligence toward the occupants of the wagon (1).

(Syllabus by the Court.)

IN BANC. Error from District Court, Atchison County.

Action by Nancy J. Judah against the Atchison, Topeka & Santa Fe Railway Company. From judgment for plaintiff, defendant brings error. *Judgment reversed.*

A. A. HURD and O. J. WOOD, for plaintiff in error.

C. D. WALKER and J. L. BERRY, for defendant in error.

SMITH, J. — This was an action by Nancy J. Judah, as mother and next of kin of Fannie Judah, to recover damages for her death. She had judgment in the District Court. Jennings D. Judah, the husband of the plaintiff below, with his two daughters, Fannie and another, were killed in a collision between a spring wagon in which they were riding and an engine pulling a passenger train of plaintiff

1. *Imputed negligence.* — See NOTE ON IMPUTED NEGLIGENCE, 11 Am. Neg. Cas. 151-156. See also numerous cases involving the question of imputed negligence in vols. 11 and 12 Am. Neg. Cas., arising out of accidents to persons riding in vehicles, caused by collision with trains at crossings.

in error. The accident happened in January, 1898, about six o'clock P. M., at a crossing a short distance west of the city of Atchison, where what is known as the Monrovia road passes over the tracks of the Missouri Pacific Railway Company, the Central Branch Union Pacific Railway Company, and the Atchison, Topeka & Santa Fe Railway Company, in the order named, beginning from the north. The wagon road runs from the north in a southwesterly direction across the tracks. Jennings D. Judah, accompanied by his two daughters, started from Atchison toward their home in the country. He was driving the team. When they reached a point several feet north of the Missouri Pacific track, which is about fifty feet north of the track of plaintiff in error, a switchman, whose watchhouse or "shanty" was about 140 feet north from the center of the Santa Fe track, south of the wagon road, and eight or nine feet north of the Missouri Pacific Railway track, heard the voices of persons approaching. About this time he saw the headlight of an engine coming from the west. A few seconds later he heard the whistle sounded eighty rods distant. Immediately he heard one of the women in the wagon exclaim, "Stop, there comes a train." He then took his lantern, went out, and saw a team of horses and a spring wagon approaching from the northeast. The team was then sixty-five feet distant from the Santa Fe track. He shouted, as the jury found, in more than a moderate tone of voice, "Hold on, you can't make the crossing." The team was going at a brisk trot, and continued at the same speed until the collision with the locomotive. Eighty rods from the crossing the engineer sounded four blasts of the whistle. The jury found that the bell was not rung. They also found that, as soon as the engineer learned that there was a team going toward the crossing, he applied the air brakes with full force. The negligence of plaintiff in error was found by the jury in answer to a particular question, as follows: "Q. If you find that deceased came to her death by or through the fault or negligence of the defendant, then state fully all the facts and things which you find from the evidence constituted the said fault or negligence of the defendant. A. Excessive rate of speed over a crossing which had an unusual amount of travel over same, and failing to provide proper and reasonable precautions." The testimony introduced by plaintiff below tended to show that the train was running at a speed of from forty to fifty miles per hour. It is an established fact that the occupants of the wagon had due warning of the approach of the train when they were at least sixty-five feet from the track of the plaintiff in error. The first alarm came from one of the women, who said, "Stop, there comes a train," and the second from the switchman who was watching the crossing. Having ample knowledge of the proximity of the train, a failure to ring the bell cannot be charged against the railway company as an act of negligence. A signal by whistle or bell in such cases is to give warning of an approaching train. When a traveler about to cross a railroad track has notice of that which a whistle or bell signifies, the giving of such warnings is a work of supererogation as to him. A failure to give notice to one already informed of a fact cannot be called negligence. Railway Co. *v.* Bell, 70 Ill. 102; Pakalinsky *v.* Railroad Co., 82 N. Y. 424, (12 Am. Neg. Cas. 396n); Railroad Co. *v.* Walz, 40 Kan. 433, 19 Pac. Rep. 787. There remains, therefore, in the case, but one question, which is whether the railway company is chargeable with negligence in running its train at a speed of from forty to fifty miles an hour. This speed, it is urged, was so great that the momentum of it could not be overcome by the engineer after he saw the team and wagon about to cross the track. Witnesses who testified for the plaintiff below stated that the train was going at about its usual speed, and it appeared not to be behind time. While there was considerable travel over this crossing, yet it was not in the corporate limits of a city, but in the country. It has been held by this court that in such cases speed cannot be made an element of negligence. In Mo. Pac. R'y Co. *v.* Moffatt, 56 Kan. 667, 670, 11 Am. Neg. Cas. 554, 44 Pac. Rep. 607, it is said: "The crossing was in an open country, where there was no statutory or municipal regulation with respect to the speed of trains. The demands of the public and the necessities of modern business require that such trains should be run at a rapid rate, and railroad companies would hardly be justified in slacking the speed at every such highway crossing to avoid the risk of a collision with some one who was passing over the same. Even if the rate of speed had been pleaded as a specific act of negligence, it could hardly be held, under the circumstances, that the speed at which the train in question was run was negligent or unlawful. The court, however, without justification, made the speed of the train an element of negligence, and the jury evidently made it a basis of recovery. In this there was error. * * * Under ordinary circumstances, in the open country, the railroad company can run as many trains and at as great a rate of speed as is consistent with the safety of its passengers." Railroad Co. *v.* Hague, 54 Kan. 284, 38 Pac. Rep. 257 (11 Am. Neg. Cas. 570n). Those in charge of the train seem to have done all they could to avert the accident. Probably nothing more would have served any useful purpose.

Counsel for defendant in error insist that the carelessness of the father, who was driving the horses, cannot be imputed to the daughter, who was riding by his side. This is an immaterial consideration, however, when it is found that the railway company was guilty of no act of negligence toward the occupants of the wagon.

The judgment of the court below will be reversed, with directions to enter judgment on the findings of the jury in favor of the defendant below. All the justices concurring.

GRAY v. ST. PAUL CITY RAILWAY COMPANY.

Supreme Court, Minnesota, October, 1902.

CHILD OF TENDER YEARS STRUCK BY STREET CAR AT STREET CROSSING — DUTY OF MOTORMAN — ORDINANCE. — 1. Where street-railway tracks occupy a street at the foot of an incline which, in conjunction with other streets, forms a system of crossings in a populous part of the city, it is the duty of the motorman in charge of a car coming down the grade to keep a lookout for young children approaching the crossings or standing near the tracks, and to take reasonable precaution to prevent injury to them, by sounding the gong, checking the speed of the train, and holding it under control (1).

2. A certain ordinance reads as follows: " No person having the control of the speed of a street-railway car passing in a street shall, on the appearance of any obstruction to his car, fail to stop the car in the shortest time and space possible." *Held*, this ordinance is not unreasonable, in that it requires the stopping of the car without regard to the safety of the train and the persons therein. It is no more than a declaration of the law, and only requires the person in charge of the car, upon the appearance of an obstruction, to stop the car as soon as possible under the circumstances, with due regard for the safety of the passengers.

3. Other assignments of error considered, and *held* to be not well taken.

(Syllabus by the Court.)

APPEAL from District Court, Ramsey County.

Action by Henry M. Gray, as administrator of the estate of Charles H. Gray, deceased, against the St. Paul City Railway Company. Verdict for plaintiff for $2,750. From an order denying a motion for a new trial, defendant appeals. *Order affirmed.*

1. *Accidents to children at crossings, etc.* — For actions arising out of accidents to children on track or at street crossings, etc., from the earliest period to 1897, see vols. 11 and 12 Am. Neg. Cas., where the same are chronologically grouped and arranged in alphabetical order of States. Subsequent actions to date are reported in vols. 1–12 AM. NEG. REP., and the current numbers of that series of Reports.

MUNN & THYGESON, for appellant.

S. P. CROSBY and CHAS. N. DOHS, for respondent.

LEWIS, J. — At the foot of Oakland avenue, in the city of St. Paul, Ramsey street, Oakland avenue, Pleasant avenue, and Garfield street cross each other; and Oakland avenue runs up a steep incline, on a grade of 3.66 feet per 100, and is occupied by defendant's street railway system, consisting of double tracks, and at the foot of the grade the tracks turn upon a curve in Ramsey street. The crossings are in a populous part of the city, and in frequent use. On the 19th day of January, 1901, at about three o'clock in the afternoon, Charles H. Gray, an infant, five years and nine months of age, was struck by one of defendant's cars at or near the crossing on the south side of Ramsey street at its intersection with Garfield street, and received injuries from which he died. This action is brought by the administrator to recover damages for the boy's death. At the trial below, plaintiff recovered a verdict of $2,750. Defendant appealed.

First. Was there any evidence reasonably tending to show that defendant was guilty of negligence? Second. Was error committed by the court in giving certain instructions to the jury? Third. Was a certain ordinance of the city admissible in evidence? Fourth. Did the court err in permitting testimony to be received as to the distance the car ran after the accident?

1. The charge of negligence against the defendant is as follows: The deceased, in company with a little girl about nine years of age, had left his home, on the north side of Ramsey street, in order to go to a store on the other side of the street-car tracks; and as the children approached the tracks the motorman of the car coming down the Oakland avenue grade could have seen the children, and should have anticipated that they would either attempt to cross the tracks ahead of the car, or that they would be in such close proximity as to be in danger, and that under such circumstances it was the duty of the motorman to have had his car under control, and checked its speed. That the car came down the hill at a rapid rate, and crossed Garfield street without giving any signal, and in consequence the boy was struck. According to the testimony of the little girl, Eleanor Lynch, she and the little boy came down the sidewalk on the north side of Oakland avenue, skipping along until they reached the curb, and then, hand in hand, walked toward the car tracks to cross the street. That she saw a west-bound car going up the hill, and that they walked on until they came upon the north track, and reached that point just as the fender of the front car of the east-bound train passed them, and she told the little boy to look

out for the car; but he, excited over a runaway which had occurred on Ramsey street, pulled his hand away from her and ran toward the passing train, and was struck by the platform of the second car. Another witness, who was in the front car of the train, testified that as the car approached the crossing she looked out over her shoulder, and noticed the children running in the street toward the car, and that they stopped on the north track just as she passed them. Several witnesses testified to the speed at which the car was running; some saying it was running rapidly; one stating that it was going as fast as a horse would ordinarily trot; and several witnesses testified that they heard no gong ring at that crossing, although they were in positions to hear it. Witnesses testified that the car did not stop at Garfield street, but finally stopped at a distance of from 120 to 160 feet east of the place where the boy was struck. Other witnesses testified that the car stopped at Garfield street to take on a passenger, and that it was running slowly when it struck the boy. The vision of the motorman as the car came down the incline was unobstructed, and the children might have been seen, not only as they walked along Oakland avenue, but as they approached the tracks upon the crossing. The motorman testified that he saw some children upon the north side of Oakland avenue, as he was going down the grade, but that he did not look to the left as he approached the crossing, and did not know whether the children he saw were this little boy and girl. In view of this testimony, we think it was a question of fact, for the jury to pass upon, whether or not, under the circumstances, the persons in charge of the car were in the exercise of such care as should be exercised at a crossing of that character under such circumstances. If it was true that the train came down the grade at a rapid rate, and crossed Garfield avenue without giving any signals or slowing up, and the motorman did not look to see whether any persons were approaching the crossing at that point, then we think the jury were justified in holding the defendant guilty of negligence. In the decision of this case we assume that there was no contributory negligence on the part of deceased, or the little girl in charge of him, or of the parents. The boy was *non sui juris*, and that question is eliminated by concessions of defendant. It can make no difference that the front part of the car had passed the children, and that the boy came in contact with the second part or rear of the train, for the evidence tended to show that they were either standing in close proximity to the cars at the time the motorman passed them, or that they were approaching it with the intent of crossing the track, either upon a walk or running. It was for the jury to say whether it was reasonably to be apprehended that such young children might run into or come in collision with the car as it was passing. In Strutzel *v.* Railway Co., 47 Minn. 543, 50 N. W. Rep. 690, the children were unlawfully crossing the street; but certainly no less degree of care would be required from the railway company in a case where an injured person was lawfully possessed of the street.

2. In the course of the court's charge the following language was used: "But on the other hand, you are instructed that it is the duty of the motorman to keep a reasonable lookout for children or others that may be not only on, but in a dangerous proximity to, the tracks, in the operation of its cars on the streets; and if you find from all the evidence that the motorman in this case, in the exercise of reasonable diligence and care, should have seen the child or children sufficiently near the track to have caused a man of reasonable prudence to believe that the child might be injured, * * * then it was the duty of such motorman to have so operated said car as to prevent the injury, or such threatened injury, if the same could have been prevented by the exercise of reasonable care." Exception is taken to this part of the charge upon the ground that it assumes the children were standing upon the track, or so dangerously near to it that the motorman should have discovered them. The first part of the charge states the proposition in the abstract, but we do not think the remainder of the charge is susceptible of the criticism made. It does not merely assume that the children were standing in a dangerous place, but its more natural import is that if the children were in a dangerous position, and the motorman could have seen them by the mere exercise of reasonable care, then it was his duty to use reasonable diligence in preventing an injury. However, if the language of the court was susceptible of the meaning put upon it by defendant, and likely to mislead the jury, it was the duty of counsel to call the court's attention to it at the time.

3. Ordinance No. 893 of the city of St. Paul was introduced in evidence against defendant's objection. The ordinance reads as follows: "No person having the control of the speed of a street-railway car passing in a street shall, on the appearance of any obstruction to his car, fail to stop the car in the shortest time and space possible." The objection is that the ordinance is unreasonable, in that it requires the person in charge of a street car to stop it under all circumstances, without regard to the safety of the train or persons therein. This ordinance, when given a reasonable construction, is no more than a declaration of the law, and its meaning is very evident. No more is required than that the person in charge of a train shall, upon the appearance of any obstruction, stop his

car as soon as possible under the circumstances, with due regard for the safety of the passengers.

4. A witness was permitted to testify that the car ran a certain distance after the accident. This was proper as bearing upon the general conduct and control of the train as it came down the hill and passed the crossing, even though the motorman made no effort to stop the car until signaled to do so by the conductor, for the bearing it might have upon whether the train stopped at the Garfield street crossing, and whether the motorman slowed up, or kept a proper lookout for persons approaching the crossings.

5. While the amount of damages, as found by the jury, would seem to be somewhat large, considering the age of the child, yet we are not disposed to disturb it, since it appears from the record that this is the second trial of this action, and that two juries have returned the same verdict. A verdict for a greater amount was sustained in O'Malley *v.* Railway Co., 43 Minn. 289, 45 N. W. Rep. 440.

Order affirmed.

DENNIS v. NEW ORLEANS AND NORTH-EASTERN RAILROAD COMPANY.

Supreme Court, Mississippi, November, 1902.

CHILD RUN OVER AND KILLED BY ENGINE AT CROSSING — EVIDENCE — QUESTION FOR JURY. — Where a child of tender years was struck and killed by an engine while crossing defendant's track at a highway crossing, it was held that on the evidence, the case should have gone to the jury, and judgment on peremptory instruction to find for defendant was reversed.

APPEAL from Circuit Court, Lauderdale County.

Action by Monroe Dennis against the New Orleans & Northeastern Railroad Company. From a judgment for defendant, plaintiff appeals. *Judgment reversed.*

"Appellant brought this suit against appellee to recover damages for the alleged negligent killing of his little girl, about three and one-half years old. The child was injured on the 25th of October, 1900, and died from the injuries the next day. The court gave a peremptory instruction to find for the defendant. From a verdict and judgment for defendant, plaintiff appeals. The evidence was, in substance, as follows: The little child was going north on a public road that crossed the railroad tracks, and just as she was about to reach the north side of the tracks she was struck on the head by the steps of the tender, and injured. The evidence shows that the tracks of the defendant and also the tracks of the Alabama & Vicksburg Railway Company run east and west parallel with and very near each other. They cross a highway, where the injury occurred, running north and south at right angles. The track of defendant is south of the Alabama & Vicksburg track, and the child was approaching the crossing from the south. The child was struck by a loose engine that was being run by the servants of and was owned by the defendant company. Situated south of these railroads, and facing east, was the store and residence of plaintiff. The north corner of the store is forty-five feet from the track of appellee, and about sixty feet from the Alabama & Vicksburg track. There was a plank fence running south from the tracks on the west side of the public road to plaintiff's store. This fence was about five feet high, with openings of several inches between the several planks. The highway was much frequented, the crossing being just outside the city limits of Meridian, and there were nine dwelling houses just north of the crossing. The tracks west of the crossing were straight for 300 or 400 yards. The engine was approaching from the west, and there was a slight up grade from that direction, and there was nothing to obstruct the view of a person approaching the crossing from the west except the plank fence and an artificial embankment about three feet high; and nothing else to prevent one seeing persons approaching the crossing from the south in the highway, the direction in which the child was going, until the store, sixty feet away, was reached. The engine was backing east, running, according to the plaintiff's evidence, at the rate of twenty five miles an hour. The defendant's witnesses say eight or ten miles per hour. Plaintiff's witness stated that no whistle was blown, and that the bell was not rung; but this is contradicted by witnesses for the defense. One witness for plaintiff testified that the child ran along the highway toward the crossing for about sixty feet, and did not stop until struck by the engine. Two witnesses for appellant testified that they stood at a distance of 180 and 150 yards west of the crossing, and could see a child about the size of the child killed while it was running along the highway south of the tracks for forty or fifty feet. A witness for plaintiff testified that he had been a fireman on defendant's road for a number of years, and that an engine running at the rate of ten miles an hour could have been stopped at from thirty to forty feet. The engineer and fireman on the engine testified that they saw the child when the engine was 150 to 200 feet from the crossing, and immediately did all they could to stop the engine; the engineer testifying that he immediately reversed the engine, and put on more steam, and blew the whistle, and that the bell was ringing. It was also shown by plaintiff that the child was dressed in white, with red ribbons on the dress, and that the accident occurred at about three or four o'clock in the afternoon."

NEVILLE & WILBOURN, for appellant.

WOODS, FEWELL & FEWELL, for appellee.

WHITFIELD, CH. J. — The case should have gone to the jury. Reversed and remanded.

CONNOR v. METROPOLITAN STREET RAILWAY COMPANY.

Supreme Court, New York, Appellate Division, First Department, December, 1902.

BOY INJURED IN COLLISION BETWEEN STREET CAR AND VEHICLE — NEGLIGENCE OF MOTORMAN — ERRONEOUS INSTRUCTION — QUESTION FOR JURY. — In an action to recover damages for injuries sustained by plaintiff, a boy about fourteen years of age, by reason of a collision between a street car and a truck on the rear of which latter vehicle he was riding, it was error to charge that if the jury found certain facts then the motorman was negligent as matter of law, as it was for the jury to determine whether or not such facts constituted negligence, taking into consideration all facts and circumstances surrounding the collision.

PRACTICE — EXCEPTIONS TO CHARGE TO JURY. — A party excepting to a charge to a jury must by some exception point to the specific proposition which the court has charged or refused to charge, or to a specific ruling on a refusal to charge to which counsel supposed himself entitled. Where several requests are made, some of which are charged and some refused, the attention of the court must be called to the ruling refusing a specific request by an exception taken to that ruling; an exception generally to the refusal of the court to charge as requested is not sufficiently specific (1).

O'BRIEN, J., *dissented.*

APPEAL by Metropolitan Street Railway Company from a judgment entered on verdict for plaintiff, Raymond Connor, by Guardian,

1. The cases of MCKINLEY v. METROPOLITAN STREET R'Y CO., *(N. Y. Sup. Ct., App. Div., First Dept., December, 1902)* and BENEDICT v. DESHEL *(N. Y. Sup. Ct., App. Div., First Dept., December, 1902)*, appear to have been handed down at the same time as the case at bar, in which the rule as to exceptions to charge to jury was discussed.

etc., and from an order denying a motion for a new trial. *Judgment reversed.*

Argued before VAN BRUNT, P. J., MORGAN, J., O'BRIEN, INGRAHAM, MCLAUGHLIN and HATCH, JJ.

CHARLES F. BROWN, for appellant.

I. NEWTON WILLIAMS, for respondent.

MCLAUGHLIN, J. — This action was brought to recover damages for personal injuries alleged to have been caused by defendant's negligence.

The plaintiff, on the 4th of August, 1899, then about fourteen years of age, was injured by a collision between one of defendant's cars and a truck on which he was riding. The testimony on the part of the plaintiff, so far as it relates to the collision, tended to show that the plaintiff sat on the rear of the truck, which was going in a northerly direction on defendant's tracks, and while in this position, one of the defendant's cars came up behind and collided with it; and before he had any chance to escape and without any fault on his part, he sustained the injuries complained of. The testimony on the part of the defendant tended to show that as the car came up behind the truck the motorman of the car signaled for the driver of the truck to leave the tracks, and in obedience thereto he did commence to leave the tracks; that while in the act of doing so the horse attached to the truck, or else the truck itself, came into collision with one of defendant's south-bound cars, and by reason thereof the truck was forced back against and came in collision with the northbound car, and thus the plaintiff was injured. It matters little which contention be taken as the true one, it is quite clear a question of fact was presented as to defendant's negligence, as well as the contributory negligence of the plaintiff, and we should have no hesitancy in affirming the judgment were it not for an error in the charge. The trial court, at plaintiff's request, charged the jury: "If the north-bound motorman, by the exercise of reasonable care, could or should have seen that there was danger of a collision between the south-bound car and the van, and yet kept his car up to within a few feet of the van, so that the van was driven back into his car, then he was negligent." The defendant excepted to the instruction thus given, and we think the exception well taken.

If the jury found that the facts stated in the request were established by the evidence, then it was for them to say whether or not such facts constituted negligence on the part of the motorman — taking into consideration all of the facts and circumstances surrounding the collision. It was error for the court to charge, as matter of law, that if they found such facts, that then the motorman was negligent. Kellegher *v.* Forty-second St. R'y, 171 N. Y. 309. It would seem as though the motorman would have a right to assume, when the driver of the truck started to leave the tracks, that he would do so in such a way as not to collide with one of the defendant's cars going in an opposite direction. This would certainly be the natural inference and one which a reasonably prudent man would have the right to make; and the fact that he acted upon this assumption, by bringing his car close to the truck, so that he might proceed with it as soon as the truck had left the tracks, did not make him negligent *per se.* At most, it was for the jury to say whether or not his act was a negligent one. That the defendant was prejudiced by this instruction was sufficiently evidenced by the verdict rendered.

For the error thus committed, the judgment and order must be reversed and a new trial ordered, with costs to the appellant to abide the event.

VAN BRUNT, P. J. and HATCH, J., concur.

INGRAHAM, J. — I concur with Mr. Justice McLaughlin, and only wish to call attention to the exception necessary to justify a review of the charge to the jury. In this case, after the charge was finished, the court said that he had been requested by the defendant to charge certain propositions which he charged, and "on behalf of the plaintiff I will charge the requests one, two, three, four, five, six, seven, eight, nine, ten, eleven, twelve, thirteen, and fourteen. Fifteenth, sixteenth, and seventeenth I decline to charge, to which you are entitled to an exception." The requests that the court charged are then stated in the record, which included the tenth request. Counsel for the defendant then, after excepting to specific portions of the charge, said: "I except to your Honor's charging the following requests to charge made by the plaintiff — first, second, third, fourth, fifth, sixth, seventh, eighth, ninth, tenth, eleventh, twelfth, and thirteenth and fourteenth." Here the court specifically charged the tenth request made by the plaintiff, and the defendant specifically excepted to the charge of that request.

By section 995 of the Code of Civil Procedure it is provided that an exception must be taken at the time when the ruling is made, unless it is taken to the charge given to the jury in which case it must be taken before the jury have rendered their verdict. This exception comes within the last clause of this section, as it was an exception taken to the charge of the court to the jury, and upon the record it appears to have been taken before the jury had rendered their verdict. It was taken to a specific charge made at the request of the plaintiff, and the exception specified the particular request that the court had charged to which the defendant excepted. It is undoubtedly the rule that to entitle a defeated party to review a proposition contained in a charge to the jury, there must be a specific exception to the charge so that the attention of the court is directed to the express proposition to which counsel desires to except; or where there is a refusal to charge a request, there must be a specific exception to the ruling of the court refusing to charge the specific request. A general exception to the charge without specifying the particular proposition to which it is desired to except manifestly raises no question upon a review of the judgment; nor where several requests to charge have been presented, to some of which the court has acceded and to others refused, does a general exception to the refusal to charge as requested present a question for review. Such an exception is too general. In Smedis *v.* Brooklyn & Rockaway Beach R. R. Co., 88 N. Y. 14, at the close of the evidence counsel for the defendant presented to the court fifteen separate requests to charge. The court charged substantially as requested, and then at the close of the charge, declined to charge except as already charged; to which refusal as to each of such requests the defendant's counsel then and there excepted. The court said: "We think, for the reason stated, that the court properly disposed of the questions raised by these requests to charge. But if the court erred in refusing to charge one or more of the propositions as requested, there is no sufficient exception to such refusal. It is well settled that where several requests to charge are submitted to the court, some of which are charged as requested, some charged in a modified form, and others not charged, an exception taken in the form in which it appears in this case cannot be sustained. The exception must be more specific and point out the particular request to which it is intended to apply."

In Newall *v.* Bartlett, 114 N. Y. 399, it appeared that at the close of the evidence the defendant's counsel presented to the court eight requests to charge the jury. Without making any ruling upon these requests the court proceeded to deliver his charge. At its close the defendant's counsel requested the court to charge upon two additional requests, which the court charged. The counsel then excepted to one instruction embodied in the charge as delivered. The case then shows that the court refused to charge the defendant's requests except as already charged, and the defendant's counsel took an exception to the refusal to charge as to each and every one of said requests. The court say: "It does not appear which of the requests had been charged, and consequently we are not advised as to which of the requests the exceptions apply. To raise any question upon the ruling of the trial court for review in this court, the exception must be specific and point out the particular request to which it is intended to apply."

In Read *v.* Nichols, 118 N. Y. 224, it appeared that at the close of the evidence the counsel for the plaintiff presented to the court thirteen separate requests to charge. Some were charged as requested, some were charged in a modified form, and others refused. At the close of the charge counsel stated that he excepted to the refusal to charge as requested by plaintiff's counsel in so far as the court did refuse, and to each of the refusals to charge as requested. It was held that this exception was not sufficiently definite and specific to present a question for review. In Huerzeller *v.* Central Crosstown R. R. Co., 139 N. Y. 490, it appeared that at the close of the evidence the trial court charged the jury, and there were many requests by both sides to charge, some of which were granted and some refused. After the charge was finished and the jury had retired, counsel for the defendant excepted to the granting of the requests on the other side, and a refusal to charge those of the defendant's counsel. There was no other exception to the charge or refusal to charge, and it was said: "It is conceded by the learned counsel for the defendant that this general exception was wholly insufficient to present any question for review in this court; and so we have uniformly held" (citing the cases to which attention has been called). To the same effect is Piper *v.* N. Y. C. & H. R. R. Co., 89 Hun, 75. This last case was reversed by the Court of Appeals (156 N. Y. 22), but that reversal was upon the ground that the plaintiff was guilty of contributory negligence, and for that reason it was held that the complaint should have been dismissed.

The rule to be adduced from these cases requires that a party excepting to a charge to a jury must by some exception point to the specific proposition which the court has charged or refused to charge, or to a specific ruling on a refusal to charge to which counsel supposed himself entitled. Where several requests are made, some of which are charged and some refused, the attention of the court must be called to the ruling refusing a specific request by an exception taken to that ruling; an exception generally to the refusal of the court to charge as requested is not sufficiently specific. In McKinley *v.* Met. St. R'y Co., decided herewith, after the requests to charge had been presented on both sides, they were ruled upon separately, and when counsel for the defendant asked the court, "And now with respect to exceptions to those portions of your honor's charge," the court, interrupting, said: "You may take them after the jury have retired; either side may do that." After the jury retired, counsel for the defendant said, "Your Honor will allow me an exception in due form to each request which is refused and to each request which is modified," to which the court answered, "Yes;" and we hold that this request was so general, if simply taken and entered upon the record without the acquiescence of the court, it might be unavailing; but that the court having interrupted counsel when about to take specific exceptions, subsequently gave him an exception to the refusal of the court to charge his requests, that method being acceptable to the court and entered in the record as such, it was sufficient to raise the question as to the right of the defendant to have his specific requests charged which the court had refused to charge. We wish to call attention to this rule, that to entitle counsel to review a charge as actually made, there must be a specific exception to the portion of the charge which is claimed as error sufficiently definite to call the attention of the trial judge to the specific portion of the charge excepted to, and that where it is sought to review the refusal of the court to charge a request, there must be a specific exception to the refusal to charge the particular request; that a general exception to the refusal to charge as requested by the party taking the exception does not present a question for review on appeal, unless the court directs such course to be pursued and authorizes the entry of the exception to be made in that form.

HATCH, J., concurs.

O'BRIEN, J. (dissenting). — I am unable to concur in the conclusion reached by the majority of the court in this case because, under the authorities, I think the exception upon which the case is reversed is not properly before us for consideration, and, therefore, is not available. At the conclusion of the charge to the jury, some seventeen requests were presented by the plaintiff, and the trial judge stated those which he would charge and the numbers of those he declined to charge, these latter not appearing in the record. The defendant then made certain requests and, finally, just before the case went to the jury, the defendant's counsel said: "I except to your Honor's charging the following requests to charge made by the plaintiff — First, second, * * * tenth, eleventh," etc. In this way only was any exception taken to the tenth charge, which is the one in question. In Passey *v.* Craighead, 89 Hun, 76, the court said: "At the close of the charge the defendant presented to the court twenty-eight requests, some of which were charged and some refused. The defendant excepted to each of the charges made by the court at the request of the plaintiff and to each qualification of those requests and to each refusal to charge either of the propositions requested by the defendant to be charged. These exceptions are wholly insufficient to present any question for review." And in the opinion written by Mr. Justice McLaughlin, in Benedict *v.* Deshel, herewith handed down, it was held that where a number of requests were made by the plaintiff and refused by the court, and the plaintiff's counsel said: "I except to each of your Honor's refusal to charge my several requests," the exception was not so taken as to present any question for review. The only difference between the form of the exception in that case and the case at bar is that here the numbers of the request were mentioned; but this did not point out any particular misstatement so as to afford the trial court the opportunity to correct any error, and it is the failure to so specify the objection made to the refusal that constitutes the vice in such exceptions.

I think, therefore, that the judgment appealed from should be affirmed, with costs.

GUBBITOSI v. ROTHSCHILD ET AL.

Supreme Court, New York, Appellate Division, First Department, November, 1902.

NEGLIGENT KILLING OF INFANT — INADEQUATE DAMAGES. — In an action to recover damages for the negligent killing of plaintiff's son, a child about six years of age, the jury awarded plaintiff $200 which, upon motion of plaintiff, the trial court set aside as inadequate. *Held*, that the trial court was not justified in setting verdict aside as inadequate.

Following Terhune *v.* Contracting Co., 72 App. Div. 1.

APPEAL from Trial Term, New York County.

Action by George Gubbitosi, as administrator of the estate of James Gubbitosi, deceased, against Isaac Rothschild and another. From an order setting aside a verdict as inadequate (74 N. Y. Supp. 775), defendants appeal. *Order reversed.*

Argued before VAN BRUNT, P. J., and HATCH, PATTERSON, INGRAHAM, and LAUGHLIN, JJ.

CARL SCHURZ PETRASCH, for appellants.

LOUIS OPPENHEIM, for respondents.

INGRAHAM, J. — The action was brought to recover damages for the negligent killing of the plaintiff's son, a boy not quite six years of age. The jury awarded the plaintiff $200, when, upon motion of the plaintiff, the court set aside this verdict and directed a new trial upon the ground that amount allowed was inadequate. No other error is alleged which would justify the court in setting aside this verdict. We have lately held, in the case of Terhune *v.* Contracting Co., 72 App. Div. 1, 76 N. Y. Supp. 255, that in an action of this character, where the jury are required to ascertain the pecuniary injury caused to the next of kin by the death of the decedent, and the verdict is limited to such a sum as the jury deem to be fair and just compensation for such pecuniary injuries to the person or persons for whose benefit the action is brought, the court is unable to say that in the case of the killing of a young child the death of the child had caused pecuniary loss to the child's parents, and that, where a substantial amount has been awarded, the trial court is not justified in setting aside the verdict on the ground that it is inadequate.

It follows that the order appealed from must be reversed, and the motion for a new trial denied, but, under the circumstances, without costs. All concur; LAUGHLIN, J., in result.

PHELPS ET UX v. WINDSOR STEAMBOAT COMPANY ET AL.

Supreme Court, North Carolina, September, 1902.

PASSENGER ON STEAMBOAT INJURED — NEGLIGENCE OF LESSEE OF BOAT — LIABILITY OF LESSOR. — In an action by a passenger on a steamboat for damages for injuries sustained by the capsizing of the boat, it was *held*, that the lessor of a steamboat which has received no special privileges or benefits from the State, and was a private corporation, was not liable for the negligence of the lessee.

APPEAL from Superior Court, Bertie County.

Action by J. T. Phelps and wife against the Windsor Steamboat Company and another. From judgment dismissing the action as to defendant Elizabeth Branning, administratrix, plaintiffs appeal. *Judgment affirmed.*

ST. LEON SCULL for appellants.

PRUDEN & PRUDEN and SHEPHERD & SHEPHERD, for appellee.

CLARK, J. — This is an action against the defendant steamboat company, alleging that, while plaintiff was a passenger on one of its boats, by negligence in the loading and operation thereof the boat was capsized, and the plaintiff was thrown into the water and injured, and her baggage was also damaged. The plaintiff joins in the action the administratrix of one John W. Branning, upon the ground that said Branning was the owner of said vessel, and had leased it to the said steamboat company. It does not appear, nor is it alleged, that he had any connection with the operation of said vessel by the other defendant.

His Honor properly dismissed the action as to Branning upon the ground that no cause of action is stated against him. In Harden *v.* Railroad Co., 129 N. C. 354, 40 S. E. Rep. 184, and the cases there cited, from Aycock *v.* Railroad Co., 89 N. C. 321, down to and inclusive of Perry *v.* Railroad Co., 129 N. C. 333, 40 S. E. Rep. 191, and City of Raleigh *v.* North Carolina R. Co., 129 N. C. 265, 40 S. E. Rep. 2 (affirmed since in Smith *v.* Railroad Co., 130 N. C. 344, 42 S. E. Rep. 139), the lessor is held liable, notwithstanding the lease, because a railroad company (the lessor in those cases) was a *quasi*-public corporation, enjoying the use of the right of eminent domain to take private property by condemnation for its right of way "because it is for a public use," and with many other special privileges and rights conferred for the public benefit, and it could not be allowed, by merely making a lease, to put off all liability for the manner in which its duties are discharged, while receiving the full benefit for valuable privileges conferred upon it in the shape of rental. This can only be done, as the authorities cited in those cases show, when the legislative power, having had opportunity to look into the solvency of the lessee, has not only authorized the lease, but has expressly released the lessor company from further responsibility. Logan *v.* Railroad Co., 116 N. C. 940, 21 S. E. Rep. 959; Anderson *v.* Railroad Co. (Mo.), 20 Am. & Eng. R. Cas. Ann., at pages 847, 848 (s. c., 61 S. W. Rep. 874); and numerous other cases cited in Harden *v.* Railroad Co., *supra.* Were it otherwise, an insolvent lessee could operate the railroad without responsibility to the public or to employees, leaving the lessor, the original corporation, to enjoy the profits of its privileges without any corresponding responsibility in return. But nothing in those cases, nor in the reason of the thing, applies to the lessor of a steamboat which has received no special privileges or benefits of great value from the State, and who indeed in this instance was a private individual. No liability attaches to said Branning because he was president of said company, unless it was alleged and shown that the lease was collusive and colorable only, and a sham to avoid personal liability, and that he had in fact leased his own property to himself. But there is no such averment, and in dismissing the action as against his estate, there was no error.

COOK, J., concurs in the conclusion.

PENGILLY v. J. I. CASE THRESHING MACHINE COMPANY.

Supreme Court, North Dakota, May, 1902.

PERSON ASSISTING EMPLOYEE OF ANOTHER INJURED WHILE UNLOADING MACHINERY — PRACTICE — NEW TRIAL — EVIDENCE — APPEAL. — 1. Where an application to the District Court for a new trial is based upon newly-discovered evidence, and also upon the ground that the evidence adduced at the trial is insufficient to justify the verdict, the same is addressed to the sound judicial discretion of the trial court. In such cases the trial court will weigh the evidence, and its decision of the application cannot be governed by any fixed rules of law. Such discretion, however, is not a personal discretion of the judge, to be exercised capriciously or arbitrarily, but is a sound legal discretion.

2. On appeal from an order made in such cases the order will be affirmed unless it appears that there was an abuse of discretion in making the same, and in such cases the reviewing court will consider and weigh the evidence only so far as may be necessary to determine the question whether the trial court acted within its discretion.

3. An order granting a new trial is in such cases rarely reversed, and then only upon grounds which are strong and convincing. Courts discriminate in favor of such orders because the same are not final, but are such as require a retrial of the facts and merits.

4. Applying the rules of law as above stated, it is *held* in this case that the order of the District Court granting a new trial must be affirmed.

(Syllabus by the Court.)

APPEAL from District Court, Walsh County.

Action by Reuben Pengilly against the J. I. Case Threshing Machine Company. Verdict for defendant. From an order granting a new trial, it appeals. *Order affirmed.*

TURNER & LEE, for appellant.

H. A. LIBBY and COCHRANE & CORLISS, for respondent.

WALLIN, Ch. J. — This action was brought to recover damages for a personal injury which plaintiff received while unloading a threshing engine from a flat car at Park River, N. D. The defendant is a manufacturer of such engines, and has an agency at Park River, at which the defendant's engines are kept for sale; and at the time in question one J. T. Smith was in charge of the agency, and was in the defendant's employ, and as such employee Smith had the supervision of the matter of unloading the engine in question. It appears that plaintiff had, previous to the arrival of the engine at Park River, ordered this or a similar engine of the defendant, and, when the engine reached Park River, Smith notified the plaintiff of the fact, and requested him to assist in unloading the same from the flat car. Plaintiff, upon such notice, and to expedite the delivery of the engine, did assist in unloading the engine, and in doing so was injured; and plaintiff alleges in his complaint that his injuries resulted from the negligence of Smith while acting as the agent of the defendant, in unloading the engine. At the close of the testimony, and at defendant's request, special findings, eight in number, were submitted to the jury by the trial court, and all of said findings were found for the plaintiff except the seventh, which was found for the defendant, and which is as follows: "Was the plaintiff, Pengilly, guilty of any want of ordinary care which contributed proximately to his injury?" The plaintiff moved, upon the minutes of the court and upon affidavits, to set aside the special verdict for a new trial of the action. The affidavits embraced evidence alleged to be newly discovered, and relating to the matter of the contributory negligence of the plaintiff. The grounds of the motion, as stated in the notice of intention, are as follows: "1. Newly-discovered evidence material to the plaintiff, and which he could not with reasonable diligence have discovered and produced at the trial. 2. Insufficiency of the evidence to justify said verdict, in that there was no evidence whatever of any negligence or carelessness on the part of the plaintiff at the time of his injury, and that such question was not in issue upon the trial." The motion was granted by an order of the District Court. The defendant has appealed from such order, and error is assigned upon it in this court.

It will be noticed that the plaintiff, in moving to vacate the verdict and for a new trial, is assailing the seventh finding of the jury, and that only. The notice of intention, by its terms, attacks the seventh finding upon two grounds, viz.: First, that there is no evidence whatever that the plaintiff, by his own negligence, contributed to the injury of which he complains; and, second, that the question of plaintiff's contributory negligence "was not in issue upon the trial." We will consider these questions in their inverse order. An inspection of the complaint shows that the plaintiff, in stating his cause of action, uses the following language: "The plaintiff further alleges that it was by or through no fault, negligence, or carelessness on his part that he met with and sustained such injury." The answer embraces a general denial of the allegations of the complaint, but contains no specific denial of the particular averment of the complaint above quoted. Upon this state of the pleadings it is contended by counsel for the plaintiff that the question of plaintiff's negligence was not involved in the controversy, and, as they argue, the jury, in finding upon that question, have introduced an issue which is extraneous, and as such should be disregarded by this court. This contention is sought to be supported by the argument that the averment in the complaint to the effect that plaintiff was free from negligence in the premises was superfluous, and hence that the same was not a material averment of fact, and therefore that the general denial contained in the answer did not raise any issue of fact upon the matter of plaintiff's contributory negligence. We agree with this contention of plaintiff's counsel in so far as they claim that it was unnecessary to insert in the complaint the averment which is above quoted. While there is a conflict of authority upon the question, the point has been settled in this State. See Gram *v.* Railroad Co., 1 N. D. 253, 46 N. W. Rep. 972. In this State the question of plaintiff's contributory negligence in this class of cases is a matter of defense, and the same forms no part of the plaintiff's case, and hence need not be referred to in the complaint. In this State, therefore, the insertion in the complaint of a statement that the plaintiff's negligence did not contribute to the injury is bad pleading in this: that it violates a well-settled rule of Code pleading forbidding the anticipation of defensive matter in a complaint. But in this case it becomes immaterial to inquire whether plaintiff's negligence was in issue under the pleadings as they were framed. Whether in issue or not, technically speaking, the issue of contributory negligence was submitted to the jury by the trial court as a matter of fact, and no objection was made to such submission. Nor does this record embrace an exception to the action of the trial court predicated upon the order submitting the question to the jury. Nor is there an exception or error assigned upon the admission of evidence relating to the matter of plaintiff's contributory negligence. Turning to the evidence relating to the matter of contributory negligence, we find in the record certain evidence offered at the trial, which, in our opinion, tended to establish the existence of contributory negligence; and it will be necessary to briefly refer to this evidence in disposing of the case. It appears that, as a means of unloading the engine, a structure was built upon an inclined plane leading from the ground to the end of the flat car. This structure, it is conceded, was properly built, and it is further conceded that Smith, who had charge of the work of unloading the engine, was a man who had previously had considerable experience in unloading such engines from flat cars. The plaintiff also had been handling threshing machines for several years prior to the accident. The engine, which was on wheels, was backed off the car, and Smith at all times had control of a certain lever called the "friction clutch lever," which worked as a brake, and by its use the speed of the descent of the engine down the incline was within Smith's control. Smith also had exclusive control of the steering appliance of the engine, whereby the wheels resting upon the car and upon the structure extended to the ground could be guided and turned either way. Smith's position was on the platform, where he could reach and control both the friction clutch lever or brake and the steering appliance. It seems that when the clutch lever or brake is set the engine would not move down the incline by the force of its weight alone, and that, in order to give it headway, it was necessary, or at least was deemed proper, to turn the fly wheel of the engine. At the time of the accident the plaintiff stood on top of one of the large wheels of the engine, called a traction or drive wheel, and was, when in that position, engaged in turning the fly wheel as a means of moving the engine down the incline leading to the ground. His testimony is to the effect that while so engaged the clutch lever or brake was suddenly and carelessly loosed by Smith, which act, he claims, resulted in a jerk of the engine, which threw the plaintiff off his balance, and caused him to swing his foot around between certain cogs, where it was injured. This is the only act of negligence charged. But while it is conceded that plaintiff did, as he claims, occupy a position on the drive or traction wheel when he was injured, and that he was then engaged in turning the fly wheel, there is a radical difference as between the witnesses upon the question whether the plaintiff was, when injured, in a proper position, and whether Smith knew, or should have known, where the plaintiff was standing at the time of the accident. Smith and one other witness testify, in substance that, while the engine was partly on the flat car and partly on the structure leading to the ground, he (Smith) had the wheels blocked so as to stop the movement of the engine, and then and there made an examination to see whether the engine was in a proper position on the platform to complete its journey to the ground with safety; and that upon such examination Smith found the conditions to be safe, and that the engine would under conditions then existing, reach the ground in safety. Smith and one other witness further testify that Smith, after making such examination, gave directions for the blocking to be removed from the wheels, and that all persons assisting him should thereafter keep away from the engine. The plaintiff testified that no such orders were at any time given by Smith. Smith further testified that, after giving the order to keep away from the engine, he at no time gave orders to plaintiff or any one else to approach the engine, or get upon any part of the same; and that he was unaware of the fact that plaintiff was standing upon the drive or traction wheel at the time he was hurt, and did not learn that fact until after the accident. The testimony of the defendant's witnesses is to the effect that under the then existing conditions the engine would have completed its descent in safety when controlled by the friction clutch lever, and that the turning of the fly wheel was unnecessary as a means of giving momentum to the engine down the incline. On the other hand, plaintiff testifies that he was, while engaged in turning the fly wheel, and when injured, acting in accordance with the orders of Smith so to do, and with Smith's knowledge and approval. Upon this evidence the jury found that the plaintiff's own negligence was the proximate cause of his injury, and, as we have said, the testimony, if believed, would perhaps warrant such finding. It is manifestly true that if the plaintiff, as defendant claims, unnecessarily, and after being told to keep away from the engine, mounted to the top of the drive wheel, and remained there while the engine was moving down the incline, he was in a place of some danger; and, further, that he was there of his own volition, and in disregard of orders to keep away. If the plaintiff was on the wheel unnecessarily, and against instructions, he would, in law, be deemed to have assnmed all the risks incident to the position he occupied; and when hurt in that position his injury, upon this theory of the evidence, must be attributed to his own want of ordinary care. The verdict, however, rested upon substantial evidence, and possibly the evidence preponderated in favor of the verdict.

But the motion for a new trial rested upon affidavits, as well as upon the evidence adduced at the trial. The plaintiff's affidavits were five in number, and two were submitted by the defendant. Plaintiff claims that the evidence as embodied in his affidavits is newly discovered, and that the same is now accessible, and would be produced at a second trial if such trial were granted. Plaintiff presents his own affidavit to show diligence, and as explanatory of the fact that the new evidence, as stated in his affidavits, was not offered at the trial. We think due diligence is fairly shown. A careful consideration of the plaintiff's affidavits discloses the fact that some of the newly-discovered evidence would, if offered, be inadmissible under the rules of evidence; but, on the other hand, some of the same would be admissible, and would be directly pertinent upon the issue of plaintiff's contributory negligence. But defendant's counsel claims that any evidence contained in plaintiff's affidavits which would be admissible at the trial, if offered, is cumulative in character, and hence cannot be considered, when presented as newly-discovered evidence, as a basis for an application for a new trial. This assumption of counsel rests upon the well-established general rule that evidence which is cumulative merely cannot, when newly discovered, furnish a ground for a new trial. But with respect to the general rule invoked by counsel it must be remembered that there is a recognized qualification of the same, which is as well supported by authority as the rule itself. The qualification or exception is this: Where the newly-discovered evidence, if cumulative, is of such a nature as to be decisive of the result, it will not be rejected as a ground of new trial merely because it can be classified technically as cumulative evidence. See Hart *v.* Brainerd, 68 Conn. 50, 35 Atl. Rep. 776; Keet *v.* Mason, 167 Mass. 154, 45 N. E. Rep. 81; Preston *v.* Otey, 88 Va. 491, 14 S. E. Rep. 68; Durant *v.* Philpot, 16 S. C. 116; Barker *v.* French, 18 Vt. 460; Anderson *v.* State, 43 Conn. 514; Kochel *v.* Bartlett, 88 Ind. 237; Cleslie *v.* Frerichs, 95 Iowa, 83, 63 N. W. Rep. 581; White *v.* Nafus, 84 Iowa, 350, 51 N. W. Rep. 5. But in this case some of the newly-discovered evidence consists of admissions made by Smith, the agent, long subsequent to the occasion of the accident, and of other admissions made by him at or about the moment when the accident occurred. The former class of admissions by defendant's agent we think would be inadmissible in evidence, and possibly the latter would be admissible as a part of the *res gestæ.* None of the admissions of Smith would be cumulative upon the matter of plaintiff's contributory negligence. But we have reached the conclusion that under the facts of this case it is not the province of this court upon an appeal from the order of the trial court granting a new trial to rule decisively either upon the weight of the newly-discovered evidence or to settle a somewhat dubious question as to whether some of such evidence falls within the rule or the exception to the rule relating to cumulative evidence. The order granting a new trial omits to state the grounds or reasons which operated upon the mind of the trial judge in making the order, and hence we are at liberty to consider all grounds upon which the application rested, and in doing so this court will take account of both the evidence offered at the trial and the newly-discovered evidence.

An examination of the grounds of the application for the order appealed from will at once develop the fact that the trial court, in disposing of the problem presented upon the application, was not governed by fixed rules of law, and in the nature of the case could not be governed by an inflexible rule of law. When motions of this nature are presented to a court, they are classified as motions addressed to the discretion of the court. In considering the evidence adduced or that newly discovered, no fixed rules of law exist which could be decisive of the result of the investigation. Under such circumstances a margin of discretion is vested in trial courts, which permits them, with a view to promoting the ends of justice, to weigh the evidence, and, within certain limitations, act upon their own judgment with reference to its weight and credibility. Nor, in such cases will the court necessarily be governed by the fact that the verdict returned has the support of an apparent preponderance of the evidence. Unrighteous verdicts sometimes are supported by apparently substantial evidence, and to meet such exceptional cases the presiding judge, who sees and hears the witnesses, is vested with a discretion to vacate such verdicts and order a new trial in furtherance of justice. The rule that governs a court of review in this class of motions — *i. e.*, those which appeal to judicial discussion — does not apply to trial courts, and hence the trial court is not debarred from granting or refusing a new trial by the mere fact that the verdict rests upon substantial or conflicting evidence. Hayne, New Trials, sec. 97. This discretion, however, is neither capricious, arbitrary, nor unrestricted. It is, on the contrary, a reasonable discretion, to be exercised with great caution, and in cases of abuse of action of the trial court will be reversed by the reviewing court in this class of cases. The duties devolving upon a court of review in this class of cases are to be distinguished from those which govern in trial courts. In the reviewing tribunal the weight and credibility of testimony will only be considered with a view to determine whether the order made in an inferior court, when acting within the domain of discretion, was or was not an abuse of discretion. See 14 Enc. Pl. & Prac. 930, 985, and cases in note 1; Taylor *v.* Architectural Co., 47 Mo. App. 257.

The rule applicable here is analogous to that applied where a new trial is sought on the grounds of improper remarks made by counsel to a jury; *i. e.*, the granting or refusing the application is within the discretion of the trial court. See Watson *v.* Railway Co., 42 Minn. 46, 43 N. W. Rep. 904, and Sunberg *v.* Babcock, 66 Iowa, 515, 24 N. W. Rep. 19. In the federal courts, as at common law, all motions for a new trial are addressed to the discretion of the trial court, and its ruling cannot be reversed. See 14 Enc. Pl. & Prac. 955. As to the application of this rule to newly-discovered evidence, see Id. 982, note 3, and Hayne, New Trials, p. 250. See also the South Dakota cases cited in Distad *v.* Shanklin, 75 N. W. Rep. 205. In the case at bar the order appealed from granted a new trial. Such orders, when based upon the insufficiency of the evidence, are rarely reversed by a reviewing court, and never except upon grounds which are strong and cogent. The reason for discriminating in favor of such orders is that they are not decisive of the case, but, on the contrary, only open the way for a reinvestigation of the entire case upon its facts and merits. See Patch *v.* Railway Co., 5 N. D. 55, 63 N. W. Rep. 207; Hicks *v.* Stone, 13 Minn. 434 (Gil. 398); Cowley *v.* Davidson, 13 Minn. 92 (Gil. 86); Morrison *v.* Mendenhall, 18 Minn. 236, 238 (Gil. 212); also 14 Enc. Pl. & Prac. 978, 987, and cases cited in note 1; also Id., p. 960.

Our conclusion is that the order appealed from should be sustained, and this court will so direct. All the judges concurring.

NEWMAN v. DELAWARE, LACKAWANNA AND WESTERN RAILROAD COMPANY.

Supreme Court, Pennsylvania, October, 1902.

COLLISION AT CROSSING — STOP, LOOK AND LISTEN — QUESTION FOR JURY. — In an action to recover damages for injuries sustained in a collision between plaintiff's vehicle and defendant's train at a grade crossing, where it appeared that plaintiff stopped to look and listen for an approaching train, at a place somewhat dangerous, and then drove on without again stopping, it was *held* that whether there was another safe and better place for plaintiff to stop, and whether he failed to observe the necessary precaution or carefulness after having once stopped, was a question for the jury, and not for the court (1).

1. *Stop, look and listen.* — See NOTES ON THE PENNSYLVANIA RULE OF STOP, LOOK AND LISTEN, in 12 Am. Neg. Cas. 569, 573.

See also NOTE ON THE RULE OF STOP, LOOK AND LISTEN, in 9 AM. NEG. REP. 408–416.

Accident at crossing — Contributory negligence — Question for jury. — In WOLCOTT *v.* NEW YORK & LONG BRANCH R. R. Co. et al. *(New Jersey Supreme Court, November, 1902)*, 53 Atl. Rep. 297, a crossing-accident case, the case is stated in the opinion by GUMMERE, Ch. J., as follows: "This suit was brought against the New York & Long Branch Railroad Company, the Central Railroad Company of New Jersey, the New Jersey Southern Railway Company, and the Pennsylvania Railroad Company, to recover damages for negligently causing the death of Paul Wolcott, the plaintiff's intestate. A nonsuit was granted in favor of the New Jersey Southern Railway Company at the close of the plaintiff's case. A verdict was directed in favor of the Central Railroad Company of New Jersey, and the question of the liability of the New York & Long Branch Railroad Company and of the Pennsylvania Railroad Company was submitted to the jury, who returned a verdict in favor of the latter company as against the plaintiff, and in favor of the plaintiff as against the New York & Long Branch Railroad Company. This rule was allowed to the Long Branch Company, and the two questions which it presents for decision are whether the evidence will support the conclusion reached by the jury that the death of

APPEAL from Court of Common Pleas, Luzerne County.

Action by Henry C. Newman against the Delaware, Lackawanna & Western Railroad Company. From an order refusing to take off a nonsuit, plaintiff appeals. *Judgment reversed.*

Argued before MCCOLLUM, Ch. J., and MITCHELL, DEAN, BROWN and MESTREZAT, JJ.

PAUL J. SHERWOOD, for appellant.

ANDREW H. MCCLINTOCK and HENRY W. PALMER (ARTHUR HILLMAN, on the brief), for appellee.

MESTREZAT, J. — About eight o'clock in the morning of February 17, 1898, Henry C. Newman, the plaintiff, was driving one horse, hitched to a buckboard, along a country highway in Lackawanna county, and approached a grade crossing of the defendant's double-track railroad. The general direction of the highway was north and south, and the plaintiff was driving south. An automatic electric signal bell stood on the left side or east side of the highway, and

the plaintiff's intestate was due to negligence of the company or of any of its employees, and, further, whether the deceased was not guilty of contributory negligence.

"On the first point the following facts are pertinent: At the crossing where the deceased was killed there are nine separate tracks, four of which are tracks of the Long Branch Company, and the remaining five tracks of the Jersey Southern. These tracks are not all parallel, those of the Jersey Southern diverging at a considerable angle from those of the Long Branch road. Although these tracks are owned by two different companies, they are all under the management and control of the New York and Long Branch Company. Approaching the tracks from the direction in which the deceased was driving, the Jersey Southern tracks are first reached, then a triangular piece of ground is encountered, lying between the two systems of tracks, and then the tracks of the New York & Long Branch road. The distance from the first track of the Southern road to the last track of the Long Branch road, measured along one side of the highway, is about eighty-two feet, and measured along the other side of the highway is 112 feet. A flagman was kept at this crossing by the New York & Long Branch company, to warn travelers along the highway of approaching trains. At the time of the accident this flagman had taken up his position in the triangular space already referred to. It was after dark, and he had his lantern in his hand. In just what part of the highway he stood was disputed. He testified that he was in the middle of the road; other witnesses say that he was on the south edge of it. After taking his position he watched for the approach of the train, which was one belonging to the Pennsylvania Railroad Company, and running over the New York & Long Branch Company tracks. He says that when he saw it appear he turned, and then saw the decedent's wagon approaching the crossing; that it was then opposite the electric-light plant, which was immediately adjacent to the first track of the Southern road, and that it (the wagon) was about to enter upon that track; that he swung his lantern and shouted a warning, but that the deceased continued on his way over the tracks until he reached the furthermost from fifteen to thirty feet north of the railroad. Painted upon the post of this signal appliance, in large letters, were the words: "Danger while the bell rings." The purpose of this bell was to give notice of a train approaching the crossing from either direction. If in working order, it began to ring when the locomotive was 2,000 feet from the crossing, and continued until the crossing was passed. The plaintiff stopped about sixty or seventy feet from the crossing, and looked and listened for a train. At this point he had an unobstructed view for a long distance to the west, but to the east, or his left, the view was obstructed by a hill which prevented him from seeing the train or engine going west on the west-bound track. The view of the railroad track to the east continues to be obstructed until the person approaching the crossing is within thirty or thirty-five feet of the crossing, and his horse is fifteen or twenty feet from the railroad. On the right or west side of the highway there is a

track of the Long Branch road, and was there run down by the train. The testimony of the decedent's wife, who was in the wagon with him, was to the effect that the lantern was not swung; that its light remained stationary.

"Whether or not a duty rested upon the Long Branch Company to protect this crossing by a flagman or not is immaterial. It assumed that duty, and, having done so, was bound to perform it with due care. Where the flagman stood, and whether he waved his lantern or not as a signal that a train was approaching, were matters in dispute. If he stood on the southern edge of the highway, not in the wagon way at all, as some of the witnesses say, and if he gave no signal with his lantern, as decedent's widow testifies, it cannot certainly be said, as matter of law, that he fully and carefully performed the duty which he had undertaken, of giving warning of the approaching train. It was for the jury to determine where he stood and what he did, and, if they found that he stood by the side of the road and gave no signal with his lantern, then to say whether he gave efficient warning to the deceased.

"Other facts, in addition to those which have been recited, enter into the consideration of the question whether the deceased was guilty of contributory negligence. The conditions which existed in the neighborhood of the crossing, on the side from which the deceased approached it, show that there was a view down the tracks of the Long Branch road, in the direction from which the train was coming, at a point 475 feet from the crossing, but that, as the distance decreased, the view was frequently interrupted by the presence of houses and other obstructions. The night was a dark one, and it does not appear that the deceased was familiar with the crossing. There were a number of electric and other lights in the neighborhood of the crossing which illumined the surroundings more or less. The evidence is in favor of the conclusion that a bell was rung on the train, but decedent's wife says she did not hear it.

"All of these facts, taken together, do not conclusively show contributory negligence on the part of the decedent. To what extent his view in the direction of the approaching train was impeded before he reached the electric-light plant is unimportant, for up to that time the train had not come in sight. This is shown by the testimony deep ravine, and on that side of the road, for about fifty feet north of the railroad, there is no fence or wall to prevent a frightened or unruly horse from backing a vehicle over the precipice. Under the testimony, the jury would have been warranted in finding that this was a dangerous place for a traveler to stop his team to listen for an approaching train. During the time the plaintiff's team was stopped, a coal train passed the crossing, going west. After it had gone a few hundred feet, and hearing no warning of an approaching train, Newman drove towards the crossing. When his horse was about fifteen or twenty feet from the west-bound track, and he and his wagon were opposite the signal bell, he again attempted to stop the horse; but being frightened by the shrill, loud whistle of a light passenger engine approaching from the east at a speed of from fifteen to eighteen miles an hour, the animal jumped to the right, toward the embankment, and, in the language of the plaintiff, "I pulled her back into the road, and she sprung right across the track, and when

of the defendant's flagman, who testified that after going upon the crossing he was "watching the train to come down the Long Branch north-bound track," and then said, "and when I saw it appearing, coming down, I turned, and I saw this wagon coming right opposite the electric-light plant." After reaching this building, his view down the track was intercepted by it until he had passed beyond it. Although the engine bell was ringing at that time it cannot certainly be said that he heard it; for his widow swears that she did not, and her opportunity for doing so was equally as good as his. After passing beyond the electric-light building, he almost immediately came to the first of the Southern Railway tracks. Assuming that he then saw the headlight of the approaching locomotive, what was he to do? Could he be at all certain that the train was not coming upon the very track he was then crossing? Was he less prudent in driving over it, and over the other tracks of the Southern road, than he would have been if he had remained on the first track until the train had passed, bearing in mind that there is nothing in the case to show that he was at all familiar with his surroundings? And, after he had crossed the Southern tracks and reached the triangular space, did he suppose that all danger had passed; that he had reached a place of safety, and could go on his way without further risk? Was he taken by surprise when he came to the tracks of the New York & Long Branch road, and, if so, was he less careful than a reasonably prudent man would have been in attempting to cross over them for the purpose of avoiding the train? All these and other questions present themselves in determining whether or not the deceased was guilty of contributory negligence. Their solution was clearly for the jury, not for the court, and the jury determined them in favor of the plaintiff.

"In our opinion, the evidence in the case fairly supports the finding of the jury, both on the question of the negligence of the defendants and on that of the contributory negligence of the plaintiff's intestate, and the rule to show cause should be discharged." (R. V. LINDABURY and JOHN S. APPLEGATE appeared for the rule; EDMUND WILSON, *contra.*)

she came upon the track this engine going west struck her and killed her." The automatic bell was not ringing, and no other signal was given of the approaching locomotive.

The learned trial judge granted a nonsuit on the ground that the plaintiff was guilty of contributory negligence. In his opinion refusing to take off the nonsuit, he says: "We think the plaintiff was clearly guilty of contributory negligence, not in pulling his horse back from the bank, for he was in a position of sudden peril, but in voluntarily or carelessly placing himself in that position, it being one of obvious danger. His duty was, not to begin to draw up his horse when the latter was within fifteen or twenty feet of the track, but to begin that operation soon enough to come to a full stop as soon as or before his horse's head was eighteen feet from the track. It was his duty to stop. Had he done so, this accident would not have happened." It therefore appears that the trial judge held, as a matter of law, the plaintiff was guilty of negligence in not stopping the second time, and at another point nearer the crossing, where he would have had a view of the tracks to the east. We are of opinion that the court erred in not submitting the question of the plaintiff's negligence to the jury. In his charge, the trial judge says: "The evidence is undisputed that the plaintiff stopped at a point where it was usual for travelers to stop, variously estimated at from sixty to one hundred feet away from the crossing." And in his opinion he also says: "As he [plaintiff] approached the railroad, he stopped at a point where it was customary for travelers to stop, and variously estimated as being from sixty to one hundred feet from the railroad; the plaintiff's own estimate being sixty or seventy feet." As conceded by the court, the testimony conclusively shows that the plaintiff stopped at the usual and customary place at which persons stop when approaching the crossing. This, of itself, prevented the court from deciding, as a matter of law, that the plaintiff was guilty of negligence. Cookson *v.* Pittsburgh & Western R'y Co., 179 Pa. St. 184, 1 Am. Neg. Rep. 176, 36 Atl. Rep. 194. In that case it was held that: "The usual and customary place of stopping by people when about to cross a railroad at a grade crossing cannot be said, as a matter of law, to be an improper or negligent place. The standard of negligence is what persons of ordinary prudence and carefulness would do under the same circumstances, and a general habit of the public to stop in a certain place is persuasive evidence that that place is the right one."

It is contended, however, by the appellee, and was held by the court, that, as the view east was obstructed at the point at which the plaintiff stopped, it was negligence *per se* for him not to stop again at some point at which he could see a train approaching from the east. The evidence, however, shows that he could not obtain a view of the tracks to the east until he was at or near the electric signal post, where a view to the west is more or less obstructed. According to the testimony, he would then be in a position made dangerous by reason of the steep embankment to the west of the highway, and where his horse was likely to be frightened by the sudden appearance of a train or the ringing of the signal bell. This case well illustrates the peril of a traveler stopping a skittish horse at that point. Newman did not drive on the track, but was carried on it by his frightened horse when he was attempting to escape the danger to himself and team by being thrown over the declivity on the west side of the road. The court, therefore, could not declare, as a matter of law, that the plaintiff did not stop at the proper place, or was negligent in not stopping a second time. This was for the jury. In Whitman *v.* Penn. R. R. Co., 156 Pa. St. 178 (12 Am. Neg. Cas. 571n), 27 Atl. Rep. 290, it is said by our Brother Mitchell, speaking for the court: "If, notwithstanding the drawbacks of the place where plaintiff stopped, it still had sufficient advantages over other places, to make it the habitual choice of travelers on that road, only a jury can say whether or not it was the best or a proper place to stop, and, even if it was, whether, considering its disadvantages, it was not negligence in the plaintiff not to stop a second time on the level before reaching the track." In Newhard *v.* Penn. R. R. Co., 153 Pa. St. 417 (12 Am. Neg. Cas. 571n), 26 Atl. Rep. 105, our Brother Dean says: "There was testimony that plaintiff stopped and listened, and while there was strong evidence that ordinary care demanded he should have stopped at a point nearer the railroad, and there also ascertained whether it was safe to cross, we think the court, under the rule laid down in North Penn. R. R. Co. *v.* Heileman, 49 Pa. St. 60, 12 Am. Neg. Cas. 569n, followed by a large number of cases since in which the question arose could not, as a matter of law, determine the fact. If there had been any evidence of negligence on part of defendant, then at just what point the plaintiff should have stopped to look and listen was for the jury to find." It was clearly the duty of the plaintiff to stop, look, and listen at a proper place; and, having observed this duty, he was also required to be especially vigilant and careful as he continued towards the crossing, as his view to the east at the place he had stopped was obstructed. If there was another safe and better place for him to stop, he should have done so. This would have been an exercise of the precaution required of him. But whether there was such a place, and he failed to observe the necessary precaution or carefulness after he had once stopped at the usual and customary place of stopping, was a question for the jury, and not for the court. "The duty of the traveler," says our Brother Mitchell, in Cookson *v.* Railway Co., *supra,* "is therefore not only to keep a vigilant and continuous lookout, but to stop if a second place affords any increased facility to discover impending danger; but whether there is any such place is a question of fact, which is for the jury, if at all in doubt." Again, in Muckinhaupt *v.* Erie R. R. Co., 196 Pa. St. 213 (8 Am. Neg. Rep. 349n), 46 Atl. Rep. 364, our Brother Fell, citing many authorities in support of the proposition, says: "But whether the place at which he stopped was the proper place at which to stop, and whether there is a second place at which he should stop, are questions of fact for the jury, and not matters of law for the court." The appellee, in support of its position, cites numerous decisions, but the facts of these cases clearly distinguish them from the case at bar. The plaintiff did not drive in front of an approaching locomotive, nor did he fail to observe the imperative rule which required him to stop, look, and listen for an approaching train. Whether he stopped at the proper place, and thereafter continued to use due vigilance in approaching the crossing, must determine whether he was negligent, and that question is for the jury. The authorities cited by appellee did not authorize the court to determine it.

On another trial of the case, it is suggested that an accurate plan of the *locus in quo,* showing such distances as can be ascertained by measurements, be furnished the jury. Disputed distances should be omitted. We are not convinced that the photographs in evidence aided the jury in their deliberations. On the contrary, as they appear in the paper book, they are in some respects misleading.

The second assignment of error is sustained, and the judgment is reversed, with a *venire de novo.*

GORSUCH v. SWAN.

Supreme Court, Tennessee, October, 1902.

RUNAWAY TEAM — *RES IPSA LOQUITUR* — BURDEN OF PROOF. — In an action for damages for death of plaintiff's intestate, who, while riding in a buggy along a highway, was fatally injured by a runaway team belonging to defendant, it was error for the court to decline to submit plaintiff's request that the burden of explanation was upon defendant, as upon

proof by plaintiff of the accident occasioned by the team of defendant running away, without a driver, on a public road, a *prima facie* case of negligence was made (1).

ERROR to Circuit Court, Knox County.

Action by T. D. Gorsuch against M. D. Swan. From judgment for defendant, plaintiff brings error. *Judgment reversed.*

WEBB, MCCLUNG & BAKER, for plaintiff in error.

CHARLES T. CATES, JR., and T. A. R. NELSON, for defendant in error.

BEARD, J. — The intestate of the plaintiff in error, while riding in a buggy on one of the public roads of Knox county, was fatally injured by a runaway team belonging to the defendant in error. This suit was brought by the administrator to recover damages upon the alleged ground that it was through the negligence of the defendant, the owner of the team, or of his servant, that this runaway occurred, and his intestate was so injured. The trial resulted in a verdict for the defendant, and the plaintiff has appealed. The trial judge said to the jury as follows: "In order that the plaintiff may recover in this case, it must be shown that the defendant or his servants were guilty of some negligence whereby this team of horses ran away and into the vehicle in which plaintiff's intestate was riding, and that such negligence was the prime, proximate, and efficient cause of her injuries." This was a correct application of the general rule that the burden of proof is on the party (the plaintiff in this case) having the affirmative of the issue; but, as the evidence in the cause clearly established the fact that the horses of the defendant, attached to his wagon, were running away, unattended by a driver, at the time they did the injury, the plaintiff submitted a proposition to meet this phase of the case, which was declined by the court. This proposition is in these words: "The fact that a team of horses hitched to a wagon are found running upon the public highway, without a driver or any one accompanying them, raises a presumption of negligence on the part of the owner of the horses that will make him liable for any injury that may directly and proximately result therefrom, unless he shall show by a preponderance of evidence that neither he nor his servant had been guilty of negligence in letting the horses get loose." It was insisted that, as the request embodied a sound rule of law, which was raised by the facts of the case, it was error in the trial judge to decline it. This presents the question whether, upon proof by the plaintiff of the accident occasioned by the team of the defendant running away, without a driver, on a public road, a *prima facie* case of negligence

1. See NOTE ON RES IPSA LOQUITUR, in 3 AM. NEG. REP. 488–496.

was made, so as, without more, to put the burden of explanatory evidence on the defendant, or, having established so much, it was the duty of the plaintiff to have gone further, and shown that there was negligence on the part of the defendant or his servant in permitting the horses to escape his control. While the authorities are not agreed, it would seem the sounder reason would authorize in such a case the application of the maxim, *res ipsa loquitur*, for it is of common experience that horses which are well broken and kept under control will not, save in exceptional cases, break away from the one in charge of them, and inflict injury. So, when a team is found running away, unattended, upon a public thoroughfare, and doing hurt to one lawfully thereon, we think from this fact alone negligence is *prima facie* fairly imputable to the owner. This was the view taken by the court in Thane *v.* Douglass, 102 Tenn. 307, 52 S. W. Rep. 155, a case which warranted the request in question, and announced a rule which should be adhered to, unless good reason can be shown for a departure from it. This view we find enforced by Judge Thompson in his Commentaries on the Law of Negligence, the first edition of which is now going through the press. In volume 1, sec. 1297, he says "that horses which are roadwise, and fit to be driven on the street or highway, and which are properly driven and cared for, do not, as a general rule, * * * run away. From this fact the conclusion is fairly deducible * * * that if a horse or a team of horses, while unattended on the street or highway, does damage, it constitutes * * * *prima facie* evidence of negligence, to charge the owner, driver or custodian, in the absence of an explanation on his part satisfactory to the jury." In support of his text he cites a number of cases, among which are Unger *v.* Railroad Co., 51 N. Y. 497, and Strup *v.* Edens, 22 Wis. 432. Both cases involved the question of the owner's liability for injury inflicted by runaway teams. In the first the Supreme Court of New York said, "The fact that the horses were unattended and unfastened in the street was, unexplained, evidence of the negligence against the defendant;" and in the second the rule is stated in these words: "The fact that the horses got loose and ran away is some evidence of negligence. It is true such a thing might occur notwithstanding due care in hitching. But such would not be the ordinary result, and, unexplained, the reasonable inference from the first would be that there had been negligence in fastening the horses." In the case at bar, in its development before the jury, it appeared that the defendant's servant had driven his master's horses to a public watering place, where, leaving them unhitched and unattended, they ran away, inflicting the injuries complained of. Yet in a great many cases it would be impossible for the plaintiff to show negligence unless the maxim of *res ipsa loquitur* was applied, while possibly in all cases it would be within the power of the owner to rebut the presumption of negligence by showing that the runaway was not the result of a lack of care, either on his part or on that of his servant; and to put this burden on him is no great hardship. Nor is there any antagonism between this holding and that of Young *v.* Bransford, 12 Lea, 232. In that case injury resulted from an explosion of the boiler used in a sawmill, while its owner was carrying on his lawful business, and this court, reversing the trial judge, held that negligence would not be imputed to the owner from the mere fact that the killing resulted from its explosion. It is there said that the reasonable rule was the one announced by Judge Wallace in Rose *v.* Transportation Co., 21 Am. Law Reg. 522, as follows: "That from the mere fact of an explosion it is competent for the jury to infer as a proposition of fact that there was some negligence in the management of the boiler, or some defect in its condition; but that it ought not to have the weight of a conclusive presumption, whether of law or fact, so as to compel the defendants, in order to avoid liability, to prove affirmatively that they were guilty of no negligence, and that the accident was unavoidable." In the course of the opinion, and after an exhaustive review of the authorities, Judge Cooper concluded " that the question of the effect of the mere proof of the killing of the plaintiff's husband by the explosion of the defendant's boiler is one of grave doubt and great importance." The reason for the court's declining to apply the maxim of *res ipsa loquitur* to such a case, and the adoption of the more restricted rule, is found in what immediately follows: "Steam, it has been well said, has come into such general use as a motive power, not only in the operations of commerce and manufactures, but even in those of agriculture, that a rule of law making those who employ it insurers of the safety of others against damages arising from its use would not only be contrary to the analogies of the law, but would impose serious restraints upon the most necessary and beneficial industries. Both the proprietor of machinery impelled by steam and the engineer in charge of such machinery have the strongest interest for watching over its safety. The property of one and the life of the other depend upon constant vigilance in this regard. These motives will ordinarily secure that degree of skill and attention which the safety of the public demand, without the aid of a rule making the proprietor liable in any event for damages from an explosion." We think that that case is thus easily distinguished from the present, where the injury results from animals generally susceptible to control, and, when looked after by their master with ordinary prudence, are unlikely to inflict injury either on the property or person of another. We, therefore, hold that the trial judge was in error in declining to give the special request. The judgment is therefore reversed, and the case is remanded for a new trial.

Other errors are assigned, but, without passing on them, we are content to rest our reversal on the one indicated.

INTERNATIONAL AND GREAT NORTHERN RAILROAD COMPANY v. GAITANES.

Court of Civil Appeals, Texas, October, 1902.

SECTION HAND INJURED UNLOADING RAILS — ASSUMPTION OF RISK. — Where plaintiff, a section hand in defendant's employ, was ordered by the section boss to assist in throwing steel rails from a hand car and was injured, it was held that the plaintiff did not assume the risk of danger, where he was inexperienced in the work, was not informed of the danger, and the danger was not obvious and apparent (1).

APPEAL from District Court, Bexar County.

Action by Thomas Gaitanes against the International & Great Northern Railroad Company. From judgment for plaintiff, defendant appeals. *Judgment affirmed.*

DENMAN, FRANKLIN & McGOWN, for appellant.

M. W. DAVIS, SAMUEL BELDEN, JR., and NAT. B. JONES, for appellee.

FLY, J. — Appellee sued appellant to recover damages alleged to have arisen from personal injuries received by him through the negligence of appellant. The trial was by jury, and resulted in a verdict and judgment for appellee in the sum of $1,500. The evidence discloses that appellee, an inexperienced person, had been in the employ of appellant for four or five days as a section hand, when he was ordered by the section boss to assist in throwing steel rails from a hand car, and in obeying the order one of the rails sprang back, and struck appellee on the legs, inflicting serious and permanent bodily injury. The uncontradicted proof established that the work of unloading rails is very dangerous, and should not be undertaken by an inexperienced laborer. Appellee was inexperienced, and appellant knew it. Appellee was ignorant of the dangers

1. See NOTE ON ASSUMPTION OF RISK, in 7 AM. NEG. REP. 97–111.

attending the work, and was not informed by appellant of the danger attending the unloading of rails. The danger was not obvious and apparent. Appellee was not employed to throw rails off cars, and did not assume the risks incident thereto. The conclusions of fact dispose of the first and third assignments of error. Neither the ninth assignment of error, nor the proposition thereunder, points out any error in the charge, and the requested charge was directly in the face of the evidence, and was properly refused. Bonnet *v.* Railway Co., 89 Tex. 72, 33 S. W. Rep. 334; Railway Co. *v.* Eberhart, 91 Tex. 321, 43 S. W. Rep. 510; Railway Co. *v.* Hannig, 91 Tex. 347, 43 S. W. Rep. 508.

The judgment is affirmed.

HOUSTON AND TEXAS CENTRAL RAILROAD COMPANY v. PHILLIO.

Supreme Court, Texas, October, 1902.

PASSENGER ASSAULTED IN STATION — LIABILITY OF CARRIER. — Where plaintiff's wife, a passenger of defendant company, was assaulted by a drunken person while in defendant's waiting room, the defendant was liable for the assault (1).

LICENSEE ASSAULTED IN STATION — CARRIER NOT LIABLE.— Where plaintiff went to defendant's depot merely to assist his wife in taking the train, and with no intention of becoming a passenger himself, and while there was assaulted by a drunken person, the defendant was not liable, as plaintiff being only a licensee, the defendant did not owe him the duty of protection against the actions of third persons.

ERROR from Court of Civil Appeals, Third Supreme Judicial District.

Action by Steve Phillio against the Houston & Texas Central Railroad Company. From a judgment of the Court of Civil Appeals affirming a judgment in favor of plaintiff (67 S. W. Rep. 915), defendant appeals. *Judgment reversed.*

FRANK ANDREWS, for plaintiff in error.

E. T. JOHNSON, T. N. GRAHAM and N. J. LEWELLYN, for defendant in error.

1. *Assaults.* — For actions arising out of assaults upon passengers, from the earliest times to 1897, see vol. 8 Am. Neg. Cas., where the same are chronologically grouped and arranged in alphabetical order of States. Subsequent actions to date are reported in vols. 1-12 AM. NEG. REP., and the current numbers of that series of Reports.

GAINES, Ch. J. — The following is the statement of this case, together with their conclusions upon the evidence, filed by the Court of Civil Appeals: "This is an action by the appellee, Steve Phillio, against the railroad company to recover damages for injuries sustained, arising from the following state of facts, which are as substantially alleged in his petition: Plaintiff and his wife went to the depot of the appellant's road in the town of Calvert for the purpose of procuring a ticket for his wife to the town of Marlin. She at the time was sick and in feeble condition. While waiting in the waiting room of the depot for the train, and after the ticket had been purchased and the baggage checked, the defendant permitted one Allen, who was alleged to be a strong, active, and robust white man, and being in a drunken and rowdy condition, to sing vulgar and indecent songs and use vulgar and indecent language in the presence of plaintiff and his wife, and, being armed with a pocketknife open in his hand, make an unjustifiable assault upon the plaintiff and his wife, by which the plaintiff and his wife were greatly intimidated, causing them to become frightened, and causing plaintiff's wife to become very nervous and sick. There are further allegations to the effect that the agent of the plaintiff at the depot at that time was present, and witnessed the assault and wrongful conduct as alleged, inflicted upon the plaintiff and his wife by Allen, or was in a position to see the same, and that no steps were taken by the agent to prevent the assault or the wrongful conduct complained of. Upon trial of the case below, verdict and judgment were in favor of the plaintiff for the sum of $400. We find that the evidence in the record substantially sustains these averments, and the judgment and verdict below are supported by the evidence found in the record." The Court of Civil Appeals found no error in the proceedings, and affirmed the judgment of the trial court.

We are of the opinion that the conclusions of that court, in so far as they pertain to the right of recovery by reason of the assault upon, and insulting conduct towards, the wife of the plaintiff, are correct, but do not concur in the proposition that the evidence showed any right of action in the plaintiff on account of the outrage of Allen upon himself personally. The wife, having entered the depot, and a ticket having been procured for her, became a passenger of the defendant company, and the duty devolved upon the company's agent to protect her against assault and insulting conduct on the part of third persons, provided he knew of such misconduct or had reasonable grounds to anticipate it. As to the plaintiff the case is different. He went to the depot merely to assist his wife in taking the train, and with no intention of becoming a passenger himself.

He was there by the implied invitation of the company, and was not a trespasser. The railway company owed him the duty which is owed by the owners of property to persons who enter upon it by their invitation and no more. That duty is to use ordinary care to see that the premises are kept in a reasonably safe condition, so that persons entering thereupon by invitation are not injured thereby. Hamilton *v.* Railway Co., 64 Tex. 251; Railway Co. *v.* East, 66 Tex. 116, 18 S. W. Rep. 224. In the case of Louis. & Nash. R. R. Co. *v.* Crunk, 119 Ind. 542, 3 Am. Neg. Cas. 229, 21 N. E. Rep. 31, the court say: "The defendant, in contracting to carry the passenger Naas in his sick and enfeebled condition, contracted an obligation which could only be carried out by Naas being carried upon the train and seated in the car. By thus contracting to carry Naas as a passenger, it took upon itself the obligation of allowing him assistants to place him upon the train and seat him in the car, and the compensation received by the defendant for conveying Naas from Mt. Vernon to his destination included as well the right to have assistants place him in the car as the carrying him after being so placed in the car, and the defendant owed the same obligation to his assistants while necessarily entering and leaving the car with Naas as it owed to Naas himself." So far as we have been able to discover, this case, in so far as it holds that the railway company owed the same duty to the assistants which it owed to the passenger, stands by itself, and unless there be a distinguishing feature in the fact that owing to the enfeebled condition of the passenger, which made it necessary for his friends to assist in boarding the train and securing a seat (which we doubt), it is in opposition to all the authorities upon the question.

Our conclusion is that, since the plaintiff was not a passenger, the defendant company did not owe him the duty of protection against the injurious actions of third persons, and that, therefore, he was not entitled to recover for the misconduct of Allen towards himself.

Therefore the judgment of the District Court and that of the Court of Civil Appeals is reversed, and the cause remanded.

STOCKWELL v. TOWN OF RUTLAND.

Supreme Court, Vermont, October, 1902.

PERSON FALLING INTO DITCH — MUNICIPAL CORPORATIONS — GOVERNMENTAL ACTS. — Where a town annexed a part of a city to a town, under a statute which provided that the public property of the city in the annexed territory should become the property of the town, and that the town should pay to the city, among other things, the cost of the water mains the city had laid in said territory, and the cost of laying the same, and a person sustained injuries by falling into an open ditch in the highway, dug for the purpose of taking up disused water pipe, it was *held* that the town was not liable, as in digging up the pipe it was acting in its governmental capacity (1).

EXCEPTIONS from Rutland County Court.

Action by Mary P. Stockwell against the town of Rutland. From judgment for plaintiff, defendant brings exceptions. *Judgment reversed.*

BUTLER & MOLONEY, for plaintiff.

JOEL C. BAKER, for defendant.

ROWELL, J. — This is case for negligence in leaving improperly lighted and guarded an open ditch in a highway, into which the plaintiff fell, dug for the purpose of taking up disused water pipe, to which the defendant acquired title under No. 190 of the Acts of 1894, annexing a part of the city of Rutland to the town of Rutland, and providing that the public property of the city in the annexed territory should become the property of the town, and that the town should pay to the city, among other things, the cost of the water mains the city had laid in said territory, and the cost of laying the same, but silent as to what use the town should make of the pipe. The court overruled defendant's motion for a verdict, treated the act as authorizing the town to secure to itself the value of the property thus transferred, and charged that, if the town was digging up the pipe to be used for highway purposes, it was not liable, however negligently the work was done, but if it was digging it up without reference to its duty to the public regarding highways, but for the purpose, in the first instance, of converting it into money for the benefit of its treasury, it would be liable, if the case was otherwise made out. The defendant says it was error to overrule its motion

1. See NOTE ON GOVERNMENTAL ACTS OF MUNICIPAL CORPORATIONS, 5 AM. NEG. REP. 289–293.

and to submit the case to the jury, for that the evidence did not tend to show that the pipe was being dug up to sell, but only to be used for highway purposes, and for that the act conferred upon the town no authority to use the pipe for its private gain and advantage, nor for any purpose outside of its governmental agency.

The distinction drawn by the charge is well settled, namely, that municipal corporations proper are not liable when acting in their public and governmental capacity, unless made so by statute, but are liable when acting in their private and nongovernmental capacity, the same as corporations aggregate and natural persons. But the question here is whether the defendant was acting in its private and nongovernmental capacity in digging up this pipe for the purpose, in the first instance, of converting it into money for the benefit of its treasury. There were thirty-seven or thirty-eight lengths of it in all, — about 450 feet, — some of it eight-inch and some of it six. The question of when a municipal corporation is acting in its private capacity, so as to make it liable, has frequently been before this court, and it is pretty well settled. Winn *v.* Village of Rutland, 52 Vt. 481, is a leading case on the subject. There the village was held liable for damage occasioned by its negligence in constructing a sewer through plaintiff's land. The decision was put upon the ground that as the village had asked for and obtained charter authority to build and maintain sewers, not for the purpose of discharging a governmental duty, but of benefiting its inhabitants, the authority carried with it an implied obligation on the part of the village to use it so as not to injure others, and that the true principle of liability was found in that obligation. In Welsh *v.* Village of Rutland, 56 Vt. 228, it is said that when municipal corporations are exercising private franchises, powers, and privileges belonging to them for their corporate benefit, or are dealing with property held by them for their corporate advantage, gain, or emolument, though inuring ultimately to the benefit of the general public, they are liable for negligent exercise of such powers, the same as individuals are. There is nothing in the case at bar to show that the defendant asked to have this territory annexed to it, but, for aught that appears, it was done without its consent and against its will. The act dealt with the town in its public and governmental capacity, and not otherwise, for all its provisions were compulsory upon it; and the town took the territory in the same capacity, and could have taken it in no other, and the pipe, being a mere incident of the transaction, followed the principal, and the town took that in its public capacity, for the State does not force things upon municipalities in their private capacity, but waits to be asked to confer them. Indeed, it has been held that the State cannot do that. In People *v.* Common Council of Detroit, 28 Mich. 228, it was held that the legislature could not compel a municipal corporation to contract a debt for local purposes against its will, any more than it could compel a private corporation or an individual to contract a debt. The court said it would be as easy to justify on principle a law that permits the rest of the community to dictate to a man what he shall eat, as to justify one that permits the people of other parts of the State, through their representatives, to dictate to a municipal corporation what it shall do in respect of private and nongovernmental matters. The same thing was held in People *v.* Mayor, etc., of City of Chicago, 51 Ill. 17, and upon much the same reasoning. People *v.* Batcheller, 53 N. Y. 128, is to the same effect; and so is Atkins *v.* Town of Randolph, 31 Vt. 226. Now, to say that the town, having been compelled to take and pay for this pipe in its public capacity, is to be treated as holding it in its private capacity, merely because, having no other use for it, we may suppose, it intends to sell it in order to reimburse its cost, would be changing the legal relation of the town to the property, and making a matter of public concern into a matter of purely private concern, and quite overleaping the true principle of liability stated in Winn *v.* Village of Rutland, *supra.* In Bates *v.* Bassett, 60 Vt. 530, 15 Atl. Rep. 200, the town of Barre, having built a new town hall, repaired its old town hall for renting, having no other use for it; and it was held that it might lawfully do that, and raise a tax to pay for it, it not being its primary object to invest money in buildings to rent, but only to make the best and most advantageous use of property already on hand. The principle of that case is applicable here, and is decisive of the case in favor of the defendant, and therefore its other exceptions need not be considered.

Reversed and remanded.

TABLE OF CASES CLASSIFIED.

[This Table shows the Cases Reported, classified according to the cause of action and the injuries sustained, so far as the facts disclose the same, and arranged under their respective heads in the order in which they appear in this volume, together with a classification of the actions against corporations under their respective titles, as, for instance: Carriers of Passengers, Carriers of Freight, Municipal Corporations, Railroad and Street Railroad Companies, Telegraph Companies, etc., and actions arising out of the relations of Landlord and Tenant, Master and Servant, etc.]

Defective Appliance.

Defective Approach.

Defective Brake.

Defective Bridge.

Defective Cable.

Defective Car.

Defective Couplers.

Defective Crane.

Defective Crossing.

Defective Derrick.

Defective Elevator.

Defective Engine.

Defective Gate.

Defective Hand-hold.

Defective Harness.

Defective Highway.

Personal Injury—NOT STATED — *continued.*

Personal Injury—NOT STATED — *continued.*

INDEX.

[The Index should be consulted with the preceding Table of Cases Classified.]

Action.

failure to execute release for damages for injuries on receipt of benefits from relief fund does not give right of action for injuries because of such failure to sign release........................Ga. 422

where property of railway company is in exclusive possession of receivers operating the road, the company is not liable for injuries sustained by an employee of such receivers..................Kan. 438

where action is prosecuted jointly against railway corporation and the receivers of same, and the corporation is not liable, the action may be dismissed as to corporation without prejudice to plaintiff's right to have judgment against receivers...........Kan. 438

insufficiency of declaration in action by an administrator for negligent killing of intestate, an employee killed in gas explosion.. Me. 461

the statute of 1891 affords a right of action for "injuries causing death," substantially like that given to employees by the employers' liability act in Massachusetts (chapter 24, Pub. St. 1887)........................Me. 461

statute requiring notice of injury caused by defect in street to be given to municipality as a condition precedent to maintaining action therefor, not applicable to action by personal representative of deceased person, whose death was caused by such defect..Minn. 294

complaint that contains no direct allegations that plaintiff's injuries were caused by any act or omission of defendant, does not allege facts constituting cause of action.. Minn. 498

where right to recover for personal injuries was predicated solely on ground of violation of city ordinance, recovery could not be had on ground of common-law negligence.........Mo. 504

no implied duty on owner of house to inform proposed tenant that house is in dangerous condition, and no action lies against owner for omission to do so, in absence of express warranty or deceit... N. J. 124

common-law right of action by husband for injury to wife to recover for loss of her services and for his medical and other expenses in healing her injuries, is not abridged or affected by statute.......................Ohio, 547

Admission.

failure to deny under oath an allegation that a principal, through an agent, did a certain act, not an admission that principal did such act...................Kan. 442

Animal.
cows tied to wagon killed by train while crossing track; contributory negligence of person in charge of cattle and team..Minn. 471
where certain stock was killed at point west of defendant's switch, which was left unfenced and treated as part of defendant's depot grounds or switching yard, it was for jury to determine whether proximate cause of killing of cattle was absence of fence, and whether such point was reasonably required by defendant for purposes stated..... Minn. 471

Annuity Table.
not error for court to illustrate to jury the method of using mortality and annuity tables by giving figure approximating that shown by the evidence to be plaintiff's age................Ga. 223

Assault.
person not a passenger assaulted by station agent, railway company not liable, the agent not acting within scope of employment......................Kan. 435
passenger assaulted and insulted at railway station, when carrier not liable.......................Ky. 288
carrier liable for assault by drunken person upon plaintiff's wife, a passenger, while in carrier's waiting room..................Tex. 637
where person merely goes to railway station to assist his wife to a train, with no intention of becoming a passenger, and while there was assaulted by drunken person, carrier not liable, the person so assaulted being only a licensee...................Tex. 637

Assisting Employee.
person assisting employee injured while unloading machinery...... N. D. 619

Assisting Passenger.
where person merely goes to railway station to assist his wife to a train, with no intention of becoming a passenger, and while there was assaulted by drunken person, carrier not liable, the person so assaulted being only a licensee....................Tex. 637

Assumption of Risk.
employee injured in defective elevator.....................Iowa, 269
employee injured by defective machinery, the danger of running which was known to him..Mass. 76
employee injured by fall of iron metal bars, he being familiar with custom of standing the bars against wall of store......Mass. 79
employee injured by unguarded laundry mangle, the risks of operation being known to employee.. Minn. 103
servant ordered, with other employees, to unload logs from flat cars, where risk of such work is open and apparent, he assumes dangers caused by negligence of fellow-servants...........Minn. 496
employee injured while moving tank in brewery............Neb. 514
an employee, although a minor, assumes risk of dangers of employment as are obvious to him, and his employer is not responsible for injuries resulting therefrom, notwithstanding latter has failed to point out such dangers..N. J. 327
a section hand injured while unloading steel rails from hand car did not assume risk of danger where he was inexperienced, was not informed of danger and the danger was not obvious and apparent.....................Tex. 636
brakeman familiar with custom of coupling cars, injured while coupling cars..............Wis. 206
brakeman assumes risks of coup-

Assumption of Risk — *continued.*
ling cars provided with different kinds of well-known appliances.. U. S. C. C. A. 398

Automatic Couplers.
Federal statute relating to automatic couplers....U. S. C. C. A. 398
what is sufficient compliance with statute requiring equipment of cars with automatic couplers.... U. S. C. C. A. 398
the Federal statute does not make it unlawful for common carriers to use locomotives engaged in interstate commerce which are not equipped with couplers...... U. S. C. C. A. 398

Automobile.
person driving along private lane tacitly open to public use, and horse frightened by automobile approaching from opposite direction....................N. Y. 157
duty of operator of automobile when driver of horse and vehicle is in peril from fright of horse.. N. Y. 157
duty of operator of automobile towards pedestrians and especially towards children of tender years.. N. Y. 158
child run over and killed by automobile....................N. Y. 158

Baggage.
passenger's merchandise checked as baggage lost or stolen in transit........................Mich. 61
note on liability of carriers for loss of passenger's baggage.........64–74

Barriers.
person injured while driving horse and buggy at approach to highway bridge; failure to maintain barriers....................Minn. 80
person injured by falling into an unprotected ravine along public highway....................Minn. 81
bicycle riders striking loose plank and falling over bridge......Pa. 180

Benevolent Fund.
failure to execute release for damages for injuries on receipt of benefits from relief fund does not give right of action for injuries because of such failure to sign release......................Ga. 422

Bicycle.
person injured by fall from bicycle alleged to have been caused by a defect in street.............Ind. 85
bicyclist running into pile of bricks in street; contributory negligence....................N. C. 92
bicyclist striking loose plank and falling over bridge...........Pa. 180

Blasting.
property damaged by rocks thrown on plaintiff's land by blasting in defendant's quarry and also from water pumped from quarry and allowed to flow on plaintiff's land........................Me. 44
doctrine of fellow-servant not applicable to case where plaintiff, a laborer in defendant's employ, was injured by blasting operations at time when he was not at work or assisting other employees...........U. S. C. C. A. 393

Boarding.
motorman in trying to board his car, which was going at slow speed, falling from same and run over by car..................Ga. 422
child, about three years old, thrown down and injured by sudden starting of street car which she had boarded................N. J. 334

Brakeman.
injured while coupling cars; directtion of verdict for railroad company sustained..............Ga. 420
baggage-master acting as brakeman injured in derailment of train; railroad company liable.....N. J. 113

Carrier of Passengers.

passenger thrown from car by sudden jolt of defendant's train and run over and killed by passing engine of another railroad company........................Ga. 232
passenger ejected from train on presentation of expired ticket... Ga. 427
notice posted at ticket office limiting time of use of certain railroad ticket, not admissible in action for ejection of passenger unless proof is given that passenger had read same or notice of its contents........................Ga. 427
collision between public hack and train at street crossing and passenger in hack injured......Kan. 29
person not a passenger assaulted by station agent; railway company not liable; the agent not acting within scope of employment.. Kan. 435
passenger assaulted and insulted at railway station; when carrier not liable........................Ky. 288
statutory requirement as to time of keeping ticket offices and waiting rooms open for passengers before schedule time of departure of trains........................Ky. 288
passenger's merchandise checked as baggage lost or stolen in transit........................Mich. 61
child, about three years old, thrown down and injured by sudden starting of street car which she had boarded...................N. J. 334
a mere fall from a street car, without any evidence to show how it was occasioned, raises no presumption of negligence on part of operators of car..........N. J. 533
lessor of steamboat, a private corporation, not liable for negligence of lessee where passenger on steamboat was injured by capsizing of boat.............N. C. 617

Carrier of Passengers — *continued.*

intending passenger injured by falling on railroad ties and beams while attempting to reach depot, a freight train blocking the crossing at station..............Okla. 353
carrier liable for assault by drunken person upon plaintiff's wife, a passenger, while in carrier's waiting room..................Tex. 637
where person merely goes to railway station to assist his wife to a train, with no intention of becoming a passenger, and while there was assaulted by drunken person, carrier not liable, the person so assaulted being only a licensee.. Tex. 637
passenger injured by stepping into hole in station platform; liability of carrier................W. Va. 580
person standing in passenger car injured by sudden start of car... U. S. C. C. A. 314
passenger injured while riding on platform or steps of car......... U. S. C. C. A. 395
note on liability for loss of passenger's baggage.................64-74

Ceiling.

tenant injured by fall of plaster from ceiling...............N. Y. 532

Cellar.

woman walking along sidewalk falling into cellar-door opening and seriously injured..........Idaho, 243
pedestrian falling into cellar opening in sidewalk.............Kan. 431
child of tender years fatally injured by falling into hatchway on defendant's premises...........Mo. 504
child falling through grating over cellar in sidewalk...........Tex. 95

Charge to Jury. — See also INSTRUCTIONS.

rule as to exceptions........N. Y. 610
erroneous instruction as to negli-

Collision — *continued.*

vehicle and train colliding at crossing; person driving killed and person riding injured......Ohio, 343

person riding in caboose of freight train by conductor's permission killed in collision; railroad company not liable............Ohio, 544

train and vehicle colliding at grade crossing.....................Pa. 626

person riding in wagon on highway fatally injured by a runaway team colliding with wagon......Tenn. 632

fireman fatally injured by being scalded by escaping steam from boiler of engine against which he was thrown by collision between two sections of train........... U. S. C. C. A. 213

Common Carrier.

passenger's merchandise checked as baggage lost or stolen in transit.. Mich. 61

valuable horse injured in transportation while in custody of connecting carrier..............Pa. 185

stipulation in contract limiting liability of carrier for damage to horse from neglig nce to $100 is against policy of State, and will not be enforced though made in a State where such a contract is valid.......................Pa. 185

the Interstate Commerce Act is not violated by holding that contract limiting liability for carrier's negligence is invalid within this State.......................Pa. 185

the Federal statute does not make it unlawful for common carriers to use locomotives engaged in interstate commerce which are not equipped with couplers...... U. S. C. C. A. 398

note on liability for loss of passenger's baggage.................64–74

note on liability of connecting carriers for negligence..........191–199

Complaint.

complaint that contains no direct allegations that plaintiff's injuries were caused by any act or omission of defendant, does not allege facts constituting cause of action.. Minn. 498

petition alleging that certain premises were not enclosed by railing, etc., as required by city ordinance, sufficient to withstand attack by general demurrer..Mo. 504

petition that states facts from which defendant's negligence may be inferred is not defective for omission of use of word "negligent" or its derivatives............Neb. 104

petition by married woman, in action for personal injury, which does not allege ownership of any separate estate or property, or that she is engaged in any business or service, other than pertaining to her husband's household, does not entitle her to recover damages on account either of loss of earnings or diminished capacity to earn money as result of injury.........Neb. 517

where petition alleges injuries to specific parts of body error to admit evidence of injuries to other parts not set out in petition..... Tex. 199

Conductor.

injured while examining defective appliance, there being no duty imposed on him to make such examination; railroad company not liable.......................Ga. 422

person standing near track to let car pass injured by coming in contact with conductor on footboard of moving open street car; railway company not liable..Md. 51

act of conductor in permitting person to ride on train against rules of railroad company, not binding on company...............Ohio, 544

Conductor — *continued.*

killed in derailment of train caused by defective car wheels; evidence as to defects and failure to inspect. . . . . Wash. 372

Conflict of Laws.

the Interstate Commerce Act is not violated by holding that contract limiting liability for carrier's negligence is invalid within this State. . . . . Pa. 185

Connecting Carrier.

valuable horse injured in transportation while in custody of connecting carrier. . . . . Pa. 185

note on liability for negligence. . 191–199

Connecting Line.

a railway company, which delivers defective freight car to a connecting line, is not liable to employee of latter, who is injured by reason of such defects, after car has been inspected by company receiving it. . . . . Kan. 275

Contract.

failure to execute release for damages for injuries on receipt of benefits from relief fund does not give right of action for injuries because of such failure to sign release. . . . . Ga. 422

whether doctrine of *respondeat superior* applies to any particular case between the original contractor and a subcontractor is determined by the contract between the parties. . . . . Minn. 488

where a party attaches his signature to a contract otherwise valid, a conclusive presumption is created, except as against fraud, that he read, understood and assented to its terms. . . . . N. J. 313

where a party sets up defense that his signature to contract has been obtained by fraud, the burden is upon him to show fraud by clear and satisfactory proof, the presumption of the law being in favor of innocence, fraud not being assumed on doubtful evidence. . . . . N. J. 313

failure of proof to show that signature to contract accepting benefits from relief fund for injuries which operated as release was obtained by fraud. . . . . N. J. 313

liability of contractor for defective work of subcontractor. . . . . . N. J. 522

stipulation in contract limiting liability of carrier for damage to horse from negligence to $100 is against policy of State, and will not be enforced though made in a State where such a contract is valid. . . . . Pa. 185

failure of proof to establish fraud in obtaining signature to release of claim for personal injuries. . . .
U. S. C. C. A. 314

Contributory Negligence.

person crossing track, at place not public crossing, run over and killed by train; failure to look for train. Ala.

person stopping within 30 feet of crossing, looking up track, and seeing track clear for about 800 feet, proceeding to cross track without again looking for train, not guilty of contributory negligence as matter of law . . . . . Cal. 1

person killed while crossing track in front of rapidly moving train at crossing used by public but at which no flagman was in attendance. . . . . Cal. 215

contributory negligence of deceased in crossing track in front of moving train bars recovery notwithstanding negligence of railroad company in failing to have flagman at crossing. . . . . Cal. 215

Contributory Negligence — *continued.*
woman injured on defective sidewalk; contributory negligence for jury.......................Iowa, 268
general denial and plea of contributory negligence not inconsistent defenses...............Kan. 442
person driving wagon killed in collision with train at crossing; failure of deceased to exercise due care.....................Me. 452
cows tied to wagon killed by train while crossing track; contributory negligence of person in charge of cattle and team..Minn. 471
where employee was killed by electric shock, evidence not conclusive that he was negligent in attempting to push loose part of derrick cable, charged with electricity, from open street into gutter.....................Minn. 488
whether a boy, between eleven and twelve years of age, was guilty of contributory negligence in crawling out of a ditch at side of track into which he had lodged while coasting, and was run over by train, was question for jury to determine.....................Mo. 499
bicycle rider running into pile of bricks in street...........N. C. 92
testimony that there were many other street crossings in same condition as one in question competent as to whether keeping it in that condition was negligence, and also on question of contributory negligence.............Pa. 176
woman familiar with dangerous place in sidewalk at street crossing injured while walking on sidewalk at night, guilty of contributory negligence.......S. D. 94
erroneous charge regarding person on track as a trespasser....Tex. 360
error to charge that burden of proof was upon plaintiff to show by preponderance of evidence

Contributory Negligence — *continued.*
that he was not guilty of contributory negligence while walking on track................Tex. 360
an infant, under five years of age, cannot be guilty of contributory negligence................Wash. 366
rule as to looking and listening applied, where woman crossing track from station in night-time was struck and fatally injured by switch engine, and her contributory negligence held to preclude recovery of damages........Wis. 389
where a passenger stands on steps of car, for purpose of expectorating, and is injured, question of contributory negligence is for jury and not for court..........
U. S. C. C. A. 395
passenger who rides on steps or platform of car, without reasonable excuse, guilty of negligence barring recovery notwithstanding negligence of railway company.............U. S. C. C. A. 395
when question of negligence for jury and when for court.........
U. S. C. C. A. 395

Coupling Cars.
brakeman injured while coupling cars; direction of verdict for railroad company sustained.....Ga. 420
brakeman familiar with custom of coupling cars, injured while coupling cars.....................Wis. 206
brakeman injured while coupling cars..............U. S. C. C. A. 398
brakeman assumes risks of coupling cars provided with different kinds of well-known appliances........
U. S. C. C. A. 398

Crossing.
person stopping within 30 feet of crossing, looking up track, and seeing track clear for about 800 feet, proceeding to cross track without again looking for train,

Crossing — *continued.*
not guilty of contributory negligence as matter of law......Cal. 1
person killed while crossing track in front of rapidly moving train at crossing used by public but at which no flagman was in attendance........................Cal. 215
where plaintiff, while driving across track at street crossing, was struck by defendant's train which failed to signal its approach, the proximate cause of injury was failure of defendant to signal at crossing.......................Cal. 414
street cars have no superior rights to other vehicles or pedestrians at regular street crossings...Fla. 417
duty of employees of street cars to keep look out for persons on track, especially at street crossings........................Fla. 417
collision between public hack and train at street crossing and passenger in hack injured......Kan. 29
in action for negligently running train at street crossing without signal, error to admit evidence of like failure of train to signal at another street crossing.....Kan. 29
where railroad company was in habit of operating gates at street crossing at certain hours, but not at time of accident, error to refer question to jury as to whether single isolated instance of failure to operate gates at that time was negligence..................Kan. 29
person driving across track at street crossing struck by street car; evidence as to looking and listening....................Kan. 599
railroad company not chargeable with negligence in running passenger train over road crossing at speed of from forty to fifty miles per hour in open country where view of traveler on highway is unobstructed........Kan. 601

Crossing — *continued.*
traveler already warned of approach of train in time to escape injury cannot complain of negligence of railroad company in failing to give signals..........Kan. 601
person riding in wagon driven by another killed in collision with train at crossing; railroad not liable......................Kan. 601
person driving wagon killed in collision with train at crossing; failure of deceased to exercise due care........................Me. 452
duty of traveler approaching crossing to look and listen for trains.. Me. 452
duty of motorman when street car approaching street crossing..... Minn. 604
child of tender years struck by street car at street crossing..... Minn. 604
where child was run over and killed by engine at crossing, the case should have gone to jury... Miss. 608
boy run over and leg injured by train at street crossing; question of negligence for jury......Neb. 3
horse standing at gate crossing frightened by train and backing wagon against engine, and person in wagon injured; question for jury whether plaintiff was negligent in not alighting from wagon....................N. J. 329
collision between train and wagon at crossing, and person driving killed.....................N. J. 626
collision between vehicle and train at crossing; person driving killed and person riding injured..Ohio, 343
rule as to looking and listening at railroad crossings..........Ohio, 343
duty of engineer of train when approaching crossings.......Ohio, 343
collision between train and vehicle at grade crossing......Pa. 626

Crossing — *continued.*

whether person exercised care in observing the rule as to stopping, looking and listening for trains before crossing track, was question for jury and not for court.. Pa. 626

notes of cases relating to pedestrians injured at crossings or on track 1-6

Crossing Street.

person injured while crossing street-car track.............Cal. 215

person crossing street struck by street car..................Fla. 417

person crossing street stepping on street-car rail and receiving electric shock; street railroad company liable................N. Y. 156

woman crossing street over tracks at railroad yard struck and injured by engine...........Ohio, 547

person crossing street struck and hands and fingers injured by street car.................Tenn. 4

Crossing Track. — See also TRACK.

person crossing track at place not public crossing, run over and killed by train; failure to look for train.......................Ala. 1

person crossing track at street crossing struck and killed by train......................Cal. 1

collision between wagon and street car......................Mass. 216

cows tied to wagon killed by train while crossing track; contributory negligence of person in charge of cattle and team..Minn. 471

rule as to looking and listening applied, where woman crossing track from station in night time was struck and fatally injured by switch engine, and her contributory negligence held to preclude recovery of damages.......Wis. 389

Damages.

statutory requirement as to pleading and proof in action for treble damages..................Conn. 8

not error for court to illustrate to jurv the method of using mortality and annuity tables by giving figure approximating that shown by the evidence to be plaintiff's age................Ga. 223

verdict for $1,250 excessive, where plaintiff, a peddler, was ejected from train on ground that his ticket had expired...........Ga. 427

where child, about five years of age, was fatally injured on turntable, verdict for $2,000 not excessive.. Idaho, 18

verdict for $12,000 for permanent injuries sustained by woman falling into cellar door opening in sidewalk, not excessive....Idaho, 243

verdict for $6,000 excessive, $3,000 being considered sufficient, for death of child, four years and four months old, whose death was caused by horse attached to wagon in which deceased was riding becoming frightened and falling on him............Iowa, 590

verdict for $4,358, where plaintiff, a woman, was permanently injured, both internally and externally, by falling into cellar opening in sidewalk, not excessive..Kan. 431

what evidence is admissible to show pecuniary value of person whose death was caused by wrongful act................Kan. 594

instruction that damages subsequent to date of writ could not be reversed in action for injury to property caused by blasting, etc.; properly given..............Me. 44

where boy, about sixteen years old, was injured by machinery at place of employment, his toes being caught in machinery, verdict

Damages — *continued.*

for $2,500 held excessive and reduced to $1,500..........Minn. 104

petition by married woman, in action for personal injury, which does not allege ownership of any separate estate or property, or that she is engaged in any business or service, other than pertaining to her husband's household, does not entitle her to recover damages on account either of loss of earnings or diminished capacity to earn money as result of injury..................Neb. 517

where it is shown that a person is affected by a serious constitutional disease, error to submit to jury question of expectancy of life, in absence of any evidence bearing upon that question..Neb. 517

award of $200 damages for negligent killing of plaintiff's son, a child about six years of age, not so inadequate as to warrant setting aside verdict.........N. Y. 616

common-law right of action by husband for injury to wife to recover for loss of her services and for medical and other expenses in healing her injuries, is not abridged or affected by statute.. Ohio, 547

verdict for $1,500 for plaintiff, a woman, who was crippled for life (her spine being broken, caused by falling over bridge, her bicycle, which she was riding, striking against loose plank), not excessive, where at time of accident she was 39 years of age, in excellent health, and earning good salary.................Pa. 180

Dangerous Approach.

intending passenger injured by falling on railroad ties and beams while attempting to reach depot, a freight train blocking the crossing at station.............Okla. 353

Dangerous Place.

where a child's foot became fastened between planking and rail of a track on a street, and the father, in trying to extricate the child, pulled him over the rail as a train of cars approached and the train passed over the child's leg, the proximate cause of the injury was the dangerous condition of the track, for which the city was liable, notwithstanding negligence of railroad company and the parent...........Wash. 366

notes of recent cases on furnishing servant safe place to work...251-268

Dangerous Premises.

boy stepping into pool of hot water; owner of premises not liable......................Ark. 508

boy trespassing in building injured by explosion of dynamite cap; owner not liable............Ky. 509

employee injured by failure of defendants to keep trapdoors to basement in building in proper repair for use...............Minn. 99

child of tender years fatally injured by falling into hatchway on defendant's premises...........Mo. 504

person injured by stepping on coal hole cover in sidewalk, liability of owner of premises.......N. J. 121

person injured by fall of chimney.. N. J. 124

no implied duty on owner of house to inform prospective tenant that house is in dangerous condition, and no action lies against owner for omission to do so, in absence of express warranty or deceit.. N. J. 124

owner of premises liable for injury to person falling on icy sidewalk, ice being formed by water discharged from roof.........N. Y. 132

boy playing along railroad path scalded by steam and hot water

Dangerous Premises — *continued.*
discharged from adjoining premises; owner of premises liable... N. Y. 511
boy injured by explosives found on vacant lot adjacent to factory.... N. Y. 512
person injured by falling on ice on sidewalk, the ice being formed by accumulation of water from drain pipe..................Pa. 132
person rightfully on premises injured by fall of brick from building in course of construction... Pa. 295
child attracted to fire on premises where children were accustomed to play; owner not liable for injuries to child, though he took no means to prevent children approaching fire.............R. I. 550
where one going upon another's premises, not as a trespasser or mere licensee, but by invitation in legal sense, as for instance, an independent contractor to do work for the owner, the owner owes the duty of reasonable care to keep premises in safe condition for such person's work, unless defects be known to such person..................W. Va. 571
notes of recent New York cases arising out of coal-hole accidents.......................121–122
notes of recent cases relating to liability for injuries to children while on dangerous and defective premises 508–513
notes of recent cases arising from injuries to trespassers........562–571

Deaf Person.
deaf person driving and person riding in vehicle listening and assisting in looking for trains...Ohio, 343

Death.
person crossing track at place not public crossing, run over and killed by train; failure to look for train.......................Ala. 1
person crossing track at street crossing struck and killed by train......................Cal. 1
person killed while crossing track in front of rapidly moving train at crossing used by public, but at which no flagman was in attendance........................Cal. 215
passenger thrown from car by sudden jolt of defendants' train and run over and killed by passing engine of another railroad company........................Ga. 232
engineer killed in collision between passenger train and freight train.. Ga. 420
engineer killed by negligence of co-employees; railroad company liable........................Ga. 421
child fatally injured while playing on turntable.............Idaho, 18
child of tender age killed on highway by horse attached to wagon in which deceased was riding, becoming frightened at iron tiles placed on highway and backing off bridge on highway and falling on child..................Iowa, 590
gas explosion demolishing brick building and wall falling on adjoining frame shop and killing plaintiff's intestate..........Kan. 594
person riding in wagon driven by another killed in collision with train at crossing; railroad not liable......................Kan. 601
person driving wagon killed in collision with train at crossing; failure of deceased to exercise due care........................Me. 452
employee killed by gas explosion.. Me. 461
employee fatally injured in saw mill due to improper setting of saw.. Mass. 78
person walking along street fatally

Death — *continued.*

injured by fall of defective and insufficiently fastened porch. . Minn. 294

contact of electric wires with derrick cables and employee killed by shock; evidence not conclusive that derrick was placed in position and operated by independent contractors. . . . . Minn. 488

where employee was killed by electric shock, evidence not conclusive that he was negligent in attempting to push loose part of derrick cable, charged with electricity, from open street into gutter. . . . . Minn. 488

child of tender years struck by street car at street crossing. . . . . Minn. 604

where child was run over and killed by engine at crossing, the case should have gone to jury. . Miss. 608

child of tender years fatally injured by falling into hatchway on defendant's premises. . . . . Mo. 504

the fact that plaintiff's intestate was found dead in proximity to defendant's ladder, which had blown down, was not a presumption that the ladder caused his death by blowing down upon him or in any other way, in the absence of any evidence of physical injury or condition of his health. . . . N. H. 520

person attempting to remove electric wire, which fell into street, killed by contact with wire. . N. J. 321

collision between train and wagon at crossing, and person driving killed. . . . . N. J. 626

person killed by fall of elevator. . . . N. Y. 143

child run over and killed by automobile. N. Y. 158

elevator operator killed; failure of evidence to show cause of accident; nonsuit. . . . . N. Y. 269

railroad employee, a boy, riding on hand car, struck and killed by train; railroad company only held to duty of reasonable care to avoid injuring plaintiff, he being a mere licensee. . . . . Ohio, 162

person riding in caboose of freight train by conductor's permission, killed in collision; railroad company not liable. . . . . Ohio, 544

boy stealing a ride jumping from street car and run over and killed by car on other track. . . . . . Tenn. 4

person killed by engine while crossing railroad bridge or trestle. . Va. 5

liability of city for death of member of fire department killed by overturning of hose cart on defective street caused by root of trees projecting across highway. . . . Wash. 203

rule as to looking and listening applied, where woman crossing track from station in night time was struck and fatally injured by switch engine, and her contributory negligence held to preclude recovery of damages. . . . . Wis. 389

fireman fatally injured by being scalded by escaping steam from boiler of engine against which he was thrown by collision between two sections of train. . . . . U. S. C. C. A. 213

notes of cases relating to pedestrians injured at crossings or on track 1-6

Declarations.

what is sufficient to set out in declaration alleging negligence. . Fla. 417

insufficiency of declaration in action by an administrator for negligent killing of intestate, an employee killed in gas explosion. . Me. 461

lack of certainty of statement of plaintiff's case in declaration although affording sufficient ground for striking out declaration on

Declarations — *continued.*

motion, cannot be taken advantage of on general demurrer.... N. J. 525

declarations of railroad superintendent, three hours after accident, as to certain car wheels, admissible against the company.. Wash. 372

Defect.

as to duty of master to furnish safe materials and machinery and servant's knowledge of defect.. Ga. 11

where there was conflicting evidence as to length of time defect in sidewalk had existed, question as to whether city had notice of defect was for jury..........Ky. 35

plaintiff, about nineteen years of age, injured by striking his toe against brick that had been raised by root of tree; city not liable... Ky. 35

township not liable for collapse of bridge, three years after its construction, unless it had notice of defect in same...........Mich. 56

where evidence tended to show defect in bridge and that it was visible and generally known for long period, question of notice to township was for jury.....Mich. 56

employee injured by sudden breaking and fall of plank in scaffolding which had been used for more than two years, no defect having been discovered in it; master not liable.......................Pa. 183

notes of recent Georgia cases involving point of servant's knowledge of defect in machinery....11–14

Defective Appliance.

employee driving wagon injured by horse becoming frightened by harness breaking............Ga. 227

error to charge that where employer has agreed to furnish employee harness sufficiently strong

Defective Appliance — *continued.*

to enable him to control a certain horse, the employer is thereby made an insurer of the quality of harness furnished...........Ga. 227

employee injured in defective elevator; assumption of risk..Iowa, 269

employee injured by falling from staging.....................Me. 46

employee's leg injured by defective appliance to machinery......Me. 47

failure of master to provide safe appliances by reason of which failure an iron crane fell and employee was injured........Minn. 96

employee moving machine injured by fly wheel which slipped off shafting; master liable.....N. J. 127

employee injured by sudden breaking and fall of plank in scaffolding which had been used for more than two years, no defect having been discovered in it; master not liable.......................Pa. 183

notes of recent cases of defective appliances 379–389

Defective Bridge.

personal injuries caused by fall of a bent under end of bridge...... Mich. 56

where evidence tended to show defect in bridge and that it was visible and generally known for long period, question of notice to township was for jury..Mich. 56

personal injuries caused by slipping of plank on bridge which was being reconstructed and over which plaintiff was crossing......Minn. 57

Defective Building.

if any liability of temporary lessee of building exists, for injuries resulting from defective construction, it is limited to such defects as an inspection would disclose, and not for an accident produced by a latent defect...........N. J. 527

Defective Car.

a railway company, which delivers defective freight car to a connecting line, is not liable to employee of latter, who is injured by reason of such defects, after car has been inspected by company receiving it........................Kan. 275

conductor of logging train killed in derailment of train caused by defective car wheels; evidence as to defects and failure to inspect... Wash. 372

Defective Construction.

if any liability of temporary lessee of building exists, for injuries resulting from defective construction, it is limited to such defects as an inspection would disclose, and not for an accident produced by a latent defect....N. J. 527

Defective Highway.

person riding in vehicle injured on defective highway...........Me. 89

horse injured by stepping on defect in highway; driver's knowledge of defect.............Mich. 291

Defective Insulation.

barn destroyed by fire caused by defective insulation of electric wire........................Kan. 442

Defective Machinery. — See also MACHINERY.

minor employee injured by defective machinery...............Ga. 11

notes of recent Georgia cases involving point of servant's knowledge of defect in machinery....11–14

Defective Porch.

person walking along street fatally injured by fall of defective and insufficiently fastened porch.... Minn. 294

Defective Premises.

woman falling over step leading to public hall..............Mass. 529

woman falling in hallway leading to room in public building...... Mass. 531

notes of recent cases arising out of liability for personal injuries sustained on defective premises.... N. J. 529–533

tenant injured by fall of plaster from ceiling..............N. Y. 532

tenant's goods damaged by water from roof of building; liability of landlord..................N. D. 539

notes of recent cases relating to liability for injuries to children while on dangerous and defective premises 508–513

Defective Sidewalk. — See also SIDEWALK.

person injured on sidewalk covered with snow and ice..........Colo. 84

woman walking along sidewalk falling into cellar-door opening and seriously injured..........Idaho. 243

woman injured by stepping on loose plank in board sidewalk.... Iowa. 87

woman injured by falling over spike protruding from plank in sidewalk......................Iowa. 88

woman injured on defective sidewalk; contributory negligence for jury.......................Iowa. 268

pedestrian falling over obstruction made by lot owner on sidewalk: city liable...................Ky. 286

woman injured by slipping on depressed sidewalk...,......Minn 79

woman injured by tripping on loose board on sidewalk..........Neb 104

woman injured on defective sidewalk.......................Neb. 517

woman walking on board sidewalk struck by loose board upon which another person had stepped..... Okla. 93

Defective Sidewalk — *continued.*

woman stepping off defective board walk at night, falling and injuring herself......................Pa. 178

woman familiar with dangerous place in sidewalk at street crossing, injured while walking on sidewalk at night, guilty of contributory negligence........S. D. 94

notes of recent actions against municipal corporations in Nebraska.. 104–108

Defective Street.

person injured while driving, his vehicle striking against fire plug in street concealed from view; notice to city.............Colo. 220

person injured by fall from bicycle alleged to have been caused by a defect in street.............Ind. 85

vehicle overturned in defective street and person riding injured; negligence of driver not imputable to plaintiff...........Minn. 79

liability of city for death of member of fire department killed by overturning of hose cart on defective street caused by root of tree projecting across highway....Wash. 203

where a child's foot became fastened between planking and rail of a track on a street, and the father, in trying to extricate the child, pulled him over the rail as a train of cars approached and the train passed over the child's leg, the proximate cause of the injury was the dangerous condition of the track for which the city was liable, notwithstanding negligence of railroad company and the parent...........Wash. 366

Defective Wheel.

conductor of logging train killed in derailment of train caused by defective car wheels; evidence as to defects and failure to inspect.... Wash. 372

Defective Work.

liability of contractor for defective work of subcontractor.....N. J. 522

buildings damaged by fire caused by defective electrical work.... N. J. 522

Defense.

general denial and plea of contributory negligence not inconsistent defenses....................Kan. 442

the fact that another may be jointly liable with city for injury to person on defective sidewalk is no excuse for city's neglect of duty.. Ky. 286

where a party sets up defense that his signature to contract has been obtained by fraud, the burden is upon him to show fraud by clear and satisfactory proof, the presumption of the law being in favor of innocence, fraud not being assumed on doubtful evidence.....................N. J. 313

Degree of Care.

degree of care required of street railroads under the statute...Fla. 417

erroneous charge as to degree of care required of railroad company towards person on track.. Tex. 360

Demurrer.

petition alleging that certain premises were not enclosed by railing, etc., as required by city ordinance, sufficient to withstand attack by general demurrer....Mo. 504

lack of certainty of statement of plaintiff's case in declaration, although affording sufficient ground for striking out declaration on motion, cannot be taken advantage of on general demurrer...................N. J. 525

Derailment.

laborer engaged in loading a car belonging to railroad company injured by reason of derailment of car.....................Ga. 223

Derailment — *continued.*

baggage-master acting as brakeman injured in derailment of train; railroad company liable....N. J. 113

Dining Car.

when dining car held not to be engaged in interstate traffic....... U. S. C. C. A. 398

Directing Verdict.

where evidence for plaintiff is insufficient to prove cause of action it is duty of court, upon request of defendant, to instruct verdict in his behalf........Neb. 514

Ditch.

person injured by falling into open ditch in highway, dug up by a town for purpose of taking up disused water pipe; town not liable as the digging up of pipe was a governmental act......Vt. 640

Driver.

public hack driver negligently driving in front of train at street crossing may be joined in action against railway company for injury sustained by passenger in hack in collision with train..Kan. 29

whether negligence of driver can be imputed to person riding with him is immaterial where railway company was not negligent towards occupants of wagon..Kan. 601

negligence of driver of vehicle in failing to give notice of defect in highway to town officers is not imputable to person riding in vehicle.....................Me. 89

vehicle overturned in defective street and person riding injured; negligence of driver not imputable to plaintiff........Minn. 79

Driving.

where plaintiff while driving across track at street crossing was struck by defendant's train which failed to signal its approach, the proximate cause of injury was failure of defendant to signal at crossing............Cal. 414

person injured while driving, his vehicle striking against fire plug in street concealed from view; notice to city..............Colo. 220

collision between vehicles on highway.......................Conn. 8

employee driving wagon injured by horse becoming frightened by harness breaking.............Ga. 227

person driving across track at street crossing struck by street car; evidence as to looking and listening....................Kan. 599

person riding in wagon driven by another killed in collision with train at crossing; railroad not liable.......................Kan. 601

horse frightened at snowplow on street-car track, running away and person driving thrown out of vehicle and injured........Me. 38

person driving wagon killed in collision with train at crossing; failure of deceased to exercise due care........................Me. 452

horse frightened by obstruction of culvert pipe on railroad right of way near highway and person driving thrown from wagon and injured; railroad company not liable.......................Me. 458

collision between wagon and street car.......................Mass. 216

horse injured by stepping on defect in highway; driver's knowledge of defect............Mich. 291

person injured while driving horse and buggy at approach to highway bridge; failure to maintain barriers..................Minn. 80

servant of customer of one of defendant's tenants driving over wooden bridge leading from alley on defendant's premises to the

Driving — *continued.*
street, injured by collapse of bridge....................Minn. 498
collision between train and wagon at crossing, and person driving killed....................N. J. 626
person injured in collision between wagon and street car......N. Y. 151
person driving along private lane tacitly open to public use and horse frightened by automobile approaching from opposite direction....................N. Y. 157
collision between vehicle and train at crossing; person driving killed and person riding injured..Ohio, 343
deaf person driving and person riding in vehicle listening and assisting in looking for trains.... Ohio, 343
horses frightened by noise of steam from trains and persons driving injured..........Pa. 329, 331
collision between train and vehicle at grade crossing...........Pa. 626
person riding in wagon on highway fatally injured by a runaway team colliding with wagon...... Tenn. 632

Dynamite.
boy trespassing in building injured by explosion of dynamite cap; owner not liable...........Ky. 509

Ejection.
passenger ejected from train on presentation of expired ticket.. Ga. 427
where brakeman threw piece of coal at boy who was stealing a ride on moving coal train, and, in trying to dodge the missile, the boy lost his hold and fell from the car, the questions whether the brakeman used reasonable means to eject the boy and whether his act was proximate cause of injury, were for jury..................N. Y. 338

Electricity.
where employee was killed by electric shock, evidence not conclusive that he was negligent in attempting to push loose part of derrick cable, charged with electricity, from open street into gutter....................Minn. 488
buildings damaged by fire caused by defective electrical work..N. J. 522

Electric Light Company.
duty of companies maintaining electric light wires and telegraph wires in public streets......N. J. 321

Electric Shock.
contact of electric wires with derrick cables and employee killed by shock; evidence not conclusive that derrick was placed in position and operated by independent contractors........Minn. 488
where employee was killed by electric shock, evidence not conclusive that he was negligent in attempting to push loose part of derrick cable, charged with electricity, from open street into gutter....................Minn. 488
person crossing street stepping on street-car rail and receiving electric shock; street-railroad company liable................N. Y. 156

Electric Wire.
boy injured by live electric wire allowed to remain on sidewalk after falling down, a policeman having moved the same but failing to warn passers-by of danger; city liable for allowing wire to remain down exposing the public to danger..................Kan. 272
barn destroyed by fire caused by defective insulation of electric wire........................Kan. 442
contact of electric wires with derrick cables and employee killed by shock; evidence not conclu-

Electric Wire — *continued.*
sive that derrick was placed in position and operated by independent contractors........Minn. 488
lineman injured while stringing telephone wires under direction of foreman, the latter also co-operating with plaintiff in the work.. N. J. 109
person attempting to remove electric wire which fell into street killed by contact with wire..N. J. 321
duty of companies maintaining electric-light wires and telegraph wires in public streets......N. J. 321
employees injured by contact with electric wires........Pa. 322; Va. 323

Elevator.
employee injured in defective elevator; assumption of risk..Iowa, 269
person killed by fall of elevator... N. Y. 143
where defendant had shown reasonable care in construction, operation and inspection of elevator, held not liable for fatal accident.. N. Y. 143
in elevator-accident case burden of proof was upon plaintiff to show death of intestate was caused by defendant's negligence....N. Y. 143
elevator operator killed; failure of evidence to show cause of accident; nonsuit..............N. Y. 269

Employee — See also MASTER AND SERVANT.
minor employee injured by defective machinery...............Ga. 11
horse becoming frightened by harness breaking and employee driving injured..................Ga. 227
brakeman injured while coupling cars.........................Ga. 420
engineer killed in collision between passenger train and freight train........................Ga. 420
notes of recent cases arising out of the relations of master and servant......................Ga. 420–423

Employee — *continued.*
engineer killed by negligence of co-employees; railroad company liable........................Ga. 421
conductor injured while examining defective appliance, there being no duty imposed on him to make such examination; railroad company not liable...............Ga. 422
motorman in trying to board his car which was going at slow speed falling from same and run over by car..................Ga. 422
while engaged in removing a "bosh plate" from furnace, employee injured by emission of fire, coke and gas forced out by pressure from blast in furnace.. Ill. 248
injured in defective elevator; assumption of risk...........Iowa, 269
injured while loading cars; liability of connecting line..........Kan. 275
railroad employee working on bridge injured by falling timbers.. Kan. 438
minor employee injured by molding machine..................La. 448
injured by falling from staging... Me. 46
injured by defective appliance to machinery..................Me. 47
killed by gas explosion........Me. 461
the statute of 1891 affords a right of action for "injuries causing death," substantially like that given to employees by the employers' liability act in Massachusetts (chapter 24, Pub. St. 1887).......................Me. 461
minor employee, familiar with surroundings, passing between machines, slipping and injured by gears of machine; master not liable.....................Mass. 74
injured by being caught in shafting of washing machine which superintendent set running while plaintiff was attending to appliances.. Mass. 75

Employee — *continued.*
injured by fall of stones negligently piled by fellow-servants....Mass. 76
injured by defective machinery, the danger of running which was known to him............Mass. 76
tripping on plank on scaffolding, falling and breaking his leg; master not liable, the scaffolding planks not being "ways or works" within statute.....Mass. 76
fatally injured in saw mill due to improper setting of saw....Mass. 78
injured by fall of iron metal bars, he being familiar with custom of standing the bars against wall of store.....................Mass. 79
failure of master to provide safe appliances by reason of which failure an iron crane fell and employee was injured........Minn. 96
railroad employee injured while clearing railroad wreck....Minn. 99
injured by failure of defendants to keep trapdoors to basement of building in proper repair for use.. Minn. 99
railroad employee clearing snow from switch struck by "kicked" car......................Minn. 100
fireman falling from pilot and foot crushed by engine.........Minn. 101
injured by foot being crushed by saw-mill machinery........Minn. 101
section man injured while engaged with others in removing hand car from track to make way for freight train..............Minn. 102
minor employee cleaning windows injured by falling from third story of factory...........Minn. 102
injured by unguarded laundry mangle the risk of operation being known to operator..Minn. 103
minor employee injured by toes being caught in revolving knives of molding machine.......Minn. 104
contact of electric wires with derrick cables and employee killed by shock; evidence not conclusive that derrick was placed in position and operated by independent contractors.......Minn. 488
where employee was killed by electric shock, evidence not conclusive that he was negligent in attempting to push loose part of derrick cable, charged with electricity, from open street into gutter...................Minn. 488
injured while unloading logs from flat cars..................Minn. 496
ordinary labor of unloading logs from flat cars is not attended with extra hazards as to require formulation of rules for employees..................Minn. 496
servant ordered, with other employees, to unload logs from flat cars, where risk of such work is open and apparent, he assumes dangers caused by negligence of fellow-servants............Minn. 496
injured while moving tank in brewery......................Neb. 514
lineman injured while stringing telephone wires under direction of foreman, the latter also cooperating with plaintiff in the work.....................N. J. 109
baggage-master acting as brakeman injured in derailment of train; railroad company liable... N. J. 113
moving machine injured by fly wheel which slipped off shafting; master liable..............N. J. 127
brakeman injured in collision..... N. J. 313
minor employee injured by circular saw......................N. J. 327
an employee, although a minor, assumes risk of dangers of employment as are obvious to him, and his employer is not responsible for injuries resulting therefrom, notwithstanding latter has failed to point out such dangers..N. J. 327

Employee — *continued.*
injured while unloading coal cars.. N. J. 525
elevator operator killed; failure of evidence to show cause of accident; nonsuit............N. Y. 269
person assisting employee injured while unloading machinery...... N. D. 619
railroad employee, a boy, riding on hand car, struck and killed by train; railroad company only held to duty of reasonable care to avoid injuring plaintiff, he being a mere licensee...........Ohio, 162
injured by sudden breaking and fall of plank in scaffolding which had been used for more than two years, no defect having been discovered in it; master not liable.. Pa. 183
injured by contact with electric wires...............Pa. 322; Va. 323
section hand injured while unloading steel rails from hand car did not assume risk of danger where he was inexperienced, was not informed of danger and the danger was not obvious and apparent.......................Tex. 636
conductor of logging train killed in derailment of train caused by defective car wheels; evidence as to defects and failure to inspect.... Wash. 372
brakeman familiar with custom of coupling cars, injured while coupling cars..............Wis. 206
injured in coal yard......Wis. 206; 208
fireman fatally injured by being scalded by escaping steam from boiler of engine against which he was thrown by collision between two sections of train........... U. S. C. C. A. 213
doctrine of fellow-servant not applicable to case where plaintiff, a laborer in defendant's employ, was injured by blasting operations at time when he was not at

Employee — *continued.*
work or assisting other employees...........U. S. C. C. A. 393
brakeman injured while coupling cars.............U. S. C. C. A. 398
notes of recent Georgia cases involving point of servant's knowledge of defect in machinery....11–14
notes of recent Massachusetts cases relating to injuries to employees.. 75–79
notes of recent master and servant cases in Minnesota............99–104
notes of recent master and servant cases in Wisconsin..........206–210
notes of recent cases on furnishing servant safe place to work.. 251–268
notes of recent cases of defective appliances 379–389
notes of recent cases on proximate cause of injury.............477–488

Employers' Liability Act.
the statute of 1891 affords a right of action for "injuries causing death," substantially like that given to employees by the employers' liability act in Massachusetts (chapter 24, Pub. St. 1887).......................Me. 461

Engine.
passenger thrown from car by sudden jolt of defendant's train and run over and killed by passing engine of another railroad company........................Ga. 232
fireman falling from pilot and foot crushed by engine.........Minn. 101
where child was run over and killed by engine at crossing, the case should have gone to jury..Miss. 608
woman crossing street over tracks at railroad yard struck and injured by engine..........Ohio, 547
person killed by engine while crossing railroad bridge or trestle.... Va.

Engine — *continued.*

rule as to looking and listening applied, where woman crossing track from station in night-time was struck and fatally injured by switch engine, and her contributory negligence held to preclude recovery of damages........Wis. 389

Engineer.

killed in collision between passenger train and freight train....Ga. 420

duty when approaching crossings.. Ohio, 343

Evidence.

where plaintiff was injured in derailment, evidence that another car was overturned on a nearby but different track, three months prior to time of plaintiff's injury was not relevant to prove defendant's negligence at time and place alleged in petition...........Ga. 223

notice posted at ticket office limiting time of use of certain railroad ticket, not admissible in action for ejection of passenger, unless proof is given that passenger had read same or notice of its contents.........................Ga. 427

in action for negligently running train at street crossing without signal, error to admit evidence of like failure of train to signal at another street crossing.....Kan. 29

what is admissible to show pecuniary value of person whose death was caused by wrongful act.........................Kan. 594

person driving across track at street crossing struck by street car; evidence as to looking and listening...................Kan. 599

when new trial will be granted on newly-discovered evidence...Me. 38

burden of proof as to due care on part of injured person........Me. 452

contact of electric wires with derrick cables and employee killed by shock; evidence not conclusive that derrick was placed in position and operated by independent contractors........Minn. 488

where employee was killed by electric shock, evidence not conclusive that he was negligent in attempting to push loose part of derrick cable, charged with electricity, from open street into gutter.......................Minn. 488

under proper precautions and necessary explanations, X-ray pictures are admissible in evidence to show condition of internal tissues of the body..Neb. 104

where evidence for plaintiff is insufficient to prove cause of action it is duty of court, upon request of defendant, to instruct verdict in his behalf................Neb. 514

where it is shown that a person is affected by a serious constitutional disease, error to submit to jury question of expectancy of life, in absence of any evidence bearing upon that question..Neb. 517

the fact that plaintiff's intestate was found dead in proximity to defendant's ladder, which had blown down, was not a presumption that the ladder caused his death by blowing down upon him or in any other way, in the absence of any evidence of physical injury or condition of his health..N. H. 520

where a party sets up defense that his signature to contract has been obtained by fraud, the burden is upon him to show fraud by clear and satisfactory proof, the presumption of the law being in favor of innocence, fraud not being assumed on doubtful evidence.....................N. J. 313

failure of proof to show that signature to contract accepting benefits from relief fund for injuries which operated as release was obtained by fraud.............N. J. 313

Evidence — *continued.*

a mere fall from a street car, without any evidence to show how it was occasioned, raises no presumption of negligence on part of operators of car..........N. J. 533
instruction as to result of X-ray examination...............N. Y. 151
an infant under the age of 12 years is presumed to be *non sui juris*, but may be overcome by evidence to the contrary............N. Y. 338
testimony that there were many other street crossings in same condition as one in question, competent as to whether keeping it in that condition was negligence, and also on question of contributory negligence......Pa. 176
where petition alleges injuries to specific parts of body error to admit evidence of injuries to other parts not set out in petition.......................Tex. 199
admission of piece of broken flange of car wheels picked up six months after derailment of train.. Wash. 372
declarations of railroad superintendent, three hours after accident, as to certain car wheels, admissible against the company... Wash. 372
failure of proof to establish fraud in obtaining signature to release of claim for personal injuries.... U. S. C. C. A. 314

Excavation.

woman injured by stepping into excavation caused by heavy rainstorm.......................Ind. 86
liability of street-railway company for personal injuries caused by an excavation made by it in the highway..................Mass. 54
girl, fourteen years of age, falling into excavation made for building purposes in street......N. Y. 513
person injured by falling into open ditch in highway, dug up by a town for purpose of taking up disused water pipe; town not liable, as the digging up of pipe was a governmental act......Vt. 640
person falling into excavation in street, city having given permission to owner of premises to make such excavation.....Wash. 203

Exceptions.

rule as to exceptions to charge to jury.......................N. Y. 610

Exhibit.

admission of piece of broken flange of car wheels picked up six months after derailment of train.. Wash. 372

Expectancy.

where it is shown that a person is affected by a serious constitutional disease, error to submit to jury question of expectancy of life, in absence of any evidence bearing upon that question..Neb. 517

Explosion.

gas explosion demolishing brick building and wall falling on adjoining frame shop and killing plaintiff's intestate..........Kan. 594
boy trespassing in building injured by explosion of dynamite cap; owner not liable.............Ky. 509
employee killed by gas explosion.. Me. 461
boy trespassing on track finding torpedo and injured by explosion; railroad company not liable......................N. H. 510
boy injured by explosives found on vacant lot adjacent to factory......................N. Y. 512
person injured while walking on sidewalk, the heating apparatus in sidewalk basement of building having exploded..........Wash. 205

Explosion — *continued.*

doctrine of fellow-servant not applicable to case where plaintiff, a laborer in defendant's employ, was injured by blasting operations at time when he was not at work or assisting other employees...........U. S. C. C. A. 393

Falling From Car.

a mere fall from a street car, without any evidence to show how it was occasioned, raises no presumption of negligence on part of operators of car.........N. J. 533

Falling From Engine.

fireman falling from pilot and foot crushed by engine.........Minn. 101

Falling From Window.

minor employee cleaning windows injured by falling from third story of factory................Minn. 102

Falling Object.

mail clerk on railroad car injured by mail grab on outside of car coming in contact with post on station platform, the mail grab being thrown upon clerk's hand.. Ga. 231

railroad employee working on bridge injured by falling timbers.. Kan. 438

employee injured by fall of stones negligently piled by fellow-servants......................Mass. 76

employee injured by fall of iron metal bars, he being familiar with custom of standing the bars against wall of store.......Mass. 79

failure of master to provide safe appliances by reason of which failure an iron crane fell and employee was injured........Minn. 96

person walking along street fatally injured by fall of defective and insufficiently fastened porch..... Minn. 294

Falling Object — *continued.*

person injured by fall of chimney.. N. J. 124

the fact that plaintiff's intestate was found dead in proximity to defendant's ladder, which had blown down, was not a presumption that the ladder caused his death by blowing down upon him or in any other way, in the absence of any evidence of physical injury or condition of his health.....................N. H. 520

child struck by fall of pipes from building material standing on sidewalk..................N. Y. 511

tenant injured by fall of plaster from ceiling...............N. Y. 532

boy, ten years of age, climbing on gate injured by fall of same on lot owned by city; nonsuit....Pa. 294

person rightfully on premises injured by fall of brick from building in course of construction.. Pa. 295

contractor for masonry work in repairing a coal tipple injured by falling timber in work of removal by carpenters; liability of owner.. W. Va. 571

Falling Wall.

gas explosion demolishing brick building and wall falling on adjoining frame shop and killing plaintiff's intestate..........Kan. 594

Fellow-servant.

if plaintiff's fellow-workmen failed to exercise due care in adjusting appliances to staging, and plaintiff was injured by falling from staging, defendant not responsible for accident..............Me. 46

employee injured by fall of stones negligently piled by fellow-servants......................Mass. 76

employee tripping on plank on scaffolding, falling and breaking his leg; master not liable, the

Fellow-servant — *continued.*

scaffolding planks not being "ways or works" within statute.. Mass. 76

servant ordered with other employees to unload logs from flat cars, where risk of such work is open and apparent, he assumes dangers caused by negligence of fellow-servants............Minn. 496

lineman injured while stringing telephone wires under direction of foreman, the latter also co-operating with plaintiff in the work......................N. J. 109

the "superior servant rule" does not prevail in New Jersey..N. J. 109

baggage-master acting as brakeman injured in derailment of train; railroad company liable....N. J. 113

liability under Utah statutes for negligence of superior servants.. U. S. C. C. A. 213

doctrine of fellow-servant not applicable to case where plaintiff, a laborer in defendant's employ, was injured by blasting operations at time when he was not at work or assisting other employees..........U. S. C. C. A. 393

Fence.

where certain stock was killed at point west of defendant's switch, which was left unfenced and treated as part of defendant's depot grounds or switching yard, it was for jury to determine whether proximate cause of killing of cattle was absence of fence, and whether such point was reasonably required by defendant for purposes stated........Minn. 471

Fire.

barn destroyed by fire caused by defective insulation of electric wire.......................Kan. 442

buildings damaged by fire caused by defective electrical work..... N. J. 522

Fire — *continued.*

child attracted to fire on premises where children were accustomed to play; owner not liable for injuries to child though he took no means to prevent children approaching fire.............R. I. 550

Fireman.

fatally injured by being scalded by escaping steam from boiler of engine against which he was thrown by collision between two sections of train..........U. S. C. C. A. 213

Fire Plug.

person injured while driving, his vehicle striking against fire plug in street concealed from view; notice to city.............Colo. 220

Flagman.

person killed while crossing track in front of rapidly moving train at crossing used by public but at which no flagman was in attendance........................Cal. 215

Foreman.

lineman injured while stringing telephone wires under direction of foreman, the latter also co-operating with plaintiff in the work......................N. J. 109

Fraud.

where a party attaches his signature to a contract otherwise valid, a conclusive presumption is created, except as against fraud, that he read, understood and assented to its terms..........N. J. 313

where a party sets up defense that his signature to contract has been obtained by fraud, the burden is upon him to show fraud by clear and satisfactory proof, the presumption of the law being in favor of innocence, fraud not being assumed on doubtful evidence.....................N. J. 313

Fraud — *continued.*

failure of proof to show that signature to contract accepting benefits from relief fund for injuries which operated as release was obtained by fraud.....N. J. 313

failure of proof to establish fraud in obtaining signature to release of claim for personal injuries... U. S. C. C. A. 314

Freight Train.

person riding in caboose of freight train by conductor's permission killed in collision; railroad company not liable............Ohio, 544

Future Damages.

instruction that damages subsequent to date of writ could not be recovered in action for injury to property caused by blasting, etc., properly given..............Me. 44

Gas.

gas explosion demolishing brick building and wall falling on adjoining frame shop and killing plaintiff's intestate..........Kan. 594

employee killed by gas explosion.. Me. 461

Gates.

where railroad company was in habit of operating gates at street crossing at certain hours, but not at time of accident, error to refer question to jury as to whether single isolated instance of failure to operate gates at that time was negligence.................Kan. 29

horse standing at gate crossing frightened by train and backing wagon against engine, and person in wagon injured; question for jury whether plaintiff was negligent in not alighting from wagon....................N. J. 329

boy, ten years of age, climbing on gate injured by fall of same on lot owned by city; nonsuit...Pa. 294

General Denial.

general denial and plea of contributory negligence not inconsistent defenses...................Kan. 442

Goods.

passenger's merchandise checked as baggage lost or stolen in transit.....................Mich. 61

tenants goods damaged by water from roof of building; liability of landlord...................N. D. 539

Governmental Act.

person injured by falling into open ditch in highway, dug up by a town for purpose of taking up disused water pipe; town not liable as the digging up of pipe was a governmental act......Vt. 640

Grand Stand.

liability of State fair corporation for injuries sustained by fall of stand at fireworks exhibition on State fair grounds...............Tex. 199

Grade Crossing.

collision between train and vehicle at grade crossing.............Pa. 626

Gutter Crossing.

person injured at gutter crossing in street........................Pa. 176

Hack.

collision between public hack and train at street crossing and passenger in hack injured......Kan. 29

driver of public hack negligently driving in front of train at street crossing may be joined in action against railway company for injury sustained by passenger in hack in collision with train..Kan. 29

Hallway.

woman falling in hallway leading to room in public building..Mass. 531

Hand Car.

railroad employee, a boy, riding on hand car, struck and killed by train; railroad company only held to duty of reasonable care to avoid injuring plaintiff, he being a mere licensee...........Ohio, 162

Harness.

error to charge that where employer has agreed to furnish employee harness sufficiently strong to enable him to control a certain horse, the employer is thereby made an insurer of the quality of harness furnished...........Ga. 227

Hatchway.

child of tender years fatally injured by falling into hatchway on defendant's premises..........Mo. 504

Highway.

collision between vehicles on highway......................Conn. 8

child of tender age killed on highway by horse attached to wagon in which deceased was riding becoming frightened at iron tiles placed on highway and backing off bridge on highway and falling on child..................Iowa, 590

person riding in vehicle injured on defective highway..........Me. 89

horse frightened by obstruction of culvert pipe on railroad right of way near highway and person driving thrown from wagon and injured; railroad company not liable........................Me. 458

person injured while driving horse and buggy at approach to highway bridge; failure to maintain barriers...................Minn. 80

person injured by falling into an unprotected ravine along public highway.................Minn. 81

person driving along private lane tacitly open to public use and horse frightened by automobile

Highway — *continued.*

approaching from opposite direction...................N. Y. 157

bicycle rider striking loose plank and falling over bridge.......Pa. 180

woman falling over stake in highway while crossing avenue...Pa. 181

person riding in wagon on highway fatally injured by a runaway team colliding with wagon......Tenn. 632

person injured by falling into open ditch in highway, dug up by a town for purpose of taking up disused water pipe; town not liable as the digging up of pipe was a governmental act......Vt. 640

liability of city for death of member of fire department killed by overturning of hose cart on defective street caused by root of tree projecting across highway....Wash. 203

Hole in Sidewalk. — See OPENING IN SIDEWALK.

Horse.

horse injured by stepping on defect in highway; driver's knowledge of defect............Mich. 291

valuable horse injured in transportation while in custody of connecting carrier..............Pa. 185

Horse Frightened.

employee driving wagon injured by horse becoming frightened by harness breaking............Ga. 227

child of tender age killed on highway by horse attached to wagon in which deceased was riding becoming frightened at iron tiles placed on highway and backing off bridge on highway and falling on child.................Iowa. 590

horse frightened at snow plow on street-car track, running away and person driving thrown out of vehicle and injured.........Me. 38

horse frightened by obstruction of culvert pipe on railroad right of

Horse Frightened — *continued.*
way near highway and person driving thrown from wagon and injured; railroad company not liable........................Me. 458
horse standing at gate crossing frightened by train and backing wagon against engine, and person in wagon injured; question for jury whether plaintiff was negligent in not alighting from wagon.....................N. J. 329
person driving along private lane tacitly open to public use and horse frightened by automobile approaching from opposite direction......................N. Y. 157
horses frightened by noise of steam from trains and persons driving injured.................Pa. 329, 331

Husband and Wife.
common-law right of action by husband for injury to wife to recover for loss of her services and for his medical and other expenses in healing her injuries, is not abridged or affected by statute.......................Ohio, 547

Ice and Snow.
owner of premises liable for injury to person falling on icy sidewalk, ice being formed by water discharged from roof.........N. Y. 132
tenant injured by slipping on ice in hallway of tenement house, the ice forming from leakage of water from closet; landlord liable.....................N. Y. 336
person injured by falling on ice on sidewalk, the ice being formed by accumulation of water from drain pipe.......................Pa. 132

Imputed Negligence.
whether negligence of driver can be imputed to person riding with him is immaterial where railway company was not negligent towards occupants of wagon..Kan. 601

Imputed Negligence — *continued.*
negligence of driver of vehicle in failing to give notice of defect in highway to town officers is not imputable to person riding in vehicle......................Me. 89
vehicle overturned in defective street and person riding injured; negligence of driver not imputable to plaintiff...........Minn. 79
while doctrine of imputed negligence does not prevail, yet where two or more persons take active part in joint enterprise, the negligence of each must be regarded as the negligence of all....Ohio, 343
the negligence of a parent cannot be imputed to a child in action brought for benefit of child and not for benefit of parent..Wash. 366

Independent Contractor.
whether doctrine of *respondeat superior* applies to any particular case between the original contractor and a subcontractor is determined by the contract between the parties...............Minn. 488
contact of electric wires with derrick cables and employee killed by shock; evidence not conclusive that derrick was placed in position and operated by independent contractors........Minn. 488
liability of contractor for defective work of subcontractor......N. J. 522
liability of State fair corporation for injuries sustained by fall of stand at fireworks exhibition on State fair grounds..........Tex. 199
contractor for masonry work in repairing a coal tipple injured by falling timber in work of removal by carpenters; liability of owner.. W. Va. 571
where one going upon another's premises, not as a trespasser or mere licensee, but by invitation in legal sense, as for instance an independent contractor or to do

Independent Contractor — *continued.*

work for the owner, the owner owes the duty of reasonable care to keep premises in safe condition for such person's work, unless defects be known to such person.................. W. Va. 571

Infant.

boy stepping into pool of hot water; owner of premises not liable.... Ark. 508

minor employee injured by defective machinery.............. Ga. 11

child fatally injured while playing on turntable.............. Idaho, 18

child, between seven and eight years of age, injured while playing on turntable........... Iowa, 27

child of tender age killed on highway by horse attached to wagon in which deceased was riding becoming frightened at iron tiles placed on highway and backing off bridge on highway and falling on child.................. Iowa, 590

boy injured by live electric wire allowed to remain on sidewalk after falling down, a policeman having moved the same but failing to warn passers-by of danger; city liable for allowing wire to remain down exposing the public to danger.................. Kan. 272

plaintiff, about nineteen years of age, injured by striking his toe against brick that had been raised by root of tree; city not liable....................... Ky. 35

girl, twelve years of age, injured by falling on sidewalk caused by loose plank in walk.......... Ky. 35

boy trespassing in building injured by explosion of dynamite cap; owner not liable............ Ky. 509

minor employee injured by molding machine................. La. 448

minor employee, familiar with surroundings passing between machines, slipping and injured by gears of machine; master not liable..................... Mass. 74

minor employee cleaning windows injured by falling from third story of factory................ Minn. 102

minor employee injured by toes being caught in revolving knives of molding machine..... Minn. 104

child of tender years struck by street car at street crossing...... Minn. 604

where child was run over and killed by engine at crossing, the case should have gone to jury... Miss. 608

whether a boy, between eleven and twelve years of age, was guilty of contributory negligence in crawling out of a ditch at side of track into which he had lodged while coasting, and was run over by train, was question for jury to determine............... Mo. 499

child coasting run over on track.. Mo. 499

child of tender years fatally injured by falling into hatchway on defendant's premises......... Mo. 504

boy run over and leg injured by train at street crossing; question of negligence for jury...... Neb. 3

boy, four years of age, injured while playing on turntable........ Neb. 300

boy riding on back of wagon jumping off wagon and run over by street car.................. N. J. 4

minor employee injured by circular saw........................ N. J. 327

an employee, although a minor, assumes risk of dangers of employment as are obvious to him, and his employer is not responsible for injuries resulting therefrom, notwithstanding latter has failed to point out such dangers.. N. J. 327

child, about three years old, thrown down and injured by sudden starting of street car which she had boarded............... N. J. 334

Infant — *continued.*

boy trespassing on track finding torpedo and injured by explosion; railroad company not liable......................N. H. 510

child run over and killed by automobile....................N. Y. 158

where brakeman threw piece of coal at boy who was stealing a ride on moving coal train, and, in trying to dodge the missile, the boy lost his hold and fell from the car, the questions whether the brakeman used reasonable means to eject the boy and whether his act was proximate cause of injury, were for jury........N. Y. 338

error to hold that boy, about 12 years old, was, as matter of law, *sui juris*, that being for the jury to determine..............N. Y. 338

an infant under the age of 12 years is presumed to be *non sui juris* but may be overcome by evidence to the contrary............N. Y. 338

child struck by fall of pipes from building material standing on sidewalk...................N. Y. 511

boy playing along railroad path scalded by steam and hot water discharged from adjoining premises; owner of premises liable.... N. Y. 511

boy injured by explosives found on vacant lot adjacent to factory... N. Y. 512

girl, fourteen years of age, falling into excavation made for building purposes in street......N. Y. 513

boy riding on rear of wagon injured in collision between street car and wagon............N. Y. 610

railroad employee, a boy, riding on hand car, struck and killed by train; railroad company only held to duty of reasonable care to avoid injuring plaintiff, he being a mere licensee............Ohio, 162

boy, ten years of age, climbing on gate, injured by fall of same, on lot owned by city; nonsuit...Pa. 294

child attracted to fire on premises where children were accustomed to play; owner not liable for injuries to child though he took no means to prevent children approaching fire..............R. I. 550

boy stealing a ride jumping from street car and run over and killed by car on other track.....Tenn. 4

child falling through grating over cellar in sidewalk..........Tex. 95

where a child's foot became fastened between planking and rail of a track on a street and the father, in trying to extricate the child, pulled him over the rail as a train of cars approached and the train passed over the child's leg, the proximate cause of the injury was the dangerous condition of the track for which the city was liable, notwithstanding negligence of railroad company and the parent................Wash. 366

an infant under five years of age cannot be guilty of contributory negligence................Wash. 366

notes of recent cases relating to liability for injuries to children while on dangerous and defective premises 508–513

notes of recent cases arising from injuries to trespassers........562–571

Inspection.

conductor injured while examining defective appliance, there being no duty imposed on him to make such examination; railroad company not liable..............Ga. 422

a railway company, which delivers defective freight car to a connecting line is not liable to employee of latter, who is injured by reason of such defects, after car has been inspected by company receiving it..................Kan. 275

Inspection — *continued.*

if any liability of temporary lessee of building exists, for injuries resulting from defective construction, it is limited to such defects as an inspection would disclose, and not for an accident produced by a latent defect.........N. J. 527
where defendant had shown reasonable care in construction, operation and inspection of elevator, held not liable for fatal accident.. N. Y. 143

Instruction.

as to duty of master to furnish safe materials and machinery, and servant's knowledge of defect... Ga. 11
error for trial judge to instruct that given facts would constitute negligence, when the facts are not such as are made by law to constitute negligence *per se*......Ga. 227
error to charge that where employer has agreed to furnish employee harness sufficiently strong to enable him to control a certain horse, the employer is thereby made an insurer of the quality of harness furnished...........Ga. 227
that damages subsequent to date of writ could not be recovered in action for injury to property caused by blasting, etc.; properly given......................Me. 44
where evidence for plaintiff is insufficient to prove cause of action it is duty of court, upon request of defendant, to instruct verdict in his behalf...............Neb. 514
as to result of X-ray examination.. N. Y. 151
rule as to exceptions to charge to jury.....................N. Y. 610
erroneous instruction as to negligence of motorman in collision between street car and wagon, question being for jury....N. Y. 610
erroneous charge as to degree of care required of railroad company towards person on track.. Tex. 360
erroneous charge regarding person on track as a trespasser.....Tex. 360
error to charge that burden of proof was upon plaintiff to show by preponderance of evidence that he was not guilty of contributory negligence while walking on track...............Tex. 360
error to give instruction based upon a fact that there was no evidence tending to prove....Va. 5
instructions and refusals to instruct as to negligence and burden of proof....................Wash. 372

Interstate Commerce Act.

the Interstate Commerce Act is not violated by holding that contract limiting liability for carrier's negligence is invalid within this State.......................Pa. 185
when dining car held not to be engaged in interstate traffic....... U. S. C. C. A. 398
the Federal statute does not make it unlawful for common carriers to use locomotives engaged in interstate commerce which are not equipped with automatic couplers..........U. S. C. C. A. 398

Invitation.

where owner invites another to come upon his premises he is required to use reasonable care to have premises in safe condition......................N. J. 124
act of conductor in permitting person to ride on train against rules of railroad company, not binding on company..........Ohio, 544
person riding in caboose of freight train by conductor's permission killed in collision; railroad company not liable...........Ohio. 544
where one going upon another's

Invitation — *continued.*
premises, not as a trespasser or mere licensee, but by invitation in legal sense, as for instance, an independent contractor to do work for the owner, the owner owes the duty of reasonable care to keep premises in safe condition for such person's work, unless defects be known to such person..................W. Va. 571

Joint Enterprise.
deaf person driving and person riding in vehicle listening and assisting in looking for trains..... Ohio, 343

Joint Liability.
the fact that another may be jointly liable with city for injury to person on defective sidewalk is no excuse for city's neglect of duty.. Ky. 286

"Kicking" Car.
railroad employee clearing snow from switch struck by "kicked" car......................Minn. 100

Knowledge of Danger. — See also NOTICE.
minor employee, familiar with surroundings passing between machines, slipping and injured by gears of machine; master not liable.....................Mass. 74
employee injured by defective machinery, the danger of running which was known to him..Mass. 76
horse injured by stepping on defect in highway; driver's knowledge of defect.................Mich. 291
woman familiar with dangerous place in sidewalk at street crossing, injured while walking on sidewalk at night, guilty of contributory negligence.......S. D. 94

Ladder.
the fact that plaintiff's intestate was found dead in proximity to defendant's ladder, which had blown down, was not a presumption that the ladder caused his death by blowing down upon him or in any other way, in the absence of any evidence of physical injury or condition of his health....................N. H. 520

Landlord and Tenant.
no implied duty on owner of house to inform prospective tenant that house is in dangerous condition, and no action lies against owner for omission to do so, in absence of express warranty or deceit... N. J. 124
tenant injured by slipping on ice in hallway of tenement house, the ice forming from leakage of water from closet; landlord liable.......................N. Y. 336
tenant injured by fall of plaster from ceiling..............N. Y. 532
tenant's goods damaged by water from roof of building; liability of landlord..................N. D. 539

Latent Defect.
if any liability of temporary lessee of building exists, for injuries resulting from defective construction, it is limited to such defects as an inspection would disclose, and not for an accident produced by a latent defect..........N. J. 527

Leakage
tenant injured by slipping on ice in hallway of tenement house, the ice forming from leakage of water from closet; landlord liable.......................N. Y. 336
tenant's goods damaged by water from roof of building; liability of landlord..................N. D. 539

Lessor and Lessee.
if any liability of temporary lessee of building exists for injuries resulting from defective construc-

Lessor and Lessee — *continued.*
tion, it is limited to such defects as an inspection would disclose, and not for an accident produced by a latent defect..........N. J. 527
lessor of steamboat, a private corporation, not liable for negligence of lessee where passenger on steamboat was injured by capsizing of boat..........N. C. 617

Licensee.
laborer engaged in loading a car belonging to railroad company injured by reason of derailment of car......................Ga. 223
only duty owner of premises owes to mere licensee is to refrain from acts willfully injurious..N. J. 124
person driving along private lane tacitly open to public use and horse frightened by automobile approaching from opposite direction......................N. Y. 157
railroad employee, a boy, riding on hand car, struck and killed by train; railroad company only held to duty of reasonable care to avoid injuring plaintiff, he being a mere licensee...........Ohio, 162
where person merely goes to railway station to assist his wife to a train, with no intention of becoming a passenger, and while there was assaulted by drunken person, carrier not liable, the person so assaulted being only a licensee...................Tex. 637
notes of recent cases arising from injuries to trespassers........562–571

Limiting Liability.
stipulation in contract limiting liability of carrier for damage to horse from negligence to $100 is against policy of State, and will not be enforced though made in a State where such a contract is valid.......................Pa. 185
note on liability of connecting carriers for negligence..........191–199

Lineman.
injured while stringing telephone wires under direction of foreman, the latter also co-operating with plaintiff in the work........N. J. 109

Loading and Unloading Cars.
railroad employee injured while loading cars; liability of connecting line...................Kan. 275
employee injured while unloading logs from flat cars........Minn. 496
employee injured while unloading coal cars..................N. J. 525
person assisting employee injured while unloading machinery..N. D. 619
a section hand injured while unloading steel rails from hand car did not assume risk of danger where he was inexperienced, was not informed of danger and the danger was not obvious and apparent.....................Tex. 636

Looking and Listening. — See STOP, LOOK AND LISTEN.

Machinery.
minor employee injured by defective machinery...............Ga. 11
minor employee injured by molding machine.....................La. 448
extent of instructions and warning of danger to workmen in charge of machines are to be gauged by the necessity because of danger.. La. 448
employee's leg injured by defective appliance to machinery......Me. 47
minor employee, familiar with surroundings passing between machines, slipping and injured by gears of machine; master not liable.....................Mass. 74
employee injured by being caught in shafting of washing machine which superintendent set running while plaintiff was attending to appliances................Mass. 75
employee injured by defective machinery, the danger of running which was known to him..Mass. 76

Machinery — *continued.*
employee fatally injured in saw mill due to improper setting of saw.... Mass. 78
failure of master to provide safe appliances by reason of which failure an iron crane fell and employee was injured........Minn. 96
employee injured by foot being crushed by saw-mill machinery.. Minn. 101
employee injured by unguarded laundry mangle, the risks of operation being known to employee.. Minn. 103
minor employee injured by toes being caught in revolving knives of molding machine..........Minn. 104
boy, four years of age, injured while playing on turntable..Neb. 300
employee moving machine injured by fly wheel which slipped off shafting; master liable......N. J. 127
minor employee injured by circular saw......................N. J. 327
person assisting employee injured while unloading machinery..N. D. 619
notes of recent Georgia cases involving point of servant's knowledge of defect in machinery....11-14

Mail Clerk.
mail clerk on railroad car injured by mail grab on outside of car coming in contact with post on station platform, the mail grab being thrown upon clerk's hand.. Ga. 231

Married Woman.
petition by married woman, in action for personal injury, which does not allege ownership of any separate estate or property, or that she is engaged in any business or service, other than pertaining to her husband's household, does not entitle her to recover damages on account either of loss of earnings or diminished capacity to earn money as result of injury..................Neb. 517

Master and Servant.
minor employee injured by defective machinery...............Ga. 11
as to duty of master to furnish safe materials and machinery and servant's knowledge of defect... Ga. 11
employee driving wagon injured by horse becoming frightened by harness breaking............Ga. 227
engineer killed in collision between passenger train and freight train.. Ga. 420
brakeman injured while coupling cars, direction of verdict for railroad company sustained......Ga. 420
notes of recent cases arising out of the relations of master and servant....................Ga. 420-423
engineer killed by negligence of co-employees; railroad company liable.......................Ga. 421
conductor injured while examining defective appliance, there being no duty imposed on him to make such examination; railroad company not liable.............Ga. 422
motorman, in trying to board his car, which was going at slow speed, falling from same and run over by car.................Ga. 422
employee, engaged in removing a "bosh plate" from furnace, injured by emission of fire, coke and gas forced out by pressure from blast in furnace.........Ill. 248
employee injured in defective elevator; assumption of risk..Iowa, 269
railroad employee injured while loading cars; liability of connecting line...................Kan. 275
a railway company, which delivers defective freight car to a connecting line, is not liable to employee of latter, who is injured by reason of such defects, after car has been inspected by company receiving it..........................Kan. 275

Master and Servant — *continued.*

railroad employee working on bridge injured by falling timbers.. Kan. 438
where property of railway company is in exclusive possession of receivers operating the road, the company is not liable for injuries sustained by an employee of such receivers.................. Kan. 438
minor employee injured by molding machine................ La. 448
extent of instructions and warning of danger to workmen in charge of machines are to be gauged by the necessity because of danger.. La. 448
employee injured by falling from staging..................... Me. 46
if plaintiff's fellow-workmen failed to exercise due care in adjusting appliances to staging, and plaintiff was injured by falling from staging, defendant not responsible for accident.............. Me. 46
employee's leg injured by defective appliance to machinery...... Me. 47
employee killed by gas explosion.. Me. 461
the statute of 1891 affords a right of action for "injuries causing death" substantially like that given to employee by the employers' liability act in Massachusetts (chapter 24, Pub. St. 1887)........................ Me. 461
minor employee, familiar with surroundings, passing between machines, slipping and injured by gears of machine; master not liable...................... Mass. 74
employee injured by being caught in shafting of washing machine which superintendent set running while plaintiff was attending to appliances................ Mass. 75
employee injured by fall of stones negligently piled by fellow-servants...................... Mass. 76
employee injured by defective machinery, the danger of running which was known to him.. Mass. 76
employee tripping on plank on scaffolding, falling and breaking his leg; master not liable, the scaffolding planks not being "ways of work" within statute.. Mass. 76
employee fatally injured in saw mill due to improper setting of saw...................... Mass. 78
employee injured by fall of iron metal bars, he being familiar with custom of standing the bars against wall of store....... Mass. 79
failure of master to provide safe appliances by reason of which failure an iron crane fell and employee was injured........ Minn. 96
railroad employee injured while clearing railroad wreck.... Minn. 99
employee injured by failure of defendants to keep trapdoors to basement of building in proper repair for use............ Minn. 99
railroad employee clearing snow from switch struck by "kicked" car...................... Minn. 100
fireman falling from pilot and foot crushed by engine........ Minn. 101
employee injured by foot being crushed by saw-mill machinery... Minn. 101
section man injured while engaged with others in removing hand car from track to make way for freight train.............. Minn. 102
minor employee cleaning windows injured by falling from third story of factory.......... Minn. 102
employee injured by unguarded laundry mangle, the risks of operation being known to employee.. Minn. 103
minor employee injured by toes being caught in revolving knives of molding machine.......... Minn. 104
contact of electric wires with derrick cables and employee killed

Master and Servant — *continued.*

by shock; evidence not conclusive that derrick was placed in position and operated by independent contractors.......Minn. 488

where employee was killed by electric shock, evidence not conclusive that he was negligent in attempting to push loose part of derrick cable, charged with electricity, from open street into gutter.....................Minn. 488

employee injured while unloading logs from flat cars........Minn. 496

ordinary labor of unloading logs from flat cars is not attended with extra hazards as to require formulation of rules for employees...................Minn. 496

servant ordered, with other employees, to unload logs from flat cars, where risk of such work is open and apparent, he assumes dangers caused by negligence of fellow-servants...........Minn. 496

employee injured while moving tank in brewery; risk of employment.......................Neb. 514

lineman injured while stringing telephone wires under direction of foreman, the latter also cooperating with plaintiff in the work......................N. J. 109

the "superior servant rule" does not prevail in New Jersey..N. J. 109

baggage-master acting as brakeman injured in derailment of train; railroad company liable.. N. J. 113

employee moving machine injured by fly wheel which slipped off shafting; master liable......N. J. 127

brakeman injured in collision.... N. J. 313

minor employee injured by circular saw...................N. J. 327

an employee, although a minor, assumes risk of dangers of employment as are obvious to him, and his employer is not responsible for injuries resulting therefrom, notwithstanding latter has failed to point out such dangers.. N. J. 327

employee injured while unloading coal cars..................N. J. 525

elevator operator killed; failure of evidence to show cause of accident; nonsuit..............N. Y. 269

person assisting employee injured while unloading machinery..N. D. 619

railroad employee, a boy, riding on hand car, struck and killed by train; railroad company only held to duty of reasonable care to avoid injuring plaintiff, he being a mere licensee............Ohio, 162

employee injured by sudden breaking and fall of plank in scaffolding which had been used for more than two years, no defect having been discovered in it; master not liable........................Pa. 183

employees injured by contact with electric wires.......Pa. 322; Va. 323

a section hand injured while unloading steel rails from hand car did not assume risk of danger where he was inexperienced, was not informed of danger and the danger was not obvious and apparent.....................Tex. 636

conductor of logging train killed in derailment of train caused by defective car wheels; evidence as to defects and failure to inspect... Wash. 372

brakeman familiar with custom of coupling cars, injured while coupling cars...............Wis. 206

employees injured in coal yard.... Wis. 206; 208

fireman fatally injured by being scalded by escaping steam from boiler of engine against which he was thrown by collision between two sections of train........... U. S. C. C. A. 213

Master and Servant — *continued.*

liability under Utah statutes for negligence of superior servants.. U. S. C. C. A. 213

doctrine of fellow-servant not applicable to case where plaintiff, a laborer in defendant's employ, was injured by blasting operations at time when he was not at work or assisting other employees.......... U. S. C. C. A. 393

brakeman injured while coupling cars.............. U. S. C. C. A. 398

notes of recent Georgia cases involving point of servant's knowledge of defect in machinery...11-14

notes of recent Massachusetts cases relating to injuries to employees.. 75-79

notes of recent master and servant cases in Minnesota............99-104

notes of recent master and servant cases in Wisconsin...........206-210

notes of recent cases on furnishing servant safe place to work... 251-268

notes of recent cases of defective appliances 379-389

notes of recent cases on proximate cause of injury...............477-488

Merchandise.

passenger's merchandise checked as baggage lost or stolen in transit........................Mich. 61

Missile.

where brakeman threw piece of coal at boy who was stealing a ride on moving coal train, and, in trying to dodge the missile, the boy lost his hold and fell from the car, the questions whether the brakeman used reasonable means to eject the boy and whether his act was proximate cause of injury, were for jury.... N. Y. 338

Mortality Table.

not error for court to illustrate to jury the method of using mortality and annuity tables by giving figure approximating that shown by the evidence to be plaintiff's age..........................Ga. 223

Mortorman.

motorman in trying to board his car, which was going at slow speed, falling from same and run over by car..................Ga. 422

duty of motorman when street car approaching street crossing..... Minn. 604

Municipal Corporations.

person injured on sidewalk covered with snow and ice..........Colo. 84

person injured while driving, his vehicle striking against fire plug in street concealed from view; notice to city.............Colo. 220

woman walking along sidewalk falling into cellar-door opening and seriously injured.....Idaho. 243

person injured by fall from bicycle alleged to have been caused by a defect in street............Ind. 85

woman injured by stepping into excavation caused by heavy rainstorm......................Ind. 86

woman injured by stepping on loose plank in board sidewalk... Iowa. 87

woman injured by falling over spike protruding from plank in sidewalk..................Iowa. 88

woman injured on defective sidewalk; contributory negligence for jury...................Iowa. 268

child of tender age killed on highway by horse attached to wagon in which deceased was riding becoming frightened at iron tiles placed on highway and backing off bridge on highway and falling on child..................Iowa. 590

boy injured by live electric wire allowed to remain on sidewalk after

Municipal Corporations — *continued.*

falling down, a policeman having moved the same but failing to warn passers-by of danger; city liable for allowing wire to remain down exposing the public to danger.................Kan. 272

pedestrian falling into cellar opening in sidewalk...........Kan. 431

girl, twelve years of age, injured by falling on sidewalk caused by loose plank in walk..........Ky. 35

where there was conflicting evidence as to length of time defect in sidewalk had existed, question as to whether city had notice of defect was for jury.........Ky. 35

plaintiff, about nineteen years of age, injured by striking his toe against brick that had been raised by root of tree; city not liable.... Ky. 35

pedestrian falling over obstruction made by lot owner on sidewalk; city liable..................Ky. 286

the fact that another may be jointly liable with city for injury to person on defective sidewalk is no excuse for city's neglect of duty.. Ky. 286

personal injuries caused by fall of a bent under end of bridge..Mich. 56

township not liable for collapse of bridge, three years after its construction, unless it had notice of defect in same............Mich. 56

where evidence tended to show defect in bridge and that it was visible and generally known for long period, question of notice to township was for jury.....Mich. 56

horse injured by stepping on defect in highway; driver's knowledge of defect.................Mich. 291

personal injuries caused by slipping of plank on bridge which was being reconstructed and over which plaintiff was crossing......Minn. 57

woman injured by slipping on depressed sidewalk..........Minn. 79

Municipal Corporation — *continued.*

vehicle overturned in defective street and person riding injured; negligence of driver not imputable to plaintiff...........Minn. 79

person injured while driving horse and buggy at approach to highway bridge; failure to maintain barriers...................Minn. 80

person injured by falling into an unprotected ravine along public highway..................Minn. 81

person walking along street fatally injured by fall of defective and insufficiently fastened porch.... Minn. 294

statute requiring notice of injury caused by defect in street to be given to municipality as a condition precedent to maintaining action therefor, not applicable to action by personal representative of deceased person, whose death was caused by such defect.. Minn. 294

person injured at street crossing covered with snow and ice..Mo. 90

woman injured by tripping on loose board on sidewalk.........Neb. 104

woman injured on defective sidewalk......................Neb. 517

person falling over piece of sewer or drain pipe on sidewalk..N. H. 91

bicycle rider running into pile of bricks in street; contributory negligence...................N. C. 92

woman walking on board sidewalk struck by loose board upon which another person had stepped..................Okla. 93

person injured at gutter crossing in street....................Pa. 176

testimony that there were many other street crossings in same condition as one in question competent as to whether keeping it in that condition was negligence, and also on question of contributory negligence.............Pa. 176

city not bound to cover its street

Municipal Corporations — *continued.*

crossings at all places and absence, therefore, of crossing at place of accident not, of itself, negligence....................Pa. 176

person falling on sidepath along township road..............Pa. 178

woman stepping off defective boardwalk at night, falling and injuring herself..............Pa. 178

bicycle rider striking loose plank and falling over bridge......Pa. 180

woman stepping into hole in pavement filled with dust.........Pa. 181

woman falling over stake in highway while crossing avenue...Pa. 181

boy, ten years of age, climbing on gate injured by fall of same, on lot owned by city; nonsuit..Pa. 294

woman familiar with dangerous place in sidewalk at street crossing, injured while walking on sidewalk at night, guilty of contributory negligence.......S. D. 94

child falling through grating over cellar in sidewalk............Tex. 95

person injured by falling into open ditch in highway, dug up by a town for purpose of taking up disused water pipe; town not liable as the digging up of pipe was a governmental act..........Vt. 640

person falling into excavation in street, city having given permission to owner of premises to make such excavation....Wash. 203

liability of city for death of member of fire department killed by overturning of hose cart on defective street caused by root of tree projecting across highway.. Wash. 203

person injured while walking on sidewalk, the heating apparatus in sidewalk basement of building having exploded..........Wash. 205

where a child's foot became fastened between planking and rail of a track on a street, and the father, in trying to extricate the child, pulled him over the rail as a train of cars approached and the train passed over the child's leg, the proximate cause of the injury was the dangerous condition of the track, for which the city was liable, notwithstanding negligence of railroad company and the parent...............Wash. 366

person tripped up by rope stretched across pavement and fastened to telephone pole to hold wharf boat during a flood......W. Va. 95

person falling into opening made for sewer pipe in sidewalk, the same being covered with snow... W. Va. 95

notes of recent Minnesota cases against municipal corporations..79–81

notes of recent cases relating to liability of municipal corporation for personal injuries............84–96

notes of recent actions against municipal corporations in Nebraska.. 104–108

notes of recent municipal corporation cases decided in Pennsylvania 178–182

Negligence.

contributory negligence of deceased in crossing track in front of movtrain bars recovery notwithstanding negligence of railroad company in failing to have flagman at crossing.................Cal. 215

what is sufficient to set out in declaration alleging negligence.. Fla. 417

presumption of negligence under statute relating to street railroads.......................Fla. 417

error for trial judge to instruct that given facts would constitute negligence, when the facts are not such as are made by law to constitute negligence *per se*.....Ga. 227

driver of public hack negligently driving in front of train at street

Negligence — *continued.*

crossing may be joined in action against railway company for injury sustained by passenger in hack in collision with train..Kan. 29

where railroad company was in habit of operating gates at street crossing at certain hours, but not at time of accident, error to refer question to jury as to whether single isolated instance of failure to operate gates at that time was negligence..................Kan. 29

railroad company not chargeable with negligence in running passenger train over road crossing at speed of from forty to fifty miles per hour in open country where view of traveler on highway is unobstructed........Kan. 601

whether negligence of driver can be imputed to person riding with him is immaterial where railway company was not negligent towards occupants of wagon..Kan. 601

no presumption of culpable negligence arises from the mere fact that an accident happened...Me. 46

petition that states facts from which defendant's negligence may be inferred is not defective for omission of use of word "negligent" or its derivatives...........Neb. 104

doctrine of *res ipsa loquitur* is applicable only when the thing shown speaks of defendant's negligence, not merely of happening of accident................N. J. 533

erroneous instruction as to negligence of motorman in collision between street car and wagon, question being for jury....N. Y. 610

deaf person driving and person riding in vehicle listening and assisting in looking for trains.... Ohio, 343

while doctrine of imputed negligence does not prevail, yet where two or more persons take active part in joint enterprise, the negligence of each must be regarded as the negligence of all....Ohio, 343

testimony that there were many other street crossings in same condition as one in question competent as to whether keeping it in that condition was negligence, and also on question of contributory negligence..............Pa. 176

city not bound to cover its street crossings at all places, and absence, therefore, of crossing at place of accident not, of itself, negligence...................Pa. 176

proof by plaintiff of accident occasioned by defendant's runaway team makes a *prima facie* case of negligence................Tenn. 632

the negligence of a parent cannot be imputed to a child in action brought for benefit of child and not for benefit of parent..Wash. 366

instructions and refusals to instruct as to negligence and burden of proof.....................Wash. 372

when question for jury and when for court..........U. S. C. C. A. 395

New Trial.

when granted on newly-discovered evidence.....................Me. 38

Noise.

horses frightened by noise of steam from trains and persons driving injured..........Pa. 329, 331

Non Sui Juris.

an infant under the age of 12 years is presumed to be *non sui juris*, but may be overcome by evidence to the contrary............N. Y. 338

Nonsuit.

motion for nonsuit should not be granted where there is any evidence to sustain allegations of complaint................Idaho, 18

Notice — *continued.*

person injured while walking on sidewalk, the heating apparatus in sidewalk basement of building having exploded...........Wash. 205

notes of recent Georgia cases involving point of servant's knowledge of defect in machinery....11–14

Obstruction.

person injured while driving, his vehicle striking against fire plug in street concealed from view; notice to city..............Colo. 220

mail clerk on railroad car injured by mail grab on outside of car coming in contact with post on station platform, the mail grab being thrown upon clerk's hand.. Ga. 231

woman injured by falling over spike protruding from plank in sidewalk......................Iowa, 88

child of tender age killed on highway by horse attached to wagon in which deceased was riding becoming frightened at iron tiles placed on highway and backing off bridge on highway and falling on child..................Iowa, 590

boy injured by live electric wire allowed to remain on sidewalk after falling down, a policeman having moved the same but failing to warn passers-by of danger; city liable for allowing wire to remain down exposing the public to danger.................Kan. 272

pedestrian falling over obstruction made by lot owner on sidewalk; city liable..................Ky. 286

horse frightened by obstruction of culvert pipe on railroad right of way near highway and person driving thrown from wagon and injured; railroad company not liable.......................Me. 458

four days not an unreasonable time for a railroad company to allow pieces of culvert pipe to be used

Obstruction — *continued.*

for repairs to remain near highway on its right of way......Me. 458

person falling over piece of sewer or drain pipe on sidewalk..N. H. 91

person attempting to remove electric wire which fell into street killed by contact with wire..N. J. 321

bicycle rider running into pile of bricks in street; contributory negligence.................N. C. 92

intending passenger injured by falling on railroad ties and beams while attempting to reach depot, a freight train blocking the crossing at station.............Okla. 353

woman falling over stake in highway while crossing avenue...Pa. 181

liability of city for death of member of fire department killed by overturning of hose cart on defective street caused by root of tree projecting across highway....Wash. 203

person tripped up by rope stretched across pavement and fastened to telephone pole to hold wharf boat during a flood......W. Va. 95

Open Car.

person standing near track to let car pass injured by coming in contact with conductor on footboard of moving open street car; railway company not liable..Md. 51

Opening in Sidewalk.

woman walking along sidewalk falling into cellar-door opening and seriously injured......Idaho, 243

pedestrian falling into cellar opening in sidewalk............Kan. 431

person injured by stepping on coalhole cover in sidewalk; liability of owner of premises......N. J. 121

woman stepping into hole in pavement filled with dust.........Pa. 181

person falling into opening made for sewer pipe in sidewalk, the same being covered with snow.. W. Va. 95

Opening in Sidewalk — *continued.*

notes of recent New York cases arising out of coal-hole accidents 121–122

Ordinance. — See also STATUTE.

requiring person having control of speed of street car to stop car in shortest time and space possible, on appearance of any obstruction to his car, not unreasonable.... Minn. 604

where right to recover for personal injuries was predicated solely on ground of violation of city ordinance, recovery could not be had on ground of common-law negligence........................ Mo. 504

petition alleging that certain premises were not enclosed by railing, etc., as required by city ordinance, sufficient to withstand attack by general demurrer.... Mo. 504

Overflow.

property damaged by rocks thrown on plaintiff's land by blasting in defendant's quarry and also from water pumped from quarry and allowed to flow on plaintiff's land........................ Me. 44

Parties.

driver of public hack negligently driving in front of train at street crossing may be joined in action against railway company for injury sustained by passenger in hack in collision with train.. Kan. 29

Passenger — See also CARRIER OF PASSENGERS.

notice posted at ticket office limiting time of use of certain railroad ticket, not admissible in action for ejection of passenger unless proof is given that passenger had read same or notice of its contents........................ Ga. 427

Passenger — *continued.*

passenger assaulted and insulted at railway station; when carrier not liable........................ Ky. 288

a mere fall from a street car, without any evidence to show how it was occasioned, raises no presumption of negligence on part of operators of car.......... N. J. 533

carrier liable for assault by drunken person upon plaintiff's wife, a passenger, while in carrier's waiting room.............. Tex. 637

passenger who rides on steps or platform of car, without reasonable excuse, guilty of negligence barring recovery notwithstanding negligence of railway company.. U. S. C. C. A. 395

note of recent cases on proximate cause of injury.............. 477–488

Pedestrian.

person crossing track, at place not public crossing, run over and killed by train; failure to look for train........................ Ala. 1

person crossing track at street crossing struck and killed by train........................ Cal. 1

person killed while crossing track in front of rapidly moving train at crossing used by public but at which no flagman was in attendance........................ Cal. 215

person injured while crossing street-car track.............. Cal. 215

person injured on sidewalk covered with snow and ice.......... Colo. 84

person crossing street struck by street car.................. Fla. 417

woman walking along sidewalk falling into cellar-door opening and seriously injured.......... Idaho. 243

woman injured by stepping into excavation caused by heavy rainstorm...................... Ind. 86

woman injured by stepping on loose plank in board sidewalk... Iowa, 87

Pedestrian — *continued.*

woman injured by falling over spike protruding from plank in sidewalk..................Iowa, 88
woman injured on defective sidewalk; contributory negligence for jury.....................Iowa, 268
boy injured by live electric wire allowed to remain on sidewalk after falling down, a policeman having moved the same but failing to warn passers-by of danger; city liable for allowing wire to remain down exposing the public to danger.................Kan. 272
falling into cellar opening in sidewalk......................Kan. 431
girl, twelve years of age, injured by falling on sidewalk caused by loose plank in walk..........Ky. 35
plaintiff, about nineteen years of age, injured by striking his toe against brick that had been raised by root of tree; city not liable.......................Ky. 35
pedestrian falling over obstruction made by lot owner on sidewalk; city liable...................Ky. 286
liability of street-railway company for personal injuries caused by an excavation made by it in the highway..................Mass. 54
personal injuries caused by slipping of plank on bridge which was being reconstructed and over which plaintiff was crossing......Minn. 57
woman injured by slipping on depressed sidewalk..........Minn. 79
person injured by falling into an unprotected ravine along public highway..................Minn. 81
person walking along street fatally injured by fall of defective and insufficiently fastened porch..... Minn. 294
person injured at street crossing covered with snow and ice..Mo. 90
woman injured by tripping on loose board on sidewalk..........Neb. 104

Pedestrian — *continued.*

woman injured on defective sidewalk......................Neb. 517
person falling over piece of sewer or drain pipe on sidewalk..N. H. 91
person injured by stepping on coalhole cover in sidewalk; liability of owner of premises......N. J. 121
owner of premises liable for injury to person falling on icy sidewalk, ice being formed by water discharged from roof.........N. Y. 132
person crossing street stepping on street-car rail and receiving electric shock; street-railroad company liable...............N. Y. 156
girl, fourteen years of age, falling into excavation made for building purposes in street.........N. Y. 513
woman crossing street over tracks at railroad yard struck and injured by engine...........Ohio, 547
woman walking on board sidewalk struck by loose board upon which another person had stepped.... Okla. 93
person injured by falling on ice on sidewalk, the ice being formed by accumulation of water from drain pipe.........................Pa. 132
person injured at gutter crossing in street....................Pa. 176
person falling on sidepath along township road...............Pa. 178
woman stepping off defective boardwalk at night, falling and injuring herself.............Pa. 178
woman stepping into hole in pavement filled with dust........Pa. 181
woman falling over stake in highway while crossing avenue...Pa. 181
woman familiar with dangerous place in sidewalk at street crossing injured while walking on sidewalk at night, guilty of contributory negligence.......S. D. 94
person crossing street struck and hands and fingers injured by street car..................Tenn. 4

Pedestrian — *continued.*

person walking on track struck by train.......................Tex. 360
person injured by falling into open ditch in highway dug up by a town for purpose of taking up disused water pipe; town not liable as the digging up of pipe was a governmental act..........Vt. 640
person killed by engine while crossing railroad bridge or trestle..Va. 5
person falling into excavation in street, city having given permission to owner of premises to make such excavation.....Wash. 203
person injured while walking on sidewalk, the heating apparatus in sidewalk basement of building having exploded..........Wash. 205
person tripped up by rope stretched across pavement and fastened to telephone pole to hold wharf boat during a flood...........W. Va. 95
person falling into opening made for sewer pipe in sidewalk, the same being covered with snow.. W. Va. 95
rule as to looking and listening applied, where woman crossing track from station in night-time was struck and fatally injured by switch engine, and her contributory negligence held to preclude recovery of damages.......Wis. 389
notes of cases relating to pedestrians injured at crossings or on track.......................... 1-6

Personal Injuries.

instruction as to result of X-ray examination..............N. Y. 151
where petition alleges injuries to specific parts of body, error to admit evidence of injuries to other parts not set out in petition.......................Tex. 199

Photographs.

under proper precautions and necessary explanations, X-ray pictures are admissible in evidence to show condition of internal tissues of the body...Neb. 104

Place Not Crossing.

person crossing track at place not public crossing, run over and killed by train; failure to look for train.......................Ala. [illegible]

Plank.

woman injured by stepping on loose plank in board sidewalk... Iowa, 87
woman injured by falling over spike protruding from plank in sidewalk.....................Iowa, 88
girl, twelve years of age, injured by falling on sidewalk caused by loose plank in walk..........Ky. 35
personal injuries caused by slipping of plank on bridge which was being reconstructed and over which plaintiff was crossing......Minn. 57
woman injured by tripping on loose board on sidewalk..........Neb. 104
woman walking on board sidewalk struck by loose board upon which another person had stepped..Okla. 93
bicycle rider striking loose plank and falling over bridge......Pa. 180
employee injured by sudden breaking and fall of plank in scaffolding which had been used for more than two years, no defect having been discovered in it; master not liable............Pa. 183

Platform.

passenger injured by stepping into hole in station platform; liability of carrier...............W. Va. 580
passenger injured while riding on platform or steps of car.......... U. S. C. C. A. 395
passenger who rides on steps or platform of car, without reasonable excuse, guilty of negligence barring recovery notwithstanding negligence of railway company.. U. S. C. C. A. 395

Pleading and Practice.

Pleading and Practice — *continued.*

Presumption.

Presumption — *continued.*

the fact that plaintiff's intestate was found dead in proximity to defendant's ladder, which had blown down, was not a presumption that the ladder caused his death by blowing down upon him or in any other way, in the absence of any evidence of physical injury or condition of his health..N. H. 520

where a party attaches his signature to a contract otherwise valid, a conclusive presumption is created, except as against fraud, that he read, understood and assented to its terms................N. J. 313

where a party sets up defense that his signature to contract has been obtained by fraud, the burden is upon him to show fraud by clear and satisfactory proof, the presumption of the law being in favor of innocence, fraud not being assumed on doubtful evidence......................N. J. 313

a mere fall from a street car, without any evidence to show how it was occasioned, raises no presumption of negligence on part of operators of car........N. J. 533

an infant under the age of 12 years is presumed to be *non sui juris*, but may be overcome by evidence to the contrary.....N. Y. 338

Principal and Agent.

failure to deny under oath an allegation that a principal, through an agent, did a certain act, not an admission that principal did such act....................Kan. 442

Private Way.

person driving along private lane tacitly open to public use and horse frightened by automobile approaching from opposite direction....................N. Y. 157

Projecting Object.

person standing near track to let car pass injured by coming in contact with conductor on footboard of moving open street car; railway company not liable..Md. 51

Property.

barn destroyed by fire caused by defective insulation of electric wire........................Kan. 442

property damaged by rocks thrown on plaintiff's land by blasting in defendant's quarry and also from water pumped from quarry and allowed to flow on plaintiff's land........................Me. 44

buildings damaged by fire caused by defective electrical work..... N. J. 522

tenant's goods damaged by water from roof of building; liability of landlord...............N. D. 539

valuable horse injured in transportation while in custody of connecting carrier...............Pa. 185

Proximate Cause.

where plaintiff, while driving across track at street crossing, was struck by defendant's train which failed to signal its approach, the proximate cause of injury was failure of defendant to signal at crossing....................Cal. 414

passenger thrown from car by sudden jolt of defendant's train and run over and killed by passing engine of another railroad company........................Ga. 232

rule as to proximate cause.....Ga. 232

where certain stock was killed at point west of defendant's switch, which was left unfenced and treated as part of defendant's depot grounds or switching yard, it was for jury to determine whether proximate cause of killing of cattle was absence of fence, and whether such point

Proximate Cause — *continued.*

was reasonably required by defendant for purposes stated..... Minn. 471
where brakeman threw piece of coal at boy who was stealing a ride on moving coal train, and, in trying to dodge the missile, the boy lost his hold and fell from the car, the questions whether the brakeman used reasonable means to eject the boy and whether his act was proximate cause of injury, were for jury... N. Y. 338
failure of petition to show that injury was the natural and probable consequence of wrongful act of defendant..................Okla. 353
where a child's foot became fastened between planking and rail of a track on a street and the father, in trying to extricate the child, pulled him over the rail as a train of cars approached and the train passed over the child's leg, the proximate cause of the injury was the dangerous condition of the track for which the city was liable, notwithstanding negligence of railroad company and the parent............Wash. 366
note of recent cases on proximate cause of injury...............477–488

Public Building.

woman falling over step leading to public hall................Mass. 529
woman falling in hallway leading to room in public building....Mass. 531
collapse of floor in building used for public purposes........N. J. 527

Questions of Law and Fact.

erroneous instruction as to negligence of motorman in collision between street car and wagon, question being for jury....N. Y. 610
whether person exercised care in observing the rule as to stopping, looking and listening for trains before crossing track, was question for jury and not for court... Pa. 626
when question of negligence for jury and when for court........ U. S. C. C. A. 395
where a passenger stands on steps of car, for purpose of expectorating, and is injured, question of contributory negligence is for jury and not for court.......... U. S. C. C. A. 395

Railroad Company.

person crossing track, at place not public crossing, run over and killed by train; failure to look for train..............Ala. 1
person crossing track at street crossing struck and killed by train.....................Cal. 1
person killed while crossing track in front of rapidly moving train at crossing used by public but at which no flagman was in attendance.......................Cal. 215
contributory negligence of deceased in crossing track in front of moving train bars recovery notwithstanding negligence of railroad company in failing to have flagman at crossing............Cal. 215
where plaintiff, while driving across track at street crossing, was struck by defendant's train which failed to signal its approach, the proximate cause of injury was failure of defendant to signal at crossing....................Cal. 414
laborer engaged in loading a car belonging to railroad company injured by reason of derailment of car......................Ga. 223
mail clerk on railroad car injured by mail grab on outside of car coming in contact with post on station platform, the mail grab being thrown upon clerk's hand.. Ga. 231

Railroad Company — *continued.*

passenger thrown from car by sudden jolt of defendant's train and run over and killed by passing engine of another railroad company........................Ga. 232

brakeman injured while coupling cars, direction of verdict for railroad company sustained......Ga. 420

engineer killed in collision between passenger train and freight train.. Ga. 420

engineer killed by negligence of co-employee; railroad company liable........................Ga. 421

conductor injured while examining defective appliance, there being no duty imposed on him to make such examination; railroad company not liable...............Ga. 422

child fatally injured while playing on turntable..............Idaho, 18

child, between seven and eight years of age, injured while playing on turntable...........Iowa, 27

collision between public hack and train at street crossing and passenger in hack injured.....Kan. 29

where railroad company was in habit of operating gates at street crossing at certain hours, but not at time of accident, error to refer question to jury as to whether single isolated instance of failure to operate gates at that time was negligence..................Kan. 29

a railway company, which delivers defective freight car to a connecting line, is not liable to employee of latter, who is injured by reason of such defects, after car has been inspected by company receiving it..........................Kan. 265

railroad employee injured while loading cars; liability of connecting line...................Kan. 275

person not a passenger assaulted by station agent; railway company not liable, the agent not acting within scope of employment... Kan. 435

railroad employee working on bridge injured by falling timbers.. Kan. 438

where property of railway company is in exclusive possession of receivers operating the road, the company is not liable for injuries sustained by an employee of such receivers..................Kan. 438

where action is prosecuted jointly against railway corporation and the receivers of same, and the corporation is not liable, the action may be dismissed as to corporation without prejudice to plaintiff's right to have judgment against receivers...........Kan. 438

railroad company not chargeable with negligence in running passenger train over road crossing at speed of from forty to fifty miles per hour in open country where view of traveler on highway is unobstructed........Kan. 601

traveler already warned of approach of train in time to escape injury cannot complain of negligence of railroad company in failing to give signals................Kan. 601

person riding in wagon driven by another killed in collision with train at crossing; railroad not liable.......................Kan. 601

passenger assaulted and insulted at railway station; when carrier not liable.......................Ky. 288

statutory requirement as to time of keeping ticket offices and waiting rooms open for passengers before schedule time of departure of trains........................Ky. 288

person driving wagon killed in collision with train at crossing; failure of deceased to exercise due care........................Me. 452

Railroad Company — *continued.*

horse frightened by obstruction of culvert pipe on railroad right of way near highway and person driving thrown from wagon and injured; railroad company not liable........................Me. 458

four days not an unreasonable time for a railroad company to allow pieces of culvert pipe, to be used for repairs, to remain near highway on its right of way......Me. 458

passenger's merchandise checked as baggage lost or stolen in transit.. Mich. 61

railroad employee injured while clearing railroad wreck....Minn. 99

railroad employee clearing snow from switch struck by "kicked" car........................Minn. 100

fireman falling from pilot and foot crushed by engine........Minn. 101

section man injured while engaged with others in removing hand car from track to make way for freight train..............Minn. 102

cows tied to wagon killed by train while crossing track; contributory negligence of person in charge of cattle and team..Minn. 471

where certain stock was killed at point west of defendant's switch, which was left unfenced and treated as part of defendant's depot grounds or switching yard, it was for jury to determine whether proximate cause of killing of cattle was absence of fence, and whether such point was reaonably required by defendant for purposes stated............Minn. 471

where child was run over and killed by engine at crossing, the case should have gone to jury..Miss. 608

child coasting run over on track.. Mo. 499

boy run over and leg injured by train at street crossing; question of negligence for jury......Neb. 3

Railroad Company — *continued.*

boy, four years of age, injured while playing on turntable..Neb. 300

boy trespassing on track finding torpedo and injured by explosion; railroad company not liable........................N. H. 510

baggage master acting as brakeman injured in derailment of train; railroad company liable .. N. J. 113

brakeman injured in collision..N. J. 313

release by acceptance of benefits from relief fund established by a railway company...........N. J. 313

horse standing at gate crossing frightened by train and backing wagon against engine, and person in wagon injured; question for jury whether plaintiff was negligent in not alighting from wagon....................N. J. 329

collision between train and wagon at crossing, and person driving killed......................N. J. 626

where brakeman threw piece of coal at boy who was stealing a ride on moving coal train, and, in trying to dodge the missile, the boy lost his hold and fell from the car, the questions whether the brakeman used reasonable means to eject the boy and whether his act was proximate cause of injury, were for jury.... N. Y. 338

railroad employee, a boy, riding on hand car, struck and killed by train; railroad company only held to duty of reasonable care to avoid injuring plaintiff, he being a mere licensee...........Ohio, 162

collision between vehicle and train at crossing; person driving killed and person riding injured..Ohio, 343

person riding in caboose of freight train by conductor's permission killed in collision; railroad company not liable...........Ohio, 544

Railroad Company — *continued.*

act of conductor in permitting person to ride on train against rules of railroad company, not binding on company..............Ohio, 544

woman crossing street over tracks at railroad yard struck and injured by engine...........Ohio, 547

intending passenger injured by falling on railroad ties and beams while attempting to reach depot, a freight train blocking the crossing at station..............Okla. 353

horses frightened by noise of steam from trains and persons driving injured..................Pa. 329, 331

collision between train and vehicle at grade crossing............Pa. 626

person walking on track struck by train......................Tex. 360

erroneous charge as to degree of care required of railroad company towards person on track.. Tex. 360

a section hand injured while unloading steel rails from hand car did not assume risk of danger where he was inexperienced, was not informed of danger and the danger was not obvious and apparent.....................Tex. 636

person killed by engine while crossing railroad bridge or trestle..Va. 5

conductor of logging train killed in derailment of train caused by defective car wheels; evidence as to defects and failure to inspect.... Wash. 372

brakeman, familiar with custom of coupling cars, injured while coupling cars...............Wis. 206

rule as to looking and listening applied, where woman crossing track from station in night-time was struck and fatally injured by switch engine, and her contributory negligence held to preclude recovery of damages........Wis. 389

fireman fatally injured by being scalded by escaping steam from boiler of engine against which he was thrown by collision between two sections of train............ U. S. C. C. A. 213

person standing in passenger car injured by sudden start of car.... U. S. C. C. A. 314

when dining car held not to be engaged in interstate traffic........ U. S. C. C. A. 398

brakeman injured while coupling cars..............U. S. C. C. A. 398

notes of cases relating to pedestrians injured at crossing or on track........................... 1-6

notes of recent cases on proximate cause of injury...............477-488

Reasonable Time.

statutory requirement as to time of keeping ticket offices and waiting rooms open for passengers before schedule time of departure of trains....................Ky. 288

four days not an unreasonable time for a railroad company to allow pieces of culvert pipe to be used for repairs to remain near highway on its right of way......Me. 458

Receiver.

where property of railway company is in exclusive possession of receivers operating the road, the company is not liable for injuries sustained by an employee of such receivers..................Kan. 438

where action is prosecuted jointly against railway corporation and the receivers of same, and the corporation is not liable, the action may be dismissed as to corporation without prejudice to plaintiff's right to have judgment against receivers...........Kan. 438

Release.

failure to execute release for damages for injuries on receipt of benefits from relief fund does not

Release — *continued.*

give right of action for injuries because of such failure to sign release....................Ga. 422

release by acceptance of benefits from relief fund established by a railway company...........N. J. 313

failure of proof to show that signature to contract accepting benefits from relief fund for injuries which operated as release was obtained by fraud...........N. J. 313

failure of proof to establish fraud in obtaining signature to release of claim for personal injuries...... U. S. C. C. A. 314

Relief Fund.

failure to execute release for damages for injuries on receipt of benefits from relief fund does not give right of action for injuries because of such failure to sign release.......................Ga. 422

release by acceptance of benefits from relief fund established by a railroad company.........N. J. 313

Res Gestæ.

declarations of railroad superintendent, three hours after accident, as to certain car wheels, admissible against the company.. Wash. 372

Res Ipsa Loquitur.

doctrine of *res ipsa loquitur* is applicable only when the thing shown speaks of defendant's negligence, not merely of happening of accident................N. J. 533

proof by plaintiff of accident occasioned by defendant's runaway team makes a *prima facie* case of negligence................Tenn. 632

Respondeat Superior.

whether doctrine of *respondeat superior* applies to any particular case between the original contractor and a sub-contractor is determined by the contract between the parties................Minn. 488

Riding.

person injured by fall from bicycle alleged to have been caused by a defect in street............Ind. 85

child of tender age killed on highway by horse, attached to wagon in which deceased was riding, becoming frightened at iron tiles placed on highway and backing off bridge on highway and falling on child..................Iowa, 590

person riding in wagon driven by another killed in collision with train at crossing; railroad not liable......................Kan. 601

whether negligence of driver can be imputed to person riding with him is immaterial where railway company was not negligent towards occupants of wagon..Kan. 601

person riding in vehicle injured on defective highway...........Me. 89

vehicle overturned in defective street and person riding injured; negligence of driver not imputable to plaintiff...........Minn. 79

horse standing at gate crossing frightened by train and backing wagon against engine, and person in wagon injured; question for jury whether plaintiff was negligent in not alighting from wagon....................N. J. 329

boy riding on rear of wagon injured in collision between street car and wagon...........N. Y. 610

bicycle rider running into pile of bricks in street; contributory negligence................N. C. 92

collision between vehicle and train at crossing; person driving killed and person riding injured..Ohio, 343

bicycle rider striking loose plank and falling over bridge......Pa. 180

person riding in wagon on highway fatally injured by a runaway team colliding with wagon......Tenn. 632

liability of city for death of member of fire department killed by over-

Riding — *continued.*

turning of hose cart on defective street caused by root of tree projecting across highway.... Wash. 203

Right of Way.

street cars have no superior rights to other vehicles or pedestrians at regular street crossings... Fla. 417

horse frightened by obstruction of culvert pipe on railroad right of way near highway and person driving thrown from wagon and injured; railroad company not liable........................ Me. 458

Risk of Employment.

servant ordered with other employees to unload logs from flat cars, where risk of such work is open and apparent, he assumes dangers caused by negligence of fellow-servants............. Minn. 496

employee injured while moving tank in brewery............ Neb. 514

Rules and Regulations.

ordinary labor of unloading logs from flat cars is not attended with extra hazards as to require formulation of rules for employees.................... Minn. 496

act of conductor in permitting person to ride on train against rules of railroad company, not binding on company............... Ohio, 544

Runaway.

horse frightened at snow plow on street-car track, running away and person driving thrown out of vehicle and injured....... Me. 38

horse frightened by obstruction of culvert pipe on railroad right of way near highway and person driving thrown from wagon and injured; railroad company not liable........................ Me. 458

person driving along private lane tacitly open to public use and

Runaway — *continued.*

horse frightened by automobile approaching from opposite direction...................... N. Y. 157

horses frightened by noise of steam from trains and persons driving injured.......... Pa. 329, 331

person riding in wagon on highway fatally injured by a runaway team colliding with wagon.. Tenn. 632

Run Over.

person crossing track at place not public crossing, run over and killed by train; failure to look for train.................... Ala. 1

passenger thrown from car by sudden jolt of defendant's train and run over and killed by passing engine of another railroad company...................... Ga. 232

motorman in trying to board his car, which was going at slow speed, falling from same and run over by car.................. Ga. 422

fireman falling from pilot and foot crushed by engine........ Minn. 101

child of tender years struck by street car at street crossing..... Minn. 604

where child was run over and killed by engine at crossing, the case should have gone to jury.. Miss. 608

child coasting run over on track.. Mo. 499

boy run over and leg injured by train at street crossing; question of negligence for jury...... Neb. 3

boy riding on back of wagon jumping off wagon and run over by street car................. N. J. 4

child run over and killed by automobile.................. N. Y. 158

boy stealing a ride jumping from street car and run over and killed by car on other track.... Tenn.

where a child's foot became fastened between planking and rail of a track on a street and the

Run Over — *continued.*

father, in trying to extricate the child, pulled him over the rail as a train of cars approached and the train passed over the child's leg, the proximate cause of the injury was the dangerous condition of the track for which the city was liable, notwithstanding negligence of railroad company and the parent............Wash. 366

notes of cases relating to pedestrians injured at crossings or on track........................... 1-6

Scaffolding.

employee injured by falling from staging......................Me. 46

employee tripping on plank on scaffolding, falling and breaking his leg; master not liable, the scaffolding planks not being "ways or works" within statute.. Mass. 76

employee injured by sudden breaking and fall of plank in scaffolding which had been used for more than two years, no defect having been discovered in it; master not liable.............Pa. 183

Scope of Employment.

conductor injured while examining defective appliance, there being no duty imposed on him to make such examination; railroad company not liable..............Ga. 422

person not a passenger assaulted by station agent; railway company not liable, the agent not acting within scope of employment.. Kan. 435

Sidewalk.

person injured on sidewalk covered with snow and ice.........Colo. 84

woman walking along sidewalk falling into cellar-door opening and seriously injured.....Idaho, 243

woman injured by stepping on loose plank in board sidewalk.. Iowa, 87

woman injured by falling over spike protruding from plank in sidewalk..................Iowa, 88

woman injured on defective sidewalk; contributory negligence for jury..................Iowa, 268

boy injured by live electric wire allowed to remain on sidewalk after falling down, a policeman having moved the same but failing to warn passers-by of danger; city liable for allowing wire to remain down exposing the public to danger.................Kan. 272

pedestrian falling into cellar opening in sidewalk............Kan. 431

girl, twelve years of age, injured by falling on sidewalk caused by loose plank in walk..........Ky. 35

where there was conflicting evidence as to length of time defect in sidewalk had existed, question as to whether city had notice of defect was for jury.........Ky. 35

plaintiff, about nineteen years of age, injured by striking his toe against brick that had been raised by root of tree; city not liable......................Ky. 35

pedestrian falling over obstruction made by lot owner on sidewalk; city liable..................Ky. 286

woman injured by slipping on depressed sidewalk...........Minn. 79

person injured at street crossing covered with snow and ice..Mo. 90

woman injured by tripping on loose board on sidewalk....Neb. 104

woman injured on defective sidewalk......................Neb. 517

person falling over piece of sewer or drain pipe on sidewalk..N. H. 91

person injured by stepping on coal-hole cover in sidewalk; liability of owner of premises..N. J. 121

owner of premises liable for injury to person falling on icy sidewalk,

Sidewalk — *continued.*

ice being formed by water discharged from roof........N. Y. 132
child struck by fall of pipes from building material standing on sidewalk..................N. Y. 511
woman walking on board sidewalk struck by loose board upon which another person had stepped.... Okla. 93
person injured by falling on ice on sidewalk, the ice being formed by accumulation of water from drain pipe.........................Pa. 132
person falling on sidewalk along township road...............Pa. 178
woman stepping off defective boardwalk at night, falling and injuring herself..............Pa. 178
woman stepping into hole in pavement filled with dust........Pa. 181
woman familiar with dangerous place in sidewalk at street crossing injured while walking on sidewalk at night, guilty of contributory negligence........S. D. 94
child falling through grating over cellar in sidewalk..........Tex. 95
person injured while walking on sidewalk, the heating apparatus in sidewalk basement of building having exploded..........Wash. 205
person tripped up by rope stretched across pavement and fastened to telephone pole to hold wharf boat during a flood......W. Va. 95
person falling into opening made for sewer pipe in sidewalk, the same being covered with snow.. W. Va. 95
notes of recent actions against municipal corporations in Nebraska 104–108
notes of recent New York cases arising out of coal-hole accidents 121–122
notes of recent municipal corporation cases decided in Pennsylvania 178–182

Signal.

where plaintiff, while driving across track at street crossing, was struck by defendant's train, which failed to signal its approach, the proximate cause of injury was failure of defendant to signal at crossing........Cal. 414
in action for negligently running train at street crossing without signal, error to admit evidence of like failure of train to signal at another street crossing..Kan. 29
traveler, already warned of approach of train in time to escape injury, cannot complain of negligence of railroad company in failing to give signals.........Kan. 601

Snow and Ice. — See Ice and Snow.

Speed.

railroad company not chargeable with negligence in running passenger trains over road crossing at speed of from forty to fifty miles per hour in open country where view of traveler on highway is unobstructed........Kan. 601

Standing Near Track.

person standing near track to let car pass injured by coming in contact with conductor on footboard of moving open street car; railway company not liable..Md. 51

State Fair.

liability of State fair corporation for injuries sustained by fall of stand at fireworks exhibition on State fair grounds..........Tex. 199

Station.

passenger assaulted and insulted at railway station, when carrier not liable.......................Ky. 288
intending passenger injured by falling on railroad ties and beams while attempting to reach depot,

Station — *continued.*

a freight train blocking the crossing at station..............Okla. 353
carrier liable for assault by drunken person upon plaintiff's wife, a passenger, while in carrier's waiting room..................Tex. 637
where person merely goes to railway station to assist his wife to a train, with no intention of becoming a passenger, and while there was assaulted by drunken person, carrier not liable, the person so assaulted being only a licensee....................Tex. 637
passenger injured by stepping into hole in station platform; liability of carrier...............W. Va. 580

Statute.

statutory requirement as to pleading and proof in action for treble damages..................Conn. 8
degree of care required of street railroads under the statute...Fla. 417
presumption of negligence under statute relating to street railroads.......................Fla. 417
statutory requirement as to time of keeping ticket offices and waiting rooms open for passengers before schedule time of departure of trains.......................Ky. 288
insufficiency of declaration in action by an administrator for negligent killing of intestate, an employee killed in gas explosion......Me. 461
the statute of 1891 affords a right of action for "injuries causing death," substantially like that given to employees by the employers' liability act in Massachusetts (chapter 24, Pub. St. 1887).......................Me. 461
employee tripping on plank on scaffolding, falling and breaking his leg; master not liable, the scaffolding planks not being "ways or works" within statute.. Mass. 76

Statute — *continued.*

statute requiring notice of injury caused by defect in street to be given to municipality as a condition precedent to maintaining action therefor, not applicable to action by personal representative of deceased person, whose death was caused by such defect.. Minn. 294
common-law right of action by husband for injury to wife to recover for loss of her services and for his medical and other expenses in healing her injuries, is not abridged or affected by statute.. Ohio, 547
the Interstate Commerce Act is not violated by holding that contract limiting liability for carrier's negligence is invalid within this State.......................Pa. 185
liability under Utah statutes for negligence of superior servants.. U. S. C. C. A. 213
what is sufficient compliance with statute requiring equipment of cars with automatic couplers.... U. S. C. C. A. 398
construction of federal statute..... U. S. C. C. A. 398
the Federal statute does not make it unlawful for common carriers to use locomotives engaged in interstate commerce which are not equipped with couplers.......... U. S. C. C. A. 398
Federal statute relating to automatic couplers....U. S. C. C. A. 398

Steam.

boy playing along railroad path scalded by steam and hot water discharged from adjoining premises; owner of premises liable.... N. Y. 511
horses frightened by noise of steam from trains and persons driving injured.................Pa. 329, 331
fireman fatally injured by being

Steam — *continued.*

scalded by escaping steam from boiler of engine against which he was thrown by collision between two sections of train........... U. S. C. C. A. 213

Steamboat.

lessor of steamboat, a private corporation, not liable for negligence of lessee where passenger on steamboat was injured by capsizing of boat...............N. C. 617

Stop, Look and Listen.

person stopping within 30 feet of crossing, looking up track, and seeing track clear for about 800 feet, proceeding to cross track without again looking for train, not guilty of contributory negligence as matter of law......Cal. 1

person driving across track at street crossing struck by street car; evidence as to looking and listening..................Kan. 599

person driving wagon killed in collision with train at crossing; failure of deceased to exercise due care.......................Me. 452

duty of traveler approaching crossing to look and listen for trains.. Me. 452

rule as to looking and listening at railroad crossings..........Ohio, 343

whether person exercised care in observing the rule as to stopping, looking and listening for trains before crossing track, was question for jury and not for court... Pa. 626

duty of person about to step upon railway track to look both ways and listen and avoid danger, is absolute...................Wis. 389

Street.

person injured while driving, his vehicle striking against fire plug in street concealed from view; notice to city.............Colo. 220

Street — *continued.*

person injured by fall from bicycle alleged to have been caused by a defect in street.............Ind. 85

vehicle overturned in defective street and person riding injured; negligence of driver not imputable to plaintiff...........Minn. 79

person walking along street fatally injured by fall of defective and insufficiently fastened porch.... Minn. 294

girl, fourteen years of age, falling into excavation made for building purposes in street..........N. Y. 513

bicycle rider running into pile of bricks in street; contributory negligence.................N. C. 92

person falling into excavation in street, city having given permission to owner of premises to make such excavation.....Wash. 203

notes of recent actions against municipal corporations in Nebraska.. 104-108

Street Car.

person injured while crossing street-car track.............Cal. 215

person crossing street struck by street car...................Fla. 417

street cars have no superior rights to other vehicles or pedestrians at regular street crossings..Fla. 417

motorman in trying to board his car, which was going at slow speed, falling from same and run over by car.................Ga. 422

person driving across track at street crossing struck by street car; evidence as to looking and listening..................Kan. 599

person standing near track to let car pass injured by coming in contact with conductor on footboard of moving open street car: railway company not liable..Md. 51

collision between wagon and street car......................Mass. 216

ordinance requiring person having control of speed of street car to

Street Car — *continued.*

stop car in shortest time and space possible on appearance of any obstruction to his car, not unreasonable................Minn. 604
duty of motorman when street car approaching street crossing..... Minn. 604
child of tender years struck by street car at street crossing.... Minn. 604
boy riding on back of wagon jumping off wagon and run over by street car.................N. J. 4
child about three years old, thrown down and injured by sudden starting of street car which she had boarded..............N. J. 334
a mere fall from a street car, without any evidence to show how it was occasioned, raises no presumption of negligence on part of operators of car..........N. J. 533
person injured in collision between wagon and street car......N. Y. 151
boy riding on rear of wagon injured in collision between street car and wagon................N. Y. 610
boy stealing a ride jumping from street car and run over and killed by car on other track......Tenn. 4
person crossing street struck and hands and fingers injured by street car.................Tenn. 4
notes of cases relating to pedestrians injured at crossings or on track.......................... 1-6
accidents while crossing street-car tracks, notes of cases........215-216

Street-car Rail.

person crossing street stepping on street-car rail and receiving electric shock; street-railroad company liable................N. Y. 156

Street Crossing.

person crossing track at street crossing struck and killed by train.......................Cal. 1

Street Crossing — *continued.*

where plaintiff, while driving across track at street crossing was struck by defendant's train, which failed to signal its approach, the proximate cause of injury was failure of defendant to signal at crossing........................Cal. 414
street cars have no superior rights to other vehicles or pedestrians at regular street crossings..Fla. 417
duty of employees of street cars to keep look-out for persons on track, especially at street crossings.......................Fla. 417
woman injured by stepping into excavation caused by heavy rainstorm......................Ind. 86
collision between public hack and train at street crossing and passenger in hack injured......Kan. 29
in action for negligently running train at street crossing without signal, error to admit evidence of like failure of train to signal at another street crossing.....Kan. 29
where railroad company was in habit of operating gates at street crossing at certain hours, but not at time of accident, error to refer question to jury as to whether single isolated instance of failure to operate gates at that time was negligence..................Kan. 29
person driving across track at street crossing struck by street car; evidence as to looking and listening...................Kan. 599
duty of motorman when street car approaching street crossing..... Minn. 604
child of tender years struck by street car at street crossing..... Minn. 604
person injured at street crossing covered with snow and ice..Mo. 90
boy run over and leg injured by train at street crossing; question of negligence for jury......Neb. 3

Street Crossing — *continued.*

person injured at gutter crossing in street....................Pa. 176

testimony that there were many other street crossings in same condition as one in question competent as to whether keeping it in that condition was negligence, and also on question of contributory negligence..............Pa. 176

city not bound to cover its street crossings at all places and absence, therefore, of crossing at place of accident not, of itself, negligence..................Pa. 176

woman falling over stake in highway while crossing avenue...Pa. 181

woman familiar with dangerous place in sidewalk at street crossing injured while walking on sidewalk at night, guilty of contributory negligence........S. D. 94

Street railroad Company.

person injured while crossing street-car track.............Cal. 215

presumption of negligence under statute relating to street railroads......................Fla. 417

degree of care required of street railroads under the statute..Fla. 417

street cars have no superior rights to other vehicles or pedestrians at regular street crossings...Fla. 417

duty of employees of street cars to keep look out for persons on track, especially at street crossings........................Fla. 417

motorman in trying to board his car, which was going at slow speed, falling from same and run over by car.................Ga. 422

person driving across track at street crossing struck by street car; evidence as to looking and listening...................Kan. 599

horse frightened at snow plow on street-car track, running away and person driving thrown out of vehicle and injured......Me. 38

person standing near track to let car pass injured by coming in contact with conductor on footboard of moving open street car; railway company not liable..Md. 51

liability of street-railway company for personal injuries caused by an excavation made by it in the highway..................Mass. 54

collision between wagon and street car.......................Mass. 216

duty of motorman when street car approaching street crossing.....Minn. 604

child of tender years struck by street car at street crossing.....Minn. 604

ordinance requiring person having control of speed of street car to stop car in shortest time and space possible, on appearance of any obstruction to his car, not unreasonable.............Minn. 604

boy riding on back of wagon jumping off wagon and run over by street car.................N. J. 4

child, about three years old, thrown down and injured by sudden starting of street car which she had boarded...............N. J. 334

person injured in collision between wagon and street car......N. Y. 151

person crossing street stepping on street-car rail and receiving electric shock; street-railroad company liable................N. Y. 156

boy riding on rear of wagon injured in collision between street car and wagon............N. Y. 610

boy stealing a ride jumping from street car and run over and killed by car on other track.....Tenn. 4

person crossing street struck and hands and fingers injured by street car.................Tenn. 4

notes of cases relating to pedestrians injured at crossings or on track.......................... 1-6

accidents while crossing street-car tracks; notes of cases........215-216

Sub-contractor.

liability of contractor for defective work of sub-contractor.....N. J. 522

Sudden Start or Stop of Car.

passenger thrown from car by sudden jolt of defendant's train and run over and killed by passing engine of another railroad company.......................Ga. 232

child, about three years old, thrown down and injured by sudden starting of street car which she had boarded................N. J. 334

person standing in passenger car injured by sudden start of car... U. S. C. C. A. 314

Sui Juris.

error to hold that boy, about 12 years old, was, as matter of law, *sui juris*, that being for the jury to determine..............N. Y. 338

Superior Servant.

the "superior servant rule" does not prevail in New Jersey..N. J. 109

liability under Utah statutes for negligence of superior servants.. U. S. C. C. A. 213

Tables.

not error for court to illustrate to jury the method of using mortality and annuity tables by giving figure approximating that shown by the evidence to be plaintiff's age................Ga. 223

Telegraph Company.

duty of companies maintaining electric-light wires and telegraph wires in public street......N. J. 321

Tenement House.

tenant injured by slipping on ice in hallway of tenement house, the ice forming from leakage of water from closet; landlord liable.......................N. Y. 336

Theft.

passenger's merchandise checked as baggage lost or stolen in transit...................Mich. 61

note on liability of carriers for loss of passenger's baggage.........64-74

Ticket.

passenger ejected from train on presentation of expired ticket... Ga. 427

notice posted at ticket office limiting time of use of certain railroad ticket, not admissible in action for ejection of passenger unless proof is given that passenger had read same or notice of its contents.....................Ga. 427

Ticket Office.

statutory requirement as to time of keeping ticket offices and waiting rooms open for passengers before schedule time of departure of trains.......................Ky. 288

Time.

statutory requirement as to time of keeping ticket offices and waiting rooms open for passengers before schedule time of departure of trains.............Ky. 288

Torpedo.

boy trespassing on track finding torpedo and injured by explosion; railroad company not liable..... N. H. 510

Track.

person crossing track at place not public crossing, run over and killed by train; failure to look for train......................Ala. 1

person crossing track at street crossing struck and killed by train.......................Cal. 1

person injured while crossing street-car track.............Cal. 215

duty of employees of street cars to keep look-out for persons on

Track — *continued.*

track, especially at street crossings........................Fla. 417
person standing near track to let car pass injured by coming in contact with conductor on footboard of moving open street car; railway company not liable..Md. 51
collision between wagon and street car........................Mass. 216
child coasting run over on track... Mo. 499
boy trespassing on track finding torpedo and injured by explosion; railroad company not liable........................N. H. 510
woman crossing street over tracks at railroad yard struck and injured by engine...........Ohio, 547
intending passenger injured by falling on railroad ties and beams while attempting to reach depot, a freight train blocking the crossing at station.............Okla. 353
person walking on track struck by train........................Tex. 360
person killed by engine while crossing railroad bridge or trestle........................Va. 5
where a child's foot became fastened between planking and rail of a track on a street, and the father, in trying to extricate the child, pulled him over the rail as a train of cars approached and the train passed over the child's leg, the proximate cause of the injury was the dangerous condition of the track for which the city was liable, notwithstanding negligence of railroad company and the parent...........Wash. 366
duty of person about to step upon railway track to look both ways and listen and avoid danger, is absolute...................Wis. 389
rule as to looking and listening applied, where woman crossing track from station in night-time was struck and fatally injured by switch engine, and her contributory negligence held to preclude recovery of damages.......Wis. 389
notes of cases relating to pedestrians injured at crossings or on track........................ 1-6
accidents while crossing street-car tracks; notes of cases........215-216
notes of recent cases arising from injuries to trespassers........562-571

Train.

person crossing track at place not public crossing, run over and killed by train; failure to look for train........................Ala. 1
person crossing track at street crossing struck and killed by train........................Cal. 1
person killed while crossing track in front of rapidly moving train at crossing used by public but at which no flagman was in attendance........................Cal. 215
where plaintiff, while driving across track at street crossing, was struck by defendant's train, which failed to signal its approach, the proximate cause of injury was failure of defendant to signal at crossing...................Cal. 414
passenger thrown from car by sudden jolt of defendant's train and run over and killed by passing engine of another railroad company........................Ga. 232
engineer killed in collision between passenger train and freight train.. Ga. 420
collision between public hack and train at street crossing and passenger in hack injured.....Kan. 29
in action for negligently running train at street crossing without signal, error to admit evidence of like failure of train to signal at another street crossing..Kan. 29
person driving wagon killed in collision with train at crossing; fail-

Train — *continued.*

ure of deceased to exercise due care........................Me. 452

cows tied to wagon killed by train while crossing track; contributory negligence of person in charge of cattle and team..Minn. 471

where child was run over and killed by engine at crossing, the case should have gone to jury..Miss. 608

child coasting run over on track... Mo. 499

boy run over and leg injured by train at street crossing; question of negligence for jury......Neb. 3

baggage-master acting as brakeman injured in derailment of train; railroad company liable... N. J. 113

horse standing at gate crossing frightened by train and backing wagon against engine, and person in wagon injured; question for jury whether plaintiff was negligent in not alighting from wagon.....................N. J. 329

collision between train and wagon at crossing, and person driving killed.....................N. J. 626

where brakeman threw piece of coal at boy who was stealing a ride on moving coal train, and, in trying to dodge the missile, the boy lost his hold and fell from the car, the questions whether the brakeman used reasonable means to eject the boy and whether his act was proximate cause of injury, were for jury.....................N. Y. 338

railroad employee, a boy, riding on hand car, struck and killed by train; railroad company only held to duty of reasonable care to avoid injuring plaintiff, he being a mere licensee..........Ohio, 162

collision between vehicle and train at crossing; person driving killed and person riding injured..Ohio, 343

duty of engineer of train when approaching crossings.......Ohio, 343

act of conductor in permitting person to ride on train against rules of railroad company, not binding on company..............Ohio, 544

horses frightened by noise of steam from trains and persons driving injured.................Pa. 329, 331

collision between train and vehicle at grade crossing...........Pa. 626

person walking on track struck by train......................Tex. 360

conductor of logging train killed in derailment of train caused by defective car wheels; evidence as to defects and failure to inspect.. Wash. 372

fireman fatally injured by being scalded by escaping steam from boiler of engine against which he was thrown by collision between two sections of train........... U. S. C. C. A. 213

person standing in passenger car injured by sudden start of car... U. S. C. C. A. 314

passenger injured while riding on platform or steps of car........ U. S. C. C. A. 395

notes of cases relating to pedestrians injured at crossings or on track......................... 1-6

notes of recent cases arising from injuries to trespassers........562-571

Train at Crossing.

intending passenger injured by falling on railroad ties and beams while attempting to reach depot, a freight train blocking the crossing at station.............Okla. 353

Trespasser.

boy trespassing in building injured by explosion of dynamite cap; owner not liable...........Ky. 509

boy trespassing on track finding torpedo and injured by explo-

Trespasser — *continued.*

sion; railroad company not liable........................N. H. 510

where brakeman threw piece of coal at boy who was stealing a ride on moving coal train, and, in trying to dodge the missile, the boy lost his hold and fell from the car, the questions whether the brakeman used reasonable means to eject the boy and whether his act was proximate cause of injury, were for jury.......................N. Y. 338

boy, ten years of age, climbing on gate injured by fall of same on lot owned by city; nonsuit....Pa. 294

child attracted to fire on premises where children were accustomed to play; owner not liable for injuries to child though he took no means to prevent children approaching fire..............R. I. 550

erroneous charge regarding person on track as a trespasser.....Tex. 360

note of recent cases on proximate cause of injury..............477-488

notes of recent cases arising from injuries to trespassers........562-571

Trustees.

liability of trustees of real property for tort....................N. J. 121

Turntable.

child fatally injured while playing on turntable..............Idaho, 18

child, between seven and eight years of age, injured while playing on turntable...........Iowa, 27

boy, four years of age, injured while playing on turntable........Neb. 300

Vehicle.

where plaintiff, while driving across track at street crossing, was struck by defendant's train which failed to signal its approach, the proximate cause of injury was failure of defendant to signal at crossing....................Cal. 414

Vehicle — *continued.*

collision between vehicles on highway......................Conn. 8

collision between public hack and train at street crossing and passenger in hack injured......Kan. 29

person driving across track at street crossing struck by street car; evidence as to looking and listening...................Kan. 599

person riding in wagon driven by another killed in collision with train at crossing; railroad not liable......................Kan. 601

person riding in vehicle injured on defective highway...........Me. 89

person driving wagon killed in collision with train at crossing: failure of deceased to exercise due care....................Me. 452

collision between wagon and street car........................Mass. 216

collision between train and wagon at crossing, and person driving killed......................N. J. 626

person injured in collision between wagon and street car......N. Y. 151

boy riding on rear of wagon injured in collision between street car and wagon............N. Y. 610

collision between vehicle and train at crossing; person driving killed and person riding injured..Ohio. 343

collision between train and vehicle at grade crossing............Pa 626

person riding in wagon on highway fatally injured by a runaway team colliding with wagon......Tenn. 632

Verdict.

verdict for $1,250 excessive where plaintiff, a peddler, was ejected from train on ground that his ticket had expired...........Ga. 427

where child, about five years of age, was fatally injured on turntable, verdict for $2,000 not excessive.. Idaho. 18

for $12,000 for permanent injuries sustained by woman falling into

Verdict — *continued.*

celiar-door opening in sidewalk. not excessive............Idaho, 243
verdict for $6,000 excessive, $3,000 being considered sufficient, for death of child, four years and four months old, whose death was caused by horse attached to wagon in which deceased was riding becoming frightened and falling on him............Iowa, 590
verdict for $4,358, where plaintiff, a woman, was permanently injured, both internally and externally, by falling into cellar opening in sidewalk, not excessive......................Kan. 431
where boy, about sixteen years old, was injured by machinery at place of employment, his toes being caught in machinery, verdict for $2,500 held excessive and reduced to $1,500..........Minn. 104
award of $200 damages for negligent killing of plaintiff's son, a child about six years of age, not so inadequate as to warrant setting it aside..............N. Y. 616
for $15,000 for plaintiff, a woman who was crippled for life (her spine being broken, caused by falling over bridge, her bicycle, which she was riding, striking against loose plank), not excessive, where at time of accident she was 39 years of age, in excellent health and earning good salary......................Pa. 180

Vice-Principal.

liability under Utah statutes for negligence of superior servants.. U. S. C. C. A. 213

Waiting Room.

statutory requirement as to time of keeping ticket offices and waiting rooms open for passengers before schedule time of departure of trains...................Ky. 288

Waiting Room — *continued.*

carrier liable for assault by drunken person upon plaintiff's wife, a passenger, while in carrier's waitin room..................Tex. 637

Wagon. — See VEHICLE.

Walking on Track.

person walking on track struck by train......................Tex. 360
erroneous charge as to degree of care required of railroad company towards person on track....Tex. 360
erroneous charge regarding person on track as a trespasser.....Tex. 360

Warning. — See also NOTICE.

traveler already warned of approach of train in time to escape injury cannot complain of negligence of railroad company in failing to give signals...............Kan. 601
extent of instructions and warning of danger to workmen in charge of machines are to be gauged by the necessity because of danger.. La. 448
minor employee, familiar with surroundings passing between machines, slipping and injured by gears of machine; master not liable.....................Mass. 74
ordinary labor of unloading logs from flat cars is not attended with extra hazards as to require formulation of rules for employees...................Minn. 496
an employee, although a minor, assumes risk of dangers of employment as are obvious to him, and his employer is not responsible for injuries resulting therefrom, notwithstanding latter has failed to point out such dangers..N. J. 327

Water.

boy stepping into pool of hot water; owner of premises not liable.....................Ark. 508

Water — *continued.*

property damaged by rocks thrown on plaintiff's land by blasting in defendant's quarry and also from water pumped from quarry and allowed to flow on plaintiff's land........................Me. 44

owner of premises liable for injury to person falling on icy sidewalk, ice being formed by water discharged from roof........N. Y. 132

boy playing along railroad path scalded by steam and hot water discharged from adjoining premises; owner of premises liable.. N. Y. 511

tenant's goods damaged by water from roof of building; liability of landlord.....................N. D. 539

person injured by falling on ice on sidewalk, the ice being formed by accumulation of water from drain pipe...................Pa. 132

Window.

minor employee cleaning windows injured by falling from third story of factory............Minn. 102

Wire.

barn destroyed by fire caused by defective insulation of electric wire.........................Kan. 442

lineman injured while stringing telephone wires under direction of foreman, the latter also co-operating with plaintiff in the work.......................N. J. 109

person attempting to remove electric wire, which fell into street. killed by contact with wire..... N. J. 321

duty of companies maintaining electric-light wires and telegraph wires in public streets......N. J. 321

employees injured by contact with electric wires.......Pa. 322; Va. 323

X-Ray.

under proper precautions and necessary explanations, X-ray pictures are admissible in evidence to show condition of internal tissues of the body..Neb. 104

instruction as to result of X-ray examination...............N. Y. 151

Lightning Source UK Ltd.
Milton Keynes UK
UKHW011835070119
335148UK00009B/439/P